The Logical Basis for Computer Programming

for

Volume I
Deductive Reasoning

ZOHAR MANNA
Computer Science Department
Stanford University

RICHARD WALDINGER
Artificial Intelligence Center
SRI International

ADDISON-WESLEY PUBLISHING COMPANY

Reading, Massachusetts • Menlo Park, California • Don Mills, Ontario
Wokingham, England • Amsterdam • Sydney • Singapore • Tokyo
Mexico City • Bogotá • Santiago • San Juan

This book is in the Addison-Wesley Series in Computer Science

Consulting Editor:
Michael A. Harrison

Library of Congress Cataloging in Publication Data

Manna, Zohar.
  The logical basis for computer programming.

  Bibliography: p. 579
  Includes index.
  Contents: v. 1. Deductive reasoning.
  1. Programming (Electronic digital computers)
  2. Logic, Symbolic and mathematical. I. Waldinger,
Richard. II. Title.
QA76.6.M35595 1984   519.7   84-20346
ISBN 0-201-18260-2 (v. 1)

Reproduced by Addison-Wesley from camera-ready copy supplied
by the authors.

ABCDEFGHIJ-HA-898765

For our families:

Nitza	*Fran*
Yonit	*Rachel*
Hagit	*Evan*
Irit	
Amit	

Preface

In recent years, mathematical logic has developed from a theoretical activity to a practical tool, playing a fundamental role for computer science similar to that played by calculus for physics and traditional engineering. Once studied only by philosophers and mathematicians, logic is now becoming a standard part of the computer science curriculum. This book is a basic introduction to the logical concepts and techniques underlying computer programming.

Goals

The language of logic has been found to be the natural tool for expressing the purposes or intended behavior of computer programs, in the same way that programming languages express the algorithms that achieve these purposes. Logical techniques play a central role in work leading to the automation of computer programming, including program synthesis, verification, debugging, and transformation. Methods derived from logic are valuable in many branches of artificial intelligence, including planning, knowledge representation, and natural-language understanding. Computer languages (such as LISP and PROLOG) that use logical sentences as programs have been more and more widely applied. A knowledge of logic is becoming a daily necessity for the computer professional.

This book is intended to make logical concepts accessible to intelligent readers without any special background in mathematics or computer programming. We require no knowledge of mathematical logic, but only an intuitive grasp of basic mathematical concepts at the level of a good high school course. Nor do we require knowledge of any programming language; the book presents the reasoning that is fundamental to all computer programming, regardless of the programming language employed.

Subject

The first of the two volumes, subtitled *Deductive Reasoning*, describes several logical structures and presents methods for the informal but rigorous and intuitively convincing proof of theorems about these structures. The second volume, subtitled *Deductive Techniques*, presents methods for the formal proof of such theorems, oriented toward the development of computer theorem-proving systems and their applications. Let us examine the contents of each volume in more detail.

In the first volume we introduce the basic notions of propositional and predicate logic, and special theories with equality and mathematical induction. We present the theories of some of the most important structures of computer science, including the integers, strings, trees, lists, sets, and tuples (arrays). Algorithms are expressed not as explicit programs but as the definitions of functions and relations within these theories. We apply logical methods to establish the correctness of such algorithms as the parsing of strings and the sorting of tuples.

In the second volume we apply the concepts of the first volume to develop some formal proof techniques. The induction principles of the various theories presented in the first volume are unified into a single well-founded induction principle. We then describe an additional theory with induction, the theory of expressions and substitutions. Within this theory, we describe the unification algorithm and prove its correctness. We also introduce special logical techniques essential in theorem-proving systems, such as skolemization and polarity. Finally, we present a deductive system for describing formal proofs; this framework incorporates the most useful logical techniques for theorem proving, including nonclausal resolution, rewriting rules, and proof by mathematical induction.

The formal proofs expressed within the deductive system of the second volume reflect the intuitive content of the informal proofs of the first volume; indeed, many of the informal proofs used as examples in the first volume are reworked formally in the second volume.

Presentation

While there are many textbooks presenting deductive systems as an object of theoretical study for the logician, there has been a need for a textbook presenting deductive systems as a practical tool for the computer scientist. Logicians construct deductive systems primarily to study their theoretical properties and limitations; although these systems may be simple and concise, it is common that intuitively evident sentences are quite difficult to prove. Computer scientists, on the other hand, are more concerned that a system be useful: Proofs of evident theorems should be easy to discover, perhaps automatically, and should reflect the intuition behind them. For this reason, the deductive systems most attractive to logicians are not the ones most useful to computer scientists.

Some of the material we present in this book does appear in the literature, but it is dispersed among many technical papers and advanced texts for the specialist, in a variety of conflicting conceptual systems and incompatible notations. We have attempted to unify these concepts and techniques in a single framework. We have been serious about making this book understandable by the general reader, including the beginning student, programmer, and computer professional.

Our presentation is laced with examples, so that the reader develops the intuition behind the formal notions. In presenting logical arguments, we have been especially careful that the gaps between steps are not too large, so that the reading will be smooth. We have adopted an English-like notation for the logical operators rather than the more mathematical, and perhaps more intimidating, conventional symbols. For further clarity, logical sentences are presented in a two-dimensional format, so that some information may be conveyed by indentation.

Conventions

Mathematical works commonly enumerate the definitions and results and refer to them later by number. We have chosen to give mnemonic names rather than numbers to such properties, so that the reader will not need to turn back so frequently. The names of these definitions and results are included in the index.

Many of the problems at the end of each chapter present new supplementary material. To indicate which problems pertain to a given portion of the text, we annotate the text with references to the appropriate problems, and we provide a page reference with each problem. In solving a problem, readers may use any result that appears in the text prior to the corresponding page reference. They may also use the results of any previous problem and previous parts of the same problem.

Curriculum

The material in both volumes may be introduced quite early in the computer science curriculum, even before the student has been exposed to a programming language. Ultimately, we believe, the subject matter of the first volume should replace calculus as a requirement for undergraduate majors.

Each volume contains more than enough material for a separate one-semester course. The first volume is intended for a very general course, because it provides the conceptual foundation for most computer science courses, including computer programming, data structures, algorithms, and programming languages. The second volume is intended for a course on theorem proving; it provides the logical basis for courses in software engineering, artificial intelligence, database theory, and the theory of computation.

Acknowledgments

The notes on which this book is based have been used (in several incarnations over the past few years) as the text for a sequence of two courses in the Computer Science Department at Stanford University and in the Applied Mathematics Department at the Weizmann Institute. The classes were attended by computer professionals from local industry as well as undergraduate and graduate students;

the students were from departments such as psychology, linguistics, and philoso-
phy as well as mathematics, electrical engineering, and computer science. Each
time we taught the course, we revised the notes in accordance with the students'
comments and their performance on the exercises. We would like to thank all the
students of the classes for their extraordinary dedication, and especially Martin
Abadi, Alex Bronstein, Andy Golding, Eric Muller, Stuart Russell, and Jonathan
Traugott.

We would also like to thank our colleagues and graduate students at Stanford University, the Weizmann Institute, and SRI International for providing the
environment that made this work possible. Particular thanks are due to Jan
Derksen, Chris Goad, David Gries, Yoni Malachi, Ben Moszkowski, Nils Nilsson,
Larry Paulson, Amir Pnueli, Daniel Sagalowicz, Bill Scherlis, John Staples, Mark
Stickel, Pierre Wolper, and Frank Yellin for their attentive reading, insightful
suggestions, and intellectual encouragement. For support of the research behind
this book, we would like to thank the National Science Foundation, the Office
of Naval Research, the Air Force Office of Scientific Research, and the Defense
Advanced Research Projects Agency. The many versions of the manuscript have
been typeset by Evelyn Eldridge-Diaz using the TeX system of Donald Knuth;
we have relied greatly on her precision, intelligence, and endurance. The help of
TeX wizards Bill Scherlis and Frank Yellin was essential.

Stanford University   Z. M.
SRI International   R. W.

Contents

PART I: MATHEMATICAL LOGIC

Chapter 1: Propositional Logic 3

1.1 Introduction 3
1.2 The Language 5
1.3 The Meaning of a Sentence 9
1.4 Properties of Sentences 14
1.5 Truth Tables 20
1.6 Semantic Trees 23
1.7 Proof by Falsification 28
1.8 Valid Sentence Schemata 33
1.9 Substitution 40
1.10 Extended Interpretation 49
1.11 Equivalence 54
      Problems 61

Chapter 2: Predicate Logic: Basic 67

2.1 Introduction 67
2.2 The Language 69
2.3 The Meaning of a Sentence 80
2.4 Semantic Rules 85
2.5 Validity 97
2.6 Universal and Existential Closure 108
      Problems 115

Chapter 3: Predicate Logic: Advanced 119

3.1 Valid Sentence Schemata 119
3.2 Equivalence 129
3.3 Safe Substitution 140
3.4 The Value Property 154
3.5 Valid Schemata with Substitution 163

3.6   Function Introduction and Elimination   178
       Problems   185

Chapter 4:   Special Theories   189

4.1   Definition of a Theory   189
4.2   Augmenting Theories   196
4.3   Relationship between Theories   199
4.4   Theory of Strict Partial Orderings   201
4.5   Theory of Equivalence Relations   208
       Problems   212

Chapter 5:   Theories with Equality   215

5.1   Theory of Equality   215
5.2   Theory of Weak Partial Orderings   229
5.3   Theory of Associated Relations   232
5.4   Theory of Groups   249
5.5   Theory of Pairs   256
5.6   Relativized Quantifiers   266
5.7   The Lexicographic Relation   271
       Problems   278

PART II: THEORIES WITH INDUCTION

Chapter 6:   Nonnegative Integers   285

6.1   Basic Properties   285
6.2   The Addition Function   291
6.3   Multiplication and Exponentiation   304
6.4   Predecessor and Subtraction   311
6.5   Decomposition Induction   316
6.6   The Weak Less-than Relation   321
6.7   The Strict Less-than Relation   327
6.8   Complete Induction   329
6.9   Quotient and Remainder   331
6.10   Proof of Complete Induction   337
6.11   The Divides Relation   340
6.12   The Least-Number Principle   351
       Problems   354

Chapter 7:   Strings   363

7.1   Basic Properties   363
7.2   The Head and Tail Functions   369
7.3   The Concatenation Function   370

7.4   The Reverse Function   374
7.5   The Decomposition Induction Principle   383
7.6   The Substring Relation   389
7.7   The Complete Induction Principle   391
7.8   Nonnegative Integers and Strings   398
7.9   String Representation of Integers   402
        Problems   409

Chapter 8:   Trees   419

8.1   Basic Properties   419
8.2   The Left and Right Functions   422
8.3   The Subtree Relation   424
8.4   Strings and Trees   430
        Problems   433

Chapter 9:   Lists   437

9.1   Basic Properties   437
9.2   The Head and Tail Functions   441
9.3   Append and Member   442
9.4   Example: Flatlist   444
9.5   Tree Representation of Lists   448
9.6   Example: Parsing   458
        Problems   464

Chapter 10:   Sets   471

10.1   Basic Properties   471
10.2   The Equality Proposition   477
10.3   The Choice and Rest Functions   481
10.4   The Union and Intersection Functions   483
10.5   The Deletion and Difference Functions   489
10.6   The Subset Relation   491
10.7   The Set Constructor   493
10.8   Cardinality   496
10.9   Singleton Sets   499
        Problems   500

Chapter 11:   Bags   505

11.1   Basic Properties   505
11.2   The Equal-Multiplicity Relation   507
11.3   Multiplicity and Equality   515
11.4   The Count Function   518
11.5   Additional Functions and Relations   519
11.6   Sum, Union, and Intersection   521
        Problems   525

Chapter 12:   Tuples   529

12.1   Basic Properties   529

12.2   Nonnegative Integers and Tuples   536

12.3   Mapping Tuples into Sets and Bags   539

12.4   The Permutation Relation   544

12.5   The Ordered Relation   550

12.6   The Sort Function   555

12.7   Recursive Definition of Functions   565

Problems   572

Related Textbooks: a Selection   579

Index of Symbols   583

General Index   585

I

Mathematical

Logic

1

Propositional Logic

1.1 INTRODUCTION

Even if we do not know whether there is life on the planet Jupiter, we know that the sentence

> There are monkeys on Jupiter
>   or
> there are no monkeys on Jupiter

is true. The truth of the sentence can be determined from its structure alone, without knowing whether its constituents are true or false. Similarly, we can determine that the sentence

> Boise, Idaho, has fewer than 200,000 inhabitants
>   or
> Boise, Idaho, does not have fewer than 200,000 inhabitants

is true without consulting an almanac. In fact, both sentences are instances of the abstract sentence

> P
>   *or*
> (*not P*)

and any sentence of this form is true, regardless of whether P is a true or a false proposition.

We shall say that an abstract sentence is *valid* if it is true regardless of the truth or falsehood of its constituent propositions. By establishing the validity of such an abstract sentence, we can conclude the truth of all its infinitely many concrete instances. For example, if we know that the abstract sentence

$$not \ \big(P \ \ and \ (not \ P)\big)$$
$$or$$
$$Q$$

is valid, we can conclude immediately that the concrete sentence

$$not \ \big([x < 0] \ \ and \ (not \ [x < 0])\big)$$
$$or$$
$$y \geq 0$$

is true, regardless of whether $x < 0$ and $y \geq 0$ are true or false.

On the other hand, any instance of an abstract sentence such as

$$P \ \ and \ (not \ P)$$

is false independently of whether P is true or false; we shall call such sentences *contradictory*. Note that a sentence $\mathcal{F}$ is valid precisely when its negation $(not \ \mathcal{F})$ is contradictory.

Many abstract sentences, such as

$$P \ \ or \ Q$$

and

$$not \ P,$$

are neither valid nor contradictory; they have both true and false instances.

Certain pairs of abstract sentences, such as

$$if \ P \ \ then \ Q$$

and

$$if \ (not \ Q) \ \ then \ (not \ P),$$

are *equivalent*, in the sense that a concrete instance of either of them is true precisely when the corresponding instance of the other is true. For example, the two concrete sentences

         If it is raining, then the streets are wet

and

> If the streets are not wet, then it is not raining

are instances of the pair above and are both true. Neither abstract sentence of the pair is valid.

The purpose of this chapter is to present a language of abstract sentences, called *propositional logic*, and to introduce techniques for determining whether a given abstract sentence is valid or contradictory and whether two given abstract sentences are equivalent. By the methods of propositional logic, we shall be able to determine the truth or falsehood of many concrete sentences merely by examining their form.

1.2   THE LANGUAGE

We first introduce the basic symbols and show how they are combined to form the (abstract) sentences of propositional logic. We present *syntactic rules*, which say what combinations of symbols are taken to be sentences in the language. We shall not yet consider what these sentences mean.

Definition (propositions)

The sentences of propositional logic are made up of the following symbols, called *propositions*:

- The *truth symbols*

     true   and   *false*

- The *propositional* symbols

     $P, \ Q, \ R, \ S, \ P_1, \ Q_1, \ R_1, \ S_1, \ P_2, \ Q_2, \ R_2, \ S_2, \ \ldots$

   (the capital letters P, Q, R, or S, possibly with a numerical subscript) ⏌

In our informal discussion, we use the script letters $\mathcal{E}$, $\mathcal{F}$, $\mathcal{G}$, and $\mathcal{H}$, possibly with a numerical subscript, to stand for sentences. However, these symbols are not part of the language of propositional logic, but are only in our informal "metalanguage," the language in which we speak about propositional logic.

Definition (sentences)

The *sentences* of propositional logic are built up from the propositions by application of the *propositional connectives*:

not,   and,   or,   if-then,   if-and-only-if,   and   *if-then-else.*

The sentences are formed according to the following rules:

- Every proposition, i.e., a truth symbol or a propositional symbol, is a sentence.

- If $\mathcal{F}$ is a sentence, then so is its *negation*

  (*not* $\mathcal{F}$).

- If $\mathcal{F}$ and $\mathcal{G}$ are sentences, then so is their *conjunction*

  ($\mathcal{F}$ *and* $\mathcal{G}$).

  We call $\mathcal{F}$ and $\mathcal{G}$ the *conjuncts* of ($\mathcal{F}$ *and* $\mathcal{G}$).

- If $\mathcal{F}$ and $\mathcal{G}$ are sentences, then so is their *disjunction*

  ($\mathcal{F}$ *or* $\mathcal{G}$).

  We call $\mathcal{F}$ and $\mathcal{G}$ the *disjuncts* of ($\mathcal{F}$ *or* $\mathcal{G}$).

- If $\mathcal{F}$ and $\mathcal{G}$ are sentences, then so is the *implication*

  (*if* $\mathcal{F}$ *then* $\mathcal{G}$).

  We call $\mathcal{F}$ the *antecedent* and $\mathcal{G}$ the *consequent* of (*if* $\mathcal{F}$ *then* $\mathcal{G}$). The sentence (*if* $\mathcal{G}$ *then* $\mathcal{F}$) is called the *converse* of the sentence (*if* $\mathcal{F}$ *then* $\mathcal{G}$).

- If $\mathcal{F}$ and $\mathcal{G}$ are sentences, then so is the *equivalence*

  ($\mathcal{F}$ *if and only if* $\mathcal{G}$).

  We call $\mathcal{F}$ the *left-hand side* and $\mathcal{G}$ the *right-hand side* of the equivalence ($\mathcal{F}$ *if and only if* $\mathcal{G}$).

- If $\mathcal{F}$, $\mathcal{G}$, and $\mathcal{H}$ are sentences, then so is the *conditional*

  (*if* $\mathcal{F}$ *then* $\mathcal{G}$ *else* $\mathcal{H}$).

  We call $\mathcal{F}$, $\mathcal{G}$, and $\mathcal{H}$ the *if-clause*, *then-clause*, and *else-clause*, respectively, of the conditional (*if* $\mathcal{F}$ *then* $\mathcal{G}$ *else* $\mathcal{H}$). ⌙

In each case, the sentences $\mathcal{F}$, $\mathcal{G}$, and $\mathcal{H}$ used to construct the more complex sentence, by one of the above rules, will be called its *components*. Thus the components of (*if* $\mathcal{F}$ *then* $\mathcal{G}$) are its antecedent $\mathcal{F}$ and its consequent $\mathcal{G}$.

Every intermediate sentence we use in building up a sentence $\mathcal{E}$, including $\mathcal{E}$ itself, is a *subsentence* of $\mathcal{E}$. Thus the subsentences of $\mathcal{E}$ are $\mathcal{E}$ itself, the components of $\mathcal{E}$, and the subsentences of these components. The subsentences of $\mathcal{E}$ other than $\mathcal{E}$ itself are the *proper subsentences* of $\mathcal{E}$.

Example

The expression

$$\mathcal{E}: \quad \Big(\big(not\ (P\ \ or\ \ Q)\big)\ \ if\ and\ only\ if\ \ \big((not\ P)\ \ and\ \ (not\ Q)\big)\Big)$$

is a sentence. For

$$P \qquad \text{and} \qquad Q$$

are sentences; hence

$$(P\ \ or\ \ Q), \quad (not\ P), \quad \text{and} \quad (not\ Q)$$

are sentences; hence

$$\big(not\ (P\ \ or\ \ Q)\big) \quad \text{and} \quad \big((not\ P)\ \ and\ \ (not\ Q)\big)$$

are sentences; hence the given expression $\mathcal{E}$,

$$\Big(\big(not\ (P\ \ or\ \ Q)\big)\ \ if\ and\ only\ if\ \ \big((not\ P)\ \ and\ \ (not\ Q)\big)\Big),$$

is a sentence. Each of the above eight sentences (including $\mathcal{E}$) is a subsentence of $\mathcal{E}$; each of the first seven sentences (excluding $\mathcal{E}$) is a proper subsentence of $\mathcal{E}$. ◢

Note that there may be more than one *occurrence* of the same subsentence in a given sentence. For example, the above sentence $\mathcal{E}$ has two occurrences of the subsentence P and two occurrences of the subsentence Q.

NOTATION

We may omit the parentheses from sentences when they are not necessary to indicate the structure of the sentence. For example, the sentence

$$\big(not\ (P\ \ and\ \ (not\ Q))\big)$$

can be written as

$$not\ (P\ \ and\ \ not\ Q),$$

with no ambiguity.

For clarity, we shall sometimes use pairs of square brackets, [and], or braces, { and }, instead of some of the parentheses. Also we often use indentation rather than parentheses to indicate the structure of a sentence. Thus the sentence $\mathcal{E}$ of the above example may be written as

$$not\ (P\ \ or\ \ Q)$$
$$if\ and\ only\ if$$
$$(not\ \ P)\ \ and\ \ (not\ \ Q).$$

The sentence

$$\mathcal{F}:\ \Big(if\ ((P\ or\ Q)\ and\ (if\ Q\ then\ R))\ then\ (if\ (P\ and\ R)\ then\ (not\ R))\Big)$$

may be written as

$$if\ \begin{bmatrix} P\ \ or\ \ Q \\ and \\ if\ Q\ \ then\ \ R \end{bmatrix}$$
$$then\ if\ (P\ \ and\ \ R)$$
$$then\ \ not\ R.$$

The reader should be aware that the Englishlike notation we use for the propositional connectives is not the conventional one. Some of the most common notations are as follows:

Our notation	Conventional notation
and	$\wedge$ or &
or	$\vee$
not	$\sim$ or $\neg$
if-then	$\supset$ or $\rightarrow$
if-and-only-if	$\equiv$ or $\leftrightarrow$

(The *if-then-else* connective is generally not included in conventional logical systems.) We have chosen to use the Englishlike notation for clarity in the text; the reader may prefer to use a more concise mathematical notation in writing. For example, the sentence $\mathcal{E}$ above can be written as

$$\Big((\sim(P\vee Q))\ \equiv\ ((\sim P)\ \wedge\ (\sim Q))\Big).$$

The sentence $\mathcal{F}$ can be written as

$$\Big(\big((P \vee Q) \wedge (Q \supset R) \big) \supset \big((P \wedge R) \supset (\sim R) \big) \Big).$$

1.3 THE MEANING OF A SENTENCE

So far we have presented the syntax or form of the sentences of propositional logic without assigning them any semantics or meaning. We now show how to assign a *truth value*,

true   or   false,

to a propositional-logic sentence. (We sharply distinguish between the truth symbols *true* and *false*, which may occur within a sentence and which are always italicized, and the truth values true and false, which are the possible meanings of a sentence and which are never italicized.) It is meaningful to talk about whether the truth value of a sentence such as $\big(P \ or \ (not \ Q)\big)$ is true or false if we know whether the truth values of the propositional symbols P and Q themselves are true or false. This information is provided by an "interpretation."

INTERPRETATIONS

Let us now define more precisely the notion of an interpretation.

Definition (interpretation)

> An *interpretation* I is an assignment of a truth value, either true or false, to each of a set of propositional symbols; the *empty interpretation* assigns a truth value to no propositional symbols at all.
>
> For any sentence $\mathcal{F}$, an interpretation I is said to be an *interpretation for* $\mathcal{F}$ if I assigns a truth value, either true or false, to each of the propositional symbols of $\mathcal{F}$.   ◢

For example, consider the sentence

$$\mathcal{F}: \quad P \ or \ (not \ Q).$$

One interpretation I_1 for $\mathcal{F}$ assigns false to P and true to Q; that is,

$$I_1: \quad \begin{array}{l} P \text{ is false} \\ Q \text{ is true.} \end{array}$$

Another interpretation I_2 for $\mathcal{F}$ assigns false to P and false to Q; that is,

$$I_2 : \begin{array}{l} P \text{ is false} \\ Q \text{ is false.} \end{array}$$

We may also say that P is false and Q is true under I_1 and that P is false and Q is false under I_2.

In general, an interpretation for a sentence may assign truth values to some symbols that do not appear in the sentence, so long as every propositional symbol that does appear is assigned a value.

For example,

$$I_3 : \begin{array}{l} P \text{ is true} \\ Q \text{ is false} \\ R \text{ is true} \end{array}$$

is also an interpretation for $\mathcal{F}$, even though R does not occur at all in $\mathcal{F}$.

Note that all occurrences of a given propositional symbol are assigned the same value by a given interpretation; e.g., in the sentence

if P then (P or Q)

the two occurrences of P are each assigned the same value.

As a natural extension, we will define an interpretation I for several sentences $\mathcal{F}_1, \mathcal{F}_2, \ldots, \mathcal{F}_n$ to be an assignment of a truth value, either true or false, to each propositional symbol that occurs in any of the sentences $\mathcal{F}_1, \mathcal{F}_2, \ldots, \mathcal{F}_n$. For example, any interpretation that assigns truth values to P, Q, and R (and perhaps to other propositional symbols) is an interpretation for

$$\mathcal{F}_1 : \quad P \text{ and } Q$$

and

$$\mathcal{F}_2 : \quad (not\, Q) \text{ or } R.$$

SEMANTIC RULES

Once we have provided an interpretation for a sentence, we can determine its truth value under that interpretation by applying certain rules.

Definition (semantic rules)

Let $\mathcal{E}$ be a sentence and I an interpretation for $\mathcal{E}$. Then the *truth value of $\mathcal{E}$* (and all of its subsentences) *under I* is determined by applying repeatedly the following *semantic rules*:

- *proposition rule*

  The truth value of each propositional symbol

  $$P, Q, R, \ldots$$

  in $\mathcal{E}$ is the same as the truth value assigned to it by $\mathcal{I}$.

- *true rule*

  The sentence

  true

  is true under $\mathcal{I}$.

- *false rule*

  The sentence

  false

  is false under $\mathcal{I}$.

- *not rule*

  The negation

  not $\mathcal{F}$

  is true if $\mathcal{F}$ is false, and false if $\mathcal{F}$ is true.

- *and rule*

  The conjunction

  $\mathcal{F}$ *and* $\mathcal{G}$

  is true if $\mathcal{F}$ and $\mathcal{G}$ are both true, and false otherwise (that is, if $\mathcal{F}$ is false or if $\mathcal{G}$ is false).

- *or rule*

  The disjunction

  $\mathcal{F}$ *or* $\mathcal{G}$

  is true if $\mathcal{F}$ is true or if $\mathcal{G}$ is true, and false otherwise (that is, if $\mathcal{F}$ and $\mathcal{G}$ are both false).

- *if-then rule*

  The implication

  if F then G

  is true if F is false or if G is true, and false otherwise (that is, if F is true and G is false).

- *if-and-only-if rule*

  The equivalence

  F if and only if G

  is true if the truth value of F is the same as the truth value of G (that is, if F and G are both true or if F and G are both false), and false otherwise (that is, if F is true and G is false or if F is false and G is true).

- *if-then-else rule*

  The truth value of the conditional

  if F then G else H

  is the truth value of G if F is true and the truth value of H if F is false.   ⌐

The semantic rules for the connectives may be summarized in the following *truth tables*:

F	*not F*
true	false
false	true

Here, if the truth value of F under I is as given by the first column, the truth value of (*not F*) is as shown in the final column.

F	G	*F and G*	*F or G*	*if F then G*	*F if and only if G*
true	true	true	true	true	true
true	false	false	true	false	false
false	true	false	true	true	false
false	false	false	false	true	true

Here, if the truth values of $\mathcal{F}$ and $\mathcal{G}$ under $\mathcal{I}$ are as given in the first two columns, the truth values of the sentences ($\mathcal{F}$ *and* $\mathcal{G}$), ($\mathcal{F}$ *or* $\mathcal{G}$), ... are as shown in the appropriate columns.

$\mathcal{F}$	$\mathcal{G}$	$\mathcal{H}$	*if* $\mathcal{F}$ *then* $\mathcal{G}$ *else* $\mathcal{H}$
true	true	true	true
true	true	false	true
true	false	true	false
true	false	false	false
false	true	true	true
false	true	false	false
false	false	true	true
false	false	false	false

Observe that according to the *or* rule, the *or* connective is "inclusive" in the sense that (P *or* Q) is true in the case in which both P and Q are true. Intuitively speaking, it is as if, in the concrete sentence

> The house will be destroyed by fire
>> or
> the house will be destroyed by earthquake,

we allow the possibility of having both.

Note also that, according to the *if-then* rule, the sentence (*if* $\mathcal{F}$ *then* $\mathcal{G}$) is true whenever its antecedent $\mathcal{F}$ is false or its consequent $\mathcal{G}$ is true, even if there is no causal relation between $\mathcal{F}$ and $\mathcal{G}$. For example, the concrete sentence

> If California is the capital of Washington,
> then the moon is made of green cheese

is regarded as a true sentence among logicians, because its antecedent is false.

To determine the truth value of a complex sentence under a given interpretation, we first apply the semantic rules to determine the truth value of each of its components; we then apply the appropriate semantic rule to determine the truth value of the entire sentence.

Example

Consider the sentence

$$\mathcal{F}: \quad \begin{array}{l} \text{if } (P \text{ and } (not\, Q)) \\ \text{then } ((not\, P) \text{ or } R) \end{array}$$

and the interpretation

$$\mathcal{I}: \quad \begin{array}{l} P \text{ is true,} \\ Q \text{ is false,} \\ R \text{ is false} \end{array}$$

for $\mathcal{F}$.

Then we can use the semantic rules to determine the truth value of the sentence $\mathcal{F}$ under this interpretation as follows:

Because Q is false, we know (by the *not* rule) that

$$(not\ Q) \text{ is true.}$$

Because P is true and $(not\ Q)$ is true, we know (by the *and* rule) that

$$\big(P\ and\ (not\ Q)\big) \text{ is true.}$$

Because P is true, we know (by the *not* rule) that

$$(not\ P) \text{ is false.}$$

Because $(not\ P)$ is false and R is false, we know (by the *or* rule) that

$$\big((not\ P)\ or\ R\big) \text{ is false.}$$

Because $\big(P\ and\ (not\ Q)\big)$ is true and $\big((not\ P)\ or\ R\big)$ is false, we know (by the *if-then* rule) that the entire sentence $\mathcal{F}$,

$$\begin{array}{l} if\ \big(P\ \ and\ (not\ Q)\big) \\ then\ \big((not\ P)\ or\ R\big), \end{array}$$

is false.   ∎

1.4   PROPERTIES OF SENTENCES

Recall that we have said that a sentence is valid if it is true and contradictory if it is false, regardless of the truth or falsehood of its constituent propositional symbols. Also, two sentences are equivalent if they are either both true or both false, regardless of the truth or falsehood of their constituent propositional symbols. Now we can define these notions precisely.

Definition (valid, satisfiable, contradictory, implies, equivalent, consistent)

A sentence $\mathcal{F}$ is *valid* if it is true under every interpretation for $\mathcal{F}$. Valid sentences of propositional logic are sometimes called *tautologies*.

A sentence $\mathcal{F}$ is *satisfiable* if it is true under some interpretation for $\mathcal{F}$.

A sentence $\mathcal{F}$ is *contradictory* (or *unsatisfiable*) if it is false under every interpretation for $\mathcal{F}$.

A sentence $\mathcal{F}$ *implies* a sentence $\mathcal{G}$ if, for any interpretation $\mathcal{I}$ for $\mathcal{F}$ and $\mathcal{G}$, if $\mathcal{F}$ is true under $\mathcal{I}$ then $\mathcal{G}$ is also true under $\mathcal{I}$.

Two sentences $\mathcal{F}$ and $\mathcal{G}$ are *equivalent* if, under every interpretation for $\mathcal{F}$ and $\mathcal{G}$, $\mathcal{F}$ has the same truth value as $\mathcal{G}$.

A set of sentences $\mathcal{F}_1$, $\mathcal{F}_2$, ... is *consistent* if there exists some interpretation for $\mathcal{F}_1$, $\mathcal{F}_2$, ... under which each $\mathcal{F}_i$ is true.

Let us illustrate these notions with some simple examples.

Examples

The sentence

$$P$$

is satisfiable, because it is true under any interpretation that assigns P to be true; however, the sentence is not valid, because it is false under any interpretation that assigns P to be false.

The sentence

$$P \ \ or \ \ (not \ P)$$

is both satisfiable and valid, because it is true under any interpretation, regardless of whether it assigns P to be true or false. In general, any valid sentence is also satisfiable.

The sentence

$$P \ \ and \ \ (not \ P)$$

is contradictory, because it is false under any interpretation, regardless of whether it assigns P to be true or false.

The sentence

$$P \ \ and \ \ Q$$

implies the sentence

$$P,$$

because, under any interpretation for which $(P \ and \ Q)$ is true, P is also true.

The two sentences

$$P \quad and \quad not\,(not\,P)$$

are equivalent, because they are each true under any interpretation that assigns P to be true, and false under any interpretation that assigns P to be false.

The two sentences

$$P \quad and \quad Q$$

are not equivalent, because they have different truth values under any interpretation that assigns different values to P and Q.

The set of sentences

$$P, \quad P \ or \ Q, \quad not\,Q$$

is consistent, because each sentence is true under the interpretation under which P is true and Q is false.

The set of sentences

$$P, \quad not\,P, \quad not\,Q$$

is inconsistent, because at least one of the sentences is false under any interpretation, regardless of whether it assigns P and Q to be true or false. If P is true, the second sentence is false; if P is false, the first sentence is false.   ◢

The notions above may all be paraphrased in terms of validity. To explain this, we introduce some informal terminology. For ordinary English sentences A and B we say that

$$A \text{ precisely when } B$$

to indicate that A is true if B is and B is true if A is. We emphasize that "precisely when," in contrast with "if and only if," is not a connective of propositional logic and that A and B are themselves English sentences, not propositional-logic sentences.

Remark (satisfiable and valid)

> A sentence $\mathcal{F}$ is satisfiable
>   precisely when
> its negation ($not\ \mathcal{F}$) is not valid.

For we have

> $\mathcal{F}$ is satisfiable

precisely when (by the definition of satisfiability)

> $\mathcal{F}$ is true under some interpretation $\mathcal{I}$

precisely when (by the *not* rule)

> ($not\ \mathcal{F}$) is false under some interpretation $\mathcal{I}$

precisely when (by the definition of validity)

> ($not\ \mathcal{F}$) is not valid.   ◢

Remark (contradictory and valid)

> A sentence $\mathcal{F}$ is contradictory
>   precisely when
> its negation ($not\ \mathcal{F}$) is valid.

For we have

> $\mathcal{F}$ is contradictory

precisely when (by the definition of contradiction)

> $\mathcal{F}$ is false under any interpretation $\mathcal{I}$

precisely when (by the *not* rule)

> ($not\ \mathcal{F}$) is true under any interpretation $\mathcal{I}$

precisely when (by the definition of validity)

> ($not\ \mathcal{F}$) is valid.   ◢

Remark (implies and valid)

For two sentences $\mathcal{F}$ and $\mathcal{G}$,

> $\mathcal{F}$ implies $\mathcal{G}$
>   precisely when
> the sentence (*if* $\mathcal{F}$ *then* $\mathcal{G}$) is valid.

For we have

> $\mathcal{F}$ implies $\mathcal{G}$

precisely when (by the definition of implication)

> for any interpretation I (for $\mathcal{F}$ and $\mathcal{G}$),
>   if $\mathcal{F}$ is true under I then $\mathcal{G}$ is also true under I
>   (that is, $\mathcal{F}$ is false under I or $\mathcal{G}$ is true under I)

precisely when (by the *if-then* rule)

> (*if* $\mathcal{F}$ *then* $\mathcal{G}$) is true under any interpretation I

precisely when (by the definition of validity)

> (*if* $\mathcal{F}$ *then* $\mathcal{G}$) is valid. ∎

Remark (equivalent and valid)

> Two sentences $\mathcal{F}$ and $\mathcal{G}$ are equivalent
>   precisely when
> the sentence ($\mathcal{F}$ *if and only if* $\mathcal{G}$) is valid.

For we have

> $\mathcal{F}$ and $\mathcal{G}$ are equivalent

precisely when (by the definition of equivalence)

> $\mathcal{F}$ and $\mathcal{G}$ have the same truth value
> under any interpretation I (for $\mathcal{F}$ and $\mathcal{G}$)

precisely when (by the *if-and-only-if* rule)

> ($\mathcal{F}$ *if and only if* $\mathcal{G}$) is true under any interpretation I

precisely when (by the definition of validity)

> ($\mathcal{F}$ *if and only if* $\mathcal{G}$) is valid. ∎

Remark (equivalent and implies)

> Two sentences $\mathcal{F}$ and $\mathcal{G}$ are equivalent
>   precisely when
> $\mathcal{F}$ implies $\mathcal{G}$ and $\mathcal{G}$ implies $\mathcal{F}$.

For we have

> $\mathcal{F}$ and $\mathcal{G}$ are equivalent

precisely when (by the definition of equivalence)

> $\mathcal{F}$ and $\mathcal{G}$ have the same truth value under any interpretation I

precisely when

> for any interpretation I,
>   if $\mathcal{F}$ is true under I then $\mathcal{G}$ is true under I and
>   if $\mathcal{G}$ is true under I then $\mathcal{F}$ is true under I

precisely when

> for any interpretation I,
>   if $\mathcal{F}$ is true under I then $\mathcal{G}$ is true under I
> and
> for any interpretation I,
>   if $\mathcal{G}$ is true under I then $\mathcal{F}$ is true under I

precisely when (by the definition of implication)

> $\mathcal{F}$ implies $\mathcal{G}$
> and
> $\mathcal{G}$ implies $\mathcal{F}$,

as we wanted to show. ⌟

Remark (consistent and satisfiable)

> A finite set of sentences $\mathcal{F}_1$, $\mathcal{F}_2$, ..., $\mathcal{F}_{n-1}$, $\mathcal{F}_n$ is consistent
>   precisely when
> their conjunction $\left(\mathcal{F}_1 \;\; and \;\; (\mathcal{F}_2 \;\; and \ldots and \;\; (\mathcal{F}_{n-1} \;\; and \;\; \mathcal{F}_n) \ldots)\right)$
> is satisfiable.

For we have that the set

> $\mathcal{F}_1$, $\mathcal{F}_2$, ..., $\mathcal{F}_{n-1}$, $\mathcal{F}_n$ is consistent

precisely when (by the definition of consistency)

$\mathcal{F}_1, \mathcal{F}_2, \ldots, \mathcal{F}_{n-1}, \mathcal{F}_n$ are all true under some interpretation $\mathcal{I}$

precisely when (by the *and* rule)

$\mathcal{F}_1, \mathcal{F}_2, \ldots, \mathcal{F}_{n-2}, (\mathcal{F}_{n-1} \ and \ \mathcal{F}_n)$ are all true
under some interpretation $\mathcal{I}$

precisely when (by the *and* rule, applied $n - 2$ more times)

$\left(\mathcal{F}_1 \ and \ \left(\mathcal{F}_2 \ and \ \ldots \ and \ (\mathcal{F}_{n-1} \ and \ \mathcal{F}_n) \ldots \right)\right)$ is true
under some interpretation $\mathcal{I}$

precisely when (by the definition of satisfiability)

$\left(\mathcal{F}_1 \ and \ \left(\mathcal{F}_2 \ and \ \ldots \ and \ (\mathcal{F}_{n-1} \ and \ \mathcal{F}_n) \ldots \right)\right)$ is satisfiable.

Because we know that satisfiability can be expressed in terms of validity, this shows that consistency can also be expressed in terms of validity. ◢

We have seen that each of the notions we have considered can be paraphrased in terms of the validity of a propositional-logic sentence. Therefore we concentrate on methods of determining whether a given sentence is valid or not.

It is not always easy to see whether a sentence is valid; for example, consider the sentence

$$
if \left[\begin{array}{l} \left[\begin{array}{l} if \ P_1 \ then \ (P_2 \ or \ P_3) \\ \quad else \ (P_3 \ or \ P_4) \end{array} \right] \ and \\ \left[\begin{array}{l} \left[\begin{array}{l} if \ P_3 \ then \ (not \ P_6) \\ \quad else \ (if \ P_4 \ then \ P_1) \end{array} \right] \ and \\ \left[\begin{array}{l} not \ (P_2 \ and \ P_5) \ and \\ (if \ P_2 \ then \ P_5) \end{array} \right] \end{array} \right] \ and \end{array} \right]
$$

then not $(if \ P_3 \ then \ P_6)$.

This sentence is actually valid, although it is difficult to recognize its validity at first glance.

1.5   TRUTH TABLES

The most straightforward way to determine whether a sentence is valid is by a complete case analysis of the possible truth values assigned to its propositional symbols. Thus if a sentence contains only the propositional symbols P and Q, we distinguish between two cases, assigning P the truth values true and false, respectively. In each case we distinguish between two further subcases, assigning Q the truth values true and false, respectively.

Thus for a sentence containing only the propositional symbols P and Q there are four possible interpretations we must consider:

P is true and Q is true;

P is true and Q is false;

P is false and Q is true;

P is false and Q is false.

If the given sentence turns out to have the truth value true under each of the four possible interpretations, the sentence is valid.

Such a process is facilitated by a *truth table*. Suppose, for example, our given sentence is

$$\mathcal{F}: \quad \begin{array}{l} not\ (P\ or\ Q) \\ if\ and\ only\ if \\ (not\ P)\ and\ (not\ Q). \end{array}$$

The corresponding *truth table* is

P	Q	P or Q	not $(P$ or $Q)$	not P	not Q	$(not\ P)$ and $(not\ Q)$	$\mathcal{F}$
true	true	true	false	false	false	false	true
true	false	true	false	false	true	false	true
false	true	true	false	true	false	false	true
false	false	false	true	true	true	true	true

In the two leftmost columns of the table we record the four possible assignments of truth values to P and Q. For each interpretation we enter in successive columns the truth or falsehood of each subsentence of $\mathcal{F}$. The truth value in each column is determined from the truth values in the previous columns by applying the semantic rule for the corresponding connective. For example, the truth values in the column headed *not* $(P$ *or* $Q)$ are obtained from the truth values in the column headed $(P$ *or* $Q)$ by applying the *not* rule. The final column exhibits the truth value of the entire sentence; because $\mathcal{F}$ is true in each case, we have determined that $\mathcal{F}$ is valid.

On the other hand, if we are given the sentence

$$\mathcal{G}: \quad \begin{array}{l} \textit{if (if P then Q)} \\ \textit{then (if (not P) then (not Q)),} \end{array}$$

the corresponding truth table is

P	Q	if P then Q	not P	not Q	if (not P) then (not Q)	$\mathcal{G}$
true	true	true	false	false	true	true
true	false	false	false	true	true	true
false	true	true	true	false	false	false
false	false	true	true	true	true	true

We can see from the final column of the truth table that the sentence $\mathcal{G}$ is not valid; it is true in three cases, but false in the case in which P is false and Q is true.

The same technique can be used to determine whether a sentence is contradictory. We compute its truth table as above; the sentence is contradictory if the final column of the table is false in every case.

Similarly, we can determine whether two sentences are equivalent by computing the truth table for each sentence separately, including for each table all the propositional symbols that occur in either sentence. The two sentences are equivalent if the corresponding entries in the final columns of the two tables are all identical.

Thus we can determine that the sentences

$$\textit{not (P or Q)} \qquad \text{and} \qquad \textit{(not P) and (not Q)}$$

are equivalent by comparing the final columns of their truth tables

P	Q	P or Q	not (P or Q)
true	true	true	false
true	false	true	false
false	true	true	false
false	false	false	true

and

P	Q	not P	not Q	(not P) and (not Q)
true	true	false	false	false
true	false	false	true	false
false	true	true	false	false
false	false	true	true	true

Alternatively, as we have remarked earlier, we can determine whether a sentence $\mathcal{F}$ is contradictory by checking whether the sentence (*not* $\mathcal{F}$) is valid; similarily, we can determine if two sentences $\mathcal{F}$ and $\mathcal{G}$ are equivalent by checking whether the sentence ($\mathcal{F}$ *if and only if* $\mathcal{G}$) is valid. Thus since we have shown earlier that the sentence

> *not* (P *or* Q)
> *if and only if*
> (*not* P) *and* (*not* Q)

is valid, this also establishes the equivalence of the two sentences

> *not* (P *or* Q)   and   (*not* P) *and* (*not* Q).

1.6   SEMANTIC TREES

Another method of testing the validity of a sentence, the *semantic-tree technique*, is often more efficient than the truth-table method. We illustrate this technique with an example.

Example

Let us test whether the sentence

> $\mathcal{G}$:   *if* (*if* P *then* Q)
> *then* (*if* (*not* P) *then* (*not* Q))

is valid. We consider the two possible truth values for P, representing the choice in tree form:

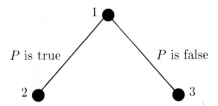

We indicate that P is true at node 2 by annotating each occurrence of P in the sentence $\mathcal{G}$ with the letter T:

> Node 2:   *if (if P then Q) then (if (not P) then (not Q))*.
>   T   T

Starting from P, we attempt to determine the truth value for larger and larger subsentences of $\mathcal{G}$. Although we know that P is true, we cannot use the *if-then* rule to determine the truth value of the antecedent, *(if P then Q)*, without also knowing the truth value of Q. Because P is true, the value of the subsentence *(not P)* is false (by the *not* rule); that is,

> Node 2:   *if (if P then Q) then (if (not P) then (not Q))*.
>   T   F T

(Note that we indicate that *(not P)* is false by annotating the connective *not* with the letter F.) Because *(not P)* is false, we can determine (by the *if-then* rule) that the consequent *(if (not P) then (not Q))* is true, even though we do not know whether *(not Q)* is true or false. Thus we have

> Node 2:   *if (if P then Q) then (if (not P) then (not Q))*.
>   T   T   F T

(Note that we indicate that an implication is true by annotating the *if* with the letter T.) Because the consequent *(if (not P) then (not Q))* is true, the entire sentence $\mathcal{G}$ is true; i.e.,

> Node 2:   *if (if P then Q) then (if (not P) then (not Q))*.
>   T   T   T   F T

We summarize the result of this analysis on the tree:

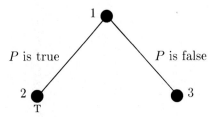

Here we have indicated that the value of $\mathcal{G}$ at node 2 is true by annotating the node with the letter T.

Now let us pursue the analysis corresponding to node 3, at which P is false.

Node 3: $if\ (if\ P\ then\ Q)\ then\ \big(if\ (not\ P)\ then\ (not\ Q)\big)$
                        F   F

Because P is false, the subsentences $(if\ P\ then\ Q)$ and $(not\ P)$ are both true (by the *if-then* and *not* rules); i.e., we have

Node 3: $if\ (if\ P\ then\ Q)\ then\ \big(if\ (not\ P)\ then\ (not\ Q)\big).$
                     T   F   T   F

Unfortunately, if the antecedent of an implication is true, we cannot use the *if-then* rule to determine the truth value of the implication without knowing whether the consequent is true or false. Thus without knowing whether $(not\ Q)$ is true or false, we cannot determine the truth value of the consequent $\big(if\,(not\ P)\ then\,(not\ Q)\big)$; and without knowing whether the consequent is true or false, we cannot determine the truth value of the entire sentence $\mathcal{G}$. Therefore our analysis at node 3 is inconclusive.

Beginning from node 3 (for the case in which P is false), we consider the two possible truth values for Q:

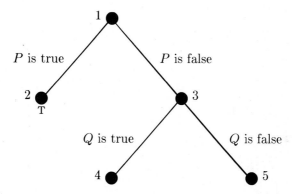

At node 4, we know that Q is true; applying the *not* and *if-then* rules, we obtain the annotated sentence

Node 4: $if\ (if\ P\ then\ Q)\ then\ \big(if\ (not\ P)\ then\ (not\ Q)\big).$
                  F   T   F   T   F   T   F   F   T

In short, the value of the sentence $\mathcal{G}$ at node 4 is false.

On the other hand, at node 5 we know that Q is false; applying the semantic rules as before yields the annotated sentence

Node 5: $if\ (if\ P\ then\ Q)\ then\ \big(if\ (not\ P)\ then\ (not\ Q)\big).$
                  T   T   F   F   T   T   F   T   F

Thus the sentence $\mathcal{G}$ is true at node 5.

Summarizing the results of our analysis, we obtain the semantic tree for the sentence $\mathcal{G}$:

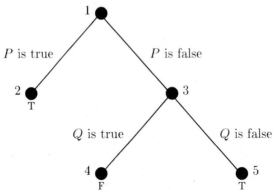

By inspection of the semantic tree we can observe that the sentence $\mathcal{G}$ is not valid. Node 4 is labeled F, indicating that the sentence $\mathcal{G}$ is false under the corresponding interpretation, in which P is false and Q is true. ⌐

If we discover that the sentence is true at the end of every branch of the tree (i.e., if every end node is labeled T), we can conclude that the sentence is valid.

Example

Let us now test whether the sentence

$$\mathcal{H}: \quad \begin{array}{l} \textit{if } Q \\ \textit{then (if } P \textit{ then } Q) \end{array}$$

is valid. We consider the two possible truth values for Q, representing the choice in tree form:

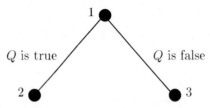

Let us indicate that Q is true at node 2 by annotating each occurrence of Q in the sentence $\mathcal{H}$ with the letter T:

Node 2: *if Q then (if P then Q).*
          T   T

Because Q is true, the consequent (*if P then Q*) is true, and hence the entire sentence is true.

We summarize the result of this analysis on the tree:

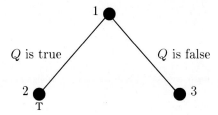

Now let us pursue the analysis corresponding to node 3, at which Q is false.

Node 3:   *if Q then (if P then Q).*
          F   F

Because its antecedent Q is false, the entire sentence is true.

Summarizing the result of this analysis, we obtain the semantic tree for the sentence $\mathcal{H}$:

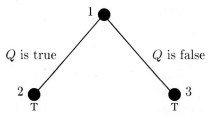

Because $\mathcal{H}$ is true at the end of each branch of the tree, we conclude that $\mathcal{H}$ is valid. ◢

Note that in the last example we were able to determine that $\mathcal{H}$ is valid without considering at all whether or not P is true. In the truth-table method, we would have had to consider separately, for each possible truth value for Q, the case in which P is true and false, even though the ultimate outcome does not depend on the truth value of P. Similarly, in the previous example, in the case in which P is true, we were able to determine that $\mathcal{G}$ is true without considering whether or not Q is true. In the truth-table method, we would have had to consider all four cases. In this way, the semantic-tree method can be more efficient than the truth-table technique.

In some cases, the discrepancy between the two methods is even more dramatic. For example, to show the validity of the sentence

$$((...(P_1 \ \textit{or} \ P_2) \ \textit{or} \ ...) \ \textit{or} \ P_{20}) \ \textit{or true},$$

which contains 20 propositional symbols, requires a truth table of $2^{20} = 1,048,576$ rows. The corresponding semantic tree contains only a single node: By the *or* rule, because the subsentence *true* is true, the entire sentence is also true; we have

$$((...(P_1 \ or \ P_2) \ or \ ...) \ or \ P_{20}) \ or \ true.$$
$$\qquad\qquad\qquad\qquad\qquad\quad \text{T} \quad\ \ \text{T}$$

1.7   PROOF BY FALSIFICATION

An alternative method for testing the validity of a sentence, which is convenient to apply by hand, is called *proof by falsification*. As usual, we illustrate the technique with an example.

Example

We want to establish the validity of the sentence

$$\mathcal{E}: \quad \begin{array}{l} \textit{if } ((not \ P) \ or \ (not \ Q)) \\ \textit{then } (not \ (P \ and \ Q)). \end{array}$$

Suppose, to the contrary, that $\mathcal{E}$ is false under some interpretation; we indicate this by annotating the *if* with the letter F:

$$\textit{if } ((not \ P) \ or \ (not \ Q)) \ \textit{then } (not \ (P \ and \ Q)).$$
$$\text{F}$$

We attempt to derive a contradiction, i.e., to show that this cannot occur.

By the *if-then* rule, the antecedent $((not \ P) \ or \ (not \ Q))$ and the consequent $(not \ (P \ and \ Q))$ must have truth values true and false, respectively, under this interpretation; that is,

$$\textit{if } ((not \ P) \ or \ (not \ Q)) \ \textit{then } (not \ (P \ and \ Q)).$$
$$\text{F} \qquad\qquad\quad \text{T} \qquad\qquad\qquad\qquad\ \text{F}$$

Again, we put T and F, respectively, under the main connectives of the antecedent and consequent.

The truth of the antecedent $((not \ P) \ or \ (not \ Q))$ does not allow us to determine the truth values of its subsentences $(not \ P)$ and $(not \ Q)$ uniquely: $(not \ P)$ could be true, $(not \ Q)$ could be true, or they both could be true. To avoid treating these cases separately, we focus our attention first on the consequent.

Because the consequent $(not \ (P \ and \ Q))$ is false, its subsentence $(P \ and \ Q)$ must be true, and hence its subsentences P and Q are both true:

$$\textit{if } ((not \ P) \ or \ (not \ Q)) \ \textit{then } (not \ (P \ and \ Q)).$$
$$\text{F} \qquad\ \text{T} \ \ \text{T} \qquad\ \ \text{T} \qquad\qquad \text{F} \ \ \text{T} \ \ \text{T} \ \ \text{T}$$

Note that when we discover the truth value of a symbol or subsentence we label all of its occurrences. Thus we have labeled each occurrence of P and Q with its truth value indication T.

At this stage, we return our attention to the antecedent. Because P and Q are both true, (*not P*) and (*not Q*) are both false. By the *or* rule, this requires that the antecedent $((not\ P)\ or\ (not\ Q))$ is also false. However, we have determined earlier that this subsentence is true, as the annotation reveals:

$$if\ ((not\ P)\ \ or\ \ (not\ Q))\ \ then\ \ (not\ (P\ \ and\ \ Q)).$$

$$\text{F} \qquad \text{F}\ \ \text{T}\ \ \text{T}_{\text{F}} \quad \text{F}\ \ \text{T} \qquad \text{F}\ \ \text{T}\ \ \text{T}\ \ \text{T}$$

We have given a conflicting annotation T_{F} (that is, T and F together) to the subsentence $((not\ P)\ \ or\ \ (not\ Q))$. Consequently, we have contradicted our original supposition, that the sentence $\mathcal{E}$ is false under some interpretation. In other words, $\mathcal{E}$ is valid.   ◢

By postponing the treatment of the antecedent in the above example, we avoided any case analysis. In general, however, we shall not always be so fortunate; it may be necessary to consider several possibilities separately, as illustrated below.

Example

Suppose we want to establish the validity of the sentence

$$\mathcal{F}:\quad \begin{array}{c} (if\ P\ \ then\ \ Q)\\ if\ and\ only\ if\\ ((not\ P)\ \ or\ \ Q). \end{array}$$

We derive a contradiction by assuming that $\mathcal{F}$ is false under some interpretation.

According to the *if-and-only-if* rule, $\mathcal{F}$ may be false for two possible reasons: Either the left subsentence, (*if P then Q*), is true and the right subsentence, $((not\ P)\ or\ Q)$, is false, or vice versa. We therefore split the annotation into two cases, corresponding to the two possibilities. In each case we must obtain a conflicting annotation.

Case: (*if P then Q*) is true and $((not\ P)\ or\ Q)$ is false

This case corresponds to the annotation

$$(if\ P\ \ then\ \ Q)\ \ if\ and\ only\ if\ \ ((not\ P)\ \ or\ \ Q).$$

$$\text{T} \qquad\qquad\qquad\qquad \text{F} \qquad\qquad\qquad \text{F}$$

There are two ways in which the left subsentence, (*if P then Q*), could be true; therefore we consider first the right subsentence, $((not\ P)\ or\ Q)$. Because

$((not\ P)\ or\ Q)$ is false, both $(not\ P)$ and Q must be false, and hence P must be true. We have

$$(if\ P\ then\ Q)\quad if\ and\ only\ if\quad ((not\ P)\quad or\quad Q).$$
$$\text{T}\ \ \text{T}\qquad\qquad \text{F}\qquad\qquad\quad \text{F}\qquad\quad\ \ \text{F}\ \ \text{T}\quad\ \text{F}\ \ \text{F}$$

Because P is true and Q is false, $(if\ P\ then\ Q)$ must also be false, contradicting our annotation for this case:

$$(if\ P\ then\ Q)\quad if\ and\ only\ if\quad ((not\ P)\quad or\quad Q).$$
$$\text{T}_\text{F}\ \ \text{T}\qquad\qquad \text{F}\qquad\qquad\quad \text{F}\qquad\quad\ \ \text{F}\ \ \text{T}\quad\ \text{F}\ \ \text{F}$$

Case: $(if\ P\ then\ Q)$ is false and $((not\ P)\ or\ Q)$ is true

This case corresponds to the annotation

$$(if\ P\ then\ Q)\quad if\ and\ only\ if\quad ((not\ P)\quad or\quad Q).$$
$$\text{F}\qquad\qquad\qquad\ \ \text{F}\qquad\qquad\qquad\qquad\ \ \text{T}$$

Because the left subsentence, $(if\ P\ then\ Q)$, is false, we have that P is true and Q is false. Hence $(not\ P)$ is false, and we have

$$(if\ P\ then\ Q)\quad if\ and\ only\ if\quad ((not\ P)\quad or\quad Q).$$
$$\text{F}\ \ \text{T}\qquad\quad \text{F}\qquad\qquad\quad \text{F}\qquad\quad\ \ \text{F}\ \ \text{T}\quad\ \text{T}\ \ \text{F}$$

However, because $(not\ P)$ and Q are both false, it follows that $((not\ P)\ or\ Q)$ is also false, contradicting the annotation we have assumed for this case:

$$(if\ P\ then\ Q)\quad if\ and\ only\ if\quad ((not\ P)\quad or\quad Q).$$
$$\text{F}\ \ \text{T}\qquad\quad \text{F}\qquad\qquad\quad \text{F}\qquad\quad\ \ \text{F}\ \ \text{T}\quad\ \text{T}_\text{F}\ \ \text{F}$$

We have shown in each case that no interpretation can falsify $\mathcal{F}$; therefore $\mathcal{F}$ is true for any interpretation, that is, $\mathcal{F}$ is valid. ⌐

Although it was not possible to avoid a case split, the above analysis still examined fewer cases than the truth-table analysis of the same sentence.

In the preceding example we were forced into a case split at the very beginning. In the next example, we are forced into a case split at a later stage.

Example

Suppose we want to establish the validity of the sentence

$$\mathcal{G}:\quad \begin{aligned} &if\ (if\ (not\ P)\ then\ Q)\\ &then\ (if\ (not\ Q)\ then\ P)\ and\ (P\ or\ Q). \end{aligned}$$

We assume that $\mathcal{G}$ is false under some interpretation. According to the *if-then* rule, this implies that the antecedent is true and the consequent is false. We annotate $\mathcal{G}$ accordingly:

$$if \; \big(if \; (not \, P) \; then \; Q\big)$$
$$\text{F} \qquad \text{T}$$

$$then \; \big(if \; (not \, Q) \; then \; P\big) \; and \; (P \; or \; Q).$$
$$\text{F}$$

The antecedent $\big(if \, (not\, P) \, then \, Q\big)$ of $\mathcal{G}$ is itself an implication. According to the *if-then* rule, it may be true in two ways: if its antecedent $(not\, P)$ is false or if its consequent Q is true (or both). If we focus on the antecedent, we cannot proceed without a case analysis.

On the other hand, the consequent of $\mathcal{G}$ is a conjunction. According to the *and* rule, it may be false for two reasons: either its first conjunct $\big(if \, (not\, Q) \, then \, P\big)$ is false or its second conjunct $(P \; or \; Q)$ is false (or both). We thus cannot focus on the consequent without a case analysis either.

We arbitrarily decide to focus on the antecedent of $\mathcal{G}$ and consider separately the two possibilities according to whether $(not\, P)$ is false or Q is true. We split the annotation into two cases, one for each possibility.

Case: $(not\, P)$ is false

We have

$$if \; \big(if \; (not \, P) \; then \; Q\big)$$
$$\text{F} \qquad \text{T} \quad \text{F}$$

$$then \; \big(if \; (not \, Q) \; then \; P\big) \; and \; (P \; or \; Q).$$
$$\text{F}$$

By the *not* rule, because $(not\, P)$ is false, P is true. We have

$$if \; \big(if \; (not \, P) \; then \; Q\big)$$
$$\text{F} \qquad \text{T} \quad \text{F} \quad \text{T}$$

$$then \; \big(if \; (not \, Q) \; then \; P\big) \; and \; (P \; or \; Q).$$
$$\text{T} \qquad \text{F} \quad \text{T}$$

Because P is true, we know (by the *if-then* and *or* rules) that the subsentence $\big(if \, (not\, Q) \, then \, P\big)$ and $(P \; or \; Q)$ of the consequent are both true, obtaining

$$if \; \big(if \; (not \, P) \; then \; Q\big)$$
$$\text{F} \qquad \text{T} \quad \text{F} \quad \text{T}$$

$$then \; \big(if \; (not \, Q) \; then \; P\big) \; and \; (P \; or \; Q).$$
$$\text{T} \qquad\qquad\quad \text{T} \quad \text{F} \quad \text{T} \; \text{T}$$

But because both conjuncts of the consequent are true, the consequent itself is true, contradicting the previous annotation of the consequent (under *and*):

$$\textit{if } \Big(\textit{if } (\textit{not } P) \ \textit{then } \ Q\Big)$$
$$\text{F} \qquad \text{T} \qquad \text{F} \ \ \text{T}$$

$$\textit{then } \Big(\textit{if } (\textit{not } Q) \ \textit{then } \ P\Big) \ \textit{and } (P \ \textit{or } \ Q).$$
$$\text{T} \qquad\qquad\qquad \text{T} \quad \text{T}_{\text{F}} \quad \text{T} \ \ \text{T}$$

Now let us consider the second case.

Case: Q is true

We have

$$\textit{if } \Big(\textit{if } (\textit{not } P) \ \textit{then } \ Q\Big)$$
$$\text{F} \qquad \text{T} \qquad\qquad \text{T}$$

$$\textit{then } \Big(\textit{if } (\textit{not } Q) \ \textit{then } \ P\Big) \ \textit{and } (P \ \textit{or } \ Q).$$
$$\text{T} \qquad\qquad\qquad \text{F} \qquad \text{T}$$

Because Q is true, the subsentence $(\textit{not } Q)$ of the consequent is false (by the *not* rule) and the second conjunct $(P \ \textit{or } Q)$ of the consequent is true (by the *or* rule). Because $(\textit{not } Q)$ is false, the first conjunct $\big(\textit{if } (\textit{not } Q) \ \textit{then } P\big)$ of the consequent is true (by the *if-then* rule); we have

$$\textit{if } \Big(\textit{if } (\textit{not } P) \ \textit{then } \ Q\Big)$$
$$\text{F} \qquad \text{T} \qquad\qquad \text{T}$$

$$\textit{then } \Big(\textit{if } (\textit{not } Q) \ \textit{then } \ P\Big) \ \textit{and } (P \ \textit{or } \ Q).$$
$$\text{T} \quad \text{F} \ \ \text{T} \qquad\qquad \text{F} \qquad \text{T} \ \ \text{T}$$

Finally, because both conjuncts of the consequent are true, the consequent itself is true (by the *and* rule), contradicting the previous annotation of the consequent:

$$\textit{if } \Big(\textit{if } (\textit{not } P) \ \textit{then } \ Q\Big)$$
$$\text{F} \qquad \text{T} \qquad\qquad \text{T}$$

$$\textit{then } \Big(\textit{if } (\textit{not } Q) \ \textit{then } \ P\Big) \ \textit{and } (P \ \textit{or } \ Q).$$
$$\text{T} \quad \text{F} \ \ \text{T} \qquad\qquad \text{T}_{\text{F}} \qquad \text{T} \ \ \text{T}$$

We have shown in each case that no interpretation can falsify $\mathcal{G}$. Therefore $\mathcal{G}$ is true under any interpretation, that is, $\mathcal{G}$ is valid. ⌐

Finally, let us see what happens if we attempt to prove by the falsification method a sentence that is not valid.

Example

Consider the sentence

$$\mathcal{H}: \quad \begin{array}{l} \textit{if } (\textit{if } P \;\; \textit{then} \;\; Q) \\ \textit{then } \big(\textit{if } (\textit{not } P) \;\; \textit{then} \;\; (\textit{not } Q)\big), \end{array}$$

and suppose that $\mathcal{H}$ is false under some interpretation. According to the *if-then* rule, this implies that the antecedent is true and the consequent is false; we have

> *if* (*if* P   *then*   Q)
> F   T
>
> *then* (*if* (*not* P)   *then*   (*not* Q)).
>   F

To avoid a case analysis we postpone treatment of the antecedent and focus on the consequent.

Because the consequent, $\big(\textit{if } (\textit{not } P) \textit{ then } (\textit{not } Q)\big)$, is false, we know (by the *if-then* rule) that its antecedent, $(\textit{not } P)$, is true and its consequent, $(\textit{not } Q)$, is false. Hence (by the *not* rule) P is false and Q is true, and we have

> *if* (*if* P   *then*   Q)
> F   T F   T
>
> *then* (*if* (*not* P)   *then*   (*not* Q)).
>   F   T F   F   T

Because P is false and Q is true, the antecedent, $(\textit{if } P \textit{ then } Q)$, is true (by the *if-then* rule), confirming our previous annotation.

We have finished the annotation without deriving a contradiction. In fact, we have found that $\mathcal{H}$ is false under the interpretation that assigns

> P to be false
> Q to be true.

Therefore $\mathcal{H}$ is not valid. ⌐

In **Problems 1.1** and **1.2**, the reader is requested to establish the validity (or nonvalidity) of some propositional-logic sentences.

1.8   VALID SENTENCE SCHEMATA

Up to now we have presented particular propositional-logic sentences and introduced methods of establishing their validity. Although we can establish the validity of a particular sentence, such as

$$P \;\; \textit{or} \;\; (\textit{not } P),$$

we cannot immediately conclude that similar sentences, such as

$$Q \ or \ (not \, Q)$$

and

$$(P \ and \ Q) \ or \ \big(not \, (P \ and \ Q)\big),$$

are also valid.

    We would prefer to be able to discuss such classes of sentences as a unit. For this purpose, we introduce "sentences" with script symbols $\mathcal{F}$, $\mathcal{G}$, $\mathcal{H}$, ..., instead of the ordinary propositional symbols P, Q, R, ... Such script symbols may stand for any sentences of propositional logic. For example, we shall say

$$\mathcal{F} \ or \ (not \, \mathcal{F})$$

is valid, to imply that the sentences

$$P \ or \ (not \, P),$$

$$Q \ or \ (not \, Q),$$

$$(P \ and \ Q) \ or \ \big(not \, (P \ and \ Q)\big),$$

and an infinite class of other sentences are all valid. Informally we shall refer to such a "sentence" as a *sentence schema*; because it contains script symbols it is not itself a legal sentence of propositional logic, but it represents an infinite class of legal sentences. These sentences are called the *instances* of the schema.

    We may check the validity of a sentence schema by any of the methods we have introduced, treating the script symbols the way we treat propositional symbols. For example, to show that the sentence schema

$$\mathcal{F} \ or \ (not \, \mathcal{F})$$

is valid by the falsification method, we assume that the sentence is false under some interpretation and annotate it accordingly:

$$\mathcal{F} \ or \ (not \, \mathcal{F}).$$
$$\;\;\;\text{F}$$

By the *or* rule, both $\mathcal{F}$ and $(not \, \mathcal{F})$ must be false:

$$\mathcal{F} \ or \ (not \, \mathcal{F}).$$
$$\text{F} \;\; \text{F} \quad\; \text{F} \;\; \text{F}$$

By the *not* rule, because the subsentence $(not \, \mathcal{F})$ is false its subsentence $\mathcal{F}$ must then be true:

$$\mathcal{F} \ or \ (not \ \mathcal{F}).$$
$$\text{T}_\text{F} \;\; \text{F} \quad\; \text{F} \;\; \text{T}_\text{F}$$

We have developed contradictory annotations for the two occurrences of $\mathcal{F}$. This shows that the given sentence schema cannot be false under any interpretation; i.e., it is valid. In other words, each instance of the schema is valid.

A CATALOG

We present a catalog of some of the most important valid sentence schemata.

- Basic valid sentences

$$\mathcal{F} \quad \textit{if and only if} \quad \mathcal{F}$$

$\mathcal{F}$ *or* (*not* $\mathcal{F}$)   *if* $\mathcal{F}$ *then* $\mathcal{F}$

if ($\mathcal{F}$ *and* $\mathcal{G}$) *then* $\mathcal{F}$ *if* $\mathcal{F}$ *then* ($\mathcal{F}$ *or* $\mathcal{G}$)

$\mathcal{F}$ *and* ($\mathcal{F}$ *or* $\mathcal{G}$) $\mathcal{F}$ *or* ($\mathcal{F}$ *and* $\mathcal{G}$)
    if and only if   *if and only if*
$\mathcal{F}$ $\mathcal{F}$

(*if* $\mathcal{F}$ *then* $\mathcal{G}$ *else* $\mathcal{G}$)
    if and only if
$\mathcal{G}$

- True-false laws

true   *not false*

$\mathcal{F}$ *or true*   *not* ($\mathcal{F}$ *and false*)

if false then $\mathcal{F}$ *if* $\mathcal{F}$ *then true*

($\mathcal{F}$ *or false*)   ($\mathcal{F}$ *and true*)
    if and only if   *if and only if*
$\mathcal{F}$ $\mathcal{F}$

(*if true then* $\mathcal{F}$)
    if and only if
$\mathcal{F}$

(*if true then F else G*)
  if and only if
F

(*if false then F else G*)
  if and only if
G

(*true if and only if F*)
  if and only if
F

(*false if and only if F*)
  if and only if
(*not F*)

- Commutativity

(*F and G*)
  if and only if
(*G and F*)

(*F or G*)
  if and only if
(*G or F*)

(*F if and only if G*)
  if and only if
(*G if and only if F*)

- Associativity

((*F and G*) *and H*)
  if and only if
(*F and* (*G and H*))

((*F or G*) *or H*)
  if and only if
(*F or* (*G or H*))

$$\left[\begin{array}{l}(\text{\textit{F if and only if G}})\\ \quad \textit{if and only if}\\ \textit{H}\end{array}\right] \textit{ if and only if } \left[\begin{array}{l}\textit{F}\\ \quad \textit{if and only if}\\ (\textit{G if and only if H})\end{array}\right]$$

- Transitivity

$$\textit{if } \left[\begin{array}{l}\textit{if F then G}\\ \textit{and}\\ \textit{if G then H}\end{array}\right]$$
then if F then H

$$\textit{if } \left[\begin{array}{l}\textit{F if and only if G}\\ \textit{and}\\ \textit{G if and only if H}\end{array}\right]$$
then F if and only if H

- Contrapositive laws

(*if F then G*)
  if and only if
(*if* (*not G*) *then* (*not F*))

(*if* (*not F*) *then G*)
  if and only if
(*if* (*not G*) *then F*)

$$(\mathcal{F} \ \textit{if and only if} \ \mathcal{G})$$
$$\textit{if and only if}$$
$$((not \ \mathcal{F}) \ \textit{if and only if} \ (not \ \mathcal{G}))$$

- Distributivity

$$(\mathcal{F} \ \textit{and} \ (\mathcal{G} \ \textit{or} \ \mathcal{H}))$$
$$\textit{if and only if}$$
$$((\mathcal{F} \ \textit{and} \ \mathcal{G}) \ \textit{or} \ (\mathcal{F} \ \textit{and} \ \mathcal{H}))$$

$$(\mathcal{F} \ \textit{or} \ (\mathcal{G} \ \textit{and} \ \mathcal{H}))$$
$$\textit{if and only if}$$
$$((\mathcal{F} \ \textit{or} \ \mathcal{G}) \ \textit{and} \ (\mathcal{F} \ \textit{or} \ \mathcal{H}))$$

$$(\textit{if} \ (\mathcal{F} \ \textit{or} \ \mathcal{G}) \ \textit{then} \ \mathcal{H})$$
$$\textit{if and only if}$$
$$\begin{bmatrix} (\textit{if} \ \mathcal{F} \ \textit{then} \ \mathcal{H}) \\ \textit{and} \\ (\textit{if} \ \mathcal{G} \ \textit{then} \ \mathcal{H}) \end{bmatrix}$$

$$(\textit{if} \ \mathcal{F} \ \textit{then} \ (\mathcal{G} \ \textit{or} \ \mathcal{H}))$$
$$\textit{if and only if}$$
$$\begin{bmatrix} (\textit{if} \ \mathcal{F} \ \textit{then} \ \mathcal{G}) \\ \textit{or} \\ (\textit{if} \ \mathcal{F} \ \textit{then} \ \mathcal{H}) \end{bmatrix}$$

$$(\textit{if} \ (\mathcal{F} \ \textit{and} \ \mathcal{G}) \ \textit{then} \ \mathcal{H})$$
$$\textit{if and only if}$$
$$\begin{bmatrix} (\textit{if} \ \mathcal{F} \ \textit{then} \ \mathcal{H}) \\ \textit{or} \\ (\textit{if} \ \mathcal{G} \ \textit{then} \ \mathcal{H}) \end{bmatrix}$$

$$(\textit{if} \ \mathcal{F} \ \textit{then} \ (\mathcal{G} \ \textit{and} \ \mathcal{H}))$$
$$\textit{if and only if}$$
$$\begin{bmatrix} (\textit{if} \ \mathcal{F} \ \textit{then} \ \mathcal{G}) \\ \textit{and} \\ (\textit{if} \ \mathcal{F} \ \textit{then} \ \mathcal{H}) \end{bmatrix}$$

$$(\textit{if} \ (\mathcal{F} \ \textit{and} \ \mathcal{G}) \ \textit{then} \ \mathcal{H})$$
$$\textit{if and only if}$$
$$(\textit{if} \ \mathcal{F} \ \textit{then} \ (\textit{if} \ \mathcal{G} \ \textit{then} \ \mathcal{H}))$$

- Laws of negation

$$not \ (not \ \mathcal{F})$$
$$\textit{if and only if}$$
$$\mathcal{F}$$

$$not \ (\mathcal{F} \ \textit{and} \ \mathcal{G})$$
$$\textit{if and only if}$$
$$((not \ \mathcal{F}) \ \textit{or} \ (not \ \mathcal{G}))$$

$$not \ (\mathcal{F} \ \textit{or} \ \mathcal{G})$$
$$\textit{if and only if}$$
$$((not \ \mathcal{F}) \ \textit{and} \ (not \ \mathcal{G}))$$

$$not \ (\textit{if} \ \mathcal{F} \ \textit{then} \ \mathcal{G})$$
$$\textit{if and only if}$$
$$(\mathcal{F} \ \textit{and} \ (not \ \mathcal{G}))$$

$$not \ (\textit{if} \ \mathcal{F} \ \textit{then} \ \mathcal{G} \ \textit{else} \ \mathcal{H})$$
$$\textit{if and only if}$$
$$(\textit{if} \ \mathcal{F} \ \textit{then} \ (not \ \mathcal{G}) \ \textit{else} \ (not \ \mathcal{H}))$$

$$not \ (\mathcal{F} \ \textit{if and only if} \ \mathcal{G})$$
$$\textit{if and only if}$$
$$(\mathcal{F} \ \textit{if and only if} \ (not \ \mathcal{G}))$$

● Reduction laws

$$(if \; \mathcal{F} \; then \; \mathcal{G})$$
$$if \; and \; only \; if$$
$$((not \; \mathcal{F}) \; or \; \mathcal{G})$$

$$(if \; \mathcal{F} \; then \; \mathcal{G} \; else \; \mathcal{H})$$
$$if \; and \; only \; if$$
$$\begin{bmatrix} (\mathcal{F} \; and \; \mathcal{G}) \\ or \\ ((not \; \mathcal{F}) \; and \; \mathcal{H}) \end{bmatrix}$$

$$(if \; \mathcal{F} \; then \; \mathcal{G} \cdot else \; \mathcal{H})$$
$$if \; and \; only \; if$$
$$\begin{bmatrix} (if \; \mathcal{F} \; then \; \mathcal{G}) \\ and \\ (if \; (not \; \mathcal{F}) \; then \; \mathcal{H}) \end{bmatrix}$$

$$(\mathcal{F} \; if \; and \; only \; if \; \mathcal{G})$$
$$if \; and \; only \; if$$
$$\begin{bmatrix} (\mathcal{F} \; and \; \mathcal{G}) \\ or \\ ((not \; \mathcal{F}) \; and \; (not \; \mathcal{G})) \end{bmatrix}$$

$$(\mathcal{F} \; if \; and \; only \; if \; \mathcal{G})$$
$$if \; and \; only \; if$$
$$\begin{bmatrix} (if \; \mathcal{F} \; then \; \mathcal{G}) \\ and \\ (if \; \mathcal{G} \; then \; \mathcal{F}) \end{bmatrix}$$

Note that many of the valid sentences above are of form

$$\mathcal{A} \; if \; and \; only \; if \; \mathcal{B}.$$

By an earlier remark this establishes that

$$\mathcal{A} \quad and \quad \mathcal{B}$$

are equivalent. Thus since the sentence schema

$$not \, (not \; \mathcal{F}) \; if \; and \; only \; if \; \mathcal{F},$$

which is one of the laws of negation, is valid, we know that the sentence schemata

$$not \, (not \; \mathcal{F}) \qquad and \qquad \mathcal{F}$$

are equivalent. In other words, any sentence of form $\big(not \, (not \; \mathcal{F})\big)$ is equivalent to the corresponding sentence of form $\mathcal{F}$. In particular, the sentences

$$not \, \big(not \, (P \; or \; Q)\big) \qquad and \qquad P \; or \; Q$$

are equivalent.

We shall say that the sentence $\big(if \, (not \; \mathcal{G}) \; then \, (not \; \mathcal{F})\big)$ is the *contrapositive* of the implication $(if \; \mathcal{F} \; then \; \mathcal{G})$. Thus the sentence

$$(if \; \mathcal{F} \; then \; \mathcal{G})$$
$$if \; and \; only \; if$$
$$(if \, (not \; \mathcal{G}) \; then \, (not \; \mathcal{F}))$$

in the catalog may be rephrased as saying that an implication is equivalent to its contrapositive.

In **Problem 1.3** the reader is asked to show that each of the connectives can be paraphrased in terms of the conditional connective *if-then-else* and the truth symbols *true* and *false*.

MULTIPLE CONJUNCTION AND DISJUNCTION

The reader may note that, because of the associative law,

$$((\mathcal{F} \ and \ \mathcal{G}) \ and \ \mathcal{H})$$
$$if \ and \ only \ if$$
$$(\mathcal{F} \ and \ (\mathcal{G} \ and \ \mathcal{H})),$$

sentences such as

$$((P \ and \ Q) \ and \ R) \ and \ S,$$

$$P \ and \ (Q \ and \ (R \ and \ S)),$$

$$P \ and \ ((Q \ and \ R) \ and \ S),$$

and so forth are equivalent. For this reason, we will sometimes write any of these sentences without parentheses, as

$$P \ and \ Q \ and \ R \ and \ S.$$

To be definite, we regard the multiple conjunction

$$\mathcal{F}_1 \ and \ \mathcal{F}_2 \ and \ \mathcal{F}_3 \ and \ \dots \ and \ \mathcal{F}_n$$

as an abbreviation for

$$((\dots((\mathcal{F}_1 \ and \ \mathcal{F}_2) \ and \ \mathcal{F}_3) \ and \ \dots) \ and \ \mathcal{F}_n).$$

Similarly, the multiple disjunction

$$\mathcal{F}_1 \ or \ \mathcal{F}_2 \ or \ \mathcal{F}_3 \ or \dots or \ \mathcal{F}_n$$

is an abbreviation for

$$((\dots((\mathcal{F}_1 \ or \ \mathcal{F}_2) \ or \ \mathcal{F}_3) \ or \ \dots) \ or \ \mathcal{F}_n).$$

We can derive the following semantic rules for these multiple connectives:

- A multiple conjunction

$$\mathcal{F}_1 \ and \ \mathcal{F}_2 \ and \ \dots \ and \ \mathcal{F}_n$$

is true precisely when each of its conjuncts $\mathcal{F}_1$, $\mathcal{F}_2$, ..., $\mathcal{F}_n$ is true.

- A multiple disjunction

$$\mathcal{F}_1 \ \ or \ \ \mathcal{F}_2 \ \ or \ \ \ldots \ \ or \ \ \mathcal{F}_n$$

is true precisely when at least one of its disjuncts $\mathcal{F}_1$, $\mathcal{F}_2$, ..., $\mathcal{F}_n$ is true.

Problems 1.4, **1.5**, and **1.6** present some puzzles to be solved with the help of propositional-logic techniques for establishing validity.

1.9   SUBSTITUTION

Let us introduce some notation for the operation of replacing subsentences of a given sentence with other subsentences. We shall use this notation throughout the book. We distinguish between "total substitution," in which all occurrences of a subsentence are replaced, and "partial substitution," in which zero, one, or more, but not necessarily all, occurrences of the subsentence are replaced.

TOTAL SUBSTITUTION

The operation ◄ allows us to replace all occurrences of a subsentence of a given sentence with another subsentence.

Definition (total substitution)

If $\mathcal{F}$, $\mathcal{G}$, and $\mathcal{H}$ are sentences, we denote by

$$\mathcal{F} \blacktriangleleft \{\mathcal{G} \leftarrow \mathcal{H}\}$$

the sentence obtained by replacing every occurrence of $\mathcal{G}$ in $\mathcal{F}$ with $\mathcal{H}$. ◢

For example,

$$\begin{bmatrix} P \ \ and \\ (Q \ \ or \ \ P) \end{bmatrix} \blacktriangleleft \ \{P \leftarrow (if \ R \ then \ S)\}$$

is

$$(if \ R \ then \ S) \ and$$
$$(Q \ or \ (if \ R \ then \ S)).$$

Note that we can make substitutions for entire subsentences, not only for propositional symbols. Thus

$$\begin{bmatrix} if\ P \\ then\ (Q\ and\ R) \end{bmatrix} \blacktriangleleft \{(Q\ and\ R) \leftarrow true\}$$

is

$$if\ P$$
$$then\ true.$$

The substitution is performed in one stage. Thus

$$[P\ and\ R] \blacktriangleleft \{P \leftarrow (P\ and\ Q)\}$$

is

$$(P\ and\ Q)\ and\ R.$$

We do not then go on to replace the newly introduced occurrence of P with $(P\ and\ Q)$.

Note also that if the subsentence to be replaced does not occur in the sentence, the substitution operation has no effect. Thus

$$[P\ and\ Q] \blacktriangleleft \{R \leftarrow S\}$$

is

$$P\ and\ Q.$$

Remark (multiple conjunction and disjunction)

In applying the substitution operator, we must recall that the multiple conjunction

$$\mathcal{F}_1\ and\ \mathcal{F}_2\ and\ \dots\ and\ \mathcal{F}_n$$

is an abbreviation for the sentence

$$(\dots(\mathcal{F}_1\ and\ \mathcal{F}_2)\ and\ \dots\ and\ \mathcal{F}_n).$$

Therefore

$$[P\ and\ Q\ and\ R] \blacktriangleleft \{(P\ and\ Q) \leftarrow S\},$$

that is,

$$[(P\ and\ Q)\ and\ R] \blacktriangleleft \{(P\ and\ Q) \leftarrow S\},$$

denotes the sentence

$$S \ and \ R.$$

But

$$[P \ and \ Q \ and \ R] \blacktriangleleft \{(Q \ and \ R) \leftarrow S\},$$

that is,

$$[(P \ and \ Q) \ and \ R] \blacktriangleleft \{(Q \ and \ R) \leftarrow S\},$$

denotes the sentence

$$(P \ and \ Q) \ and \ R$$

itself.

A similar remark applies to the multiple disjunction

$$\mathcal{F}_1 \ or \ \mathcal{F}_2 \ or \ \ldots \ or \ \mathcal{F}_n. \quad \lrcorner$$

The substitution operation ◀ has the following simple properties:

$$\mathcal{F} \blacktriangleleft \{\mathcal{F} \leftarrow \mathcal{H}\} \quad \text{is} \quad \mathcal{H}$$

$$\mathcal{F} \blacktriangleleft \{\mathcal{G} \leftarrow \mathcal{H}\} \quad \text{is} \quad \mathcal{F} \quad \text{if} \quad \mathcal{G} \ \text{does not occur in} \ \mathcal{F}.$$

The substitution operator ◀ can be distributed over the components of a sentence. More precisely, we have

$$(not \ \mathcal{F}) \blacktriangleleft \{\mathcal{G} \leftarrow \mathcal{H}\} \quad \text{is} \quad not \ (\mathcal{F} \blacktriangleleft \{\mathcal{G} \leftarrow \mathcal{H}\})$$

if $(not \ \mathcal{F})$ is distinct from $\mathcal{G}$;

$$(\mathcal{F}_1 \ and \ \mathcal{F}_2) \blacktriangleleft \{\mathcal{G} \leftarrow \mathcal{H}\} \quad \text{is} \quad (\mathcal{F}_1 \blacktriangleleft \{\mathcal{G} \leftarrow \mathcal{H}\}) \ and \ (\mathcal{F}_2 \blacktriangleleft \{\mathcal{G} \leftarrow \mathcal{H}\})$$

if $(\mathcal{F}_1 \ and \ \mathcal{F}_2)$ is distinct from $\mathcal{G}$; and so on for the other connectives.

PARTIAL SUBSTITUTION

The analogous operation ◁ allows us to replace some, but not necessarily all, occurrences of a subsentence of a given sentence with another sentence.

Definition (partial substitution)

If $\mathcal{F}$, $\mathcal{G}$, and $\mathcal{H}$ are sentences, we denote by

$$\mathcal{F} \blacktriangleleft \{\mathcal{G} \leftarrow \mathcal{H}\}$$

any one of the sentences obtained by replacing zero, one, or more occurrences of $\mathcal{G}$ in $\mathcal{F}$ with $\mathcal{H}$. ◢

Thus in contrast to the total substitution operator

$$\mathcal{F} \blacktriangleleft \{\mathcal{G} \leftarrow \mathcal{H}\},$$

the partial substitution operator $\mathcal{F} \blacktriangleleft \{\mathcal{G} \leftarrow \mathcal{H}\}$ does not necessarily denote a particular sentence, but may denote any of several sentences.

For example, the partial substitution

$$[P \ \ or \ \ P] \blacktriangleleft \{P \leftarrow Q\}$$

may denote any of the following sentences:

$P \ \ or \ \ P$	(replacing zero occurrences of P);
$Q \ \ or \ \ P$	(replacing the first occurrence of P);
$P \ \ or \ \ Q$	(replacing the second occurrence of P);
$Q \ \ or \ \ Q$	(replacing both occurrences of P).

Thus, the partial substitution above could represent any of four sentences. If we wish to specify further which occurrences are to be replaced, we must do so in words.

Remark

For any sentences $\mathcal{F}$, $\mathcal{G}$, and $\mathcal{H}$, the sentence denoted by the total substitution

$$\mathcal{F} \blacktriangleleft \{\mathcal{G} \leftarrow \mathcal{H}\}$$

is one of the sentences that the partial substitution

$$\mathcal{F} \blacktriangleleft \{\mathcal{G} \leftarrow \mathcal{H}\}$$

may denote. This is because the sentence obtained by replacing all occurrences of $\mathcal{G}$ in $\mathcal{F}$ with $\mathcal{H}$ is one of the sentences obtained by replacing zero, one, or more occurrences of $\mathcal{G}$ in $\mathcal{F}$ with $\mathcal{H}$. ◢

The partial substitution operator ◁ is *invertible* in the sense that one of the possible results of the partial substitution

$$(\mathcal{F} \triangleleft \{\mathcal{G} \leftarrow \mathcal{H}\}) \triangleleft \{\mathcal{H} \leftarrow \mathcal{G}\}$$

is $\mathcal{F}$ itself. For example,

$$P \ \ or \ \ Q$$

is one of the possible results of

$$[[P \ \ or \ \ Q] \triangleleft \{P \leftarrow Q\}] \triangleleft \{Q \leftarrow P\}.$$

The total substitution operator ◂, on the other hand, is not invertible. For example,

$$[[P \ \ or \ \ Q] \blacktriangleleft \{P \leftarrow Q\}] \blacktriangleleft \{Q \leftarrow P\}$$

is

$$P \ \ or \ \ P,$$

not $(P \ or \ Q)$.

The two operators together do have the property that one of the possible results of the substitution

$$(\mathcal{F} \blacktriangleleft \{\mathcal{G} \leftarrow \mathcal{H}\}) \triangleleft \{\mathcal{H} \leftarrow \mathcal{G}\}$$

is $\mathcal{F}$ itself. For example, one of the possible results of

$$[[P \ \ or \ \ Q] \blacktriangleleft \{P \leftarrow Q\}] \triangleleft \{Q \leftarrow P\}$$

is

$$P \ \ or \ \ Q.$$

CONCISE NOTATION

Sometimes we find it convenient to use the following more concise substitution notation:

- *Total substitution*

  If

  $$\mathcal{F}[\mathcal{G}]$$

is a sentence (which may or may not contain an occurrence of a subsentence $\mathcal{G}$), then

$$\mathcal{F}[\mathcal{H}]$$

denotes the sentence obtained by replacing every occurrence of $\mathcal{G}$ in $\mathcal{F}[\mathcal{G}]$ with the sentence $\mathcal{H}$.

For example, if $\mathcal{F}[P]$ is

> P *and*
> $(Q$ *or* $P)$,

then $\mathcal{F}[if\ R\ then\ S]$ denotes the sentence

> $(if\ R\ then\ S)$ *and*
> $Q\ or\ (if\ R\ then\ S)$.

- *Partial substitution*

  If

  $$\mathcal{F}\langle\mathcal{G}\rangle$$

  is a sentence (which may or may not contain an occurrence of a subsentence $\mathcal{G}$), then

  $$\mathcal{F}\langle\mathcal{H}\rangle$$

  denotes any of the sentences obtained by replacing zero, one, or more occurrences of $\mathcal{G}$ in $\mathcal{F}\langle\mathcal{G}\rangle$ with the sentence $\mathcal{H}$.

For example, if $\mathcal{F}\langle P\rangle$ is

> $(P\ or\ Q)$,

then $\mathcal{F}\langle Q\rangle$ denotes either of the sentences

> $(P\ or\ Q)$ or $(Q\ or\ Q)$.

MULTIPLE SUBSTITUTION

The above notions may be extended to allow us to replace more than one subsentence of a given sentence at the same time.

Definition (multiple substitution)

Suppose $\mathcal{F}$, $\mathcal{G}_1$, ..., $\mathcal{G}_n$, and $\mathcal{H}_1$, ..., $\mathcal{H}_n$ are sentences, where $\mathcal{G}_1$, ..., $\mathcal{G}_n$ are distinct.

- *Total substitution*

  We denote by

  $$\mathcal{F} \blacktriangleleft \begin{Bmatrix} \mathcal{G}_1 \leftarrow \mathcal{H}_1 \\ \vdots \\ \mathcal{G}_n \leftarrow \mathcal{H}_n \end{Bmatrix}$$

  the sentence obtained by replacing simultaneously every occurrence of each subsentence $\mathcal{G}_i$ in $\mathcal{F}$ with the corresponding sentence $\mathcal{H}_i$.

- *Partial substitution*

  We denote by

  $$\mathcal{F} \triangleleft \begin{Bmatrix} \mathcal{G}_1 \leftarrow \mathcal{H}_1 \\ \vdots \\ \mathcal{G}_n \leftarrow \mathcal{H}_n \end{Bmatrix}$$

  any of the sentences obtained by replacing simultaneously zero, one, or more occurrences of some of the subsentences $\mathcal{G}_i$ in $\mathcal{F}$ with the corresponding sentence $\mathcal{H}_i$. ⌙

Example

The total substitution

$$\begin{bmatrix} if\ P \\ then\ if\ (Q\ or\ P) \\ then\ (Q\ or\ R) \end{bmatrix} \blacktriangleleft \begin{Bmatrix} P \leftarrow R \\ (Q\ or\ R) \leftarrow (not\ R) \end{Bmatrix}$$

denotes the sentence

$$if\ R \\ then\ if\ (Q\ or\ R) \\ then\ (not\ R).$$

The two occurrences of P were replaced by R and the occurrence of $(Q\ or\ R)$ is replaced by $(not\ R)$.

The partial substitution

$$\begin{bmatrix} if\ P \\ then\ if\ (Q\ or\ P) \\ \quad then\ (Q\ or\ R) \end{bmatrix} \blacktriangleleft \begin{Bmatrix} P \leftarrow R, \\ (Q\ or\ R) \leftarrow (not\ R) \end{Bmatrix}$$

may denote any of several sentences, including

> *if R*
> *then if (Q or P)*   (replacing the first occurrence of P)
>   *then (Q or R)*

> *if P*
> *then if (Q or P)*   (replacing the occurrence of $(Q\ or\ R)$)
>   *then (not R)*

> *if R*
> *then if (Q or P)*   (replacing the first occurrence of P
>   *then (not R)*   and the occurrence of $(Q\ or\ R)$)

> *if R*
> *then if (Q or R)*   (replacing both the occurrence of P
>   *then (not R)*   and the occurrence of $(Q\ or\ R)$).

Altogether, the partial substitution may denote any of eight sentences.   ⌐

Note that the replacements of a multiple substitution are performed simultaneously in a single stage. Thus, the result of the total substitution

$$P \blacktriangleleft \begin{Bmatrix} P \leftarrow Q \\ Q \leftarrow R \end{Bmatrix}$$

is the sentence

> Q

rather than the sentence R. Though the occurrence of P was replaced by Q, the newly introduced occurrence of Q was not subsequently replaced by R. In contrast, the result of the repeated total substitution

$$[P \blacktriangleleft \{P \leftarrow Q\}] \blacktriangleleft \{Q \leftarrow R\}$$

is

> R.

The reader may wonder what sentence is denoted by the total substitution

$$[P\ or\ Q] \blacktriangleleft \begin{Bmatrix} P \leftarrow R \\ (P\ or\ Q) \leftarrow S \end{Bmatrix}$$

Here, the subsentence P occurs in the subsentence $(P \text{ or } Q)$, and both subsentences are to be replaced. By convention, we assume that the outermost subsentence, in this case $(P \text{ or } Q)$, is the one to be replaced. Thus, the result of the above total substitution is the sentence

$$S$$

rather than the sentence $(R \text{ or } Q)$.

Remark (multiple conjunction and disjunction)

In applying the substitution operators, we again recall that a multiple conjunction

$$\mathcal{F}_1 \text{ and } \mathcal{F}_2 \text{ and } \ldots \text{ and } \mathcal{F}_n$$

is an abbreviation for the sentence

$$(\ldots(\mathcal{F}_1 \text{ and } \mathcal{F}_2) \text{ and } \ldots \text{ and } \mathcal{F}_n).$$

Therefore

$$[P \text{ and } Q \text{ and } R] \blacktriangleleft \left\{ \begin{array}{l} (P \text{ and } Q) \leftarrow S \\ (Q \text{ and } R) \leftarrow S \end{array} \right\},$$

that is,

$$[(P \text{ and } Q) \text{ and } R] \blacktriangleleft \left\{ \begin{array}{l} (P \text{ and } Q) \leftarrow S \\ (Q \text{ and } R) \leftarrow S \end{array} \right\},$$

denotes the sentence

$$S \text{ and } R,$$

not the sentence $(P \text{ and } S)$.

A similar convention applies to multiple disjunction.   ⌟

We can also extend the concise substitution notation to multiple substitution:

- *Total substitution*

    If

    $$\mathcal{F}[\mathcal{G}_1, \ldots, \mathcal{G}_n]$$

    is a sentence, then

    $$\mathcal{F}[\mathcal{H}_1, \ldots, \mathcal{H}_n]$$

denotes the sentence obtained by replacing every occurrence of each sentence $\mathcal{G}_i$ in $\mathcal{F}[\mathcal{G}_1, \ldots, \mathcal{G}_n]$ with the corresponding sentence $\mathcal{H}_i$.

- *Partial substitution*

    If

    $$\mathcal{F}\langle \mathcal{G}_1, \ldots, \mathcal{G}_n \rangle$$

    is a sentence, then

    $$\mathcal{F}\langle \mathcal{H}_1, \ldots, \mathcal{H}_n \rangle$$

    denotes any of the sentences obtained by replacing zero, one, or more occurrences of some of the subsentences $\mathcal{G}_i$ in $\mathcal{F}\langle \mathcal{G}_1, \ldots, \mathcal{G}_n \rangle$ with the corresponding sentence $\mathcal{H}_i$.

Example

If $\mathcal{F}[P, (Q \text{ } or \text{ } R)]$ is

> *if P*
> *then if (Q or P)*
> *then (Q or R),*

then $\mathcal{F}[R, (not \text{ } R)]$ denotes the sentence

> *if R*
> *then if (Q or R)*
> *then (not R).*

On the other hand, if $\mathcal{F}\langle P, (Q \text{ } or \text{ } R) \rangle$ is

> *if P*
> *then if (Q or P)*
> *then (Q or R),*

then $\mathcal{F}\langle R, (not \text{ } R) \rangle$ may denote any of the eight sentences mentioned earlier. ⌙

The reader is requested to apply the total and partial substitution operator in **Problem 1.7**.

1.10   EXTENDED INTERPRETATION

When we are given an interpretation, we sometimes need to extend it to assign truth values to particular propositional symbols. We introduce notation for this here.

Definition (extended interpretation)

If I is an interpretation, P an arbitrary propositional symbol, and τ a truth value (either true or false), then the *extended interpretation*

$$\langle P \leftarrow \tau \rangle \circ I$$

is the interpretation that assigns the value τ to P and that assigns, to all propositional symbols other than P, the same truth values that I assigns them.   ◢

In other words, I and $\langle P \leftarrow \tau \rangle \circ I$ assign the same truth value to any propositional symbol other than P.

Note that, in the above definition, I may already assign a truth value to P. In this case, this truth value is superseded in the extended interpretation by the new assignment $P \leftarrow \tau$. Clearly, if I assigns no truth value to some propositional symbol other than P, neither does the extended interpretation.

Example

Consider the interpretation I under which

> Q is true
> R is false.

Then the extended interpretation

$$\langle P \leftarrow \text{false} \rangle \circ I$$

is the interpretation under which

> P is false
> Q is true
> R is false.

Furthermore, the extended interpretation

$$\langle Q \leftarrow \text{false} \rangle \circ I$$

is the interpretation under which

> Q is false
> R is false.

The original assignment for Q under I has been superseded.   ◢

We may extend an interpretation several times in succession. For an interpretation I, propositional symbols $P_1, P_2, \ldots, P_n$, and truth values $\tau_1, \tau_2, \ldots, \tau_n$, the notation

$$\langle P_1 \leftarrow \tau_1 \rangle \circ \langle P_2 \leftarrow \tau_2 \rangle \circ \ldots \circ \langle P_n \leftarrow \tau_n \rangle \circ I$$

is an abbreviation for the *multiply extended interpretation*

$$\langle P_1 \leftarrow \tau_1 \rangle \circ (\langle P_2 \leftarrow \tau_2 \rangle \circ \ldots \circ (\langle P_n \leftarrow \tau_n \rangle \circ I)...).$$

Remark

Because P_1 and P_2 are distinct, the multiply extended interpretations

$$\langle P_1 \leftarrow \tau_1 \rangle \circ \langle P_2 \leftarrow \tau_2 \rangle \circ I \quad \text{and} \quad \langle P_2 \leftarrow \tau_2 \rangle \circ \langle P_1 \leftarrow \tau_1 \rangle \circ I$$

are identical for any truth values τ_1 and τ_2. On the other hand, if τ_1 and τ_2 are distinct truth values, the multiply extended interpretations

$$\langle P \leftarrow \tau_1 \rangle \circ \langle P \leftarrow \tau_2 \rangle \circ I \quad \text{and} \quad \langle P \leftarrow \tau_2 \rangle \circ \langle P \leftarrow \tau_1 \rangle \circ I$$

are different; the former is identical to

$$\langle P \leftarrow \tau_1 \rangle \circ I,$$

while the latter is identical to

$$\langle P \leftarrow \tau_2 \rangle \circ I.$$

Example

Consider again the interpretation I under which

> Q is true
> R is false.

Then

$$\langle P \leftarrow \text{true} \rangle \circ \langle Q \leftarrow \text{false} \rangle \circ \langle P \leftarrow \text{false} \rangle \circ I$$

is the interpretation under which

> P is true
> Q is false
> R is false.

Here, conflicting assignments to P appear in the multiply extended interpretation, but the leftmost assignment, $P \leftarrow$ true, supersedes the rightmost assignment, $P \leftarrow$ false. Also, the assignment $Q \leftarrow$ false in the extended interpretation supersedes the original assignment to Q under I. ⌐

AGREEMENT

We now introduce a relationship between two interpretations.

Definition (agreement)

Two interpretations I and J *agree on* a sentence $\mathcal{F}$ if either

the value of $\mathcal{F}$ under I is the same as the value of $\mathcal{F}$ under J
    or
neither I nor J is an interpretation for $\mathcal{F}$. ⌐

Example

Consider the two interpretations I and J under which

$$I : \begin{array}{l} P \text{ is true} \\ Q \text{ is false} \end{array} \quad \text{and} \quad J : \begin{array}{l} P \text{ is false} \\ Q \text{ is false} \end{array}$$

Then I and J agree on the sentence

Q,

because the value of Q is false under each interpretation. Also, I and J agree on the sentence

R,

because neither is an interpretation for R. On the other hand, I and J do not agree on the sentence

P,

because P is true under I but false under J.

Furthermore, I and J agree on the sentence

$(P \ and \ Q)$,

because the sentence is false under each interpretation. Also, I and J agree on the sentence

$$((P \text{ or } Q) \text{ and } R),$$

because neither is an interpretation for the sentence.

On the other hand, I and J do not agree on the sentence

$$(P \text{ or } Q),$$

because the sentence is true under I but false under J. ⌐

We can now establish a basic property of the agreement relationship.

Proposition (agreement)

> If two interpretations for a sentence $\mathcal{F}$
> agree on each propositional symbol of $\mathcal{F}$,
> then they agree on $\mathcal{F}$ itself. ⌐

The proposition is intuitively straightforward: We apply the same semantic rules in determining the truth value of $\mathcal{F}$ under each interpretation, yielding the same truth value at each stage.

Example

Consider the sentence

$$\mathcal{F}: \quad P \text{ or } Q$$

and the interpretations

$$
\begin{array}{lll}
 & P \text{ is true} & \quad\quad P \text{ is true} \\
I: & Q \text{ is false} \quad \text{and} \quad J: & Q \text{ is false} \\
 & R \text{ is true} & \quad\quad R \text{ is false.}
\end{array}
$$

Because I and J agree on the propositional symbols P and Q of $\mathcal{F}$, we can infer by the *agreement* proposition that they agree on $\mathcal{F}$ itself. ⌐

The following observation relates the notion of agreement with that of extended interpretation:

Remark

Suppose $\mathcal{F}$ is a sentence and $\mathcal{I}$ is an interpretation for $\mathcal{F}$. Let $P_1, P_2, \ldots, P_n$ be propositional symbols that do not occur in $\mathcal{F}$, and $\tau_1, \tau_2, \ldots, \tau_n$ be arbitrary truth values. Then

the multiply extended interpretation

$$\mathcal{J}: \quad \langle P_1 \leftarrow \tau_1 \rangle \circ \langle P_2 \leftarrow \tau_2 \rangle \circ \ldots \circ \langle P_n \leftarrow \tau_n \rangle \circ \mathcal{I}$$

and $\mathcal{I}$ itself agree on $\mathcal{F}$.

For consider an arbitrary propositional symbol P in $\mathcal{F}$. We know that P is distinct from any of the symbols $P_1, P_2, \ldots,$ and P_n. Therefore (by the definition of extended interpretation) $\mathcal{I}$ and $\mathcal{J}$ agree on P. Hence (by the above *agreement* proposition) $\mathcal{I}$ and $\mathcal{J}$ also agree on $\mathcal{F}$. ◣

1.11   EQUIVALENCE

We have defined two sentences $\mathcal{F}$ and $\mathcal{G}$ to be equivalent if they have the same truth value under any interpretation for $\mathcal{F}$ and $\mathcal{G}$. In this section, we discuss some of the properties of the equivalence relationship.

IMPLICATION AND VALIDITY

We have already established some connection between the notions of implication and validity; in particular, we have shown (in an earlier remark) that, for any two sentences $\mathcal{F}$ and $\mathcal{G}$,

> $\mathcal{F}$ implies $\mathcal{G}$
>   precisely when
> (*if* $\mathcal{F}$ *then* $\mathcal{G}$) is valid.

In this section we establish a further connection between these two notions.

Proposition (implication and validity)

For any two sentences $\mathcal{F}$ and $\mathcal{G}$,

> if $\mathcal{F}$ implies $\mathcal{G}$
> then if $\mathcal{F}$ is valid
>   then $\mathcal{G}$ is valid. ◣

Proof

Suppose

$\mathcal{F}$ implies $\mathcal{G}$

and

$\mathcal{F}$ is valid;

we would like to show that then

$\mathcal{G}$ is valid.

To show that $\mathcal{G}$ is valid, it suffices to show that, for an arbitrary interpretation I for $\mathcal{G}$,

$\mathcal{G}$ is true under I.

We know that $\mathcal{F}$ is true under any interpretation for $\mathcal{F}$, but if some propositional symbols occur in $\mathcal{F}$ and not in $\mathcal{G}$, then I will not necessarily be an interpretation for $\mathcal{F}$. We extend I to form an interpretation for $\mathcal{F}$ as follows:

Suppose P_1, P_2, ..., P_n are all the propositional symbols that occur in $\mathcal{F}$ but not in $\mathcal{G}$, and let τ_1, τ_2, ..., τ_n be arbitrary truth symbols, either true or false. Then the extended interpretation

$$J: \quad \langle P_1 \leftarrow \tau_1 \rangle \circ \langle P_2 \leftarrow \tau_2 \rangle \circ \ldots \circ \langle P_n \leftarrow \tau_n \rangle \circ I$$

is an interpretation for $\mathcal{F}$ as well as for $\mathcal{G}$.

Because we have supposed that $\mathcal{F}$ is valid, we know that

$\mathcal{F}$ is true under J.

Because we have supposed that $\mathcal{F}$ implies $\mathcal{G}$, we can infer (by the definition) that

$\mathcal{G}$ is true under J.

Because P_1, P_2, ..., P_n do not occur in $\mathcal{G}$, we know (by the definition of J) that

I and J agree on the propositional symbols of $\mathcal{G}$.

Therefore (by the *agreement* proposition)

I and J agree on $\mathcal{G}$;

that is, $\mathcal{G}$ has the same truth value under I and J. Since we have established that $\mathcal{G}$ is true under J, we can conclude that

$\mathcal{G}$ is true under I,

as we wanted to show. ⌐

EQUIVALENCE AND VALIDITY

We now show a similar property of the equivalence relation. We have already
shown in earlier remarks that

> two sentences $\mathcal{F}$ and $\mathcal{G}$ are equivalent
>   precisely when
> the sentence ($\mathcal{F}$ *if and only if* $\mathcal{G}$) is valid

and

> two sentences $\mathcal{F}$ and $\mathcal{G}$ are equivalent
>   precisely when
> $\mathcal{F}$ implies $\mathcal{G}$ and $\mathcal{G}$ implies $\mathcal{F}$.

We also have the following result:

Proposition (equivalence and validity)

> For any two sentences $\mathcal{F}$ and $\mathcal{G}$,
>
> > if $\mathcal{F}$ and $\mathcal{G}$ are equivalent,
> > then $\mathcal{F}$ is valid
> >   precisely when
> > $\mathcal{G}$ is valid. ⌐

Proof

> Suppose that
>
> > $\mathcal{F}$ and $\mathcal{G}$ are equivalent;

then

> $\mathcal{F}$ implies $\mathcal{G}$ and $\mathcal{G}$ implies $\mathcal{F}$.

Therefore (by the previous *implication-and-validity* proposition)

> if $\mathcal{F}$ is valid,   and   if $\mathcal{G}$ is valid,
> then $\mathcal{G}$ is valid   then $\mathcal{F}$ is valid.

In other words,

      $\mathcal{F}$ is valid
         precisely when
      $\mathcal{G}$ is valid,

as we wanted to show. ⏌

The converse of the above proposition is not true: It is possible to find sentences $\mathcal{F}$ and $\mathcal{G}$ such that $\mathcal{F}$ is valid precisely when $\mathcal{G}$ is valid, but $\mathcal{F}$ and $\mathcal{G}$ are not equivalent. This can occur when $\mathcal{F}$ and $\mathcal{G}$ are not valid but are false under different interpretations. For example, the sentence P is valid precisely when the sentence Q is valid, because neither sentence is valid; but P and Q are certainly not equivalent, because there are interpretations under which one is true and the other is false.

SUBSTITUTIVITY OF EQUIVALENCE

The equivalence relationship is important because two sentences that are equivalent may in some sense be treated interchangeably. This is made precise in the following result:

Proposition (substitutivity of equivalence)

For any sentences $\mathcal{G}$, $\mathcal{H}$, and $\mathcal{F}\langle\mathcal{G}\rangle$, the sentence

     if $\left(\mathcal{G}\ \textit{if and only if}\ \mathcal{H}\right)$
     then $\left(\mathcal{F}\langle\mathcal{G}\rangle\ \textit{if and only if}\ \mathcal{F}\langle\mathcal{H}\rangle\right)$

is valid. ⏌

In other words, the sentence

     $\left(\mathcal{G}\ \textit{if and only if}\ \mathcal{H}\right)$

implies the sentence

     $\left(\mathcal{F}\langle\mathcal{G}\rangle\ \textit{if and only if}\ \mathcal{F}\langle\mathcal{H}\rangle\right).$

In particular (by the *implication-and-validity* proposition),

     if $\left(\mathcal{G}\ \textit{if and only if}\ \mathcal{H}\right)$ is valid,
     then $\left(\mathcal{F}\langle\mathcal{G}\rangle\ \textit{if and only if}\ \mathcal{F}\langle\mathcal{H}\rangle\right)$ is valid.

Thus (by an earlier remark), we have the following result:

Corollary (substitutivity of equivalence)

For any sentences $\mathcal{G}$, $\mathcal{H}$, and $\mathcal{F}\langle\mathcal{G}\rangle$,

if $\mathcal{G}$ and $\mathcal{H}$ are equivalent,
then $\mathcal{F}\langle\mathcal{G}\rangle$ and $\mathcal{F}\langle\mathcal{H}\rangle$ are equivalent.   ⌐

Thus if two sentences are equivalent, we may replace zero, one, or more occurrences of one of them with the other, obtaining an equivalent sentence.

The proposition itself is intuitively clear, because, for any interpretation $\mathcal{I}$ such that

($\mathcal{G}$ *if and only if* $\mathcal{H}$) is true under $\mathcal{I}$,

we know (by the *if-and-only-if* rule) that

$\mathcal{G}$ and $\mathcal{H}$ have the same truth value under $\mathcal{I}$.

But $\mathcal{F}\langle\mathcal{G}\rangle$ and $\mathcal{F}\langle\mathcal{H}\rangle$ differ only in that certain occurrences of $\mathcal{G}$ in $\mathcal{F}\langle\mathcal{G}\rangle$ have been replaced by $\mathcal{H}$. Therefore in determining the truth value of $\mathcal{F}\langle\mathcal{G}\rangle$ and $\mathcal{F}\langle\mathcal{H}\rangle$ under $\mathcal{I}$, we obtain the same result in each case. The precise proof of the proposition involves concepts we have not yet introduced and is therefore omitted here.

As an important special case of the proposition, we may conclude that the corresponding sentence for total substitution,

if $\left(\mathcal{G}\ \ \textit{if and only if}\ \ \mathcal{H}\right)$
then $\left(\mathcal{F}[\mathcal{G}]\ \textit{if and only if}\ \mathcal{F}[\mathcal{H}]\right)$,

is valid. This is because the result of a total substitution is one of the possible results of a partial substitution.

Example

We know that the sentence

$\mathcal{G}:$ *not* $(P\ \ and\ \ Q)$

is equivalent to the sentence

$\mathcal{H}:$ $(not\ P)\ \ or\ \ (not\ Q)$.

Therefore, by the above corollary, the sentence

$\mathcal{F}\langle\mathcal{G}\rangle:$ $\begin{array}{l} not\ (P\ \ and\ \ Q) \\ or \\ R\ \ and\ \ not\ (P\ \ and\ \ Q) \end{array}$

is equivalent to the sentence

$$\mathcal{F}\langle \mathcal{H} \rangle : \quad \begin{array}{l} (not\ P)\ \ or\ \ (not\ Q) \\ or \\ R\ \ and\ \ not\ (P\ \ and\ \ Q), \end{array}$$

obtained by replacing the first occurrence of $\mathcal{G}$ in $\mathcal{F}\langle \mathcal{G} \rangle$ with $\mathcal{H}$. Note that we did not replace the second occurrence of $\mathcal{G}$ in $\mathcal{F}\langle \mathcal{G} \rangle$, although we could have. ◢

CHAINS OF EQUIVALENCES

We have noted (in the catalog) that the equivalence connective is transitive; i.e., the sentence

$$if\ \begin{bmatrix} \mathcal{F}\ if\ and\ only\ if\ \mathcal{G} \\ and \\ \mathcal{G}\ if\ and\ only\ if\ \mathcal{H} \end{bmatrix}$$

$$then\ (\mathcal{F}\ if\ and\ only\ if\ \mathcal{H})$$

is valid. In particular, the equivalence relationship between sentences is transitive; that is,

if $\mathcal{F}$ and $\mathcal{G}$ are equivalent
　　and
　$\mathcal{G}$ and $\mathcal{H}$ are equivalent,
then $\mathcal{F}$ and $\mathcal{H}$ are equivalent.

This provides another way of proving the validity of certain sentences, called the *chain-of-equivalence* method.

Suppose we would like to prove the validity of a sentence $\mathcal{F}$. We attempt to find a sequence of sentences $\mathcal{F}_1, \mathcal{F}_2, \ldots, \mathcal{F}_n$ such that

$\mathcal{F}$ is equivalent to $\mathcal{F}_1$,

$\mathcal{F}_1$ is equivalent to $\mathcal{F}_2$,

$$\vdots$$

$\mathcal{F}_{n-1}$ is equivalent to $\mathcal{F}_n$,

and

$\mathcal{F}_n$ is known to be valid.

Then we can conclude that

$\mathcal{F}$ is valid.

For because $\mathcal{F}$ is equivalent to $\mathcal{F}_1$ and $\mathcal{F}_1$ is equivalent to $\mathcal{F}_2$, we infer (by the transitivity of the equivalence relationship) that

$\mathcal{F}$ is equivalent to $\mathcal{F}_2$.

And because $\mathcal{F}_2$ is also equivalent to $\mathcal{F}_3$, we infer (by the transitivity of the equivalence relationship again) that

$\mathcal{F}$ is equivalent to $\mathcal{F}_3$.

In this way, by repeated use of the transitivity of the equivalence relationship, we infer that

$\mathcal{F}$ is equivalent to $\mathcal{F}_n$.

Then, because $\mathcal{F}_n$ is known to be valid, we may infer (by the *equivalence-and-validity* proposition) that

$\mathcal{F}$ is valid.

Example

Suppose we would like to show the validity of the sentence

$$\mathcal{F}: \quad \begin{array}{l} \textit{if not}\,(\textit{not}\,P) \\ \textit{then}\,\,\big(P\,\,\textit{and}\,\,(P\,\,\textit{or}\,\,R)\big). \end{array}$$

- The sentence

$$\mathcal{F}_1: \quad \begin{array}{l} \textit{if } P \\ \textit{then}\,\,\big(P\,\,\textit{and}\,\,(P\,\,\textit{or}\,\,R)\big) \end{array}$$

  is equivalent to $\mathcal{F}$, by the substitutivity of equivalence, because $\mathcal{F}_1$ is obtained from $\mathcal{F}$ by replacing the antecedent $\big(\textit{not}\,(\textit{not}\,P)\big)$ with P, and (by our catalog)

  $\textit{not}\,(\textit{not}\,P)$ is equivalent to P.

- The sentence

$$\mathcal{F}_2: \quad \begin{array}{l} \textit{if } P \\ \textit{then}\,\,P \end{array}$$

  is equivalent to $\mathcal{F}_1$, by the substitutivity of equivalence again, because $\mathcal{F}_2$ is obtained from $\mathcal{F}_1$ by replacing the consequent $\big(P\,\,\textit{and}\,\,(P\,\,\textit{or}\,\,R)\big)$ with P, and (by our catalog)

  $P\,\,\textit{and}\,\,(P\,\,\textit{or}\,\,R)$ is equivalent to P.

- The sentence $\mathcal{F}_2$ is known (by our catalog) to be valid.

Thus we can use the chain-of-equivalence method to conclude that

$\mathcal{F}$ is valid,

because $\mathcal{F}$ is equivalent to $\mathcal{F}_1$, $\mathcal{F}_1$ is equivalent to $\mathcal{F}_2$, and $\mathcal{F}_2$ is known to be valid.

We may present such a proof by the chain-of-equivalence method more concisely as follows:

We have

$$\mathcal{F}: \quad \begin{array}{l} \textit{if not (not P)} \\ \textit{then } \left(P \textit{ and } (P \textit{ or } R)\right) \end{array}$$

is equivalent (by the substitutivity of equivalence, because *not (not P)* is equivalent to P) to

$$\mathcal{F}_1: \quad \begin{array}{l} \textit{if P} \\ \textit{then } \left(P \textit{ and } (P \textit{ or } R)\right) \end{array}$$

which is equivalent (by the substitutivity of equivalence, because $\left(P \textit{ and } (P \textit{ or } R)\right)$ is equivalent to P) to

$$\mathcal{F}_2: \quad \begin{array}{l} \textit{if P} \\ \textit{then } P, \end{array}$$

which is valid; therefore $\mathcal{F}$ is valid. ◢

In **Problem 1.8** the reader is requested to discover a chain of equivalences to prove the validity of several sentences.

PROBLEMS

As mentioned in the preface, in solving a problem, the reader may use any result or technique that appears in the text prior to the page reference for the problem. For example, in solving Problem 1.1, one may use any result or technique that appears before the problem reference on page 33 or earlier. Also, the reader may use the results of any previous problem, and the results of previous parts of the same problem. For example, in solving Problem 2.2(c) of Chapter 2, the reader may use the results of Problems 2.1, 2.2(a), and 2.2(b), as well as any of the results of the problems of Chapter 1.

Problem 1.1 (Validity)   page 33

Consider the following sentences:

(a) $(\textit{if P then Q}) \textit{ or } (\textit{if Q then P})$

(b) $(not\,Q)$ or not $\begin{bmatrix} if\ P\ then\ (not\,Q) \\ and \\ P \end{bmatrix}$

(c) $(if\ P\ then\ (not\,Q))$ if and only if $not\,(P\ and\ Q)$

(d) $\begin{bmatrix} if\ (P\ or\ Q) \\ then\ R \end{bmatrix}$ if and only if $\begin{bmatrix} if\ P\ then\ R \\ and \\ if\ Q\ then\ R \end{bmatrix}$

(e) $\begin{bmatrix} if\ P \\ then\ (Q\ and\ R) \end{bmatrix}$ if and only if $\begin{bmatrix} if\ P\ then\ Q \\ or \\ if\ P\ then\ R \end{bmatrix}$

(f) $\begin{bmatrix} if\ P \\ then\ (if\ Q\ then\ R) \end{bmatrix}$ if and only if $\begin{bmatrix} if\ (P\ and\ Q) \\ then\ R \end{bmatrix}$

(g) $\begin{bmatrix} if\ P \\ then\ (Q\ or\ R) \end{bmatrix}$ if and only if $\begin{bmatrix} if\ (P\ and\ (not\,Q)) \\ then\ R \end{bmatrix}$

(h) $\begin{bmatrix} P\ and \\ if\ Q\ then\ R \end{bmatrix}$ if and only if $\begin{bmatrix} if\ ((not\,P)\ or\ Q) \\ then\ (P\ and\ R) \end{bmatrix}$

(i) $\begin{bmatrix} P \\ if\ and\ only\ if \\ (Q\ if\ and\ only\ if\ R) \end{bmatrix}$ if and only if $\begin{bmatrix} (P\ if\ and\ only\ if\ Q) \\ if\ and\ only\ if \\ R \end{bmatrix}$

(j) $\begin{bmatrix} if\ P \\ then\ Q\ and\ R \\ else\ (not\,Q)\ and\ S \end{bmatrix}$ if and only if $\begin{bmatrix} if\ Q \\ then\ P\ and\ R \\ else\ (not\,P)\ and\ S \end{bmatrix}$

Some of these sentences are valid; some are not. Find which sentences are not valid and produce interpretations under which they are false. Prove the validity of the other sentences, using any of the following methods: truth tables, semantic trees, and proof by falsification. Use each method at least once.

Problem 1.2 (Frightful sentence)   page 33

Establish the validity of the following sentence:

$$
\text{if } \left[\left[\begin{array}{l} \left[\begin{array}{l} \textit{if } P_1 \textit{ then } (P_2 \textit{ or } P_3) \\ \qquad \textit{else } (P_3 \textit{ or } P_4) \end{array} \right] \textit{ and} \\ \\ \left[\begin{array}{l} \left[\begin{array}{l} \textit{if } P_3 \textit{ then } (\textit{not } P_6) \\ \qquad \textit{else } (\textit{if } P_4 \textit{ then } P_1) \end{array} \right] \textit{ and} \\ \\ \left[\begin{array}{l} \textit{not } (P_2 \textit{ and } P_5) \textit{ and} \\ (\textit{if } P_2 \textit{ then } P_5) \end{array} \right] \end{array} \right] \end{array} \right] \textit{ and} \right]
$$

then not (if P_3 then P_6).

Problem 1.3 (**Conditional connective**)   page 39

The valid sentence schema

> (*not* $\mathcal{F}$)
>   *if and only if*
> (*if* $\mathcal{F}$ *then false else true*)

suggests that the negation connective *not* can be "paraphrased" in terms of the conditional connective *if-then-else* and the truth symbols *true* and *false*. Show that the other connectives (i.e., *and*, *or*, *if-then*, and *if-and-only-if*) can be paraphrased in the same way, using a sentence containing only *if-then-else*, *true*, and *false*.

Problem 1.4 (**Tardy bus**)   page 40

Suppose the following three statements are given:

A_1: If Bill takes the bus, then if the bus is late, Bill misses his appointment.

A_2: If Bill misses his appointment and Bill feels downcast, Bill shouldn't go home.

A_3: If Bill doesn't get the job, then Bill feels downcast and Bill should go home.

Assuming these statements are all true, which of the following statements are also true?

G_1: If Bill takes the bus and the bus is late, then Bill does get the job.

G_2: If Bill misses his appointment and Bill should go home, then Bill does get the job.

G_3: If the bus is late, then either Bill does not take the bus or Bill does not miss his appointment.

G_4: If the bus is late or if Bill misses his appointment, then Bill feels downcast.

G_5: If Bill should go home and Bill takes the bus, then Bill does not feel downcast if the bus is late.

Let P_1 stand for "Bill takes the bus," P_2 for "the bus is late," P_3 for "Bill misses his appointment," P_4 for "Bill feels downcast," P_5 for "Bill gets the job," and P_6 for "Bill should go home." For each of the sentences G_i ($i = 1, 2, 3, 4, 5$), consider the sentence

$$if \ (A_1 \ \ and \ A_2 \ \ and \ A_3) \ \ then \ G_i,$$

expressed in propositional logic in terms of the propositional symbols P_1, P_2, P_3, P_4, P_5, and P_6. If the sentence is valid, give a proof. Otherwise, give an interpretation under which it is false.

Note the difference between the inclusive "or" and the exclusive "either-or." The inclusive or is (P or Q), and is true in particular in the case in which both P and Q are true; the exclusive either-or is

$$((P \ \ or \ Q) \ \ \ and \ \ \ not \ (P \ \ and \ \ Q))$$

and is false in particular in the case in which both P and Q are true.

Problem 1.5 (Love)   page 40

Use propositional logic to answer the following questions. (This problem is by R. Smullyan.)

(a) Suppose the following two statements are true:

    (1) I love Pat or I love Quincy.

    (2) If I love Pat, then I love Quincy.

Does it necessarily follow that I love Pat? Does it necessarily follow that I love Quincy?

(b) Suppose someone asks me,

    "Is it really true that if you love Pat, then you also love Quincy?"

I reply,

    "If it is true, then I love Pat."

Does it follow that I love Pat? Does it follow that I love Quincy?

(c) Suppose someone asks me,

    "Is it really true that if you love Pat, then you also love Quincy?"

I reply,

"If it is true, then I love Pat, and if I love Pat, then it is true."

Which one do I necessarily love?

(d) This time we are given three people, Pat, Quincy, and Ray. Suppose the following facts are given:

(1) I love at least one of the three.

(2) If I love Pat but not Ray, then I also love Quincy.

(3) I love both Ray and Quincy or I love neither one.

(4) If I love Ray, then I also love Pat.

Which of the three do I love?

Hint: Let P stand for "I love Pat," Q for "I love Quincy," and R for "I love Ray." Then determine the validity of the appropriate propositional-logic sentence. For example, in part (a) we are actually asked if the sentences

$$if \begin{bmatrix} P & or & Q \\ & and & \\ if & P & then & Q \end{bmatrix} \quad \text{and} \quad if \begin{bmatrix} P & or & Q \\ & and & \\ if & P & then & Q \end{bmatrix}$$
$$then \ P \qquad\qquad\qquad\qquad then \ Q$$

are valid.

Problem 1.6 (The land of the liars and truth tellers)   page 40

Use propositional logic to solve the following problem.

A certain country is inhabited entirely by people who either always tell the truth or always tell lies and who will respond to questions with only a yes or a no.

A tourist comes to a fork in the road, where one branch leads to a restaurant and the other does not. There is no sign indicating which branch to take, but there is an inhabitant, Mr. X, standing at the fork.

What single yes/no question can the hungry tourist ask to find the way to the restaurant?

Hint: Let P stand for "Mr. X always tells the truth" and Q stand for "The left-hand branch leads to the restaurant." We must find a propositional-logic sentence $\mathcal{F}$ in terms of P and Q such that, whether or not Mr. X tells the truth, his answer to the question "Is $\mathcal{F}$ true?" will be yes precisely when Q is true. Construct the truth table that $\mathcal{F}$ must have, in terms of P and Q, and then design an appropriate sentence $\mathcal{F}$ accordingly.

Problem 1.7 (Substitution)   page 49

Let $\mathcal{F}$ be the sentence

$$\mathcal{F}: \begin{bmatrix} P \ and \ Q \\ or \\ if \ R \ then \ (P \ and \ Q \ and \ R) \end{bmatrix}.$$

Apply the following substitutions. (Give three possible results of applying each partial substitution.)

(a) $\mathcal{F} \triangleleft \{(P \ and \ Q) \leftarrow P\}$ (b) $\mathcal{F} \triangleleft \{(P \ and \ Q) \leftarrow P\}$

(c) $\mathcal{F} \triangleleft \begin{Bmatrix} P \leftarrow S \\ (P \ and \ Q) \leftarrow P \end{Bmatrix}$ (d) $\mathcal{F} \triangleleft \begin{Bmatrix} P \leftarrow S \\ (P \ and \ Q) \leftarrow P \end{Bmatrix}.$

Problem 1.8 (Chain of equivalences)   page 61

Use a chain of equivalences to establish the validity of the sentences (b), (d), (e), and (j) of Problem 1.1, if they are valid at all. In your proof you may use the substitutivity of equivalence and any of the valid sentences or equivalent sentences from the catalog, but no other valid sentences.

2

Predicate Logic: Basic

2.1   INTRODUCTION

By our study of propositional logic we have determined that a sentence such as

> The monkeys on Jupiter are red
> or
> the monkeys on Jupiter are not red

is true without needing to investigate Jovian biology: The sentence is an instance of the valid propositional-logic sentence

> P or $(not\ P)$,

taking P to be the proposition "The monkeys on Jupiter are red."

There are some sentences, however, that we can tell to be true by their form, but that are not instances of any valid sentences in propositional logic. For example, we can tell that the sentences

> There are red rocks on Jupiter
> or
> all the rocks on Jupiter are not red

and

> There is an odd perfect number
>   or
> all perfect numbers are not odd

are true without launching a spacecraft or even knowing the definition of a perfect number. The propositional-logic language is too coarse and primitive to express the concept of an object, a property of an object (such as being a rock or a perfect number), or a relationship between several objects.

The predicate-logic language we are about to introduce extends propositional logic by enabling us to speak about objects and the relationships between them. In this language, the two sentences above can both be regarded as instances of the abstract sentence

$$\mathcal{F}: \quad \begin{array}{l} (\textit{for some } x)\big[p(x) \ \textit{ and } \ q(x)\big] \\ \quad \textit{or} \\ (\textit{for all } x)\big[\textit{if } p(x) \ \textit{ then } \ \textit{not } q(x)\big]. \end{array}$$

For the "rocks" sentence, we take $p(x)$ to be "x is a rock on Jupiter" and $q(x)$ to be "x is red." Under this interpretation, the intuitive meaning of the abstract sentence $\mathcal{F}$ becomes

> ($\textit{for some } x$)[x is a rock on Jupiter $\textit{and}$ x is red]
> $\textit{or}$
> ($\textit{for all } x$)[$\textit{if}$ x is a rock on Jupiter $\textit{then}$ $\textit{not}$ (x is red)],

which is a non-English rewording of the original rocks sentence.

For the "numbers" sentence, we take $p(x)$ to be "x is a perfect number" and $q(x)$ to be "x is odd." Under this interpretation, the intuitive meaning of the abstract sentence $\mathcal{F}$ becomes

> ($\textit{for some } x$)[x is a perfect number $\textit{and}$ x is odd]
> $\textit{or}$
> ($\textit{for all } x$)[$\textit{if}$ x is a perfect number $\textit{then}$ $\textit{not}$ (x is odd)].

Both of the interpreted sentences are true; in fact, any instance of the abstract sentence $\mathcal{F}$ is true regardless of the meaning assigned to $p(x)$ and $q(x)$.

On the other hand, not every instance of the abstract sentence

$$\mathcal{G}: \quad \begin{array}{l} (\textit{for all } x)p(x) \\ \quad \textit{or} \\ (\textit{for all } x)[\textit{not } p(x)] \end{array}$$

is true. For example, if we take $p(x)$ to be "x is a rhesus monkey," the intuitive meaning of the sentence $\mathcal{G}$ becomes

> (*for all x*)[*x* is a rhesus monkey]
>   *or*
> (*for all x*)[*not* (*x* is a rhesus monkey)];

that is,

> Everything is a rhesus monkey
>   *or*
> everything is not a rhesus monkey.

Since it is not true that everything is a rhesus monkey, but it is also not true that everything is not a rhesus monkey (in fact, there actually do exist some rhesus monkeys), the entire sentence is false.

The purpose of this section is to adapt the propositional-logic language to speak of objects and the relationships between them and to extend the notion of validity accordingly. The new language, along with the extended notion of validity, is called *predicate logic*. We then introduce augmented methods to show the validity of predicate-logic sentences.

2.2   THE LANGUAGE

We begin by introducing the language of predicate logic. We present *syntactic rules*, which say which expressions are taken to be predicate-logic sentences without saying what these sentences mean.

THE SENTENCES

We begin by introducing the symbols of predicate logic.

Definition (symbols)

The sentences of predicate logic are made up of the following symbols:

- The *truth symbols*

    true   and   *false*

- The *constant symbols* (or *constants*)

    $a, \ b, \ c, \ a', \ b', \ c', \ a_1, \ b_1, \ c_1, \ a_2, \ b_2, \ c_2, \ \ldots$

    (i.e., the letters a, b, and c, possibly with a prime or a numerical subscript)

- The *variable symbols* (or *variables*)

    $u, \; v, \; w, \; x, \; y, \; z, \; u', \; v', \; w', \; x', \; y', \; z', \; u_1, \; v_1, \; \ldots$

- The *function symbols*

    $f, \; g, \; h, \; f_1, \; g_1, \; h_1, \; f_2, \; \ldots$

    Each function symbol has an associated positive integer called its *arity*, indicating how many arguments the function should take.

- The *predicate symbols*

    $p, \; q, \; r, \; p_1, \; q_1, \; r_1, \; p_2, \; \ldots$

    Each predicate symbol also has an associated *arity*. ⌐

A function or predicate symbol of arity n will also be called an *n-ary* function or predicate symbol. Also, 1-ary, 2-ary, and 3-ary symbols are called *unary*, *binary*, and *ternary*, respectively.

Intuitively, the constants and variables will denote objects, and the function and predicate symbols will denote functions and relations, respectively, on these objects. Note that the propositional symbols P, Q, R, $\ldots$ of propositional logic are not in the language of predicate logic.

We build the language from these symbols in three stages: First we define the terms of the language, then we define its propositions, and finally we define its sentences.

Definition (terms)

The *terms* of predicate logic are the expressions that denote objects. They are built up according to the following rules:

- The constants a, b, c, $\ldots$ are terms.

- The variables u, v, w, $\ldots$ are terms.

- If t_1, t_2, $\ldots, t_n$ are terms, where $n \geq 1$ and f is a function symbol of arity n, then the *application*

    $f(t_1, t_2, \ldots, t_n)$

    is a term.

- If $\mathcal{F}$ is a sentence and s and t are terms, then the *conditional*

  if $\mathcal{F}$ then s else t

  is a term. Note that this rule depends on the concept of "sentence," which has not yet been defined. ⌐

Example

Assume the function symbol f is binary, i.e., of arity 2, and the function symbol g is ternary, i.e., of arity 3. Then

a is a term (since a is a constant);

x is a term (since x is a variable);

$f(a, x)$ is a term (since a and x are terms and f is a binary function symbol);

$g\bigl(x,\ f(a, x),\ a\bigr)$ is also a term (since x, $f(a, x)$, and a are terms and g is a ternary function symbol). ⌐

An example of a conditional term is postponed until after the definition of "sentence."

Note that it is impossible for $f(a, x)$ and $f(y)$ both to be terms, because f must have a unique arity. However, it is possible that in one discussion we will assume that f has arity 2 and in another discussion assume that f has arity 1, if there is no chance of confusion.

Definition (propositions)

The *propositions* of predicate logic are intended to represent relations between objects. They are constructed according to the following rules:

- The truth symbols

  true   and   *false*

  are propositions.

- If $t_1, t_2, \ldots, t_n$ are terms, where $n \geq 1$ and p is a predicate symbol of arity n, then

  $p(t_1, t_2, \ldots, t_n)$

  is a proposition. ⌐

For example, if p is a ternary predicate symbol, then

$$p(a,\ x,\ f(a,x))$$

is a proposition (since a, x, and $f(a,x)$ are terms and p is a ternary predicate symbol).

Definition (sentences)

The *sentences* of predicate logic are built from its propositions, just as in propositional logic, according to the following rules:

- Every proposition is a sentence.

- If $\mathcal{F}$ is a sentence, then so is its *negation*

    (*not* $\mathcal{F}$).

- If $\mathcal{F}$ and $\mathcal{G}$ are sentences, then so are their *conjunction*,

    ($\mathcal{F}$ *and* $\mathcal{G}$),

    and their *disjunction*,

    ($\mathcal{F}$ *or* $\mathcal{G}$).

- If $\mathcal{F}$ and $\mathcal{G}$ are sentences, then so are the *implication*,

    (*if* $\mathcal{F}$ *then* $\mathcal{G}$),

    and the *equivalence*,

    ($\mathcal{F}$ *if and only if* $\mathcal{G}$).

- If $\mathcal{F}$, $\mathcal{G}$, and $\mathcal{H}$ are sentences, then so is the *conditional*,

    (*if* $\mathcal{F}$ *then* $\mathcal{G}$ *else* $\mathcal{H}$).

- If x is any variable and $\mathcal{F}$ is a sentence, then

    ((*for all* x)$\mathcal{F}$)

    and

    ((*for some* x)$\mathcal{F}$)

    are sentences. The prefixes "*for all*" and "*for some*" are called the *universal quantifier* and the *existential quantifier*, respectively; the occurrence of $\mathcal{F}$ is said to be the *scope* of the corresponding quantifier. ⌐

We illustrate the definition with an example.

Example

Assume the function symbols f and g and the predicate symbol q are binary, i.e., of arity 2, and the predicate symbol p is ternary, i.e., of arity 3. Then

$$p(a,\ x,\ f(a,x))$$

is a sentence (since it is a proposition);

$$q(g(b,x),\ y)$$

is a sentence (since it is a proposition);

$$((\textit{for some } y)q(g(b,x),\ y))$$

is a sentence (since the scope of the existential quantifier (*for some y*) is a sentence);

$$(p(a,\ x,\ f(a,x))\ \textit{ and }\ ((\textit{for some } y)q(g(b,x),\ y)))$$

is a sentence (since both conjuncts are sentences);

$$((\textit{for all } x)(p(a,\ x,\ f(a,x))\ \textit{ and }\ ((\textit{for some } y)q(g(b,x),\ y))))$$

is a sentence (since the scope of the universal quantifier (*for all x*) is a sentence). ⌟

For clarity, we shall display sentences with brackets, braces, two dimensions, and indentation, omitting parentheses when not necessary to indicate the structure of a sentence. This is merely an informal convention that does not really extend the language of predicate logic.

Example

The sentence

$$((\textit{for all } x)(p(a,\ x,\ f(a,x))\ \textit{ and }\ ((\textit{for some } y)q(g(b,x),\ y))))$$

may be written informally as

$$(\textit{for all } x)\left[\begin{array}{c} p(a,\ x,\ f(a,x)) \\ \textit{and} \\ (\textit{for some } y)q(g(b,x),\ y) \end{array}\right].$$

The sentence

$$((\textit{for all } y)((\textit{for all } x)((\textit{for all } z)(\textit{if } q(y,z)\ \textit{ then }\ (\textit{if } r(x)\ \textit{ then }$$
$$((\textit{for some } u)p(y,z,u)))))))$$

may be written informally as

$$(\textit{for all } y) \begin{bmatrix} \textit{if } q(y,z) \\ \textit{then } \textit{if } r(x) \\ \qquad \textit{then } (\textit{for some } u)p(y,z,u) \end{bmatrix}$$
$$(\textit{for all } x)$$
$$(\textit{for all } z)$$

Note that we have defined *and* and *or* to apply to two arguments. As in propositional logic, we may extend these connectives to apply to several arguments. Thus the multiple conjunction

$$\mathcal{F}_1 \textit{ and } \mathcal{F}_2 \textit{ and } \mathcal{F}_3 \textit{ and } \dots \textit{ and } \mathcal{F}_n$$

is an abbreviation for

$$((\dots((\mathcal{F}_1 \textit{ and } \mathcal{F}_2) \textit{ and } \mathcal{F}_3)\dots) \textit{ and } \mathcal{F}_n),$$

and the multiple disjunction

$$\mathcal{F}_1 \textit{ or } \mathcal{F}_2 \textit{ or } \mathcal{F}_3 \textit{ or } \dots \textit{ or } \mathcal{F}_n$$

is an abbreviation for

$$((\dots((\mathcal{F}_1 \textit{ or } \mathcal{F}_2) \textit{ or } \mathcal{F}_3)\dots) \textit{ or } \mathcal{F}_n).$$

Now that we have defined sentences, the terms employing the *if-then-else* construct are completely characterized. For example, the conditional

$$\textit{if } (\textit{for all } x)p(a,b,x)$$
$$\textit{then } f(a,x)$$
$$\textit{else } g(b,y)$$

is a term, since $(\textit{for all } x)p(a,b,x)$ is a sentence and $f(a,x)$ and $g(b,y)$ are terms.

Remark (*if-then-else*)

We have used the same *if-then-else* construct as an operator to construct conditional terms and as a connective to construct conditional sentences. Which meaning we intend will be apparent from the *then* and *else* clauses of the expression. For example,

$$\textit{if } (\textit{for all } x)p(a,b,x)$$
$$\textit{then } f(a,x)$$
$$\textit{else } g(b,y)$$

is a term, because $f(a,x)$ and $g(b,y)$ are terms, while

$$\textit{if } (\textit{for all } x)p(a,b,x)$$
$$\textit{then } (\textit{for some } y)q(x,y)$$
$$\textit{else } r(y)$$

is a sentence, because *(for some y)*$q(x, y)$ and $r(y)$ are sentences. ⌐

On some occasions we need a phrase that includes both terms and sentences.

Definition (**expressions**)

An *expression* of predicate logic is either a sentence or a term. ⌐

Thus both x and $p(x)$ are expressions.

As in propositional logic, we introduce terminology for the components of an expression.

Definition (**subterms, subsentences, subexpressions**)

Every intermediate term we use in building up a term t (including t itself) or a sentence $\mathcal{F}$ is called a *subterm* of t or $\mathcal{F}$, respectively.

Also, every intermediate sentence we use in building up a term t or a sentence $\mathcal{F}$ (including $\mathcal{F}$ itself) is called a *subsentence* of t or $\mathcal{F}$, respectively.

Together the subterms and subsentences of a term t (including t itself) are called the *subexpressions* of t. Similarly, the subterms and subsentences of a sentence $\mathcal{F}$ (including $\mathcal{F}$ itself) are called the *subexpressions* of $\mathcal{F}$.

A *proper* subterm, *proper* subsentence, or *proper* subexpression of an expression $\mathcal{E}$ is one that is distinct from $\mathcal{E}$ itself. ⌐

A single subexpression of a given expression may have more than one occurrence in the given expression.

Example

In the conditional term

$$t: \quad \begin{array}{l} \textit{if } (\textit{for all } x)q(x,\ f(a)) \\ \textit{then } f(a) \\ \textit{else } b \end{array}$$

the subterms are

$$x, \quad a, \quad f(a), \quad b, \quad \text{and} \quad t \text{ itself.}$$

The subsentences are

$$q\big(x,\ f(a)\big)\quad \text{and}\quad (\textit{for all } x)q\big(x,\ f(a)\big).$$

Here t has two occurrences of the subterm x, two occurrences of the subterm a, and two occurrences of the subterm $f(a)$. All of these subterms and subsentences are the subexpressions of t.

In the sentence

$$\mathcal{F}:\quad\begin{array}{l} p\big(a,\ x,\ f(a,x)\big)\\ \quad and\\ (\textit{for some } y)q\big(g(b,x),\ y\big),\end{array}$$

the subterms are

$$a,\quad x,\quad f(a,x),\quad b,\quad g(b,x),\quad \text{and}\quad y.$$

The subsentences are

$$p\big(a,\ x,\ f(a,x)\big),\quad q\big(g(b,x),\ y\big),\quad (\textit{for some } y)q\big(g(b,x),\ y\big),$$

and $\mathcal{F}$ itself. ⌐

Our English like notation for quantifiers is not the conventional one; the standard system is as follows:

Our notation	Conventional notation
(*for all x*)	$(\forall x)$
(*for some x*)	$(\exists x)$

Also, the conventional phrase for "proposition" is "atomic formula" and for "sentence" is "well-formed formula." Thus the sentence we write as

$$\begin{array}{l}(\textit{for all } y)\\ (\textit{for all } x)\\ (\textit{for all } z)\end{array}\left[\begin{array}{l}\textit{if } q(y,z)\ \textit{and}\ r(a)\\ \textit{then if } r(x)\ \textit{or}\ q(a,x)\\ \qquad\textit{then } (\textit{for some } u)p(y,z,u)\end{array}\right]$$

might be written conventionally as

$$(\forall y)(\forall x)(\forall z)\big[\big(q(y,z)\wedge r(a)\big)\supset\big((r(x)\vee q(a,x))\supset(\exists u)p(y,z,u)\big)\big].$$

As in propositional logic, we have adopted the English like notation for clarity in the text; the reader may choose to use the more conventional notation in writing.

FREE AND BOUND VARIABLES

We have now introduced the terms and sentences of predicate logic. Before we can

begin to consider the meanings of these expressions, however, we must introduce
the technical notions of "bound" and "free" variable. In the next section we
shall introduce interpretations for predicate logic and discuss how to determine
the value of a predicate logic expression under a given interpretation, just as we
have done earlier for propositional logic. The distinction between free and bound
occurrences of variables will then become very important, because the values of
the free occurrences will be assigned by the interpretation, while the values of the
bound occurrences will be independent of the interpretation.

Because the definitions of bound and free variables can be confusing at first,
we begin with an example.

In the sentence

$$(\textit{for all } x) \begin{bmatrix} p(x,y) \\ \quad and \\ (\textit{for some } y)q(y,x) \end{bmatrix}$$

there are two occurrences of x in the scope of the universal quantifier (*for all x*);
these occurrences of x are therefore said to be "bound" by the quantifier (*for all x*).
On the other hand, the first occurrence of y, in $p(x,y)$, is not within the scope
of any quantifier of form (*for all y*) or (*for some y*); it is therefore said to be a
"free" occurrence of y. The final occurrence of y, in $q(y,x)$, is a bound occurrence,
because it is within the scope of the quantifier (*for some y*). The occurrences of
the symbols x and y within the quantifiers (*for all x*) and (*for some y*) themselves
are considered to be neither bound nor free.

Note that the same occurrence of a variable x can be within the scope of more
than one quantifier (*for all x*) or (*for some x*). For example, in the sentence

$$(\textit{for all } x) \begin{bmatrix} p(x,y) \\ \quad and \\ (\textit{for some } x)(\textit{for all } y)q(y,x) \end{bmatrix}$$

the final occurrence of x, in $q(y,x)$, is in the scope of both the inner quantifier
(*for some x*) and the outer quantifier (*for all x*). However, we do not regard x as
being bound by both quantifiers, but only by the inner quantifier (*for some x*).
Again, the occurrences of the symbols x and y within the quantifiers (*for all x*)
and (*for some y*) themselves are considered to be neither bound nor free.

Now let us be more precise.

Definition (bound and free occurrences)

Let x be a variable and $\mathcal{E}$ be an expression (i.e., a sentence or term) of
predicate logic. Consider an occurrence of x in $\mathcal{E}$ that is not the variable
of a quantifier (*for all x*) or (*for some x*).

The occurrence of x is *bound in* $\mathcal{E}$ if it is within the scope of a quantifier (*for all x*) or (*for some x*) in $\mathcal{E}$; it is *bound by* the innermost quantifier (*for all x*) or (*for some x*) that contains the occurrence of x within its scope.

The occurrence of x is *free in* $\mathcal{E}$ if it is not within the scope of any quantifier (*for all x*) or (*for some x*) in $\mathcal{E}$.

The occurrences of x in the quantifiers (*for all x*) and (*for some x*) themselves are neither bound nor free.   ⌐   •

Example

Consider the sentence

$$\mathcal{E}: \quad (\textit{for all } x) \begin{bmatrix} p(x,y) \\ \textit{and} \\ (\textit{for some } y)q(y,z) \end{bmatrix}.$$

The occurrence of x in $p(x,y)$ is bound in $\mathcal{E}$, by the quantifier (*for all x*). The occurrence of z, in $q(y,z)$, is free in $\mathcal{E}$. The occurrence of y in $p(x,y)$ is free, while the occurrence of y in $q(y,z)$ is bound, by the quantifier (*for some y*).   ⌐

Note that an occurrence of a variable is always free in an expression with no quantifiers. Also, it is quite possible for an occurrence of a variable x to be bound in a term, because we admit conditional terms (*if $\mathcal{F}$ then s else t*), where $\mathcal{F}$ is a sentence which may contain quantifiers (*for all x*) or (*for some x*).

Remark

If $\mathcal{F}$ is a subexpression of an expression $\mathcal{E}$, an occurrence of a variable in $\mathcal{F}$ can be free in $\mathcal{F}$ but bound in $\mathcal{E}$. For example, if $\mathcal{E}$ is the sentence

$$\mathcal{E}: \quad (\textit{for all } x)(\textit{for some } y)p(x,y)$$

and $\mathcal{F}$ is its subsentence

$$\mathcal{F}: \quad (\textit{for some } y)p(x,y),$$

the occurrence of x is free in $\mathcal{F}$, because it is within the scope of no quantifier (*for all x*) or (*for some x*) in $\mathcal{F}$. The same occurrence of x, however, is bound in $\mathcal{E}$, because it is within the scope of the quantifier (*for all x*) in $\mathcal{E}$.   ⌐

The preceding definition (of bound and free occurrences) determines whether a particular occurrence of a variable is bound or free in an expression. We now define whether the variable itself is bound or free in the expression, independent of any particular occurrence of the variable.

Definition (bound and free variables)

The variable x is *bound in* an expression $\mathcal{E}$ if there is at least one bound occurrence of x in $\mathcal{E}$, and *free in* $\mathcal{E}$ if there is at least one free occurrence of x in $\mathcal{E}$. ⌟

Example

Consider the sentence $\mathcal{E}$,

$$(for\ all\ x) \begin{bmatrix} p(x,y) \\ and \\ (for\ some\ y)q(y,z) \end{bmatrix},$$

of the preceding example. The variable x is bound in $\mathcal{E}$, because it has a bound occurrence, in $p(x,y)$; the variable z is free in $\mathcal{E}$, because it has a free occurrence, in $q(y,z)$; the variable y is both bound and free in $\mathcal{E}$, because it has a bound occurrence, in $q(y,z)$, and a free occurrence, in $p(x,y)$. ⌟

Note that a variable may be both bound and free in an expression $\mathcal{E}$ if it has at least one bound occurrence and at least one free occurrence in $\mathcal{E}$.

Definition (closed sentence)

A sentence is *closed* if it has no free occurrences of any variable. ⌟

Example

The sentence

$$(for\ all\ x)p(x,y)$$

is not closed, because the occurrence of y is free. On the other hand, the sentence

$$(for\ all\ x)(for\ some\ y)p(x,y)$$

is closed. ⏌

As we shall see, the "free symbols" of an expression are those whose meanings must be assigned by an interpretation. They are defined as follows:

Definition (free symbols)

> The *free symbols* of an expression $\mathcal{E}$ are the free variables of $\mathcal{E}$ and all the constant, function, and predicate symbols of $\mathcal{E}$. ⏌

Thus the free symbols of the sentence

$$(for\ all\ x) \begin{bmatrix} p(x,\ y) \\ and \\ (for\ some\ y)q(y,\ f(a,z)) \end{bmatrix}$$

are the free variables y and z, the constant a, the function symbol f, and the predicate symbols p and q. The variable x, which only occurs bound, is not a free symbol of the sentence.

2.3   THE MEANING OF A SENTENCE

In defining validity for propositional logic, we first defined the notion of the truth of a sentence under an interpretation, which assigned truth values to all the propositional symbols of the sentence. In this section, we will extend this notion to the sentences of predicate logic in an analogous way. But since these sentences involve terms, an interpretation must include a "domain," a set of objects that provides a meaning for the terms.

The precise notion of an interpretation will be defined shortly, but first we give an informal preview of the meaning of predicate logic sentences.

MOTIVATION

An interpretation for a sentence must assign a meaning to each of the sentence's free symbols. It will assign domain elements to the constants and the free variables, functions (over the domain) to the function symbols, and relations (over the domain) to the predicate symbols.

For example, consider the closed sentence

$$\mathcal{G} : \quad \begin{array}{l} \textit{if (for all x)(for some y)}p(x, y) \\ \textit{then } p(a, \, f(a)). \end{array}$$

Any interpretation for this sentence must specify a domain and assign meanings to the constant a, the unary function symbol f, and the binary predicate symbol p. Because the sentence has no free variables, the interpretation does not need to assign meanings to any variables.

Consider the interpretation I, in which we take the domain D to be the integers and under which

a is 0;

f is the "successor" function,
    that is, the function f_I such that $f_I(d)$ is $d + 1$;

p is the "greater-than" relation,
    that is, the relation p_I such that $p_I(d_1, d_2)$ is $d_1 > d_2$.

The intuitive meaning provided for the consequent $p(a, f(a))$ of $\mathcal{G}$ under this interpretation is the inequality

$$0 > 0 + 1.$$

More precisely, the value of the term $f(a)$ is 1 (because $0 + 1$ is 1), and hence the value of the consequent $p(a, f(a))$ is false (because $0 > 1$ is false).

If we could determine the truth value of the antecedent

$$\textit{(for all x)(for some y)}p(x, \, y),$$

we could apply the *if-then* semantic rule of propositional logic to determine the truth value of the whole sentence. However, the antecedent contains quantifiers; to determine its truth value we must introduce two new semantic rules for the universal and existential quantifier, respectively.

According to one of these rules, a sentence of form *(for all x)* $\mathcal{F}$ will be true under a given interpretation if the subsentence $\mathcal{F}$ is true under the interpretation for every possible assignment of a domain element d to x. According to the other rule, a sentence of the form *(for some x)* $\mathcal{F}$ will be true under a given interpretation if there exists an assignment of a domain element d to x such that $\mathcal{F}$ is true under the interpretation.

Thus the antecedent

$$\textit{(for all x)(for some y)}p(x, \, y)$$

will be given the intuitive meaning

> For every integer d
>> there exists an integer d'
>>> such that $d > d'$.

This is true (e.g., for any d, we could take d' to be $d - 1$).

Thus under the above interpretation $\mathcal{I}$, the entire sentence will be given the intuitive meaning

> If for every integer d
>> there exists an integer d'
>>> such that $d > d'$,
> then $0 > 0 + 1$.

Because its antecedent is true and its consequent is false, the entire sentence

> *if (for all x)(for some y)p(x, y)*
> *then p(a, f(a))*

is false under $\mathcal{I}$.

On the other hand, suppose we consider the interpretation J, which differs from $\mathcal{I}$ only in that, under J,

> f is the "predecessor" function,
>> that is, the function f_J such that $f_J(d)$ is $d - 1$;

> p is the "inequality" relation,
>> that is, the relation p_J such that $p_J(d_1, d_2)$ is $d_1 \neq d_2$.

Under the interpretation J, the intuitive meaning of the sentence $\mathcal{G}$ is

> If for every integer d
>> there exists an integer d'
>>> such that $d \neq d'$,
> then $0 \neq 0 - 1$.

This is a true statement about the integers: Its antecedent

> For every integer d
>> there exists an integer d'
>>> such that $d \neq d'$

is true again (e.g., for any d, take d' to be $d + 1$), but its consequent

$$0 \neq 0 - 1$$

is also true; therefore (by the *if-then* rule) the entire implication is true under J.

To be valid, a closed sentence must be true under every possible interpretation. Thus although the above sentence $\mathcal{G}$ is true under the interpretation J, it is not valid, because it is false under the interpretation I.

Next consider the sentence

$$\mathcal{H}: \quad \begin{array}{l} \textit{if } (\textit{for all } x)p(x,\ f(x)) \\ \textit{then } (\textit{for some } y)p(a,\ y). \end{array}$$

This sentence is true under both of the above interpretations, I and J.

Under I, the intuitive meaning of the sentence $\mathcal{H}$ is

> If for every integer d
> $d > d + 1$,
> then there exists an integer d'
> such that $0 > d'$.

Here the antecedent is false and the consequent is true, and therefore (by the *if-then* rule) the entire sentence is true under I.

Under J, the intuitive meaning of the sentence $\mathcal{H}$ is

> If for every integer d
> $d \neq d - 1$,
> then there exists an integer d'
> such that $0 \neq d'$.

Here both the antecedent and the consequent are true, so the entire sentence is also true, under J.

In fact, this sentence is valid: It is true under every interpretation, as we shall see in a later section.

INTERPRETATIONS

Let us now define the notion of interpretation for predicate logic more precisely.

Definition (interpretation)

Let D be an arbitrary nonempty set.

An *interpretation I over the domain D* assigns values to each of a set of constant, variable, function, and predicate symbols, as follows:

- To each constant a in the set, an element a_I of D.

- To each variable x in the set, an element x_I of D.

- To each function symbol f of arity n in the set, an n-ary function $f_I(d_1, d_2, \ldots, d_n)$; the function f_I is defined on arguments d_1, d_2, $\ldots, d_n$ in D, and its value $f_I(d_1, d_2, \ldots, d_n)$ belongs to D.

- To each predicate symbol p of arity n in the set, an n-ary relation $p_I(d_1, d_2, \ldots, d_n)$; the relation p_I is defined on arguments d_1, d_2, $\ldots, d_n$ in D, and its value $p_I(d_1, d_2, \ldots, d_n)$ is either true or false.

For any expression $\mathcal{E}$ in predicate logic, an interpretation I is said to be an *interpretation for* $\mathcal{E}$ if I assigns a value to each of the free symbols of $\mathcal{E}$, i.e., to each of the constant, function, and predicate symbols and each of the free variables of $\mathcal{E}$. ◢

We have required that the domain of an interpretation be a nonempty set; otherwise we would not be able to assign any values to the constants and variables of an expression.

In general, an interpretation for an expression $\mathcal{E}$ may assign a value to some symbols that are not free in $\mathcal{E}$, i.e., constant, variable, function, or predicate symbols that do not occur in $\mathcal{E}$ at all, or variables that occur only bound in $\mathcal{E}$.

Example

Consider the sentence

$$\mathcal{E}: \quad \begin{array}{l} \textit{if } p(x, f(x)) \\ \textit{then (for some } y)p(a, y). \end{array}$$

Note that $\mathcal{E}$ has a free variable x.

Let I be the interpretation for $\mathcal{E}$ over the domain of the real numbers under which

a is $\sqrt{2}$,

x is π,

f is the "division by 2" function (that is, $f_I(d)$ is $d/2$), and

p is the "greater than or equal" relation (that is, $p_I(d_1, d_2)$ is $d_1 \geq d_2$).

Then the intuitive meaning of the sentence under I is

> If $\pi \geq \pi/2$,
> then there exists a real number d
> such that $\sqrt{2} \geq d$.

Note that the interpretation assigns no value to the variable y, which occurs bound but not free in $\mathcal{E}$.

Now let J be the interpretation for $\mathcal{E}$ over the set of all people under which

> a is Queen Elizabeth,
>
> b is Napoleon,
>
> x is George Washington,
>
> f is the "mother" function (that is, $f_J(d)$ is the mother of d), and
>
> p is the "child" relation (that is, $p_J(d_1, d_2)$ is "d_1 is the child of d_2").

Then the intuitive meaning of the sentence under J is

> If George Washington is the child of George Washington's mother,
> then there exists a person y
> such that Queen Elizabeth is the child of y.

Note that the interpretation assigns a value (Napoleon) to the constant b even though b does not occur in the sentence. ⌟

2.4   SEMANTIC RULES

Once we have provided an interpretation I for an expression (i.e., a sentence or term) $\mathcal{E}$, we can determine its value. For a sentence, this value is a truth value, either true or false; for a term, this value is an object in the domain D of the interpretation. As in propositional logic, the association of a value to an expression is done "recursively"; i.e., the value of the expression is determined from the values of its components, by applying the following semantic rules.

BASIC RULES

We first present the rules that apply to symbols other than quantifiers.

Definition (basic semantic rules)

Let $\mathcal{E}$ be an expression and I an interpretation for $\mathcal{E}$ over a nonempty domain D.

Then the *value of $\mathcal{E}$ under I* is determined by applying repeatedly the following *semantic rules*:

- *Constant rule*

  The value of a constant

  $$a$$

  is the domain element a_I.

- *Variable rule*

  The value of a variable

  $$x$$

  is the domain element x_I.

- *Application rule*

  The value of an application

  $$f(t_1, t_2, \ldots, t_n)$$

  is the domain element $f_I(d_1, d_2, \ldots, d_n)$, where f_I is the function assigned to f and $d_1, d_2, \ldots, d_n$ are the values of the terms $t_1, t_2, \ldots, t_n$, under I.

- *if-then-else term rule*

  The value of a conditional term

  $$if \;\mathcal{F}\; then \; s \; else \; t$$

  is the value of the term s if the sentence $\mathcal{F}$ is true and the value of the term t if $\mathcal{F}$ is false, under I.

- *true and false rules*

  The values of the truth symbols

  $$true \quad and \quad false$$

  are the truth values true and false, respectively.

- *Proposition rule*

  The value of a proposition

  $$p(t_1, t_2, \ldots, t_n)$$

  is the truth value $p_I(d_1, d_2, \ldots, d_n)$, either true or false, where p_I is the relation assigned to p and $d_1, d_2, \ldots, d_n$ are the values of the terms $t_1, t_2, \ldots, t_n$, under I.

The rules for the logical connectives are the same as for propositional logic:

- *not rule*

  The value of the negation

  $$not\ \mathcal{F}$$

  is true if the sentence $\mathcal{F}$ is false and false if $\mathcal{F}$ is true, under I.

We omit the rules for the other logical connectives *and, or, if-then, if-and-only-if,* and *if-then-else.* ◢

Before we give the semantic rules for the two quantifiers (*for all x*) and (*for some x*), which are somewhat more complex, let us give an example that does not require these rules.

Example

Consider the sentence

$$\mathcal{E}: \quad \begin{array}{l} not\ p(y,\ f(y)) \\ \quad or \\ p(a,\ f(f(a))) \end{array}$$

and let I be the interpretation over the domain of nonnegative integers under which

       a is 0,

       y is 2,

       f is the successor function (that is, $f_I(d)$ is $d+1$), and

       p is the less-than relation (that is, $p_I(d_1, d_2)$ is $d_1 < d_2$).

In other words, the interpretation I gives $\mathcal{E}$ the intuitive meaning

     not $2 < 2 + 1$
      or
     $0 < (0 + 1) + 1$.

We can use the semantic rules to determine the value of the first disjunct *not* $p(y, f(y))$ under this interpretation as follows:

We know (by the *variable* rule) that

> the value of y is 2.

Because y is 2 and f is the successor function, we know (by the *application* rule) that

> the value of $f(y)$ is 2+1, that is, 3.

Because y is 2, $f(y)$ is 3, and p is the less-than relation $<$, we know (by the *proposition* rule) that

> the value of $p(y, f(y))$ is $2 < 3$, that is, true.

Because $p(y, f(y))$ is true, we know (by the *not* rule) that

> the value of *not* $p(y, f(y))$ is false.

On the other hand, we can determine the value of the second disjunct $p(a, f(f(a)))$ under the interpretation $\mathcal{I}$ as follows:

We know (by the *constant* rule) that

> the value of a is 0.

Because a is 0 and f is the successor function, we know (by the *application* rule) that

> the value of $f(a)$ is $0 + 1$, that is, 1.

Because $f(a)$ is 1 and f is the successor function, we know (by the *application* rule) that

> the value of $f(f(a))$ is $1 + 1$, that is, 2.

Because a is 0, $f(f(a))$ is 2, and p is the less-than relation $<$, we know (by the *proposition* rule) that

> the value of $p(a, f(f(a)))$ is $0 < 2$, that is, true.

Finally, because under the interpretation $\mathcal{I}$ the first disjunct *not* $p(y, f(y))$ is false and the second disjunct $p(a, f(f(a)))$ is true, we know (by the *or* rule)

> the value of the entire sentence $\mathcal{E}$, that is,
> *not* $p(y, f(y))$
> > *or*
> $p(a, f(f(a)))$,

is true. ⌟

A problem arises when we attempt to express the value of a quantified sentence, of form (*for all x*)$\mathcal{F}$ or (*for some x*)$\mathcal{F}$, in terms of the value of its component $\mathcal{F}$, analogously to the other semantic rules. For example, if $\mathcal{E}$ is the sentence

$$(\textit{for all } x)p(x, y),$$

an interpretation I for $\mathcal{E}$ will assign a domain element to y and a relation to p, but may make no assignment to x, since x is not a free variable in $\mathcal{E}$. Consequently, we cannot determine a truth value for the subsentence $p(x, y)$ under the interpretation I.

Moreover, even if the interpretation of the sentence (*for all x*)$p(x, y)$ assigns some domain element to the variable x, we would like to ignore this assignment and to say that the sentence is true if $p(x, y)$ is true no matter what domain element is assigned to x. To make this idea precise requires that we introduce the notion of an "extended interpretation" for predicate logic. This interpretation assigns new values to symbols of a given interpretation, just as, in propositional logic, the extended interpretation assigns new values to the propositional symbols of a given interpretation.

EXTENDED INTERPRETATION

We show how to extend an interpretation by assigning a new value to a symbol.

Definition (extended interpretation)

Let I be any interpretation over a domain D.

For any variable x and element d of the domain D, the *extended interpretation*

$$\langle x \leftarrow d \rangle \circ I$$

of I is the interpretation over D under which:

- The variable x is assigned the domain element d.

- Each variable y other than x is assigned the domain element y_I, its original value under I. (If y has no value under I, it has no value under $\langle x \leftarrow d \rangle \circ I$ either.)

- Each constant a, function symbol f, and predicate symbol p are assigned their original values a_I, f_I, and p_I under I. (If the symbol has no value under I, it has no value under $\langle x \leftarrow d \rangle \circ I$ either.)

Similarly, for any constant a (or n-ary function symbol f or n-ary predicate symbol p, respectively) and for any domain element d (or n-ary function k or n-ary relation r over D, respectively), the extended interpretation

$$\langle a \leftarrow d \rangle \circ I$$

(or $\langle f \leftarrow k \rangle \circ I$ or $\langle p \leftarrow r \rangle \circ I$, respectively) of I is the interpretation over D under which:

- The constant a (or function symbol f or predicate symbol p, respectively) is assigned the domain element d (or function k or relation r, respectively).

- Each symbol other than a (or f or p, respectively) is assigned its original value under I. (If the symbol has no value under I, it has no value under the extended interpretation either.)

Note that the original interpretation I may already assign some value to the symbol x (or a, f, or p). If I does make such an assignment, it is superseded under the extended interpretation.

Example

Suppose that I is an interpretation over the domain of integers under which

x is 1
y is 2.

Then the extended interpretation

$$\langle x \leftarrow 3 \rangle \circ I$$

will still assign 2 to y but will now assign 3 to x; in other words, under $\langle x \leftarrow 3 \rangle \circ I$

x is 3
y is 2.

Example

Suppose I is an interpretation over the integers, f is a binary function symbol, and $+$ is the addition function over the integers. Then

$$\langle f \leftarrow + \rangle \circ I$$

is the interpretation over the integers under which

f is the addition function $+$

but any other symbol is assigned its original value under I. ◢

Although ultimately we shall need to consider extended interpretations for constant, function, and predicate symbols, in the semantic rules for quantifiers it is the extended interpretation $\langle x \leftarrow d \rangle \circ I$ for variables that will be used. Henceforth, we discuss only such extended interpretations, with the understanding that what we say may be applied to constant, function, and predicate symbols as well.

As in propositional logic, we may extend an interpretation several times in succession. For an interpretation I over a domain D, variables $x_1, x_2, \ldots, x_n$, and domain elements $d_1, d_2, \ldots, d_n$ in D, the notation

$$\langle x_1 \leftarrow d_1 \rangle \circ \langle x_2 \leftarrow d_2 \rangle \circ \ldots \circ \langle x_n \leftarrow d_n \rangle \circ I$$

is an abbreviation for the *multiply extended interpretation*

$$\langle x_1 \leftarrow d_1 \rangle \circ (\langle x_2 \leftarrow d_2 \rangle \circ \ldots \circ (\langle x_n \leftarrow d_n \rangle \circ I)...).$$

Note that, if x and y are distinct variables, the multiply extended interpretations

$$\langle x \leftarrow d \rangle \circ \langle y \leftarrow e \rangle \circ I \qquad \text{and} \qquad \langle y \leftarrow e \rangle \circ \langle x \leftarrow d \rangle \circ I$$

are identical for any domain elements d and e. On the other hand, if d and e are distinct domain elements, the multiply extended interpretations

$$\langle x \leftarrow d \rangle \circ \langle x \leftarrow e \rangle \circ I \qquad \text{and} \qquad \langle x \leftarrow e \rangle \circ \langle x \leftarrow d \rangle \circ I$$

are different; the former is identical to

$$\langle x \leftarrow d \rangle \circ I,$$

while the latter is identical to

$$\langle x \leftarrow e \rangle \circ I.$$

Remark

The extended interpretation has the property that,

> if I is an interpretation for a sentence of form
> *(for all x)*$\mathcal{F}$ or   *(for some x)*$\mathcal{F}$,
> then $\langle x \leftarrow d \rangle \circ I$ is an interpretation for $\mathcal{F}$.

Although the sentence $\mathcal{F}$ may have a free variable x that does not occur free in *(for all x)*$\mathcal{F}$ or *(for some x)*$\mathcal{F}$, an assignment of the domain element d to x is provided by the extended interpretation $\langle x \leftarrow d \rangle \circ I$. ⌐

RULES FOR QUANTIFIERS

We are finally ready to present the semantic rules that determine the truth values of sentences $\mathcal{E}$ of form *(for all x)*$\mathcal{F}$ and *(for some x)*$\mathcal{F}$ under an interpretation I. In each case, the value of $\mathcal{E}$ under I is determined from the values of its component $\mathcal{F}$, not under I but under certain extended interpretations of I.

Definition (semantic rules for quantifiers)

- *for-all rule*

Let I be an interpretation for a sentence *(for all x)*$\mathcal{F}$ over a domain D.

Then the value of a universally quantified sentence

> *(for all x)*$\mathcal{F}$

is true under I if

> for every domain element d in D
> the value of $\mathcal{F}$ is true under the extended interpretation
> $\langle x \leftarrow d \rangle \circ I$.

On the other hand, the value of the sentence is false under I if

> there exists a domain element d in D
> such that the value of $\mathcal{F}$ is false under the extended interpretation
> $\langle x \leftarrow d \rangle \circ I$.

- *for-some rule*

Let I be an interpretation for a sentence *(for some x)*$\mathcal{F}$ over a domain D.

Then the value of an existentially quantified sentence

$$(for\ some\ x)\mathcal{F}$$

is true under I if

there exists a domain element d in D
such that the value of $\mathcal{F}$ is true under the extended interpretation
$\langle x \leftarrow d \rangle \circ I$.

On the other hand, the value of the sentence is false under I if

for every domain element d in D
the value of $\mathcal{F}$ is false under the extended interpretation
$\langle x \leftarrow d \rangle \circ I$. ◢

Example

Consider the sentence

$$\mathcal{G}: \quad (for\ some\ x)p(x,\ y)$$

and let I be the interpretation over the positive integers under which

y is 2
p is the less-than relation $<$.

We claim that $\mathcal{G}$ is true under I.

To show this, we must show (by the *for-some* rule) that

there exists a domain element d in D
such that the value of
$p(x,\ y)$
is true under the extended interpretation $\langle x \leftarrow d \rangle \circ I$.

To show this, let us take d to be 1. Then, because p is the less-than relation, x is 1, and y is 2 under the extended interpretation $\langle x \leftarrow 1 \rangle \circ I$, we know (by the *proposition* rule) that

the value of
$p(x,\ y)$
is $1 < 2$, that is, true, under $\langle x \leftarrow 1 \rangle \circ I$,

as we wanted to show.

Therefore, the given sentence $\mathcal{G}$ is true under I. ◢

Example

Consider the sentence

$$\mathcal{H}: \quad \begin{array}{l} \textit{if (for all x)(for some y)}p(x,\,y) \\ \textit{then } p(a,\,f(a)), \end{array}$$

and let $\mathcal{I}$ be the interpretation over the positive real numbers under which

  a is 1
  f is the square-root function $\sqrt{\ }$
  p is the inequality relation $\neq$.

We claim that the sentence $\mathcal{H}$ is false under this interpretation. To show this, we show that, under $\mathcal{I}$, the antecedent

$$(\textit{for all x})(\textit{for some y})p(x,\,y)$$

is true and the consequent

$$p(a,\,f(a))$$

is false.

To show that the antecedent is true under $\mathcal{I}$, we must show (by the *for-all* rule) that

  for every domain element d in D
  the value of the subsentence
    $(\textit{for some y})p(x,\,y)$
  is true under the extended interpretation $\langle x \leftarrow d \rangle \circ \mathcal{I}$.

For this purpose, we show (by the *for-some* rule) that

  for every domain element d in D
  there exists a domain element d' in D
  such that the value of
    $p(x,\,y)$
  is true under the extended interpretation $\langle y \leftarrow d' \rangle \circ \langle x \leftarrow d \rangle \circ \mathcal{I}$.

However, for an arbitrary domain element d, let us take d' to be $d+1$. Then because p is the inequality relation $\neq$, x is d, and y is $d+1$, we know (by the *proposition* rule) that

  the value of
    $p(x,\,y)$
  is $d \neq d+1$, that is, true, under $\langle y \leftarrow d+1 \rangle \circ \langle x \leftarrow d \rangle \circ \mathcal{I}$,

as we wanted to show. Therefore

> the value of the antecedent
> $(for\ all\ x)(for\ some\ y)p(x,\ y)$
> is true under $\mathcal{I}$.

On the other hand, because p is the inequality relation $\neq$, a is 1, and f is the square-root function, we know (by the *proposition* rule) that

> the value of the consequent
> $p(a,\ f(a))$
> is $1 \neq \sqrt{1}$, that is, false, under $\mathcal{I}$.

Since the antecedent is true and the consequent is false, the entire implication $\mathcal{H}$ is false under $\mathcal{I}$. ⌟

In **Problem 2.1**, the reader is requested to determine the truth values of several sentences under particular interpretations.

AGREEMENT

We now discuss a relationship between two interpretations.

Definition (agreement)

Two interpretations *agree on* a symbol (i.e., a variable, constant, function, or predicate symbol) if either

> they both assign the same value to the symbol
> or
> neither assigns any value to the symbol.

Two interpretations $\mathcal{I}$ and $\mathcal{J}$ *agree on* an expression $\mathcal{E}$ if either

> the value of $\mathcal{E}$ under $\mathcal{I}$ is the same as the value of $\mathcal{E}$ under $\mathcal{J}$
> or
> neither $\mathcal{I}$ nor $\mathcal{J}$ is an interpretation for $\mathcal{E}$. ⌟

Example

Consider the interpretation I over the integers under which

$$I: \quad \begin{array}{l} a \text{ is } 0 \\ b \text{ is } 2 \\ x \text{ is } -1 \\ f \text{ is the successor function (that is, } f_I(d) = d+1) \end{array}$$

and the interpretation J over the integers under which

$$J: \quad \begin{array}{l} a \text{ is } 0 \\ x \text{ is } 1 \\ f \text{ is the predecessor function (that is, } f_J(d) = d-1). \end{array}$$

Then I and J agree on the constant a, because the value of a is 0 under each interpretation. Also, I and J agree on the predicate symbol p, because neither assigns any value to this symbol. On the other hand, I and J do not agree on the variable x, because the value of x is -1 under I but 1 under J.

Furthermore, I and J agree on the expression $f(x)$, because the value of $f(x)$ is $(-1)+1$, that is, 0, under I and $1-1$, that is, 0, under J. Also, I and J agree on the expression $f(y)$, because neither is an interpretation for this expression. On the other hand, I and J do not agree on the expression $f(b)$, because I is an interpretation for $f(b)$ but J is not. ⌐

The *agreement* proposition for predicate logic is analogous to that for propositional logic.

Proposition (agreement)

> If two interpretations (over the same domain) for an expression $\mathcal{E}$
>   agree on each free symbol of $\mathcal{E}$,
> then they agree on $\mathcal{E}$ itself. ⌐

The proposition is intuitively straightforward: We apply the same semantic rules in determining the value of $\mathcal{E}$ under each interpretation, yielding the same value at each stage.

The following observation relates the notion of agreement with that of a multiply extended interpretation. This observation is analogous to one we made for propositional logic.

Remark (multiply extended interpretation)

Suppose $\mathcal{E}$ is an expression and I is an interpretation for $\mathcal{E}$ over a domain D. Let $x_1, x_2, \ldots, x_n$ be variables that do not occur free in $\mathcal{E}$, and let $d_1, d_2, \ldots, d_n$ be arbitrary domain elements in D. Then the multiply extended interpretation

$$J = \langle x_1 \leftarrow d_1 \rangle \circ \langle x_2 \leftarrow d_2 \rangle \circ \ldots \circ \langle x_n \leftarrow d_n \rangle \circ I$$

and I itself agree on $\mathcal{E}$. ◢

2.5   VALIDITY

In predicate logic, we define validity only for closed sentences, i.e., sentences with no free variables. The definition is the same as it is for propositional-logic sentences.

Definition (valid)

A closed sentence $\mathcal{F}$ is *valid* if it is true under every interpretation for $\mathcal{F}$. ◢

ESTABLISHING VALIDITY

In this volume, we do not introduce formal methods for proving the validity of closed sentences of predicate logic; these methods are presented in a subsequent volume. However, we can use the semantic rules and common sense to convince ourselves that sentences are valid.

Example

Suppose we want to show the validity of the following *duality of quantifiers* sentence

$$\mathcal{E}: \quad \begin{array}{l} not \ (for \ all \ x)p(x) \\ \quad if \ and \ only \ if \\ (for \ some \ x)[not \ p(x)]. \end{array}$$

By the *if-and-only-if* rule, it suffices to show that

$$not \ (for \ all \ x)p(x)$$

and

$$(for\ some\ x)[not\ p(x)]$$

have the same truth value under any interpretation, i.e., that the former sentence is true precisely when the latter sentence is true.

Consider an arbitrary interpretation I for $\mathcal{E}$. We have that

$$not\ (for\ all\ x)p(x)\ \text{is true under } I$$

precisely when (by the *not* rule)

$$(for\ all\ x)p(x)\ \text{is false under } I$$

precisely when (by the *for-all* rule)

there exists a domain element d
such that $p(x)$ is false under $\langle x \leftarrow d \rangle \circ I$

precisely when (by the *not* rule)

there exists a domain element d
such that $\big(not\ p(x)\big)$ is true under $\langle x \leftarrow d \rangle \circ I$

precisely when (by the *for-some* rule)

$$(for\ some\ x)[not\ p(x)]\ \text{is true under } I,$$

as desired. ◢

This sentence and the similar valid sentence

$$not\ (for\ some\ x)p(x)$$
$$if\ and\ only\ if$$
$$(for\ all\ x)[not\ p(x)]$$

are said to express the *duality* between the universal and existential quantifiers.

Example

Suppose we would like to show the validity of the sentence

$$\mathcal{F}: \quad \begin{array}{l} if\ (for\ some\ x)\big[p(x)\ \ and\ \ r(x)\big] \\ then\ \big[(for\ some\ x)p(x)\ \ and\ \ (for\ some\ x)r(x)\big]. \end{array}$$

It suffices (by the *if-then* rule) to show that, for any interpretation I for $\mathcal{F}$, if the antecedent

$$(for\ some\ x)[p(x)\ \ and\ \ r(x)]$$

is true under I, then the consequent

$$(for\ some\ x)p(x)\ \ and\ \ (for\ some\ x)r(x)$$

must also be true under I.

Consider an arbitrary interpretation I for $\mathcal{F}$ and assume that the antecedent

$$(for\ some\ x)[p(x)\ and\ r(x)]$$

is true under I. Then (by the *for-some* rule)

there exists a domain element d such that
    $p(x)\ \ and\ \ r(x)$
is true under $\langle x \leftarrow d \rangle \circ I$.

Hence (by the *and* rule)

there exists a domain element d such that
    $p(x)$
and
    $r(x)$
are both true under $\langle x \leftarrow d \rangle \circ I$.

Hence (by common sense)

there exists a domain element d such that
    $p(x)$
is true under $\langle x \leftarrow d \rangle \circ I$
 and
there exists a domain element d such that
    $r(x)$
is true under $\langle x \leftarrow d \rangle \circ I$.

Hence (by the *for-some* rule, applied twice)

the subsentence
    $(for\ some\ x)p(x)$
is true under I
 and
the subsentence
    $(for\ some\ x)r(x)$
is true under I.

Hence (by the *and* rule)

the consequent of $\mathcal{F}$,
    $(for\ some\ x)p(x)\ \ and\ \ (for\ some\ x)r(x),$
is true under I,

as desired. ⌐

The reader may be surprised that the commonsense principles applied in establishing the validity of simple predicate logic sentences are the same as the intuitive meanings of the sentences themselves. This circularity is only apparent: In these arguments, we are not establishing the correctness of the commonsense principles, but only that the abstract symbols we have devised behave in accordance with our intuition.

Let us illustrate an indirect approach to showing the validity of a sentence. In this approach, we assume that the sentence is not valid and derive a contradiction.

Example

Suppose we want to show the validity of the sentence

$$\mathcal{G}: \quad \begin{array}{l} \textit{if (for some y)(for all x)q(x, y)} \\ \textit{then (for all x)(for some y)q(x, y).} \end{array}$$

Assume that $\mathcal{G}$ is not valid, i.e., that it is false under some interpretation $\mathcal{I}$. We try to derive a contradiction.

We have (by the *if-then* rule) that the antecedent,

$$\textit{(for some y)(for all x)q(x, y),}$$

is true under $\mathcal{I}$ and the consequent,

$$\textit{(for all x)(for some y)q(x, y),}$$

is false under $\mathcal{I}$.

Because the antecedent is true under $\mathcal{I}$, we have (by the *for-some* rule) that there exists a domain element e such that

$$(1) \quad \begin{array}{l} \textit{(for all x)q(x, y)} \\ \text{is true under } \langle y \leftarrow e \rangle \circ \mathcal{I}. \end{array}$$

Because the consequent is false under $\mathcal{I}$, we have (by the *for-all* rule) that there exists a domain element d such that

$$(2) \quad \begin{array}{l} \textit{(for some y)q(x, y)} \\ \text{is false under } \langle x \leftarrow d \rangle \circ \mathcal{I}. \end{array}$$

From (1) above, we can conclude (by the *for-all* rule) that

$$(3) \quad \begin{array}{l} \text{for every domain element } e' \\ q(x, y) \\ \text{is true under } \langle x \leftarrow e' \rangle \circ \langle y \leftarrow e \rangle \circ \mathcal{I}. \end{array}$$

From (2) above, we can conclude (by the *for-some* rule) that

> for every domain element d'
>
> (4) $q(x, y)$
>
> is false under $\langle y \leftarrow d' \rangle \circ \langle x \leftarrow d \rangle \circ I$.

In particular, in (3) above we can take the domain element e' to be d; and in (4) above, we can take the domain element d' to be e. We obtain, respectively,

> (5) $q(x, y)$
>
> is true under $\langle x \leftarrow d \rangle \circ \langle y \leftarrow e \rangle \circ I$

and

> (6) $q(x, y)$
>
> is false under $\langle y \leftarrow e \rangle \circ \langle x \leftarrow d \rangle \circ I$.

Because x and y are distinct, the interpretations

$$\langle x \leftarrow d \rangle \circ \langle y \leftarrow e \rangle \circ I$$

and

$$\langle y \leftarrow e \rangle \circ \langle x \leftarrow d \rangle \circ I$$

are identical, and hence (5) and (6) contradict each other.

We have contradicted our original assumption, that the sentence $\mathcal{G}$,

> *if* (*for some y*)(*for all x*) $q(x, y)$
> *then* (*for all x*)(*for some y*) $q(x, y)$,

is false under some interpretation I; therefore the sentence is valid. ⌙

ESTABLISHING NONVALIDITY

To be valid, a sentence must be true under any interpretation. Consequently, to show that a sentence is not valid, it suffices to discover a single interpretation under which the sentence is false.

Example

Let us show that the sentence

$$\mathcal{F}' : \quad \begin{aligned} &\textit{if } \big[(\textit{for some x})p(x) \ \textit{ and } \ (\textit{for some x})r(x)\big] \\ &\textit{then } (\textit{for some x})[p(x) \ \textit{ and } \ r(x)], \end{aligned}$$

which is the converse of the sentence $\mathcal{F}$ from a previous example, is not valid.

To show this, we need only discover a single interpretation I under which $\mathcal{F}'$ is false. Let I be the interpretation over all the integers under which

p is the "positive" relation   (that is, $p_I(d)$ is $d > 0$)
r is the "negative" relation   (that is, $r_I(d)$ is $d < 0$).

The intuitive meaning of the sentence $\mathcal{F}'$ under I is

If there exists an integer x such that $x > 0$ and
    there exists an integer x such that $x < 0$,
then there exists an integer x such that $x > 0$ and $x < 0$.

In other words, the sentence asserts that the existence of a positive integer x and the existence of a negative integer x guarantee the existence of a single integer x that is both positive and negative.

In fact, $\mathcal{F}'$ is false under the interpretation I. To show this, it suffices (by the *if-then* rule and the *and* rule) to show that

(for some x)$p(x)$ is true under I,

(for some x)$r(x)$ is true under I,

but

(for some x)$\bigl[p(x)$ *and* $r(x)\bigr]$ is false under I.

We have (by the *proposition* rule) that

$p(x)$ is true under $\langle x \leftarrow 1 \rangle \circ I$

and

$r(x)$ is true under $\langle x \leftarrow -1 \rangle \circ I$.

Therefore (by the *for-some* rule)

(for some x)$p(x)$ is true under I

and

(for some x)$r(x)$ is true under I.

On the other hand, for any integer d we know that d cannot be both positive and negative. Therefore

$(p(x)$ *and* $r(x))$ is false under $\langle x \leftarrow d \rangle \circ I$, and hence (by the *for-some* rule)

$$(for \ some \ x)\big[p(x) \ \ and \ \ r(x)\big] \text{ is false under } I,$$

as we wanted to show. ◢

Example (mother of us all)

Let us show that the sentence

$$\mathcal{G}' : \quad \begin{array}{l} if \ (for \ all \ x)(for \ some \ y) \ q(x, \ y) \\ then \ \ (for \ some \ y)(for \ all \ x) \ q(x, \ y), \end{array}$$

which is the converse of the sentence $\mathcal{G}$ of a previous example, is not valid.

Let I be the interpretation over the set of all people (living or dead) under which

q is the "mother" relation
(that is, $q_I(d_1, d_2)$ is "d_2 is the mother of d_1").

The intuitive meaning of the sentence under this interpretation is

if for every person x,
there exists a person y
such that y is the mother of x,
then there exists a person y
such that for every person x,
y is the mother of x,

that is,

if every person has a mother,
then there exists one mother of us all.

By applying the semantic rules for predicate logic, as in the previous example, we can establish that the antecedent of $\mathcal{G}'$ is true and the consequent of $\mathcal{G}'$ is false under I; therefore the entire sentence $\mathcal{G}'$ is false under I. Because we have found an interpretation I under which $\mathcal{G}'$ is false, we can conclude that $\mathcal{G}'$ is not valid. ◢

Example

Suppose we want to show that the sentence

$$\mathcal{H} : \quad \begin{array}{l} (for \ all \ x) \\ (for \ all \ y) \end{array} \left[\begin{array}{l} if \ p(x, x) \\ then \ if \ p(x, y) \\ \qquad then \ p(y, y) \end{array} \right]$$

is not valid. To establish this, it suffices to discover an interpretation $\mathcal{I}$ for $\mathcal{H}$ such that $\mathcal{H}$ is false under $\mathcal{I}$. For this purpose, we must (by two applications of the *for-all* rule) find domain elements d and e such that the quantifier-free subsentence

$$\mathcal{H'}: \quad \begin{array}{l} if \ p(x,x) \\ then \ if \ p(x,y) \\ \qquad then \ p(y,y) \end{array}$$

is false under the extended interpretation

$$\mathcal{I'}: \quad \langle x \leftarrow d \rangle \circ \langle y \leftarrow e \rangle \circ \mathcal{I}.$$

It suffices (by two applications of the *if-then* rule) to construct $\mathcal{I}$ and find domain elements d and e such that

$$p(x,x) \text{ and } p(x,y) \text{ are true under } \mathcal{I'}$$

and

$$p(y,y) \text{ is false under } \mathcal{I'}.$$

Let $\mathcal{I}$ be the interpretation over the set $\{A, B\}$ of two elements under which p is the relation $p_{\mathcal{I}}$ such that

$$p_{\mathcal{I}}(A, A) \text{ and } p_{\mathcal{I}}(A, B) \text{ are true}$$

and

$$p_{\mathcal{I}}(B, A) \text{ and } p_{\mathcal{I}}(B, B) \text{ are false.}$$

This relation can be illustrated by the following diagram:

In this representation each node corresponds to a domain element. An arc labeled $p_{\mathcal{I}}$ leading from one node to another indicates that the binary relation $p_{\mathcal{I}}$ holds between the corresponding domain elements; the absence of an arc indicates that the relation does not hold. A circular arc, leading from the node to itself, indicates that the relation $p_{\mathcal{I}}$ holds between the corresponding element and itself. This diagram notation is a convenient way to describe a binary relation over a finite set.

Let d and e be the domain elements A and B, respectively. Then the extended interpretation $\mathcal{I'}$ is

$$\langle x \leftarrow A \rangle \circ \langle y \leftarrow B \rangle \circ \mathcal{I},$$

and the truth values of

$$p(x,x), \quad p(x,y), \quad \text{and} \quad p(y,y)$$

under I' are

$$p_I(A,A), \quad p_I(A,B), \quad \text{and} \quad p_I(B,B),$$

respectively. Therefore

$$p(x,x) \text{ and } p(x,y) \text{ are true under } I'$$

and

$$p(y,y) \text{ is false under } I',$$

as we wanted to show. ⌐

Remark

Note that we could not have used an interpretation over a domain $\{A\}$ of a single element to show that the sentence $\mathcal{H}$ of the previous example is not valid. In fact, $\mathcal{H}$ is true under any such interpretation.

To show this, it suffices (by two applications of the *for-all* rule) to establish that, for any domain elements d and e, the quantifier-free subsentence

$$\mathcal{H'}: \quad \begin{array}{l} \textit{if } p(x,x) \\ \quad \textit{then if } p(x,y) \\ \qquad \textit{then } p(y,y) \end{array}$$

is true under the extended interpretation $I' : \langle x \leftarrow d \rangle \circ \langle x \leftarrow e \rangle \circ I$. But since we have only one element in our domain, we are forced to take d and e to be the same element A. Therefore, the truth values of $p(x,x)$, $p(x,y)$, and $p(y,y)$ under I' are all identical to $p_I(A,A)$. Hence (by two applications of the *if-then* rule, whether or not $p_I(A,A)$ is true), $\mathcal{H'}$ is true under I', as we wanted to show. ⌐

EXAMPLES OF VALID SENTENCES

We present some examples of valid sentences, dividing them into separate categories.

- Instances of valid propositional-logic sentences

  (for all x)p(x)
     or
  not (for all x)p(x)

  $$(\textit{for all } y)\begin{bmatrix} \textit{if } (\textit{for some } x)q(x,y) \\ \textit{then } (\textit{for some } x)q(x,y) \end{bmatrix}$$

- Removal and introduction of quantifiers

  if (for all x)p(x)
  then p(a)

  if p(a)
  then (for some y)p(y)

- Renaming of variables

  (for all x)p(x)
    if and only if
  (for all y)p(y)

  (for some x)p(x)
    if and only if
  (for some y)p(y)

- Reversal of quantifiers

  $$\begin{bmatrix} (\textit{for all } x) \\ (\textit{for all } y) \end{bmatrix}q(x,y)$$
  if and only if
  $$\begin{bmatrix} (\textit{for all } y) \\ (\textit{for all } x) \end{bmatrix}q(x,y)$$

  $$\begin{bmatrix} (\textit{for some } x) \\ (\textit{for some } y) \end{bmatrix}q(x,y)$$
  if and only if
  $$\begin{bmatrix} (\textit{for some } y) \\ (\textit{for some } x) \end{bmatrix}q(x,y)$$

  if (for some y)(for all x)q(x,y)
  then (for all x)(for some y)q(x,y)

- Redundant quantifiers

  $$\begin{bmatrix} (\textit{for all } x) \\ (\textit{for all } x) \end{bmatrix}p(x)$$
  if and only if
  (for all x)p(x)

  $$\begin{bmatrix} (\textit{for some } x) \\ (\textit{for some } x) \end{bmatrix}p(x)$$
  if and only if
  (for some x)p(x)

- Duality of quantifiers

  not (for all x)p(x)
    if and only if
  (for some x)[not p(x)]

  not (for some x)p(x)
    if and only if
  (for all x)[not p(x)]

● Distribution of quantifiers

$(for\ all\ x)[p(x)\ and\ r(x)]$
 if and only if
$(for\ all\ x)p(x)\ and\ (for\ all\ x)r(x)$

$(for\ some\ x)[p(x)\ or\ r(x)]$
 if and only if
$(for\ some\ x)p(x)\ or\ (for\ some\ x)r(x)$

$(for\ some\ x)[if\ p(x)\ then\ r(x)]$
 if and only if
$if\ (for\ all\ x)p(x)\ then\ (for\ some\ x)r(x)$

● Distribution of conditionals

$$(for\ all\ x)\begin{bmatrix} p(if\ r(x)\ then\ a\ else\ b) \\ if\ and\ only\ if \\ if\ r(x)\ then\ p(a)\ else\ p(b) \end{bmatrix}$$

$$(for\ all\ x)\begin{bmatrix} p(f(if\ r(x)\ then\ a\ else\ b)) \\ if\ and\ only\ if \\ p(if\ r(x)\ then\ f(a)\ else\ f(b)) \end{bmatrix}$$

The validity of some of these sentences has been established earlier. The reader is requested to establish the validity or nonvalidity of several sentences in **Problem 2.2**. Also, the reader is requested to construct sentences that are true over some domains but false over others in **Problem 2.3**.

ADDITIONAL CONCEPTS

There are several additional concepts that are related to validity but not of such importance to us here.

Definition (satisfiable, contradictory, consistent)

A closed sentence $\mathcal{F}$ is *satisfiable* if it is true under some interpretation for $\mathcal{F}$.

A closed sentence $\mathcal{F}$ is *contradictory* (or *unsatisfiable*) if it is false under every interpretation for $\mathcal{F}$.

A set of closed sentences $\mathcal{F}_1, \mathcal{F}_2, \ldots,$ is *consistent* if there exists some interpretation for $\mathcal{F}_1, \mathcal{F}_2, \ldots,$ under which each $\mathcal{F}_i$ is true. ⌐

As in propositional logic, these notions can each be paraphrased in terms of validity. For example,

> a closed sentence $\mathcal{F}$ is contradictory,
> i.e., false under every interpretation for $\mathcal{F}$,

precisely when

> ($not\ \mathcal{F}$) is valid.

Example

The sentence

$$\mathcal{F}:\quad (for\ some\ x)p(x)$$

is satisfiable: It is true under the interpretation $\mathcal{I}$ over the integers such that $p_\mathcal{I}(d)$ is the relation $d = 0$. Note that there are interpretations under which $\mathcal{F}$ is false, e.g., the interpretation $\mathcal{J}$ over the integers such that $p_\mathcal{J}(d)$ is false for every integer d. Therefore $\mathcal{F}$ is not valid.

The sentence

$$\mathcal{G}:\quad \begin{array}{c} (for\ all\ x)p(x) \\ and \\ (for\ some\ x)[not\ p(x)] \end{array}$$

is contradictory; it is false under every interpretation. ⌙

2.6   UNIVERSAL AND EXISTENTIAL CLOSURE

We have defined validity and the other logical concepts only for closed sentences. We now define two operations that add quantifiers to a given sentence to produce a closed sentence.

Definition (closure)

Suppose that $x_1,\ x_2,\ \ldots, x_n$ is a complete list of the distinct free variables of a sentence $\mathcal{F}$ (in the order in which they first occur). Then:

- The *universal closure of* $\mathcal{F}$, denoted by ($for\ all\ *$)$\mathcal{F}$, is the closed sentence

$$(for\ all\ x_1)(for\ all\ x_2)\ldots(for\ all\ x_n)\mathcal{F}.$$

- The *existential closure of $\mathcal{F}$*, denoted by *(for some ∗)*$\mathcal{F}$, is the closed sentence

$$(for\ some\ x_1)(for\ some\ x_2)\ldots(for\ some\ x_n)\mathcal{F}. \quad \rfloor$$

Example

The free variables of the sentence

$$\mathcal{F}:\quad (for\ some\ z)\begin{bmatrix} q(y,z)\quad or\quad r(x)\\ and\\ (for\ all\ w)p(y,z,w)\end{bmatrix},$$

in order of first occurrence, are y and x; therefore the universal closure of $\mathcal{F}$, that is, *(for all ∗)*$\mathcal{F}$, is

$$(for\ all\ y)(for\ all\ x)(for\ some\ z)\begin{bmatrix} q(y,z)\quad or\quad r(x)\\ and\\ (for\ all\ w)p(y,z,w)\end{bmatrix},$$

and the existential closure of $\mathcal{F}$, that is, *(for some ∗)*$\mathcal{F}$, is

$$(for\ some\ y)(for\ some\ x)(for\ some\ z)\begin{bmatrix} q(y,z)\quad or\quad r(x)\\ and\\ (for\ all\ w)p(y,z,w)\end{bmatrix}.$$

In our usual two-dimensional format, we may write the universal closure *(for all ∗)*$\mathcal{F}$ of $\mathcal{F}$ as

$$\begin{matrix}(for\ all\ y)\\(for\ all\ x)\end{matrix}(for\ some\ z)\begin{bmatrix} q(y,z)\quad or\quad r(x)\\ and\\ (for\ all\ w)p(y,z,w)\end{bmatrix}$$

and the existential closure *(for some ∗)*$\mathcal{F}$ of $\mathcal{F}$ as

$$\begin{matrix}(for\ some\ y)\\(for\ some\ x)\end{matrix}(for\ some\ z)\begin{bmatrix} q(y,z)\quad or\quad r(x)\\ and\\ (for\ all\ w)p(y,z,w)\end{bmatrix}. \quad \rfloor$$

Although the closure operators, *(for all ∗)* and *(for some ∗)*, are merely abbreviations and not legitimate symbols of predicate logic, they may be seen to obey semantic rules resembling those for quantifiers. We present each rule in a separate proposition.

Proposition (semantic rule for universal closure)

Suppose $\mathcal{F}$ is a sentence and I is an interpretation, over a domain D, for the universal closure *(for all $*$)$\mathcal{F}$* of $\mathcal{F}$.

Let $x_1, x_2, \ldots, x_n$ be a complete list of the distinct free variables of $\mathcal{F}$, in order of occurrence.

Then

> the value of the universal closure
> *(for all $*$)$\mathcal{F}$*
> is true under I *(closure)*

precisely when

> for any domain elements $d_1, d_2, \ldots, d_n$ of D,
> the value of $\mathcal{F}$ is true under the extended interpretation
> $\langle x_1 \leftarrow d_1 \rangle \circ \langle x_2 \leftarrow d_2 \rangle \circ \ldots \circ \langle x_n \leftarrow d_n \rangle \circ I$ *(extension)*

precisely when

> for every interpretation J for $\mathcal{F}$ that agrees with I
> on the free symbols of *(for all $*$)$\mathcal{F}$*,
> $\mathcal{F}$ is true under J.   *(agreement)*

We have named the three conditions of the rule for ease in referring to them later.

Note that, in the proposition, I is an interpretation for the universal closure *(for all $*$)$\mathcal{F}$* of $\mathcal{F}$, but I need not be an interpretation for $\mathcal{F}$ itself, because the free variables $x_1, x_2, \ldots, x_n$ of $\mathcal{F}$ are not free in the universal closure and therefore need not be assigned any values under I.

Note also that, since *(for all $*$)$\mathcal{F}$* contains no free variables, the "free symbols" referred to in the agreement condition are precisely the constant, function, and predicate symbols of $\mathcal{F}$. The interpretations J referred to in the *agreement* condition must agree with I on these symbols, but need not agree with I on the variables $x_1, x_2, \ldots, x_n$.

Finally, note that the multiply extended interpretation $\langle x_1 \leftarrow d_1 \rangle \circ \langle x_2 \leftarrow d_2 \rangle \circ \ldots \circ \langle x_n \leftarrow d_n \rangle \circ I$ referred to in the *extension* condition is one of the interpretations J for $\mathcal{F}$ mentioned in the *agreement* condition. In other words, this interpretation agrees with I on the free symbols of *(for all $*$)$\mathcal{F}$*.

Example

Consider the sentence

$$\mathcal{F}: \quad q(x_1, x_2) \ \ or \ \ not \ q(x_1, x_2).$$

The free variables of $\mathcal{F}$, in order of first occurrence, are x_1 and x_2. The universal closure of $\mathcal{F}$ is

$$(\textit{for all } *)\mathcal{F}: \quad \begin{matrix} (\textit{for all } x_1) \\ (\textit{for all } x_2) \end{matrix} \Big[q(x_1, x_2) \quad \textit{or} \quad \textit{not } q(x_1, x_2) \Big].$$

The only free symbol of $(\textit{for all } *)\mathcal{F}$ is the predicate symbol q. An interpretation I over a domain D for $(\textit{for all } *)\mathcal{F}$ must assign a relation q_I to q, but it need not assign any domain elements to x_1 or x_2.

According to the proposition,

> $(\textit{for all } *)\mathcal{F}$ is true under I

precisely when

> for any domain elements d_1 and d_2 of D,
> $\mathcal{F}$ is true under $\langle x_1 \leftarrow d_1 \rangle \circ \langle x_2 \leftarrow d_2 \rangle \circ I$

precisely when

> for every interpretation J for $\mathcal{F}$ that agrees with I on the predicate symbol q, $\mathcal{F}$ is true under J.   ⌟

The proposition may be justified by appealing to the semantic rules for the universal and existential quantifiers and to the *agreement* proposition.

Proof (semantic rule for universal closure)

Let I be an arbitrary interpretation over a domain D for $(\textit{for all } *)\mathcal{F}$. Let us prove each part of the proposition separately.

Closure condition ⇔ extension condition

We have the *closure* condition

> the value of the universal closure $(\textit{for all } *)\mathcal{F}$, that is,
> $\quad (\textit{for all } x_1)(\textit{for all } x_2) \ldots (\textit{for all } x_n)\mathcal{F}$,
> is true under I

precisely when (by the *for-all* rule)

> for every domain element d_1 of D,
> $\quad (\textit{for all } x_2) \ldots (\textit{for all } x_n)\mathcal{F}$
> is true under $\langle x_1 \leftarrow d_1 \rangle \circ I$

precisely when (by $n-1$ further applications of the *for-all* rule)

> for every domain element d_n of D,
>
> $\vdots$
>
> for every domain element d_2 of D,
> for every domain element d_1 of D,
> $\mathcal{F}$ is true under
> $$\langle x_n \leftarrow d_n \rangle \circ \ldots \circ \langle x_2 \leftarrow d_2 \rangle \circ \langle x_1 \leftarrow d_1 \rangle \circ \mathcal{I}$$

precisely when (because $x_1, x_2, \ldots, x_n$ are distinct)

> for any domain elements $d_1, d_2, \ldots, d_n$ of D,
> $\mathcal{F}$ is true under
> $$\langle x_1 \leftarrow d_1 \rangle \circ \langle x_2 \leftarrow d_2 \rangle \circ \ldots \circ \langle x_n \leftarrow d_n \rangle \circ \mathcal{I},$$

which is the *extension* condition.

For the second part of the proposition, we need to establish each direction separately.

Extension condition $\Rightarrow$ agreement condition

Suppose the *extension* condition holds, that is,

> for any domain elements $d_1, d_2, \ldots, d_n$ of D,
> $\mathcal{F}$ is true under the extended interpretation
> $$\langle x_1 \leftarrow d_1 \rangle \circ \langle x_2 \leftarrow d_2 \rangle \circ \ldots \circ \langle x_n \leftarrow d_n \rangle \circ \mathcal{I}.$$

We would like to show the *agreement* condition holds, that is,

> for every interpretation J for $\mathcal{F}$ that agrees with $\mathcal{I}$
> on the free symbols of *(for all $*$)*$\mathcal{F}$,
> $\mathcal{F}$ is true under J.

Let J be any such interpretation; we show that $\mathcal{F}$ is true under J. Let $e_1, e_2, \ldots, e_n$ be the values under J of the free variables $x_1, x_2, \ldots, x_n$ of $\mathcal{F}$. Then, by the *extension* condition, which we have supposed to be true, $\mathcal{F}$ is true under the extended interpretation

$$\mathcal{I}': \quad \langle x_1 \leftarrow e_1 \rangle \circ \langle x_2 \leftarrow e_2 \rangle \circ \ldots \circ \langle x_n \leftarrow e_n \rangle \circ \mathcal{I}.$$

We have assumed that J agrees with $\mathcal{I}$ on the free symbols of *(for all $*$)*$\mathcal{F}$, i.e., on the constant, function, and predicate symbols of $\mathcal{F}$. Hence (by the definition of $\mathcal{I}'$), J agrees with $\mathcal{I}'$ on the free symbols of *(for all $*$)*$\mathcal{F}$. By the way $e_1, e_2, \ldots, e_n$ were selected, J also agrees with $\mathcal{I}'$ on the free variables $x_1, x_2, \ldots, x_n$ of $\mathcal{F}$. In other words, J agrees with $\mathcal{I}'$ on all the free symbols of $\mathcal{F}$ and hence (by the *agreement* proposition) on $\mathcal{F}$ itself.

Thus, since we have established that $\mathcal{F}$ is true under I', we may conclude that $\mathcal{F}$ is also true under J, as we wanted to show. This establishes the *agreement* condition.

Agreement condition $\Rightarrow$ *extension condition*

Suppose the *agreement* condition holds; that is,

> for every interpretation J for $\mathcal{F}$ that agrees with I
> on the free symbols of *(for all $*$)$\mathcal{F}$*,
> $\mathcal{F}$ is true under J.

We would like to show that the *extension* condition holds; that is,

> for any domain elements $d_1, d_2, \ldots, d_n$ of D,
> $\mathcal{F}$ is true under the extended interpretation
> $$I': \quad \langle x_1 \leftarrow d_1 \rangle \circ \langle x_2 \leftarrow d_2 \rangle \circ \ldots \circ \langle x_n \leftarrow d_n \rangle \circ I.$$

Consider arbitrary domain elements $d_1, d_2, \ldots, d_n$ in D. Because I' agrees with I on all the free symbols of *(for all $*$)$\mathcal{F}$*, it follows by the *agreement* condition, which we have supposed to be true, that

> $\mathcal{F}$ is true under I',

as we wanted to show. This establishes the *extension* condition. ⌐

The semantic rule for the existential closure is analogous.

Proposition (semantic rule for existential closure)

Suppose $\mathcal{F}$ is a sentence and I is an interpretation, over a domain D, for the existential closure *(for some $*$)$\mathcal{F}$* of $\mathcal{F}$.

Let $x_1, x_2, \ldots, x_n$ be a complete list of the distinct free variables of $\mathcal{F}$, in order of occurrence.

Then

> the value of the existential closure
> *(for some $*$)$\mathcal{F}$*
> is true under I (*closure*)

precisely when

> there exist domain elements $d_1, d_2, \ldots, d_n$ of D such that
> the value of $\mathcal{F}$ is true under the extended interpretation
> $$\langle x_1 \leftarrow d_1 \rangle \circ \langle x_2 \leftarrow d_2 \rangle \circ \ldots \circ \langle x_n \leftarrow d_n \rangle \circ I \quad (\textit{extension})$$

precisely when

> there exists an interpretation J for $\mathcal{F}$ that agrees with I
> on the free symbols of $(for \; some \; *)\mathcal{F}$ such that
> $\mathcal{F}$ is true under J.   (*agreement*) ⌐

The proof of the *existential-closure* rule is analogous to that for the *universal-closure* rule, but uses the *for-some* rule in place of the *for-all* rule.

The semantic rules for universal and existential closure allow us to establish the following proposition:

Proposition (validity and satisfiability of closures)

For any sentence $\mathcal{F}$

> the universal closure $(for \; all \; *)\mathcal{F}$ is valid
>   precisely when
> $\mathcal{F}$ is true under every interpretation for $\mathcal{F}$;   (*validity*)

> the existential closure $(for \; some \; *)\mathcal{F}$ is satisfiable
>   precisely when
> $\mathcal{F}$ is true under some interpretation for $\mathcal{F}$.   (*satisfiability*) ⌐

We prove only the validity part.

Proof (validity of closures)

We establish each direction separately.

(⇐)

Suppose $\mathcal{F}$ is true under every interpretation; we would like to show that its universal closure $(for \; all \; *)\mathcal{F}$ is valid, i.e., true under any interpretation.

Consider an arbitrary interpretation I of the sentence $(for \; all \; *)\mathcal{F}$. To show that $(for \; all \; *)\mathcal{F}$ is true under I, it suffices (by the *universal-closure* rule) to show that $\mathcal{F}$ is true under any interpretation J that agrees with I on the free symbols of $(for \; all \; *)\mathcal{F}$; but this follows from our assumption that $\mathcal{F}$ is true under any interpretation.

$(\Rightarrow)$

Suppose *(for all* $*$*)*$\mathcal{F}$ is valid; we would like to show that $\mathcal{F}$ is true under every interpretation for $\mathcal{F}$.

Consider an arbitrary interpretation J for $\mathcal{F}$. Then J is also an interpretation for *(for all* $*$*)*$\mathcal{F}$, and J clearly agrees with itself on the free symbols of *(for all* $*$*)*$\mathcal{F}$. Because *(for all* $*$*)*$\mathcal{F}$ is valid, it is true under J. Therefore (by the *universal-closure* rule) $\mathcal{F}$ is also true under J, as we wanted to show.   ⌐

PROBLEMS

Problem 2.1 (interpretations)   page 95

Consider the sentences

(a) $p(x, a)$

(b) $p(a, x)$ *and* $p\big(x, f(x)\big)$

(c) *(for some* y*)*$p(y, x)$

(d) *(for some* y*)*$\big[p(y, a)$ *or* $p\big(f(y), y\big)\big]$

(e) *(for all* x*)*(for some* y*)*$p(x, y)$

(f) *(for some* y*)*(for all* x*)*$p(x, y)$.

Let I be the interpretation over the nonnegative integers under which

  a is 0

  x is 1

  f is the successor function (that is, $f_I(d)$ is $d + 1$)

  p is the less-than relation (that is, $p_I(d_1, d_2)$ is $d_1 < d_2$).

Let J be the interpretation over all the integers (nonnegative and negative) under which

  a is 0

  x is -1

  y is 0

f is the successor function

p is the less-than relation.

Determine the truth values of each of the above sentences under the interpretation $\mathcal{I}$ and under the interpretation $\mathcal{J}$.

Problem 2.2 (validity)   page 107

Some of the following sentences are valid; others are not. For each sentence give either an informal argument showing its validity or an interpretation under which its value is false.

(a) *(for some x)*$\big[$*if p(x) then r(x)*$\big]$
      if and only if
      if (for all x)p(x) then (for some x)r(x)

(b) *if (for all x)[p(x) or r(x)]*
      then $\big[$*(for all x)p(x) or (for all x)r(x)*$\big]$

(c) *if* $\big[$*(for all x)p(x) or (for all x)r(x)*$\big]$
      then (for all x)[p(x) or r(x)]

(d) *(for some x)*$\big[$*p(x) if and only if r(x)*$\big]$
      if and only if
      [(for some x)p(x)] if and only if [(for some x)r(x)]

(e) *(for some x)* $\begin{bmatrix} \textit{if } p(x) \textit{ then } p(a) \\ \textit{and} \\ \textit{if } p(x) \textit{ then } p(b) \end{bmatrix}$

(f) *(for some x)(for all y)* $\begin{bmatrix} \textit{if } (q(x,y) \textit{ and not } q(y,x)) \\ \textit{then } (q(x,x) \textit{ if and only if } q(y,y)) \end{bmatrix}$

(g) *(for some x)*$\big[$*p(x) and q(x)*$\big]$
      or
      (for all x)$\big[$*if p(x) then not q(x)*$\big]$

(h) *(for all x)* $\begin{bmatrix} p(\textit{if } r(x) \textit{ then } a \textit{ else } b) \\ \textit{if and only if} \\ \textit{if } r(x) \textit{ then } p(a) \textit{ else } p(b) \end{bmatrix}$.

Problem 2.3 (domains of two or three elements)   page 107

(a) Find a sentence that is true for any interpretation whose domain has
    precisely two elements, but false for some interpretation whose domain
    has three elements.

(b) Find a sentence that is true for any interpretation whose domain has
    precisely three elements, but false for some interpretation whose domain
    has four elements.

Give an informal justification for your answers.

3

Predicate Logic: Advanced

In the previous chapter we introduced methods for establishing validity and other properties of particular predicate-logic sentences. It is often more convenient to treat an entire class of sentences as a single unit, or "schema." This is the subject of the present chapter.

3.1 VALID SENTENCE SCHEMATA

We have given examples of particular valid sentences of predicate logic such as

> *not (for all x)p(x)*
>   *if and only if*
> *(for some x)[not p(x)].*

We cannot directly conclude from the above sentence that a different sentence of the same form, such as

> *not (for all x)[(for some y)q(x, y)]*
>   *if and only if*
> *(for some x)[not (for some y)q(x, y)],*

is also valid.

It is more useful to establish at once that entire classes of sentences are valid. For example, in a single argument we can establish that, for any sentence $\mathcal{F}$, the universal closure of the sentence

$$not \; (for \; all \; x) \mathcal{F}$$
$$if \; and \; only \; if$$
$$(for \; some \; x)[not \; \mathcal{F}]$$

is valid. This accomplished, we can immediately infer that the above two particular sentences are valid: In the first case, we take $\mathcal{F}$ to be $p(x)$; in the second, we
take $\mathcal{F}$ to be $(for \; some \; y)q(x, y)$. As in propositional logic, we shall refer to such
a "sentence," containing script symbols $\mathcal{F}$, $\mathcal{G}$, $\mathcal{H}$, ..., as a *sentence schema*; we
shall refer to the particular sentences it represents as *instances* of the schema.

Note that we generally speak about establishing the validity of the universal
closure of a sentence schema, rather than of the schema itself, because a particular
sentence $\mathcal{F}$, $\mathcal{G}$, or $\mathcal{H}$ may have some free variables, and we have only defined
validity for closed sentences.

VALIDITY OF SENTENCE SCHEMA

We can establish the validity of a sentence schema by the same style of argument
we used for particular sentences.

Example

Suppose we want to show the validity of the universal closure of the sentence
schema

$$not \; (for \; all \; x) \mathcal{F}$$
$$if \; and \; only \; if$$
$$(for \; some \; x)[not \; \mathcal{F}].$$

In other words, we would like to show that

$$(for \; all \; *) \begin{bmatrix} not \; (for \; all \; x) \mathcal{F} \\ if \; and \; only \; if \\ (for \; some \; x)[not \; \mathcal{F}] \end{bmatrix}$$

is valid. It suffices (by the *validity-of-closures* proposition) to show that the
subsentence

$$\mathcal{E} : \quad \begin{array}{l} not \; (for \; all \; x) \mathcal{F} \\ if \; and \; only \; if \\ (for \; some \; x)[not \; \mathcal{F}] \end{array}$$

is true under every interpretation. For this purpose, we may (by the *if-and-only-if* rule) show that

$$not\ (for\ all\ x)\mathcal{F}$$

and

$$(for\ some\ x)[not\ \mathcal{F}]$$

have the same truth value under any interpretation, i.e., that the former sentence is true precisely when the latter sentence is true.

Consider an arbitrary interpretation I for $\mathcal{E}$. We have that

$$not\ (for\ all\ x)\mathcal{F}\ \text{is true under}\ I$$

precisely when (by the *not* rule)

$$(for\ all\ x)\mathcal{F}\ \text{is false under}\ I$$

precisely when (by the *for-all* rule)

> there exists a domain element d such that
> $\mathcal{F}$ is false under $\langle x \leftarrow d \rangle \circ I$

precisely when (by the *not* rule)

> there exists a domain element d such that
> $(not\ \mathcal{F})$ is true under $\langle x \leftarrow d \rangle \circ I$

precisely when (by the *for-some* rule)

$$(for\ some\ x)[not\ \mathcal{F}]\ \text{is true under}\ I,$$

as desired. ⌐

The reader may have noticed that the proof of the validity of the sentence schema in the above example resembles the earlier proof of the validity of the particular sentence

$$not\ (for\ all\ x)p(x)$$
$$if\ and\ only\ if$$
$$(for\ some\ x)\big[not\ p(x)\big],$$

which is an instance of the sentence schema.

CATALOG OF VALID SENTENCE SCHEMATA

By similar methods, we can establish the validity of the universal closures of the following sentence schemata.

- Reversal of quantifiers

(for all x)(for all y)$\mathcal{F}$ *(for some x)(for some y)$\mathcal{F}$*
     if and only if   *if and only if*
(for all y)(for all x)$\mathcal{F}$ *(for some y)(for some x)$\mathcal{F}$*

             if (for some y)(for all x)$\mathcal{F}$
            then (for all x)(for some y)$\mathcal{F}$

- Duality of quantifiers

not (for all x)$\mathcal{F}$ *not (for some x)$\mathcal{F}$*
    if and only if   *if and only if*
(for some x)[not $\mathcal{F}$]   *(for all x)[not $\mathcal{F}$]*

- Distribution of quantifiers (equivalences)

(for all x)[$\mathcal{F}$ and $\mathcal{G}$]   *(for some x)[$\mathcal{F}$ or $\mathcal{G}$]*
     if and only if   *if and only if*
(for all x)$\mathcal{F}$ and (for all x)$\mathcal{G}$ *(for some x)$\mathcal{F}$ or (for some x)$\mathcal{G}$*

           (for some x)[if $\mathcal{F}$ then $\mathcal{G}$]
                if and only if
       if (for all x)$\mathcal{F}$ then (for some x)$\mathcal{G}$

- Distribution of quantifiers (implications)

if (for some x)[$\mathcal{F}$ and $\mathcal{G}$] $\left[\begin{array}{l}\textit{(for all x)}\mathcal{F}\\ \textit{or}\\ \textit{(for all x)}\mathcal{G}\end{array}\right.$
        $\left[\begin{array}{l}\textit{(for some x)}\mathcal{F}\\ \textit{and}\\ \textit{(for some x)}\mathcal{G}\end{array}\right.$ *if*
then   *then (for all x)[$\mathcal{F}$ or $\mathcal{G}$]*

   if $\left[\begin{array}{l}\textit{if (for some x)}\mathcal{F}\\ \textit{then (for all x)}\mathcal{G}\end{array}\right]$ *if (for all x)[if $\mathcal{F}$ then $\mathcal{G}$]*
then (for all x)[if $\mathcal{F}$ then $\mathcal{G}$]   *then* $\left[\begin{array}{l}\textit{if (for all x)}\mathcal{F}\\ \textit{then (for all x)}\mathcal{G}\end{array}\right]$

     The reader is requested in **Problem 3.1** to establish the validity of some of these schemata.

Note that under the headings *reversal of quantifiers* and *distribution of quantifiers*, certain of the sentences are implications rather than equivalences. In fact, the universal closures of the converses of each of these implications are not valid.

For example, consider the implication under the heading *reversal of quantifiers*,

> *if (for some y)(for all x)$\mathcal{F}$*
> *then (for all x)(for some y)$\mathcal{F}$.*

The converse is the sentence schema

> *if (for all x)(for some y)$\mathcal{F}$*
> *then (for some y)(for all x)$\mathcal{F}$.*

In a previous example (the *mother-of-us-all* example), we have discussed a particular instance of this schema,

> *if (for all x)(for some y)q(x, y)*
> *then (for some y)(for all x)q(x, y).*

We have seen that this sentence is not valid; e.g., it is false under the interpretation over the domain of all people under which the predicate symbol q is taken to be the "mother" relation.

The reader is requested in **Problem 3.1** to construct such interpretations for the converses of some other implications in this section.

VALID PROPOSITIONAL-LOGIC SENTENCES

A useful if obvious class of valid sentences is the universal closures of predicate-logic sentences that are instances of valid propositional-logic sentences. For example, consider the valid propositional-logic sentence

> *if P*
> *then P or Q.*

An instance of this sentence in predicate logic is obtained by replacing the propositional symbols P and Q with arbitrary predicate-logic sentences. Thus, taking P and Q to be $p(x)$ and *(for some y)q(x, y)*, respectively, we obtain the predicate-logic sentence

> *if p(x)*
> *then p(x) or (for some y)q(x, y).*

This sentence is not closed (it has the free variable x), but its universal closure is the valid predicate-logic sentence

$$(\textit{for all } x) \left[\begin{array}{l} \textit{if } p(x) \\ \textit{then } p(x) \;\; \textit{or} \;\; (\textit{for some } y)q(x,y) \end{array} \right].$$

The validity of such predicate-logic sentences is established in the following result.

Proposition (instances of valid propositional-logic sentences)

If a propositional-logic sentence $\mathcal{E}$ is valid,
then the universal closure of a predicate-logic instance of $\mathcal{E}$ is valid. ◢

Proof

Let $\mathcal{E}$ be a valid propositional-logic sentence, and let $\mathcal{E}_0$ be the instance of $\mathcal{E}$ obtained by replacing the propositional symbols P, Q, R, ... of $\mathcal{E}$ by predicate-logic sentences $\mathcal{F}_0$, $\mathcal{G}_0$, $\mathcal{H}_0$, ..., respectively.

To show that $(\textit{for all } *)\mathcal{E}_0$ is valid in predicate logic, it suffices (by the *universal-closure* proposition) to show that $\mathcal{E}_0$ is true under every predicate-logic interpretation. Consider an arbitrary interpretation $\mathcal{I}_0$ for $\mathcal{E}_0$; we would like to show that $\mathcal{E}_0$ is true under $\mathcal{I}_0$.

Consider the truth values of the subsentences $\mathcal{F}_0$, $\mathcal{G}_0$, $\mathcal{H}_0$, ... of $\mathcal{E}_0$ under $\mathcal{I}_0$, and let $\mathcal{I}$ be the propositional-logic interpretation that assigns the same truth values to the corresponding propositional symbols P, Q, R, ... of $\mathcal{E}$; then $\mathcal{I}$ is an interpretation for $\mathcal{E}$. Also the truth value of $\mathcal{E}$ under $\mathcal{I}$ is the same as the truth value for $\mathcal{E}_0$ under $\mathcal{I}_0$, because the semantic rules for the logic connectives *not, and, or,* ... are the same in propositional logic and predicate logic. Since $\mathcal{E}$ is valid, $\mathcal{E}$ is true under $\mathcal{I}$; therefore $\mathcal{E}_0$ is also true under $\mathcal{I}_0$, as we wanted to show. ◢

VALIDITY UNDER SIDE CONDITIONS

Certain sentence schemata are not valid in general but are valid if particular conditions are found to hold. The universal closures of the following sentence schemata are valid under the following side condition:

The variable x does not occur free in the sentence $\mathcal{G}$.

- Redundant quantifiers

$$(for\ all\ x)\mathcal{G}$$
$$if\ and\ only\ if$$
$$\mathcal{G}$$

$$(for\ some\ x)\mathcal{G}$$
$$if\ and\ only\ if$$
$$\mathcal{G}$$

- Distribution of quantifiers

$$(for\ all\ x)[\mathcal{F}\ and\ \mathcal{G}]$$
$$if\ and\ only\ if$$
$$(for\ all\ x)\mathcal{F}\ and\ \mathcal{G}$$

$$(for\ some\ x)[\mathcal{F}\ or\ \mathcal{G}]$$
$$if\ and\ only\ if$$
$$(for\ some\ x)\mathcal{F}\ or\ \mathcal{G}$$

$$(for\ all\ x)[\mathcal{F}\ or\ \mathcal{G}]$$
$$if\ and\ only\ if$$
$$(for\ all\ x)\mathcal{F}\ or\ \mathcal{G}$$

$$(for\ some\ x)[\mathcal{F}\ and\ \mathcal{G}]$$
$$if\ and\ only\ if$$
$$(for\ some\ x)\mathcal{F}\ and\ \mathcal{G}$$

$$(for\ all\ x)[if\ \mathcal{F}\ then\ \mathcal{G}]$$
$$if\ and\ only\ if$$
$$if\ (for\ some\ x)\mathcal{F}\ then\ \mathcal{G}$$

$$(for\ some\ x)[if\ \mathcal{F}\ then\ \mathcal{G}]$$
$$if\ and\ only\ if$$
$$if\ (for\ all\ x)\mathcal{F}\ then\ \mathcal{G}$$

$$(for\ all\ x)[if\ \mathcal{G}\ then\ \mathcal{F}]$$
$$if\ and\ only\ if$$
$$if\ \mathcal{G}\ then\ (for\ all\ x)\mathcal{F}$$

$$(for\ some\ x)[if\ \mathcal{G}\ then\ \mathcal{F}]$$
$$if\ and\ only\ if$$
$$if\ \mathcal{G}\ then\ (for\ some\ x)\mathcal{F}$$

$$(for\ all\ x)\begin{bmatrix} if\ \mathcal{G} \\ then\ \mathcal{E} \\ else\ \mathcal{F} \end{bmatrix}$$
$$if\ and\ only\ if$$
$$\begin{bmatrix} if\ \mathcal{G} \\ then\ (for\ all\ x)\mathcal{E} \\ else\ (for\ all\ x)\mathcal{F} \end{bmatrix}$$

$$(for\ some\ x)\begin{bmatrix} if\ \mathcal{G} \\ then\ \mathcal{E} \\ else\ \mathcal{F} \end{bmatrix}$$
$$if\ and\ only\ if$$
$$\begin{bmatrix} if\ \mathcal{G} \\ then\ (for\ some\ x)\mathcal{E} \\ else\ (for\ some\ x)\mathcal{F} \end{bmatrix}$$

The side condition that x does not occur free in $\mathcal{G}$, which we imposed in asserting the validity of the above sentences, is essential. Let us illustrate this point for the first *redundant-quantifiers* sentence.

Example (necessity for side condition)

The universal closure of the *redundant-quantifiers* sentence

$$(for\ all\ x)\mathcal{G}$$
$$if\ and\ only\ if$$
$$\mathcal{G}$$

is asserted to be valid under the side condition that the variable x does not occur free in the sentence $\mathcal{G}$. Thus, taking $\mathcal{G}$ to be the sentence

$$(for\ some\ y)q(z, y),$$

in which x does not occur free, we can conclude that the universal closure of

$$(for\ all\ x)(for\ some\ y)q(z, y)$$
$$if\ and\ only\ if$$
$$(for\ some\ y)q(z, y)$$

is valid.

On the other hand, taking $\mathcal{G}$ to be the sentence

$$p(x),$$

in which the variable x is free, violating the side condition, we cannot conclude that the universal closure of

$$(for\ all\ x)p(x)$$
$$if\ and\ only\ if$$
$$p(x)$$

is valid; indeed, it is not.

To show this, it suffices (by the *validity-of-closures* proposition) to exhibit a single interpretation under which the sentence is false. Let $\mathcal{I}$ be the interpretation over the set $\{A, B\}$ of two elements under which

$$p_\mathcal{I}(A)\ \text{is true}\quad \text{and}\quad p_\mathcal{I}(B)\ \text{is false}$$
$$x_\mathcal{I}\ \text{is A.}$$

Because $p_\mathcal{I}(B)$ is false, we have that

$$p(x)\ \text{is false under the extended interpretation}\ \langle x \leftarrow B \rangle \circ \mathcal{I}$$

and therefore (by the *for-all* rule) that

$$(for\ all\ x)p(x)\ \text{is false under}\ \mathcal{I}.$$

Because $p_\mathcal{I}(A)$ is true and $x_\mathcal{I}$ is A, we have that

$$p(x)\ \text{is true under}\ \mathcal{I}.$$

Therefore (by the *if-and-only-if* rule)

$$\begin{bmatrix} (for\ all\ x)p(x) \\ \quad if\ and\ only\ if \\ p(x) \end{bmatrix}\ \text{is false under}\ \mathcal{I},$$

as we wanted to show. ⌐

Note that, for any sentence $\mathcal{G}'$, the variable x is not free in $(for\ all\ x)\mathcal{G}'$. Therefore, taking $\mathcal{G}$ to be $(for\ all\ x)\mathcal{G}'$ in the above *redundant-quantifiers* sentence, we have, as a special case, that the universal closure of the sentence schema

$$(for\ all\ x)(for\ all\ x)\mathcal{G}'$$
$$if\ and\ only\ if$$
$$(for\ all\ x)\mathcal{G}'$$

is valid, with no side conditions.

Let us illustrate how the side conditions come into play in showing the validity of the above sentences.

Example

Suppose we would like to show that the universal closure of the *distribution-of-quantifiers* equivalence

$$(for\ some\ x)[\mathcal{F}\ \ and\ \ \mathcal{G}]$$
$$if\ and\ only\ if$$
$$(for\ some\ x)\mathcal{F}\ \ and\ \ \mathcal{G}$$

is valid, where x is not free in $\mathcal{G}$. By the *validity-of-closures* proposition, it suffices to show that the equivalence itself is true under any interpretation $\mathcal{I}$. However,

the left-hand side of the equivalence, that is,
$$(for\ some\ x)[\mathcal{F}\ \ and\ \ \mathcal{G}],$$
is true under $\mathcal{I}$

precisely when (by the *for-some* rule)

there exists a domain element d such that the subsentence
$$\mathcal{F}\ \ and\ \ \mathcal{G}$$
is true under the extended interpretation $\langle x \leftarrow d \rangle \circ \mathcal{I}$

precisely when (by the *and* rule)

there exists a domain element d such that
$$\mathcal{F}$$
is true under $\langle x \leftarrow d \rangle \circ \mathcal{I}$
and
$$\mathcal{G}$$
is true under $\langle x \leftarrow d \rangle \circ \mathcal{I}$

precisely when (because x does not occur free in $\mathcal{G}$)

> there exists a domain element d such that
> $$\mathcal{F}$$
> is true under $\langle x \leftarrow d \rangle \circ \mathcal{I}$
> and
> $$\mathcal{G}$$
> is true under $\mathcal{I}$

precisely when (by the *for-some* rule)

> $$(for\ some\ x)\mathcal{F}$$
> is true under $\mathcal{I}$
> and
> $$\mathcal{G}$$
> is true under $\mathcal{I}$

precisely when (by the *and* rule)

> $(for\ some\ x)\mathcal{F}\ and\ \mathcal{G}$,
> that is, the right-hand side of the equivalence, is true under $\mathcal{I}$.

We have shown that the left-hand side of the equivalence is true under $\mathcal{I}$ precisely when the right-hand side is true under $\mathcal{I}$; therefore (by the *if-and-only-if* rule) the equivalence

> $(for\ some\ x)[\mathcal{F}\ and\ \mathcal{G}]$
> *if and only if*
> $(for\ some\ x)\mathcal{F}\ and\ \mathcal{G}$

is true under $\mathcal{I}$, as we wanted to show.

In showing the validity of the above sentence, we have used the fact that

> $\mathcal{G}$ is true under $\langle x \leftarrow d \rangle \circ \mathcal{I}$

precisely when

> $\mathcal{G}$ is true under $\mathcal{I}$,

which holds because we have assumed the side condition that x does not occur free in $\mathcal{G}$.   ⌐

The reader is requested to establish the validity of some of the above sentence schemata in **Problem 3.2** and to illustrate that the side condition is essential in each case.

3.2   EQUIVALENCE

The notions of implication and equivalence are the same for predicate logic as for propositional logic.

Definition (implication, equivalence)

> A sentence $\mathcal{F}$ *implies* a sentence $\mathcal{G}$ if,
>   for any interpretation I for $\mathcal{F}$ and $\mathcal{G}$,
>   if $\mathcal{F}$ is true under I, then $\mathcal{G}$ is true under I.
>
> Two sentences $\mathcal{F}$ and $\mathcal{G}$ are *equivalent* if,
>   under every interpretation for $\mathcal{F}$ and $\mathcal{G}$,
> $\mathcal{F}$ has the same truth value as $\mathcal{G}$.   ◢

Note that we do not require $\mathcal{F}$ and $\mathcal{G}$ to be closed sentences.

IMPLICATION, EQUIVALENCE, AND VALIDITY

A simple relationship between implication and validity and between equivalence and validity is expressed by the following observations:

Remark

> For any two sentences $\mathcal{F}$ and $\mathcal{G}$ in predicate logic
>
> $\mathcal{F}$ implies $\mathcal{G}$
> precisely when
>   *(for all* ∗*)*[*if* $\mathcal{F}$ *then* $\mathcal{G}$] is valid.

Also

> $\mathcal{F}$ is equivalent to $\mathcal{G}$
> precisely when
>   *(for all* ∗*)*[$\mathcal{F}$ *if and only if* $\mathcal{G}$] is valid.

Consider the first observation. We have

   $\mathcal{F}$ implies $\mathcal{G}$

precisely when (by the definition)

> for any interpretation I (for $\mathcal{F}$ and $\mathcal{G}$),
>> if $\mathcal{F}$ is true under I
>> then $\mathcal{G}$ is true under I

precisely when (by the *if-then* rule)

> for any interpretation I,
>> (*if* $\mathcal{F}$ *then* $\mathcal{G}$) is true under I

precisely when (by the *validity-of-closures* proposition)

> (*for all* ∗)[*if* $\mathcal{F}$ *then* $\mathcal{G}$] is valid,

as we wanted to show.

The proof of the second observation is similar and uses the *if-and-only-if* rule. ⌙

Example

We have mentioned that the closed sentence

> *not* (*for all* x)$p(x)$
> *if and only if*
> (*for some* x)[*not* $p(x)$],

which expresses part of the duality of quantifiers, is valid. This implies (by the above remark) that the sentences

> *not* (*for all* x)$p(x)$ and   (*for some* x)[*not* $p(x)$]

are equivalent.

Similarly, because the universal closure of

> *not* (*for all* x)$q(x, y)$
> *if and only if*
> (*for some* x)$\big[$*not* $q(x, y)\big]$

is valid, the two sentences

> *not* (*for all* x)$q(x, y)$ and   (*for some* x)[*not* $q(x, y)$]

are equivalent.

In fact, we have determined that the universal closure of the corresponding schema

> not (for all x)$\mathcal{F}$
> if and only if
> (for some x)[not $\mathcal{F}$]

is valid. Therefore for any sentence $\mathcal{F}$, the two sentences

> not (for all x)$\mathcal{F}$ and   (for some x)[not $\mathcal{F}$]

are equivalent. ◢

We now consider a further connection between implication and validity and between equivalence and validity.

Proposition (implication and validity)

For any two sentences $\mathcal{F}$ and $\mathcal{G}$,

> if $\mathcal{F}$ implies $\mathcal{G}$,
> then   if   (for all ∗)$\mathcal{F}$ is valid,
>   then (for all ∗)$\mathcal{G}$ is valid. ◢

Proposition (equivalence and validity)

For any two sentences $\mathcal{F}$ and $\mathcal{G}$,

> if $\mathcal{F}$ is equivalent to $\mathcal{G}$,
> then   (for all ∗)$\mathcal{F}$ is valid
>   precisely when
>   (for all ∗)$\mathcal{G}$ is valid. ◢

The proofs of these propositions are analogous to the proofs of the corresponding results in propositional logic and are requested as an exercise (**Problem 3.3**). The converses do not hold.

EQUIVALENT PROPOSITIONAL-LOGIC SENTENCES

We have observed that the universal closure of any instance of a valid propositional-logic sentence is valid in predicate logic. It is also true that corresponding instances of equivalent propositional-logic sentences are equivalent in predicate logic. This is expressed more precisely as follows.

Proposition (instances of equivalent propositional-logic sentences)

> If two propositional-logic sentences $\mathcal{F}$ and $\mathcal{G}$ are equivalent,
> then corresponding predicate-logic instances of $\mathcal{F}$ and $\mathcal{G}$
> are equivalent. ⌐

Before proving the proposition we consider an example.

Example

We have seen that the sentences

$$\begin{array}{c} \textit{if } P \\ \textit{then } Q \end{array} \quad \text{and} \quad \begin{array}{c} \textit{if not } Q \\ \textit{then not } P \end{array}$$

are equivalent in propositional logic; the latter is the contrapositive of the former. The proposition therefore implies that the predicate-logic instances of these sentences,

$$\begin{array}{c} \textit{if } p(x) \\ \textit{then } (\textit{for some } y)q(x,y) \end{array} \quad \text{and} \quad \begin{array}{c} \textit{if not } (\textit{for some } y)q(x,y) \\ \textit{then not } p(x) \end{array}$$

(obtained by replacing P and Q with $p(x)$ and $(\textit{for some } y)q(x,y)$, respectively), are equivalent in predicate logic. ⌐

Now let us prove the proposition.

Proof

Suppose $\mathcal{F}$ and $\mathcal{G}$ are equivalent propositional-logic sentences, and let $\mathcal{F}_0$ and $\mathcal{G}_0$ be corresponding predicate-logic instances of $\mathcal{F}$ and $\mathcal{G}$. We want to show that $\mathcal{F}_0$ is equivalent to $\mathcal{G}_0$.

Because $\mathcal{F}$ and $\mathcal{G}$ are equivalent, the propositional-logic sentence

$$\mathcal{F} \textit{ if and only if } \mathcal{G}$$

is valid (in propositional logic). Consequently, the universal closure of its predicate-logic instance,

$$\mathcal{F}_0 \textit{ if and only if } \mathcal{G}_0,$$

is valid (in predicate logic). Therefore (by our earlier remark)

$$\mathcal{F}_0 \text{ is equivalent to } \mathcal{G}_0. \quad ⌐$$

PROPERTIES OF CLOSURES

The universal and existential closures of $\mathcal{F}$ exhibit the following duality property, which reflects the duality between universal and existential quantifiers.

Proposition (duality of closures)

> For any sentence $\mathcal{F}$,
>
> $$not \ (for \ all \ *)\mathcal{F} \quad \text{is equivalent to} \quad (for \ some \ *)[not \ \mathcal{F}]$$
>
> and
>
> $$not \ (for \ some \ *)\mathcal{F} \quad \text{is equivalent to} \quad (for \ all \ *)[not \ \mathcal{F}].$$ ◢

Proof

To prove the first statement, let $\mathcal{F}$ be a sentence and I be any interpretation for $not \ (for \ all \ *)\mathcal{F}$ and hence for $(for \ some \ *)[not \ \mathcal{F}]$. Let $x_1, x_2, \ldots, x_n$ be the free variables of $\mathcal{F}$.

Then

$$not \ (for \ all \ *)\mathcal{F} \text{ is true under } I$$

precisely when (by the *not* rule)

$$(for \ all \ *)\mathcal{F} \text{ is false under } I$$

precisely when (by the *universal-closure* rule)

> there exist domain elements $d_1, d_2, \ldots, d_n$ such that $\mathcal{F}$ is false under $\langle x_1 \leftarrow d_1 \rangle \circ \langle x_2 \leftarrow d_2 \rangle \circ \ldots \circ \langle x_n \leftarrow d_n \rangle \circ I$

precisely when (by the *not* rule)

> there exist domain elements $d_1, d_2, \ldots, d_n$ such that $(not \ \mathcal{F})$ is true under $\langle x_1 \leftarrow d_1 \rangle \circ \langle x_2 \leftarrow d_2 \rangle \circ \ldots \circ \langle x_n \leftarrow d_n \rangle \circ I$

precisely when (by the *existential-closure* rule)

$$(for \ some \ *)[not \ \mathcal{F}] \text{ is true under } I.$$

In short, for an arbitrary interpretation I, $not \ (for \ all \ *)\mathcal{F}$ is true under I precisely when $(for \ some \ *)[not \ \mathcal{F}]$ is true under I. Thus the two schemata are equivalent.

The proof of the second equivalence is similar. ⌟

Several other properties of the universal and existential closures reflect the properties of the corresponding universal and existential quantifiers.

Proposition (distribution of closures)

For any sentences $\mathcal{F}$ and $\mathcal{G}$ the following sentences are valid:

(for all ∗)[$\mathcal{F}$ and $\mathcal{G}$]
   if and only if
 (for all ∗)$\mathcal{F}$ and (for all ∗)$\mathcal{G}$
	(for some ∗)[$\mathcal{F}$ or $\mathcal{G}$]
	   if and only if
	 (for some ∗)$\mathcal{F}$ or (for some ∗)$\mathcal{G}$

if (for some ∗)[$\mathcal{F}$ and $\mathcal{G}$]

$$\text{then} \begin{bmatrix} (for\ some\ \ast)\mathcal{F} \\ and \\ (for\ some\ \ast)\mathcal{G} \end{bmatrix}$$

$$\text{if} \begin{bmatrix} (for\ all\ \ast)\mathcal{F} \\ or \\ (for\ all\ \ast)\mathcal{G} \end{bmatrix}$$

then (for all ∗)[$\mathcal{F}$ or $\mathcal{G}$]

if (for all ∗)[if $\mathcal{F}$ then $\mathcal{G}$]

$$\text{then} \begin{bmatrix} if\ (for\ all\ \ast)\mathcal{F} \\ then\ (for\ all\ \ast)\mathcal{G} \end{bmatrix}$$

$$\text{if} \begin{bmatrix} if\ (for\ some\ \ast)\mathcal{F} \\ then\ (for\ some\ \ast)\mathcal{G} \end{bmatrix}$$

then (for some ∗)[if $\mathcal{F}$ then $\mathcal{G}$]. ⌟

The proof is requested in **Problem 3.4**.

REPLACEMENT OF EQUIVALENT SENTENCES

If two sentences are equivalent, they may be used interchangeably, in a sense made precise in the following proposition.

Proposition (replacement of equivalent sentences)

For any sentences $\mathcal{G}$, $\mathcal{G}'$, and $\mathcal{F}$, let $\mathcal{F}'$ be the result of replacing zero, one, or more occurrences of $\mathcal{G}$ in $\mathcal{F}$ with $\mathcal{G}'$. Then

    if $\mathcal{G}$ and $\mathcal{G}'$ are equivalent,
    then $\mathcal{F}$ and $\mathcal{F}'$ are equivalent. ⌟

A rigorous proof is technical (and is omitted), but the intuitive justification is straightforward. In determining the truth values of $\mathcal{F}$ and $\mathcal{F}'$ under a given interpretation $\mathcal{I}$, the respective results will be the same at each stage. Although $\mathcal{F}'$ may have occurrences of $\mathcal{G}'$ where $\mathcal{F}$ has occurrences of $\mathcal{G}$, the corresponding subsentences $\mathcal{G}$ and $\mathcal{G}'$ are themselves equivalent, and hence yield the same truth values under any interpretation.

Let us illustrate the proposition with two examples.

Example

Consider the sentences

$$\mathcal{G}: \quad p(x) \;\; and \;\; p(x)$$

and

$$\mathcal{G}': \quad p(x).$$

Then, because $\mathcal{G}$ and $\mathcal{G}'$ are instances of the equivalent propositional-logic sentences $(P \; and \; P)$ and P,

$\mathcal{G}$ and $\mathcal{G}'$ are equivalent.

Consider now the sentence

$$\mathcal{F}: \quad (for \; all \; x)(for \; some \; y) \begin{bmatrix} p(x) \;\; and \;\; p(x) \\ or \\ r(y, \; z) \end{bmatrix}$$

and the sentence

$$\mathcal{F}': \quad (for \; all \; x)(for \; some \; y) \begin{bmatrix} p(x) \\ or \\ r(y, \; z) \end{bmatrix},$$

obtained by replacing one occurrence of $\mathcal{G}$ in $\mathcal{F}$ with $\mathcal{G}'$. Then, according to the proposition,

$\mathcal{F}$ and $\mathcal{F}'$ are equivalent. ⌟

Example

Consider the sentences

$$\mathcal{G}: \quad p(x)$$

and

$$\mathcal{G}': \quad p(x) \;\; and \;\; (p(x) \;\; or \;\; q(y)).$$

Then because $\mathcal{G}$ and $\mathcal{G}'$ are instances of the equivalent propositional-logic sentences P and $(P \;\; and \;\; (P \;\; or \;\; Q))$,

$\mathcal{G}$ and $\mathcal{G}'$ are equivalent.

Consider now the sentence

$$\mathcal{F}: \quad (for \;\; all \;\; x)(for \;\; some \;\; y) \begin{bmatrix} p(x) \\ or \\ p(x) \end{bmatrix}$$

and the sentence

$$\mathcal{F}': \quad (for \;\; all \;\; x)(for \;\; some \;\; y) \begin{bmatrix} p(x) \;\; and \;\; (p(x) \;\; or \;\; q(y)) \\ or \\ p(x) \end{bmatrix},$$

obtained by replacing one occurrence of $\mathcal{G}$ in $\mathcal{F}$ with $\mathcal{G}'$. Then, according to the proposition,

$\mathcal{F}$ and $\mathcal{F}'$ are equivalent.

Note that only one of the two occurrences of $\mathcal{G}$ in $\mathcal{F}$ is replaced. ⌟

RENAMING OF BOUND VARIABLES

A consequence of the semantic rule for quantifiers is that the variable x in a quantified sentence $(for \;\; all \;\; x)\mathcal{F}$ or $(for \;\; some \;\; x)\mathcal{F}$ is a "dummy," in the sense that we can systematically replace it with a new variable, i.e., one not occurring in $\mathcal{F}$, without changing the meaning of the sentence. For example, the two sentences

$$(for \;\; all \;\; x)p(x) \quad and \quad (for \;\; all \;\; y)p(y)$$

are equivalent: Whether we choose to use x or y has no effect on the meaning of the sentence. Because the variables x and y are quantified, the truth values of the sentences under an interpretation do not depend on what domain element, if any, the interpretation assigns to these variables.

In contrast, the two sentences

$$p(x) \quad and \quad p(y),$$

in which x and y occur free, are not equivalent. If the two variables x and y are assigned different elements under an interpretation, the two sentences $p(x)$ and $p(y)$ may have different truth values under the interpretation.

We can also rename the variable x of quantifiers *(for all x)* or *(for some x)* that do not occur at the top level of the sentence. Let us explain this with an example.

Example

The sentence

$$\mathcal{G}: \quad (\textit{for all } x)\big[p(u) \ \ \textit{and} \ \ r(x)\big]$$

is equivalent to the sentence

$$\mathcal{G}': \quad (\textit{for all } y)\big[p(u) \ \ \textit{and} \ \ r(y)\big],$$

obtained by renaming the variable x of the quantifier *(for all x)* to y.

Consequently, the sentence

$$\mathcal{F}: \quad \begin{array}{l} (\textit{for all } z)\big[p(z) \ \ \textit{and} \ \ r(x)\big] \\ \quad \textit{and} \\ \textit{if } p(u) \ \ \textit{then} \ \ (\textit{for all } x)\big[p(u) \ \ \textit{and} \ \ r(x)\big] \end{array}$$

is equivalent to the sentence

$$\mathcal{F}': \quad \begin{array}{l} (\textit{for all } z)\big[p(z) \ \ \textit{and} \ \ r(x)\big] \\ \quad \textit{and} \\ \textit{if } p(u) \ \ \textit{then} \ \ (\textit{for all } y)\big[p(u) \ \ \textit{and} \ \ r(y)\big], \end{array}$$

obtained by replacing the occurrence of $\mathcal{G}$ in $\mathcal{F}$ with the equivalent sentence $\mathcal{G}'$. ⌙

It is important that, in renaming the variable of a quantifier, we choose a new variable, i.e., one that does not already occur in the replaced subsentence. The reason for this will be illustrated in the following two examples.

Example

Consider the sentence

$$\mathcal{F}: \quad (\textit{for all } x)p(x, y).$$

This sentence is not equivalent to the sentence

$$\mathcal{F}': \quad (\textit{for all } y)p(y, y),$$

obtained by renaming the variable x of the quantifier (*for all x*) to the variable y, which already occurs free in the replaced subsentence.

In particular, under any interpretation over a domain with two or more elements that assigns p to be the equality relation, $\mathcal{F}$ is given the intuitive meaning

for every x, $x = y$,

which is false, while $\mathcal{F}'$ is given the intuitive meaning

for every y, $y = y$,

which is true. ⌐

In the example above, we renamed the quantified variable to a variable that already has a free occurrence in the sentence. Similar problems may occur if we rename the quantified variable to a variable that only occurs bound in the sentence.

Example

Consider the sentence

$\mathcal{F}$:   (*for all x*)(*for all y*)$p(x, y)$;

this sentence is not equivalent to the sentence

$\mathcal{F}'$:   (*for all y*)(*for all y*)$p(y, y)$,

obtained by renaming the variable x of the quantifier (*for all x*) to the variable y, which already occurs bound in the replaced subsentence.

In particular, under any interpretation over a domain with two or more elements that assigns p to be the equality relation, $\mathcal{F}$ is given the intuitive meaning

for every x and y, $x = y$,

which is false, while $\mathcal{F}'$, which is equivalent to

(*for all y*)$p(y, y)$,

is given the intuitive meaning

for every y, $y = y$,

which is true. ⌐

In general, we can establish the following result:

Proposition (renaming of bound variables, special case)

Let $(for \ldots x)\mathcal{G}$ be a sentence, where $(for \ldots x)$ is a quantifier, either $(for\ all\ x)$ or $(for\ some\ x)$.

Let x' be a variable that does not occur in $(for \ldots x)\mathcal{G}$ and $\mathcal{G}'$ be the result of replacing every free occurrence of x in $\mathcal{G}$ with x'.

Let $\mathcal{F}$ be a sentence and let $\mathcal{F}'$ be the result of replacing one or more occurrences of $(for \ldots x)\mathcal{G}$ in $\mathcal{F}$ with $(for \ldots x')\mathcal{G}'$.

Then

$\mathcal{F}$ and $\mathcal{F}'$ are equivalent.   ⌐

Later we shall present a more general version of the proposition; hence we refer to this proposition as a "special case."

Proof

We first show that, under the conditions of the proposition,

$(for\ all\ x)\mathcal{G}$ is equivalent to $(for\ all\ x')\mathcal{G}'$.

But for any interpretation I for these two sentences,

$(for\ all\ x)\mathcal{G}$ is true under I

precisely when (by the *for-all* rule)

for every domain element d,
$\mathcal{G}$ is true under $\langle x \leftarrow d \rangle \circ I$

precisely when (because x' does not occur in $\mathcal{G}$)

for every domain element d,
$\mathcal{G}$ is true under $\langle x \leftarrow d \rangle \circ \langle x' \leftarrow d \rangle \circ I$

precisely when (because $\mathcal{G}'$ is obtained from $\mathcal{G}$ by replacing every free occurrence of x with x')

for every domain element d,
$\mathcal{G}'$ is true under $\langle x \leftarrow d \rangle \circ \langle x' \leftarrow d \rangle \circ I$

precisely when (because x does not occur free in $\mathcal{G}'$)

for every domain element d,
$\mathcal{G}'$ is true under $\langle x' \leftarrow d \rangle \circ I$

precisely when (by the *for-all* rule)

$$(\textit{for all } x')\mathcal{G}' \text{ is true under } \mathcal{I}.$$

Thus

$$(\textit{for all } x)\mathcal{G} \text{ is equivalent to } (\textit{for all } x')\mathcal{G}'.$$

The desired result, that $\mathcal{F}$ is equivalent to $\mathcal{F}'$, follows, because $\mathcal{F}'$ is the result of replacing one or more occurrences of $(\textit{for all } x)\mathcal{G}$ in $\mathcal{F}$ with the equivalent sentence $(\textit{for all } x')\mathcal{G}'$. ◢

Remark (nested quantifiers)

It is often confusing when a sentence contains nested quantifiers over the same variable. For example, in the sentence

$$\mathcal{F}: \quad (\textit{for all } x)\big[p(x) \quad \textit{and} \quad (\textit{for some } x)q(x,y)\big],$$

the second quantifier, $(\textit{for some } x)$, is within the scope of the first quantifier, $(\textit{for all } x)$. Consequently the occurrence of the variable x in $p(x)$ is bound by the first quantifier, $(\textit{for all } x)$, but the occurrence of x in $q(x,y)$ is bound by the second quantifier, $(\textit{for some } x)$.

Using the above *renaming-of-bound-variables* proposition, we can rename the variable x of the second quantifier, $(\textit{for some } x)$, to x', obtaining the equivalent sentence

$$\mathcal{F}': \quad (\textit{for all } x)\big[p(x) \quad \textit{and} \quad (\textit{for some } x')q(x',y)\big].$$

Although $\mathcal{F}$ and $\mathcal{F}'$ are equivalent, $\mathcal{F}'$ may be easier to understand, because it is clearer which quantifier binds each variable in $\mathcal{F}'$. ◢

3.3 SAFE SUBSTITUTION

We now introduce a notion of substitution for predicate logic analogous to the one we used for propositional logic. Because this notion is surprisingly complex, we begin with examples showing that more straightforward definitions of substitution do not exhibit the desired properties.

BOUND AND FREE SUBEXPRESSIONS

In our chapter on propositional logic, we observed that the equivalence connective *if-and-only-if* has the substitutivity property: For any propositional-logic sentences $\mathcal{G}$, $\mathcal{H}$, and $\mathcal{F}\langle\mathcal{G}\rangle$, the sentence

> *if $\mathcal{G}$ if and only if $\mathcal{H}$*
> *then $\mathcal{F}\langle\mathcal{G}\rangle$ if and only if $\mathcal{F}\langle\mathcal{H}\rangle$*

is valid, where $\mathcal{F}\langle\mathcal{H}\rangle$ is the result of replacing zero, one, or more occurrences of $\mathcal{G}$ in $\mathcal{F}\langle\mathcal{G}\rangle$ with $\mathcal{H}$.

We would like to extend the substitution operator to predicate logic so that the universal closure of the corresponding predicate-logic sentence

(∗)
> *if $\mathcal{G}$ if and only if $\mathcal{H}$*
> *then $\mathcal{F}\langle\mathcal{G}\rangle$ if and only if $\mathcal{F}\langle\mathcal{H}\rangle$*

is valid. Unfortunately, if we naively adopt the propositional-logic definition of substitution, this is not the case, as is illustrated by the following examples.

Our first observation leads us to distinguish between "bound" and "free" subexpressions of a given expression and to define the substitution operator so that only "free" subexpressions are replaced.

Example (replacing bound subexpressions)

Consider the sentences

> $\mathcal{G}:$ $p(x),$
>
> $\mathcal{H}:$ $q(x),$

and

> $\mathcal{F}\langle\mathcal{G}\rangle:$ *(for all x)$p(x)$.*

Suppose we define the predicate-logic substitution operator so that $\mathcal{F}\langle\mathcal{H}\rangle$ is

> *(for all x)$q(x)$,*

that is, the result of replacing the occurrence of $p(x)$ in *(for all x)$p(x)$* with $q(x)$. Then, according to the desired substitutivity-of-equivalence property (∗) above, the universal closure of the implication

> *if $p(x)$ if and only if $q(x)$*
> *then (for all x)$p(x)$ if and only if (for all x)$q(x)$*

should be valid; but this is not the case.

To show this, it suffices, by the *validity-of-closures* proposition, to exhibit a single interpretation under which the implication itself is false.

Consider the interpretation $\mathcal{I}$ over the domain $\{A, B\}$ under which

> x is A

> p is true for both domain elements, that is,
> $p_I(A)$ is true and $p_I(B)$ is true

> q is true only for A, that is,
> $q_I(A)$ is true and $q_I(B)$ is false.

Then the antecedent

> $p(x)$ *if and only if* $q(x)$

has been given the intuitive meaning

> true if and only if A is A,

which is true, while the consequent

> *(for all* x)$p(x)$ *if and only if* *(for all* x)$q(x)$

has been given the intuitive meaning

> true if and only if every domain element is A,

which is false.

Therefore, the implication

> *if* $p(x)$ *if and only if* $q(x)$
> *then* *(for all* x)$p(x)$ *if and only if* *(for all* x)$q(x)$

is false under $\mathcal{I}$, as we intended to show.   ⏋

In the above example, the problem was that the variable x, which is free in $p(x)$, is bound in *(for all* x)$p(x)$ and thus has a different meaning in $p(x)$ and in *(for all* x)$p(x)$.

To phrase the definition of substitution for predicate logic to avoid the sort of mishap illustrated in the above example, we need to introduce some special terminology. We extend the notion of bound and free variables to subexpressions, either terms or sentences.

Definition (bound subexpressions)

Consider an occurrence of a subexpression t in an expression $\mathcal{E}$.

The occurrence of t is *bound in* $\mathcal{E}$ if

> some occurrence of a variable x is free in the occurrence of t,
> but the same occurrence of x is bound in $\mathcal{E}$.　◢

In other words, the occurrence of x is not within the scope of any quantifier
(*for ... x*) in t, but the occurrence of t is within the scope of some quantifier
(*for ... x*) in $\mathcal{E}$.

Example

Consider the subsentence

$$t: \quad p(x)$$

of the sentence

$$\mathcal{E}: \quad (for\ all\ x)p(x).$$

The occurrence of $p(x)$ is bound in (*for all x*)$p(x)$, because $p(x)$ has a free occurrence of x that is bound in (*for all x*)$p(x)$.　◢

A sentence may have bound occurrences in a term if that term contains the
conditional connective *if-then-else*.

Example

Consider the subsentence

$$t: \quad p(x)$$

of the term

$$\mathcal{E}: \quad \begin{array}{l} if\ (for\ all\ x)p(x) \\ then\ \ a \\ else\ \ f(x). \end{array}$$

The occurrence of $p(x)$ is bound in $\mathcal{E}$, because the free occurrence of x in $p(x)$ is
bound in $\mathcal{E}$, by the quantifier (*for all x*).　◢

Definition (free subexpressions)

> Consider an occurrence of a subexpression t in an expression $\mathcal{E}$.
>
> The occurrence of t is free in $\mathcal{E}$ if,
>
>> in that occurrence of t,
>> every free occurrence of a variable is also free in $\mathcal{E}$.   ⌐

In other words, if the occurrence of x is not within the scope of any quantifier (*for* ... *x*) in the occurrence of t, then it is also not within the scope of any quantifier (*for* ... *x*) in $\mathcal{E}$.

Example

> Consider the subsentence
>
>> $t:$ $q(y, z)$
>
> of the sentence
>
>> $\mathcal{E}:$ $q(y, z)$ *and* (*for all y*)$q(u, y)$.
>
> The occurrence of $q(y, z)$ is free in $\mathcal{E}$, because the free occurrences of y and z in $q(y, z)$ are also free in $\mathcal{E}$.   ⌐

A subexpression may have both bound and free occurrences in one expression.

Example

> Consider the subterm
>
>> $t:$ $f(y)$
>
> of the sentence
>
>> $\mathcal{E}:$ (*for some y*)$p(f(y))$
>> *or*
>> $q(f(y))$.
>
> The first occurrence of the term $f(y)$, in $p(f(y))$, is bound in $\mathcal{E}$, because the free occurrence of y in this occurrence of $f(y)$ is bound in $\mathcal{E}$, by the quantifier (*for some y*).
>
> The second occurrence of the term $f(y)$, in $q(f(y))$, is free in $\mathcal{E}$, because the free occurrence of y in this occurrence of $f(y)$ is also free in $\mathcal{E}$, and there are no other free occurrences of variables in the term.   ⌐

Remark

If I is an interpretation for an expression $\mathcal{E}$, and if the expression t has a free occurrence in $\mathcal{E}$, then I is also an interpretation for t. For instance, the term $f(y)$ has a free occurrence in the sentence $p\big(f(y)\big)$. Therefore every interpretation for $p\big(f(y)\big)$ is also an interpretation for $f(y)$, because it must assign values to f and y.

On the other hand, if I is an interpretation for an expression $\mathcal{E}$ and if the subexpression t has only bound occurrences in $\mathcal{E}$, then I need not be an interpretation for t. For instance, the subsentence $p\big(f(y)\big)$ has only bound occurrences in the sentence $(for\ all\ y)p\big(f(y)\big)$. Therefore an interpretation for $(for\ all\ y)p\big(f(y)\big)$ need not be an interpretation for $p\big(f(y)\big)$, because it may assign no value to y. ◢

In attempting to formulate a definition of substitution for predicate logic that would enable us to retain a substitutivity-of-equivalence property, we observed that the universal closure of the sentence

$$if\ p(x)\ \ if\ and\ only\ if\ q(x)$$
$$then\ \ (for\ all\ x)p(x)\ \ if\ and\ only\ if\ (for\ all\ x)q(x)$$

is not valid. Here the sentence $(for\ all\ x)q(x)$ was formed by replacing the (bound) occurrence of $p(x)$ in $(for\ all\ x)p(x)$ with $q(x)$. In formulating the notion of substitution for predicate logic, we shall require that only free occurrences of subexpressions may be replaced. In this way, we avoid such counterexamples to the substitutivity of equivalence.

CAPTURING

Even if we phrase the definition of substitution so that only free occurrences of subexpressions can be replaced, other problems arise.

Example (capturing)

Consider the sentences

$$\mathcal{G}:\quad p(x)$$

$$\mathcal{H}:\quad q(y)$$

and

$$\mathcal{F}\langle\mathcal{G}\rangle:\quad (for\ all\ y)p(x).$$

Suppose we define the substitution operator so that $\mathcal{F}\langle\mathcal{H}\rangle$ is

(*for all y*)*q*(*y*),

that is, the result of replacing the (free) occurrence of $p(x)$ in (*for all y*)*p*(*x*) with $q(y)$. Then, according to the desired substitutivity-of-equivalence property (∗) above, the universal closure of the implication

> *if p(x) if and only if q(y)*
> *then (for all y)p(x) if and only if (for all y)q(y)*

should be valid; but this is not the case.

To show this, it suffices, by the *validity-of-closures* proposition, to exhibit a single interpretation under which the implication itself is false.

Consider the interpretation $\mathcal{I}$ over the domain {A, B} under which

> x is A
>
> y is A
>
> p is true for both domain elements, that is,
> $p_{\mathcal{I}}(\text{A})$ is true and $p_{\mathcal{I}}(\text{B})$ is true
>
> q is true only for A, that is,
> $q_{\mathcal{I}}(\text{A})$ is true and $q_{\mathcal{I}}(\text{B})$ is false.

Then the antecedent

> *p(x) if and only if q(y)*

has been given the intuitive meaning

> true if and only if A is A,

which is true, while the consequent

> (*for all y*)*p*(*x*) *if and only if* (*for all y*)*q*(*y*)

has been given the intuitive meaning

> true if and only if every domain element is A,

which is false.

Therefore the implication

> *if p(x) if and only if q(y)*
> *then (for all y)p(x) if and only if (for all y)q(y)*

is false under I, as we intended to show. ◢

In the example above, although the subsentence $p(x)$ is free in the surrounding sentence *(for all y)p(x)*, the newly introduced occurrence of $q(y)$ in *(for all y)q(y)* is bound. The occurrence of y, which is free in $q(y)$, is bound in *(for all y)q(y)*; therefore its meaning has been changed by the substitution operation. We shall say that y has been "captured" by the quantifier *(for all y)*. The definition of substitution for predicate logic will be formulated so that quantified variables are renamed, if necessary, to avoid such capturing.

SAFE SUBSTITUTION

We are now ready to present our "safe" substitution operator for predicate logic expressions, which avoids both the above mishaps, i.e., the replacement of bound subexpressions and the capturing of free variables. We distinguish between "total safe substitution," in which all free occurrences of a subexpression are replaced, and "partial safe substitution," in which zero, one, or more, but not necessarily all, free occurrences are replaced.

Definition (total safe substitution)

Suppose $\mathcal{F}$, $\mathcal{G}$, and $\mathcal{H}$ are expressions, where $\mathcal{G}$ and $\mathcal{H}$ are either both terms or both sentences.

We denote by

$$\mathcal{F} \blacktriangleleft \{\mathcal{G} \leftarrow \mathcal{H}\}$$

the expression obtained as follows:

- Replace every free occurrence of $\mathcal{G}$ in $\mathcal{F}$ with $\mathcal{H}$,

but

- if any free variable y in $\mathcal{H}$ is about to be captured by a quantifier *(for ... y)* in $\mathcal{F}$ as a result of the above replacement, rename the variable y of this quantifier to a new variable y' before performing the replacement; y' is taken to be a variable that does not already occur in $\mathcal{F}$, $\mathcal{G}$, or $\mathcal{H}$.

We shall say that $\mathcal{F} \blacktriangleleft \{\mathcal{G} \leftarrow \mathcal{H}\}$ is the result of *safely replacing* every free occurrence of $\mathcal{G}$ in $\mathcal{F}$ with $\mathcal{H}$. ◢

Example

The result of the total safe substitution

$$\begin{bmatrix} (for\ all\ x)\big[p(x)\ \ and\ \ r(y)\big] \\ and \\ if\ p(x)\ \ then\ \ (for\ all\ y)\big[p(x)\ \ and\ \ r(y)\big] \end{bmatrix} \blacktriangleleft \{p(x) \leftarrow q(y)\}$$

is the sentence

$$(for\ all\ x)\big[p(x)\ \ and\ \ r(y)\big]$$
$$and$$
$$if\ q(y)\ \ then\ \ (for\ all\ y')\big[q(y)\ \ and\ \ r(y')\big].$$

Note that the first occurrence of $p(x)$, which is bound, is not replaced by the substitution; the other two occurrences of $p(x)$, which are free, must be replaced. Also note that the variable y of the quantifier $(for\ all\ y)$ has been renamed to the new variable y', to avoid capturing the free variable y in $q(y)$. The first occurrence of y, in the subsentence $r(y)$, is not renamed, because it is not within the scope of the quantifier $(for\ all\ y)$.   **⌐**

The result of applying the substitution $\mathcal{F} \blacktriangleleft \{\mathcal{G} \leftarrow \mathcal{H}\}$ is not unique, because, to avoid capturing a free variable, we may rename the variable y of the quantifier $(for\ ...\ y)$ to any new variable y'. However, any two results of applying the substitution are equivalent, because either can be obtained from the other by renaming of bound variables.

The corresponding partial substitution operator ◁, described as follows, is analogous to the total substitution operator ◀.

Definition (partial safe substitution)

Suppose $\mathcal{F}$, $\mathcal{G}$, and $\mathcal{H}$ are expressions, where $\mathcal{G}$ and $\mathcal{H}$ are either both terms or both sentences.

We denote by

$$\mathcal{F} \triangleleft \{\mathcal{G} \leftarrow \mathcal{H}\}$$

any of the expressions obtained as follows:

- Replace zero, one, or more free occurrences of $\mathcal{G}$ in $\mathcal{F}$ with $\mathcal{H}$,

but

- if any free variable y in $\mathcal{H}$ is about to be captured by a quantifier $(for\ ...\ y)$ in $\mathcal{F}$ as a result of the above replacement, rename the variable y of this quantifier to a new variable y' before performing the replacement.

We shall say that $\mathcal{F} \triangleleft \{\mathcal{G} \leftarrow \mathcal{H}\}$ is the result of *safely replacing* zero, one, or more free occurrences of $\mathcal{G}$ in $\mathcal{F}$ with $\mathcal{H}$. ∎

As in propositional logic, the partial substitution operator $\mathcal{F} \triangleleft \{\mathcal{G} \leftarrow \mathcal{H}\}$ may denote any of several sentences. Moreover, two distinct results of applying the partial substitution operator (as opposed to the total substitution operator) are not necessarily equivalent.

Example

The partial safe substitution

$$\begin{bmatrix} (\textit{for all } y)p\big(f(x),\, y\big) \\ \textit{and} \\ (\textit{for some } z)r\big(z,\, f(x)\big) \end{bmatrix} \triangleleft \{f(x) \leftarrow z\}$$

may denote any of the following four sentences:

$(\textit{for all } y)p\big(f(x),\, y\big)$ $(\textit{for all } y)p(z,\, y)$
  and   and
$(\textit{for some } z)r\big(z,\, f(x)\big)$ $(\textit{for some } z)r\big(z,\, f(x)\big)$

$(\textit{for all } y)p\big(f(x),\, y\big)$ $(\textit{for all } y)p(z,\, y)$
  and   and
$(\textit{for some } z')r(z',\, z)$ $(\textit{for some } z')r(z',\, z)$

Note that there are two occurrences of $f(x)$ in the original sentence, both free. In the first result, we replaced neither occurrence of $f(x)$. In the second result, we replaced the first occurrence of $f(x)$; in the third result, we replaced the second occurrence of $f(x)$; in the fourth result, we replaced both occurrences of $f(x)$. Also, in the third and fourth results, we were forced to rename the variable z of the quantifier (*for some z*) to the new variable z', to avoid capturing the newly introduced free variable z. ∎

We may extend our concise substitution notation from propositional logic to apply to safe substitution in predicate logic expressions.

Suppose $\mathcal{G}$ and $\mathcal{H}$ are expressions that are either both terms or both sentences.

- *Total safe substitution*

    If $\mathcal{F}[\mathcal{G}]$ is an expression,
    then $\mathcal{F}[\mathcal{H}]$ denotes the expressions obtained by safely replacing every
        free occurrence of the subexpression $\mathcal{G}$ in $\mathcal{F}[\mathcal{G}]$ with the expres-
        sion $\mathcal{H}$.

- *Partial safe substitution*

    If $\mathcal{F}\langle\mathcal{G}\rangle$ is an expression,
    then $\mathcal{F}\langle\mathcal{H}\rangle$ denotes any of the expressions obtained by safely replac-
        ing zero, one, or more free occurrences of $\mathcal{G}$ in $\mathcal{F}\langle\mathcal{G}\rangle$ with the
        expression $\mathcal{H}$.

The reader should be aware that we may use the concise substitution notation
even if $\mathcal{G}$ does not occur free in $\mathcal{F}[\mathcal{G}]$ or $\mathcal{F}\langle\mathcal{G}\rangle$; in this case, $\mathcal{F}[\mathcal{H}]$ and $\mathcal{F}\langle\mathcal{H}\rangle$ are
identical to $\mathcal{F}[\mathcal{G}]$ and $\mathcal{F}\langle\mathcal{G}\rangle$, respectively.

Remark

Suppose $\mathcal{G}$ and $\mathcal{H}$ are expressions that are either both terms or both sentences. Then if $\mathcal{G}$ has at least one free occurrence in an expression $\mathcal{F}[\mathcal{G}]$, the
newly introduced occurrences of $\mathcal{H}$ are free in $\mathcal{F}[\mathcal{H}]$. Similarly, if at least one free
occurrence of $\mathcal{G}$ in an expression $\mathcal{F}\langle\mathcal{G}\rangle$ is replaced by $\mathcal{H}$, the newly introduced
occurrences of $\mathcal{H}$ are free in $\mathcal{F}\langle\mathcal{H}\rangle$.

This is true because, in applying the substitution operators, we rename the
variable of any quantifier that would otherwise capture a free variable of the newly
introduced expression $\mathcal{H}$. ◢

MULTIPLE SAFE SUBSTITUTION

The above notions may be extended to allow simultaneous multiple replacements
in predicate-logic expressions as follows:

Definition (multiple safe substitution)

Suppose $\mathcal{F}$, $\mathcal{G}_1$, ..., $\mathcal{G}_n$, and $\mathcal{H}_1$, ..., $\mathcal{H}_n$ are expressions, where $\mathcal{G}_1$, ...,
$\mathcal{G}_n$ are distinct and, for each i, $\mathcal{G}_i$ and $\mathcal{H}_i$ are either both terms or both
sentences.

- *Total safe substitution*

  We denote by

  $$\mathcal{F} \blacktriangleleft \left\{ \begin{array}{l} \mathcal{G}_1 \leftarrow \mathcal{H}_1 \\ \vdots \\ \mathcal{G}_n \leftarrow \mathcal{H}_n \end{array} \right\}$$

  the expression obtained as follows:

  - Replace simultaneously every free occurrence of each subexpression $\mathcal{G}_i$ in $\mathcal{F}$ with the corresponding expression $\mathcal{H}_i$,

  but

  - if any free variable y in $\mathcal{H}_1, \ldots,$ or $\mathcal{H}_n$ is about to be captured by a quantifier (*for ... y*) in $\mathcal{F}$ as a result of one of the above replacements, rename the variable y of this quantifier to a new variable y' before performing the replacement.

  We shall say that

  $$\mathcal{F} \blacktriangleleft \left\{ \begin{array}{l} \mathcal{G}_1 \leftarrow \mathcal{H}_1 \\ \vdots \\ \mathcal{G}_n \leftarrow \mathcal{H}_n \end{array} \right\}$$

  is the result of *safely replacing* every free occurrence of each of the $\mathcal{G}_i$ in $\mathcal{F}$ with the corresponding $\mathcal{H}_i$.

- *Partial safe substitution*

  Furthermore, we denote by

  $$\mathcal{F} \triangleleft \left\{ \begin{array}{l} \mathcal{G}_1 \leftarrow \mathcal{H}_1 \\ \vdots \\ \mathcal{G}_n \leftarrow \mathcal{H}_n \end{array} \right\}$$

  any one of the expressions obtained as follows:

  - Replace simultaneously zero, one, or more free occurrences of some of the subexpressions $\mathcal{G}_i$ in $\mathcal{F}$ with the corresponding expression $\mathcal{H}_i$,

  but

  - if any free variable y in $\mathcal{H}_1, \ldots,$ or $\mathcal{H}_n$ is about to be captured by a quantifier (*for ... y*) in $\mathcal{F}$ as a result of one of the above

replacements, rename the variable y of this quantifier to a new
variable y' before performing the replacement.

We shall say that

$$\mathcal{F} \triangleleft \left\{ \begin{array}{c} \mathcal{G}_1 \leftarrow \mathcal{H}_1 \\ \vdots \\ \mathcal{G}_n \leftarrow \mathcal{H}_n \end{array} \right\}$$

is the result of *safely replacing* zero, one, or more free occurrences of
some of the $\mathcal{G}_i$ in $\mathcal{F}$ with the corresponding $\mathcal{H}_i$.　⌐

We can also extend the concise substitution notation to multiple safe substitution of predicate logic expressions.

- *Total safe substitution*

    If $\mathcal{F}[\mathcal{G}_1, \ldots, \mathcal{G}_n]$ is an expression,
    then $\mathcal{F}[\mathcal{H}_1, \ldots, \mathcal{H}_n]$ denotes the sentence obtained by safely replac-
    ing every free occurrence of each of the subexpressions $\mathcal{G}_i$ in
    $\mathcal{F}[\mathcal{G}_1, \ldots, \mathcal{G}_n]$ with the corresponding expression $\mathcal{H}_i$.

- *Partial safe substitution*

    If $\mathcal{F}\langle \mathcal{G}_1, \ldots, \mathcal{G}_n \rangle$ is an expression,
    then $\mathcal{F}\langle \mathcal{H}_1, \ldots, \mathcal{H}_n \rangle$ denotes any of the sentences obtained by safely re-
    placing zero, one, or more free occurrences of some of the subex-
    pressions $\mathcal{G}_i$ in $\mathcal{F}\langle \mathcal{G}_1, \ldots, \mathcal{G}_n \rangle$ with the corresponding expression
    $\mathcal{H}_i$.

Example

The result of the multiple total safe substitution

$$\begin{bmatrix} \textit{if } (\textit{for all } z)\big[p(x) \textit{ and } q(y, z)\big] \\ \textit{then } p\big(f(y)\big) \\ \textit{else } (\textit{for some } z)(\textit{for all } x)\big[q\big(f(y), z\big) \textit{ or } p(x)\big] \end{bmatrix} \triangleleft \left\{ \begin{array}{l} p(x) \leftarrow q\big(a, f(y)\big) \\ f(y) \leftarrow z \\ p\big(f(y)\big) \leftarrow \textit{false} \end{array} \right\}$$

is

$$\begin{bmatrix} \textit{if } (\textit{for all } z)\big[q\big(a, f(y)\big) \textit{ and } q(y, z)\big] \\ \textit{then } \textit{false} \\ \textit{else } (\textit{for some } z')(\textit{for all } x)\big[q(z, z') \textit{ or } p(x)\big] \end{bmatrix}.$$

Note that, as in propositional logic, multiple substitutions are applied simultaneously in a single stage. Thus though the first occurrence of $p(x)$ was replaced

by $q(a,\ f(y))$, the newly introduced occurrence of $f(y)$ was not subsequently replaced by z.

Again, in case of a conflict between two expressions, the outermost subexpression is always the one to be replaced. Thus the first occurrence of $f(y)$ in the given sentence is not replaced by z, because it occurs in a subsentence $p(f(y))$, which is replaced by *false* as a result of the substitution.

As is also the case in a single substitution, we do not replace the second occurrence of $p(x)$, since it is bound. Also, we are forced to rename the variable z of the quantifier (*for some* z) to z', to avoid capturing the free occurrence of z introduced by the replacement of the occurrence of $f(y)$ in $q(f(y),\ z)$ with z.

In our concise notation, we would say that, if the given sentence is

$$\mathcal{F}\big[p(x),\ f(y),\ p(f(y))\big],$$

then the resulting sentence is

$$\mathcal{F}\big[q(a, f(y)),\ z,\ \textit{false}\big].\quad \lrcorner$$

The next example illustrates the multiple partial safe substitution.

Example

The multiple partial safe substitution

$$\begin{bmatrix}(\textit{for all } y)\big[\textit{if } p(f(x))\ \textit{then}\ q(y)\big]\\ \textit{and}\\ \textit{if } \big(\textit{not}\, p(f(x))\big)\ \textit{then}\ r(y,\ f(y))\end{bmatrix} \triangleleft \left\{\begin{matrix} f(x) \leftarrow g(y)\\ p(f(x)) \leftarrow \textit{false} \end{matrix}\right\}$$

denotes any of several sentences, including

$$(\textit{for all } y)\big[\textit{if false then}\ q(y)\big]$$
$$\textit{and}$$
$$\textit{if } \big(\textit{not}\, p(f(x))\big)\ \textit{then}\ r(y, f(y)),$$

obtained by replacing the first occurrence of $p(f(x))$ with *false*;

$$(\textit{for all } y')\big[\textit{if } p(g(y))\ \textit{then}\ q(y')\big]$$
$$\textit{and}$$
$$\textit{if } (\textit{not false})\ \textit{then}\ r(y,\ f(y)),$$

obtained by replacing the first occurrence of $f(x)$ with $g(y)$ and the second occurrence of $p(f(x))$ with *false*; and

$$(\textit{for all } y')\big[\textit{if } p(g(y))\ \textit{then}\ q(y')\big]$$
$$\textit{and}$$
$$\textit{if } \big(\textit{not}\, p(g(y))\big)\ \textit{then}\ r(y,\ f(y)),$$

obtained by replacing both occurrences of $f(x)$ with $g(y)$.

Recall that we are not required to apply all the replacements in a multiple partial substitution; thus in the first result we replace no occurrences of $f(x)$; in the last result we replace no occurrences of $p(f(x))$. Note that, in the last two cases, we were forced to rename the variable y of the quantifier (*for all y*) to y', to avoid capturing the newly introduced free occurrence of y in $g(y)$.

In our concise notation, we would say that, if the given sentence is

$$\mathcal{F}\langle f(x),\ p(f(x))\rangle,$$

then the three resulting sentences are among those denoted by

$$\mathcal{F}\langle g(y),\ \textit{false}\rangle. \quad \lrcorner$$

Some further examples of the safe substitution operator are requested in **Problem 3.5**.

3.4   THE VALUE PROPERTY

The substitution operator exhibits the property that, under a given interpretation, the value of the entire expression is unchanged if a subexpression is replaced by another of the same value. This is expressed more precisely by the following result.

THE GENERAL PROPERTY

We first give the property in its general form.

Proposition (value)

Suppose $\mathcal{G}$ and $\mathcal{H}$ are two terms or two sentences.

- *Total value*

    Suppose $\mathcal{F}[\mathcal{G}]$ is an expression.

Let I be an interpretation for $\mathcal{G}$ and $\mathcal{F}[\mathcal{G}]$, and let J be an interpretation for $\mathcal{H}$ and $\mathcal{F}[\mathcal{H}]$, such that

> the value of $\mathcal{G}$ under I
> is the same as
> the value of $\mathcal{H}$ under J

and

> I and J agree on any free symbol that occurs in $\mathcal{F}[\mathcal{G}]$ somewhere other than in the replaced occurrences of $\mathcal{G}$.

Then

> the value of $\mathcal{F}[\mathcal{G}]$ under I
> is the same as
> the value of $\mathcal{F}[\mathcal{H}]$ under J.

- *Partial value*

Suppose $\mathcal{F}\langle\mathcal{G}\rangle$ is an expression.

Let I be an interpretation for $\mathcal{G}$ and $\mathcal{F}\langle\mathcal{G}\rangle$, and let J be an interpretation for $\mathcal{H}$ and $\mathcal{F}\langle\mathcal{H}\rangle$, such that

> the value of $\mathcal{G}$ under I
> is the same as
> the value of $\mathcal{H}$ under J

and

> I and J agree on any free symbol that occurs in $\mathcal{F}\langle\mathcal{G}\rangle$ somewhere other than in the replaced occurrences of $\mathcal{G}$.

Then

> the value of $\mathcal{F}\langle\mathcal{G}\rangle$ under I
> is the same as
> the value of $\mathcal{F}\langle\mathcal{H}\rangle$ under J. ◢

Note that we require that I and J agree on free symbols that occur in $\mathcal{F}\langle\mathcal{G}\rangle$ somewhere outside the replaced occurrences of $\mathcal{G}$. This means that, if not all occurrences of $\mathcal{G}$ are replaced in applying a partial substitution, I and J must agree on the free symbols of $\mathcal{G}$ as well.

Example

Suppose I is an interpretation for

$$\mathcal{F}[x]: \quad p(x)$$

and J is an interpretation for

$$\mathcal{F}[a]: \quad p(a)$$

such that

> the value of x under I
> is the same as
> the value of a under J,

and

> I and J agree on p.

Then, by the *total value* property,

> the value of $p(x)$ under I
> is the same as
> the value of $p(a)$ under J.   ⌟

Example

Suppose I is an interpretation for

$$\mathcal{F}\langle x \rangle: \quad p(x,\, x)$$

and J is an interpretation for

$$\mathcal{F}\langle a \rangle: \quad p(x,\, a)$$

such that

> the value of x under I
> is the same as
> the value of a under J,

and

> I and J agree on p.

Then we cannot conclude by the *partial value* property that

> the value of $p(x,\, x)$ under I
> is the same as
> the value of $p(x,\, a)$ under J.

The problem here is that not all free occurrences of x in $p(x, x)$ were replaced in forming $p(x, a)$, and we are not given that I and J agree on x.

In fact, consider two interpretations I and J over the integers. Under the first interpretation,

$$I : \quad \begin{array}{l} x \text{ is } 1 \\ p \text{ is the equality relation } = \end{array}$$

Under the second interpretation,

$$J : \quad \begin{array}{l} x \text{ is } 2 \\ a \text{ is } 1 \\ p \text{ is the equality relation } = \end{array}$$

Note that the value of x under I is the same as the value of a under J and that I and J agree on p.

Nevertheless, the truth values of $p(x, x)$ under I and of $p(x, a)$ under J are different: Under I the intuitive meaning of $p(x, x)$ is $1 = 1$, while under J the intuitive meaning of $p(x, a)$ is $2 = 1$. Thus we have exhibited interpretations that violate the agreement condition for the value property and for which the conclusion of the property is false. ⌐

Example

Suppose that K is an interpretation over a domain, that d is a domain element, and that k is a unary function over the domain.

Then we have

the value of $f(y)$ under
$$I : \langle y \leftarrow d \rangle \circ \langle f \leftarrow k \rangle \circ K$$
is (by the semantic rules) $k(d)$

and

the value of z under
$$J : \langle z \leftarrow k(d) \rangle \circ \langle y \leftarrow d \rangle \circ K$$
is (by the semantic rules) $k(d)$.

Hence

the value of $f(y)$ under I
is the same as
the value of z under J.

Consider the sentences

$$\mathcal{F}\big[f(y)\big]: \quad q\big(y,\, f(y)\big)$$

and

$$\mathcal{F}[z]: \quad q(y, z),$$

the result of replacing $f(y)$ with z in $\mathcal{F}\big[f(y)\big]$.

Assume that $\mathcal{K}$ assigns some value to q. Then because

$\mathcal{I}$ and $\mathcal{J}$ agree on the symbols q and y,

which are the free symbols that occur in $\mathcal{F}\big[f(y)\big]$ somewhere other than in the replaced subexpression $f(y)$, we have (by the *total value* property) that

the value of $q\big(y,\, f(y)\big)$ under $\mathcal{I}$
   is the same as
the value of $q(y,\, z)$ under $\mathcal{J}$. ◢

A detailed proof of the value property is technical; we present only a rough outline of the proof of the total value property.

Proof (total value)

Suppose that the value of $\mathcal{G}$ under $\mathcal{I}$ is the same as the value of $\mathcal{H}$ under $\mathcal{J}$ and that $\mathcal{I}$ and $\mathcal{J}$ satisfy the agreement condition. We would like to prove that the value of $\mathcal{F}[\mathcal{G}]$ under $\mathcal{I}$ is the same as the value of $\mathcal{F}[\mathcal{H}]$ under $\mathcal{J}$. For this purpose we show that, in determining the value of $\mathcal{F}[\mathcal{G}]$ under $\mathcal{I}$ and the value of $\mathcal{F}[\mathcal{H}]$ under $\mathcal{J}$, the corresponding results are the same at each stage.

We first observe that the renaming of bound variables that we perform during safe substitution to avoid capturing has no effect on the value of $\mathcal{F}[\mathcal{G}]$ under $\mathcal{I}$. It therefore suffices to show that the value of $\mathcal{F}[\mathcal{G}]$ under $\mathcal{I}$ after renaming is the same as the value of $\mathcal{F}[\mathcal{H}]$ under $\mathcal{J}$. The renaming ensures that the newly introduced occurrences of $\mathcal{H}$ in $\mathcal{F}[\mathcal{H}]$ are free.

At a certain stage in determining the value of $\mathcal{F}[\mathcal{G}]$ under $\mathcal{I}$, we need to determine the value of $\mathcal{G}$ under an extended interpretation

$$\mathcal{I}': \quad \langle y_1 \leftarrow d_1 \rangle \circ \langle y_2 \leftarrow d_2 \rangle \circ \ldots \circ \langle y_n \leftarrow d_n \rangle \circ \mathcal{I}.$$

Here $y_1, y_2, \ldots, y_n$ are the variables of the quantifiers (*for* ... y_1), (*for* ... y_2), ..., (*for* ... y_n) that contain some free occurrence of $\mathcal{G}$ within their scopes. Because that occurrence of $\mathcal{G}$ is free, we know that none of the variables $y_1, y_2, \ldots, y_n$

actually occurs free in $\mathcal{G}$, and therefore the value of $\mathcal{G}$ under the extended interpretation I' is the same as the value of $\mathcal{G}$ under I.

At the corresponding stage in determining the value of $\mathcal{F}[\mathcal{H}]$ under J, we need to determine the value of $\mathcal{H}$ under an extended interpretation

$$J': \quad \langle y_1 \leftarrow d_1 \rangle \circ \langle y_2 \leftarrow d_2 \rangle \circ \ldots \circ \langle y_n \leftarrow d_n \rangle \circ J,$$

for the corresponding newly introduced occurrence of $\mathcal{H}$. Because the newly introduced occurrence of $\mathcal{H}$ is free, we know that none of the variables y_1, y_2, $\ldots$, y_n actually occurs free in $\mathcal{H}$, and therefore the value of $\mathcal{H}$ under the extended interpretation J' is the same as the value $\mathcal{H}$ under J.

We have supposed that the value of $\mathcal{G}$ under I is the same as the value of $\mathcal{H}$ under J; therefore the results of these corresponding stages are the same.

At other stages in determining the value of $\mathcal{F}[\mathcal{G}]$ under I, we need to determine the value of some free symbol of $\mathcal{F}[\mathcal{G}]$ under an extended interpretation of I, where that symbol occurs somewhere other than in the replaced occurrences of $\mathcal{G}$; at the corresponding stages in determining the value of $\mathcal{F}[\mathcal{H}]$ under J, we need to determine the value of precisely the same free symbol under the corresponding extended interpretation of J. But we have supposed that the values of these free symbols are the same under I and J and, hence, under their corresponding extended interpretations. Therefore the results of these corresponding stages are the same.

The proof of the partial value property is similar. ⌐

SPECIAL CASES

We seldom require the most general version of the value property. Usually, we use one of the following special cases.

Corollary (instance)

> Suppose x is a variable, $\mathcal{F}[x]$ is an expression, and t is a term.
> Let J be an interpretation for $\mathcal{F}[x]$ and t and let d be the value
> of t under J.

Then

> the value of $\mathcal{F}[x]$ under $I : \langle x \leftarrow d \rangle \circ J$
>   is the same as
> the value of $\mathcal{F}[t]$ under J. ⌐

We shall say that $\mathcal{F}[t]$ is an *instance* of $\mathcal{F}[x]$ (or, in general, that $\mathcal{F}[t_1, t_2, \ldots, t_n]$ is an *instance* of $\mathcal{F}[x_1, x_2, \ldots, x_n]$).

Proof

By our supposition,

> the value of x under $I : \langle x \leftarrow d \rangle \circ J$
> is the same as
> the value of t under J.

Also

> I and J agree on any free symbol that occurs in $\mathcal{F}[x]$ somewhere other than in the replaced occurrences of x,

because

$$I : \langle x \leftarrow d \rangle \circ J \qquad \text{and} \qquad J$$

agree on all symbols other than x, and all free occurrences of x in $\mathcal{F}[x]$ are replaced.

Therefore (by the total value property)

> the value of $\mathcal{F}[x]$ under I
> is the same as
> the value of $\mathcal{F}[t]$ under J.   ⌐

Note that the corresponding corollary does not necessarily hold for the partial substitution operator ◄, as illustrated in the following counterexample.

Example

Suppose $\mathcal{F}\langle x \rangle$ is the sentence $p(x, x)$, t is the constant a, and $\mathcal{F}\langle t \rangle$ is the sentence $p(x, a)$, in which only one of the occurrences of x has been replaced. Let J be an interpretation for $p(x, x)$ and a, and let d be the value for a under J.

Then

> the value of $p(x, x)$ under $I : \langle x \leftarrow d \rangle \circ J$
> is not necessarily the same as
> the value of $p(x, a)$ under J.

For instance, take J to be an interpretation over the domain $\{A, B\}$ of two distinct elements under which

> a is A
> x is B
> p is the equality relation $=$.

Then d is A and

>the value of $p(x, x)$ under $I : \langle x \leftarrow \text{A} \rangle \circ J$ is A $=$ A, that is, true,

but

>the value of $p(x, a)$ under J is B $=$ A, that is, false.

The partial value property does not apply because not all the free occurrences of x have been replaced, and I and J do not agree on x. ⌐

Another consequence of the value property is as follows.

Corollary (variable)

Suppose x is a variable, $\mathcal{F}[x]$ is an expression, and y is a variable that does not occur free in $\mathcal{F}[x]$.

Let K be an interpretation for $\mathcal{F}[x]$ and let d be an arbitrary domain element.

Then

>the value of $\mathcal{F}[x]$ under $I : \langle x \leftarrow d \rangle \circ K$
>>is the same as
>
>the value of $\mathcal{F}[y]$ under $J : \langle y \leftarrow d \rangle \circ K$. ⌐

Proof

We have

>the value of x under $I : \langle x \leftarrow d \rangle \circ K$
>>is the same as
>
>the value of y under $J : \langle y \leftarrow d \rangle \circ K$.

Also

>I and J agree on any free symbol of $\mathcal{F}[x]$
>that occurs somewhere other than in the replaced occurrences of x,

because all free occurrences of x are replaced and y does not occur free in $\mathcal{F}[x]$.

Therefore (by the total value property)

the value of $\mathcal{F}[x]$ under I
is the same as
the value of $\mathcal{F}[x]$ under J.   ⌐

The corresponding result for the partial substitution operator does not hold. The reader is requested in **Problem 3.6** to illustrate this with a counterexample.

The final special case is obtained from the value property by taking I and J to be the same interpretation.

Corollary (same interpretation)

Suppose $\mathcal{G}$ and $\mathcal{H}$ are two terms or two sentences.

Let I be an interpretation for $\mathcal{G}$ and $\mathcal{H}$ such that

the value of $\mathcal{G}$ under I
is the same as
the value of $\mathcal{H}$ under I.

- *Total value*

If I is an interpretation for an expression $\mathcal{F}[\mathcal{G}]$ (and hence for $\mathcal{F}[\mathcal{H}]$), then

the value of $\mathcal{F}[\mathcal{G}]$ under I
is the same as
the value of $\mathcal{F}[\mathcal{H}]$ under I.

- *Partial value*

If I is an interpretation for an expression $\mathcal{F}\langle\mathcal{G}\rangle$ (and hence for $\mathcal{F}\langle\mathcal{H}\rangle$), then

the value of $\mathcal{F}\langle\mathcal{G}\rangle$ under I
is the same as
the value of $\mathcal{F}\langle\mathcal{H}\rangle$ under I.   ⌐

The proof is straightforward because I agrees with I on any symbol.

The total value property and its corollaries may be extended to multiple safe substitutions in a straightforward way.

3.5 VALID SCHEMATA WITH SUBSTITUTION

Now that we have introduced the safe substitution operator and established the value property for predicate logic, we can present the substitutivity of equivalence and the general renaming of bound variables and augment our catalog of valid sentence schemata.

SUBSTITUTIVITY OF EQUIVALENCE

The safe substitution operator has been defined carefully so that certain properties, including an analog of the substitutivity of equivalence from propositional logic, will be true in predicate logic.

Proposition (substitutivity of equivalence)

> For any sentences $\mathcal{G}$, $\mathcal{H}$, and $\mathcal{F}\langle\mathcal{G}\rangle$, the universal closure of
>
>   *if $\mathcal{G}$ if and only if $\mathcal{H}$*
>   *then $\mathcal{F}\langle\mathcal{G}\rangle$ if and only if $\mathcal{F}\langle\mathcal{H}\rangle$*
>
> is valid. ◢

Before proving the proposition we give an example.

Example

Consider the sentence

$$\mathcal{F}\langle p(x)\rangle: \quad (\textit{for all } y) \begin{bmatrix} \textit{if } p(x) \\ \textit{then } r(x,y) \end{bmatrix}.$$

The result of replacing the free occurrence of $p(x)$ in $\mathcal{F}\langle p(x)\rangle$ with $q(y)$ is the sentence

$$\mathcal{F}\langle q(y)\rangle: \quad (\textit{for all } y') \begin{bmatrix} \textit{if } q(y) \\ \textit{then } r(x,y') \end{bmatrix}.$$

Then, by the *substitutivity-of-equivalence* proposition, we may conclude that the universal closure of

  if $p(x)$ if and only if $q(y)$

$$\textit{then } \left[(\textit{for all } y) \begin{bmatrix} \textit{if } p(x) \\ \textit{then } r(x,y) \end{bmatrix} \textit{ if and only if } (\textit{for all } y') \begin{bmatrix} \textit{if } q(y) \\ \textit{then } r(x,y') \end{bmatrix} \right]$$

is valid.   ⌙

As an important special case of the proposition, we have that the universal closure of

> if $\mathcal{G}$ if and only if $\mathcal{H}$
> then $\mathcal{F}[\mathcal{G}]$ if and only if $\mathcal{F}[\mathcal{H}]$

is valid. This is because the result of a total substitution is one of the possible results of a partial substitution.

Let us now establish the proposition.

Proof (substitutivity of equivalence)

It suffices (by the *validity-of-closures* proposition) to show that, for an arbitrary interpretation $\mathcal{I}$, if the antecedent

> $\mathcal{G}$ if and only if $\mathcal{H}$

is true under $\mathcal{I}$, then the consequent

> $\mathcal{F}\langle\mathcal{G}\rangle$ if and only if $\mathcal{F}\langle\mathcal{H}\rangle$

is also true under $\mathcal{I}$.

Suppose that the antecedent ($\mathcal{G}$ *if and only if* $\mathcal{H}$) is true under $\mathcal{I}$. Then we have (by the *if-and-only-if* rule) that

> the value of $\mathcal{G}$ under $\mathcal{I}$
> is the same as
> the value of $\mathcal{H}$ under $\mathcal{I}$.

Therefore (by the *same-interpretation* corollary to the *value* proposition)

> the value of $\mathcal{F}\langle\mathcal{G}\rangle$ under $\mathcal{I}$
> is the same as
> the value of $\mathcal{F}\langle\mathcal{H}\rangle$ under $\mathcal{I}$.

In other words (by the *if-and-only-if* rule again),

> $\mathcal{F}\langle\mathcal{G}\rangle$ if and only if $\mathcal{F}\langle\mathcal{H}\rangle$

is true under $\mathcal{I}$, as we wanted to show.   ⌙

RENAMING OF BOUND VARIABLES

We have already established a special case of the *renaming-of-bound-variables* proposition; we now present the more general result. This version is stated in terms of the safe substitution operator.

Proposition (renaming of bound variables)

Let $(for \ \ldots \ x)\mathcal{G}[x]$ be a sentence and let x' be any variable that does not occur free in $(for \ \ldots \ x)\mathcal{G}[x]$.

Let $\mathcal{F}$ be a sentence and let $\mathcal{F}'$ be the result of replacing one or more occurrences of $(for \ \ldots \ x)\mathcal{G}[x]$ in $\mathcal{F}$ with $(for \ \ldots \ x')\mathcal{G}[x']$.

Then

$\mathcal{F}$ and $\mathcal{F}'$ are equivalent. ◢

The special case of this proposition, which we treated earlier, required that x' not occur at all in the replaced subsentence $(for \ \ldots \ x)\mathcal{G}[x]$. This version requires only that x' not occur free in the replaced subsentence. Here, if x' does occur bound in the replaced subsentence $\mathcal{G}[x]$, those occurrences will be renamed automatically in $\mathcal{G}[x']$ by the action of the safe substitution operator, if necessary to avoid capturing.

We introduced the special case earlier because we needed it to define safe substitution, while we needed safe substitution to express this general renaming of bound variables.

Before establishing the proposition, we illustrate it with examples.

Example

Consider the sentence

$$\mathcal{F}: \quad (for \ all \ y)\big[p(x',y) \ \ and \ \ (for \ some \ x)q(y,x)\big]$$

and its subsentence

$$(for \ \ldots \ x)\mathcal{G}[x]: \quad (for \ some \ x)q(y,x).$$

Note that x' does not occur free in $(for \ \ldots \ x)\mathcal{G}[x]$. (In fact, it does not occur at all in $(for \ \ldots \ x)\mathcal{G}[x]$, although it does occur free in $\mathcal{F}$.)

Then, according to the proposition, we may replace the occurrence of the subsentence $(for \ ... \ x)\mathcal{G}[x]$ in $\mathcal{F}$ with

$$(for \ ... \ x')\mathcal{G}[x'] : \quad (for \ some \ x')q(y, x'),$$

obtaining a sentence

$$\mathcal{F}' : \quad (for \ all \ y)\big[p(x', y) \ and \ (for \ some \ x')q(y, x')\big]$$

that is equivalent to $\mathcal{F}$.   ⌐

In the next example, we rename the bound variable to a variable that actually does occur bound in the replaced subsentence.

Example

Consider the sentence

$$\mathcal{F} : \quad (for \ all \ y) \left[p(x', y) \ and \ (for \ some \ x) \begin{bmatrix} if \ q(y, x) \\ then \ (for \ all \ x')q(x, x') \end{bmatrix} \right]$$

and its subsentence

$$(for \ ... \ x)\mathcal{G}[x] : \quad (for \ some \ x) \begin{bmatrix} if \ q(y, x) \\ then \ (for \ all \ x')q(x, x') \end{bmatrix}.$$

Note that x' does not occur free in $(for \ ... \ x)\mathcal{G}[x]$, although it does occur bound in this subsentence.

Then, according to the proposition, we may replace the occurrence of $(for \ ... \ x)\mathcal{G}[x]$ in $\mathcal{F}$ with

$$(for \ ... \ x')\mathcal{G}[x'] : \quad (for \ some \ x') \begin{bmatrix} if \ q(y, x') \\ then \ (for \ all \ x'')q(x', x'') \end{bmatrix},$$

obtaining a sentence

$$\mathcal{F}' : \quad (for \ all \ y) \left[p(x', y) \ and \ (for \ some \ x') \begin{bmatrix} if \ q(y, x') \\ then \ (for \ all \ x'')q(x', x'') \end{bmatrix} \right]$$

that is equivalent to $\mathcal{F}$.

Note that the variable x' of the quantifier $(for \ all \ x')$ in $\mathcal{G}[x]$ was renamed to a new variable x'' in $\mathcal{G}[x']$, by the action of the safe substitution operator.   ⌐

The prohibition against free occurrences of x' in the replaced subsentence $(for \ ... \ x)\mathcal{G}[x]$ is essential, as illustrated by the following example.

Example

Consider the sentence

$$\mathcal{F}: \quad (\textit{for some } x)q(x', x)$$

and take the subsentence $(\textit{for } ... \, x)\mathcal{G}[x]$ to be $\mathcal{F}$ itself. Note that x' does occur free in $(\textit{for } ... \, x)\mathcal{G}[x]$, contrary to the restriction imposed by the proposition.

Indeed, if we replace the occurrence of $(\textit{for } ... \, x)\mathcal{G}[x]$ with $(\textit{for } ... \, x')\mathcal{G}[x']$, we obtain a sentence

$$\mathcal{F}': \quad (\textit{for some } x')q(x', x')$$

that is not equivalent to $\mathcal{F}$. The occurrence of x' in $(\textit{for } ... \, x)\mathcal{G}[x]$ is not renamed by the safe substitution operator, because it is free, not bound. ⌐

The proof of the proposition relies on the value property and the replacement of equivalent sentences.

Proof (renaming of bound variables)

To show that $\mathcal{F}$ and $\mathcal{F}'$ are equivalent, it suffices (by the *replacement-of-equivalent-sentences* proposition) to show that

$$(\textit{for } ... \, x)\mathcal{G}[x]$$

is equivalent to

$$(\textit{for } ... \, x')\mathcal{G}[x'].$$

We consider only the case in which $(\textit{for } ... \, x)$ is the universal quantifier $(\textit{for all } x)$. To establish that $(\textit{for all } x)\mathcal{G}[x]$ is equivalent to $(\textit{for all } x')\mathcal{G}[x']$, we show that they have the same truth value under any interpretation. But for an arbitrary interpretation $\mathcal{I}$, we have

$$(\textit{for all } x)\mathcal{G}[x] \quad \text{is true under} \quad \mathcal{I}$$

precisely when (by the *for-all* rule)

> for every domain element d,
> $\mathcal{G}[x]$ is true under $\langle x \leftarrow d \rangle \circ \mathcal{I}$

precisely when (by the *variable* corollary to the *value* proposition, because x' is not free in $\mathcal{G}[x]$)

> for every domain element d,
> $\mathcal{G}[x']$ is true under $\langle x' \leftarrow d \rangle \circ \mathcal{I}$

precisely when (by the *for-all* rule)

　　　(for all x′) $\mathcal{G}[x′]$　is true under　$\mathcal{I}$,

as we wanted to show.

　　　The case in which *(for ... x)* is the existential quantifier *(for some x)* is similar. ⏌

QUANTIFIER INSTANTIATION

The following classes of valid sentence schemata are described in terms of the total safe substitution operator.

Proposition (quantifier instantiation)

　　　For any variable x, sentence $\mathcal{F}[x]$, and term t, the universal closures of the sentences :

　　　　　if (for all x) $\mathcal{F}[x]$
　　　　　then $\mathcal{F}[t]$　　　　　　　　　　　　　　　　*(universal)*

　　　　　if $\mathcal{F}[t]$
　　　　　then (for some x) $\mathcal{F}[x]$　　　　　　　　　*(existential)*

　　are valid. ⏌

We first illustrate the proposition with an example.

Example

　　　Consider the sentence

　　　　　$\mathcal{F}[x]$:　$p(x, a)$.

The result of replacing the free occurrence of x in $\mathcal{F}[x]$ with the term a is the sentence

　　　　　$\mathcal{F}[a]$:　$p(a, a)$.

　　　According to the *universal* part of the proposition, taking t to be a, the sentence

　　　　　if (for all x) $\mathcal{F}[x]$　　　*if (for all x)* $p(x, a)$
　　　　　then $\mathcal{F}[a]$　　　：　　*then* $p(a, a)$

is valid.

On the other hand, according to the *existential* part of the proposition, the sentence

$$\begin{array}{ll} \textit{if } \mathcal{F}[a] & \textit{if } p(a,a) \\ \textit{then } (\textit{for some } x)\mathcal{F}[x] & \textit{then } (\textit{for some } x)p(x,a) \end{array} :$$

is also valid. ◢

Let us give an intuitive justification of the quantifier-instantiation proposition. We prove each part separately.

Proof (universal quantifier instantiation)

We establish the validity of the universal closure of the sentence

$$\begin{array}{l} \textit{if } (\textit{for all } x)\mathcal{F}[x] \\ \textit{then } \mathcal{F}[t]. \end{array}$$

We distinguish between two cases, according to whether or not x occurs free in $\mathcal{F}$. We establish the desired conclusion separately in each case.

Case: x occurs free in $\mathcal{F}[x]$.

By the *validity-of-closures* proposition, to show the validity of the closure of the sentence it suffices to show that the sentence itself is true under any interpretation $\mathcal{I}$. Let $\mathcal{I}$ be an arbitrary interpretation for the above implication. Suppose that

the antecedent $(\textit{for all } x)\mathcal{F}[x]$ is true under $\mathcal{I}$.

We would like to show that

the consequent $\mathcal{F}[t]$ is also true under $\mathcal{I}$.

Because in this case x occurs free in $\mathcal{F}[x]$, we know that the newly introduced occurrences of t are free in $\mathcal{F}[t]$. Therefore, because $\mathcal{I}$ is an interpretation for $\mathcal{F}[t]$, $\mathcal{I}$ is also an interpretation for t. Let the domain element d be the value of t under $\mathcal{I}$.

Because the antecedent $(\textit{for all } x)\mathcal{F}[x]$ is true under the interpretation $\mathcal{I}$, we have (by the *for-all* rule) that, for any domain element e,

$\mathcal{F}[x]$ is true under $\langle x \leftarrow e \rangle \circ \mathcal{I}$.

In particular, taking e to be the domain element d, we know

$\mathcal{F}[x]$ is true under $\langle x \leftarrow d \rangle \circ \mathcal{I}$.

But by the *instance* corollary of the *value* proposition,

> the value of $\mathcal{F}[x]$ under $\langle x \leftarrow d \rangle \circ I$
> is the same as
> the value of $\mathcal{F}[t]$ under I.

Therefore

> $\mathcal{F}[t]$ is true under I,

as we wanted to show.

Case: x does not occur free in $\mathcal{F}[x]$.

In this case, the quantifier *(for all x)* in the sentence *(for all x)*$\mathcal{F}[x]$ is redundant; that is, *(for all x)*$\mathcal{F}[x]$ is equivalent to $\mathcal{F}[x]$. Furthermore, in this case, $\mathcal{F}[t]$ is identical to $\mathcal{F}[x]$. Therefore, by the *replacement-of-equivalent-sentences* proposition, the sentence is equivalent to

> *if* $\mathcal{F}[x]$
> *then* $\mathcal{F}[x]$.

But the universal closure of any instance of a valid propositional-logic sentence is valid in predicate logic.

Because we have established the validity of the universal closure of the sentence in each case, we know it is valid whether or not x occurs free in $\mathcal{F}[x]$. ◢

We could establish the *existential* part of the proposition in the same way as the *universal* part. It is more instructive, however, to use the result we have just obtained in establishing the new result.

Proof (existential quantifier instantiation)

Let $\mathcal{F}[x]$ be an arbitrary sentence.

By the *universal* part of the proposition, we know that, for any sentence $\mathcal{G}[x]$, the universal closure of the sentence

> *if* *(for all x)*$\mathcal{G}[x]$
> *then* $\mathcal{G}[t]$

is valid. In particular, taking $\mathcal{G}[x]$ to be the sentence *(not* $\mathcal{F}[x]$*)*, we have that $\mathcal{G}[t]$ is the sentence *(not* $\mathcal{F}[t]$*)*, and therefore the universal closure of the sentence

$(*)$

> *if* *(for all x)*$\big[$*not* $\mathcal{F}[x]$$\big]$
> *then not* $\mathcal{F}[t]$

is valid.

By the duality between universal and existential quantifiers, the subsentence

$$(for\ all\ x)\big[not\ \mathcal{F}[x]\big]$$

is equivalent to

$$not\ (for\ some\ x)\mathcal{F}[x].$$

Hence (by the *replacement-of-equivalent-sentences* proposition), the sentence itself is equivalent to

$$if\ not\ (for\ some\ x)\mathcal{F}[x]$$
$$then\ not\ \mathcal{F}[t].$$

By propositional logic then, the sentence is equivalent to its contrapositive

$$if\ \mathcal{F}[t]$$
$$then\ (for\ some\ x)\mathcal{F}[x],$$

which is the desired sentence.

We have shown that the original sentence (∗),

$$if\ (for\ all\ x)\big[not\ \mathcal{F}[x]\big]$$
$$then\ not\ \mathcal{F}[t],$$

is equivalent to the desired sentence

$$if\ \mathcal{F}[t]$$
$$then\ (for\ some\ x)\mathcal{F}[x].$$

But the universal closure of the sentence (∗) has been shown to be valid; therefore (by the *equivalence-and-validity* proposition) the universal closure of the desired sentence is valid as well. ⌙

Let us illustrate the proposition with an example that requires renaming in applying the safe substitution operator.

Example

Consider the sentence

$$\mathcal{F}[x]:\quad \begin{array}{l} (for\ all\ y)p(x,\ y) \\ and \\ p(y,\ x). \end{array}$$

The result of safely replacing the two free occurrences of x in $\mathcal{F}[x]$ with the term $g(y)$ is the sentence

$$\mathcal{F}[g(y)]: \quad \begin{array}{c} (\textit{for all } y')p(g(y),\ y') \\ \textit{and} \\ p(y,\ g(y)). \end{array}$$

Note that the variable y of the quantifier (*for all y*) was renamed y' to avoid capturing the free variable y in a newly introduced occurrence of $g(y)$. The free occurrence of y, in $p(y,\ x)$, was not renamed.

According to the *universal* part of the proposition, the universal closure of the sentence

$$\begin{array}{c} \textit{if } (\textit{for all } x)\mathcal{F}[x] \\ \textit{then } \mathcal{F}[g(y)] \end{array} : \quad \begin{array}{c} \textit{if } (\textit{for all } x) \left[\begin{array}{c} (\textit{for all } y)p(x,\ y) \\ \textit{and} \\ p(y,\ x) \end{array}\right] \\ \textit{then} \left[\begin{array}{c} (\textit{for all } y')p(g(y),\ y') \\ \textit{and} \\ p(y,\ g(y)) \end{array}\right] \end{array}$$

is valid.

⌐

The renaming required by the safe substitution operator is essential to ensure the truth of the proposition; this is illustrated by the following example.

Example (necessity for renaming)

Consider the sentence

$$\mathcal{F}[x]: \quad (\textit{for some } y)p(x,\ y).$$

The result of safely replacing the (free) occurrence of x in $\mathcal{F}[x]$ with the term y is the sentence

$$\mathcal{F}[y]: \quad (\textit{for some } y')p(y,\ y'),$$

where the variable y of the quantifier (*for some y*) was renamed y'.

According to the *universal* part of the proposition, the universal closure of the sentence

$$\begin{array}{c} \textit{if } (\textit{for all } x)\mathcal{F}[x] \\ \textit{then } \mathcal{F}[y] \end{array} : \quad \begin{array}{c} \textit{if } (\textit{for all } x)(\textit{for some } y)p(x,\ y) \\ \textit{then } (\textit{for some } y')p(y,\ y') \end{array}$$

is valid.

However, if we had neglected to rename the variable y during the substitution, we would have obtained the sentence

> *if (for all x)(for some y)p(x, y)*
> *then (for some y)p(y, y),*

which is not valid. In particular, consider the interpretation over the integers under which

> p is the less-than relation $<$.

Under this interpretation the sentence has the intuitive meaning

> if for every integer x
>   there exists an integer y such that $x < y$,
> then there exists an integer y such that $y < y$,

which is false because its antecedent is true and its consequent is false.   ◢

Let us discuss one point that can be confusing in applying the *existential* part of the proposition.

Remark (existential quantifier instantiation)

In a previous example we considered the sentence

> $\mathcal{F}[x]:$ $p(x, a)$

and its instance

> $\mathcal{F}[a]:$ $p(a, a)$

and concluded, by the *existential* part of the proposition, that the sentence

> *if $p(a, a)$*
> *then (for some x)p(x, a)*

is valid.

Suppose instead we consider the sentence

> $\mathcal{F}[x]:$ $p(a, x)$.

The corresponding instance is again the sentence

> $\mathcal{F}[a]:$ $p(a, a)$.

According to the *existential* part of the proposition, we can conclude that the sentence

> *if* $p(a, a)$
> *then* (*for some* x)$p(a, x)$

is valid.

Finally, if we consider instead the sentence

> $\mathcal{F}[x]$: $p(x, x)$,

the corresponding instance is again the sentence

> $\mathcal{F}[a]$: $p(a, a)$,

and we may conclude, by the *existential* part of the proposition, that the sentence

> *if* $p(a, a)$
> *then* (*for some* x)$p(x, x)$

is valid.

In short, the *existential* part of the proposition allows us to conclude that all of the following sentences are valid:

> *if* $p(a, a)$ *if* $p(a, a)$
> *then* (*for some* x)$p(x, a)$ *then* (*for some* x)$p(a, x)$

> *if* $p(a, a)$
> *then* (*for some* x)$p(x, x)$.

In other words, the sentence $p(a, a)$ implies each of the three sentences (*for some* x)$p(x, a)$,   (*for some* x)$p(a, x)$,   and   (*for some* x)$p(x, x)$. ⌐

The *quantifier-instantiation* proposition is stated in terms of the total substitution operator; in fact, the corresponding result for the partial substitution operator does not hold, as the reader is requested to show in **Problem 3.7(a)**.

The *quantifier-instantiation* proposition can be generalized to apply to more than one variable. More precisely, we have the following result.

Proposition (quantifier instantiation, multiple)

For any distinct variables $x_1, x_2, \ldots, x_n$, sentence $\mathcal{F}[x_1, x_2, \ldots, x_n]$, and terms $t_1, t_2, \ldots, t_n$, the universal closures of the sentences

> *if (for all x_1)(for all x_2) ... (for all x_n)$\mathcal{F}[x_1, x_2, \ldots, x_n]$*
> *then $\mathcal{F}[t_1, t_2, \ldots, t_n]$*   (*universal*)
>
> *if $\mathcal{F}[t_1, t_2, \ldots, t_n]$*
> *then (for some x_1)(for some x_2) ... (for some x_n)$\mathcal{F}[x_1, x_2, \ldots, x_n]$*
>   (*existential*)

are valid.

Note that we do not require that the variables x_1, x_2, ..., x_n actually occur in $\mathcal{F}[x_1, x_2, \ldots, x_n]$, nor that they include all the free variables in $\mathcal{F}[x_1, x_2, \ldots, x_n]$.

The proof is by repeated application of the *quantifier-instantiation* proposition for one variable.

Proof

For the *universal* part it suffices (by the *validity-of-closures* proposition) to show that the implication is true under any interpretation, i.e., that its antecedent

$$(\text{for all } x_1)(\text{for all } x_2) \ldots (\text{for all } x_n)\mathcal{F}[x_1, x_2, \ldots, x_n]$$

implies its consequent

$$\mathcal{F}[t_1, t_2, \ldots, t_n].$$

We have that the antecedent

$$(\text{for all } x_1)(\text{for all } x_2) \ldots (\text{for all } x_n)\mathcal{F}[x_1, x_2, \ldots, x_n]$$

implies (by one application of the *universal* part of the *quantifier-instantiation* proposition)

$$(\text{for all } x_2) \ldots (\text{for all } x_n)\mathcal{F}[t_1, x_2, \ldots, x_n].$$

But (by $n - 1$ further applications of the *universal* part of the proposition) this sentence implies the desired consequent

$$\mathcal{F}[t_1, t_2, \ldots, t_n].$$

The proof of the *existential* part is similar.

CLOSURE INSTANTIATION

Another version of the quantifier-instantiation proposition applies to the universal and existential closures of a given sentence.

Proposition (closure instantiation)

For any distinct variables x_1, x_2, ..., x_n, sentence $\mathcal{F}[x_1, x_2, ..., x_n]$, and terms $t_1, t_2, ..., t_n$, the sentences

$$\begin{array}{ll} \textit{if (for all }*)\mathcal{F}[x_1, x_2, \ldots, x_n] & \textit{(universal)} \\ \textit{then (for all }*)\mathcal{F}[t_1, t_2, \ldots, t_n] & \end{array}$$

$$\begin{array}{ll} \textit{if (for some }*)\mathcal{F}[t_1, t_2, \ldots, t_n] & \textit{(existential)} \\ \textit{then (for some }*)\mathcal{F}[x_1, x_2, \ldots, x_n] & \end{array}$$

are valid. ◢

Note that we do not require that the variables x_1, x_2, ..., x_n actually occur in $\mathcal{F}[x_1, x_2, ..., x_n]$, nor do we assume that they include all the free variables in $\mathcal{F}[x_1, x_2, ..., x_n]$. We do not need to refer to the universal closures of the two sentences, because they are already closed.

We illustrate the proposition with one example.

Example

Consider the sentence

$$\mathcal{F}[x_1,\ x_2]: \quad \begin{array}{l} \textit{(for all } y)p(x_1,\ y) \\ \quad \textit{and} \\ p(x_2,\ z). \end{array}$$

Then the result of safely replacing the free occurrences of x_1 and x_2 with the terms $g(y)$ and z, respectively, in $\mathcal{F}[x_1,\ x_2]$ is the sentence

$$\mathcal{F}\big[g(y),\ z\big]: \quad \begin{array}{l} \textit{(for all } y')p\big(g(y),\ y'\big) \\ \quad \textit{and} \\ p(z,\ z). \end{array}$$

According to the *universal* part of the proposition, the sentence

$$\text{if } (for\ all\ *)\mathcal{F}[x_1,\ x_2] \atop \text{then } (for\ all\ *)\mathcal{F}\big[g(y),\ z\big] \quad :$$

$$\begin{array}{l} (for\ all\ x_1) \\ if\ (for\ all\ x_2) \\ (for\ all\ z) \end{array} \left[\begin{array}{l} (for\ all\ y)p(x_1,\ y) \\ and \\ p(x_2,\ z) \end{array}\right]$$

$$then\ \begin{array}{l} (for\ all\ y) \\ (for\ all\ z) \end{array} \left[\begin{array}{l} (for\ all\ y')p\big(g(y),\ y'\big) \\ and \\ p(z,\ z) \end{array}\right]$$

is valid.

We establish the *universal* part of the proposition. The proof relies on the *multiple* version of the *quantifier-instantiation* proposition.

Proof (universal closure instantiation)

Recall that we have established (in the *multiple* version of the *quantifier-instantiation* proposition) that the universal closure

$$(for\ all\ *)\left[\begin{array}{l} if\ (for\ all\ x_1)(for\ all\ x_2)\dots(for\ all\ x_n)\mathcal{F}[x_1, x_2,\ \dots, x_n] \\ then\ \ \mathcal{F}[t_1, t_2,\ \dots, t_n] \end{array}\right]$$

is valid. This implies (by the *distribution-of-closures* proposition) that the sentence

(†) $$if\ (for\ all\ *)(for\ all\ x_1)(for\ all\ x_2)\dots(for\ all\ x_n)\mathcal{F}[x_1, x_2.\ \dots, x_n] \\ then\ (for\ all\ *)\mathcal{F}[t_1, t_2,\ \dots, t_n]$$

is valid.

By the *reversal-of-quantifiers* schema for predicate logic, we observe that the antecedent

(1) $(for\ all\ *)(for\ all\ x_1)(for\ all\ x_2)\dots,(for\ all\ x_n)\mathcal{F}[x_1, x_2,\ \dots, x_n]$

of the above sentence is equivalent to

(‡) $(for\ all\ x_1)(for\ all\ *)(for\ all\ x_2)\dots(for\ all\ x_n)\mathcal{F}[x_1, x_2,\ \dots, x_n].$

Note that

(2) $(for\ all\ *)(for\ all\ x_2)\dots(for\ all\ x_n)\mathcal{F}[x_1, x_2,\ \dots, x_n]$

is a closed subsentence. In particular, x_1 does not occur free in this subsentence and therefore the first quantifier, $(for\ all\ x_1)$, of (‡) is redundant and can be dropped by the *redundant-quantifier* schema of predicate logic. In other words,

(1) is equivalent to (2).

By the same reasoning, the subsequent quantifiers $(for\ all\ x_2), (for\ all\ x_3)$, $\dots, (for\ all\ x_n)$ of (2) can be dropped; in other words,

(1) is equivalent to $(for\ all\ *)\mathcal{F}[x_1, x_2, \dots, x_n]$.

Consequently, the entire implication (†),

$if\ (for\ all\ *)(for\ all\ x_1)(for\ all\ x_2) \dots (for\ all\ x_n)\mathcal{F}[x_1, x_2, \dots, x_n]$
$then\ (for\ all\ *)\mathcal{F}[t_1, t_2, \dots, t_n]$,

is equivalent to the desired sentence

$if\ (for\ all\ *)\mathcal{F}[x_1, x_2, \dots, x_n]$
$then\ (for\ all\ *)\mathcal{F}[t_1, t_2, \dots, t_n]$.

Since (†) has been shown to be valid, the desired sentence is also valid. ⌐

The proof of the *existential* part of the proposition is left as an exercise (**Problem 3.8**).

The *closure-instantiation* proposition is stated in terms of the total substitution operator. In fact, the corresponding result for the partial substitution operator does not hold, as the reader is requested to show in **Problem 3.7(b)**.

3.6   FUNCTION INTRODUCTION AND ELIMINATION

We complete our discussion of predicate logic with a property that will be very useful later in allowing us to define new functions. We establish that, although the two sentence schemata

$\mathcal{F}:$ $(for\ all\ x)(for\ some\ y)\mathcal{H}[x,\ y]$

and

$\mathcal{G}:$ $(for\ all\ x)\mathcal{H}[x,\ g(x)]$

are not equivalent, they are true for nearly the same interpretations and hence may be regarded as "almost equivalent."

Before we make this property precise, we must introduce the following result concerning functions and relations.

Lemma (function-relation)

Let D be a set and $R(d, e)$ be a relation between elements of D. Then

(†)   for every element d of D,
         there exists an element e of D such that
           $R(d, e)$ is true

precisely when

(‡)   there exists a unary function k over D such that,
         for every element d of D,
           $R\big(d, k(d)\big)$ is true. ⌐

Note that this is a property, not of the sentences of predicate logic, but of actual functions and relations over a set. In particular, $R(d, e)$ is not a sentence but an actual relation; k is not a function symbol but an actual function.

We illustrate the lemma with an example.

Example

Suppose D is the set of integers and let $R(d, e)$ be the less-than relation, which holds precisely when $d < e$. Then, according to the lemma, the condition (†), i.e. (in this case),

         for every integer d,
         there exists an integer e such that
           $d < e$

is true precisely when the condition (‡), that is,

         there exists a unary function k such that,
         for every integer d,
           $d < k(d)$,

is true. In fact, in this case, both conditions are true, taking k in (‡) to be, say, the successor function $k(d) = d + 1$. ⌐

We now establish the lemma.

Proof

We prove each direction separately.

$(\dagger) \Rightarrow (\ddagger)$

Suppose ($\dagger$) holds; we define a unary function k as follows. Consider an arbitrary element d of D. Let e be an element such that $R(d, e)$ is true. (The existence of such an element is guaranteed by ($\dagger$).) Take $k(d)$ to be e. Thus for every element d of D, the relation $R(d, k(d))$ is true, that is, ($\ddagger$) holds.

$(\ddagger) \Rightarrow (\dagger)$

Suppose ($\ddagger$) holds; let k be a unary function over D such that, for every element d of D, the relation $R(d, k(d))$ is true. (The existence of such a function is guaranteed by ($\ddagger$).) For an arbitrary element d of D, take e to be $k(d)$; then $R(d, e)$ is true, that is, ($\dagger$) holds.   ⌟

The main result of this section applies the lemma to sentences of predicate logic.

Proposition (function introduction and elimination)

Let

$$\mathcal{F}: \quad (for\ all\ x)(for\ some\ y)\mathcal{H}[x, y]$$

be a sentence, where x and y are distinct variables.

Let

$$\mathcal{G}: \quad (for\ all\ x)\mathcal{H}[x, g(x)]$$

be the sentence obtained by dropping the quantifier (*for some y*) from $\mathcal{F}$ and replacing all the free occurrences of y in $\mathcal{H}[x, y]$ with the term $g(x)$, where g is a unary function symbol that does not occur in $\mathcal{F}$.

Then

> if $\mathcal{F}$ is true under an interpretation I for $\mathcal{F}$,
> then $\mathcal{G}$ is true under some interpretation I_g for $\mathcal{G}$,
> where I and I_g agree on all symbols except perhaps g
>
> *(function introduction)*

and

> if $\mathcal{G}$ is true under an interpretation J for $\mathcal{G}$,
> then $\mathcal{F}$ is also true under J.
>
> *(function elimination)*

Example

Consider the sentence

$$\mathcal{F}: \quad (for \; all \; x)(for \; some \; y)p(x, y)$$

and consider an interpretation $\mathcal{I}$ over the integers under which

p is the less-than relation (that is, $p_\mathcal{I}(d, e)$ is $d < e$).

Then the intuitive meaning of $\mathcal{F}$ under $\mathcal{I}$ is

for every integer x,
there exists an integer y such that
$x < y$,

which is true.

For the unary function symbol g, the corresponding sentence is

$$\mathcal{G}: \quad (for \; all \; x)p(x, g(x)).$$

Then, according to the *function-introduction* proposition, $\mathcal{G}$ is true under some interpretation $\mathcal{I}_g$ for $\mathcal{G}$ that agrees with $\mathcal{I}$ on all symbols except perhaps g. In fact, consider the extended interpretation

$$\mathcal{I}_g: \quad \langle g \leftarrow k \rangle \circ \mathcal{I},$$

where k is the successor function, that is, $k(d) = d + 1$. Then $\mathcal{I}_g$ does agree with $\mathcal{I}$ on all symbols except perhaps g. Also, the intuitive meaning of $\mathcal{G}$ under $\mathcal{I}_g$ is

for every integer x,
$x < x + 1$,

which is true.

On the other hand, consider the interpretation $\mathcal{J}$ over the integers under which

p is the less-than relation

g is the successor function.

Then the intuitive meaning of $\mathcal{G}$ under $\mathcal{J}$ is

for every integer x,
$x < x + 1$,

which is true.

According to the *function-elimination* proposition, therefore, $\mathcal{F}$ is also true under the same interpretation J. In fact, the intuitive meaning of $\mathcal{F}$ under J is

> for every integer x,
> there exists an integer y such that
> > $x < y$,

which is true. ⅃

Remark ("almost equivalent")

If the proposition had told us that $\mathcal{F}$ and $\mathcal{G}$ are true under precisely the same interpretations, we would have established that $\mathcal{F}$ and $\mathcal{G}$ are equivalent. Since the proposition tells us that $\mathcal{F}$ and $\mathcal{G}$ are true under interpretations that may differ only on g, we say that $\mathcal{F}$ and $\mathcal{G}$ are "almost equivalent." In fact, $\mathcal{F}$ and $\mathcal{G}$ are not necessarily equivalent.

To see this, consider the sentences of the previous example,

$$\mathcal{F}: \quad (for\ all\ x)(for\ some\ y)p(x,\ y)$$

and

$$\mathcal{G}: \quad (for\ all\ x)p\big(x,\ g(x)\big).$$

Let K be interpretation over the integers under which

> p is the less-than relation
>
> g is the predecessor function (that is, $g_K(d) = d - 1$).

Then the intuitive meaning of $\mathcal{F}$ under K is

> for every integer x,
> there exists an integer y such that
> > $x < y$,

which is true. But the intuitive meaning of $\mathcal{G}$ under K is

> for every integer x,
> > $x < x - 1$,

which is false. Because we have found an interpretation under which $\mathcal{F}$ and $\mathcal{G}$ have different truth values, we may conclude that they are not equivalent. ⅃

We prove each part of the proposition separately.

Proof (function introduction)

Suppose I is an interpretation under which $\mathcal{F}$ is true; that is,

$(\textit{for all } x)(\textit{for some } y)\mathcal{H}[x, y]$ is true under I.

We would like to show that then $\mathcal{G}$, that is,

$(\textit{for all } x)\mathcal{H}[x, g(x)]$,

is true under some interpretation I_g that agrees with I on all symbols except perhaps g.

We have (by the *for-all* rule)

for every domain element d,
$(\textit{for some } y)\mathcal{H}[x, y]$ is true under $\langle x \leftarrow d \rangle \circ I$.

Then (by the *for-some* rule)

for every domain element d,
there exists a domain element e such that
$\mathcal{H}[x, y]$ is true under $\langle y \leftarrow e \rangle \circ \langle x \leftarrow d \rangle \circ I$.

Then (by the *function-relation* lemma)

there exists a unary function k over the domain such that,
for every domain element d,
$\mathcal{H}[x, y]$ is true under $I' : \langle y \leftarrow k(d) \rangle \circ \langle x \leftarrow d \rangle \circ I$.

Therefore (by the *total-value* proposition, because the value of y under the interpretation I' above, that is, $k(d)$, is the same as the value of $g(x)$ under the interpretation I'' below),

there exists a unary function k over the domain such that,
for every domain element d,
$\mathcal{H}[x, g(x)]$ is true under $I'' : \langle x \leftarrow d \rangle \circ \langle g \leftarrow k \rangle \circ I$.

Take k to be any such function and let I_g be the interpretation $\langle g \leftarrow k \rangle \circ I$; note that I_g is an interpretation for $\mathcal{G}$ that agrees with I on all symbols except perhaps g. Then

for every domain element d,
$\mathcal{H}[x, g(x)]$ is true under $\langle x \leftarrow d \rangle \circ I_g$.

Therefore (by the *for-all* rule)

$(\textit{for all } x)\mathcal{H}[x, g(x)]$ is true under I_g, that is, $\mathcal{G}$ is true under some interpretation I_g for $\mathcal{G}$ that agrees with I on all symbols except perhaps g, as we wanted to show. ⏌

We now give the proof of the *function-elimination* part of the proposition.

Proof (function elimination)

Suppose J is an interpretation under which $\mathcal{G}$ is true, that is,

$$(\text{for all } x)\mathcal{H}[x, \, g(x)] \text{ is true under } J.$$

We would like to show that then $\mathcal{F}$, that is,

$$(\text{for all } x)(\text{for some } y)\mathcal{H}[x, \, y],$$

is also true under J.

Consider an arbitrary domain element d. We have (by the *for-all* rule)

$$\mathcal{H}[x, \, g(x)] \text{ is true under } J' : \langle x \leftarrow d \rangle \circ J.$$

Let e be the value of $g(x)$ under J'. Then (by the *total-value* proposition, because the value of $g(x)$ under the interpretation J' above, that is, e, is the same as the value of y under the interpretation J'' below),

$$\mathcal{H}[x, \, y] \text{ is true under } J'' : \langle x \leftarrow d \rangle \circ \langle y \leftarrow e \rangle \circ J.$$

In short, we have

> for every domain element d,
> there exists a domain element e such that
> $\mathcal{H}[x, \, y]$ is true under $J'' : \langle x \leftarrow d \rangle \circ \langle y \leftarrow e \rangle \circ J.$

Then (by the *for-some* rule)

> for every domain element d,
> $(\text{for some } y)\mathcal{H}[x, \, y]$ is true under $\langle x \leftarrow d \rangle \circ J.$

Therefore (by the *for-all* rule)

$$(\text{for all } x)(\text{for some } y)\mathcal{H}[x, \, y] \text{ is true under } J,$$

that is, $\mathcal{F}$ is true under J, as we wanted to show. ⏌

PROBLEMS

Problem 3.1 (validity of sentence schemata)   page 123

Show that the universal closures of the following sentences are valid for any sentences $\mathcal{F}$ and $\mathcal{G}$. For those sentences that are implications, show that the universal closures of their converses are not valid for some sentences $\mathcal{F}$ and $\mathcal{G}$.

(a)   *(for some x)[if $\mathcal{F}$ then $\mathcal{G}$]*
                if and only if
            if (for all x)$\mathcal{F}$ then (for some x)$\mathcal{G}$

(b)   *if [(for all x)$\mathcal{F}$ or (for all x)$\mathcal{G}$]*
            then (for all x)[$\mathcal{F}$ or $\mathcal{G}$]

(c)   *if [if (for some x)$\mathcal{F}$ then (for all x)$\mathcal{G}$]*
            then (for all x)[if $\mathcal{F}$ then $\mathcal{G}$]

Problem 3.2 (validity with side conditions)   page 128

Show that the universal closures of the following sentences are valid for any sentences $\mathcal{F}$ and $\mathcal{G}$ such that x is not free in $\mathcal{G}$. Show that the universal closures of these sentences are not valid for some sentences $\mathcal{F}$ and $\mathcal{G}$ such that x does occur free in $\mathcal{G}$.

(a)   *(for all x)[$\mathcal{F}$ or $\mathcal{G}$]*
                if and only if
            (for all x)$\mathcal{F}$ or $\mathcal{G}$

(b)   *(for some x)[if $\mathcal{F}$ then $\mathcal{G}$]*
                if and only if
            if (for all x)$\mathcal{F}$ then $\mathcal{G}$

(c)   *(for all x)[if $\mathcal{G}$ then $\mathcal{F}$]*
                if and only if
            if $\mathcal{G}$ then (for all x)$\mathcal{F}$

Problem 3.3 (implication, equivalence, and validity)   page 131

Show for any two sentences $\mathcal{F}$ and $\mathcal{G}$:

(a)   Implication and validity

            if $\mathcal{F}$ implies $\mathcal{G}$

then if (*for all* *)$\mathcal{F}$ is valid
then (*for all* *)$\mathcal{G}$ is valid.

(b) Equivalence and validity

if $\mathcal{F}$ is equivalent to $\mathcal{G}$
then (*for all* *)$\mathcal{F}$ is valid
precisely when
(*for all* *)$\mathcal{G}$ is valid.

Problem 3.4 (distribution of closures) page 134

Establish the validity of the sentences

(a) (*for all* *)[$\mathcal{F}$ *and* $\mathcal{G}$]
if and only if
(*for all* *)$\mathcal{F}$ *and* (*for all* *)$\mathcal{G}$

(b) (*for some* *)[$\mathcal{F}$ *or* $\mathcal{G}$]
if and only if
(*for some* *)$\mathcal{F}$ *or* (*for some* *)$\mathcal{G}$

(c) *if* (*for some* *)[$\mathcal{F}$ *and* $\mathcal{G}$]
then $\begin{bmatrix} (\textit{for some } *)\mathcal{F} \\ \textit{and} \\ (\textit{for some } *)\mathcal{G} \end{bmatrix}$

(d) *if* $\begin{bmatrix} (\textit{for all } *)\mathcal{F} \\ \textit{or} \\ (\textit{for all } *)\mathcal{G} \end{bmatrix}$
then (*for all* *)[$\mathcal{F}$ *or* $\mathcal{G}$]

(e) *if* (*for all* *)[*if* $\mathcal{F}$ *then* $\mathcal{G}$]
then $\begin{bmatrix} \textit{if } (\textit{for all } *)\mathcal{F} \\ \textit{then } (\textit{for all } *)\mathcal{G} \end{bmatrix}$

(f) *if* $\begin{bmatrix} \textit{if } (\textit{for some } *)\mathcal{F} \\ \textit{then } (\textit{for some } *)\mathcal{G} \end{bmatrix}$
then (*for some* *)[*if* $\mathcal{F}$ *then* $\mathcal{G}$].

Problem 3.5 (safe substitution) page 154

Apply the following substitutions. Give three possible results of applying the partial substitution.

(a) $\begin{bmatrix} p(x) \ \ and \\ (\textit{for all } y)q(x,y) \ \ and \\ (\textit{for some } x)q(x,y) \ \ and \\ (\textit{for all } y)[p(x) \ \ and \ (\textit{for some } y)q(x,y)] \ \ and \\ (\textit{for all } z)q(x,z) \end{bmatrix}$ ◀ $\{x \leftarrow y\}$

(b) $\begin{bmatrix} p(f(x)) \ \ and \\ (\textit{for all } y)[p(f(x)) \ and \ q(y)] \ \ and \\ q(f(x)) \ \ and \\ (\textit{for some } x)q(f(x)) \ \ and \\ p(f(y)) \end{bmatrix}$ ◀ $\left\{ \begin{array}{l} p(f(x)) \leftarrow q(y) \\ f(x) \leftarrow g(x,y) \end{array} \right\}$

(c)
$$\begin{bmatrix} p\big(f(x)\big) \ \ and \\ (for\ all\ y)\big[p\big(f(x)\big)\ and\ q(y)\big]\ \ and \\ q\big(f(x)\big)\ \ and \\ (for\ some\ x)q\big(f(x)\big)\ \ and \\ p\big(f(y)\big) \end{bmatrix} \lhd \left\{ \begin{aligned} p\big(f(x)\big) &\leftarrow q(y) \\ f(x) &\leftarrow g(x,y) \end{aligned} \right\}.$$

Problem 3.6 (value property)   page 162

Show that the *variable* corollary to the *value* proposition does not hold for the partial substitution operator. In other words, it is not necessarily the case that

for a variable x, an expression $\mathcal{F}\langle x\rangle$, a variable y that does not occur free in $\mathcal{F}\langle x\rangle$, an interpretation $\mathcal{K}$ for $\mathcal{F}\langle x\rangle$, and an arbitrary domain element d,

the value of $\mathcal{F}\langle x\rangle$ under $I : \langle x \leftarrow d\rangle \circ \mathcal{K}$
is the same as
the value of $\mathcal{F}\langle y\rangle$ under $J : \langle y \leftarrow d\rangle \circ \mathcal{K}$.

Problem 3.7 (instantiation and partial substitution)   pages 174, 178

If we replace the total substitution operator with the partial substitution operator, the corresponding *quantifier-instantiation* and *closure-instantiation* propositions do not necessarily hold.

(a) For each of the following sentences, find a subsentence $\mathcal{F}\langle x\rangle$, a term t, and an interpretation under which the entire sentence is false.

$$\begin{array}{ll} if\ (for\ all\ x)\mathcal{F}\langle x\rangle & if\ \mathcal{F}\langle t\rangle \\ then\ \ \mathcal{F}\langle t\rangle & then\ (for\ some\ x)\mathcal{F}\langle x\rangle \end{array}$$

(b) For each of the following sentences, find a subsentence $\mathcal{F}\langle x_1, x_2, \ldots, x_n\rangle$, terms $t_1, t_2, \ldots, t_n$, and an interpretation under which the entire sentence is false.

$$\begin{array}{ll} if\ (for\ all\ *)\mathcal{F}\langle x_1, x_2, \ldots, x_n\rangle & if\ (for\ some\ *)\mathcal{F}\langle t_1, t_2, \ldots, t_n\rangle \\ then\ (for\ all\ *)\mathcal{F}\langle t_1, t_2, \ldots, t_n\rangle & then\ (for\ some\ *)\mathcal{F}\langle x_1, x_2, \ldots, x_n\rangle. \end{array}$$

Problem 3.8 (existential closure instantiation)   page 178

The *existential* part of the *closure-instantiation* proposition states that

for any distinct variables x_1, x_2, $\ldots$, x_n, sentence $\mathcal{F}[x_1, x_2, \ldots, x_n]$, and
terms t_1, t_2, $\ldots$, t_n, the sentence

> *if (for some $*$)$\mathcal{F}[t_1, t_2, \ldots, t_n]$*
> *then (for some $*$)$\mathcal{F}[x_1, x_2, \ldots, x_n]$*

is valid.

Prove this proposition in two different ways:

(a) Use the *universal* part of the proposition and the duality between the
universal and existential closures.

(b) Prove the *existential* part directly, without using the *universal* part of
the proposition.

4

Special
Theories

Most of the sentences we will be interested in proving are not valid sentences of predicate logic, i.e., they are not true under every interpretation, but they are true under certain specific interpretations. For example, a sentence such as "For every integer x, $x + 0 = x$," which might be written in predicate logic as $(\textit{for all } x)p(f(x,a), \ x)$, is not valid, but it is certainly true under an interpretation over the integers that assigns

a to be 0

f to be the *addition* function

p to be the *equality* relation.

Our problem is to describe the language for the sentences we wish to consider and the interpretations under which we intend these sentences to be true. For this purpose, we introduce the general notion of a "theory."

4.1   DEFINITION OF A THEORY

A *theory* consists of a language and a set of sentences (called *axioms*). The *language* of a theory is the language of predicate logic in which we restrict the constant, function, and predicate symbols to a specific *vocabulary*, i.e., a particular subset of the symbols allowed in general predicate logic.

Definition (vocabulary)

The *vocabulary* of a theory is

- A particular subset

    $c_1, \ c_2, \ c_3, \ \ldots$

    of the constants of predicate logic

- A particular subset

    $f_1, \ f_2, \ f_3, \ \ldots$

    of the function symbols of predicate logic

- A particular subset

    $p_1, \ p_2, \ p_3, \ \ldots$

    of the predicate symbols of predicate logic.   ⌐

Each of the three subsets of the vocabulary of a theory may be finite or infinite, empty or nonempty.

For example, in the theory of the nonnegative integers we shall develop, we begin by considering a single constant symbol a, corresponding to the domain element 0; a single unary function symbol $f(x)$, corresponding to the successor function $d + 1$ over the domain; and a single binary predicate symbol $p(x, y)$, corresponding to the equality relation $d_1 = d_2$ over the domain. Later we augment the theory by introducing new constant, function, and predicate symbols to the vocabulary, e.g., those corresponding to the domain element 1, the binary function $d_1 + d_2$ over the domain, and the binary relation $d_1 < d_2$ over the domain.

The *terms*, *sentences*, and *expressions* of a theory are those terms, sentences, and expressions of predicate logic whose constant, function, and predicate symbols all belong to the vocabulary of the theory.

A theory consists not only of a vocabulary but also of a set of axioms.

Definition (axioms)

The *axioms* of a theory are a set of closed sentences

    $\mathcal{A}_1, \ \mathcal{A}_2, \ \mathcal{A}_3, \ \ldots$

of the theory. We will say that the theory is *defined* by its axioms.   ⌐

Note that we do not require that the given set of axioms be finite.

Example (family theory)

Suppose we would like to define a theory of family relationships. In the "family" interpretation I we have in mind, the domain is the set of people, and, intuitively speaking,

$f(x)$ is the father of x

$g(x)$ is the mother of x

$p(x, y)$ means y is a parent of x

$q(x, y)$ means y is a grandfather of x

$r(x, y)$ means y is a grandmother of x.

(More precisely, $p_I(d, e)$ holds if e is a parent of d, and so forth.)

Thus the vocabulary of the theory consists of the function symbols f and g, the predicate symbols p, q, and r, and no constant symbols at all.

The axioms of the theory are the following set of closed sentences:

$\mathcal{F}_1:$ $(\textit{for all } x)p\big(x,\ f(x)\big)$ $(\textit{father})$

(Everyone's father is his or her parent.)

$\mathcal{F}_2:$ $(\textit{for all } x)p\big(x,\ g(x)\big)$ $(\textit{mother})$

(Everyone's mother is his or her parent.)

$\mathcal{F}_3:$ $\begin{array}{l}(\textit{for all } x)\\(\textit{for all } y)\end{array}\left[\begin{array}{l}\textit{if } p(x, y)\\\textit{then } q\big(x,\ f(y)\big)\end{array}\right]$ $(\textit{grandfather})$

(The father of one's parent is his or her grandfather.)

$\mathcal{F}_4:$ $\begin{array}{l}(\textit{for all } x)\\(\textit{for all } y)\end{array}\left[\begin{array}{l}\textit{if } p(x, y)\\\textit{then } r\big(x,\ g(y)\big)\end{array}\right]$ $(\textit{grandmother})$

(The mother of one's parent is his or her grandmother.)   ◢

Let us consider the relationship between the axioms of a theory and the specific interpretation we have in mind.

Definition (model, validity, consistency)

An interpretation I is a *model* for a theory if each axiom $\mathcal{A}_i$ of the theory is true under I.

A closed sentence S of a theory is *valid* in the theory if S is true under every model for the theory.

A sentence S *implies* a sentence T in the theory if, whenever S is true under a model for the theory, T is also true under the model.

Two sentences S and T are *equivalent* in the theory if S and T have the same truth value under every model for the theory.

A theory is *consistent* if there is at least one model for the theory. ⌐

As an immediate consequence of the definition, we have that every axiom for a theory is valid in the theory. Also, if a theory is inconsistent, it has no models, and therefore every sentence is "vacuously" valid in the theory.

In defining a theory, we make sure that the interpretation we have in mind is a model for the theory. In general, however, there are many models for a theory.

Example (models)

The "family" interpretation we had in mind is a model for the family theory defined by the axioms $\mathcal{F}_1$, $\mathcal{F}_2$, $\mathcal{F}_3$, and $\mathcal{F}_4$ in the example above because each of the axioms is true under the family interpretation. However, there are many other models for this theory.

Consider the "number" interpretation I over the domain of the nonnegative integers under which, intuitively speaking,

$$f(x) \quad \text{is} \quad 2x$$

$$g(x) \quad \text{is} \quad 3x$$

$$p(x, y) \quad \text{is} \quad y = 2x \quad \text{or} \quad y = 3x$$

$$q(x, y) \quad \text{is} \quad y = 4x \quad \text{or} \quad y = 6x$$

$$r(x, y) \quad \text{is} \quad y = 6x \quad \text{or} \quad y = 9x.$$

(More precisely, $f_I(d)$ is $2d$, and so forth.) Each of the above axioms $\mathcal{F}_1$, $\mathcal{F}_2$, $\mathcal{F}_3$, and $\mathcal{F}_4$ is true under the interpretation I. For instance, the intuitive meaning of the *mother* axiom $\mathcal{F}_2$,

$$(\textit{for all } x)p\big(x,\, g(x)\big),$$

is

> for every integer x,
> $$3x = 2x \quad \text{or} \quad 3x = 3x,$$

and the intuitive meaning of the *grandfather* axiom $\mathcal{F}_3$,

> $$(\textit{for all } x) \begin{bmatrix} \textit{if } p(x,\, y) \\ \textit{then } q\big(x,\, f(y)\big) \end{bmatrix},$$
> $(\textit{for all } y)$

is

> for every integer x and y,
> $$\text{if} \quad y = 2x \quad \text{or} \quad y = 3x,$$
> $$\text{then} \quad 2y = 4x \quad \text{or} \quad 2y = 6x.$$

Therefore the "number" interpretation $\mathcal{I}$ is a model for the family theory. ◢

For a given closed sentence to be valid in a theory, it must be true under every model for the theory. To establish validity in a theory, we may apply the same techniques we used in predicate logic itself.

Example (validity)

Suppose we would like to establish the validity of the sentence

> $\mathcal{F}:\quad (\textit{for all } x)(\textit{for some } z)r(x,\, z)$
>
> (Everyone has a grandmother)

in the above "family" theory. Let us give an informal argument based on the semantic rules and our common sense.

Let $\mathcal{I}$ be an arbitrary model for the family theory. Then each of the axioms $\mathcal{F}_1$, $\mathcal{F}_2$, $\mathcal{F}_3$, and $\mathcal{F}_4$ is true under $\mathcal{I}$.

Because the *father* axiom $\mathcal{F}_1$, that is,

> $(\textit{for all } x)p\big(x,\, f(x)\big),$

is true under $\mathcal{I}$, we know (by the *for-all* rule) that

> for every domain element d,
> $$p\big(x,\, f(x)\big)$$
>
> is true under the extended interpretation $\langle x \leftarrow d \rangle \circ \mathcal{I}$.

Therefore (by the *value* property), we know that

for every domain element d,

(†) $p(x, y)$

is true under $\langle x \leftarrow d \rangle \circ \langle y \leftarrow f_I(d) \rangle \circ I$,

where f_I is the function assigned to f by I.

Because the *grandmother* axiom $\mathcal{F}_4$, that is,

$$(\textit{for all } x) \begin{bmatrix} \textit{if } p(x, y) \\ \textit{then } r\big(x, g(y)\big) \end{bmatrix},$$
$$(\textit{for all } y)$$

is true under I, we know (by the *for-all* rule) that,

for all domain elements d and e, the subsentence

(‡) $\begin{array}{l} \textit{if } p(x, y) \\ \textit{then } r\big(x, g(y)\big) \end{array}$

is true under $\langle x \leftarrow d \rangle \circ \langle y \leftarrow e \rangle \circ I$.

Consider an arbitrary domain element d. Taking e to be the domain element $f_I(d)$, we have that

the implication (‡)
is true under the interpretation $\langle x \leftarrow d \rangle \circ \langle y \leftarrow f_I(d) \rangle \circ I$.

Because the implication (‡) and its antecedent (†), $p(x, y)$ are both true under $\langle x \leftarrow d \rangle \circ \langle y \leftarrow f_I(d) \rangle \circ I$, its consequent

$r\big(x, g(y)\big)$

is also true under $\langle x \leftarrow d \rangle \circ \langle y \leftarrow f_I(d) \rangle \circ I$.

Therefore (by the *value* property), the sentence

$r(x, z)$

is true under $\langle x \leftarrow d \rangle \circ \langle z \leftarrow g_I\big(f_I(d)\big) \rangle \circ I$.

Hence (by the *for-some* rule),

$(\textit{for some } z)r(x, z)$

is true under $\langle x \leftarrow d \rangle \circ I$.

Because d is an arbitrary domain element, we know (by the *for-all* rule) that the sentence $\mathcal{F}$, that is,

$(\textit{for all } x)(\textit{for some } z)r(x, z),$

is true under I.

Because I was taken to be an arbitrary model for the family theory, this means that $\mathcal{F}$ is valid in the family theory.   ⏌

Up to now we have been very careful to avoid confusing a symbol in a sentence and its value under an interpretation. For example, we never consider hybrid objects such as $f(a, d)$, in which f is a function symbol, a is a constant symbol, and d is a domain element. Such a construct is neither an expression in predicate logic nor an element in the domain of an interpretation. Our pedantry in this respect, unfortunately, has made our proofs of validity more cumbersome than necessary. Informal arguments may be made more concise and given more intuitive content if we agree to confuse symbols and their meanings under an intended interpretation. The argument in the above example, for instance, can be abbreviated if we say that x "is" a person and $f(x)$ "is" x's father, even though we are confusing symbols and their meanings in this way. We shall call such a style of proof an "intuitive argument."

Example (intuitive argument)

Suppose again we would like to give an intuitive argument to establish the validity of the sentence

$$\mathcal{F}: \quad (\textit{for all } x)(\textit{for some } z)r(x, z),$$

that is, "Everyone has a grandmother," in the family theory.

Consider an arbitrary person x. By the *father* axiom, $\mathcal{F}_1$, we know that the father $f(x)$ of x is a parent of x; that is,

$$(\dagger) \quad p\big(x, f(x)\big).$$

By the *grandmother* axiom, $\mathcal{F}_4$, we have (taking y to be $f(x)$), that

$$(\ddagger) \quad \begin{aligned} &\textit{if } p\big(x, f(x)\big) \\ &\textit{then } r\big(x, g\big(f(x)\big)\big) \end{aligned}$$

Hence, by $(\dagger)$ and $(\ddagger)$, we know that the mother $g\big(f(x)\big)$ of the father $f(x)$ of x is a grandmother of x; that is,

$$r\big(x, g\big(f(x)\big)\big).$$

Therefore, we know by predicate logic that

$$(\textit{for some } z)r(x, z).$$

Because this has been shown to be true for an arbitrary person x, we can conclude

> *(for all x)(for some z)r(x, z)*

is a valid sentence of the family theory. ⌐

Because such intuitive arguments are shorter and easier to follow than arguments with explicit interpretations, we shall use them from now on, except in situations in which it is important to preserve the distinction between an expression and its meaning. Whenever such an intuitive argument is given, a precise proof could be substituted.

In **Problem 4.1**, the reader is asked to give an intuitive argument in the family theory.

4.2   AUGMENTING THEORIES

The sentence $\mathcal{F}$,

> *(for all x)(for some z)r(x, z)*,

which we have established in the preceding example, will be true under any model for the family theory. In particular, it will be true under the "number" interpretation we gave earlier. The sentence $\mathcal{F}$ then has the intuitive meaning

> for every integer x,
>> there exists an integer z such that
>> $z = 6x$ or $z = 9x$.

In showing that the sentence is valid in the theory, we are showing that it is true under all the models of the theory at once.

Our family theory is "incomplete" in the sense that there are many properties of family relationships that are not valid in the theory. For example, we cannot show that

> $\mathcal{G}:$ *(for all x)[not p(x, x)]*
>
> (No one is his or her own parent.)

is valid. Even though this sentence is true under the "family" interpretation we have in mind, it is not true under all models of the theory. In particular, it is not true under the "number" interpretation, for which it has the intuitive meaning

> for every integer x,
>> it is not so that
>> $x = 2x$ or $x = 3x$.

In fact, this sentence is false when x is taken to be 0.

If we want to develop a theory in which $\mathcal{G}$ is valid, we can add $\mathcal{G}$ to the axioms, obtaining an augmented theory defined by the axioms

$$\mathcal{F}_1, \ \mathcal{F}_2, \ \mathcal{F}_3, \ \mathcal{F}_4, \ \text{and} \ \mathcal{G}.$$

The "family" interpretation would still be a model for this new theory, but the "number" interpretation would not.

On the other hand, if we have the "number" interpretation in mind, we may consider adding $(not\ \mathcal{G})$, that is,

$$not\ (for\ all\ x)[not\ p(x,\ x)],$$

or, equivalently,

$$\mathcal{G}':\quad (for\ some\ x)p(x,\ x),$$

as an axiom, obtaining an alternative theory defined by

$$\mathcal{F}_1, \ \mathcal{F}_2, \ \mathcal{F}_3, \ \mathcal{F}_4, \ \text{and} \ \mathcal{G}'.$$

The "family" interpretation would not be a model for this theory, since no one is his or her own parent, but the "number" interpretation would be a model.

If a theory is augmented by a new axiom that contains symbols not in the original vocabulary, we extend the vocabulary of the augmented theory accordingly.

Note that, in adding new axioms to a theory, we may reduce its collection of models. In particular, if a new axiom is not true under one of the original models, that interpretation will no longer be a model for the augmented theory.

In forming or augmenting a theory, we must be careful that the axioms are consistent, i.e., that there is at least one model for the theory.

Example (inconsistency)

In our original formulation of the "family" theory defined by the axioms

$$\mathcal{F}_1, \ \mathcal{F}_2, \ \mathcal{F}_3, \ \text{and} \ \mathcal{F}_4,$$

we did not account for the possibility of "first" people such as Adam. We might be tempted to add to our theory an axiom

$$\mathcal{A}:\quad (for\ all\ y)[not\ p(a,\ y)] \hspace{4cm} (Adam)$$

$$(\text{Person } a \text{ has no parents.})$$

However, the augmented theory defined by the axioms

$$\mathcal{F}_1, \quad \mathcal{F}_2, \quad \mathcal{F}_3, \quad \mathcal{F}_4, \quad \text{and} \quad \mathcal{A}$$

is inconsistent; i.e., there is no model for this theory.

To see this, suppose I is a model for the augmented theory. Then the "father" axiom $\mathcal{F}_1$, that is,

$$(\textit{for all } x)p\big(x,\ f(x)\big),$$

is true under I. We know (by the *universal quantifier-instantiation* proposition) that the implication

> *if* $(\textit{for all } x)p\big(x,\ f(x)\big)$
> *then* $p\big(a,\ f(a)\big)$

is true under any interpretation, including I. Therefore (by the *if-then* rule)

$$p\big(a,\ f(a)\big)$$

is true under I.

We also know (by the *existential quantifier-instantiation* proposition) that the sentence

> *if* $p\big(a,\ f(a)\big)$
> *then* $(\textit{for some } y)p(a,\ y)$

is true under any interpretation, including I. Therefore (by the *if-then* rule)

$$(\textit{for some } y)p(a,\ y)$$

is true under I.

Note that this sentence is equivalent (by the duality between the quantifiers) to the sentence

$$\textit{not } (\textit{for all } y)\big[\textit{not}\, p(a,\ y)\big],$$

which is exactly the negation of the new *Adam* axiom. Hence this axiom cannot be true under I, contradicting our original supposition that I is a model for the augmented theory. ◢

We have seen that, if a theory is inconsistent, it has no models, and therefore every sentence is (vacuously) valid in the theory. For this reason, although there is nothing essentially wrong with inconsistent theories, they are not very interesting. By demonstrating the existence of a model for a given set of axioms, we can ensure that the theory it defines is consistent.

4.3   RELATIONSHIP BETWEEN THEORIES

In this section we relate theories defined by different sets of axioms.

Definition (containment, equivalence)

If the vocabulary of a theory A is a subset of the vocabulary of theory B, and each of the valid sentences of the theory A is also valid in the theory B, we shall say that the theory A is *contained in* the theory B.

If a theory A is contained in a theory B, and B is also contained in A, we shall say that A and B are *equivalent* theories. ⌐

Thus two equivalent theories have the same vocabulary and the same valid sentences.

Proposition (containment)

Suppose that the vocabulary of a theory A is a subset of the vocabulary of a theory B and that each axiom of A is valid in B.

Then the theory A is contained in the theory B. ⌐

Proof

Because each axiom of A is valid in B, we know (by the definition of validity in a theory) that each axiom of A is true under every model for B. Hence (by the definition of a model) every model for B is also a model for A.

Consider an arbitrary closed sentence S that is valid in A; we show that then S is valid in B as well.

Because S is valid in A, we know (by the definition of validity in a theory) that S is true under every model for A. But we have just shown that every model for B is also a model for A. Therefore, S is true under every model for B, and hence (by the definition of validity in a theory again) S is valid in B, as we wanted to show. ⌐

The *containment* proposition has several immediate consequences.

Proposition (monotonicity)

Suppose that the vocabulary of a theory A is a subset of the vocabulary of the theory B and that each axiom of A is also an axiom of B.

Then the theory A is contained in the theory B. ⌐

Proof

Because every axiom of A is an axiom of B, every axiom of A is valid in B. Therefore (by the *containment* proposition) A is contained in B, as we wanted to show. ⌐

Proposition (equivalence)

Suppose that the theories A and B have the same vocabulary, that every axiom of A is valid in B, and that every axiom in B is valid in A.

Then the theory A is equivalent to the theory B. ⌐

Proof

By the *containment* proposition, each of these theories is contained in the other. Therefore (by the definition of equivalence between theories) they are equivalent. ⌐

The equivalence proposition directly implies the following corollary.

Corollary (equivalence)

Suppose that the closed sentence S is valid in a theory A.

Let B be the theory obtained from A by introducing S as an additional axiom.

Then the theory A is equivalent to the theory B. ⌐

In other words, once we have established the validity of a sentence in a theory, we may add it as a new axiom without changing the resulting theory. In practice, we shall freely use previously established valid sentences of a theory in the proofs of the validity of other sentences.

Proof

Each axiom of A is an axiom of B and hence is valid in B. Each axiom of B is either an axiom of A, and hence is valid in A, or is the sentence S, which has been supposed to be valid in A. Therefore (by the *equivalence* proposition) A is equivalent to B. ⌐

In the balance of this chapter, we introduce several special theories that are of importance in their own right.

4.4 THEORY OF STRICT PARTIAL ORDERINGS

For a given binary predicate symbol p, the *theory of the strict partial ordering p* is the theory whose vocabulary consists of the symbol p, defined by the axioms:

$$
\boxed{
\begin{array}{ll}
S_1: & \begin{array}{l}(\textit{for all } x)\\ (\textit{for all } y)\\ (\textit{for all } z)\end{array} \left[\begin{array}{l}\textit{if } p(x,\, y) \ \textit{ and } \ p(y,\, z)\\ \textit{then } p(x,\, z)\end{array}\right] \qquad (\textit{transitivity})\\[2em]
S_2: & (\textit{for all } x)\big[\textit{not } p(x,\, x)\big] \qquad\qquad\qquad\qquad (\textit{irreflexivity})
\end{array}
}
$$

We surround these sentences with a box to indicate that they are axioms.

Under any model for the theory defined by S_1 and S_2, we shall say that p denotes a *strict partial ordering*.

In this theory, we shall use the conventional notation $x \prec y$ rather than $p(x,\, y)$. We can thus rewrite S_1 and S_2 as

$$
\boxed{
\begin{array}{ll}
S_1: & \begin{array}{l}(\textit{for all } x)\\ (\textit{for all } y)\\ (\textit{for all } z)\end{array} \left[\begin{array}{l}\textit{if } x \prec y \ \textit{ and } \ y \prec z\\ \textit{then } x \prec z\end{array}\right] \qquad (\textit{transitivity})\\[2em]
S_2: & (\textit{for all } x)[\textit{not } (x \prec x)] \qquad\qquad\qquad\quad (\textit{irreflexivity})
\end{array}
}
$$

The reader should understand that here $x \prec y$ is merely an informal notation for $p(x,\, y)$.

Let us consider two models for the theory of the strict partial ordering $\prec$.

Examples (strict partial orderings)

- *The less-than relation*

Consider an interpretation I over the integers that assigns the less-than relation $<$ to the binary predicate symbol $\prec$. Then I is a model for the theory of the strict partial ordering $\prec$, because the *transitivity* and *irreflexivity* axioms for $\prec$ both hold under I. The intuitive meaning of these axioms under this interpretation are

> for every integer d_1, d_2, and d_3,
>   if $d_1 < d_2$ and $d_2 < d_3$
>   then $d_1 < d_3$

and

> for every integer d,
>   not $d < d$,

which are both true.

- *A finite relation*

Consider an interpretation over a domain $\{A, B, C, D\}$ that assigns to $\prec$ the binary relation illustrated by the following diagram:

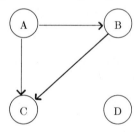

Recall that, in this representation, an arc leading directly from one element d to another e indicates that the relation holds between these elements; that is, $d \prec_I e$ is true. Thus we have

$$A \prec_I B, \quad B \prec_I C, \quad \text{and} \quad A \prec_I C.$$

The absence of an arc indicates that the relation does not hold between the corresponding elements. Thus

$$\text{not } B \prec_I D, \quad \text{not } B \prec_I B, \quad \text{and so forth.}$$

The reader may confirm that the *transitivity* and *irreflexivity* axioms for $\prec$ hold under I; therefore I is a model for the theory of the strict partial ordering $\prec$. $\quad\lrcorner$

Now let us consider two interpretations that are not models for the theory of the strict partial ordering $\prec$.

Examples (not strict partial orderings)

- *The inequality relation*

Consider an interpretation I over the integers that assigns the inequality relation $\neq$ to the binary predicate symbol $\prec$. Then I is not a model for the theory of the strict partial ordering $\prec$. The *irreflexivity* axiom for $\prec$ does hold under I; its intuitive meaning is

> for every integer d,
>   not $d \neq d$,

which is true. On the other hand, the *transitivity* axiom for $\prec$ does not hold under I; its intuitive meaning is

> for every integer d_1, d_2, and d_3,
>   if $d_1 \neq d_2$ and $d_2 \neq d_3$
>   then $d_1 \neq d_3$,

which is false if d_1 and d_3 are the same integer and d_2 is a different integer.

- *A finite interpretation*

Consider an interpretation I over a domain $\{A, B, C\}$ that assigns to $\prec$ the binary relation illustrated by the following diagram:

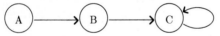

Then I is not a model for the theory of the strict partial ordering $\prec$. The *transitivity* axiom for $\prec$ does not hold under I, for we have

$$A \prec_I B \quad \text{and} \quad B \prec_I C \quad \text{but not} \quad A \prec_I C.$$

Also, the *irreflexivity* axiom for $\prec$ does not hold, for we have

$$C \prec_I C. \quad \blacksquare$$

In **Problem 4.2**, the reader is asked to construct interpretations for the theory of the strict partial ordering $\prec$ over a finite domain under which one of the axioms is true and the other is not.

ASYMMETRY

Now let us establish the validity of a sentence in the theory.

Proposition (asymmetry of strict partial orderings)

In the theory of the strict partial ordering $\prec$, the sentence

$$S_3 : \quad \begin{array}{l} (\textit{for all } x) \\ (\textit{for all } y) \end{array} \begin{bmatrix} \textit{if } x \prec y \\ \textit{then not } (y \prec x) \end{bmatrix} \qquad\qquad (\textit{asymmetry})$$

is valid.   ⌟

This means that S_3 is true under all models for the theory defined by S_1 and S_2. In other words, for any interpretation under which S_1 and S_2 are true, S_3 is also true. We give an intuitive argument.

Proof

Suppose that, contrary to the *asymmetry* sentence S_3, there exist elements x and y such that both $x \prec y$ and $y \prec x$. Then, by the *transitivity* axiom S_1, we have $x \prec x$. But this contradicts the *irreflexivity* axiom S_2.   ⌟

Remark (asymmetry implies irreflexivity)

We have established that, in the theory defined by the *transitivity* axiom S_1 and the *irreflexivity* axiom S_2, the *asymmetry* sentence S_3 is valid.

On the other hand, note that the *asymmetry* sentence S_3,

$$\begin{array}{l} (\textit{for all } x) \\ (\textit{for all } y) \end{array} \begin{bmatrix} \textit{if } x \prec y \\ \textit{then not } (y \prec x) \end{bmatrix},$$

by itself implies the *irreflexivity* sentence S_2. For, taking y to be x, we obtain

$$(\textit{for all } x) \begin{bmatrix} \textit{if } x \prec x \\ \textit{then not } (x \prec x) \end{bmatrix}.$$

But (by propositional logic)

$$\begin{array}{l} \textit{if } x \prec x \\ \textit{then not } (x \prec x) \end{array} \quad \text{is equivalent to} \quad \textit{not } (x \prec x).$$

Therefore (by the *replacement-of-equivalent-sentences* proposition)

$$(\textit{for all } x) \begin{bmatrix} \textit{if } x \prec x \\ \textit{then not } (x \prec x) \end{bmatrix}$$

is equivalent to

$$(for\ all\ x)\big[not\ (x \prec x)\big],$$

which is the *irreflexivity* sentence S_2.

Therefore in the theory whose vocabulary consists of the symbol $\prec$ and whose sole axiom is the *asymmetry* axiom S_3, the *irreflexivity* sentence S_2 is valid. Hence (by the *monotonicity* proposition for theories) in the theory (with the same vocabulary) defined by the *transitivity* axiom S_1 and the *asymmetry* axiom S_3, the *irreflexivity* sentence S_2 is also valid.

We have established that, in the theory whose axioms are S_1 and S_2, the sentence S_3 is valid; and, in the theory whose axioms are S_1 and S_3, the sentence S_2 is valid. Also, both theories have the same vocabulary. Consequently (by the *equivalence* proposition for theories),

> the theory defined by S_1 and S_2
> is equivalent to
> the theory defined by S_1 and S_3;

the valid sentences of these two theories are the same. ⌐

Up to now we have been discussing a theory whose only axioms are the *transitivity* axiom S_1 and the *irreflexivity* axiom S_2. Consider a theory in which these properties are true for some binary predicate symbol q. In other words, whatever the axioms of the theory are, the sentences

$$\begin{matrix} (for\ all\ x) \\ (for\ all\ y) \\ (for\ all\ z) \end{matrix} \begin{bmatrix} if\ q(x,\ y)\ and\ q(y,\ z) \\ then\ q(x,\ z) \end{bmatrix}$$

and

$$(for\ all\ x)\big[not\ q(x,\ x)\big]$$

are valid. We shall say that, in such a theory, q denotes a *strict partial ordering*. Of course, it is possible to have a theory with many binary predicate symbols, each denoting a strict partial ordering.

INVERSE RELATION

In practice, people often use the sentence $x \succ y$ synonymously with $y \prec x$. This can be reflected in our theory by adding $\succ$ as a new predicate symbol, with an additional axiom to define it. More precisely, we augment our theory of the strict partial ordering $\prec$ by introducing a new binary predicate symbol $\succ$, called the *inverse* of $\prec$, into the vocabulary. This symbol is defined by the new special axiom

$$S_4 : \quad \begin{array}{l} (\textit{for all } x) \\ (\textit{for all } y) \end{array} \left[\begin{array}{l} x \succ y \\ \quad \textit{if and only if} \\ y \prec x \end{array} \right] \qquad (\textit{inverse})$$

As before, $x \succ y$ is merely an informal notation for an ordinary predicate symbol such as $q(x, y)$.

Whenever we augment a theory by introducing a new axiom, we run the risk of making our theory inconsistent. If so, the augmented theory will have no model, and therefore any sentence will be valid.

In this case, it is clear that there do exist models for the augmented theory, obtained by introducing the new axiom S_4 into the strict partial ordering theory. In fact, any model for the original theory may be extended to a model for the augmented theory, in a sense made precise in the following result.

Proposition (consistency of the inverse axiom)

If I is any model for the theory of the strict partial ordering $\prec$,
there exists a model J of the theory augmented by the *inverse* axiom
for $\succ$.

Furthermore, J agrees with I except perhaps on the predicate symbol
$\succ$.   ◢

Proof

Let I be any model for the theory of the strict partial ordering $\prec$ and suppose that the predicate symbol $\prec$ is assigned the binary relation $\prec_I$ under I.

Let J be the interpretation that agrees with I except that it assigns to the predicate symbol $\succ$ the inverse relation of $\prec_I$; in other words, for every domain element d and e,

$$d \succ_J e \text{ precisely when } e \prec_I d.$$

We claim that J is a model for the augmented theory; i.e., the three axioms S_1, S_2, and S_4 are true under J.

By the *agreement* proposition, each of the axioms S_1 and S_2 of the original theory is true under J, because J agrees with I on all symbols other than $\succ$, and $\succ$ does not occur in S_1 or S_2.

We would like to show that the additional axiom S_4 is also true under J. But we have that S_4, that is,

$$(\textit{for all } x) \quad \begin{bmatrix} x \succ y \\ \quad \textit{if and only if} \\ y \prec x \end{bmatrix},$$
$$(\textit{for all } y)$$

is true under J

precisely when (by the *for-all* rule)

for all domain elements d and e, the sentence
$x \succ y$
   if and only if
$y \prec x$
is true under the extended interpretation $\langle x \leftarrow d \rangle \circ \langle y \leftarrow e \rangle \circ J$

precisely when (by the *if-and-only-if* and *proposition* rules)

for all domain elements d and e,
$d \succ_J e$
   has the same truth value as
$e \prec_J d$

precisely when (by the definition of J)

for all domain elements d and e,
$e \prec_I d$
   has the same truth value as
$e \prec_I d,$

which is true. ⌟

Another way of showing that the augmented theory has a model is simply to describe one. For example, consider the interpretation over the nonnegative integers that assigns the less-than relation $<$ to the predicate symbol $\prec$, and the greater-than relation $>$ to the predicate symbol $\succ$. The reader may confirm that all three axioms S_1, S_2, and S_4 for the augmented theory are true under this interpretation. The above proposition establishes a more powerful result, however, because it shows that any model for the original theory may be extended to a model for the augmented theory by providing the appropriate assignment for the new symbol $\succ$.

In the future, we shall often omit the proof of consistency when we augment a theory.

4.5   THEORY OF EQUIVALENCE RELATIONS

For any binary predicate symbol p, the *theory of the equivalence relation p* is defined by the axioms:

$$\mathcal{Q}_1: \quad \begin{matrix} (\textit{for all } x) \\ (\textit{for all } y) \\ (\textit{for all } z) \end{matrix} \begin{bmatrix} \textit{if } p(x,\,y) \ \textit{ and } \ p(y,\,z) \\ \textit{then } \ p(x,\,z) \end{bmatrix} \qquad (\textit{transitivity})$$

$$\mathcal{Q}_2: \quad \begin{matrix} (\textit{for all } x) \\ (\textit{for all } y) \end{matrix} \begin{bmatrix} \textit{if } p(x,\,y) \\ \textit{then } \ p(y,\,x) \end{bmatrix} \qquad (\textit{symmetry})$$

$$\mathcal{Q}_3: \quad (\textit{for all } x)\bigl[p(x,\,x)\bigr] \qquad\qquad (\textit{reflexivity})$$

Under any model for the theory defined by $\mathcal{Q}_1$, $\mathcal{Q}_2$, and $\mathcal{Q}_3$, we shall say that p denotes an *equivalence relation*.

The convention for an equivalence relation is to write $x \approx y$ rather than $p(x,\,y)$. In other words, we shall use the symbol $\approx$ informally, rather than the predicate symbol p, to denote a relation for which $\mathcal{Q}_1$, $\mathcal{Q}_2$, and $\mathcal{Q}_3$ hold. We shall thus write $\mathcal{Q}_1$, $\mathcal{Q}_2$, and $\mathcal{Q}_3$ as

$$\mathcal{Q}_1: \quad \begin{matrix} (\textit{for all } x) \\ (\textit{for all } y) \\ (\textit{for all } z) \end{matrix} \begin{bmatrix} \textit{if } x \approx y \ \textit{ and } \ y \approx z \\ \textit{then } \ x \approx z \end{bmatrix} \qquad (\textit{transitivity})$$

$$\mathcal{Q}_2: \quad \begin{matrix} (\textit{for all } x) \\ (\textit{for all } y) \end{matrix} \begin{bmatrix} \textit{if } x \approx y \\ \textit{then } \ y \approx x \end{bmatrix} \qquad (\textit{symmetry})$$

$$\mathcal{Q}_3: \quad (\textit{for all } x)\bigl[x \approx x\bigr] \qquad\qquad (\textit{reflexivity})$$

Let us consider some models for the theory of the equivalence relation $\approx$.

Examples (equivalence relations)

● *The congruence-modulo-2 relation*

Consider an interpretation $\mathcal{I}$ over the integers that assigns to $\approx$ the "congruence modulo 2" relation $\approx_2$, that is, for every integer d_1 and d_2,

$$d_1 \approx_2 d_2$$

precisely when

$$\begin{bmatrix} d_1 \text{ and } d_2 \text{ are both even} \\ \text{or} \\ d_1 \text{ and } d_2 \text{ are both odd} \end{bmatrix}.$$

Thus $2 \approx_2 6$ but not $1 \approx_2 2$.

The reader may confirm that the *transitivity*, *symmetry*, and *reflexivity* axioms $\mathcal{Q}_1$, $\mathcal{Q}_2$ and $\mathcal{Q}_3$ are each true under this interpretation.

• *A finite relation*

Consider an interpretation I over a domain $\{A, B, C, D, E, F, G\}$ that assigns $\approx$ to be the binary relation illustrated by the following diagram:

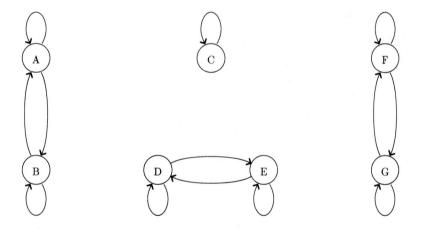

The reader may confirm that the *transitivity*, *symmetry*, and *reflexivity* axioms $\mathcal{Q}_1$, $\mathcal{Q}_2$, and $\mathcal{Q}_3$ each hold under the interpretation I; therefore I is a model for the theory of the equivalence relation $\approx$. ⌐

Now let us consider some finite interpretations that are not models for the theory of the equivalence relation $\approx$.

Examples (nonequivalence relations)

• *A nontransitive relation*

Over the domain $\{A, B, C\}$, consider the interpretation I that assigns to $\approx$ the binary relation $\approx_I$ illustrated by the following diagram:

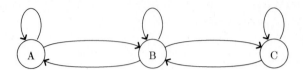

Then I is not a model for the theory of the equivalence relation $\approx$, because the *transitivity* axiom Q_1 does not hold under I. In particular, we have

$$A \approx_I B \quad \text{and} \quad B \approx_I C \quad \text{but not} \quad A \approx_I C.$$

The reader may confirm that the *symmetry* and *reflexivity* axioms do hold under I.

- *A nonsymmetric relation*

Over the domain $\{A, B\}$, consider the interpretation I that assigns to $\approx$ the binary relation $\approx_I$ illustrated by the following diagram:

Then I is not a model for the theory of the equivalence relation $\approx$, because the *symmetry* axiom Q_2 does not hold under I; we have

$$A \approx_I B \quad \text{but not} \quad B \approx_I A.$$

The reader may confirm that the *transitivity* and *reflexivity* axioms do hold under I.

- *An irreflexive relation*

Over the domain $\{A\}$, consider the interpretation I that assigns to $\approx$ the binary relation $\approx_I$ illustrated by the following diagram:

In other words, $\approx_I$ is the empty relation, which holds for no domain elements at all.

Then I is not a model for the theory of the equivalence relation $\approx$, because the *reflexivity* axiom Q_3 does not hold under $\approx_I$; we have

$$\text{not A} \approx_I A.$$

The reader may note that the *transitivity* and *symmetry* axioms Q_1 and Q_2 do hold under I, because their antecedents are always false under I. ⌐

The above three examples illustrate that the axioms for the equivalence relation $\approx$ are independent; in other words, none of them is implied by the other two. For in each example we presented an interpretation under which two of the axioms are true and the third is false. If the two axioms implied the third, all three axioms would be true.

In **Problem 4.3**, the reader is asked to find the "bug" in a fallacious proof that one of the axioms for the theory of equivalence is implied by the other two.

DOUBLE TRANSITIVITY

From the axioms for the equivalence relation $\approx$, we can show the following result.

Proposition (double transitivity)

The sentence

$$\begin{array}{l} (\textit{for all } u) \\ (\textit{for all } v) \\ (\textit{for all } x) \\ (\textit{for all } y) \end{array} \left[\begin{array}{l} \textit{if } u \approx v \ \textit{ and} \\ \quad u \approx x \ \textit{ and} \\ \quad v \approx y \\ \textit{then } x \approx y \end{array} \right] \qquad (\textit{double transitivity})$$

is valid in the theory of the equivalence relation $\approx$. ⌐

We give an intuitive justification.

Proof

Suppose that for arbitrary elements u, v, x, and y,

$$u \approx v, \quad u \approx x, \quad \text{and} \quad v \approx y$$

are all true; we attempt to show that then

$$x \approx y$$

is true.

Because $u \approx v$ and $v \approx y$, we have, by the *transitivity* axiom $\mathcal{Q}_1$, that

$$u \approx y.$$

Because $u \approx x$, we have, by the *symmetry* axiom $\mathcal{Q}_2$, that

$$x \approx u.$$

Finally, because $x \approx u$ and $u \approx y$, we have, by the *transitivity* axiom $\mathcal{Q}_1$ again, that

$$x \approx y,$$

which is the desired conclusion.   ⌐

PROBLEMS

Problem 4.1 (family theory)   page 196

In the family theory show that

if Alice is the parent of her own father,
then Alice's father is his own grandfather.

(First express the sentence in logic, then give an intuitive argument to show it is valid in the family theory. Let the constant a denote Alice.)

Problem 4.2 (strict partial ordering)   page 203

Construct two interpretations over a finite domain $\{A, B, C\}$ under which

(a)   The *transitivity* axiom S_1 is true but the *irreflexivity* axiom S_2 is false.

(b)   The *irreflexivity* axiom S_2 is true but the *transitivity* axiom S_1 is false.

Problem 4.3 (equivalence relation)   page 211

Consider the following "proof" that, in the theory of the equivalence relation $\approx$, the *transitivity* axiom $\mathcal{Q}_1$ and the *symmetry* axiom $\mathcal{Q}_2$ imply the *reflexivity* axiom $\mathcal{Q}_3$.

We would like to show that, for an arbitrary element x,

$$x \approx x.$$

Let y be any element such that

$$x \approx y.$$

Then (by the *symmetry* axiom $\mathcal{Q}_2$) we have

$$y \approx x.$$

Therefore (by the *transitivity* axiom Q_1, because $x \approx y$ and $y \approx x$) we have

$$x \approx x,$$

as we wanted to show.

We have already shown that the three axioms for the theory of equivalence are independent, i.e., that no two of them imply the third. Find the fallacious step in the above argument.

5

Theories with Equality

The equality relation is an important tool that requires special treatment. We want to define a theory of equality under whose intended models a binary predicate symbol p is assigned the equality relation over the domain; i.e., the sentence $p(t_1, t_2)$ is true under a model I precisely when the terms t_1 and t_2 have the same value under I.

5.1   THEORY OF EQUALITY

The usual convention is to write $x = y$ rather than $p(x, y)$ to denote the equality relation in the theory of equality. The reader should understand that here $x = y$ is merely an informal notation for $p(x, y)$, where p is a binary predicate symbol. It is not to be confused with our use of the notation $d_1 = d_2$, in giving the intuitive meanings for sentences, to indicate that d_1 and d_2 are the same domain elements.

THE THEORY

The vocabulary of the theory of equality consists of the binary predicate symbol $=$ and an unspecified set of other constant, function, and predicate symbols.

Although our previous theories have been defined by finite sets of axioms, the theory we devise requires a possibly infinite axiom set.

- *Basic axioms*

$\mathcal{E}_1:$ *(for all x)* *(for all y)* *(for all z)* $\left[\text{if } x = y \text{ and } y = z \atop \text{then } x = z\right]$ (*transitivity*)

$\mathcal{E}_2:$ *(for all x)* *(for all y)* $\left[\text{if } x = y \atop \text{then } y = x\right]$ (*symmetry*)

$\mathcal{E}_3:$ *(for all x)*$[x = x]$ (*reflexivity*)

- *Substitutivity axiom schemata*

For every k-ary function symbol f in the vocabulary and for each i from 1 through k,

$$
\mathcal{E}_4: \quad \begin{array}{l} \textit{(for all } z_1) \\ \vdots \\ \textit{(for all x)(for all } z_{i-1}) \\ \textit{(for all y)(for all } z_{i+1}) \\ \vdots \\ \textit{(for all } z_k) \end{array} \left[\begin{array}{l} \text{if } x = y \\ \text{then } f(z_1, \ldots, z_{i-1}, x, z_{i+1}, \ldots, z_k) = \\ \qquad f(z_1, \ldots, z_{i-1}, y, z_{i+1}, \ldots, z_k) \end{array}\right]
$$

(*functional substitutivity for f*)

For every ℓ-ary predicate symbol q (other than $=$) in the vocabulary and for each j from 1 through ℓ,

$$
\mathcal{E}_5: \quad \begin{array}{l} \textit{(for all } z_1) \\ \vdots \\ \textit{(for all x)(for all } z_{j-1}) \\ \textit{(for all y)(for all } z_{j+1}) \\ \vdots \\ \textit{(for all } z_\ell) \end{array} \left[\begin{array}{l} \text{if } x = y \\ \text{then } q(z_1, \ldots, z_{j-1}, x, z_{j+1}, \ldots, z_\ell) \\ \qquad \text{if and only if} \\ \qquad q(z_1, \ldots, z_{j-1}, y, z_{j+1}, \ldots, z_\ell) \end{array}\right]
$$

(*predicate substitutivity for q*)

Thus both the *functional-substitutivity* axiom schema $\mathcal{E}_4$ and the *predicate-substitutivity* axiom schema $\mathcal{E}_5$ actually represent sets of axioms, one or more for each function and predicate symbol. If there are infinitely many function or predicate symbols in our vocabulary, there will be infinitely many *functional-substitutivity* or *predicate-substitutivity* axioms. We exclude the instances of the *predicate-substitutivity* axiom for =, in which q is the equality symbol =, because these instances follow from the other axioms.

Example

For a binary function g, the corresponding instances of the *functional-substitutivity* axiom schema $\mathcal{E}_4$ are

$$\begin{array}{l}(\textit{for all } x)\\(\textit{for all } y)\\(\textit{for all } z_2)\end{array}\left[\begin{array}{l}\textit{if } x = y\\\textit{then } g(x, z_2) = g(y, z_2)\end{array}\right]$$

and

$$\begin{array}{l}(\textit{for all } x)\\(\textit{for all } y)\\(\textit{for all } z_1)\end{array}\left[\begin{array}{l}\textit{if } x = y\\\textit{then } g(z_1, x) = g(z_1, y)\end{array}\right].$$

For a unary predicate p, the corresponding instance of the *predicate-substitutivity* axiom schema $\mathcal{E}_5$ is

$$\begin{array}{l}(\textit{for all } x)\\(\textit{for all } y)\end{array}\left[\begin{array}{l}\textit{if } x = y\\\textit{then } p(x)\\\qquad\textit{if and only if}\\\qquad p(y)\end{array}\right].$$

Note that the axioms for the theory of equality include the *transitivity, symmetry,* and *reflexivity* axioms from the theory of equivalence relations; in other words, = is an equivalence relation. This means that (by the *containment* proposition) the theory of the equivalence relation = is contained in the theory of the equality relation =, and any sentence valid in the former theory is also valid in the latter. In particular, we have that the *double-transitivity* property is valid in the theory of equality.

Proposition (double transitivity)

The sentence

$$\mathcal{E}_6 : \begin{array}{l}(\textit{for all } u)\\(\textit{for all } v)\\(\textit{for all } x)\\(\textit{for all } y)\end{array}\left[\begin{array}{l}\textit{if } u = v \textit{ and}\\\quad u = x \textit{ and}\\\quad v = y\\\textit{then } x = y\end{array}\right] \qquad (\textit{double transitivity})$$

is valid in the theory of equality.

The models for the theory of equality exhibit the following property.

Proposition (semantic rule for equality)

Suppose that the model I for the theory of equality is an interpretation for the terms t_1 and t_2.

If

> the value of t_1 under I
> is the same as
> the value of t_2 under I,

then

> $t_1 = t_2$ is true under I.   ◢

We shall refer to this result as the "= rule."

Proof

Suppose that the terms t_1 and t_2 each have the same value, the domain element d, under I. We would like to show that the sentence $t_1 = t_2$ is true under I.

Let $=_I$ be the binary relation assigned to the equality predicate symbol $=$ under I. Then (by the *proposition* semantic rule, because the values of t_1 and t_2 under I are each d)

> the value of $t_1 = t_2$ under I is $d =_I d$.

We would like to show that

> $d =_I d$ is true.

We have assumed that I is a model for the theory of equality. In particular, the *reflexivity* axiom $\mathcal{E}_3$,

> (*for all x*)$[x = x]$,

is true under I. Hence (by the *universal quantifier-instantiation* proposition), the sentence

> $t_1 = t_1$ is true under I.

We know (according to the *proposition* semantic rule, because the value of t_1 under I is d) that

> the value of $t_1 = t_1$ under I is $d =_I d$.

Therefore

$$d =_I d \text{ is true,}$$

as we wanted to show. ◣

We had wanted to formulate a theory of equality under whose models the binary predicate symbol $=$ would be assigned the equality relation over the domain; i.e., under any model I for the theory, the sentence $t_1 = t_2$ is true under I precisely when the terms t_1 and t_2 have the same value under I. In fact, this is not the case for the theory of equality we have formulated.

The above semantic rule establishes that the implication holds in one direction; i.e., if the terms t_1 and t_2 have the same value under I, then the sentence $t_1 = t_2$ is true under I.

The converse of the implication, however, is not true: There are some "abnormal" models I for the theory of equality under which some terms t_1 and t_2 have distinct values under I, but the sentence $t_1 = t_2$ is true under I nevertheless. This is illustrated by the following example.

Example (abnormal model for equality)

Consider an interpretation I over a domain $\{A, B\}$ of two elements that assigns

a to be A
b to be B

and each predicate symbol (including the equality symbol $=$) to be the relation that is true for all domain elements. (We do not care what functions are assigned to function symbols under I.)

This is a model for the theory of equality; each of the axioms $\mathcal{E}_1$ through $\mathcal{E}_5$ is true under I. For instance, to show that the *symmetry* axiom $\mathcal{E}_2$ is true under I, it suffices to show that, for every domain element d and e, the subsentence

if $x = y$
then $y = x$

is true under the extended interpretation $\langle x \leftarrow d \rangle \circ \langle y \leftarrow e \rangle \circ I$. But since the equality symbol $=$ is assigned the binary relation that is true for all domain elements, including e and d, the consequent $y = x$ of the implication, and hence the implication itself, is true under the extended interpretation.

The truth under I of the other axioms for equality may be established similarly. Under I, the terms a and b have distinct values A and B, respectively, but the sentence $a = b$ is true. ◢

The above example illustrates that the converse of the semantic rule for equality (the $=$ rule) is not true. In other words, there are some models for the theory of equality under which the equality predicate symbol $=$ is not assigned the normal equality relation over the domain. Such "abnormal" models cannot be avoided in predicate logic, but they do not disturb us because the sentences we shall want to prove concerning the equality relation will be true under the abnormal models as well as the normal models.

SUBSTITUTIVITY OF EQUALITY

The most important property of the theory of equality is given in the following proposition.

Proposition (substitutivity of equality)

Suppose s, t, and $\tau\langle s \rangle$ are terms; then the universal closure of

$$
\begin{aligned}
&\textit{if } s = t \\
&\textit{then } \tau\langle s \rangle = \tau\langle t \rangle
\end{aligned}
\qquad\qquad (\textit{term})
$$

is valid in the theory of equality.

Suppose s and t are terms and $\mathcal{F}\langle s \rangle$ is a sentence; then the universal closure of

$$
\begin{aligned}
&\textit{if } s = t \\
&\textit{then } \left(\mathcal{F}\langle s \rangle \textit{ if and only if } \mathcal{F}\langle t \rangle \right)
\end{aligned}
\qquad\qquad (\textit{sentence})
$$

is valid in the theory of equality. ◢

Recall that, for any term $\tau\langle s \rangle$, the term $\tau\langle t \rangle$ denotes the result of safely replacing zero, one, or more free occurrences of s in $\tau\langle s \rangle$ with t. Similarly for sentences $\mathcal{F}\langle s \rangle$.

Let us consider an example.

Example

According to the *term* part of the proposition, the sentence

$$(\textit{for all } x) \begin{bmatrix} \textit{if } x = f(y) \\ \textit{then } h\big(g(x,\, x)\big) \ = \ h\big(g(f(y),\, x)\big) \end{bmatrix}$$
$$(\textit{for all } y)$$

is valid in the theory of equality, because $h\big(g(f(y),\, x)\big)$ is the result of safely replacing one of the free occurrences of x in $h\big(g(x,\, x)\big)$ with $f(y)$.

Also, according to the *sentence* part of the proposition, the sentence

$$(\textit{for all } x) \begin{bmatrix} \textit{if } x = f(y) \\ \textit{then } \begin{bmatrix} (\textit{for some } y)p(x,\, y) \\ \textit{if and only if} \\ (\textit{for some } y')p\big(f(y),\, y'\big) \end{bmatrix} \end{bmatrix}$$
$$(\textit{for all } y)$$

is valid in the theory of equality, because $(\textit{for some } y')p\big(f(y),\, y'\big)$ is the result of safely replacing the free occurrence of x in $(\textit{for some } y)p(x,\, y)$ with $f(y)$. Note that we have renamed the bound variable y to y'. ⌐

The truth of the proposition is intuitively clear, but the general proof is rather technical. We illustrate the idea behind the proof using the particular term and sentence of the above example.

Proof (substitutivity of equality, special case)

The proof relies on repeated application of the *functional-* and *predicate-substitutivity* axiom schemata $\mathcal{E}_4$ and $\mathcal{E}_5$.

Term part

For arbitrary elements x and y, we suppose that

$$x = f(y)$$

and show that then

$$h\big(g(x,\, x)\big) \ = \ h\big(g(f(y),\, x)\big).$$

We know (by the *functional-substitutivity* equality axiom for g, because $x = f(y)$) that

$$g(x,\, x) \ = \ g(f(y),\, x).$$

Therefore (by the *functional-substitutivity* equality axiom for h) we have

$$h\big(g(x, \, x)\big) \; = \; h\big(g(f(y), \, x)\big),$$

as we wanted to show.

Sentence part

For arbitrary elements x and y, we suppose that

$$x = f(y)$$

and show that then

> *(for some y)$p(x, \, y)$*
> *if and only if*
> *(for some y')$p\big(f(y), \, y'\big)$.*

We actually show only one direction of this equivalence, namely, that

> *if (for some y)$p(x, \, y)$*
> *then (for some y')$p\big(f(y), \, y'\big)$.*

Suppose that

$$(for \; some \; y)p(x, \, y)$$

and let z be an element such that

$$p(x, \, z).$$

We know (by the *predicate-substitutivity* equality axiom for p, because $x = f(y)$) that

$$p\big(f(y), \, z\big).$$

Therefore (by the *existential quantifier-instantiation* proposition) we have

$$(for \; some \; y')p\big(f(y), \, y'\big),$$

as we wanted to show.

The proof of the other direction of the equivalence is similar.   ⌟

REPLACEMENT

We now use the *substitutivity-of-equality* proposition to establish another important property of the theory of equality.

Proposition (replacement)

Suppose x is a variable, t is a term, and $\mathcal{F}[x]$ is a sentence, where x does not occur free in t.

Then

$$(\textit{for all } x)\big[\textit{if } x = t \ \textit{ then } \ \mathcal{F}[x]\big] \quad \text{is equivalent to} \quad \mathcal{F}[t] \qquad (\textit{universal})$$

and

$$(\textit{for some } x)\big[x = t \ \textit{ and } \ \mathcal{F}[x]\big] \quad \text{is equivalent to} \quad \mathcal{F}[t] \qquad (\textit{existential})$$

in the theory of equality. ⌐

The proof depends on the following observation about the total and partial substitution operator.

Remark (invertibility of substitution)

Suppose $\mathcal{F}$ is a sentence and s and t are terms. Then $\mathcal{F}$ is equivalent to one of the sentences denoted by

$$\big(\mathcal{F} \blacktriangleleft \{s \leftarrow t\}\big) \triangleleft \{t \leftarrow s\}.$$

In other words, $\mathcal{F}$ is equivalent to a sentence $\mathcal{F}'$ obtained from $\mathcal{F} \blacktriangleleft \{s \leftarrow t\}$ by replacing zero, one, or more free occurrences of t with s.

For in obtaining $\mathcal{F} \blacktriangleleft \{s \leftarrow t\}$ from $\mathcal{F}$ we replace all the free occurrences of s in $\mathcal{F}$ (if any) with occurrences of t, and perhaps rename some bound variables. The newly introduced occurrences of t are free in $\mathcal{F} \blacktriangleleft \{s \leftarrow t\}$. If we replace those occurrences of t in $\mathcal{F} \blacktriangleleft \{s \leftarrow t\}$ with s, we obtain a sentence $\mathcal{F}'$ identical to $\mathcal{F}$, except that perhaps some of the bound variables have been renamed. At any rate, $\mathcal{F}'$ is certain to be equivalent to $\mathcal{F}$.

As in propositional logic, we cannot use the total substitution operator $\blacktriangleleft$ in place of the partial substitution operator $\triangleleft$ in stating the invertibility property, because $\mathcal{F}$ may have free occurrences of t as well as of s. For example,

$$\big(p(x, y) \blacktriangleleft \{x \leftarrow y\}\big) \blacktriangleleft \{y \leftarrow x\}$$

is $p(x, x)$, not $p(x, y)$. ⌐

We now can prove the proposition.

Proof (replacement)

We first establish the *universal* part.

It suffices to show that if either side of the equivalence is true (under a given interpretation), the other side is also true. We show each direction separately.

($\Rightarrow$)

Suppose

$$(for\ all\ x)\big[if\ x = t\ \ then\ \ \mathcal{F}[x]\big]$$

is true. We would like to show that then

$$\mathcal{F}[t]$$

is also true.

We have (by the *universal quantifier-instantiation* proposition applied to our supposition, taking x to be t)

$$if\ t = t\ \ then\ \ \mathcal{F}[t]$$

is true. Note that replacing x with t had no effect on the term t in $x = t$, because x does not occur free in t.

Because (by the *reflexivity* axiom $\mathcal{E}_3$ for equality)

$$t = t$$

is true, we have that

$$\mathcal{F}[t]$$

is true, as we wanted to show.

($\Leftarrow$)

Suppose

$$\mathcal{F}[t]$$

is true; we would like to show that then

$$(for\ all\ x)\big[if\ x = t\ \ then\ \ \mathcal{F}[x]\big]$$

is also true.

Consider an arbitrary element x and suppose that

$$x = t;$$

hence (by the *symmetry* axiom $\mathcal{E}_2$ for equality)

$$t = x.$$

We would like to show that then

$$\mathcal{F}[x]$$

is true.

Note (by the above *invertibility* property of substitution) that $\mathcal{F}[x]$ is equivalent to one of the sentences denoted by $\mathcal{F}[t] \triangleleft \{t \leftarrow x\}$. Because $t = x$ and $\mathcal{F}[t]$ are true, we know (by the *substitutivity-of-equality* proposition) that $\mathcal{F}[t] \triangleleft \{t \leftarrow x\}$ is true. Therefore

$$\mathcal{F}[x]$$

is also true, as we wanted to show.

The proof of the *existential* part relies on the *universal* part. We would like to show

$$(for\ some\ x)\big[x = t\ \ and\ \ \mathcal{F}[x]\big] \quad \text{is equivalent to} \quad \mathcal{F}[t],$$

which is true precisely when

$$not\ (for\ some\ x)\big[x = t\ \ and\ \ \mathcal{F}[x]\big] \quad \text{is equivalent to} \quad \big(not\ \mathcal{F}[t]\big)$$

precisely when (by the duality of quantifiers)

$$(for\ all\ x)\big[not\ (x = t\ \ and\ \ \mathcal{F}[x])\big] \quad \text{is equivalent to} \quad \big(not\ \mathcal{F}[t]\big)$$

precisely when (by propositional logic)

$$(for\ all\ x)\big[if\ x = t\ \ then\ \ (not\ \mathcal{F}[x])\big] \quad \text{is equivalent to} \quad \big(not\ \mathcal{F}[t]\big).$$

But this follows from the *universal* part of the proposition, taking $\big(not\ \mathcal{F}[x]\big)$ in place of $\mathcal{F}[x]$. ◢

We can similarly establish a more general version of the proposition, in which n variables $x_1,\ x_2,\ \ldots,\ x_n$ in a sentence $\mathcal{F}[x_1, x_2,\ \ldots, x_n]$ are replaced by n terms $t_1, t_2,\ \ldots, t_n$, as follows.

Proposition (general replacement)

Suppose that $x_1,\ x_2,\ \ldots,\ x_n$ are variables, $t_1,\ t_2,\ \ldots,\ t_n$ are terms, and $\mathcal{F}[x_1, x_2,\ \ldots, x_n]$ is a sentence, where none of the variables $x_1,\ x_2,\ \ldots,\ x_n$ occurs free in any of the terms $t_1,\ t_2,\ \ldots,\ t_n$.

Then

$$
\begin{array}{l}
(\textit{for all } x_1) \\
(\textit{for all } x_2) \\
\qquad \vdots \\
(\textit{for all } x_n)
\end{array}
\left[
\begin{array}{l}
\textit{if } x_1 = t_1 \;\; \textit{and} \\
\quad\; x_2 = t_2 \;\; \textit{and} \\
\qquad \vdots \\
\quad\; x_n = t_n \\
\textit{then } \; \mathcal{F}[x_1, x_2, \ldots, x_n]
\end{array}
\right]
\qquad (\textit{universal})
$$

is equivalent to

$$
\mathcal{F}[t_1, \; t_2, \; \ldots, \; t_n]
$$

and

$$
\begin{array}{l}
(\textit{for some } x_1) \\
(\textit{for some } x_2) \\
\qquad \vdots \\
(\textit{for some } x_n)
\end{array}
\left[
\begin{array}{l}
x_1 = t_1 \;\; \textit{and} \\
x_2 = t_2 \;\; \textit{and} \\
\qquad \vdots \\
x_n = t_n \;\; \textit{and} \\
\mathcal{F}[x_1, x_2, \ldots, x_n]
\end{array}
\right]
\qquad (\textit{existential})
$$

is equivalent to

$$
\mathcal{F}[t_1, t_2, \ldots, t_n]
$$

in the theory of equality. ◢

We omit the proof.

The replacement proposition would not hold if we referred to the partial substitution operator instead of the total substitution operator; the reader is requested to show this in **Problem 5.1**.

The reader is also requested (in **Problem 5.2**) to show the validity of the following properties of conditional terms in the theory of equality:

$$
(\textit{if true then } a \textit{ else } b) = a \qquad\qquad\qquad (\textit{true})
$$

$$
(\textit{if false then } a \textit{ else } b) = b \qquad\qquad\qquad (\textit{false})
$$

$$
(\textit{for all } x)
\left[
\begin{array}{l}
f(\textit{if } p(x) \textit{ then } a \textit{ else } b) \\
\quad = \\
\textit{if } p(x) \textit{ then } f(a) \textit{ else } f(b)
\end{array}
\right]
\qquad (\textit{distributivity})
$$

COMPOSITION INTRODUCTION

We now introduce a result that will allow us to define a new function equal to the composition of two previously defined functions.

Proposition (composition introduction)

Suppose a model I for the theory of equality assigns a value to the unary function symbols g and h.

Then for any unary function symbol f, there exists a model I_f for the theory of equality under which

$$(for\ all\ x)\big[f(x) = g(h(x))\big]$$

is true, where I_f and I agree on all symbols except perhaps f. ⌐

The proof relies on the *function-introduction* proposition of predicate logic.

Proof

To prove that there exists a suitable interpretation I_f under which

$$(for\ all\ x)\big[f(x) = g(h(x))\big]$$

is true, it suffices (by the *function-introduction* proposition) to establish that

$$(for\ all\ x)(for\ some\ y)\big[y = g(h(x))\big]$$

is true under I.

Consider an arbitrary domain element d; we would like to show (by the *for-all* rule) that

$$(for\ some\ y)\big[y = g(h(x))\big]$$

is true under the extended interpretation $\langle x \leftarrow d\rangle \circ I$.

Let e be the value of $g(h(x))$ under I; then it suffices to show (by the *for-some* rule) that

$$y = g(h(x))$$

is true under the extended interpretation $\langle y \leftarrow e\rangle \circ \langle x \leftarrow d\rangle \circ I$. But this holds (by the $=$ rule) because y and $g(h(x))$ have the same value under the extended interpretation. ⌐

We can similarly establish a more general version of the proposition, in which g is an n-ary function symbol that is composed with n function symbols

h_1, h_2, ..., h_n, each of which may itself have more than one argument. For example, suppose that a model I for the theory of equality assigns a value to a binary function symbol g, a binary function symbol h_1, and a unary function symbol h_2. Then for any ternary function symbol f, the general proposition guarantees the existence of an interpretation I_f under which

$$\begin{array}{l}(\textit{for all } x_1) \\ (\textit{for all } x_2) \\ (\textit{for all } x_3)\end{array}\Big[f(x_1,\ x_2,\ x_3)\ =\ g\big(h_1(x_1,\ x_2),\ h_2(x_3)\big)\Big]$$

is true, where I_f and I agree on all symbols except perhaps f.

The precise statement and proof of the more general version of the proposition are omitted.

THEORY WITH EQUALITY

Often we wish to define theories whose models assign special meanings to certain constant, function, and predicate symbols in addition to the equality predicate symbol $=$. For this purpose we may provide *special* axioms for the theory, as well as the equality axioms $\mathcal{E}_1$ through $\mathcal{E}_5$. A theory that is defined by a set of axioms that includes the equality axioms is called a *theory with equality*.

In general, when we describe a model I for a theory with equality, we will assume (unless stated otherwise) that the equality symbol $=$ is assigned the normal equality relation, that is,

$x = y$ is true under I precisely when x_I is identical to y_I.

Under such a model all the equality axioms are satisfied.

In any theory with equality there is exactly one equality relation. This is expressed precisely in the following result. (The proof is requested in **Problem 5.3.**)

Proposition (uniqueness of equality)

In any theory with equality, let $r(x, y)$ be a binary predicate symbol such that the equality axioms $\mathcal{E}_1$ through $\mathcal{E}_5$ are valid for r. (In other words, r satisfies the *transitivity, symmetry*, and *reflexivity* axioms and the *functional-* and *predicate-substitutivity* axiom schemata.)

Then r and the equality symbol $=$ denote the same relation; i.e., the sentence

$$(for\ all\ x) \begin{bmatrix} r(x,\ y) \\ \quad if\ and\ only\ if \\ x = y \end{bmatrix} \qquad (uniqueness)$$
$(for\ all\ y)$

is valid in the theory. ⌙

We give four examples of theories with equality: the theories of weak partial orderings, associated relations, groups, and pairs.

5.2   THEORY OF WEAK PARTIAL ORDERINGS

Our first example of a theory with equality is the *theory of a weak partial ordering*. The vocabulary of this theory consists of a binary predicate symbol, which we denote by $\preceq$, as well as the equality symbol $=$. The meaning of the symbol $\preceq$ is defined by the following special axioms:

$$\mathcal{W}_1: \quad \begin{matrix} (for\ all\ x) \\ (for\ all\ y) \\ (for\ all\ z) \end{matrix} \begin{bmatrix} if\ x \preceq y\ \ and\ \ y \preceq z \\ then\ \ x \preceq z \end{bmatrix} \qquad (transitivity)$$

$$\mathcal{W}_2: \quad \begin{matrix} (for\ all\ x) \\ (for\ all\ y) \end{matrix} \begin{bmatrix} if\ x \preceq y\ \ and\ \ y \preceq x \\ then\ \ x = y \end{bmatrix} \qquad (antisymmetry)$$

$$\mathcal{W}_3: \quad (for\ all\ x)[x \preceq x] \qquad\qquad\qquad\qquad (reflexivity)$$

As in any theory of equality, we also have the *transitivity*, *symmetry*, and *reflexivity* axioms $\mathcal{E}_1$, $\mathcal{E}_2$, and $\mathcal{E}_3$ for equality. Because the binary predicate symbol $\preceq$ is in our vocabulary, we have two instances of the *predicate-substitutivity* axiom schema $\mathcal{E}_5$:

$$\begin{matrix} (for\ all\ x) \\ (for\ all\ y) \\ (for\ all\ z) \end{matrix} \begin{bmatrix} if\ x = y \\ then\ \ x \preceq z \\ \qquad\quad if\ and\ only\ if \\ \quad y \preceq z \end{bmatrix} \qquad (left\ substitutivity\ for\ \preceq)$$

and

$$\begin{matrix} (for\ all\ x) \\ (for\ all\ y) \\ (for\ all\ z) \end{matrix} \begin{bmatrix} if\ x = y \\ then\ \ z \preceq x \\ \qquad\quad if\ and\ only\ if \\ \quad z \preceq y \end{bmatrix} \qquad (right\ substitutivity\ for\ \preceq)$$

We require no instances of the *functional-substitutivity* axiom schema $\mathcal{E}_4$, because we have no function symbols in our vocabulary.

The *transitivity* axiom $\mathcal{W}_1$, the *antisymmetry* axiom $\mathcal{W}_2$, and the *reflexivity* axiom $\mathcal{W}_3$ for the weak partial ordering $\preceq$ are independent; i.e., none of them is implied by the other two. The reader is requested to show this (in **Problem 5.4**) by constructing, for each of these axioms, a model for the theory of equality under which the axiom is false but the other two axioms are true.

The following result establishes that the equality relation of this theory can be paraphrased in terms of the weak partial ordering $\preceq$.

Proposition (splitting)

The sentence

$$(\textit{for all } x) \atop (\textit{for all } y) \left[{x = y \atop \textit{if and only if} \atop x \preceq y \;\; \textit{and} \;\; y \preceq x} \right] \qquad (\textit{splitting})$$

is valid in the theory of the weak partial ordering $\preceq$. ⌐

We give an intuitive justification.

Proof

Consider arbitrary elements x and y; it suffices (by propositional logic) to show that

> *if* $x = y$
> *then* $x \preceq y$ *and* $y \preceq x$

and

> *if* $x \preceq y$ *and* $y \preceq x$
> *then* $x = y$.

The latter sentence follows from the *antisymmetry* axiom $\mathcal{W}_2$.

To show the former sentence, suppose that

> $x = y$;

we would like to show that

> $x \preceq y$ *and* $y \preceq x$.

We know (by the *left-substitutivity* equality axiom for $\preceq$, taking z to be x) that

> *if* $x = y$
> *then* $x \preceq x$
> > *if and only if*
> > $y \preceq x$

and (by the *right-substitutivity* axiom for $\preceq$, taking z to be x) that

> *if* $x = y$
> *then* $x \preceq x$
> > *if and only if*
> > $x \preceq y$.

Therefore, because $x = y$ and (by the *reflexivity* axiom $\mathcal{W}_3$) $x \preceq x$, we have (by propositional logic)

$$x \preceq y \ \ and \ \ y \preceq x,$$

as we wanted to show. ◢

As in the theory of strict partial orderings, we may augment our theory of the weak partial ordering $\preceq$ by introducing a new binary predicate symbol $\succeq$, denoting the *inverse* relation of $\preceq$. It is defined by the new special axiom:

$$\mathcal{W}_4: \quad \begin{array}{l} (for\ all\ x) \\ (for\ all\ y) \end{array} \left[\begin{array}{l} x \succeq y \\ \quad if\ and\ only\ if \\ y \preceq x \end{array} \right] \qquad (inverse)$$

Because the augmented theory contains a new predicate symbol $\succeq$ in its vocabulary, we automatically provide the corresponding instances of the *predicate-substitutivity* axiom schema $\mathcal{E}_5$ for equality:

$$\begin{array}{l} (for\ all\ x) \\ (for\ all\ y) \\ (for\ all\ z) \end{array} \left[\begin{array}{l} if\ x = y \\ then\ x \succeq z \\ \quad if\ and\ only\ if \\ y \succeq z \end{array} \right] \qquad (left\ substitutivity\ for\ \succeq)$$

$$\begin{array}{l} (for\ all\ x) \\ (for\ all\ y) \\ (for\ all\ z) \end{array} \left[\begin{array}{l} if\ x = y \\ then\ z \succeq x \\ \quad if\ and\ only\ if \\ z \succeq y \end{array} \right] \qquad (right\ substitutivity\ for\ \succeq)$$

As before, we can establish that the augmented theory is consistent.

5.3   THEORY OF ASSOCIATED RELATIONS

Let us now relate the theories of weak and strict partial orderings. For this purpose, we introduce a second theory with equality, the *theory of associated relations.*

The vocabulary of this theory consists of the equality predicate symbol $=$ and

- A binary predicate symbol $x \prec y$, denoting an arbitrary binary relation

- A binary predicate symbol $x < y$, denoting the *irreflexive restriction* of $\prec$

- A binary predicate symbol $x \preceq y$, denoting the *reflexive closure* of $\prec$.

The reader should realize that $\prec$, $<$, and $\preceq$ are informal notations for binary predicate symbols of predicate logic, such as $p_{17}(x, y)$, $q_{31}(x, y)$, and $r_{57}(x, y)$.

The predicate symbols $<$ and $\preceq$ are defined in terms of the predicate symbol $\prec$ by the following special axioms:

$$
\mathcal{R}_1 : \quad
\begin{array}{l} (\textit{for all } x) \\ (\textit{for all } y) \end{array}
\left[
\begin{array}{l}
x < y \\
\quad \textit{if and only if} \\
x \prec y \;\; \textit{and} \;\; \textit{not } (x = y)
\end{array}
\right]
\quad (\textit{irreflexive restriction})
$$

$$
\mathcal{R}_2 : \quad
\begin{array}{l} (\textit{for all } x) \\ (\textit{for all } y) \end{array}
\left[
\begin{array}{l}
x \preceq y \\
\quad \textit{if and only if} \\
x \prec y \;\; \textit{or} \;\; x = y
\end{array}
\right]
\quad (\textit{reflexive closure})
$$

Because the theory of relations is a theory with equality, we also have the *transitivity*, *symmetry*, and *reflexivity* axioms $\mathcal{E}_1$, $\mathcal{E}_2$, and $\mathcal{E}_3$ for equality, as well as those instances of the *predicate-substitutivity* axiom schema $\mathcal{E}_5$ that apply to the predicate symbols. For the predicate symbol $\prec$ we have

$$
\begin{array}{l} (\textit{for all } x) \\ (\textit{for all } y) \\ (\textit{for all } z) \end{array}
\left[
\begin{array}{l}
\textit{if } x = y \\
\textit{then } x \prec z \\
\qquad \textit{if and only if} \\
\qquad y \prec z
\end{array}
\right]
\quad \textit{and} \quad
\begin{array}{l} (\textit{for all } x) \\ (\textit{for all } y) \\ (\textit{for all } z) \end{array}
\left[
\begin{array}{l}
\textit{if } x = y \\
\textit{then } z \prec x \\
\qquad \textit{if and only if} \\
\qquad z \prec y
\end{array}
\right]
$$

(*left and right predicate substitutivity for* $\prec$)

For the predicate symbol $<$ we have

$$
\begin{array}{c}
(\textit{for all } x) \\
(\textit{for all } y) \\
(\textit{for all } z)
\end{array}
\left[
\begin{array}{l}
\textit{if } x = y \\
\textit{then } x \prec z \\
\qquad \textit{if and only if} \\
\quad y \prec z
\end{array}
\right]
\quad \text{and} \quad
\begin{array}{c}
(\textit{for all } x) \\
(\textit{for all } y) \\
(\textit{for all } z)
\end{array}
\left[
\begin{array}{l}
\textit{if } x = y \\
\textit{then } z \prec x \\
\qquad \textit{if and only if} \\
\quad z \prec y
\end{array}
\right]
$$

(*left and right predicate substitutivity for* $\prec$)

For the predicate symbol $\preceq$ we have

$$
\begin{array}{c}
(\textit{for all } x) \\
(\textit{for all } y) \\
(\textit{for all } z)
\end{array}
\left[
\begin{array}{l}
\textit{if } x = y \\
\textit{then } x \preceq z \\
\qquad \textit{if and only if} \\
\quad y \preceq z
\end{array}
\right]
\quad \text{and} \quad
\begin{array}{c}
(\textit{for all } x) \\
(\textit{for all } y) \\
(\textit{for all } z)
\end{array}
\left[
\begin{array}{l}
\textit{if } x = y \\
\textit{then } z \preceq x \\
\qquad \textit{if and only if} \\
\quad z \preceq y
\end{array}
\right]
$$

(*left and right predicate substitutivity for* $\preceq$)

Example

Consider a finite interpretation I over the domain of two elements $\{A, B\}$ under which

- The predicate symbol $\preceq$ is the relation $\preceq_I$ illustrated by the following diagram:

- The predicate symbol $\prec$ is the relation $\prec_I$ illustrated by the following diagram:

- The predicate symbol $\preceq$ is the relation $\preceq_I$ illustrated by the following diagram:

The relation $\prec_I$ is identical to the relation $\preceq_I$, except that $A \prec_I A$ is not true; thus no node is linked to itself. The relation $\preceq_I$ is identical to the relation $\preceq_I$, except that $B \preceq_I B$ is true; thus each node is linked to itself. The reader may confirm that the definitions $\mathcal{R}_1$ of the irreflexive restriction $\prec$ and $\mathcal{R}_2$ of the reflexive closure $\preceq$ are satisfied under this interpretation. ⌐

IRREFLEXIVITY AND REFLEXIVITY

In this theory we can show that the irreflexive restriction is indeed irreflexive and that the reflexive closure is indeed reflexive.

Proposition (irreflexivity and reflexivity)

In the theory of associated relations the sentences

$$(for\ all\ x)\big[not\ (x \prec x)\big] \hspace{3cm} (irreflexivity\ of \prec)$$

and

$$(for\ all\ x)[x \preceq x] \hspace{3.5cm} (reflexivity\ of \preceq)$$

are valid. ⌐

We give an intuitive justification. Let us first show the irreflexivity of $\prec$.

Proof (irreflexivity of $\prec$)

For an arbitrary domain element x, we have (by the *reflexivity* axiom $\mathcal{E}_3$ for equality)

$$x = x$$

and therefore (by propositional logic)

$$not\ (x \prec x\ \ and\ \ not\ (x = x))$$

or, equivalently (by the definition $\mathcal{R}_1$ of the irreflexive restriction $\prec$),

$$not\ (x \prec x),$$

as we wanted to show. ⌐

Now let us show the reflexivity of $\preceq$.

Proof (reflexivity of $\preceq$)

For an arbitrary domain element x, we have (by the *reflexivity* axiom $\mathcal{E}_3$ for equality)

$$x = x$$

—

and therefore (by propositional logic)

$$x \prec x \ \ or \ \ x = x$$

or, equivalently (by the definition $\mathcal{R}_2$ of the reflexive closure $\preceq$),

$$x \preceq x,$$

as we wanted to show. ◢

We can also establish that, in the theory of associated relations, a relation $\prec$ is irreflexive precisely when it is identical to its irreflexive restriction $\prec$ and is reflexive precisely when it is identical to its reflexive closure $\preceq$.

Proposition (irreflexivity and reflexivity conditions)

In the theory of associated relations, the sentences

$$
\begin{array}{l}
(for\ all\ x)[not\ (x \prec x)] \\
\quad if\ and\ only\ if \\
(for\ all\ x) \\
(for\ all\ y)
\left[
\begin{array}{l}
x \prec y \\
\quad if\ and\ only\ if \\
x \prec y
\end{array}
\right]
\end{array}
\qquad (irreflexivity\ condition)
$$

and

$$
\begin{array}{l}
(for\ all\ x)[x \prec x] \\
\quad if\ and\ only\ if \\
(for\ all\ x) \\
(for\ all\ y)
\left[
\begin{array}{l}
x \prec y \\
\quad if\ and\ only\ if \\
x \preceq y
\end{array}
\right]
\end{array}
\qquad (reflexivity\ condition)
$$

are valid. ◢

We prove the first part of the proposition. The proof of the second part is similar and is left as an exercise (**Problem 5.5**).

Proof (irreflexivity condition)

We have that

$$
(for\ all\ x) \atop (for\ all\ y)
\left[
\begin{array}{l}
x \prec y \\
\quad if\ and\ only\ if \\
x \prec y
\end{array}
\right]
$$

is equivalent (by the definition $\mathcal{R}_1$ of the reflexive restriction $\prec$) to

$$(\textit{for all } x) \quad \left[\begin{array}{l} x \prec y \\ \textit{if and only if} \\ x \preceq y \ \textit{and} \ \textit{not} \ (x = y) \end{array} \right]$$
$$(\textit{for all } y)$$

is equivalent (by propositional logic) to

$$(\textit{for all } x) \left[\begin{array}{l} \textit{if } \ x \prec y \\ \textit{then} \ \ \textit{not} \ (x = y) \end{array} \right]$$
$$(\textit{for all } y)$$

is equivalent (by propositional and predicate logic) to

$$(\textit{for all } y)(\textit{for all } x) \left[\begin{array}{l} \textit{if } \ x = y \\ \textit{then} \ \ \textit{not} \ (x \prec y) \end{array} \right]$$

is equivalent (by the *universal-replacement* proposition for equality) to

$$(\textit{for all } y)[\textit{not} \ (y \prec y)]$$

is equivalent (renaming the bound variable) to

$$(\textit{for all } x)[\textit{not} \ (x \prec x)],$$

as we wanted to show.   ⌐

Examples

We consider three models for the theory of associated relations that illustrate the above proposition.

- *The strict less-than relation*

    Consider the interpretation over the integers under which

    ■ The predicate symbol $\prec$ is the strict less-than relation $<$, which is irreflexive.

    ■ The predicate symbol $\preceq$ is also the strict less-than relation $<$.

    ■ The predicate symbol $\underset{\sim}{\prec}$ is the weak less-than relation $\leq$.

    The reader may confirm that this interpretation is a model for the theory of associated relations. Under this interpretation the relation $\prec$ is irreflexive and hence (as the proposition predicts) is identical to its irreflexive restriction $\preceq$.

- *The weak less-than relation*

    Consider the interpretation over the integers under which

- The predicate symbol $\preceq$ is the weak less-than relation $\leq$, which is reflexive.

- The predicate symbol $\preceq$ is also the weak less-than relation $\leq$.

- The predicate symbol $\prec$ is the strict less-than relation $<$.

The reader may confirm that this interpretation is a model for the theory of associated relations. Under this interpretation the relation $\preceq$ is reflexive and hence (as the proposition predicts) is identical to its reflexive closure $\preceq$.

• *The finite model*

The reader may confirm that, under the finite model I for the theory over the domain of two elements $\{A, B\}$ we presented in the previous example, the relation $\preceq$ is identical to neither its irreflexive restriction $\prec$ nor its reflexive closure $\preceq$ and hence (as the proposition predicts) is neither irreflexive nor reflexive. ⌐

ASYMMETRY AND ANTISYMMETRY

We now show that, if the relation $\preceq$ is antisymmetric, its irreflexive restriction $\prec$ is asymmetric; and if the relation $\preceq$ is asymmetric, its reflexive closure $\preceq$ is antisymmetric.

Proposition (asymmetry and antisymmetry)

• *Asymmetry of $\prec$*

In the theory of associated relations augmented by the axiom

$$(\text{for all } x) \left[\begin{array}{l} \text{if } x \preceq y \ \text{ and } \ y \preceq x \\ \text{then } \ x = y \end{array} \right] \qquad (\text{antisymmetry of } \preceq)$$
$$(\text{for all } y)$$

the sentence

$$(\text{for all } x) \left[\begin{array}{l} \text{if } x \prec y \\ \text{then } \ \text{not } (y \prec x) \end{array} \right] \qquad (\text{asymmetry of } \prec)$$
$$(\text{for all } y)$$

is valid.

• *Antisymmetry of $\preceq$*

In the theory of associated relations augmented by the axiom

$$(\text{for all } x) \left[\begin{array}{l} \text{if } x \preceq y \\ \text{then } \ \text{not } (y \preceq x) \end{array} \right] \qquad (\text{asymmetry of } \preceq)$$
$$(\text{for all } y)$$

the sentence

$$(\textit{for all } x) \begin{bmatrix} \textit{if } x \preceq y \textit{ and } y \preceq x \\ \textit{then } x = y \end{bmatrix} \qquad (\textit{antisymmetry of } \preceq)$$

is valid. ⌐

We give an intuitive justification. We first show that, if $\preceq$ is antisymmetric, its irreflexive restriction $\prec$ is asymmetric.

Proof (asymmetry of $\prec$)

Suppose that $\preceq$ is antisymmetric and that, contrary to the *asymmetry* property of $\prec$, there exist domain elements x and y such that

$$x \prec y \textit{ and } y \prec x.$$

Then (by the definition $\mathcal{R}_1$ of the irreflexive restriction $\prec$)

$$x \prec y \textit{ and } not\,(x = y)$$
$$and$$
$$y \prec x \textit{ and } not\,(y = x).$$

Because $x \prec y$ and $y \prec x$, we have (by the *antisymmetry* axiom for $\prec$)

$$x = y.$$

But this contradicts our conclusion that $not\,(x = y)$. ⌐

We now show that, if $\prec$ is asymmetric, its reflexive closure $\preceq$ is antisymmetric.

Proof (antisymmetry of $\preceq$)

Suppose that $\prec$ is asymmetric and that, for arbitrary domain elements x and y,

$$x \preceq y \textit{ and } y \preceq x.$$

We would like to show that then

$$x = y.$$

We have (by the definition $\mathcal{R}_2$ of the reflexive closure $\preceq$)

$$x \prec y \textit{ or } x = y$$
$$and$$
$$y \prec x \textit{ or } y = x$$

or, equivalently (by the *symmetry* axiom $\mathcal{E}_2$ for equality and by propositional logic),

$$(x \prec y \; and \; y \prec x) \; or \; x = y.$$

We know (by the *asymmetry* axiom for $\prec$ and by propositional logic)

$$not \, (x \prec y \; and \; y \prec x).$$

Therefore (by propositional logic)

$$x = y,$$

as we wanted to show. ⌐

TRANSITIVITY

We next show that if $\prec$ is antisymmetric and transitive, its irreflexive restriction $\prec$ is transitive; and if $\prec$ is transitive, its reflexive closure $\preceq$ is transitive.

Proposition (transitivity)

- *Transitivity of* $\prec$

In the theory of associated relations augmented by the axioms

$$\begin{matrix} (for \; all \; x) \\ (for \; all \; y) \end{matrix} \left[\begin{matrix} if \; x \prec y \; and \; y \prec x \\ then \; x = y \end{matrix} \right] \qquad (antisymmetry \; of \; \prec)$$

and

$$\begin{matrix} (for \; all \; x) \\ (for \; all \; y) \\ (for \; all \; z) \end{matrix} \left[\begin{matrix} if \; x \prec y \; and \; y \prec z \\ then \; x \prec z \end{matrix} \right] \qquad (transitivity \; of \; \prec)$$

the sentence

$$\begin{matrix} (for \; all \; x) \\ (for \; all \; y) \\ (for \; all \; z) \end{matrix} \left[\begin{matrix} if \; x \prec y \; and \; y \prec z \\ then \; x \prec z \end{matrix} \right] \qquad (transitivity \; of \; \prec)$$

is valid.

- *Transitivity of* $\preceq$

In the theory of associated relations augmented by the axiom

$$\begin{matrix} (for \; all \; x) \\ (for \; all \; y) \\ (for \; all \; z) \end{matrix} \left[\begin{matrix} if \; x \prec y \; and \; y \prec z \\ then \; x \prec z \end{matrix} \right] \qquad (transitivity \; of \; \prec)$$

the sentence

$$\begin{matrix} (\textit{for all } x) \\ (\textit{for all } y) \\ (\textit{for all } z) \end{matrix} \begin{bmatrix} \textit{if } x \preceq y \ \textit{ and } \ y \preceq z \\ \textit{then } \ x \preceq z \end{bmatrix} \qquad (\textit{transitivity of } \preceq)$$

is valid. ⌟

We give an intuitive justification. We first show that, if $\prec$ is antisymmetric and transitive, its irreflexive restriction $\prec$ is transitive.

Proof (transitivity of $\prec$)

Suppose that $\prec$ is antisymmetric and transitive and that, for arbitrary domain elements x, y, and z,

$$x \prec y \ \textit{ and } \ y \prec z$$

or, equivalently (by the definition $\mathcal{R}_1$ of the irreflexive restriction $\prec$),

$$x \preceq y \ \textit{ and } \ \textit{not} \ (x = y)$$
$$\textit{and}$$
$$y \preceq z \ \textit{ and } \ \textit{not} \ (y = z).$$

We would like to show that then

$$x \prec z$$

or, equivalently (by the definition $\mathcal{R}_1$ of the irreflexive restriction $\prec$ again),

$$x \preceq z \ \textit{ and } \ \textit{not} \ (x = z).$$

Because $x \preceq y$ and $y \preceq z$, we have (by the *transitivity* axiom for $\preceq$)

$$x \preceq z,$$

which is the first conjunct of our desired result.

It remains to show *not* $(x = z)$. Suppose, to the contrary, that

$$x = z.$$

Then, because $x \preceq y$, we have (by the *left-substitutivity* equality axiom for $\preceq$)

$$z \preceq y.$$

Therefore (by the *antisymmetry* axiom for $\preceq$, because we have established that $y \preceq z$)

$$y = z,$$

contradicting our earlier conclusion that

$$not\ (y = z).\quad \lrcorner$$

Now let us show that if $\prec$ is transitive, its reflexive closure $\preceq$ is also transitive.

Proof (transitivity of $\preceq$)

Suppose that $\prec$ is transitive and that, for arbitrary domain elements x, y, and z,

$$x \preceq y \ \ and \ \ y \preceq z.$$

We would like to show that then

$$x \preceq z.$$

Our proof distinguishes among three cases, depending on whether $x = y$, $y = z$, or neither.

Case: $x = y$

Then (by the *symmetry* axiom $\mathcal{E}_2$ for equality)

$$y = x.$$

Therefore (by the *left-substitutivity* equality axiom for $\preceq$, because $y \preceq z$)

$$x \preceq z,$$

as we wanted to show.

Case: $y = z$

Therefore (by the *right-substitutivity* equality axiom for $\preceq$, because $x \preceq y$)

$$x \preceq z,$$

as we wanted to show.

Case: $not\ (x = y)\ \ and\ \ not\ (y = z)$

We know

$$x \preceq y \ \ and \ \ y \preceq z$$

or, equivalently (by the definition $\mathcal{R}_2$ of the reflexive closure $\preccurlyeq$),

$$x \prec y \;\; or \;\; x = y$$
$$and$$
$$y \prec z \;\; or \;\; y = z.$$

Therefore (by propositional logic, because *not* $(x = y)$ and *not* $(y = z)$)

$$x \prec y \;\; and \;\; y \prec z.$$

Therefore (by the *transitivity* axiom for $\prec$)

$$x \prec z.$$

Hence (by propositional logic)

$$x \prec z \;\; or \;\; x = z$$

or, equivalently (by the definition $\mathcal{R}_2$ of the reflexive closure $\preccurlyeq$),

$$x \preccurlyeq z,$$

as we wanted to show. ⌐

Remark

To establish that the reflexive restriction $\prec$ is transitive, we had to assume that the given relation $\prec$ is antisymmetric as well as transitive. In fact, there are transitive, non-antisymmetric relations $\prec$ whose irreflexive restrictions $\prec$ are not transitive, as the reader may confirm. ⌐

STRICT AND WEAK PARTIAL ORDERINGS

Let us combine the preceding three propositions together to establish that the irreflexive restriction of a weak partial ordering is a strict partial ordering and that the reflexive closure of a strict partial ordering is a weak partial ordering.

Proposition (strict and weak partial orderings)

- *Strict partial ordering*

In the theory of the weak partial ordering $\prec$ augmented by the axiom

$$(\textit{for all } x) \quad \begin{bmatrix} x \prec y \\ \textit{if and only if} \\ x \preceq y \ \textit{ and } \ not \, (x = y) \end{bmatrix} \qquad (\textit{irreflexive restriction of } \preceq)$$

the irreflexive restriction $\prec$ of $\preceq$ is a strict partial ordering.

- *Weak partial ordering*

In the theory of the strict partial ordering $\prec$ augmented by the axiom

$$(\textit{for all } x) \quad \begin{bmatrix} x \preceq y \\ \textit{if and only if} \\ x \prec y \ \textit{ or } \ x = y \end{bmatrix} \qquad (\textit{reflexive closure of } \prec)$$

the reflexive closure $\preceq$ of $\prec$ is a weak partial ordering. ⌟

We prove each part separately.

Proof (strict partial ordering)

In the theory of the weak partial ordering $\preceq$ augmented by the definition of its irreflexive restriction $\prec$, we would like to show that $\prec$ is a strict partial ordering.

Because $\preceq$ is a weak partial ordering, it satisfies the *transitivity* axiom $\mathcal{W}_1$ and the *antisymmetry* axiom $\mathcal{W}_2$. Therefore we know (by the *transitivity* proposition) that its irreflexive restriction $\prec$ is transitive; i.e., it satisfies the *transitivity* axiom $\mathcal{S}_1$.

We also know (by the *irreflexivity* proposition) that the irreflexive restriction $\prec$ is always irreflexive; i.e., it satisfies the *irreflexivity* axiom $\mathcal{S}_2$.

Therefore because $\prec$ satisfies the *transitivity* and *irreflexivity* axioms, it is a strict partial ordering. ⌟

Incidentally, in the above proof we did not use the *reflexivity* axiom $\mathcal{W}_3$ for $\preceq$.

Let us now prove the second part of the proposition.

Proof (weak partial ordering)

In the theory of the strict partial ordering $\prec$ augmented by the definition of its reflexive closure $\preceq$, we would like to show that $\preceq$ is a weak partial ordering.

Because $\prec$ is a strict partial ordering, it satisfies the *transitivity* axiom $\mathcal{S}_1$ and the *asymmetry* property $\mathcal{S}_3$.

Because $\prec$ is transitive, we know (by the *transitivity* proposition) that its reflexive closure $\preceq$ is transitive; i.e., it satisfies the *transitivity* axiom $\mathcal{W}_1$.

Because $\prec$ is asymmetric, we know (by the *antisymmetry* proposition) that its reflexive closure $\preceq$ is antisymmetric; i.e., it satisfies the *antisymmetry* axiom $\mathcal{W}_2$.

We also know (by the *reflexivity* proposition) that a reflexive closure $\preceq$ is always reflexive; i.e., it satisfies the *reflexivity* axiom $\mathcal{W}_3$.

Therefore because $\preceq$ satisfies the *transitivity, antisymmetry,* and *reflexivity* axioms, it is a weak partial ordering. ◢

MIXED TRANSITIVITY

We now introduce two *mixed-transitivity* conditions for the reflexive closure $\preceq$ that are equivalent to the transitivity of the given relation $\prec$ in the theory of associated relations.

Proposition (mixed transitivity of $\preceq$)

In the theory of associated relations, the following sentences are equivalent:

$$(\text{for all } x)\ (\text{for all } y)\ (\text{for all } z) \begin{bmatrix} \text{if } x \prec y \ \text{and} \ y \prec z \\ \text{then} \ \ x \prec z \end{bmatrix} \qquad (\text{transitivity of } \prec)$$

$$(\text{for all } x)\ (\text{for all } y)\ (\text{for all } z) \begin{bmatrix} \text{if } x \preceq y \ \text{and} \ y \prec z \\ \text{then} \ \ x \prec z \end{bmatrix} \quad (\text{left mixed transitivity of } \preceq)$$

$$(\text{for all } x)\ (\text{for all } y)\ (\text{for all } z) \begin{bmatrix} \text{if } x \prec y \ \text{and} \ y \preceq z \\ \text{then} \ \ x \prec z \end{bmatrix} \quad (\text{right mixed transitivity of } \preceq) \qquad ◢$$

Proof

It suffices (by propositional logic) to establish each of the following directions in the theory of associated relations:

($\Rightarrow$ *left*):   The transitivity of $\prec$ implies the left mixed transitivity of $\preceq$.

($\Leftarrow$ *left*):   The left mixed transitivity of $\preceq$ implies the transitivity of $\prec$.

($\Rightarrow$ *right*):   The transitivity of $\prec$ implies the right mixed transitivity of $\preceq$.

($\Leftarrow$ *right*):   The right mixed transitivity of $\preceq$ implies the transitivity of $\prec$.

We give the proof of ($\Rightarrow$ *left*); the proofs of the other three parts are left as an exercise (**Problem 5.6(a)**).

Proof of ($\Rightarrow$ *left*)

We assume the transitivity of $\prec$ and establish the left mixed transitivity of $\preceq$.

For arbitrary elements x, y, and z, suppose that

$$x \preceq y \ \ and \ \ y \prec z.$$

We would like to conclude that then

$$x \prec z.$$

Because $x \preceq y$, we know (by the definition $\mathcal{R}_2$ of the reflexive closure $\preceq$)

$$x \prec y \ \ or \ \ x = y.$$

The proof distinguishes between these two cases.

Case: $x \prec y$

Then (by the transitivity of $\prec$, because $x \prec y$ and $y \prec z$) we have

$$x \prec z,$$

which is our desired conclusion.

Case: $x = y$

Then (by the *symmetry* axiom $\mathcal{E}_2$ for equality)

$$y = x.$$

Therefore (by the *left-substitutivity* equality axiom of $\prec$, because $y \prec z$) we have

$$x \prec z,$$

which is our desired conclusion.   ◢

We can also establish two *mixed-transitivity* conditions for $\prec$, which are equivalent to the transitivity of $\prec$ in the theory of associated relations augmented by the *antisymmetry* axiom for $\prec$.

Proposition (mixed transitivity of $\prec$)

In the theory of associated relations augmented by the antisymmetry axiom for $\preceq$,

$$\begin{array}{l}(\textit{for all } x) \\ (\textit{for all } y)\end{array}\left[\begin{array}{l}\textit{if } x \preceq y \ \textit{and} \ y \preceq x \\ \textit{then} \ x = y\end{array}\right],$$

the following three sentences are equivalent:

$$\begin{array}{l}(\textit{for all } x) \\ (\textit{for all } y) \\ (\textit{for all } z)\end{array}\left[\begin{array}{l}\textit{if } x \preceq y \ \textit{and} \ y \preceq z \\ \textit{then} \ x \preceq z\end{array}\right] \qquad (\textit{transitivity of } \preceq)$$

$$\begin{array}{l}(\textit{for all } x) \\ (\textit{for all } y) \\ (\textit{for all } z)\end{array}\left[\begin{array}{l}\textit{if } x \prec y \ \textit{and} \ y \preceq z \\ \textit{then} \ x \prec z\end{array}\right] \qquad (\textit{left mixed transitivity of } \prec)$$

$$\begin{array}{l}(\textit{for all } x) \\ (\textit{for all } y) \\ (\textit{for all } z)\end{array}\left[\begin{array}{l}\textit{if } x \preceq y \ \textit{and} \ y \prec z \\ \textit{then} \ x \prec z\end{array}\right] \qquad (\textit{right mixed transitivity of } \prec) \qquad \blacksquare$$

The proof is similar to that of the *mixed-transitivity* proposition for $\preceq$ and is left as an exercise (**Problem 5.6(b)**). The reader is also asked (in **Problem 5.6(c)**) to show that the antisymmetry axiom for $\preceq$ is essential to the proposition.

TOTAL RELATIONS

Consider the theory of associated relations augmented by the axiom

$$\begin{array}{l}(\textit{for all } x) \\ (\textit{for all } y)\end{array}\left[x \preceq y \ \textit{or} \ y \preceq x \ \textit{or} \ x = y\right] \qquad (\textit{totality})$$

We shall call this the *theory of total associated relations*. In general, in any theory with equality, if a predicate symbol q satisfies the *totality* property, i.e., if the sentence

$$\begin{array}{l}(\textit{for all } x) \\ (\textit{for all } y)\end{array}\left[q(x, y) \ \textit{or} \ q(y, x) \ \textit{or} \ x = y\right]$$

is valid, we shall say that q denotes a *total* relation.

In the theory of associated relations, the above *totality* axiom is equivalent (by the definition of the reflexive closure $\preceq$ and the *symmetry* axiom $\mathcal{E}_2$ for equality) to the sentence

$$\begin{array}{l}(\textit{for all } x) \\ (\textit{for all } y)\end{array}\left[x \preceq y \ \textit{or} \ y \preceq x\right] \qquad (\textit{totality})$$

We shall use these two *totality* properties interchangeably.

Let us consider some models for the theory of total associated relations.

Examples

- *The strict less-than relation*

    Consider an interpretation over the integers under which the predicate symbol $\prec$ is the strict less-than relation $<$. Then the *totality* axiom is true under this interpretation; that is,

    > for all integers x and y,
    > $x < y$ or $y < x$ or $x = y$.

In other words, the strict less-than relation is *total*.

- *The proper-divides relation*

    Consider the interpretation over the integers under which

    - The predicate symbol $\prec$ is the proper-divides relation $\prec_{div}$, that is, the relation such that, for all integers d and e,

        $d \prec_{div} e$ if d divides e and $d \neq e$.

    - The predicate symbol $\prec$ is also the proper-divides relation $\prec_{div}$.

    - The predicate symbol $\preceq$ is the divides relation $\preceq_{div}$, that is, the relation such that, for all integers d and e,

        $d \preceq_{div} e$ if d divides e.

    The reader may confirm that this interpretation is a model for the theory of associated relations (recalling that an integer divides itself). However, the *totality* axiom is not true for $\prec_{div}$ under the interpretation. For instance, taking x and y to be 2 and 3, respectively, we have

    $$not\,(2 \prec_{div} 3), \quad not\,(3 \prec_{div} 2), \quad and \quad not\,(2 = 3).$$

In other words, $\prec_{div}$ is not a total relation. ⌐

Let us establish a proposition in the theory of total associated relations.

Proposition (total asymmetry)

Consider the theory of associated relations augmented by the axioms

$$\begin{array}{l}(\textit{for all } x) \\ (\textit{for all } y)\end{array}\left[\begin{array}{l}\textit{if } x \prec y \\ \textit{then } \ not\ (y \prec x)\end{array}\right] \qquad\qquad (\textit{asymmetry of } \prec)$$

and

$$\begin{array}{l}(\textit{for all } x) \\ (\textit{for all } y)\end{array}\left[x \prec y \ \ or \ \ y \prec x \ \ or \ \ x = y\right] \qquad\qquad (\textit{totality of } \prec)$$

In this theory the sentence

$$\begin{array}{l}(\textit{for all } x) \\ (\textit{for all } y)\end{array}\left[\begin{array}{l}not\ (x \prec y) \\ \quad \textit{if and only if} \\ y \preceq x\end{array}\right] \qquad\qquad (\textit{total asymmetry})$$

is valid. ◢

Proof

For arbitrary elements x and y, we have

$$not\ (x \prec y)$$

is equivalent (by the definition $\mathcal{R}_1$ of the irreflexive restriction) to

$$not\ (x \prec y \ \ and \ \ not\ (x = y))$$

is equivalent (by propositional logic) to

(†) $not\ (x \prec y) \ \ or \ \ x = y.$

On the other hand,

$$y \preceq x$$

is equivalent (by the definition $\mathcal{R}_2$ of the reflexive closure) to

$$y \prec x \ \ or \ \ y = x$$

is equivalent (by the *symmetry* axiom $\mathcal{E}_2$ for equality) to

(‡) $y \prec x \ \ or \ \ x = y.$

It remains to show that (†) is equivalent to (‡). Suppose (†), that is,

$$not\ (x \prec y) \ \ or \ \ x = y.$$

Then (by the *totality* axiom for $\prec$)

$$y \prec x \quad or \quad x = y.$$

But this is the condition (‡).

On the other hand, suppose (‡), that is,

$$y \prec x \quad or \quad x = y.$$

Then (by the *asymmetry* axiom for $\prec$)

$$not \ (x \prec y) \quad or \quad x = y.$$

But this is the condition (†).

This concludes the proof. ⌐

5.4   THEORY OF GROUPS

Our third example of a theory with equality is the theory of groups. The vocabulary of this theory consists of the equality predicate symbol $=$ and

- A binary function symbol $x \circ y$, denoting the *group operation*

- A constant symbol e, denoting the *identity* element

- A unary function symbol x^{-1}, denoting the *inverse* function.

Again the reader should understand that the symbols $x \circ y$, e, and x^{-1} are conventional notations for standard symbols of predicate logic, such as $f_{17}(x, y)$, a_3, and $g_{101}(x)$.

The theory of groups is defined by the following special axioms:

$\mathcal{G}_1:$	$(for\ all\ x)\left[x \circ e = x\right]$	(*right identity*)
$\mathcal{G}_2:$	$(for\ all\ x)\left[x \circ x^{-1} = e\right]$	(*right inverse*)
$\mathcal{G}_3:$	$\begin{array}{l}(for\ all\ x)\\(for\ all\ y)\\(for\ all\ z)\end{array}\left[(x \circ y) \circ z = x \circ (y \circ z)\right]$	(*associativity*)

Because group theory is a theory with equality, we also have the *transitivity*, *symmetry*, and *reflexivity* axioms $\mathcal{E}_1$, $\mathcal{E}_2$, and $\mathcal{E}_3$ for equality, as well as those instances of the *functional-substitutivity* axiom schema $\mathcal{E}_4$ that apply to the functions $x \circ y$ and x^{-1} of group theory:

$$
\begin{array}{l}
(\textit{for all } x) \\
(\textit{for all } y) \\
(\textit{for all } z)
\end{array}
\left[
\begin{array}{l}
\textit{if } x = y \\
\textit{then } x \circ z = y \circ z
\end{array}
\right]
\qquad (\textit{left substitutivity for } \circ)
$$

$$
\begin{array}{l}
(\textit{for all } x) \\
(\textit{for all } y) \\
(\textit{for all } z)
\end{array}
\left[
\begin{array}{l}
\textit{if } x = y \\
\textit{then } z \circ x = z \circ y
\end{array}
\right]
\qquad (\textit{right substitutivity for } \circ)
$$

$$
\begin{array}{l}
(\textit{for all } x) \\
(\textit{for all } y)
\end{array}
\left[
\begin{array}{l}
\textit{if } x = y \\
\textit{then } x^{-1} = y^{-1}
\end{array}
\right]
\qquad (\textit{substitutivity for inverse})
$$

Because $x \circ y$ is a binary function and x^{-1} is a unary function, we have two instances of the *functional-substitutivity* axiom for $x \circ y$ and one for x^{-1}. Because we have no predicate symbols other than $=$, we have no instances of the *predicate-substitutivity* axiom schema $\mathcal{E}_5$.

Let us consider some models for this theory.

Examples

• *The plus model*

One model for the theory is the *plus interpretation* $\mathcal{I}$ over the integers, under which

- The group operation $x \circ y$ is the plus function $x_{\mathcal{I}} + y_{\mathcal{I}}$.

- The identity symbol e is the integer 0.

- The inverse function symbol x^{-1} is the unary minus function $-x_{\mathcal{I}}$.

• *The times model*

Another model for the theory is the *times interpretation* $\mathcal{J}$ over the positive real numbers, under which

- The group operation $x \circ y$ is the times function $x_{\mathcal{J}} \cdot y_{\mathcal{J}}$.

- The identity symbol e is the number 1.

- The inverse function x^{-1} is the reciprocal function $1/x_{\mathcal{J}}$.

The reader may confirm that each of these interpretations is a model for the theory of groups. In other words, each of the above axioms is true under both interpretations. For instance, the *right-inverse axiom*

$$(for\ all\ x)[x \circ x^{-1} = e]$$

is true under the times interpretation because, for every positive real number r,

$$r \cdot \left(1/r\right) = 1.$$

Note that there is no model for the theory of groups over all the real numbers under which $x \circ y$ is the times function and e is 1. Because whatever unary function $g(r)$ over the reals is assigned to the inverse function symbol x^{-1} under such an interpretation, it cannot be the case that

$$0 \cdot g(0) = 1.$$

Therefore, the *right-inverse* axiom cannot be true under the interpretation.   ⌐

In the theory of groups, we can prove many properties from very few axioms.

Since group theory is a theory with equality, we know (by the *monotonicity* proposition) that those sentences in our language that are valid in the theory of equality are also valid in the theory of groups. For instance, we have (by the *substitutivity-of-equality* proposition) that, for all terms s and t and any sentence $\mathcal{F}\langle s \rangle$ in the theory of groups, the universal closure of

> *if* $s = t$
> *then* $(\mathcal{F}\langle s \rangle$ *if and only if* $\mathcal{F}\langle t \rangle)$

is valid in the theory of groups (where $\mathcal{F}\langle t \rangle$ is the result of replacing zero, one, or more occurrences of s in $\mathcal{F}\langle s \rangle$ with t).

Let us show the validity of a sentence in group theory.

Proposition (right cancellation)

The sentence

$$\begin{matrix}(for\ all\ x) \\ (for\ all\ y) \\ (for\ all\ z)\end{matrix} \left[\begin{matrix}if\ x \circ z = y \circ z \\ then\ x = y\end{matrix}\right] \qquad (right\ cancellation)$$

is valid in the theory of groups.   ⌐

Proof

Suppose that, for arbitrary elements x, y, and z,

(1) $x \circ z = y \circ z$.

We would like to show that $x = y$.

By (1) and the *left-substitutivity* equality axiom for the group operation $\circ$,

(2) $(x \circ z) \circ z^{-1} = (y \circ z) \circ z^{-1}$.

By the *associativity* axiom $\mathcal{G}_3$ for $\circ$,

(3) $(x \circ z) \circ z^{-1} = x \circ (z \circ z^{-1})$

and

(4) $(y \circ z) \circ z^{-1} = y \circ (z \circ z^{-1})$.

By the substitutivity of equality applied to (2) and (3), we may replace $(x \circ z) \circ z^{-1}$ with $x \circ (z \circ z^{-1})$ in (2), to obtain

(5) $x \circ (z \circ z^{-1}) = (y \circ z) \circ z^{-1}$.

Similarly, by the substitutivity of equality applied to (4) and (5), we may replace $(y \circ z) \circ z^{-1}$ with $y \circ (z \circ z^{-1})$ in (5), to obtain

(6) $x \circ (z \circ z^{-1}) = y \circ (z \circ z^{-1})$.

By the *right-inverse* axiom $\mathcal{G}_2$, we have

(7) $z \circ z^{-1} = e$.

By the substitutivity of equality applied to (6) and (7), replacing both occurrences of $(z \circ z^{-1})$ with e in (6), we obtain

(8) $x \circ e = y \circ e$.

By the *right-identity* axiom $\mathcal{G}_1$, we have

(9) $x \circ e = x$

and

(10) $y \circ e = y$.

By two applications of the substitutivity of equality applied to (8), (9), and (10), replacing $x \circ e$ with x in (8) and replacing $y \circ e$ with y in the result, we obtain

(11) $x = y$.

This is the desired conclusion. ⌐

Some other valid sentences of group theory are

$$(for\ all\ x)[e \circ x = x] \qquad\qquad (left\ identity)$$

$$(for\ all\ x)[x^{-1} \circ x = e] \qquad\qquad (left\ inverse)$$

$$\begin{matrix}(for\ all\ x) \\ (for\ all\ y) \\ (for\ all\ z)\end{matrix} \begin{bmatrix} if\ z \circ x = z \circ y \\ then\ x = y \end{bmatrix} \qquad\qquad (left\ cancellation)$$

$$(for\ all\ x) \begin{bmatrix} if\ x \circ x = x \\ then\ x = e \end{bmatrix} \qquad\qquad (nonidempotence)$$

The proofs of the validity of these properties in group theory are left as an exercise (**Problem 5.7**).

Once we have proved these properties for groups, we know that they are true under all models for groups. For example, because the *nonidempotence* property above is valid in group theory and because the *plus* interpretation over the integers is a model for group theory, we can conclude that

> for every nonnegative integer x,
> if $x + x = x$,
> then $x = 0$.

Similarly, because the *times* interpretation over the positive real numbers is a model for group theory, we can conclude that

> for every positive real number x,
> if $x \cdot x = x$,
> then $x = 1$.

COMMUTATIVITY

Not every property of plus and times is valid in group theory. For example, even though plus is commutative, that is,

$$x + y = y + x$$

is true for all integers x and y, and times is also commutative, that is,

$$x \cdot y = y \cdot x$$

is true for all positive real numbers, the group operation $\circ$ is not commutative, i.e., the corresponding sentence

$$\begin{matrix} (for\ all\ x) \\ (for\ all\ y) \end{matrix} \Big[x \circ y = y \circ x \Big]$$

is not valid in group theory. To see this, it suffices to find a single model for group theory under which the commutativity sentence is not true.

Example (permutation model)

Consider the set Π of all permutations on the set of three elements $S = \{A, B, C\}$. These are the unary functions that map distinct elements of S into distinct elements of S; there are precisely six of them:

- The *identity* π_0, which leaves all elements fixed; that is,

$$\pi_0(A) = A \qquad \pi_0(B) = B \qquad \pi_0(C) = C.$$

- The *transpositions* π_A, π_B, and π_C, which leave one element fixed but interchange the other two; that is,

$$\pi_A(A) = A \qquad \pi_A(B) = C \qquad \pi_A(C) = B$$
$$\pi_B(A) = C \qquad \pi_B(B) = B \qquad \pi_B(C) = A$$
$$\pi_C(A) = B \qquad \pi_C(B) = A \qquad \pi_C(C) = C.$$

- The *cycles* π_+ and π_-, which alter all the elements; that is,

$$\pi_+(A) = B \qquad \pi_+(B) = C \qquad \pi_+(C) = A$$
$$\pi_-(A) = C \qquad \pi_-(B) = A \qquad \pi_-(C) = B.$$

For all permutations π and π', let the *composition permutation* $\pi \otimes \pi'$ be the permutation obtained by applying first π and then π'; in other words, for any element s of S,

$$(\pi \otimes \pi')(s) = \pi'\big(\pi(s)\big).$$

The *composition function* maps any two permutations π and π' into their composition permutation $\pi \otimes \pi'$. For example,

$$[\pi_A \otimes \pi_C](A) \;=\; \pi_C\big(\pi_A(A)\big) \;=\; \pi_C(A) \;=\; B$$
$$[\pi_A \otimes \pi_C](B) \;=\; \pi_C\big(\pi_A(B)\big) \;=\; \pi_C(C) \;=\; C$$
$$[\pi_A \otimes \pi_C](C) \;=\; \pi_C\big(\pi_A(C)\big) \;=\; \pi_C(B) \;=\; A.$$

Note that, for each element s of S, $[\pi_A \otimes \pi_C](s) = \pi_+(s)$; thus $\pi_A \otimes \pi_C = \pi_+$.

For any permutation π, let the *inverse permutation* $\tilde{\pi}$ be defined so that, for any elements s and s' of S,

$$\pi(s) = s' \text{ precisely when } \tilde{\pi}(s') = s.$$

The *inverse function* maps any permutation π into its inverse permutation $\tilde{\pi}$. For example,

since $\pi_+(A) = B$, we have $\tilde{\pi}_+(B) = A$;

since $\pi_+(B) = C$, we have $\tilde{\pi}_+(C) = B$;

since $\pi_+(C) = A$, we have $\tilde{\pi}_+(A) = C$.

Note that, for each element s of S, $\tilde{\pi}_+(s) = \pi_-(s)$; thus $\tilde{\pi}_+ = \pi_-$.

Now consider the *permutation interpretation* K over the set Π of permutations of elements of S, under which

- The function symbol $x \circ y$ is the composition function $x_K \otimes y_K$.

- The constant e is the identity permutation π_0.

- The function symbol x^{-1} is the inverse function $\tilde{x}_K$.

In **Problem 5.8**, the reader is requested to confirm that K is a model for the theory of groups, i.e., that the *right-identity* axiom $\mathcal{G}_1$, the *right-inverse* axiom $\mathcal{G}_2$, and the *associativity* axiom $\mathcal{G}_3$ are true under K.

On the other hand, the *commutativity* property

$$\begin{matrix} (\textit{for all } x) \\ (\textit{for all } y) \end{matrix} \left[x \circ y = y \circ x \right]$$

is not true under K. For we have already observed that

$$\pi_A \otimes \pi_C = \pi_+.$$

On the other hand,

$$[\pi_C \otimes \pi_A](A) = \pi_A(\pi_C(A)) = \pi_A(B) = C$$

$$[\pi_C \otimes \pi_A](B) = \pi_A(\pi_C(B)) = \pi_A(A) = A$$

$$[\pi_C \otimes \pi_A](C) = \pi_A(\pi_C(C)) = \pi_A(C) = B.$$

Thus, for each element s of S, $[\pi_C \otimes \pi_A](s) = \pi_-(s)$; that is,

$$\pi_C \otimes \pi_A = \pi_-.$$

Because $\pi_+ \neq \pi_-$, we have

$$\pi_A \otimes \pi_C \neq \pi_C \otimes \pi_A,$$

showing that the composition function on permutations of S is not commutative. ◢

Because we have found a model for group theory under which the *commutativity* property is not true, we have shown that the property is not valid in the theory. If we wish to consider only those models for group theory under which the group operation $x \circ y$ is commutative, we can augment the theory of groups by adding the new axiom

$$\mathcal{G}_4: \quad \begin{matrix} (\textit{for all } x) \\ (\textit{for all } y) \end{matrix} \Big[x \circ y \;=\; y \circ x \Big] \qquad\qquad (\textit{commutativity})$$

The new theory is called the theory of *commutative* (or *abelian*) *groups*. All the valid sentences of group theory are also valid (by the *containment* proposition) in this augmented theory. For the theory of commutative groups, the *plus* and *times* interpretations are still models but the permutation interpretation is not.

5.5   THEORY OF PAIRS

Another example of a theory with equality is the theory of pairs. Intuitively speaking, in this theory we have certain basic elements, called *atoms*, from which we construct pairs of form $\langle x_1, x_2 \rangle$, where each component x_1 and x_2 is an atom. For example, if the atoms are A, B, and C, then

$$\langle A, B \rangle, \quad \langle B, A \rangle, \quad \text{and } \langle C, A \rangle$$

are all pairs. The intended domain consists of both the atoms and the pairs of atoms.

The vocabulary of the theory of pairs consists of the equality predicate symbol $=$ and of

- A unary predicate symbol $atom(x)$

- A unary predicate symbol $pair(x)$

- A binary function symbol $\langle x_1, x_2 \rangle$, denoting the *pairing* function.

The predicate symbol $atom(x)$ is true if x is an atom and false if x is a pair; $pair(x)$ is true if x is a pair and false if x is an atom. The value of the pairing function $\langle x_1, x_2 \rangle$ is the pair whose first element is the atom x_1 and whose second element is the atom x_2.

Again, do not be confused; we are not adding a new notation $\langle x_1, x_2 \rangle$ to the formal language of predicate logic; we are merely adopting informally the familiar mathematical notation for a pair to represent a standard predicate-logic binary function symbol, such as $f_{101}(x_1, x_2)$.

The theory of pairs is defined by the special axioms:

$$\mathcal{P}_1: \quad (\textit{for all } x) \begin{bmatrix} pair(x) \\ \textit{if and only if} \\ (\textit{for some } x_1) \\ (\textit{for some } x_2) \end{bmatrix} \begin{bmatrix} atom(x_1) \ \ and \ \ atom(x_2) \\ and \\ x = \langle x_1, x_2 \rangle \end{bmatrix} \qquad (pair)$$

In other words, every pair is of form $\langle x_1, x_2 \rangle$, where x_1 and x_2 are atoms.

$$\mathcal{P}_2: \quad (\textit{for all } x)\big[not \ (atom(x) \ \ and \ \ pair(x))\big] \qquad (disjoint)$$

In other words, no domain element is both an atom and a pair.

$$\mathcal{P}_3: \quad \begin{matrix} (\textit{for all } x_1)(\textit{for all } x_2) \\ (\textit{for all } y_1)(\textit{for all } y_2) \end{matrix} \begin{bmatrix} if \begin{bmatrix} atom(x_1) \ \ and \ \ atom(x_2) \\ and \\ atom(y_1) \ \ and \ \ atom(y_2) \end{bmatrix} \\ then \ \ if \ \langle x_1, x_2 \rangle = \langle y_1, y_2 \rangle \\ then \ \ x_1 = y_1 \ \ and \ \ x_2 = y_2 \end{bmatrix}$$

$$(uniqueness)$$

In other words, a pair can be constructed in only one way from two atoms.

Remark (pairs of nonatoms)

Note that the axioms do not specify the result of applying the pairing function $\langle x_1, x_2 \rangle$ if x_1 or x_2 is itself a pair rather than an atom. Although expressions of this form are legal in the language of the theory of pairs and although they must have some values under any interpretation, the axioms do not determine these values. Thus if x_1 and x_2 are not both atoms under a given model, the term $\langle x_1, x_2 \rangle$ might have the value A or $\langle$A, B$\rangle$ or $\langle$B, C$\rangle$. We simply do not care what the value of the pairing function is in this case. ◢

Because the theory of pairs is a theory with equality, we also have the *transitivity*, *symmetry*, and *reflexivity* axioms $\mathcal{E}_1$, $\mathcal{E}_2$, and $\mathcal{E}_3$ for equality. Because the pairing function $\langle x_1, x_2 \rangle$ is in our vocabulary, we include the corresponding instances of the *functional-substitutivity* axiom schema $\mathcal{E}_4$ for equality:

$$
\begin{array}{l}
(\textit{for all } x_1) \\
(\textit{for all } x_1') \\
(\textit{for all } x_2)
\end{array}
\left[
\begin{array}{l}
\textit{if } x_1 = x_1' \\
\textit{then } \langle x_1, x_2 \rangle = \langle x_1', x_2 \rangle
\end{array}
\right]
$$

(*left functional substitutivity for pairing*)

$$
\begin{array}{l}
(\textit{for all } x_1) \\
(\textit{for all } x_2) \\
(\textit{for all } x_2')
\end{array}
\left[
\begin{array}{l}
\textit{if } x_2 = x_2' \\
\textit{then } \langle x_1, x_2 \rangle = \langle x_1, x_2' \rangle
\end{array}
\right]
$$

(*right functional substitutivity for pairing*)

We must also include the instances of the *predicate-substitutivity* axiom schema $\mathcal{E}_5$ for equality that apply to the *atom* predicate,

$$
\begin{array}{l}
(\textit{for all } x) \\
(\textit{for all } y)
\end{array}
\left[
\begin{array}{l}
\textit{if } x = y \\
\textit{then } atom(x) \\
\qquad\qquad \textit{if and only if} \\
\qquad atom(y)
\end{array}
\right]
\qquad (\textit{predicate substitutivity for atom})
$$

and to the *pair* predicate,

$$
\begin{array}{l}
(\textit{for all } x) \\
(\textit{for all } y)
\end{array}
\left[
\begin{array}{l}
\textit{if } x = y \\
\textit{then } pair(x) \\
\qquad\qquad \textit{if and only if} \\
\qquad pair(y)
\end{array}
\right]
\qquad (\textit{predicate substitutivity for pair})
$$

because these symbols are in our vocabulary.

Example (pairs of integers)

Consider the interpretation $\mathcal{I}$ over the set of integers and pairs of integers under which

- The unary predicate symbol $atom(x)$ is the relation that is true if $x_{\mathcal{I}}$ is an integer and false if $x_{\mathcal{I}}$ is a pair.

- The unary predicate symbol $pair(x)$ is the relation that is true if $x_{\mathcal{I}}$ is a pair and false if $x_{\mathcal{I}}$ is an integer.

- The binary function symbol $\langle x_1, x_2 \rangle$ is any function k such that $k(d_1, d_2)$ is the pair $\langle d_1, d_2 \rangle$, for all integers d_1 and d_2; we do not care what the value of $k(d_1, d_2)$ is if d_1 or d_2 is itself a pair.

The reader may confirm that $\mathcal{I}$ is a model for the theory of pairs. $\blacksquare$

THE FIRST AND SECOND FUNCTIONS

Let us now augment our theory of pairs by adding to our vocabulary two unary function symbols *first* and *second*. Intuitively speaking, $first(x)$ and $second(x)$ are the first and second elements, respectively, of the pair x. The axioms that define these functions follow:

$$P_4 : \quad \begin{array}{l} (for\ all\ x_1) \\ (for\ all\ x_2) \end{array} \left[\begin{array}{l} if\ atom(x_1)\ \ and\ atom(x_2) \\ then\ \ first(\langle x_1,\ x_2 \rangle) = x_1 \end{array} \right] \qquad (first)$$

$$P_5 : \quad \begin{array}{l} (for\ all\ x_1) \\ (for\ all\ x_2) \end{array} \left[\begin{array}{l} if\ atom(x_1)\ \ and\ atom(x_2) \\ then\ \ second(\langle x_1,\ x_2 \rangle) = x_2 \end{array} \right] \qquad (second)$$

Note that the axioms do not specify the values of an expression of the form $first(x)$ or $second(x)$ if x is an atom rather than a pair. We do not care what value is assigned to such an expression under a model for the augmented theory.

For clarity we shall refer to the theory of pairs without the definitions of *first* and *second* as the "original" theory and to the theory of pairs with the definitions of *first* and *second* as the "augmented" theory. By the *containment* proposition, every sentence valid in the original theory is also valid in the augmented theory.

Because the augmented theory contains two new function symbols in its vocabulary, we automatically provide the corresponding instances of the *functional-substitutivity* axiom schema $\mathcal{E}_4$ for equality:

$$\begin{array}{l} (for\ all\ x) \\ (for\ all\ y) \end{array} \left[\begin{array}{l} if\ x = y \\ then\ first(x) = first(y) \end{array} \right] \quad (functional\ substitutivity\ for\ first)$$

$$\begin{array}{l} (for\ all\ x) \\ (for\ all\ y) \end{array} \left[\begin{array}{l} if\ x = y \\ then\ second(x) = second(y) \end{array} \right]$$
$$(functional\ substitutivity\ for\ second)$$

As we have remarked, when we augment a theory by introducing new axioms we run the risk of making our theory inconsistent: No model will satisfy the augmented set of axioms, and therefore any sentence will be valid in the augmented theory. Here, however, we can establish that the definitions of the *first* and *second* functions do not introduce an inconsistency.

Proposition (consistency of first and second)

If I is any model for the original theory of pairs, there exists a model J for the augmented theory of pairs.

Furthermore, J and I agree on all symbols except perhaps the function symbols *first* and *second*. ⌐

We give the proof in some detail.

Proof

We shall establish that the sentences

$$\mathcal{F}_1: \quad (\textit{for all } x)(\textit{for some } y)\genfrac{}{}{0pt}{}{(\textit{for all } x_1)}{(\textit{for all } x_2)}\left[\begin{array}{l}\textit{if } x = \langle x_1,\, x_2\rangle \\ \textit{then if } atom(x_1) \ \textit{ and } \ atom(x_2) \\ \qquad \textit{then } \ y = x_1\end{array}\right]$$

and

$$\mathcal{F}_2: \quad (\textit{for all } x)(\textit{for some } y)\genfrac{}{}{0pt}{}{(\textit{for all } x_1)}{(\textit{for all } x_2)}\left[\begin{array}{l}\textit{if } x = \langle x_1,\, x_2\rangle \\ \textit{then if } atom(x_1) \ \textit{ and } \ atom(x_2) \\ \qquad \textit{then } \ y = x_2\end{array}\right]$$

are valid in the original theory of pairs. Before we do this, however, let us see why these sentences help us establish the proposition.

If $\mathcal{F}_1$ is valid in the original theory of pairs, then by the *function-introduction* proposition of predicate logic, the sentence

$$\mathcal{G}_1: \quad (\textit{for all } x)\genfrac{}{}{0pt}{}{(\textit{for all } x_1)}{(\textit{for all } x_2)}\left[\begin{array}{l}\textit{if } x = \langle x_1,\, x_2\rangle \\ \textit{then if } atom(x_1) \ \textit{ and } \ atom(x_2) \\ \qquad \textit{then } \ first(x) = x_1\end{array}\right]$$

is true under some interpretation I', where I and I' agree on all symbols except perhaps the function symbol *first*. Equivalently (rearranging the quantifiers),

$$\genfrac{}{}{0pt}{}{(\textit{for all } x_1)}{(\textit{for all } x_2)}(\textit{for all } x)\left[\begin{array}{l}\textit{if } x = \langle x_1,\, x_2\rangle \\ \textit{then if } atom(x_1) \ \textit{ and } \ atom(x_2) \\ \qquad \textit{then } \ first(x) = x_1\end{array}\right]$$

is true under I'. Equivalently (by the *replacement* property of the theory of equality), the definition of *first*, that is,

$$\genfrac{}{}{0pt}{}{(\textit{for all } x_1)}{(\textit{for all } x_2)}\left[\begin{array}{l}\textit{if } atom(x_1) \ \textit{ and } \ atom(x_2) \\ \textit{then } first(\langle x_1,\, x_2\rangle) = x_1\end{array}\right]$$

,

is true under I'.

Similarly, if $\mathcal{F}_2$ is also valid in the theory of pairs, then, by the *function-introduction* proposition, there exists an interpretation J such that the definition of *second*, that is,

$$(for\ all\ x_1) \begin{bmatrix} if\ atom(x_1)\ and\ atom(x_2) \\ then\ second(\langle x_1,\ x_2 \rangle) = x_2 \end{bmatrix}$$
$$(for\ all\ x_2)$$

is true under J, where J and I' agree on all symbols except perhaps the function symbol *second*.

We now show that J satisfies the required conditions of the proposition.

We know that J and I' agree on all symbols except perhaps the function symbol *second*, and that I' and I agree on all symbols except perhaps the function symbol *first*; therefore J and I agree on all symbols except perhaps the two function symbols *first* and *second*.

We have assumed that I is a model for the original theory of pairs. Also, the function symbols *first* and *second* do not occur in axioms for the original theory. Because I and J agree on all symbols except perhaps *first* and *second*, we know (by the *agreement* proposition) that J is also a model for the original theory.

We have constructed I' so that the definition of *first* is true under I'. Because J and I' agree on all symbols except perhaps the function symbol *second* and because *second* does not occur in the definition of *first*, we know (by the *agreement* proposition again) that the definition of *first* is true under J.

We have constructed J so that the definition of *second* is true under J.

In short, J is a model for the augmented theory of pairs, and J and I agree on all symbols except perhaps *first* and *second*, as we wanted to show.

It remains to establish the validity of the sentences $\mathcal{F}_1$ and $\mathcal{F}_2$ in the original theory. Let us show the validity of $\mathcal{F}_1$; the proof of $\mathcal{F}_2$ is similar.

Proof of $\mathcal{F}_1$

We would like to show that

$$(for\ all\ x)(for\ some\ y)\genfrac{}{}{0pt}{}{(for\ all\ x_1)}{(for\ all\ x_2)} \begin{bmatrix} if\ x = \langle x_1,\ x_2 \rangle \\ then\ if\ atom(x_1)\ and\ atom(x_2) \\ then\ y = x_1 \end{bmatrix}$$

is valid in the original theory of pairs.

Consider an arbitrary element x. The proof distinguishes between two cases, depending on whether or not x is a pair.

Case: $pair(x)$

Then (by the *pair* axiom $\mathcal{P}_1$)

$$(\textit{for some } y_1) \atop (\textit{for some } y_2) \left[{atom(y_1) \textit{ and } atom(y_2) \atop \textit{and} \atop x = \langle y_1, y_2 \rangle} \right].$$

(Note that we have renamed the bound variables x_1 and x_2 in the axiom to y_1 and y_2, respectively.) Let y_1 and y_2 be arbitrary elements such that

$$atom(y_1) \textit{ and } atom(y_2)$$
$$\textit{and}$$
$$x = \langle y_1, y_2 \rangle,$$

that is (by the *symmetry* axiom of equality),

$$\langle y_1, y_2 \rangle = x.$$

Take y to be the atom y_1; it suffices to show that

$$(\textit{for all } x_1) \atop (\textit{for all } x_2) \left[{\textit{if } x = \langle x_1, x_2 \rangle \atop \textit{then if } atom(x_1) \textit{ and } atom(x_2) \atop \textit{then } y_1 = x_1} \right].$$

Now let x_1 and x_2 be arbitrary elements such that

$$x = \langle x_1, x_2 \rangle$$

and

$$atom(x_1) \textit{ and } atom(x_2).$$

We would like to show that

$$y_1 = x_1.$$

Because $\langle y_1, y_2 \rangle = x$ and $x = \langle x_1, x_2 \rangle$, we have (by the *transitivity* axiom for equality)

$$\langle y_1, y_2 \rangle = \langle x_1, x_2 \rangle.$$

Therefore (by the *uniqueness* axiom $\mathcal{P}_3$ for pairs), because $atom(x_1)$, $atom(x_2)$, $atom(y_1)$, and $atom(y_2)$, we have

$$y_1 = x_1 \textit{ and } y_2 = x_2.$$

In particular, $y_1 = x_1$, as we wanted to show.

Case: not pair(x)

Then (by the *pair* axiom P_1)

$$not \begin{matrix} (for\ some\ y_1) \\ (for\ some\ y_2) \end{matrix} \begin{bmatrix} atom(y_1)\ \ and\ \ atom(y_2) \\ and \\ x = \langle y_1,\ y_2 \rangle \end{bmatrix}$$

or, equivalently (by the duality of quatifiers),

$$(*) \qquad \begin{matrix} (for\ all\ y_1) \\ (for\ all\ y_2) \end{matrix} not \begin{bmatrix} atom(y_1)\ \ and\ \ atom(y_2) \\ and \\ x = \langle y_1,\ y_2 \rangle \end{bmatrix}.$$

Take y to be any element and consider arbitrary elements x_1 and x_2; we would like to show that

$$if\ x = \langle x_1,\ x_2 \rangle$$
$$then\ if\ atom(x_1)\ \ and\ \ atom(x_2)$$
$$then\ y = x_1$$

or, equivalently (by propositional logic),

$$if \begin{bmatrix} atom(x_1)\ \ and\ \ atom(x_2) \\ and \\ x = \langle x_1,\ x_2 \rangle \end{bmatrix}$$
$$then\ y = x_1.$$

By condition $(*)$, taking y_1 and y_2 to be x_1 and x_2, respectively, we have that

$$not \begin{bmatrix} atom(x_1)\ \ and\ \ atom(x_2) \\ and \\ x = \langle x_1,\ x_2 \rangle \end{bmatrix}.$$

Therefore (by propositional logic), because its antecedent is false, the desired implication is true.

We have established the desired result whether or not $pair(x)$ is true; this concludes the proof of $\mathcal{F}_1$. The proof of $\mathcal{F}_2$ is similar. ◢

To ensure consistency, we must establish such a proposition every time we augment a theory by defining new function symbols. However, we shall often omit these propositions.

We can easily establish the validity of the following sentences in the theory of pairs:

For the *first* function we have

$$(\textit{for all } x) \begin{bmatrix} \textit{if } pair(x) \\ \textit{then } atom\,(first(x)) \end{bmatrix} \qquad (\textit{sort of first})$$

For the *second* function we have

$$(\textit{for all } x) \begin{bmatrix} \textit{if } pair(x) \\ \textit{then } atom\,(second(x)) \end{bmatrix} \qquad (\textit{sort of second})$$

Often we refer to a unary predicate symbol, which characterizes a set of domain elements, as a "sort." The above properties are called the *sort* properties of the *first* and *second* function, respectively, because they establish that if a given element x is of sort *pair*, then $first(x)$ and $second(x)$ are elements of sort *atom*.

THE DECOMPOSITION PROPERTY

In the augmented theory of pairs we can establish the following result.

Proposition (decomposition)

The sentence

$$(\textit{for all } x) \begin{bmatrix} \textit{if } pair(x) \\ \textit{then } x \;=\; \langle first(x),\; second(x) \rangle \end{bmatrix} \quad (\textit{decomposition})$$

is valid in the augmented theory of pairs. ⏌

In other words, any pair is the result of pairing its first and second elements.

Proof

For an arbitrary element x, suppose that

$$pair(x).$$

We would like to show that

$$x \;=\; \langle first(x),\; second(x) \rangle.$$

stands for

(for

which stands for

(for

We can app

Definition (m

For any un
$\mathcal{F}[x_1, x_2, \ldots, x_i$

(for
(for

(for

stands for

(for
(for

(for

and

(for
(for

(for

stands for

(for
(for

(for

We know (by the *pair* axiom $\mathcal{P}_1$) that

$$(\text{for some } x_1) \atop (\text{for some } x_2) \left[{atom(x_1) \ \ and \ \ atom(x_2) \atop {and \atop x = \langle x_1, \, x_2 \rangle}} \right].$$

Let x_1 and x_2 be elements such that

$$atom(x_1) \ \ and \ \ atom(x_2)$$
$$and$$
$$x = \langle x_1, \, x_2 \rangle.$$

Then (by the *symmetry* axiom for equality)

$$\langle x_1, \, x_2 \rangle = x.$$

We have (by the definitions of *first* and *second*)

$$if \ \ atom(x_1) \ \ and \ \ atom(x_2)$$
$$then \ \ first(\langle x_1, \, x_2 \rangle) = x_1$$

and

$$if \ \ atom(x_1) \ \ and \ \ atom(x_2)$$
$$then \ \ second(\langle x_1, \, x_2 \rangle) = x_2.$$

Therefore (by propositional logic, because $atom(x_1)$ and $atom(x_2)$)

$$first(\langle x_1, \, x_2 \rangle) = x_1$$

and

$$second(\langle x_1, \, x_2 \rangle) = x_2,$$

that is (by the *functional-substitutivity* equality axiom for *first* and *second*, because $\langle x_1, \, x_2 \rangle = x$),

$$first(x) = x_1$$

and

$$second(x) = x_2.$$

Therefore (by the *symmetry* axiom for equality)

$$x_1 = first(x)$$

and

$$x_2 = second(x).$$

Finally (
function, bec:

x

and therefore
function)

x

as we wanted

We now intro
breviate sent
quantifiers to
entire domair

Definition (

For any

(*f*

(*f*

Examples

For a bir

(*f*

stands for

(*f*

The sent

(*f*

Examples

The sentence

$$(\text{for all atom } x_1) \atop (\text{for all atom } x_2) \left[\mathit{first}(\langle x_1,\ x_2\rangle) = x_1 \right]$$

stands for

$$(\text{for all } x_1) \atop (\text{for all } x_2) \left[\begin{array}{l} \textit{if } atom(x_1) \ \textit{ and } \ atom(x_2) \\ \textit{then } \mathit{first}(\langle x_1,\ x_2\rangle) = x_1 \end{array} \right].$$

The sentence

$$(\text{for some pair } x) \atop (\text{for some pair } y) \left[x \prec y \ \textit{ and } \ y \prec x \right]$$

stands for

$$(\text{for some } x) \atop (\text{for some } y) \left[\begin{array}{l} pair(x) \ \textit{ and } \ pair(y) \\ \textit{and} \\ x \prec y \ \textit{ and } \ y \prec x \end{array} \right].$$

The sentence

$$(\text{for all pair } x){(\text{for some atom } x_1) \atop (\text{for some atom } x_2)} \left[x = \langle x_1,\ x_2\rangle \right]$$

stands for

$$(\text{for all } x) \left[\begin{array}{l} \textit{if } pair(x) \\ \textit{then } {(\text{for some atom } x_1) \atop (\text{for some atom } x_2)} \left[x = \langle x_1,\ x_2\rangle \right] \end{array} \right],$$

which stands for

$$(\text{for all } x) \left[\begin{array}{l} \textit{if } pair(x) \\ \textit{then } {(\text{for some } x_1) \atop (\text{for some } x_2)} \left[\begin{array}{l} atom(x_1) \ \textit{ and } \ atom(x_2) \\ \textit{and} \\ x = \langle x_1,\ x_2\rangle \end{array} \right] \end{array} \right].$$

The relativized quantifier notation can make the sentences in our theory of pairs somewhat clearer. For example, the definition $\mathcal{P}_1$ of the *pair* relation, which was originally written as

$$(\text{for all } x) \left[\begin{array}{l} pair(x) \\ \quad \textit{if and only if} \\ {(\text{for some } x_1) \atop (\text{for some } x_2)} \left[\begin{array}{l} atom(x_1) \ \textit{ and } \ atom(x_2) \\ \textit{and} \\ x = \langle x_1,\ x_2\rangle \end{array} \right] \end{array} \right],$$

can now be abbreviated as

$$(\textit{for all } x) \begin{bmatrix} pair(x) \\ \textit{if and only if} \\ (\textit{for some atom } x_1) \\ (\textit{for some atom } x_2) \end{bmatrix} \begin{bmatrix} x = \langle x_1, x_2 \rangle \end{bmatrix} .$$

The *uniqueness* axiom P_3 for pairs, which was originally written as

$$\begin{matrix} (\textit{for all } x_1)(\textit{for all } x_2) \\ (\textit{for all } y_1)(\textit{for all } y_2) \end{matrix} \begin{bmatrix} \textit{if} \begin{bmatrix} atom(x_1) \ and \ atom(x_2) \\ and \\ atom(y_1) \ and \ atom(y_2) \end{bmatrix} \\ \textit{then if } \langle x_1, x_2 \rangle = \langle y_1, y_2 \rangle \\ \textit{then } x_1 = y_1 \ and \ x_2 = y_2 \end{bmatrix} ,$$

can now be abbreviated as

$$\begin{matrix} (\textit{for all atom } x_1)(\textit{for all atom } x_2) \\ (\textit{for all atom } y_1)(\textit{for all atom } y_2) \end{matrix} \begin{bmatrix} \textit{if } \langle x_1, x_2 \rangle = \langle y_1, y_2 \rangle \\ \textit{then } x_1 = y_1 \ and \ x_2 = y_2 \end{bmatrix} .$$

The definitions P_4 and P_5 of the *first* and *second* functions can now be abbreviated as

$$\begin{matrix} (\textit{for all atom } x_1) \\ (\textit{for all atom } x_2) \end{matrix} \begin{bmatrix} first(\langle x_1, x_2 \rangle) = x_1 \end{bmatrix}$$

and

$$\begin{matrix} (\textit{for all atom } x_1) \\ (\textit{for all atom } x_2) \end{matrix} \begin{bmatrix} second(\langle x_1, x_2 \rangle) = x_2 \end{bmatrix} .$$

The *decomposition* proposition may be written as

$$(\textit{for all pair } x) \begin{bmatrix} x = \langle first(x), \ second(x) \rangle \end{bmatrix} .$$

When we need to prove a sentence expressed in terms of relativized quantifiers, we can always abandon the abbreviation, rephrase the sentence in terms of ordinary quantifiers, and use the ordinary rules of predicate logic. Alternatively, we can introduce rules for proving sentences with relativized quantifiers and often retain the abbreviation. The new rules resemble some of the ordinary rules.

In particular, we have, for all unary predicate symbols p and q and sentences $\mathcal{F}$,

• *Reversal of quantifiers*

$$\begin{matrix} (\textit{for all } p \ x) \\ (\textit{for all } q \ y) \end{matrix} \mathcal{F} \qquad \text{is equivalent to} \qquad \begin{matrix} (\textit{for all } q \ y) \\ (\textit{for all } p \ x) \end{matrix} \mathcal{F}$$

and

$$\begin{matrix} (for\ some\ p\ x) \\ (for\ some\ q\ y) \end{matrix} \mathcal{F} \quad \text{is equivalent to} \quad \begin{matrix} (for\ some\ q\ y) \\ (for\ some\ p\ x) \end{matrix} \mathcal{F}.$$

- *Duality of quantifiers*

$$(for\ all\ p\ x)[not\ \mathcal{F}] \quad \text{is equivalent to} \quad not\ (for\ some\ p\ x)\mathcal{F}$$

and

$$(for\ some\ p\ x)[not\ \mathcal{F}] \quad \text{is equivalent to} \quad not\ (for\ all\ p\ x)\mathcal{F}.$$

Let us justify the last of these equivalences.

Proposition (duality of relativized quantifiers)

For any unary predicate symbol p and sentence $\mathcal{F}$,

$$(for\ some\ p\ x)[not\ \mathcal{F}] \quad \text{is equivalent to} \quad not\ (for\ all\ p\ x)\mathcal{F}. \quad \lrcorner$$

Proof

We have

$$(for\ some\ p\ x)[not\ \mathcal{F}]$$

is an abbreviation of

$$(for\ some\ x) \begin{bmatrix} p(x) \\ and \\ not\ \mathcal{F} \end{bmatrix},$$

which is equivalent (by propositional logic) to

$$(for\ some\ x)\ not\ \begin{bmatrix} if\ p(x) \\ then\ \mathcal{F} \end{bmatrix},$$

which is equivalent (by the duality property of ordinary quantifiers) to

$$not\ (for\ all\ x) \begin{bmatrix} if\ p(x) \\ then\ \mathcal{F} \end{bmatrix},$$

which may be abbreviated as

$$not\ (for\ all\ p\ x)\mathcal{F}.$$

This establishes the desired equivalence.   ⌟

The reader is requested (in **Problem 5.9**) to prove two additional equivalences concerning relativized quantifiers.

Remark (pitfall)

We must be careful not to apply properties of ordinary quantifiers blindly to relativized quantifiers. For example, the sentence

> *if (for all x)q(x)*
> *then (for some x)q(x)*

is valid. However, for any unary predicate symbol p, the analogous sentence with relativized quantifiers,

> *if (for all p x)q(x)*
> *then (for some p x)q(x),*

is not valid. The sentence stands for the sentence

> *if (for all x)[if p(x) then q(x)]*
> *then (for some x)[p(x) and q(x)],*

which is false under any interpretation in which $p(x)$ is always false. For the antecedent of this implication is true vacuously, but its consequent is false.

On the other hand, the sentence is true under any interpretation in which $p(x)$ is not always false.

Exercising due care, we may apply to relativized quantifiers results that have been established for ordinary quantifiers.   ⌟

5.7   THE LEXICOGRAPHIC RELATION

We now augment our theory of pairs further by adding two binary-predicate symbols $x_1 \prec y_1$ and $x \prec_{lex} y$ to our vocabulary. In our intended models, for an arbitrary binary relation $\prec$ over the atoms, $\prec_{lex}$ denotes a relation over the pairs, called the *lexicographic relation (corresponding to $\prec$)*, defined by the following axiom:

$$
\begin{array}{ll}
\begin{aligned}
&(\textit{for all atom } x_1)(\textit{for all atom } x_2) \\
&(\textit{for all atom } y_1)(\textit{for all atom } y_2)
\end{aligned}
&
\left[
\begin{array}{l}
\langle x_1,\, x_2 \rangle \prec_{lex} \langle y_1,\, y_2 \rangle \\
\quad \textit{if and only if} \\
\left[
\begin{array}{l}
x_1 \prec y_1 \\
\quad \textit{or} \\
x_1 = y_1 \ \ \textit{and} \ \ x_2 \prec y_2
\end{array}
\right]
\end{array}
\right]
\end{array}
$$

$$
(\textit{lexicographic relation})
$$

Intuitively speaking, the lexicographic relation between two pairs initially compares the first elements x_1 and y_1 of the pairs; if these are equal, it compares the second elements x_2 and y_2. The lexicographic relation $\prec_{lex}$ depends on the relation $\prec$; for each binary relation there corresponds a different lexicographic relation.

As usual, because the augmented theory provides two new predicate symbols, $\prec$ and $\prec_{lex}$, in its vocabulary, we automatically provide the corresponding instances of the predicate substitutivity axiom schema $\mathcal{E}_5$ for equality.

We shall call the theory of pairs augmented by the above definition the *theory of the lexicographic relation $\prec_{lex}$ (corresponding to $\prec$).*

Example

Consider any interpretation $\mathcal{I}$ over the set of integers and pairs of integers that is a model for the theory of pairs, under which

- The binary predicate symbol $\prec$ is a relation $p_{\mathcal{I}}(d_1, e_1)$ such that, for any integers d_1 and e_1,

  $p_{\mathcal{I}}(d_1, e_1)$ is true if $d_1 < e_1$

  $p_{\mathcal{I}}(d_1, e_1)$ is false otherwise, that is, if $d_1 \geq e_1$.

  In other words, $p_{\mathcal{I}}$ is the less-than relation $<$ on the integers. We do not care if $p_{\mathcal{I}}(d, e)$ is true or false if either of its arguments d or e is a pair rather than an integer.

- The binary predicate symbol $\prec_{lex}$ is a relation $<_{lex}$ such that, for any integers d_1, d_2, e_1, and e_2,

  $\langle d_1,\, d_2 \rangle <_{lex} \langle e_1,\, e_2 \rangle$ is true if $d_1 < e_1$

  $\langle d_1,\, d_2 \rangle <_{lex} \langle e_1,\, e_2 \rangle$ is true if $d_1 = e_1$ and $d_2 < e_2$

  $\langle d_1,\, d_2 \rangle <_{lex} \langle e_1,\, e_2 \rangle$ is false if $d_1 > e_1$

  $\langle d_1,\, d_2 \rangle <_{lex} \langle e_1,\, e_2 \rangle$ is false if $d_1 = e_1$ and $d_2 \geq e_2$.

We do not care if $d <_{lex} e$ is true or false if either of its arguments d or e is an integer rather than a pair.

According to the definition of the relation $<_{lex}$,

$\langle 1,\ 100 \rangle <_{lex} \langle 2,\ 2 \rangle$ is true because $1 < 2$

$\langle 1,\ 2 \rangle <_{lex} \langle 1,\ 3 \rangle$ is true because $1 = 1$ and $2 < 3$

$\langle 2,\ 100 \rangle <_{lex} \langle 1,\ 100 \rangle$ is false because $2 > 1$

$\langle 100,\ 0 \rangle <_{lex} \langle 100,\ -1 \rangle$ is false because $100 = 100$ and $0 \geq -1$.

The relations assigned to $\prec$ and $\prec_{lex}$ must be defined for all elements of the domain of the interpretation; thus the relation assigned to $\prec$ under I must have a value for pairs (as well as for integers), and the relation assigned to $\prec_{lex}$ must have a value for integers (as well as for pairs); but these assignments are arbitrary.

The reader may confirm that I is a model for the theory of the lexicographic relation $\prec_{lex}$. ⌟

We can now establish that certain properties of the binary relation $\prec$ over the atoms are inherited by the corresponding lexicographic relation $\prec_{lex}$ over the pairs, including transitivity, asymmetry, and irreflexivity.

Proposition (transitivity)

Consider the theory of the lexicographic relation $\prec_{lex}$ corresponding to a relation $\prec$, and augmented by the *transitivity* axiom for $\prec$ over atoms, that is,

$$\begin{array}{l}(\textit{for all atom } x_1) \\ (\textit{for all atom } y_1) \\ (\textit{for all atom } z_1)\end{array} \left[\begin{array}{l}\textit{if } x_1 \prec y_1 \ \textit{ and } \ y_1 \prec z_1 \\ \textit{then } x_1 \prec z_1\end{array}\right] \qquad (\textit{transitivity of } \prec)$$

In this theory, the lexicographic relation $\prec_{lex}$ is transitive over pairs, i.e., the sentence

$$\begin{array}{l}(\textit{for all pair } x) \\ (\textit{for all pair } y) \\ (\textit{for all pair } z)\end{array} \left[\begin{array}{l}\textit{if } x \prec_{lex} y \ \textit{ and } \ y \prec_{lex} z \\ \textit{then } x \prec_{lex} z\end{array}\right] \qquad (\textit{transitivity of } \prec_{lex})$$

is valid. ⌟

Proof

Suppose x, y, and z are pairs, that is,

$$pair(x) \ and \ pair(y) \ and \ pair(z),$$

and that

$$x \prec_{lex} y \ and \ y \prec_{lex} z.$$

We would like to establish that then

$$x \prec_{lex} z.$$

Because x, y, and z are pairs, we know (by the definition of the *pair* relation) that they can be decomposed into atoms, i.e., there exist elements x_1, x_2, y_1, y_2, z_1, and z_2 such that

$$atom(x_1) \ and \ atom(x_2)$$
$$and$$
$$x = \langle x_1, \ x_2 \rangle$$

$$atom(y_1) \ and \ atom(y_2)$$
$$and$$
$$y = \langle y_1, \ y_2 \rangle$$

$$atom(z_1) \ and \ atom(z_2)$$
$$and$$
$$z = \langle z_1, \ z_2 \rangle.$$

Therefore (by the *left* and *right predicate-substitutivity* equality axioms for $\prec_{lex}$, applied six times) we know

$$\langle x_1, \ x_2 \rangle \prec_{lex} \langle y_1, \ y_2 \rangle \quad and \quad \langle y_1, \ y_2 \rangle \prec_{lex} \langle z_1, \ z_2 \rangle$$

and would like to show

$$\langle x_1, \ x_2 \rangle \prec_{lex} \langle z_1, \ z_2 \rangle.$$

Because x_1, x_2, y_1, y_2, z_1, and z_2 are all atoms, we know (by the definition of the lexicographic relation) that

$$
(\dagger) \quad
\begin{matrix}
x_1 \prec y_1 \\
or \\
x_1 = y_1 \ and \ x_2 \prec y_2
\end{matrix}
\quad and \quad
\begin{matrix}
y_1 \prec z_1 \\
or \\
y_1 = z_1 \ and \ y_2 \prec z_2
\end{matrix}
$$

and would like to show that

$$
(\ddagger) \quad
\begin{matrix}
x_1 \prec z_1 \\
or \\
x_1 = z_1 \ and \ x_2 \prec z_2.
\end{matrix}
$$

Our proof distinguishes among four cases, depending on whether $x_1 \prec y_1$ and whether $y_1 \prec z_1$.

Case: $x_1 \prec y_1$ *and* $y_1 \prec z_1$

Then (by the *transitivity* axiom for $\prec$)

$$x_1 \prec z_1.$$

Therefore (by propositional logic)

$$x_1 \prec z_1$$
$$or$$
$$x_1 = z_1 \;\; and \;\; x_2 \prec z_2,$$

which is our desired conclusion (‡).

Case: $x_1 \prec y_1$ *and* $not\,(y_1 \prec z_1)$

Then (by our earlier conclusion (†), because *not* $(y_1 \prec z_1)$)

$$y_1 = z_1.$$

Therefore (by the *right-substitutivity* equality axiom for $\prec$, because $x_1 \prec y_1$)

$$x_1 \prec z_1.$$

Hence (by propositional logic)

$$x_1 \prec z_1$$
$$or$$
$$x_1 = z_1 \;\; and \;\; x_2 \prec z_2,$$

which is our desired conclusion (‡).

Case: $not\,(x_1 \prec y_1)$ *and* $y_1 \prec z_1$

This case is similar to the previous case.

Case: $not\,(x_1 \prec y_1)$ *and* $not\,(y_1 \prec z_1)$

Then (by our earlier conclusion (†))

$$x_1 = y_1 \;\; and \;\; x_2 \prec y_2$$

and

$$y_1 = z_1 \;\; and \;\; y_2 \prec z_2.$$

We know (by the *transitivity* axiom for equality, because $x_1 = y_1$ and $y_1 = z_1$) that

$$x_1 = z_1.$$

We also know (by the *transitivity* axiom for $\prec$, because $x_2 \prec y_2$ and $y_2 \prec z_2$) that

$$x_2 \prec z_2.$$

Therefore (by propositional logic)

$$x_1 \prec z_1$$
$$or$$
$$x_1 = z_1 \;\; and \;\; x_2 \prec z_2,$$

which is our desired conclusion (‡). ⌐

The asymmetry of the relation $\prec$ over the atoms is inherited by the corresponding lexicographic relation $\prec_{lex}$ over the pairs.

Proposition (asymmetry)

Consider the theory of the lexicographic relation $\prec_{lex}$ corresponding to a relation $\prec$, augmented by the *asymmetry* axiom for $\prec$ over the atoms, that is,

$$(\textit{for all atom } x_1) \begin{bmatrix} \textit{if } x_1 \prec y_1 \\ \textit{then } not\,(y_1 \prec x_1) \end{bmatrix} \qquad (\textit{asymmetry of } \prec)$$
$$(\textit{for all atom } y_1)$$

In this theory the lexicographic relation $\prec_{lex}$ is asymmetric over the pairs, i.e., the sentence

$$(\textit{for all pair } x) \begin{bmatrix} \textit{if } x \prec_{lex} y \\ \textit{then } not\,(y \prec_{lex} x) \end{bmatrix} \qquad (\textit{asymmetry of } \prec_{lex})$$
$$(\textit{for all pair } y)$$

is valid. ⌐

The proof is left as an exercise (**Problem 5.10**).

Also, the irreflexivity of the relation $\prec$ over the atoms is inherited by the corresponding lexicographic relation $\prec_{lex}$ over the pairs.

Proposition (irreflexivity)

Consider the theory of the lexicographic relation $\prec_{lex}$ corresponding to a relation $\prec$, augmented by the *irreflexivity* axiom for $\prec$ over the atoms, that is,

$$(for\ all\ atom\ x)\big[not\ (x \prec x)\big] \qquad (irreflexivity\ of \prec)$$

In this theory, the lexicographic relation $\prec_{lex}$ is irreflexive over the pairs; i.e., the sentence

$$(for\ all\ pair\ x)\big[not\ (x \prec_{lex} x)\big] \qquad (irreflexivity\ of \prec_{lex})$$

is valid. ⌐

Proof

Suppose x is a pair, that is,

$$pair(x),$$

and that, contrary to the proposition,

$$x \prec_{lex} x.$$

We would like to derive a contradiction.

Because x is a pair, we know (by the definition of the *pair* relation) that it is constructed from atoms; i.e., there exist elements x_1 and x_2 such that

$$atom(x_1)\ \ and\ \ atom(x_2)$$
$$and$$
$$x = \langle x_1,\ x_2 \rangle.$$

Therefore (by the *left* and *right predicate-substitutivity* equality axioms for $\prec_{lex}$, because $x \prec_{lex} x$)

$$\langle x_1,\ x_2 \rangle \prec_{lex} \langle x_1,\ x_2 \rangle.$$

Because x_1 and x_2 are both atoms, we know (by the definition of the lexicographic relation $\prec_{lex}$) that

$$x_1 \prec x_1$$
$$or$$
$$x_1 = x_1\ \ and\ \ x_2 \prec x_2.$$

But this is a contradiction, because (by the *irreflexivity* axiom for $\prec$)

$$not\ (x_1 \prec x_1)$$

and

$$not \ (x_2 \prec x_2).$$ ⌟

PROBLEMS

Problem 5.1 (replacement)   page 226

Show that the *replacement* proposition would not hold if we had applied the partial substitution operator rather than the total substitution operator. More precisely,

(a) *Universal*

Find a term t and a sentence $\mathcal{F}\langle x \rangle$ such that

$$(for \ all \ x)\big[if \ x = t \ \ then \ \ \mathcal{F}\langle x \rangle\big]$$

is not equivalent to $\mathcal{F}\langle t \rangle$.

(b) *Existential*

Find a term t and a sentence $\mathcal{F}\langle x \rangle$ such that

$$(for \ some \ x)[x = t \ \ and \ \ \mathcal{F}\langle x \rangle]$$

is not equivalent to $\mathcal{F}\langle t \rangle$.

Problem 5.2 (conditional terms)   page 226

Establish the validity of the following sentences in the theory of equality:

(a) *True*

$$(if \ true \ \ then \ a \ \ else \ b) = a$$

(b) *False*

$$(if \ false \ \ then \ a \ \ else \ b) = b$$

(c) *Distributivity*

$$(for \ all \ x) \begin{bmatrix} f\,(if \ p(x) \ \ then \ a \ \ else \ b) \\ = \\ if \ p(x) \ \ then \ f(a) \ \ else \ f(b) \end{bmatrix}.$$

Problem 5.3 (uniqueness of equality)   page 229

Prove the *uniqueness-of-equality* proposition:

In any theory with equality, let $r(x, y)$ be a binary predicate symbol such that the equality axioms $\mathcal{E}_1$ through $\mathcal{E}_5$ are valid for r.

Then the sentence

$$(\textit{for all } x) \atop (\textit{for all } y) \left[\begin{array}{l} r(x, y) \\ \quad \textit{if and only if} \\ x = y \end{array} \right]$$

is valid in the theory.

Problem 5.4 (weak partial ordering)   page 230

Prove that the *transitivity* axiom $\mathcal{W}_1$, the *antisymmetry* axiom $\mathcal{W}_2$, and the *reflexivity* axiom $\mathcal{W}_3$ for the theory of a weak partial ordering $\preceq$ are independent; i.e., for each of these axioms, there is a model for the theory of equality under which the axiom is false but the other two axioms are true.

Problem 5.5 (reflexivity condition)   page 235

In the theory of associated relations, establish that the *reflexivity-condition* property

$$(\textit{for all } x)[x \prec\!\!\!- x]$$
$$\textit{if and only if}$$
$$(\textit{for all } x) \atop (\textit{for all } y) \left[\begin{array}{l} x \prec\!\!\!- y \\ \quad \textit{if and only if} \\ x \preceq y \end{array} \right]$$

is valid. In other words, a relation $\prec\!\!\!-$ is reflexive precisely when it is identical to its reflexive closure.

Problem 5.6 (mixed transitivity)   pages 245, 246

In the theory of associated relations,

(a) Prove the ($\Leftarrow$ *left*), ($\Rightarrow$ *right*), and ($\Leftarrow$ *right*) parts of the *mixed-transitivity* proposition for $\preceq$.

(b) Prove the *mixed-transitivity* proposition for $\prec$.

(c) Show that, in the *mixed-transitivity* proposition for $\prec$, the condition that the given relation $\prec\!\!\!-$ be antisymmetric is essential. In particular, find a non-antisymmetric, transitive relation that does not satisfy the left mixed-transitivity condition.

Problem 5.7 (group theory)   page 253

Prove informally the validity of the following properties in the theory of groups:

(a) *Left identity*

$$(for\ all\ x)[e \circ x = x]$$

[*Hint*: For an arbitrary element x, show that $(e \circ x) \circ x^{-1} = x \circ x^{-1}$.]

(b) *Left inverse*

$$(for\ all\ x)[x^{-1} \circ x = e]$$

[*Hint*: For an arbitrary element x, show that $(x^{-1} \circ x) \circ x^{-1} = e \circ x^{-1}$.]

(c) *Left cancellation*

$$\begin{matrix}(for\ all\ x)\\(for\ all\ y)\\(for\ all\ z)\end{matrix}\left[\begin{matrix}if\ z \circ x = z \circ y\\then\ \ x = y\end{matrix}\right]$$

[*Hint*: For arbitrary elements x, y, and z such that $z \circ x = z \circ y$, show that $(z^{-1} \circ z) \circ x = (z^{-1} \circ z) \circ y$.]

(d) *Nonidempotence*

$$(for\ all\ x)\left[\begin{matrix}if\ x \circ x = x\\then\ \ x = e\end{matrix}\right].$$

Note: The order in which these sentences are presented is significant; the proof of each may rely on the validity of the previous sentences.

Problem 5.8 (permutation interpretation)   page 255

Show that the permutation interpretation K is a model for the theory of groups; i.e., show that

(a) The *right-identity* axiom $\mathcal{G}_1$

(b) The *right-inverse* axiom $\mathcal{G}_2$

(c) The *associativity* axiom $\mathcal{G}_3$

are true under K.

Problem 5.9 (relativized quantifiers)   page 271

For all unary predicate symbols p and sentences $\mathcal{F}$ and $\mathcal{G}$, prove the following:

(a) *Reversal*

$$\begin{matrix} (for\ some\ p\ x) \\ (for\ some\ q\ y) \end{matrix} \mathcal{F} \quad \text{is equivalent to} \quad \begin{matrix} (for\ some\ q\ y) \\ (for\ some\ p\ x) \end{matrix} \mathcal{F}$$

(b) *Distributivity*

$$(for\ all\ p\ x)[\mathcal{F}\ and\ \mathcal{G}] \quad \text{is equivalent to} \quad \begin{matrix} (for\ all\ p\ x)\mathcal{F} \\ and \\ (for\ all\ p\ x)\mathcal{G} \end{matrix}.$$

Problem 5.10 (asymmetry of $\prec_{lex}$)   page 276

Prove the *asymmetry* proposition for $\prec_{lex}$; that is,

In the theory of the lexicographic relation $\prec_{lex}$ corresponding to a relation $\prec$, augmented by the *asymmetry* axiom for $\prec$ over the atoms, the lexicographic relation $\prec_{lex}$ is asymmetric over the pairs, i.e., the sentence

$$\begin{matrix} (for\ all\ pair\ x) \\ (for\ all\ pair\ y) \end{matrix} \left[\begin{matrix} if\ x \prec_{lex} y \\ then\ \ not\ (y \prec_{lex} x) \end{matrix} \right]$$

is valid.

II

Theories

with

Induction

6

Nonnegative Integers

The most important special theories for us will be those defined in terms of the *principle of mathematical induction*. This principle is represented here as an axiom schema, an infinite set of axioms, like the functional- and predicate-substitutivity axioms for equality. Theories with induction include those of the nonnegative integers, strings, trees, lists, sets, and other fundamental structures. We begin with the nonnegative integers, which are the most familiar and the most important.

6.1   BASIC PROPERTIES

The vocabulary of the theory of the nonnegative integers consists of

- A constant symbol 0, denoting the integer *zero*

- A unary function symbol x^+, denoting the *successor* function

- A unary predicate symbol *integer*(x).

The reader should understand that 0 is an informal notation for a constant symbol (such as a or b) and is not to be confused with the actual integer zero, which is a domain element. Under the intended model for the theory, the symbol 0 will be assigned the integer zero as its value.

Also the symbol x^+ is an informal notation for a unary function symbol (such as $f(x)$ or $g(x)$). Under the intended model for the theory, the function symbol

x^+ will be assigned the successor function, i.e., the function that maps the integer d into the integer $d + 1$.

Because the vocabulary of the theory includes the constant symbol 0 and the function symbol x^+, the terms of the theory include

$$0, \quad 0^+, \quad (0^+)^+, \quad ((0^+)^+)^+, \quad \ldots .$$

Conventionally, 0^+ is abbreviated as 1, $(0^+)^+$ as 2, $((0^+)^+)^+$ as 3, and so forth. The symbols 1, 2, 3, ... are merely informal abbreviations for these terms; they are not notations for constant symbols. Under the intended model they denote the actual domain elements one, two, three, ...

The predicate symbol *integer*(x) is intended to be true if x is assigned a nonnegative integer, and false otherwise. In the simplest models for the theory, all the domain elements will be nonnegative integers, and hence *integer*(x) will always be true. Later, however, we shall introduce elements into our domain that are not nonnegative integers; the predicate symbol *integer*(x) will then be used to distinguish between the nonnegative integers and the other domain elements.

The theory of the nonnegative integers is a theory with equality and the following special axioms:

● The *generation* axioms

integer(0)	(*zero*)
(*for all integer* x)$[integer(x^+)]$	(*successor*)

● The *uniqueness* axioms

(*for all integer* x)$[not\ (x^+ = 0)]$	(*zero*)
(*for all integer* x) $\left[\begin{array}{l} if\ x^+ = y^+ \\ then\ \ x = y \end{array}\right.$ (*for all integer* y)	(*successor*)

• The *induction* principle

> For each sentence $\mathcal{F}[x]$ in the theory, the universal closure of the sentence
>
> $$if \begin{bmatrix} \mathcal{F}[0] \\ \quad and \\ (for\ all\ integer\ x) \begin{bmatrix} if\ \mathcal{F}[x] \\ then\ \ \mathcal{F}[x^+] \end{bmatrix} \\ then\ \ (for\ all\ integer\ x)\mathcal{F}[x] \end{bmatrix} \quad (induction)$$
>
> is an axiom.

The two generation axioms have the intuitive meaning that any element that can be constructed from the zero element 0 and the successor function x^+ is a nonnegative integer. Thus $0,\ 0^+,\ (0^+)^+,\ \ldots$ all denote nonnegative integers.

The two uniqueness axioms have the intuitive meaning that each nonnegative integer can be constructed in at most one way from the zero element 0 and the successor function x^+. Thus $0,\ 0^+,\ (0^+)^+,\ \ldots$ denote distinct nonnegative integers.

Note that the axioms for the theory include two *zero* axioms and two *successor* axioms. In referring to them later we shall always discriminate between them by speaking of the *zero* generation axiom or the *zero* uniqueness axiom and of the *successor* generation axiom or the *successor* uniqueness axiom.

The induction principle is actually an axiom schema, because it represents a set of axioms, one for each sentence $\mathcal{F}[x]$ in the theory. The sentence $\mathcal{F}[x]$ is called the *inductive sentence*. The subsentence

$$\mathcal{F}[0]$$

is called the *base case* of the induction. The subsentence

$$(for\ all\ integer\ x) \begin{bmatrix} if\ \mathcal{F}[x] \\ then\ \ \mathcal{F}[x^+] \end{bmatrix}$$

is called the *inductive step*; the subsentences $\mathcal{F}[x]$ and $\mathcal{F}[x^+]$ of the inductive step are called the *induction hypothesis* and the *desired conclusion*, respectively. The variable x is called the *inductive variable*.

The inductive sentence $\mathcal{F}[x]$ may have free variables other than x. The induction principle asserts that the universal closure of the implication is true under every model of the theory. This implies that the implication itself is true under every model.

The induction principle may be paraphrased intuitively as follows:

> To prove that a sentence $\mathcal{F}[x]$ is true for every nonnegative integer x, it suffices to prove the base case
>
> $\mathcal{F}[0]$ is true
>
> and the inductive step
>
> > for an arbitrary nonnegative integer x,
> > if $\mathcal{F}[x]$ is true,
> > then $\mathcal{F}[x+1]$ is also true.

The induction principle states that, to prove a sentence about all the non-negative integers, it suffices to show that the sentence is true for 0 and that, whenever it is true for a nonnegative integer x, it is also true for the successor x^+. Therefore it is true for 0^+ (by one application of the inductive step), for $(0^+)^+$ (by another application of the inductive step), and so forth.

In **Problem 6.11**, the reader is requested to show that a schema obtained by renaming a bound variable in the induction principle, which is therefore apparently equivalent to the induction principle, is actually not valid. (This exercise is included as one of the last problems in this chapter because of its theoretical nature.)

Since the theory of the nonnegative integers is a theory with equality, we include the *transitivity, symmetry,* and *reflexivity* axioms for equality. Because the only function symbol in the vocabulary is the successor x^+, we include only the one corresponding instance of the *functional-substitutivity* axiom schema for the successor function,

$$(\textit{for all } x) \begin{bmatrix} \textit{if } x = y \\ \textit{then } x^+ = y^+ \end{bmatrix} \qquad (\textit{functional substitutivity})$$
$$(\textit{for all } y)$$

Because the vocabulary includes the predicate symbol *integer*(x), we include the corresponding instance of the *predicate-substitutivity* axiom schema,

$$(\textit{for all } x) \begin{bmatrix} \textit{if } x = y \\ \textit{then } \textit{integer}(x) \\ \qquad \textit{if and only if} \\ \textit{integer}(y) \end{bmatrix} \qquad (\textit{predicate substitutivity})$$
$$(\textit{for all } y)$$

In this chapter, when we speak about the validity of a sentence, we shall always mean validity in the theory of the nonnegative integers. Let us show the validity of a sentence in this theory.

Proposition (decomposition)

The sentence

$$(for\ all\ integer\ x) \begin{bmatrix} if\ not\ (x = 0) \\ then\ (for\ some\ integer\ y) [x = y^+] \end{bmatrix}$$

$$(decomposition)$$

is valid (in the theory of the nonnegative integers). ⌐

Proof

The proof employs the instance of the induction principle in which the inductive sentence is taken to be

$$\mathcal{F}[x]: \quad \begin{aligned} &if\ not\ (x = 0) \\ &then\ (for\ some\ integer\ y) [x = y^+] \end{aligned}.$$

To prove

$$(for\ all\ integer\ x)\,\mathcal{F}[x],$$

it suffices, by the induction principle and propositional logic, to establish the base case,

$$\mathcal{F}[0],$$

and the inductive step,

$$(for\ all\ integer\ x) \begin{bmatrix} if\ \mathcal{F}[x] \\ then\ \mathcal{F}[x^+] \end{bmatrix}.$$

We establish the base case and the inductive step separately.

Base Case

We want to prove

$$\mathcal{F}[0]: \quad \begin{aligned} &if\ not\ (0 = 0) \\ &then\ (for\ some\ integer\ y) [0 = y^+] \end{aligned}.$$

Because (by the *reflexivity* axiom for equality) $0 = 0$, the antecedent

$$not\ (0 = 0)$$

of this implication is false and therefore the entire sentence is true.

Inductive Step

We want to prove

$$(\textit{for all integer } x) \left[\begin{array}{l} \textit{if } \mathcal{F}[x] \\ \textit{then } \mathcal{F}[x^+] \end{array} \right],$$

that is,

$$(\textit{for all integer } x) \left[\begin{array}{l} \textit{if } \left[\begin{array}{l} \textit{if not } (x = 0) \\ \textit{then } (\textit{for some integer } y)[x = y^+] \end{array} \right] \\ \textit{then } \left[\begin{array}{l} \textit{if not } (x^+ = 0) \\ \textit{then } (\textit{for some integer } y)[x^+ = y^+] \end{array} \right] \end{array} \right].$$

Consider an arbitrary nonnegative integer x, that is, an element x such that

$$integer(x).$$

We assume the induction hypothesis

$$\mathcal{F}[x] : \quad \begin{array}{l} \textit{if not } (x = 0) \\ \textit{then } (\textit{for some integer } y) \left[x = y^+ \right] \end{array}$$

and would like to show the desired conclusion

$$\mathcal{F}[x^+] : \quad \begin{array}{l} \textit{if not } (x^+ = 0) \\ \textit{then } (\textit{for some integer } y) \left[x^+ = y^+ \right]. \end{array}$$

It suffices to show the consequent,

$$(\textit{for some integer } y) \left[x^+ = y^+ \right],$$

of the desired conclusion $\mathcal{F}[x^+]$.

Because we have supposed $integer(x)$ and we know (by the *reflexivity* axiom for equality) that $x^+ = x^+$, we have

$$\begin{array}{l} integer(x) \\ \quad and \\ x^+ = x^+. \end{array}$$

Therefore (by the *existential quantifier-instantiation* proposition, taking y to be x) we have

$$(\textit{for some } y) \left[\begin{array}{l} integer(y) \\ \quad and \\ x^+ = y^+ \end{array} \right]$$

or, in terms of our relative quantifier notation,

$$(for\ some\ integer\ y)\big[x^+ = y^+\big],$$

as we wanted to show.

Since we have established both the base case and the inductive step, the proof is complete. ⌐

The above proof has the unusual feature that it requires the induction principle but makes no use of the induction hypothesis in the inductive step. Nevertheless, the principle is essential in this proof. If the principle were deleted from the theory of the nonnegative integers, there would be models for the resulting theory under which the *decomposition* proposition would be false. The reader is requested to construct such a model in **Problem 6.12(a)**. (This exercise, like Problem 6.11, is included as one of the last problems in this chapter because of its theoretical nature.)

6.2   THE ADDITION FUNCTION

Suppose we augment our theory of the nonnegative integers by formulating two special axioms that define a binary function symbol $x + y$, denoting, under the intended model, the *addition* (*plus*) function over the nonnegative integers. As usual, $x + y$ is merely a conventional notation for a standard binary function symbol of predicate logic, such as $f_{97}(x, y)$.

The axioms for addition are as follows:

$$(for\ all\ integer\ x)\big[x + 0 = x\big] \qquad\qquad (right\ zero)$$

$$\begin{array}{l}(for\ all\ integer\ x)\\ (for\ all\ integer\ y)\end{array}\big[x + y^+ = (x + y)^+\big] \qquad (right\ successor)$$

As usual, when we introduce a new function symbol into a theory with equality, we automatically provide the corresponding instances of the *functional-substitutivity* axiom schema for addition, that is,

$$\begin{array}{l}(for\ all\ x)\\ (for\ all\ y)\\ (for\ all\ z)\end{array}\left[\begin{array}{l}if\ x = y\\ then\ x + z = y + z\end{array}\right] \qquad (left\ functional\ substitutivity)$$

and

$$\begin{array}{l}(\textit{for all } x) \\ (\textit{for all } y) \\ (\textit{for all } z)\end{array} \left[\begin{array}{l}\textit{if } x = y \\ \textit{then } z + x = z + y\end{array}\right] \qquad (\textit{right functional substitutivity})$$

The *right-zero* and *right-successor* axioms for addition are in the form of a typical "recursive" definition for the function. The *right-zero* axiom defines the function for the case in which its second argument is 0. The *right-successor* axiom defines the function for the case in which its second argument is of form y^+; the value of $x + y^+$ is defined in terms of the value of $x + y$. Because (by the *decomposition* proposition) the second argument must either be 0 or of form y^+, the two axioms cover all possibilities.

As we have seen before, whenever we add new axioms to a theory, we run the risk of making it inconsistent. Usually we disregard this issue and assume that the axioms we provide do not introduce inconsistencies. Subsequently (in Chapter 12), however, we shall show that the axioms for addition, and other sets of axioms of the same recursive form, preserve the consistency of the theory.

It may not be obvious that the *right-zero* and *right-successor* axioms actually define the addition function we are familiar with in everyday life. We cannot prove this within the theory, but we can try to convince ourselves that it is so by showing that the function defined by the axioms satisfies the properties we expect the addition function to have.

In our augmented theory we can establish the validity of the following properties of addition:

$$\begin{array}{l}(\textit{for all integer } x) \\ (\textit{for all integer } y)\end{array} \Big[\textit{integer}(x + y)\Big] \qquad\qquad (\textit{sort})$$

$$(\textit{for all integer } x)\big[x + 1 \ = \ x^+\big] \qquad\qquad (\textit{right one})$$

$$(\textit{for all integer } x)\big[0 + x \ = \ x\big] \qquad\qquad (\textit{left zero})$$

$$\begin{array}{l}(\textit{for all integer } x) \\ (\textit{for all integer } y)\end{array}\big[(x + 1) + y = (x + y) + 1\big] \qquad (\textit{left successor})$$

$$\begin{array}{l}(\textit{for all integer } x) \\ (\textit{for all integer } y)\end{array}\big[x + y = y + x\big] \qquad\qquad (\textit{commutativity})$$

The *sort* property establishes that the result $x + y$ of adding two nonnegative integers is also a nonnegative integer.

Recall that, in the *right-one* property, 1 is merely an abbreviation for 0^+, the binary function symbol $+$ in the term $x+1$ denotes the addition function, and the unary function symbol $^+$ in the term x^+ denotes the successor function. Once we have established the *right-one* property, we can use the more conventional expression $t + 1$, rather than t^+, to denote the successor of t. For example, in the *left-successor* property, we write $x + 1$ and $(x + y) + 1$, in terms of the addition function, rather than x^+ and $(x + y)^+$, in terms of the successor function.

The order in which the properties are presented is significant; some of their proofs make use of earlier properties on the list. We will give proofs for the last four of these properties, illustrating various features of mathematical proofs; the proof for the first one is routine and is left as an exercise (**Problem 6.1(a)**).

PROOF WITHOUT INDUCTION

We begin with the *right-one* property; its proof does not require the induction principle.

Proposition (right one)

The sentence

$$(\textit{for all integer } x)\left[x + 1 \; = \; x^+\right]$$

is valid.　⌙

Proof

Consider an arbitrary nonnegative integer x, that is, an element x such that

$integer(x).$

We would like to prove that

$x + 1 \; = \; x^+.$

Because 1 is an abbreviation for 0^+, we actually want to show

$x + 0^+ \; = \; x^+.$

Because $integer(x)$ and (by the *zero* generation axiom) $integer(0)$, we have (by the *right-successor* axiom for addition)

(†) $x + 0^+ \; = \; (x + 0)^+.$

Because *integer*(x), we have (by the *right-zero* axiom for addition)

$$x + 0 \ = \ x.$$

Therefore, by the *functional-substitutivity* equality axiom for the successor function,

(‡) $(x + 0)^+ \ = \ x^+.$

Finally, by (†), (‡), and the *transitivity* axiom for equality, we obtain

$$x + 0^+ \ = \ x^+,$$

as we wanted to show.   ◢

Let us discuss some features of the above proof.

Remark (universal instantiation)

In the proof we have made free use of the *universal quantifier-instantiation* proposition of predicate logic without mentioning it. For example, consider the point in the proof where we deduced (‡). We used the *functional-substitutivity* equality axiom for the successor function, which reads (after renaming the bound variables to avoid confusion)

$$(\textit{for all } u) \left[\begin{matrix} \textit{if } u = v \\ \textit{then } u^+ = v^+ \end{matrix} \right].$$
$$(\textit{for all } v)$$

For this purpose we implicitly applied the *universal quantifier-instantiation* proposition, taking u to be $x + 0$ and v to be x, to conclude that

$$\textit{if } x + 0 = x$$
$$\textit{then } (x + 0)^+ = x^+.$$

Because we had earlier deduced that

$$x + 0 = x,$$

we could then conclude (‡), that is, that

$$(x + 0)^+ = x^+.$$

In the future, we shall often use the *universal quantifier-instantiation* proposition without explicit indication.   ◢

Remark (sort conditions)

In the above proof, before we could apply the *right-successor* axiom for addition to conclude (†), that

$$x + 0^+ = (x + 0)^+,$$

it was necessary to establish the "sort conditions" that x and 0 are both nonnegative integers, that is,

$$integer(x) \quad \text{and} \quad integer(0).$$

This is because the axiom reads (after renaming the bound variables to avoid confusion)

$$\begin{array}{l} (\textit{for all integer } u) \\ (\textit{for all integer } v) \end{array} \left[u + v^+ = (u + v)^+ \right]$$

or, abandoning the relative quantifier notation,

$$\begin{array}{l} (\textit{for all } u) \\ (\textit{for all } v) \end{array} \left[\begin{array}{l} \textit{if } integer(u) \;\; \textit{and} \;\; integer(v) \\ \textit{then } u + v^+ = (u + v)^+ \end{array} \right].$$

In other words, the axiom applies only if u and v are nonnegative integers. In particular, taking u to be x and v to be 0, we have

$$\begin{array}{l} \textit{if } integer(x) \;\; \textit{and} \;\; integer(0) \\ \textit{then } x + 0^+ = (x + 0)^+. \end{array}$$

Then, because $integer(x)$ and $integer(0)$, we can conclude that

$$x + 0^+ = (x + 0)^+,$$

as we did in the proof.

For the same reason, before we could apply the *right-zero* axiom for addition, to conclude that

$$x + 0 = x,$$

it was necessary to establish that x is a nonnegative integer, that is,

$$integer(x).$$

In future proofs we shall not always bother to establish such sort conditions, i.e., that the terms we construct denote nonnegative integers, since these aspects of a proof tend to be repetitive and straightforward. Sort conditions may be assumed without proof in all the exercises, unless otherwise requested. ⌟

Remark (equality)

We shall assume henceforth that the reader is so familiar with the theory of equality that we do not need to mention its properties explicitly during a proof.

Thus we may abbreviate the above argument, showing that $x + 0^+ = x^+$, as follows:

for an arbitrary nonnegative integer x,

$$x + 0^+ \;=\; (x + 0)^+$$
$$\text{(by the } \textit{right-successor} \text{ axiom for addition)}$$

$$=\; x^+$$
$$\text{(by the } \textit{right-zero} \text{ axiom for addition).}$$

Here we have not mentioned the *functional-substitutivity* and *transitivity* axioms for equality. ⌐

We have established the *right-one* property, i.e., that

$$(\textit{for all integer } x)\big[x + 1 = x^+\big].$$

In particular, for any term t, we may conclude (by the *universal quantifier-instantiation* proposition) that

$$t + 1 = t^+$$

is true. Hence (by the substitutivity of equality) any sentence $\mathcal{F}\langle t^+ \rangle$ containing a term t^+ is equivalent to the corresponding sentence $\mathcal{F}\langle t + 1 \rangle$ containing instead the term $t + 1$. Therefore as we have remarked earlier, we may now use the conventional notation $t + 1$ freely in place of our original notation t^+, to denote the successor of t.

Remark (computation of addition)

The axioms for the addition function can be used to prove properties of the function, such as the above *right-one* property. Furthermore, the axioms actually suggest a way to compute the function, in terms of the constant 0 and the successor function x^+. In other words, the axioms can be regarded as a "program" for performing addition. This is illustrated by the following example.

For example, we would like to compute $3 + 2$, that is, $((0^+)^+)^+ + (0^+)^+$. In other words, we would like to find a term equal to $((0^+)^+)^+ + (0^+)^+$ expressed solely in terms of the constant 0 and the successor function x^+, not the addition function $x + y$. We have

$$((0^+)^+)^+ + (0^+)^+ = (((0^+)^+)^+ + 0^+)^+$$
$$\text{(by the } right\text{-}successor \text{ axiom)}$$

$$= ((((0^+)^+)^+ + 0)^+)^+$$
$$\text{(by the } right\text{-}successor \text{ axiom again)}$$

$$= ((((0^+)^+)^+)^+)^+$$
$$\text{(by the } right\text{-}zero \text{ axiom).}$$

In short,

$$((0^+)^+)^+ + (0^+)^+ = ((((0^+)^+)^+)^+)^+,$$

that is,

$$3 + 2 = 5.$$

In the computation we have applied properties of equality without mentioning them explicitly. We have also disregarded the *sort* conditions, e.g., that $integer(0)$ and $integer(0^+)$ are true. ◢

A SIMPLE INDUCTION PROOF

The proof of the *right-one* property did not require induction; let us now consider a proof that does make use of the induction principle.

Proposition (left zero)

The sentence

$$(\textit{for all integer } x)\big[0 + x = x\big]$$

is valid. ◢

Proof

The proof employs the instance of the induction principle in which the inductive sentence is taken to be

$$\mathcal{F}[x]: \quad 0 + x = x.$$

To prove

$$(for\ all\ integer\ x)\mathcal{F}[x],$$

it suffices, by the induction principle, to establish the base case,

$$\mathcal{F}[0],$$

and the inductive step,

$$(for\ all\ integer\ x) \begin{bmatrix} if\ \mathcal{F}[x] \\ then\ \mathcal{F}[x+1] \end{bmatrix}.$$

(Note that here we use the more familiar notation $x + 1$ rather than x^+.)

We establish the base case and the inductive step separately.

Base Case

We want to prove

$$\mathcal{F}[0]: \quad 0 + 0 = 0.$$

But this is an instance of the *right-zero* axiom,

$$(for\ all\ integer\ x)[x + 0 = x],$$

for the addition function.

Inductive Step

We want to prove

$$(for\ all\ integer\ x) \begin{bmatrix} if\ \mathcal{F}[x] \\ then\ \mathcal{F}[x+1] \end{bmatrix}.$$

For an arbitrary nonnegative integer x, we assume the induction hypothesis

$$\mathcal{F}[x]: \quad 0 + x = x$$

and attempt to establish the desired conclusion

$$\mathcal{F}[x+1]: \quad 0 + (x+1) = x+1.$$

But we have

$$0 + (x+1) = (0+x) + 1$$
$$\text{(by the } right\text{-}successor \text{ axiom for addition)}$$

$$= x + 1$$
$$\text{(by our induction hypothesis).} \quad \lrcorner$$

CHOICE OF VARIABLES

The principle of mathematical induction states that

for all sentences $\mathcal{F}[x]$ in the theory of the nonnegative integers, the universal closure of

$$if \begin{bmatrix} \mathcal{F}[0] \\ \quad and \\ (for\ all\ integer\ x) \begin{bmatrix} if\ \mathcal{F}[x] \\ then\ \ \mathcal{F}[x+1] \end{bmatrix} \end{bmatrix}$$

then $(for\ all\ integer\ x)\mathcal{F}[x]$

is an axiom.

Note that x can be taken to be any variable; thus we can apply the principle to prove sentences $(for\ all\ integer\ x)\mathcal{F}[x]$ by "induction on x," $(for\ all\ integer\ y)\mathcal{F}[y]$ by "induction on y," or $(for\ all\ integer\ z)\mathcal{F}[z]$ by "induction on z," and so forth.

The following proposition illustrates a proof by induction on y.

Proposition (left successor)

The sentence

$$\begin{matrix} (for\ all\ integer\ x) \\ (for\ all\ integer\ y) \end{matrix} \Big[(x+1) + y\ =\ (x+y) + 1 \Big]$$

is valid.   ◢

Proof

Consider an arbitrary nonnegative integer x; we attempt to prove

$(for\ all\ integer\ y)\big[(x+1) + y = (x+y) + 1\big].$

The proof is by induction on y; we take the inductive sentence to be

$\mathcal{F}[y]:\quad (x+1) + y\ =\ (x+y) + 1.$

To prove

$(for\ all\ integer\ y)\mathcal{F}[y],$

it suffices, by the induction principle, to establish the base case,

$$\mathcal{F}[0],$$

and the inductive step,

$$(\textit{for all integer } y) \begin{bmatrix} \textit{if } \mathcal{F}[y] \\ \textit{then } \mathcal{F}[y+1] \end{bmatrix}.$$

We establish the base case and the inductive step separately.

Base Case

We would like to prove

$$\mathcal{F}[0]: \quad (x+1)+0 \ = \ (x+0)+1.$$

But we have

$$(x+1)+0 \ = \ x+1$$
$$\text{(by the } \textit{right-zero} \text{ axiom for addition)}$$

$$= \ (x+0)+1$$
$$\text{(by the } \textit{right-zero} \text{ axiom for addition again).}$$

Inductive Step

For an arbitrary nonnegative integer y, we assume the induction hypothesis

$$\mathcal{F}[y]: \quad (x+1)+y \ = \ (x+y)+1$$

and attempt to prove the desired conclusion

$$\mathcal{F}[y+1]: \quad (x+1)+(y+1) \ = \ \bigl(x+(y+1)\bigr)+1.$$

But we have

$$(x+1)+(y+1) \ = \ \bigl((x+1)+y\bigr)+1$$
$$\text{(by the } \textit{right-successor} \text{ axiom for addition)}$$

$$= \ \bigl((x+y)+1\bigr)+1$$
$$\text{(by our induction hypothesis)}$$

$$= \ \bigl(x+(y+1)\bigr)+1$$
$$\text{(by the } \textit{right-successor} \text{ axiom for}$$
$$\text{addition again).} \quad \lrcorner$$

Note that in the above proof the inductive sentence $\mathcal{F}[y]$, that is,

$$(x+1)+y \ = \ (x+y)+1,$$

contained free occurrences of x as well as y.

Remark (choice of variables)

The proof illustrates some of the strategic aspects of the use of the induction principle. It might seem more straightforward to attempt the proof by induction on x, taking the inductive sentence to be

$$\mathcal{F}[x]: \quad (\textit{for all integer } y)\big[(x+1)+y = (x+y)+1\big].$$

In such a proof, we would first attempt to establish the base case

$$\mathcal{F}[0]: \quad (\textit{for all integer } y)\big[(0+1)+y = (0+y)+1\big].$$

Considering an arbitrary nonnegative integer y, we would try to prove

$$(0+1)+y = (0+y)+1$$

or, equivalently (by two applications of the *left-zero* property for addition),

$$1+y = y+1.$$

For this purpose, we would have to prove that

$$(\textit{for all integer } y)[1+y = y+1],$$

requiring an additional application of the induction principle, on y. An attempt to establish the inductive step of such a proof would lead to similar obstructions.

In other words, a decision to use induction on x, rather than on y, in proving the *left-successor* property of addition would lead to a needlessly complicated proof. In general, part of the strategic aspect of using the induction principle is deciding on which variable to do induction. ⏌

USE OF EARLIER RESULTS

Once we have established the validity of a sentence in the theory of the nonnegative integers, we can use it in the proofs of other sentences, just as we would use an axiom. The proof of the following *commutativity* property relies on the validity of the *left-zero* property,

$$(\textit{for all integer } x)\big[0+x = x\big],$$

and the *left-successor* property,

$$(\textit{for all integer } x)\atop(\textit{for all integer } y)\big[(x+1)+y := (x+y)+1\big],$$

which we established in the preceding sections.

Proposition (commutativity)

The sentence

$$\begin{array}{l}(\textit{for all integer } x) \\ (\textit{for all integer } y)\end{array} \big[x + y \ = \ y + x\big].$$

is valid.   ⌟

Proof

Consider an arbitrary nonnegative integer x; we would like to prove

$$(\textit{for all integer } y)\big[x + y \ = \ y + x\big].$$

The proof is by induction on y; we take the inductive sentence to be

$$\mathcal{F}[y]: \quad x + y \ = \ y + x.$$

To prove

$$(\textit{for all integer } y)\,\mathcal{F}[y],$$

it suffices, by the induction principle, to establish the base case,

$$\mathcal{F}[0],$$

and the inductive step,

$$(\textit{for all integer } y) \begin{bmatrix} \textit{if } \mathcal{F}[y] \\ \textit{then } \mathcal{F}[y+1] \end{bmatrix}.$$

Base Case

We would like to prove

$$\mathcal{F}[0]: \quad x + 0 \ = \ 0 + x.$$

But we have

$$x + 0 \ = \ x$$
$$(\text{by the } \textit{right-zero} \text{ axiom for addition})$$

$$= \ 0 + x$$
$$(\text{by the } \textit{left-zero} \text{ property of addition}).$$

Inductive Step

For an arbitrary nonnegative integer y, we assume the induction hypothesis

$$\mathcal{F}[y]: \quad x + y = y + x$$

and attempt to establish the desired conclusion

$$\mathcal{F}[y + 1]: \quad x + (y + 1) = (y + 1) + x.$$

But we have

$$x + (y + 1) = (x + y) + 1$$
$$\text{(by the } \textit{right-successor} \text{ axiom for addition)}$$

$$= (y + x) + 1$$
$$\text{(by our induction hypothesis)}$$

$$= (y + 1) + x$$
$$\text{(by the } \textit{left-successor} \text{ property of addition).} \quad \lrcorner$$

The proof of the *commutativity* proposition for addition above made use of the *left-zero* and the *left-successor* properties of addition, whose validity we established earlier. Had we attempted to prove the *commutativity* proposition without having proved the other two properties first, we would have had to include the proof of the two required properties within the proof of the proposition, making the combined proof rather unwieldy.

We can also establish the validity of the following properties of the addition function:

$$\begin{array}{l} (\textit{for all integer } x) \\ (\textit{for all integer } y) \left[(x + y) + z = x + (y + z) \right] \\ (\textit{for all integer } z) \end{array} \qquad (\textit{associativity})$$

$$\begin{array}{l} (\textit{for all integer } x) \\ (\textit{for all integer } y) \left[\begin{array}{l} \textit{if } z + x = z + y \\ \textit{then } x = y \end{array} \right] \\ (\textit{for all integer } z) \end{array} \qquad (\textit{left cancellation})$$

$$\begin{array}{l} (\textit{for all integer } x) \\ (\textit{for all integer } y) \left[\begin{array}{l} \textit{if } x + z = y + z \\ \textit{then } x = y \end{array} \right] \\ (\textit{for all integer } z) \end{array} \qquad (\textit{right cancellation})$$

$$\begin{array}{l} (\textit{for all integer } x) \\ (\textit{for all integer } y) \end{array} \left[\begin{array}{l} \textit{if } x + y = 0 \\ \textit{then } x = 0 \ \textit{and} \ y = 0 \end{array} \right] \qquad (\textit{annihilation})$$

The proofs are left as an exercise (**Problem 6.1**).

Note that once we have established the *associativity* property of addition we can freely use the conventional notation $r + s + t$, rather than $(r + s) + t$ or $r + (s + t)$, because both terms have the same value.

6.3   MULTIPLICATION AND EXPONENTIATION

In this section we extend the theory by defining two new functions. We shall also illustrate some of the strategic aspects of using the induction principle.

MULTIPLICATION

Let us further augment our theory of the nonnegative integers by introducing special axioms that define a binary function symbol $x \cdot y$, denoting, under the intended model, the *multiplication* (*times*) function over the nonnegative integers.

The axioms for multiplication are as follows:

$$(for\ all\ integer\ x)\big[x \cdot 0\ =\ 0\big] \qquad\qquad (right\ zero)$$

$$(for\ all\ integer\ x) \atop (for\ all\ integer\ y) \big[x \cdot (y + 1)\ =\ x \cdot y + x\big] \qquad (right\ successor)$$

We write $x \cdot y + x$ as an abbreviation of $(x \cdot y) + x$.

As before, we introduce the corresponding instances of the *functional-substitutivity* equality axiom schema for multiplication automatically:

$$(for\ all\ x) \atop (for\ all\ y) \atop (for\ all\ z) \left[{if\ x = y \atop then\ x \cdot z = y \cdot z} \right] \qquad (left\ functional\ substitutivity)$$

$$(for\ all\ x) \atop (for\ all\ y) \atop (for\ all\ z) \left[{if\ x = y \atop then\ z \cdot x = z \cdot y} \right] \qquad (right\ functional\ substitutivity)$$

Note also that we retain the special axioms that define the addition function.

In our augmented theory we can establish the validity of the following properties of multiplication:

$$(\textit{for all integer } x) \atop (\textit{for all integer } y) \left[integer(x \cdot y) \right] \qquad (\textit{sort})$$

$$(\textit{for all integer } x) \left[x \cdot 1 \; = \; x \right] \qquad (\textit{right one})$$

$$(\textit{for all integer } x) \left[0 \cdot x \; = \; 0 \right] \qquad (\textit{left zero})$$

$$(\textit{for all integer } x) \atop (\textit{for all integer } y) \left[(x+1) \cdot y \; = \; x \cdot y + y \right] \qquad (\textit{left successor})$$

$$(\textit{for all integer } x) \left[1 \cdot x \; = \; x \right] \qquad (\textit{left one})$$

From these properties we can establish the associativity, commutativity, and distributivity of multiplication:

$$\begin{array}{l}(\textit{for all integer } x) \\ (\textit{for all integer } y) \\ (\textit{for all integer } z) \end{array} \left[x \cdot (y+z) \; = \; x \cdot y + x \cdot z \right] \quad (\textit{right distributivity})$$

$$\begin{array}{l}(\textit{for all integer } x) \\ (\textit{for all integer } y) \\ (\textit{for all integer } z) \end{array} \left[(x \cdot y) \cdot z \; = \; x \cdot (y \cdot z) \right] \qquad (\textit{associativity})$$

$$(\textit{for all integer } x) \atop (\textit{for all integer } y) \left[x \cdot y \; = \; y \cdot x \right] \qquad (\textit{commutativity})$$

$$\begin{array}{l}(\textit{for all integer } x) \\ (\textit{for all integer } y) \\ (\textit{for all integer } z) \end{array} \left[(x+y) \cdot z \; = \; x \cdot z + y \cdot z \right] \qquad (\textit{left distributivity})$$

The proofs of all these properties are left as an exercise (**Problem 6.2**). As usual, the order in which the properties are presented is significant: Some of their proofs make use of earlier properties on the list.

EXPONENTIATION

Suppose we augment our theory of the nonnegative integers further by formulating two special axioms that define a binary function symbol x^y, denoting, under the intended model, the *exponentiation* function over the nonnegative integers.

The axioms for exponentiation are as follows:

$$(\textit{for all integer } x)\left[x^0 \; = \; 1\right] \hspace{4cm} (\textit{exp zero})$$

$$\begin{array}{l}(\textit{for all integer } x)\\(\textit{for all integer } y)\end{array}\left[x^{y+1} \; = \; x^y \cdot x\right] \hspace{2.5cm} (\textit{successor})$$

(Note that, under these axioms, 0^0 is taken to be 1, not 0.) As usual, we automatically introduce the instances of the *functional-substitutivity* equality axiom schema for exponentiation.

From these axioms we can establish the validity of the following properties of exponentiation:

$$\begin{array}{l}(\textit{for all integer } x)\\(\textit{for all integer } y)\end{array}\left[integer(x^y)\right] \hspace{3cm} (\textit{sort})$$

$$(\textit{for all integer } x)\left[x^1 \; = \; x\right] \hspace{4cm} (\textit{exp one})$$

$$(\textit{for all integer } y)\left[\begin{array}{l}\textit{if} \;\; not \, (y = 0)\\ \textit{then} \;\; 0^y = 0\end{array}\right] \hspace{2.5cm} (\textit{base zero})$$

$$\begin{array}{l}(\textit{for all integer } x)\\(\textit{for all integer } y)\\(\textit{for all integer } z)\end{array}\left[x^{y+z} \; = \; (x^y) \cdot (x^z)\right] \hspace{2cm} (\textit{exp plus})$$

$$\begin{array}{l}(\textit{for all integer } x)\\(\textit{for all integer } y)\\(\textit{for all integer } z)\end{array}\left[x^{y \cdot z} \; = \; (x^y)^z\right] \hspace{2.5cm} (\textit{exp times})$$

The proofs of these properties are left as an exercise (**Problem 6.3**).

THE NEED FOR GENERALIZATION

In proving a property by mathematical induction, it is frequently necessary to prove a stronger, more general property instead. This phenomenon is illustrated in the proof of the following proposition.

Proposition (alternative exponentiation)

Suppose we define a new ternary function, denoted by *exp3*, by the following two axioms:

$$(\textit{for all integer } x)\atop(\textit{for all integer } z)\Big\}\Big[exp3(x,\ 0,\ z)\ =\ z\Big] \qquad\qquad (\textit{zero})$$

$$\left.\begin{matrix}(\textit{for all integer } x)\\(\textit{for all integer } y)\\(\textit{for all integer } z)\end{matrix}\right\}\Big[exp3(x,\ y+1,\ z)\ =\ exp3(x,\ y,\ x\cdot z)\Big] \quad (\textit{successor})$$

Then the sentence

$$(\textit{for all integer } x)\atop(\textit{for all integer } y)\Big\}\Big[exp3(x,\ y,\ 1)\ =\ x^y\Big]$$

is valid.   ⌐

Before we prove the proposition, let us explain the $exp3$ function. For any nonnegative integers x, y, and z, the function is defined in such a way that

$$exp3(x,\ y,\ z)\ =\ x^y\cdot z.$$

Following the axioms, to compute $exp3(x,\ y,\ z)$ we multiply z by x precisely y times.

Example (computation of exp3)

We have

$$\begin{aligned}exp3(3,\ 2,\ 4)\ &=\ exp3\big(3,\ (0+1)+1,\ 4\big)\\ &\qquad\text{(because 2 is an abbreviation for }(0+1)+1)\\[6pt] &=\ exp3(3,\ 0+1,\ 3\cdot 4)\\ &\qquad\text{(by the }\textit{successor}\text{ axiom for }exp3)\\[6pt] &=\ exp3(3;\ 0,\ 3\cdot 3\cdot 4)\\ &\qquad\text{(by the }\textit{successor}\text{ axiom for }exp3\text{ again)}\\[6pt] &=\ 3\cdot 3\cdot 4\\ &\qquad\text{(by the }\textit{zero}\text{ axiom for }exp3).\end{aligned}$$

In other words

$$exp3(3,\ 2,\ 4)\ =\ 3\cdot 3\cdot 4\ =\ 3^2\cdot 4.\qquad ⌐$$

The proposition suggests that we can use the axioms for $exp3(x,\ y,\ z)$ as an alternative method for computing x^y, simply by taking z to be 1 and computing $exp3(x,\ y,\ 1)$.

Let us prove the proposition.

Proof (alternative exponentiation)

Rather than proving the original desired sentence,

$$(\textit{for all integer } x) \atop (\textit{for all integer } y) \Big[exp3(x,\ y,\ 1)\ =\ x^y\Big],$$

we prove instead the stronger, more general sentence

$$(\textit{for all integer } x) \atop (\textit{for all integer } y) \atop (\textit{for all integer } z) \Big[exp3(x,\ y,\ z)\ =\ x^y \cdot z\Big],$$

which fully characterizes the *exp3* function.

Once we have proved this sentence, we can infer the original desired sentence easily. For consider arbitrary nonnegative integers x and y; we have

$$exp3(x,\ y,\ 1)\ =\ x^y \cdot 1$$
$$\text{(by the more general sentence)}$$

$$=\ x^y$$
$$\text{(by the \textit{right-one} property of multiplication).}$$

To prove the more general sentence, consider an arbitrary nonnegative integer x; we would like to show

$$(\textit{for all integer } y) \atop (\textit{for all integer } z) \Big[exp3(x,\ y,\ z)\ =\ x^y \cdot z\Big].$$

The proof is by induction on y, taking the inductive sentence to be

$$\mathcal{F}[y]:\quad (\textit{for all integer } z)\Big[exp3(x,\ y,\ z)\ =\ x^y \cdot z\Big].$$

Base Case

We would like to prove

$$\mathcal{F}[0]:\quad (\textit{for all integer } z)\Big[exp3(x,\ 0,\ z)\ =\ x^0 \cdot z\Big].$$

For an arbitrary nonnegative integer z, we have

$$exp3(x,\ 0,\ z)\ =\ z$$
$$\text{(by the \textit{zero} axiom for \textit{exp3}).}$$

But on the other hand, we have

$$x^0 \cdot z\ =\ 1 \cdot z$$
$$\text{(by the \textit{exp-zero} axiom for exponentiation)}$$

$$= z$$
(by the *left-one* property of multiplication).

Inductive Step

For an arbitrary nonnegative integer y, we assume the induction hypothesis

$$\mathcal{F}[y]: \quad (\textit{for all integer } z)\left[exp3(x,\ y,\ z)\ =\ x^y \cdot z\right]$$

and attempt to show the desired conclusion

$$\mathcal{F}[y+1]: \quad (\textit{for all integer } z')\left[exp3(x,\ y+1,\ z')\ =\ (x^{y+1}) \cdot z'\right].$$

(Here we have renamed the bound variable z of the desired conclusion to z', to avoid confusion with the variable z in the induction hypothesis.)

For an arbitrary nonnegative integer z', we have

$$exp3(x,\ y+1,\ z')\ =\ exp3(x,\ y,\ x \cdot z')$$
(by the *successor* axiom for $exp3$).

But on the other hand, we have

$$(x^{y+1}) \cdot z'\ =\ (x^y \cdot x) \cdot z'$$
(by the *successor* axiom for exponentiation)

$$=\ x^y \cdot (x \cdot z')$$
(by the *associativity* property of multiplication)

$$=\ exp3(x,\ y,\ x \cdot z')$$
(by the induction hypothesis, taking z to be $x \cdot z'$).

In short, we have established that

$$exp3(x,\ y+1,\ z')\ =\ (x^{y+1}) \cdot z',$$

as we wanted to show. ⌐

The proof of the above proposition illustrates some of the strategic aspects of discovering a proof by induction.

Remark (generalization)

We proved the original desired property

$$\begin{matrix} (\textit{for all integer } x) \\ (\textit{for all integer } y) \end{matrix}\left[exp3(x,\ y,\ 1)\ =\ x^y\right]$$

by establishing the more general property

$$\begin{array}{l}(\textit{for all integer } x)\\(\textit{for all integer } y)\\(\textit{for all integer } z)\end{array}\Big[exp3(x,\ y,\ z)\ =\ x^y\cdot z\Big].$$

Had we attempted to prove the original property without first generalizing, the above proof would not have gone through. In other words, we cannot establish the original property directly.

For in establishing the inductive step in the proof of the original property, we would assume the induction hypothesis,

$$\mathcal{F}'[y]:\quad exp3(x,\ y,\ 1)\ =\ x^y,$$

and attempt to prove the desired conclusion,

$$\mathcal{F}'[y+1]:\quad exp3(x,\ y+1,\ 1)\ =\ x^{y+1}.$$

It suffices to show (by the *successor* axioms for *exp3* and exponentiation) that

$$exp3(x,\ y,\ x\cdot 1)\ =\ x^y\cdot x.$$

The desired conclusion is concerned with $exp3(x,\ y,\ x\cdot 1)$, that is, $exp3(x,\ y,\ x)$, while the induction hypothesis gives us information only about $exp3(x,\ y,\ 1)$.

Thus in attempting to prove the original weaker property, we have a correspondingly weaker induction hypothesis, one that is no longer general enough to imply the desired conclusion. By proving the more general property, we have the advantage of the correspondingly more general induction hypothesis. For the *alternative exponentiation* proposition, it is paradoxically easier to prove the more general, stronger property than it is to prove the weaker special case.

In proving such a property by induction, it often requires ingenuity to discover a generalization that enables the proof to go through. Sometimes an unsuccessful attempt to prove the original property will suggest the required generalization. ⌐

Generalization is also required to solve **Problem 6.4**, which concerns the *factorial* function $x!$.

Remark (treatment of quantifiers)

In proving the property

$$\begin{array}{l}(\textit{for all integer } x)\\(\textit{for all integer } y)\\(\textit{for all integer } z)\end{array}\Big[exp3(x,\ y,\ z)\ =\ x^y\cdot z\Big],$$

we treated each of the quantifiers differently:

- To dispose of the quantifier (*for all integer x*), we considered an arbitrary nonnegative integer at the beginning of the proof.

- To dispose of (*for all integer y*), we performed induction on y.

- To dispose of (*for all integer z*), we allowed the quantifier to remain in the inductive sentence $\mathcal{F}[y]$ and considered arbitrary nonnegative integers z both in the base case and in the inductive step.

This treatment of the quantifiers is essential. To see this, the reader may attempt to prove the property differently, e.g., by induction on x, taking the inductive sentence to be

$$\begin{array}{l} (\textit{for all integer } y) \\ (\textit{for all integer } z) \end{array} \Big[exp3(x,\, y,\, z) = x^y \cdot z \Big].$$

The proof will be considerably more complex.

Had we originally been given the quantifiers in a different order, say,

$$\begin{array}{l} (\textit{for all integer } z) \\ (\textit{for all integer } y) \\ (\textit{for all integer } x) \end{array} \Big[exp3(x,\, y,\, z) \;=\; x^y \cdot z \Big],$$

we would have needed to reorder them. ⌐

6.4   PREDECESSOR AND SUBTRACTION

Before we define the predecessor and subtraction functions, let us introduce a useful unary predicate symbol.

POSITIVE

We augment our theory by defining a unary predicate symbol $positive(x)$, denoting, under the intended model, the relation that is true for positive integers and false for zero. It is defined by the axiom

$$(\textit{for all } x) \begin{bmatrix} positive(x) \\ \quad \textit{if and only if} \\ integer(x) \;\; \textit{and} \;\; not\,(x = 0) \end{bmatrix} \qquad (\textit{positive})$$

Using this predicate symbol in relativized quantifiers enables us to abbreviate many properties. For example, we can express the *decomposition* property for the nonnegative integers, that is,

$$(\textit{for all integer } x) \begin{bmatrix} \textit{if} \ \ not \ (x = 0) \\ then \ \ (\textit{for some integer } y)[x = y + 1] \end{bmatrix},$$

as

$$\begin{matrix} (\textit{for all positive } x) \\ (\textit{for some integer } y) \end{matrix} \Big[x = y + 1 \Big].$$

From the *zero* uniqueness axiom, it follows that

$$(\textit{for all integer } x)\big[positive(x + 1)\big] \qquad\qquad (\textit{sort})$$

PREDECESSOR

Suppose we augment our theory by introducing special axioms to define a unary function symbol x^-, denoting, under the intended model, the *predecessor* function over the nonnegative integers, i.e., the function that maps the positive integer d into the integer $d - 1$. The axiom for the predecessor function is

$$\boxed{(\textit{for all integer } x)\big[(x + 1)^- = x\big] \qquad\qquad (\textit{predecessor})}$$

As usual, we automatically introduce the corresponding instance of the *functional-substitutivity* equality axiom schema for the predecessor function.

Remark (the value of 0^-)

Note that the above axioms do not specify the value of the term 0^-. Although this term is legal in the language, the axioms do not force it to have any particular value.

For example, we might have many different models for the extended theory over the nonnegative integers, each assigning a different value to the term 0^-. Thus 0^- might be assigned the nonnegative integer 27 under one model, the nonnegative integer 32 under another model, and the nonnegative integer 0 under a third model. This vagueness is intentional; we do not care what the value of 0^- is under a model for the extended theory. ⌟

In the augmented theory, we can prove the following properties of the predecessor function:

$$(\textit{for all positive } x)\left[integer(x^-)\right] \qquad\qquad (\textit{sort})$$

$$(\textit{for all positive } x)\left[x \;=\; x^- + 1\right] \qquad\qquad (\textit{decomposition})$$

The proof of the *sort* property is omitted; the proof of the *decomposition* property is left as an exercise (**Problem 6.5(a)**). Our earlier *decomposition* property

$$\begin{matrix}(\textit{for all positive } x)\\(\textit{for some integer } y)\end{matrix}\left[x = y+1\right]$$

follows immediately from this one by the *existential quantifier-instantiation* proposition.

SUBTRACTION

Suppose we augment our theory further by formulating special axioms that define a binary function symbol $x - y$, denoting the *subtraction* (*minus*) function under the intended model for the nonnegative integers.

The axioms for the subtraction function are as follows:

$$(\textit{for all integer } x)\left[x - 0 \;=\; x\right] \qquad\qquad (\textit{right zero})$$

$$\begin{matrix}(\textit{for all integer } x)\\(\textit{for all integer } y)\end{matrix}\left[(x+1) - (y+1) \;=\; x - y\right] \qquad (\textit{successor})$$

As usual, we automatically introduce the corresponding two instances of the *functional-substitutivity* equality axiom schema for the subtraction function.

Example (computation of minus)

To illustrate the axioms, we show the computation of the value of $3 - 2$. We have

$$3 - 2 \;=\; \left(((0+1)+1)+1\right) \;-\; \left((0+1)+1\right)$$

$$=\; \left((0+1)+1\right) \;-\; (0+1)$$
$$\text{(by the } \textit{successor} \text{ axiom)}$$

$$=\; (0+1) - 0$$
$$\text{(by the } \textit{successor} \text{ axiom again)}$$

$$= 0 + 1$$

(by the *right-zero* axiom)

$$= 1.$$

In short,

$$3 - 2 = 1. \quad \lrcorner$$

Remark (unspecified values)

Note that these axioms do not specify the value of terms of form $s - t$, where the value of s is less than the value of t. Although such terms are legal in the language, the axioms do not force them to have any particular value.

For example, we might have many different models for the extended theory over the nonnegative integers, each assigning a different nonnegative integer to the term $2 - 3$, that is, $\big((0+1)+1\big) - \big(((0+1)+1)+1\big)$. However, according to the *successor* axiom, the value assigned to the term $\big((0+1)+1\big) - \big(((0+1)+1)+1\big)$ must be the same as the value assigned to $(0+1) - \big((0+1)+1\big)$, whatever that is. $\quad \lrcorner$

In the augmented theory, we can prove the following properties of subtraction:

$$(\textit{for all positive } x)[x - 1 \ = \ x^-] \hspace{3cm} (\textit{right one})$$

$$\begin{aligned}(\textit{for all integer } x)\\(\textit{for all integer } y)\end{aligned}\Big[(x + y) - y \ = \ x\Big] \hspace{2cm} (\textit{addition})$$

The proofs of these properties are left as an exercise (**Problem 6.5**).

Note that in the *right-one* property the function symbol $-$ in the term $x - 1$ denotes the binary subtraction function, while the function symbol $^-$ in the term x^- denotes the unary predecessor function. Once we have established this property, we may use the more conventional notation $t - 1$, in place of t^-, to denote the predecessor of t.

MONUS

We have remarked that the axioms for the subtraction function do not specify any properties of terms of form $s - t$ if, under the intended interpretation, s is less than t. Let us define a new binary function symbol $x \doteq y$, denoting a function *monus*, which differs from the subtraction function in that the value of $s \doteq t$ is 0 if s is less than t.

The monus function is defined by the following axioms:

$$(\textit{for all integer } x)\big[x \doteq 0 \; = \; x\big] \qquad\qquad (\textit{right zero})$$

$$(\textit{for all integer } y)\big[0 \doteq y \; = \; 0\big] \qquad\qquad (\textit{left zero})$$

$$\begin{array}{l}(\textit{for all integer } x)\\(\textit{for all integer } y)\end{array}\Big[\big((x+1) \doteq (y+1)\big) \; = \; x \doteq y\Big] \qquad (\textit{successor})$$

Example (computation of monus)

We have

$$2 \doteq 3 \; = \; \big((0+1)+1\big) \; \doteq \; \big(((0+1)+1)+1\big)$$

$$= \; (0+1) \; \doteq \; \big((0+1)+1\big)$$
$$\text{(by the } \textit{successor} \text{ axiom)}$$

$$= \; 0 \; \doteq \; (0+1)$$
$$\text{(by the } \textit{successor} \text{ axiom again)}$$

$$= \; 0$$
$$\text{(by the } \textit{left-zero} \text{ axiom).}$$

In short,

$$2 \doteq 3 \; = \; 0. \quad \blacksquare$$

Note that two of the axioms for the monus function, the *right-zero* and *successor* axioms, are the same as the two axioms for the minus function. Therefore any property we can prove about minus we can also prove about monus. But monus has an additional *left-zero* axiom, so we can prove properties about monus that we cannot prove about minus. For instance, we can prove that $x \doteq y$ is always a nonnegative integer, that is,

$$\begin{array}{l}(\textit{for all integer } x)\\(\textit{for all integer } y)\end{array}\Big[\textit{integer}(x \doteq y)\Big] \qquad\qquad (\textit{sort})$$

The corresponding sentence for the minus function,

$$\begin{array}{l}(\textit{for all integer } x)\\(\textit{for all integer } y)\end{array}\Big[\textit{integer}(x - y)\Big],$$

is not valid in our theory. For example, if the domain of a model includes all the integers and s is less than t, then $s - t$ can be a negative integer under that model.

6.5   DECOMPOSITION INDUCTION

Using the definition of the predecessor function, we can prove an alternative version of the induction principle.

Proposition (decomposition induction principle)

For each sentence $\mathcal{F}[x]$, the universal closure of the sentence

$$
if \begin{bmatrix} \mathcal{F}[0] \\ and \\ (for\ all\ positive\ x) \begin{bmatrix} if\ \mathcal{F}[x-1] \\ then\ \mathcal{F}[x] \end{bmatrix} \end{bmatrix}
$$

$$
then\ (for\ all\ integer\ x)\,\mathcal{F}[x] \qquad (decomposition\ induction)
$$

is valid. ⌐

The sentence $\mathcal{F}[x]$ is called the *inductive sentence*. The subsentence

$$\mathcal{F}[0]$$

of the decomposition induction principle is called the *base case* of the principle. The subsentence

$$
(for\ all\ positive\ x) \begin{bmatrix} if\ \mathcal{F}[x-1] \\ then\ \mathcal{F}[x] \end{bmatrix}
$$

is called the *inductive step*; the subsentences $\mathcal{F}[x-1]$ and $\mathcal{F}[x]$ of the inductive step are called the *induction hypothesis* and the *desired conclusion*, respectively. The variable x is called the *inductive variable*.

The decomposition version of the induction principle may be paraphrased informally as follows:

> To prove that a sentence $\mathcal{F}[x]$ is true for every nonnegative integer x, it suffices to prove the base case
>
> $\mathcal{F}[0]$ is true

and the inductive step

> for an arbitrary positive integer x,
>   if $\mathcal{F}[x-1]$ is true
>   then $\mathcal{F}[x]$ is also true.

When we need to distinguish the original version of the induction principle from this *decomposition* version, we shall refer to the original version as the *generator* induction principle. Collectively, we may refer to both of these as *stepwise* induction principles.

The only difference between the decomposition version of the induction principle and the generator version is that in the decomposition version we infer $\mathcal{F}[x]$ from $\mathcal{F}[x-1]$, where x is positive, while in the generator version we infer $\mathcal{F}[x+1]$ from $\mathcal{F}[x]$, where x is nonnegative.

Rather than merely establishing the validity of the decomposition induction principle, we establish a stronger result, that the two versions of the induction principle are in some sense interchangeable. To make this notion precise, we introduce a new "predecessor theory."

Definition (predecessor theory)

The *predecessor theory* is obtained from the basic (unaugmented) theory of the nonnegative integers as follows:

- Omit the generator version of the induction principle.

- Add the following axioms:

$$(\textit{for all } x) \left[\begin{array}{l} positive(x) \\ \quad \textit{if and only if} \\ integer(x) \;\; and \;\; not \, (x = 0) \end{array} \right] \qquad (positive)$$

$$(\textit{for all integer } x) \left[(x+1) - 1 \; = \; x \right] \qquad (predecessor)$$

$$(\textit{for all positive } x) \left[x \; = \; (x-1)+1 \right] \qquad (decomposition)$$

The additional axioms are simply the definition of the *predecessor* function and its *decomposition* property. Note that the predecessor theory has no induction principle at all.

Proposition (decomposition vs. generator induction)

In the predecessor theory, for an arbitrary sentence $\mathcal{F}[x]$,

the decomposition induction principle
is equivalent to
the generator induction principle. ⌐

Let us first show that this proposition implies the validity of the decomposition induction principle in the augmented theory of the nonnegative integers.

Proof (decomposition induction)

The above *positive* and *predecessor* sentences, which were added as axioms to the predecessor theory, have also been taken as axioms in the (augmented) theory of the nonnegative integers. The *decomposition* sentence, which was also added as an axiom to the predecessor theory, has been shown to be valid in the theory of the nonnegative integers. In short, all the axioms of the predecessor theory are valid in the theory of the nonnegative integers; that is, the predecessor theory is contained in the theory of the nonnegative integers. Hence (by the *decomposition-vs.-generator* proposition) the two versions of the induction principle are equivalent in the theory of the nonnegative integers as well. Because in the theory of the nonnegative integers, for any sentence $\mathcal{F}[x]$, the generator induction principle is an axiom, the decomposition induction principle is valid. ⌐

Now let us establish the equivalence between the two induction principles in the predecessor theory.

Proof (decomposition vs. generator)

Consider an arbitrary sentence $\mathcal{F}[x]$ in the predecessor theory. The base cases $\mathcal{F}[0]$ and the consequents (*for all integer x*)$\mathcal{F}[x]$ are identical in the two versions of the induction principle. Therefore it suffices to show that the inductive steps of the two versions are equivalent, i.e., the decomposition inductive step,

$$(\textit{for all positive } x) \begin{bmatrix} \textit{if} & \mathcal{F}[x-1] \\ \textit{then} & \mathcal{F}[x] \end{bmatrix},$$

is equivalent to the generator inductive step,

$$(\textit{for all integer } x) \begin{bmatrix} \textit{if} & \mathcal{F}[x] \\ \textit{then} & \mathcal{F}[x+1] \end{bmatrix}.$$

We prove each direction of the equivalence separately.

Decomposition inductive step ⇒ generator inductive step

Suppose the decomposition inductive step,

$$(\textit{for all positive } x') \begin{bmatrix} \textit{if } \mathcal{F}[x'-1] \\ \textit{then } \mathcal{F}[x'] \end{bmatrix},$$

is true; to avoid confusion with the generator inductive step, we have renamed the bound variable x to x' (where x' does not occur in $\mathcal{F}[x]$). Consider an arbitrary nonnegative integer x and suppose that

$$\mathcal{F}[x]$$

is true; we would like to show that

$$\mathcal{F}[x+1]$$

is also true.

It suffices by the above decomposition inductive step (taking x' to be $x+1$) to show that

$$positive(x+1) \quad \text{and} \quad \mathcal{F}\big[(x+1)-1\big].$$

We know (by the *sort* property of the *positive* relation) that

$$positive(x+1).$$

Also (by the *predecessor* axiom of the predecessor theory)

$$x \;=\; (x+1)-1.$$

Therefore (by the substitutivity of equality, because $\mathcal{F}[x]$ is true)

$$\mathcal{F}\big[(x+1)-1\big]$$

is true, as we wanted to show.

Generator inductive step ⇒ decomposition inductive step

Suppose the generator inductive step,

$$(\textit{for all integer } x) \begin{bmatrix} \textit{if } \mathcal{F}[x] \\ \textit{then } \mathcal{F}[x+1] \end{bmatrix},$$

is true. Consider an arbitrary positive integer x' and suppose that

$$\mathcal{F}[x'-1]$$

is true; we would like to show that

$$\mathcal{F}[x']$$

is also true.

We have (by the generator inductive step, taking x to be $x' - 1$)

> *if* $\mathcal{F}[x' - 1]$
> *then* $\mathcal{F}[(x' - 1) + 1]$.

Therefore, because $\mathcal{F}[x' - 1]$, we obtain

$$\mathcal{F}[(x' - 1) + 1].$$

We have (by the *decomposition* axiom of the predecessor theory, because x' is positive)

$$(x' - 1) + 1 \ = \ x'.$$

Therefore (by the substitutivity of equality) we conclude

$$\mathcal{F}[x'],$$

as we wanted to show. ◢

We have seen that the *decomposition-vs.-generator* proposition implies the validity of the decomposition induction principle in the theory of the nonnegative integers. It also implies that we can actually replace the generator induction principle with the decomposition version in the theory of the nonnegative integers, obtaining an equivalent theory, provided we add as special axioms the definition of the predecessor function, its *decomposition* property, and the definition of the *positive* relation. The definition of the predecessor function and *positive* relation are required because we use them in the statement of the decomposition induction principle; the *decomposition* property is required because it cannot be proved from the decomposition version of the induction principle, but only from the generator version. The reader is requested to show this in **Problem 6.12(b)**. (This exercise is included as one of the last problems in the chapter because of its theoretical nature.)

Because the decomposition induction principle is valid in the theory of the nonnegative integers, we can use either the generator or the decomposition version of the induction principle in establishing the validity of a sentence in the theory. Which version is more convenient to use in a proof depends on how we choose to formulate our axioms and properties. If these tend to refer to the successor $x + 1$, the generator version will be more convenient; if they refer to the predecessor $x - 1$, the decomposition version will be more convenient. In this book we typically use the successor function; therefore the generator version is usually easier to use.

In the following section we introduce new axioms using the predecessor function $x - 1$; the decomposition version of the induction principle will be more convenient in proving propositions from these axioms.

6.6   THE WEAK LESS-THAN RELATION

Suppose we augment our theory further by formulating two axioms that define a binary predicate symbol $x \leq y$, denoting the *weak less-than relation* under the intended model for the nonnegative integers.

The axioms for the weak less-than relation are as follows:

$$
(\textit{for all integer } x) \begin{bmatrix} x \leq 0 \\ \quad \textit{if and only if} \\ x = 0 \end{bmatrix} \qquad (\textit{right zero})
$$

$$
\begin{matrix} (\textit{for all integer } x) \\ (\textit{for all positive } y) \end{matrix} \begin{bmatrix} x \leq y \\ \quad \textit{if and only if} \\ x = y \ \textit{ or } \ x \leq y - 1 \end{bmatrix} \qquad (\textit{right predecessor})
$$

As usual, because we are introducing a new binary predicate symbol $\leq$ into a theory with equality, we automatically add the corresponding two instances of the *predicate-substitutivity* equality axiom schema for the weak less-than relation.

Example (computation of $\leq$)

Let us use the axioms to compute the truth value of $0 \leq 1$, that is, $0 \leq 0 + 1$. We have

$$0 \leq 0 + 1$$

precisely when (by the above *right predecessor* axiom, because *not* $(0 + 1 = 0)$)

$$0 = 0 + 1 \quad \textit{or} \quad 0 \leq (0 + 1) - 1$$

precisely when (because *not* $(0 = 0 + 1)$)

$$0 \leq (0 + 1) - 1$$

precisely when (by the definition of the predecessor function)

$$0 \leq 0$$

precisely when (by the above *right-zero* axiom)

$$0 = 0,$$

which is true.   ◢

We can now establish the following proposition in the augmented theory:

Proposition (left addition)

The sentence

$$(\textit{for all integer } x) \ (\textit{for all integer } y) \left[\begin{array}{l} x \le y \\ \textit{if and only if} \\ (\textit{for some integer } z)\,[x + z = y] \end{array} \right]$$

is valid.   ◢

The proof will employ the decomposition version of the induction principle.

Proof

By predicate logic, it suffices to establish the validity of the two sentences

$(\Rightarrow)$ $(\textit{for all integer } x) \ (\textit{for all integer } y) \left[\begin{array}{l} \textit{if } x \le y \\ \textit{then } (\textit{for some integer } z)\,[x + z = y] \end{array} \right]$

and

$(\Leftarrow)$ $(\textit{for all integer } x) \ (\textit{for all integer } y) \left[\begin{array}{l} \textit{if } (\textit{for some integer } z)\,[x + z = y] \\ \textit{then } x \le y \end{array} \right].$

We prove only the $(\Rightarrow)$ part here; the proof of the $(\Leftarrow)$ part is left as an exercise (**Problem 6.6(a)**).

To prove the $(\Rightarrow)$ part, consider an arbitrary nonnegative integer x; we would like to show

$$(\textit{for all integer } y) \left[\begin{array}{l} \textit{if } x \le y \\ \textit{then } (\textit{for some integer } z)\,[x + z = y] \end{array} \right].$$

The proof is by decomposition induction on y, taking the inductive sentence to be

$$\mathcal{F}[y]: \quad \begin{array}{l} \textit{if } x \le y \\ \textit{then } (\textit{for some integer } z)\,[x + z = y]. \end{array}$$

Base Case

We would like to show

$$\mathcal{F}[0] : \quad \begin{array}{l} if \ x \leq 0 \\ then \ (for \ some \ integer \ z)\big[x + z = 0\big]. \end{array}$$

Suppose that

$$x \leq 0.$$

Then (by the *right-zero* axiom for the weak less-than relation $\leq$)

$$x = 0$$

and hence (by the *right-zero* axiom for addition)

$$x + 0 = 0.$$

Therefore (by the *existential quantifier-instantiation* proposition, taking z to be 0)

$$(for \ some \ integer \ z)\big[x + z = 0\big],$$

establishing the desired base case.

Inductive Step

For an arbitrary positive integer y, assume the induction hypothesis

$$\mathcal{F}[y - 1] : \quad \begin{array}{l} if \ x \leq y - 1 \\ then \ (for \ some \ integer \ z)\big[x + z \ = \ y - 1\big]. \end{array}$$

We would like to establish the desired conclusion

$$\mathcal{F}[y] : \quad \begin{array}{l} if \ x \leq y \\ then \ (for \ some \ integer \ z')\big[x + z' \ = \ y\big]. \end{array}$$

(We have renamed the bound variable z of the desired conclusion $\mathcal{F}[y]$ to z', to avoid confusion with the variable z of the induction hypothesis.)

We suppose that

$$x \leq y$$

and would like to show that

$$(for \ some \ integer \ z')\big[x + z' \ = \ y\big].$$

Because $x \leq y$ and y is positive, we have (by the *right-predecessor* axiom for the weak less-than relation $\leq$)

$$x = y \ \ or \ \ x \leq y - 1.$$

We treat each case separately.

Case: $x = y$

Then (by the *right-zero* axiom for addition)

$$x + 0 = y$$

and (by the *existential quantifier-instantiation* proposition, taking z' to be 0)

$$(\textit{for some integer } z')\big[x + z' \ = \ y\big],$$

which is the desired result.

Case: $x \le y - 1$

Then (by our induction hypothesis $\mathcal{F}[y - 1]$)

$$(\textit{for some integer } z)\big[x + z \ = \ y - 1\big].$$

Consider a nonnegative integer z such that

$$x + z \ = \ y - 1.$$

Then (by the *functional-substitutivity* axiom for the successor function)

$$(x + z) + 1 \ = \ (y - 1) + 1.$$

Hence (by the *right-successor* axiom for addition and by the decomposition property of the *predecessor* relation, because y is positive) we have

$$x + (z + 1) \ = \ y.$$

Finally (by the *existential quantifier-instantiation* proposition, taking z' to be $z + 1$) we obtain

$$(\textit{for some integer } z')\big[x + z' \ = \ y\big],$$

which is our desired result.

Because we have proved the desired result in each case, we have established the inductive step. ∎

Remark (generator vs. decomposition induction)

It was convenient to use the decomposition version of the induction principle in the above proposition because we had defined the weak less-than relation $\le$ by the *right-predecessor* axiom

$$(\textit{for all integer } x) \quad \begin{bmatrix} x \leq y \\ \textit{if and only if} \\ x = y \ \textit{ or } \ x \leq y - 1 \end{bmatrix}$$
$$(\textit{for all positive } y)$$

Had we instead used the alternative *right-successor* axiom for $\leq$,

$$(\textit{for all integer } x) \quad \begin{bmatrix} x \leq y + 1 \\ \textit{if and only if} \\ x = y + 1 \ \textit{ or } \ x \leq y \end{bmatrix} \qquad (\textit{right successor})$$
$$(\textit{for all integer } y)$$

to define the relation, it would have been more natural to use the generator version of the induction principle in the proof.

As an exercise (**Problem 6.6(b)**), we request the reader to prove the *left-addition* proposition for the weak less-than relation using the *right-successor* axiom for the relation rather than the *right-predecessor* axiom.   ◢

The weak less-than relation we have defined can be shown to be a weak partial ordering; in other words, we can establish the validity of the three weak partial-ordering axioms for $\leq$:

$$(\textit{for all integer } x)$$
$$(\textit{for all integer } y) \quad \begin{bmatrix} \textit{if } x \leq y \ \textit{ and } \ y \leq z \\ \textit{then } \ x \leq z \end{bmatrix} \qquad (\textit{transitivity})$$
$$(\textit{for all integer } z)$$

$$(\textit{for all integer } x) \quad \begin{bmatrix} \textit{if } x \leq y \ \textit{ and } \ y \leq x \\ \textit{then } \ x = y \end{bmatrix} \qquad (\textit{antisymmetry})$$
$$(\textit{for all integer } y)$$

$$(\textit{for all integer } x)[x \leq x] \qquad (\textit{reflexivity})$$

We can also establish the following properties of the weak less-than relation:

$$(\textit{for all integer } x)\big[0 \leq x\big] \qquad (\textit{left zero})$$

$$(\textit{for all integer } x)$$
$$(\textit{for all integer } y) \Big[x \leq x + y\Big] \qquad (\textit{right addition})$$

$$(\textit{for all integer } x)$$
$$(\textit{for all integer } y) \Big[x \leq y \ \textit{ or } \ y \leq x\Big] \qquad (\textit{totality})$$

This last property states that $\leq$ is actually a total weak partial ordering.

The predicate symbol $\geq$ denotes the *weak greater-than relation*, which is the inverse of the weak less-than relation $\leq$. It is defined by the following axiom:

$$(\textit{for all integer } x) \begin{bmatrix} x \geq y \\ \quad \textit{if and only if} \\ y \leq x \end{bmatrix} \qquad (\textit{weak greater-than})$$
$(\textit{for all integer } y)$

EXPRESSING PROPERTIES OF FUNCTIONS

We can now express the properties of several other functions in terms of the weak less-than relation. For the subtraction function, we can establish the following properties:

$$(\textit{for all integer } x) \begin{bmatrix} \textit{if } x \leq y \\ \textit{then } \textit{integer}(y - x) \end{bmatrix} \qquad (\textit{sort})$$
$(\textit{for all integer } y)$

$$(\textit{for all integer } x) \begin{bmatrix} \textit{if } x \leq y \\ \textit{then } x + (y - x) \; = \; y \end{bmatrix} \qquad (\textit{decomposition})$$
$(\textit{for all integer } y)$

$$(\textit{for all integer } x) \qquad \begin{bmatrix} \textit{if } x \leq y \\ \quad \textit{then} \begin{bmatrix} x + z = y \\ \quad \textit{if and only if} \\ z = y - x \end{bmatrix} \end{bmatrix} \qquad (\textit{cancellation})$$
$(\textit{for all integer } y)$
$(\textit{for all integer } z)$

For the monus function we can express the following properties:

$$(\textit{for all integer } x) \begin{bmatrix} \textit{if } y \leq x \\ \textit{then } x \div y \; = \; x - y \end{bmatrix} \qquad (\textit{subtraction})$$
$(\textit{for all integer } y)$

$$(\textit{for all integer } x) \begin{bmatrix} \textit{if } x \leq y \\ \textit{then } x \div y = 0 \end{bmatrix} \qquad (\textit{less-than})$$
$(\textit{for all integer } y)$

We can augment our theory further by introducing two binary function symbols $max(x, y)$ and $min(x, y)$, denoting the *maximum* and *minimum*, respectively, of the nonnegative integers x and y. The axioms that define these functions are as follows:

$$
\begin{array}{l}
\textit{(for all integer x)} \\
\textit{(for all integer y)}
\end{array}
\left[max(x,\, y) = \begin{bmatrix} \textit{if } x \leq y \\ \textit{then } y \\ \textit{else } x \end{bmatrix} \right]
\qquad (\textit{maximum})
$$

$$
\begin{array}{l}
\textit{(for all integer x)} \\
\textit{(for all integer y)}
\end{array}
\left[min(x,\, y) = \begin{bmatrix} \textit{if } x \leq y \\ \textit{then } x \\ \textit{else } y \end{bmatrix} \right]
\qquad (\textit{minimum})
$$

From these axioms we can establish the following properties of the maximum and minimum functions:

$$
\begin{array}{l}
\textit{(for all integer x)} \\
\textit{(for all integer y)}
\end{array}
\begin{bmatrix} max(x,\, y) \geq x \\ and \\ max(x,\, y) \geq y \end{bmatrix}
\qquad (\textit{greater-than})
$$

$$
\begin{array}{l}
\textit{(for all integer x)} \\
\textit{(for all integer y)}
\end{array}
\begin{bmatrix} min(x,\, y) \leq x \\ and \\ min(x,\, y) \leq y \end{bmatrix}
\qquad (\textit{less-than})
$$

$$
\begin{array}{l}
\textit{(for all integer x)} \\
\textit{(for all integer y)} \\
\textit{(for all integer z)}
\end{array}
\begin{bmatrix} min\big(x,\, max(y,\, z)\big) \\ = \\ max\big(min(x,\, y),\, min(x,\, z)\big) \end{bmatrix}
\qquad (\textit{minimax})
$$

$$
\begin{array}{l}
\textit{(for all integer x)} \\
\textit{(for all integer y)} \\
\textit{(for all integer z)}
\end{array}
\begin{bmatrix} max\big(x,\, min(y,\, z)\big) \\ = \\ min\big(max(x,\, y),\, max(x,\, z)\big) \end{bmatrix}
\qquad (\textit{maximin})
$$

The reader is requested to establish the *greater-than* and *minimax* properties in **Problem 6.7**.

6.7 THE STRICT LESS-THAN RELATION

We have established (in the *strict partial-ordering* proposition of the theory of associated relations) that if $\preceq$ is a weak partial ordering, its irreflexive restriction $\prec$, defined by the axiom

$$
\begin{array}{l}
\textit{(for all x)} \\
\textit{(for all y)}
\end{array}
\begin{bmatrix} x \prec y \\ \textit{if and only if} \\ x \preceq y \ \ and \ \ not\,(x = y) \end{bmatrix},
$$

is a strict partial ordering, i.e., it is transitive and irreflexive.

We have already remarked that the weak less-than relation $\leq$ is a weak partial ordering. Let us augment the theory further to define a new binary predicate symbol $<$, denoting the (*strict*) *less-than relation,* by the following axiom:

$$
\begin{array}{ll}
\textit{(for all integer x)} & \left[\begin{array}{l} x < y \\ \quad \textit{if and only if} \\ x \leq y \ \ \textit{and not} \ (x = y) \end{array}\right] \\
\textit{(for all integer y)} &
\end{array}
\qquad (\textit{less-than})
$$

In other words, $<$ denotes the irreflexive restriction of the weak less-than relation $\leq$. Then we know that $<$ is a strict partial ordering in the augmented theory; i.e., the sentences

$$
\begin{array}{l}
\textit{(for all integer x)} \\
\textit{(for all integer y)} \\
\textit{(for all integer z)}
\end{array}
\left[\begin{array}{l} \textit{if } x < y \ \textit{ and } y < z \\ \textit{then } x < z \end{array}\right]
\qquad (\textit{transitivity})
$$

$$
\textit{(for all integer x)} \left[\textit{not } (x < x)\right]
\qquad (\textit{irreflexivity})
$$

are valid. Therefore any property we can prove in the theory of the strict partial orderings is valid in our augmented theory of the nonnegative integers. For example, the *asymmetry* property

$$
\begin{array}{l}
\textit{(for all integer x)} \\
\textit{(for all integer y)}
\end{array}
\left[\begin{array}{l} \textit{if } x < y \\ \textit{then } \textit{not } (y < x) \end{array}\right]
\qquad (\textit{asymmetry})
$$

is valid.

We have defined the strict less-than predicate symbol $<$ to denote the irreflexive restriction of the weak less-than relation $\leq$. We can also show that the weak less-than predicate symbol $\leq$ denotes the reflexive closure of $<$, that is,

$$
\begin{array}{l}
\textit{(for all integer x)} \\
\textit{(for all integer y)}
\end{array}
\left[\begin{array}{l} x \leq y \\ \quad \textit{if and only if} \\ x < y \ \textit{ or } \ x = y \end{array}\right]
\qquad (\textit{reflexive closure})
$$

The less-than relation $<$ can be shown to be total, that is,

$$
\begin{array}{l}
\textit{(for all integer x)} \\
\textit{(for all integer y)}
\end{array}
\left[x < y \ \textit{ or } \ y < x \ \textit{ or } \ x = y\right]
\qquad (\textit{totality})
$$

It follows (by the *total-asymmetry* proposition of the theory of associated relations, because $<$ is asymmetric and total) that

$$
\begin{array}{l}
\textit{(for all integer x)} \\
\textit{(for all integer y)}
\end{array}
\left[\begin{array}{l} \textit{not } (x < y) \\ \quad \textit{if and only if} \\ y \leq x \end{array}\right]
\qquad (\textit{total asymmetry})
$$

The predicate symbol $>$, denoting the corresponding (*strict*) *greater-than relation*, is defined by the axiom

$$\begin{array}{l} (\textit{for all integer } x) \\ (\textit{for all integer } y) \end{array} \left[\begin{array}{l} x > y \\ \quad \textit{if and only if} \\ y < x \end{array} \right] \qquad\qquad (\textit{greater-than})$$

We can also establish the following properties of the strict less-than relation:

$$\begin{array}{l} (\textit{for all integer } x) \\ (\textit{for all integer } y) \end{array} \left[\begin{array}{l} x < y \\ \quad \textit{if and only if} \\ (\textit{for some positive } z)[x + z = y] \end{array} \right] \qquad (\textit{left addition})$$

$$(\textit{for all positive } x) \big[0 < x \big] \qquad\qquad\qquad\qquad\quad (\textit{left zero})$$

$$(\textit{for all integer } x) \big[\textit{not } (x < 0) \big] \qquad\qquad\qquad\quad (\textit{right zero})$$

$$(\textit{for all integer } x) \big[x < x + 1 \big] \qquad\qquad\qquad\quad (\textit{adjacent})$$

$$\begin{array}{l} (\textit{for all integer } x) \\ (\textit{for all positive } y) \end{array} \big[x < x + y \big] \qquad\qquad\qquad (\textit{right addition})$$

$$\begin{array}{l} (\textit{for all integer } x) \\ (\textit{for all integer } y) \end{array} \left[\begin{array}{l} x < y + 1 \\ \quad \textit{if and only if} \\ x \leq y \end{array} \right] \qquad\qquad (\textit{right successor})$$

$$\begin{array}{l} (\textit{for all integer } x) \\ (\textit{for all integer } y) \end{array} \left[\begin{array}{l} x < y \\ \quad \textit{if and only if} \\ x + 1 \leq y \end{array} \right] \qquad\qquad (\textit{left successor})$$

6.8   COMPLETE INDUCTION

Using the less-than relation $<$, we can state and prove an alternative version of the induction principle, which is often much more convenient to use.

Proposition (complete induction principle)

For each sentence $\mathcal{F}[x]$, the universal closure of the sentence

$$if\ (for\ all\ integer\ x)\ \begin{bmatrix} if\ (for\ all\ integer\ x') \begin{bmatrix} if\ x' < x \\ then\ \mathcal{F}[x'] \end{bmatrix} \\ then\ \mathcal{F}[x] \end{bmatrix}$$

$$then\ (for\ all\ integer\ x)\mathcal{F}[x]$$

$$(complete\ induction)$$

where x' does not occur free in $\mathcal{F}[x]$, is valid.   ⌐

As usual, the sentence $\mathcal{F}[x]$ is called the *inductive sentence* and the variable x is called the *inductive variable*. The antecedent of the principle,

$$(for\ all\ integer\ x)\ \begin{bmatrix} if\ (for\ all\ integer\ x') \begin{bmatrix} if\ x' < x \\ then\ \mathcal{F}[x'] \end{bmatrix} \\ then\ \mathcal{F}[x] \end{bmatrix},$$

is called the *inductive step*; the subsentences

$$(for\ all\ integer\ x')\begin{bmatrix} if\ x' < x \\ then\ \mathcal{F}[x'] \end{bmatrix} \qquad and \qquad \mathcal{F}[x]$$

of the inductive step are called the *induction hypothesis* and the *desired conclusion*, respectively.

The complete induction principle may be paraphrased informally as follows:

To prove that a sentence $\mathcal{F}[x]$ is true for every nonnegative integer x, it suffices to prove the inductive step

for an arbitrary nonnegative integer x,
 if $\mathcal{F}[x']$ is true for every nonnegative integer x'
  such that $x' < x$,
 then $\mathcal{F}[x]$ is also true.

In other words, to prove that a sentence $\mathcal{F}[x]$ is true for every nonnegative integer x, it suffices to show that, for an arbitrary nonnegative integer x, if

$$\mathcal{F}[0], \quad \mathcal{F}[1], \quad \mathcal{F}[2], \quad \ldots, \quad and \quad \mathcal{F}[x-1]$$

are all true, then

$$\mathcal{F}[x]$$

is also true.

Let us postpone the proof of the complete induction principle until we have had a chance to illustrate its application.

6.9   QUOTIENT AND REMAINDER

Suppose we augment our theory by defining two binary function symbols, $quot(x, y)$ and $rem(x, y)$. Under the intended model for the nonnegative integers, these symbols denote the *quotient* and *remainder*, respectively, of dividing a nonnegative integer x by a positive integer y. The axioms for the quotient of dividing x by y are

$$(\textit{for all integer } x) \begin{bmatrix} \textit{if } x < y \\ \textit{then } quot(x, y) = 0 \end{bmatrix} \qquad (\textit{less-than})$$
$$(\textit{for all positive } y)$$

$$(\textit{for all integer } x) \Big[quot(x + y, y) \; = \; quot(x, y) + 1 \Big] \qquad (\textit{addition})$$
$$(\textit{for all positive } y)$$

The axioms for the remainder of dividing x by y are

$$(\textit{for all integer } x) \begin{bmatrix} \textit{if } x < y \\ \textit{then } rem(x, y) = x \end{bmatrix} \qquad (\textit{less-than})$$
$$(\textit{for all positive } y)$$

$$(\textit{for all integer } x) \Big[rem(x + y, y) \; = \; rem(x, y) \Big] \qquad (\textit{addition})$$
$$(\textit{for all positive } y)$$

Note that the axioms for the quotient and remainder do not specify the values of terms of form $quot(s, 0)$ or $rem(s, 0)$. Again, although such terms are legal in the language, the axioms do not allow us to prove any properties about them.

From these axioms, we can establish the usual *sort* properties for the quotient function,

$$(\textit{for all integer } x) \Big[integer\big(quot(x, y)\big) \Big] \qquad (\textit{sort})$$
$$(\textit{for all positive } y)$$

and for the remainder function,

$$(\textit{for all integer } x) \Big[integer\big(rem(x, y)\big) \Big] \qquad (\textit{sort})$$
$$(\textit{for all positive } y)$$

The reader is requested to prove these properties in **Problem 6.8.**

The following proposition expresses a relationship between the quotient and remainder functions.

Proposition (quotient-remainder)

The sentence

$$(\textit{for all integer } x) \atop (\textit{for all positive } y) \left[{x \; = \; y \cdot quot(x, \, y) + rem(x, \, y) \atop \textit{and} \atop rem(x, \, y) < y} \right]$$

(*quotient-remainder*)

is valid. ⌐

The proof illustrates the use of the complete induction principle.

Proof

We actually prove the equivalent sentence

$$(\textit{for all positive } y) \atop (\textit{for all integer } x) \left[{x \; = \; y \cdot quot(x, \, y) + rem(x, \, y) \atop \textit{and} \atop rem(x, \, y) < y} \right]$$

(obtained by reversing the quantifiers).

Consider an arbitrary positive integer y. We would like to show that

$$(\textit{for all integer } x) \left[{x \; = \; y \cdot quot(x, \, y) + rem(x, \, y) \atop \textit{and} \atop rem(x, \, y) < y} \right].$$

The proof is by complete induction on x; we take the inductive sentence to be

$$\mathcal{F}[x]: \quad {x \; = \; y \cdot quot(x, \, y) + rem(x, \, y) \atop \textit{and} \atop rem(x, \, y) < y.}$$

To prove (*for all integer* x)$\mathcal{F}[x]$, it suffices only to establish the inductive step.

Inductive Step

We would like to show

$$(\textit{for all integer } x) \left[\textit{if } (\textit{for all integer } x') \left[{\textit{if } x' < x \atop \textit{then } \mathcal{F}[x']} \right] \atop \textit{then } \mathcal{F}[x] \right].$$

For an arbitrary nonnegative integer x, we assume the induction hypothesis

$$(\textit{for all integer } x') \left[{\textit{if } x' < x \atop \textit{then } \mathcal{F}[x']} \right]$$

and attempt to show the desired conclusion

$$\mathcal{F}[x],$$

that is,

$$x = y \cdot quot(x, y) + rem(x, y)$$
$$and$$
$$rem(x, y) < y.$$

Following the way the quotient and remainder are defined, we distinguish between two subcases, depending on whether or not $x < y$.

Case: $x < y$

Then (by the *less-than* axioms for the quotient and remainder, because y is positive) we have

$$quot(x, y) = 0 \quad and \quad rem(x, y) = x.$$

The desired conclusion $\mathcal{F}[x]$ then reduces to

$$x = y \cdot 0 + x$$
$$and$$
$$x < y.$$

The first conjunct follows from the *right-zero* axiom for multiplication and the *left-zero* property of addition; the second conjunct is the assumption for this subcase.

Case: $not\ (x < y)$

Then (by the *total-asymmetry* property of the less-than relation)

$$y \leq x$$

and hence (by the *decomposition* property of the weak less-than relation)

$$y + (x - y) = x,$$

that is (by the *commutativity* property of addition),

$$x = (x - y) + y.$$

Hence (by *addition* axioms for the quotient and remainder, because y is positive) we have

$$quot(x, y) = quot\big((x - y) + y,\ y\big) = quot(x - y,\ y) + 1$$

and

$$rem(x, y) \;=\; rem\big((x-y)+y, \; y\big) \;=\; rem(x-y, \; y).$$

We would like to show $\mathcal{F}[x]$, that is,

$$x \;=\; y \cdot quot(x, \; y) + rem(x, \; y)$$
$$and$$
$$rem(x, \; y) < y,$$

which expands (in this case) to

$$x \;=\; y \cdot \big(quot(x-y, \; y)+1\big) + rem(x-y, \; y)$$
$$and$$
$$rem(x-y, \; y) < y.$$

This can be transformed (by the *right-successor* axiom for multiplication) into

$$x = \big(y \cdot quot(x-y, \; y)+y\big) + rem(x-y, \; y)$$
$$and$$
$$rem(x-y, \; y) < y.$$

This can be transformed further (by the *commutativity* and *associativity* properties of addition) into

$$x \;=\; \big(y \cdot quot(x-y, \; y) + rem(x-y, \; y)\big) + y$$
$$and$$
$$rem(x-y, \; y) < y.$$

Therefore (by the *cancellation* property of subtraction, because, in this case, $y \leq x$) it suffices to establish

$$x - y \;=\; y \cdot quot(x-y, \; y) + rem(x-y, \; y)$$
$$and$$
$$rem(x-y, \; y) < y,$$

which is precisely $\mathcal{F}[x-y]$.

We have assumed as our induction hypothesis that

$$(for \; all \; integer \; x') \begin{bmatrix} if \; x' < x \\ then \; \mathcal{F}[x'] \end{bmatrix}.$$

In particular, taking x' to be $x - y$, we have

$$if \; x-y < x$$
$$then \; \mathcal{F}[x-y].$$

Because $(x - y) + y = x$ and y is positive, it follows (by the *left-addition* property of the less-than relation $<$) that

$$x - y < x,$$

and thus we have the desired result $\mathcal{F}[x - y]$.

Because we have completed the proof of the inductive step, we have established the *quotient-remainder* proposition. ◢

Remark (Why not stepwise induction?)

Note that the above proposition would be awkward to prove by stepwise induction rather than complete induction. In the inductive step we showed that, to prove our desired conclusion $\mathcal{F}[x]$, it suffices (in the case in which *not* $(x < y)$) to establish the condition

$$\mathcal{F}[x - y].$$

This turned out to be implied by our induction hypothesis

$$(for\ all\ integer\ x')\ \begin{bmatrix} if\ x' < x \\ then\ \mathcal{F}[x'] \end{bmatrix},$$

taking x' to be $x - y$, since in this case $x - y < x$.

Had we attempted the proof by, say, the decomposition version of stepwise induction, our induction hypothesis would have been simply

$$\mathcal{F}[x - 1].$$

This does not necessarily imply $\mathcal{F}[x-y]$, because we do not know that $y = 1$. The induction hypothesis of the complete-induction proof tells us not only $\mathcal{F}[x - 1]$ but the entire conjunction of

$$\mathcal{F}[0], \quad \mathcal{F}[1], \quad \ldots, \quad \mathcal{F}[x - 2], \quad and \quad \mathcal{F}[x - 1]. ◢$$

Remark (Where is the base case?)

The reader may be puzzled to note that, although the earlier stepwise induction principle requires us to prove a base case and an inductive step, the complete induction principle requires only an induction step. At first glance, it may seem as if we are getting something for nothing in using complete induction.

This appearance is misleading: In proving the inductive step for complete induction,

$$(for\ all\ integer\ x)\left[\begin{array}{l} if\ (for\ all\ integer\ x')\left[\begin{array}{l} if\ x' < x \\ then\ \mathcal{F}[x'] \end{array}\right] \\ then\ \mathcal{F}[x] \end{array}\right],$$

we must actually consider the possibility that the arbitrary nonnegative integer x is 0. In this case our induction hypothesis is

$$(for\ all\ integer\ x')\left[\begin{array}{l} if\ x' < 0 \\ then\ \mathcal{F}[x'] \end{array}\right].$$

Because (by the *right-zero* property for the less-than relation $<$) there are no nonnegative integers x' such that $x' < 0$, we can never make use of the induction hypothesis in this case. Therefore we must prove the desired conclusion $\mathcal{F}[x]$, that is, $\mathcal{F}[0]$, without the help of the induction hypothesis, just as in the base case of a stepwise induction proof.

In the *quotient-remainder* proposition above, for instance, we had to prove the inductive step

$$(for\ all\ integer\ x)\left[\begin{array}{l} if\ (for\ all\ integer\ x')\left[\begin{array}{l} if\ x' < x \\ then\ \mathcal{F}[x'] \end{array}\right] \\ then\ \mathcal{F}[x] \end{array}\right].$$

In this proof, we treated separately the case in which $x < y$. Because we have taken y to be positive, this case includes the possibility that $x = 0$. The case was handled without appealing to the induction hypothesis.   **⌟**

The proposition we have just established states that, for any nonnegative integer x and positive integer y, the quotient $quot(x, y)$ and the remainder $rem(x, y)$ exhibit the *quotient-remainder* relationship

$$x = y \cdot quot(x, y) + rem(x, y)$$
$$and$$
$$rem(x, y) < y.$$

It can actually be shown that $quot(x, y)$ and $rem(x, y)$ are unique, in the sense that, for all nonnegative integers u and v satisfying the *quotient-remainder* relationship

$$x = y \cdot u + v$$
$$and$$
$$v < y,$$

we have

$$u = quot(x, y) \quad and \quad v = rem(x, y).$$

The proof is requested as an exercise (**Problem 6.8(c)**).

6.10 PROOF OF COMPLETE INDUCTION

We are now ready to give the proof of the complete induction principle.

Proof (complete induction)

For an arbitrary sentence $\mathcal{F}[x]$, suppose that

$$(*) \qquad (\textit{for all integer } x) \left[\begin{array}{l} \textit{if } (\textit{for all integer } x') \left[\begin{array}{l} \textit{if } x' < x \\ \textit{then } \mathcal{F}[x'] \end{array} \right] \\ \textit{then } \mathcal{F}[x] \end{array} \right]$$

is true; we would like to show that then

$$(\dagger) \qquad (\textit{for all integer } x)\mathcal{F}[x]$$

is true.

We actually prove an alternative property

$$(\ddagger) \qquad (\textit{for all integer } y)\mathcal{F}'[y],$$

where $\mathcal{F}'[y]$ is

$$\mathcal{F}'[y]: \quad (\textit{for all integer } x') \left[\begin{array}{l} \textit{if } x' < y \\ \textit{then } \mathcal{F}[x'] \end{array} \right]$$

and y is a new variable. Intuitively speaking, $\mathcal{F}'[y]$ is the conjunction of

$$\mathcal{F}[0], \quad \mathcal{F}[1], \quad \mathcal{F}[2], \quad \ldots, \quad \textit{and} \quad \mathcal{F}[y-1].$$

Proof that $(\ddagger) \Rightarrow (\dagger)$

To show that the alternative property $(\ddagger)$, that is, (*for all integer* $y)\mathcal{F}'[y]$, implies the original property $(\dagger)$, that is, (*for all integer* $x)\mathcal{F}[x]$, suppose that

$$(\textit{for all integer } y)\mathcal{F}'[y],$$

and consider an arbitrary nonnegative integer x; we attempt to show that

$$\mathcal{F}[x]$$

is true.

From the supposition (taking y to be $x + 1$) we have $\mathcal{F}'[x + 1]$, that is,

$$\textit{(for all integer } x')\begin{bmatrix} \textit{if } x' < x + 1 \\ \textit{then } \mathcal{F}[x'] \end{bmatrix}.$$

In particular (taking x' to be x), we have

$$\textit{if } x < x + 1$$
$$\textit{then } \mathcal{F}[x].$$

By the *adjacent* property of the less-than relation $<$, we know $x < x+1$. Therefore we conclude

$$\mathcal{F}[x],$$

as we wanted to show.

Proof that $(*) \Rightarrow (\ddagger)$

The proof of $(\ddagger)$,

$$\textit{(for all integer } y)\mathcal{F}'[y],$$

is by the original generator version of the stepwise induction principle; we take the inductive sentence to be $\mathcal{F}'[y]$.

Base Case

We would like to show $\mathcal{F}'[0]$, that is,

$$\textit{(for all integer } x')\begin{bmatrix} \textit{if } x' < 0 \\ \textit{then } \mathcal{F}[x'] \end{bmatrix}.$$

But, for an arbitrary nonnegative integer x', we have (by the *right-zero* property of the less-than relation $<$)

$$\textit{not } (x' < 0).$$

Therefore the entire implication is true.

Inductive Step

For an arbitrary nonnegative integer y, we assume the induction hypothesis (for the stepwise induction principle)

$$\mathcal{F}'[y]: \quad \textit{(for all integer } x')\begin{bmatrix} \textit{if } x' < y \\ \textit{then } \mathcal{F}[x'] \end{bmatrix}$$

and establish the desired conclusion (for the stepwise induction principle)

$$\mathcal{F}'[y+1]: \quad (\textit{for all integer } x') \begin{bmatrix} \textit{if } x' < y+1 \\ \textit{then } \mathcal{F}[x'] \end{bmatrix}.$$

Consider an arbitrary nonnegative integer x' such that

$$x' < y+1;$$

we would like to show that

$$\mathcal{F}[x'].$$

Since $x' < y+1$, we have (by the *right-successor* property of the less-than relation $<$) that $x' \leq y$ or, equivalently (because $\leq$ is the reflexive closure of $<$),

$$x' < y \ \textit{or} \ x' = y.$$

We treat each subcase separately.

Case: $x' < y$

By our induction hypothesis $\mathcal{F}'[y]$, we have

$$\textit{if } x' < y$$
$$\textit{then } \mathcal{F}[x'].$$

Therefore, because (in this case) $x' < y$, we obtain the desired result

$$\mathcal{F}[x'].$$

Case: $x' = y$

In this case we would like to show $\mathcal{F}[y]$. From our initial supposition $(*)$ (taking x to be y) we have

$$\textit{if } (\textit{for all integer } x') \begin{bmatrix} \textit{if } x' < y \\ \textit{then } \mathcal{F}[x'] \end{bmatrix}$$
$$\textit{then } \mathcal{F}[y].$$

Therefore it suffices to show

$$(\textit{for all integer } x') \begin{bmatrix} \textit{if } x' < y \\ \textit{then } \mathcal{F}[x'] \end{bmatrix};$$

but this is precisely our induction hypothesis $\mathcal{F}'[y]$.

Because we have completed the base case and the inductive step of the stepwise induction proof, we have established the validity of the complete induction principle. ⌟

As the proof of the above proposition illustrates, any sentence we can prove by complete induction we can also prove by stepwise induction, but the stepwise-induction proof may be more complex.

Some further applications of the complete induction principle are illustrated in the next section.

6.11   THE DIVIDES RELATION

In this section we introduce a new relation over the nonnegative integers and further illustrate the usefulness of the complete induction principle.

DIVIDES

Suppose we augment our theory by defining a new binary predicate symbol $x \preceq_{div} y$, denoting the *divides* relation, which holds when x divides y with no remainder. (The conventional symbol for this relation is $x|y$.)

The axiom for the divides relation is

$$
\boxed{
\begin{array}{l}
(\text{for all integer } x) \\
(\text{for all integer } y)
\end{array}
\left[
\begin{array}{l}
x \preceq_{div} y \\
\quad \text{if and only if} \\
(\text{for some integer } z)\left[x \cdot z = y\right]
\end{array}
\right]
}
\qquad (\text{divides})
$$

From this axiom we can establish the validity of the following properties of the divides relation:

$$(\text{for all integer } x)\left[x \preceq_{div} 0\right] \qquad\qquad (\text{right zero})$$

$$(\text{for all positive } y)\left[not \ (0 \preceq_{div} y)\right] \qquad\qquad (\text{left zero})$$

$$
\begin{array}{l}
(\text{for all integer } x) \\
(\text{for all integer } y) \\
(\text{for all integer } z)
\end{array}
\left[
\begin{array}{l}
x \preceq_{div} y \ \ and \ \ x \preceq_{div} z \\
\quad \text{if and only if} \\
x \preceq_{div} y \ \ and \ \ x \preceq_{div} (y + z)
\end{array}
\right]
\qquad (\text{addition})
$$

$$(\textit{for all integer } x) \atop \begin{array}{l}(\textit{for all integer } y)\\(\textit{for all integer } z)\end{array} \left[\begin{array}{l} \textit{if } x \preceq_{div} y \ \textit{ or } \ x \preceq_{div} z \\ \textit{then } x \preceq_{div} (y \cdot z) \end{array} \right] \qquad (\textit{multiplication})$$

$$\begin{array}{l}(\textit{for all positive } x)\\(\textit{for all integer } y)\end{array} \left[\begin{array}{c} x \preceq_{div} y \\ \textit{if and only if} \\ rem(y, \ x) = 0 \end{array} \right] \qquad (\textit{remainder})$$

We can also show that the divides relation is a weak partial ordering; in other words, we can establish the validity of the three weak-partial-ordering axioms for the divides relation, that is,

$$\begin{array}{l}(\textit{for all integer } x)\\(\textit{for all integer } y)\\(\textit{for all integer } z)\end{array} \left[\begin{array}{l} \textit{if } x \preceq_{div} y \ \textit{ and } \ y \preceq_{div} z \\ \textit{then } x \preceq_{div} z \end{array} \right] \qquad (\textit{transitivity})$$

$$\begin{array}{l}(\textit{for all integer } x)\\(\textit{for all integer } y)\end{array} \left[\begin{array}{l} \textit{if } x \preceq_{div} y \ \textit{ and } \ y \preceq_{div} x \\ \textit{then } x = y \end{array} \right] \qquad (\textit{antisymmetry})$$

$$(\textit{for all integer } x)\left[x \preceq_{div} x \right] \qquad (\textit{reflexivity})$$

Note that we cannot establish the *totality* property for the divides relation; in other words, the sentence

$$\begin{array}{l}(\textit{for all integer } x)\\(\textit{for all integer } y)\end{array} \left[x \preceq_{div} y \ \textit{ or } \ y \preceq_{div} x \ \textit{ or } \ x = y \right]$$

is not valid. For instance, none of $2 \preceq_{div} 3$, $3 \preceq_{div} 2$, or $2 = 3$ is true.

Note that the definition of the divides relation does not immediately suggest a method of computing the relation, i.e., of determining whether $s \preceq_{div} t$ for terms s and t denoting particular nonnegative integers. For this purpose it is necessary (according to the definition) to decide whether

$$(\textit{for some integer } z)[s \cdot z = t].$$

But since there are infinitely many nonnegative integers z to be tested, this is impossible.

There are other properties of the divides relation that do suggest methods to compute it. For example, we can establish the validity of the following properties:

$$\begin{array}{l}\textit{(for all integer } x)\\\textit{(for all positive } y)\end{array}\left[\begin{array}{l}\textit{if } x > y\\\textit{then not } (x \preceq_{div} y)\end{array}\right] \qquad (\textit{greater-than})$$

$$\begin{array}{l}\textit{(for all integer } x)\\\textit{(for all integer } y)\end{array}\left[\begin{array}{l}\textit{if } x \leq y\\\textit{then }\left[\begin{array}{c}x \preceq_{div} y\\\textit{if and only if}\\x \preceq_{div} (y - x)\end{array}\right]\end{array}\right] \qquad (\textit{subtraction})$$

These two properties, together with the *right-zero* and *left-zero* properties above, suggest a method for computing the divides relation.

Example (computation of $\preceq_{div}$)

Suppose we would like to determine whether 2 divides 4. We have

$$2 \preceq_{div} 4$$

precisely when (by the *subtraction* property, because $2 \leq 4$)

$$2 \preceq_{div} (4 - 2)$$

precisely when

$$2 \preceq_{div} 2$$

precisely when (by the *subtraction* property, because $2 \leq 2$)

$$2 \preceq_{div} (2 - 2)$$

precisely when

$$2 \preceq_{div} 0,$$

which is true (by the *right-zero* property). Note that we could have used the *reflexivity* property to determine that $2 \preceq_{div} 2$ is true, giving a shorter computation.

On the other hand, suppose we would like to determine whether 2 divides 3. We have

$$2 \preceq_{div} 3$$

precisely when (by the *subtraction* property, because $2 \leq 3$)

$$2 \preceq_{div} (3 - 2)$$

precisely when

$$2 \preceq_{div} 1,$$

which is false (by the *greater-than* property, because $2 > 1$ and 1 is positive). ⌐

In **Problem 6.9**, the reader is requested to show the validity of the *right-zero*, *left-zero*, *greater-than*, and *subtraction* properties of the divides relation and to show that these properties in fact constitute an alternative definition for the relation.

The *proper-divides* relation, denoted by $\prec_{div}$, is the irreflexive restriction of $\preceq_{div}$, defined by the axiom

$$(\textit{for all integer } x) \quad \begin{bmatrix} x \prec_{div} y \\ \quad \textit{if and only if} \\ x \preceq_{div} y \ \textit{ and } \ \textit{not } (x = y) \end{bmatrix} \qquad (\textit{proper divides})$$
$$(\textit{for all integer } y)$$

Because we have established that $\preceq_{div}$ is a weak partial ordering, we know immediately (by the *strict partial ordering* proposition of the theory of associated relations) that its irreflexive restriction $\prec_{div}$ is a strict partial ordering, i.e., it is transitive and irreflexive.

The proper divides relation $\prec_{div}$ may also be shown to satisfy the following property

$$(\textit{for all positive } x) \quad \begin{bmatrix} x \prec_{div} y \\ \quad \textit{if and only if} \\ (\textit{for some integer } z) \begin{bmatrix} x \cdot z = y \ \textit{ and} \\ \textit{not } (z = 1) \end{bmatrix} \end{bmatrix}$$
$$(\textit{for all positive } y)$$

$$(\textit{multiplication})$$

GREATEST COMMON DIVISOR

Let us further augment our system by defining a binary function symbol $gcd(x\,y)$ intended to denote the *greatest common divisor* of x and y. The axioms for the greatest-common-divisor function are

$$(\textit{for all integer } x)\big[gcd(x, 0) = x\big] \qquad (\textit{zero})$$

$$(\textit{for all integer } x) \atop (\textit{for all positive } y) \big[gcd(x, y) \ = \ gcd\big(y, \ rem(x, y)\big)\big] \qquad (\textit{remainder})$$

We illustrate the use of the axioms to compute the greatest common divisor of two particular nonnegative integers.

Example (computation of gcd)

Suppose we would like to determine the greatest common divisor of 6 and 9, assuming we can compute the remainder function *rem*. We have

$$gcd(6,\ 9) \ = \ gcd\big(9,\ rem(6,9)\big)$$
(by the *remainder* axiom, because 9 is positive)

$$= \ gcd(9,\ 6)$$

$$= \ gcd\big(6,\ rem(9,6)\big)$$
(by the *remainder* axiom, because 6 is positive)

$$= \ gcd(6,\ 3)$$

$$= \ gcd\big(3,\ rem(6,3)\big)$$
(by the *remainder* axiom, because 3 is positive)

$$= \ gcd(3,\ 0)$$

$$= \ 3$$
(by the *zero* axiom).

In short,

$$gcd(6,\ 9) \ = \ 3. \quad \lrcorner$$

Remark (consistency)

As usual when we introduce new axioms, we run the risk of making the theory inconsistent. Here the risk is greater than usual, because these axioms do not fit the same form as our previous recursive definitions. Typically, in defining a function f we have used a *successor* axiom, which expresses the value of $f(x, y+1)$ in terms of the value of $f(x, y)$. Here the *remainder* axiom expresses the value of $gcd(x, y)$, for positive y, in terms of the value of $gcd\big(y, rem(x, y)\big)$. The augmented theory is in fact consistent, but we omit discussion of this issue. $\quad \lrcorner$

It may not be clear at this point why the function defined by these axioms is called the "greatest common divisor." The following proposition establishes that $gcd(x, y)$ is a "common divisor" of x and y; later we shall observe that it is indeed the "greatest" of the common divisors.

Proposition (common divisor)

The sentence

$$(\textit{for all integer } x) \atop (\textit{for all integer } y) \begin{bmatrix} gcd(x,\ y) \preceq_{div} x \\ and \\ gcd(x,\ y) \preceq_{div} y \end{bmatrix}$$

is valid. ⏌

In other words, $gcd(x,\ y)$ divides both x and y.

Proof

We actually prove (rearranging the quantifiers) the equivalent sentence

$$(\textit{for all integer } y) \atop (\textit{for all integer } x) \begin{bmatrix} gcd(x,\ y) \preceq_{div} x \\ and \\ gcd(x,\ y) \preceq_{div} y \end{bmatrix}.$$

The proof is by complete induction on y, taking the inductive sentence to be

$$\mathcal{F}[y]: \quad (\textit{for all integer } x) \begin{bmatrix} gcd(x,\ y) \preceq_{div} x \\ and \\ gcd(x,\ y) \preceq_{div} y \end{bmatrix}.$$

To prove $(\textit{for all integer } y)\mathcal{F}[y]$, it suffices to establish the inductive step.

Inductive Step

We would like to show

$$(\textit{for all integer } y) \begin{bmatrix} if\ (\textit{for all integer } y') \begin{bmatrix} if\ y' < y \\ then\ \ \mathcal{F}[y'] \end{bmatrix} \\ then\ \ \mathcal{F}[y] \end{bmatrix}.$$

For an arbitrary nonnegative integer y, we assume the induction hypothesis

$$(\textit{for all integer } y') \begin{bmatrix} if\ y' < y \\ then\ \ \mathcal{F}[y'] \end{bmatrix}$$

and attempt to show the desired conclusion

$$\mathcal{F}[y],$$

that is,

$$(for\ all\ integer\ x)\ \begin{bmatrix} gcd(x,\ y) \preceq_{div} x \\ and \\ gcd(x,\ y) \preceq_{div} y \end{bmatrix}.$$

Consider an arbitrary nonnegative integer x; we would like to show that

$$gcd(x,\ y) \preceq_{div} x$$
$$and$$
$$gcd(x,\ y) \preceq_{div} y.$$

Following the axioms for the *gcd* function, we distinguish between two subcases, depending on whether or not $y = 0$.

Case: $y = 0$

Then (by the *zero* axiom for the *gcd*) we have

$$gcd(x,\ y)\ =\ x.$$

The statement we would like to show then reduces to

$$x \preceq_{div} x\ \ and\ \ x \preceq_{div} 0.$$

The first conjunct follows from the *reflexivity* property of the divides relation, and the second from the *right-zero* property.

Case: *not* $(y = 0)$

In other words, y is positive. Then (by the *remainder* axiom for *gcd*)

$$gcd(x,\ y)\ =\ gcd\big(y,\ rem(x,y)\big).$$

We would like to show

$$gcd(x,\ y) \preceq_{div} x$$
$$and$$
$$gcd(x,\ y) \preceq_{div} y,$$

which (in this case) may be expanded to

$$gcd\big(y,\ rem(x,y)\big) \preceq_{div} x$$
$$and$$
$$gcd\big(y,\ rem(x,y)\big) \preceq_{div} y.$$

We know (by the *quotient-remainder* proposition, because y is positive) that

$$x\ =\ y \cdot quot(x,y) + rem(x,y).$$

Therefore the statement we would like to show may be expanded further, to

$$gcd\big(y,\, rem(x,y)\big) \preceq_{div} \big(y \cdot quot(x,y) + rem(x,y)\big)$$
and
$$gcd\big(y,\, rem(x,y)\big) \preceq_{div} y.$$

Thus (by the *addition* property of the divides relation) it suffices to establish

$$gcd\big(y,\, rem(x,y)\big) \preceq_{div} y \cdot quot(x,y)$$
and
$$gcd\big(y,\, rem(x,y)\big) \preceq_{div} rem(x,y)$$
and
$$gcd\big(y,\, rem(x,y)\big) \preceq_{div} y.$$

Hence (by the *multiplication* property of the divides relation) it suffices to establish

$$\begin{bmatrix} gcd\big(y,\, rem(x,y)\big) \preceq_{div} y \\ or \\ gcd\big(y,\, rem(x,y)\big) \preceq_{div} quot(x,y) \end{bmatrix}$$
and
$$gcd\big(y,\, rem(x,y)\big) \preceq_{div} rem(x,y)$$
and
$$gcd\big(y,\, rem(x,y)\big) \preceq_{div} y,$$

which is equivalent (by propositional logic) to

$$gcd\big(y,\, rem(x,y)\big) \preceq_{div} y$$
(∗)   *and*
$$gcd\big(y,\, rem(x,y)\big) \preceq_{div} rem(x,y).$$

We have assumed as our induction hypothesis that

$$(for\ all\ integer\ y') \begin{bmatrix} if\ y' < y \\ then\ \mathcal{F}[y'] \end{bmatrix}.$$

In particular (taking y' to be $rem(x,y)$), we have

$$if\ rem(x,y) < y$$
$$then\ \mathcal{F}\big[rem(x,y)\big].$$

Since (by the *quotient-remainder* proposition, because y is positive in this case)

$$rem(x,y) < y,$$

we have $\mathcal{F}[rem(x, y)]$, that is,

$$(\textit{for all integer } x') \begin{bmatrix} gcd\big(x',\ rem(x,y)\big) \preceq_{div} x' \\ \quad and \\ gcd\big(x',\ rem(x,y)\big) \preceq_{div} rem(x,y) \end{bmatrix}.$$

(Note that we have renamed the bound variable x of the induction hypothesis to be x', to avoid capturing the free occurrence of x in $rem(x, y)$.) In particular (taking x' to be y), we obtain

$$gcd\big(y,\ rem(x,y)\big) \preceq_{div} y$$
$$and$$
$$gcd\big(y,\ rem(x,y)\big) \preceq_{div} rem(x,y),$$

which is the statement $(*)$ we were trying to establish.

Because we have established the desired result in both cases, we have completed the proof. ⌙

Note that the proof of the inductive step for the case in which $y = 0$ was completed without appealing to the induction hypothesis. This would have been the base case in a stepwise induction proof.

Remark (Why not stepwise induction?)

The above proof would be awkward to carry out by stepwise induction rather than complete induction. In the inductive step we attempted to prove our desired conclusion $\mathcal{F}[y]$, which is of form

$$(\textit{for all integer } x)\mathcal{G}[x,\ y],$$

where

$$\mathcal{G}[x,\ y]: \quad \begin{array}{l} gcd(x,\ y) \preceq_{div} x \\ \quad and \\ gcd(x,\ y) \preceq_{div} y. \end{array}$$

For an arbitrary nonnegative integer x, we found (in the case in which $not\ (y = 0)$) that to establish $\mathcal{G}[x,\ y]$ it suffices to establish the corresponding condition $(*)$,

$$\mathcal{G}[y,\ rem(x,y)].$$

We were then able to apply our induction hypothesis,

$$(\textit{for all integer } y') \begin{bmatrix} \textit{if } y' < y \\ \textit{then } (\textit{for all integer } x)\mathcal{G}[x,\ y'] \end{bmatrix},$$

to establish (renaming x to x' and taking y' to be $rem(x, y)$, since $rem(x, y) < y$) that

$$(\textit{for all integer } x') \mathcal{G}[x', \; rem(x, y)].$$

This gives the desired condition $(*)$, taking x' to be y.

Had we attempted the proof by, say, the decomposition version of stepwise induction, our induction hypothesis would have been simply

$$(\textit{for all integer } x) \mathcal{G}[x, \; y - 1].$$

This does not necessarily give us the condition $(*)$, that is, $\mathcal{G}[y, \; rem(x, y)]$, because $rem(x, y)$ can be any nonnegative integer less than y. Similar difficulties would be encountered if the proof were attempted by the generator version of stepwise induction. A successful stepwise-induction proof requires a more complex inductive sentence. ◢

The proof of the *common-divisor* proposition illustrates some of the strategic aspects of performing a proof by induction.

Remark (generalization)

The proof of the *common-divisor* proposition did not require us to generalize the sentence to be proved, but it can be used to illustrate the need for generalization. Suppose, instead of being given the sentence

$$\begin{matrix}(\textit{for all integer } x) \\ (\textit{for all integer } y)\end{matrix} \Big[gcd(x, \, y) \preceq_{div} x \quad and \quad gcd(x, \, y) \preceq_{div} y \Big]$$

to prove, we had been given only the left conjunct,

$$\begin{matrix}(\textit{for all integer } x) \\ (\textit{for all integer } y)\end{matrix} \Big[gcd(x, \, y) \preceq_{div} x \Big].$$

Although this is a weaker sentence, we would not be able to establish it by imitating the above proof.

For suppose we reverse the quantifiers and attempt to prove

$$\begin{matrix}(\textit{for all integer } y) \\ (\textit{for all integer } x)\end{matrix} \Big[gcd(x, \, y) \preceq_{div} x \Big]$$

by complete induction on y, taking the inductive sentence to be

$$\mathcal{F}[y] : \quad (\textit{for all integer } x) \big[gcd(x, \, y) \preceq_{div} x \big].$$

The desired conclusion of the inductive step would also be

$$(\textit{for all integer } x) \big[gcd(x, \, y) \preceq_{div} x \big].$$

For an arbitrary nonnegative integer x, we would succeed in showing (in the case in which *not* $(y = 0)$) that, to establish the subsentence

$$gcd(x,\, y) \preceq_{div} x,$$

it suffices to establish the sentence $(*)$,

$$gcd\bigl(y,\, rem(x,y)\bigr) \preceq_{div} y$$
$$\text{and}$$
$$gcd\bigl(y,\, rem(x,y)\bigr) \preceq_{div} rem(x,y),$$

as in our original proof.

However, because we are attempting to show a weaker sentence, our induction hypothesis is the correspondingly weaker sentence

$$(\text{for all integer } y') \left[\begin{matrix} \text{if } y' < y \\ \text{then } (\text{for all integer } x)\bigl[gcd(x,\, y') \preceq_{div} x\bigr] \end{matrix} \right].$$

Our weaker induction hypothesis would allow us to show (taking y' to be $rem(x,y)$ and x to be y, because $rem(x,y) < y$) that

$$gcd\bigl(y,\, rem(x,y)\bigr) \preceq_{div} y,$$

which is the first conjunct of the sentence $(*)$ we need to establish. We could not show the second conjunct, that

$$gcd\bigl(y,\, rem(x,y)\bigr) \preceq_{div} rem(x,y).$$

In fact, if initially we were only given the single condition

$$(\text{for all integer } x) \atop (\text{for all integer } y) \left[gcd(x,\, y) \preceq_{div} x \right]$$

to prove, we would have had to discover the second condition ourselves and prove a more general, stronger statement consisting of the conjunction of the two conditions together, as we did in the proposition. This generalization process may require some ingenuity. ◢

The proposition we have just established states that, for all nonnegative integers x and y, the nonnegative integer $gcd(x,\, y)$ is indeed a common divisor of x and y, i.e., it exhibits the common-divisor relationship

$$gcd(x,\, y) \preceq_{div} x \quad \text{and} \quad gcd(x,\, y) \preceq_{div} y.$$

It can also be shown that $gcd(x,\, y)$ is the "greatest" common divisor of x and y, where "greatest" means greatest with respect to the divides relation $\preceq_{div}$.

In other words, for every nonnegative integer z, if z is a common divisor of x and y, that is, if

$$z \preceq_{div} x \quad and \quad z \preceq_{div} y,$$

then $gcd(x, y)$ is "greater" than z, that is,

$$z \preceq_{div} gcd(x, y).$$

The proof of this property is left as an exercise (**Problem 6.10**).

We have defined the greatest-common-divisor function $gcd(x, y)$ in terms of the rather unnatural looking *zero* and *remainder* axioms; we can then establish that $gcd(x, y)$ is indeed a greatest common divisor of x and y. In an alternative augmentation of the theory, we can define the function by axioms that express the desired property, that $gcd(x, y)$ is a greatest common divisor of x and y, as follows:

$$
\begin{array}{ll}
\begin{array}{l}(\textit{for all integer } x) \\ (\textit{for all integer } y)\end{array}
\left[\begin{array}{l} gcd(x,\, y) \preceq_{div} x \\ \quad and \\ gcd(x,\, y) \preceq_{div} y \end{array}\right]
& (\textit{common divisor}) \\[3em]
\begin{array}{l}(\textit{for all integer } x) \\ (\textit{for all integer } y) \\ (\textit{for all integer } z)\end{array}
\left[\begin{array}{l} \textit{if } z \preceq_{div} x \ \textit{ and } \ z \preceq_{div} y \\ \textit{then } z \preceq_{div} gcd(x,\, y) \end{array}\right]
& (\textit{greatest})
\end{array}
$$

and then prove the original *zero* and *remainder* axioms as properties. These alternative axioms, however, do not suggest a method for computing the *gcd* function.

6.12 THE LEAST-NUMBER PRINCIPLE

In this section, we establish a basic property of the nonnegative integers, which turns out to be equivalent to the complete induction principle.

Propostion (least-number principle)

For each sentence $\mathcal{G}[x]$, the universal closure of the sentence *if (for some integer x) $\mathcal{G}[x]$*

then (for some integer x) $\begin{bmatrix} \mathcal{G}[x] \\ and \\ (for\ all\ integer\ x') \begin{bmatrix} if\ x' < x \\ then\ not\ \mathcal{G}[x'] \end{bmatrix} \end{bmatrix}$

(least number)

where x' does not occur free in $\mathcal{F}[x]$, is valid. ⌐

In other words, if a statement $\mathcal{G}[x]$ is true for some nonnegative integer x, there must be a least nonnegative integer x' for which it is true.

Proof

Consider an arbitrary sentence $\mathcal{G}[x]$.

Recall the complete induction principle asserted that, for each sentence $\mathcal{F}[x]$, the universal closure of the sentence

if (for all integer x) $\begin{bmatrix} if\ (for\ all\ integer\ x') \begin{bmatrix} if\ x' < x \\ then\ \mathcal{F}[x'] \end{bmatrix} \\ then\ \mathcal{F}[x] \end{bmatrix}$

then (for all integer x) $\mathcal{F}[x]$

is valid. If we take $\mathcal{F}[x]$ to be *not* $\mathcal{G}[x]$, we obtain

if (for all integer x) $\begin{bmatrix} if\ (for\ all\ integer\ x') \begin{bmatrix} if\ x' < x \\ then\ not\ \mathcal{G}[x'] \end{bmatrix} \\ then\ not\ \mathcal{G}[x] \end{bmatrix}$

then (for all integer x) $\left[not\ \mathcal{G}[x]\right]$.

Using the propositional-logic equivalence

$\begin{bmatrix} if\ \mathcal{H}_1 \\ then\ not\ \mathcal{H}_2 \end{bmatrix}$ *if and only if not* $\begin{bmatrix} \mathcal{H}_1 \\ and \\ \mathcal{H}_2 \end{bmatrix}$,

we obtain the equivalent sentence

if (for all integer x) not $\begin{bmatrix} (for\ all\ integer\ x') \begin{bmatrix} if\ x' < x \\ then\ not\ \mathcal{G}[x'] \end{bmatrix} \\ and \\ \mathcal{G}[x] \end{bmatrix}$

then (for all integer x) $\left[not\ \mathcal{G}[x]\right]$.

By the duality between the universal and existential quantifiers, this is equivalent
to

$$
\text{if } not \ (\text{for some integer } x) \left[\begin{array}{l} (\text{for all integer } x') \left[\begin{array}{l} \text{if } x' < x \\ \text{then } not \ \mathcal{G}[x'] \end{array} \right] \\ \text{and} \\ \mathcal{G}[x] \end{array} \right]
$$

$$
\text{then } not \ (\text{for some integer } x) \, \mathcal{G}[x].
$$

Because any sentence is equivalent to its contrapositive, that is,

$$
\left[\begin{array}{l} \text{if } not \ \mathcal{H}_1 \\ \text{then } not \ \mathcal{H}_2 \end{array} \right] \quad \text{if and only if} \quad \left[\begin{array}{l} \text{if } \mathcal{H}_2 \\ \text{then } \mathcal{H}_1 \end{array} \right]
$$

is valid in propositional logic, we obtain

$$
\text{if } (\text{for some integer } x) \, \mathcal{G}[x]
$$

$$
\text{then } (\text{for some integer } x) \left[\begin{array}{l} (\text{for all integer } x') \left[\begin{array}{l} \text{if } x' < x \\ \text{then } not \ \mathcal{G}[x'] \end{array} \right] \\ \text{and} \\ \mathcal{G}[x] \end{array} \right]
$$

or equivalently, reversing the conjuncts,

$$
\text{if } (\text{for some integer } x) \, \mathcal{G}[x]
$$

$$
\text{then } (\text{for some integer } x) \left[\begin{array}{l} \mathcal{G}[x] \\ \text{and} \\ (\text{for all integer } x') \left[\begin{array}{l} \text{if } x' < x \\ \text{then } not \ \mathcal{G}[x'] \end{array} \right] \end{array} \right].
$$

This is precisely the least-number principle for the sentence $\mathcal{G}[x]$. ⌐

Note that the proof of the validity of the least-number principle required only
the complete induction principle and properties of propositional and predicate
logic; it made no mention of other properties of the less-than relation $<$ or of the
nonnegative integers. We can actually establish that the least-number principle
and the complete induction principle are equivalent in predicate logic; this is
done in greater generality in a subsequent chapter on the well-founded induction
principle (in Volume II).

PROBLEMS

Problem 6.1 (addition)   pages 293, 304

Establish the validity of the following sentences in the theory of the nonnegative integers, augmented by the axioms for addition:

(a) *Sort*

$$(\textit{for all integer } x) \atop (\textit{for all integer } y) \left[integer(x+y) \right]$$

(b) *Associativity*

$$(\textit{for all integer } x) \atop (\textit{for all integer } y) \atop (\textit{for all integer } z) \left[(x+y)+z \; = \; x+(y+z) \right]$$

(c) *Left cancellation*

$$(\textit{for all integer } x) \atop (\textit{for all integer } y) \atop (\textit{for all integer } z) \left[\begin{matrix} if \; z+x = z+y \\ then \; x = y \end{matrix} \right]$$

(d) *Right cancellation*

$$(\textit{for all integer } x) \atop (\textit{for all integer } y) \atop (\textit{for all integer } z) \left[\begin{matrix} if \; x+z = y+z \\ then \; x = y \end{matrix} \right]$$

(e) *Annihilation*

$$(\textit{for all integer } x) \atop (\textit{for all integer } y) \left[\begin{matrix} if \; x+y = 0 \\ then \; x = 0 \; and \; y = 0 \end{matrix} \right]$$

As usual, you may use in your proof any property that is stated in the text earlier than the page reference for the problem, even if that property is given without proof; and you may use the results of any previous problem, even if you haven't solved that problem yourself.

Problem 6.2 (multiplication)   page 305

Establish the validity of the following sentences in the theory of the nonnegative integers, augmented by the axioms for addition and multiplication:

(a)   *Sort*

$$\begin{matrix} \textit{(for all integer } x) \\ \textit{(for all integer } y) \end{matrix} \Big[integer(x \cdot y) \Big]$$

(b)   *Right one*

$$\textit{(for all integer } x) \big[x \cdot 1 \; = \; x \big]$$

(c)   *Left zero*

$$\textit{(for all integer } x) \Big[0 \cdot x \; = \; 0 \Big]$$

(d)   *Left successor*

$$\begin{matrix} \textit{(for all integer } x) \\ \textit{(for all integer } y) \end{matrix} \Big[(x+1) \cdot y \; = \; x \cdot y + y \Big]$$

(e)   *Left one*

$$\textit{(for all integer } x) \big[1 \cdot x \; = \; x \big]$$

(f)   *Right distributivity*

$$\begin{matrix} \textit{(for all integer } x) \\ \textit{(for all integer } y) \\ \textit{(for all integer } z) \end{matrix} \Big[x \cdot (y+z) \; = \; x \cdot y + x \cdot z \Big]$$

(g)   *Associativity*

$$\begin{matrix} \textit{(for all integer } x) \\ \textit{(for all integer } y) \\ \textit{(for all integer } z) \end{matrix} \Big[(x \cdot y) \cdot z \; = \; x \cdot (y \cdot z) \Big]$$

(h)   *Commutativity*

$$\begin{matrix} \textit{(for all integer } x) \\ \textit{(for all integer } y) \end{matrix} \Big[x \cdot y \; = \; y \cdot x \Big]$$

(i)   *Left distributivity*

$$\begin{matrix} \textit{(for all integer } x) \\ \textit{(for all integer } y) \\ \textit{(for all integer } z) \end{matrix} \Big[(x+y) \cdot z \; = \; x \cdot z + y \cdot z \Big].$$

Problem 6.3 (exponentiation)   page 306

Establish the validity of the following sentences in the theory of the nonnegative integers, augmented by the axioms for addition, multiplication, and exponentiation:

(a)   *Sort*

$$(\textit{for all integer } x) \atop (\textit{for all integer } y)\left[integer(x^y)\right]$$

(b)   *Exp one*

$$(\textit{for all integer } x)\left[x^1 \; = \; x\right]$$

(c)   *Base zero*

$$(\textit{for all integer } y)\left[\begin{matrix} \textit{if } \; not \; (y = 0) \\ then \; 0^y = 0 \end{matrix}\right]$$

(d)   *Exp plus*

$$(\textit{for all integer } x) \atop (\textit{for all integer } y) \atop (\textit{for all integer } z)\left[x^{y+z} \; = \; (x^y) \cdot (x^z)\right]$$

(e)   *Exp times*

$$(\textit{for all integer } x) \atop (\textit{for all integer } y) \atop (\textit{for all integer } z)\left[x^{y \cdot z} \; = \; (x^y)^z\right].$$

Problem 6.4 (factorial)   page 310

Suppose we augment our theory of the nonnegative integers by formulating two axioms that define a unary function symbol $x!$, denoting the *factorial* function under the intended model for the nonnegative integers. The axioms are

$$0! \; = \; 1 \tag{\textit{zero}}$$

$$(\textit{for all integer } x)\left[(x+1)! \; = \; (x+1) \cdot (x!)\right] \tag{\textit{successor}}$$

For example,

$$3! \; = \; 3 \cdot (2!) \; = \; 3 \cdot 2 \cdot (1!) \; = \; 3 \cdot 2 \cdot 1 \cdot (0!) \; = \; 3 \cdot 2 \cdot 1 \cdot 1 \; = \; 6.$$

Let us introduce an alternative definition of the factorial function by formulating two additional axioms that define a binary function symbol $fact2(x, y)$, as follows:

$$(\textit{for all integer } y)\big[fact2(0, y) \;=\; y\big] \qquad\qquad (\textit{equal})$$

$$\begin{array}{l}(\textit{for all integer } x) \\ (\textit{for all integer } y)\end{array} \left[\begin{array}{l} fact2(x + 1, \; y) \\ = \\ fact2\big(x, \; (x+1)\cdot y\big) \end{array}\right] \qquad (\textit{successor})$$

Prove that the sentence

$$(\textit{for all integer } x)\big[fact2(x, \; 1) \;=\; x!\big] \qquad (\textit{alternative definition})$$

is valid. [*Hint*: Prove a more general property.]

Problem 6.5 (predecessor and subtraction)   pages 313, 314

Establish the validity of the following sentences in the theory of the nonnegative integers augmented by the axioms for the addition, predecessor, and subtraction functions and the *positive* relation:

(a)   *Decomposition*

$$(\textit{for all positive } x)\big[x \;=\; (x^-) + 1\big]$$

(b)   *Right one*

$$(\textit{for all positive } x)[x - 1 \;=\; x^-]$$

(c)   *Addition*

$$\begin{array}{l}(\textit{for all integer } x) \\ (\textit{for all integer } y)\end{array}\Big[(x + y) - y \;=\; x\Big]$$

(d)   *Negative*

$$\begin{array}{l}(\textit{for all integer } x) \\ (\textit{for all integer } y)\end{array}\Big[x - (y + x) \;=\; 0 - y\Big].$$

Problem 6.6 (weak less-than)   pages 322, 325

(a) In the augmented theory of the nonnegative integers, establish the validity of the ($\Leftarrow$) part of the *left-addition* property for the weak less-than relation, that is,

$$\begin{array}{l}(\textit{for all integer } x) \\ (\textit{for all integer } y)\end{array}\left[\begin{array}{l} \textit{if } (\textit{for some integer } z)[x + z = y] \\ \textit{then } x \le y \end{array}\right].$$

(b) Suppose that the weak less-than relation $\leq$ is defined by the *right-zero* axiom and the *right-successor* axiom,

$$(for\ all\ integer\ x) \atop (for\ all\ integer\ y) \left[\begin{matrix} x \leq y + 1 \\ if\ and\ only\ if \\ x = y + 1 \ \ or \ \ x \leq y \end{matrix} \right],$$

instead of the *right-predecessor* axiom. In this augmented theory of the nonnegative integers, establish the validity of the *left-addition* property for the weak less-than relation, that is,

$$(for\ all\ integer\ x) \atop (for\ all\ integer\ y) \left[\begin{matrix} x \leq y \\ if\ and\ only\ if \\ (for\ some\ integer\ z)\left[x + z = y \right] \end{matrix} \right].$$

Problem 6.7 (max and min)   page 327

In the augmented theory of the nonnegative integers, establish the validity of the following properties of the maximum and minimum functions:

(a) *Greater-than*

$$(for\ all\ integer\ x) \atop (for\ all\ integer\ y) \left[\begin{matrix} max(x,\ y) \geq x \\ and \\ max(x,\ y) \geq y \end{matrix} \right]$$

(b) *Minimax*

$$(for\ all\ integer\ x) \atop (for\ all\ integer\ y) \left[min\big(x,\ max(y,\ z)\big) \ = \ max\big(min(x,\ y),\ min(x,\ z)\big) \right].$$

Problem 6.8 (quotient-remainder)   pages 331, 337

In the augmented theory of the nonnegative integers, establish the validity of the following properties of the quotient and remainder functions:

(a) *Sort for quotient*

$$(for\ all\ integer\ x) \atop (for\ all\ positive\ y) \left[integer\big(quot(x,\ y)\big) \right]$$

(b) *Sort for remainder*

$$(for\ all\ integer\ x) \atop (for\ all\ positive\ y) \left[integer\big(rem(x,\ y)\big) \right]$$

(c)   *Uniqueness*

$$
\begin{array}{l}
\textit{(for all integer } x) \\
\textit{(for all integer } y) \\
\textit{(for all integer } u) \\
\textit{(for all integer } v)
\end{array}
\; \textit{if} \;
\begin{bmatrix}
x = y \cdot u + v \\
\textit{and} \\
v < y
\end{bmatrix}
\; \textit{then} \;
\begin{bmatrix}
u = quot(x,\, y) \\
\textit{and} \\
v = rem(x,\, y)
\end{bmatrix} .
$$

Problem 6.9 (divides relation)   page 343

In the theory of the nonnegative integers augmented by the definition of the divides relation, establish the validity of the following sentences:

(a)   *Right zero*

$$(\textit{for all integer } x)[x \preceq_{div} 0]$$

(b)   *Left zero*

$$(\textit{for all positive } y)\big[not\,(0 \preceq_{div} y)\big]$$

(c)   *Greater than*

$$
\begin{array}{l}
\textit{(for all integer } x) \\
\textit{(for all positive } y)
\end{array}
\begin{bmatrix}
\textit{if } x > y \\
\textit{then } \; not\,(x \preceq_{div} y)
\end{bmatrix}
$$

(d)   *Subtraction*

$$
\begin{array}{l}
\textit{(for all integer } x) \\
\textit{(for all integer } y)
\end{array}
\begin{bmatrix}
\textit{if } x \le y \\
\textit{then}
\begin{bmatrix}
x \preceq_{div} y \\
\textit{if and only if} \\
x \preceq_{div} (y - x)
\end{bmatrix}
\end{bmatrix} .
$$

Show also that these properties constitute an alternative definition for the divides relation. In other words, in the theory of the nonnegative integers augmented by the above four properties, establish the validity of the original definition of $\preceq_{div}$:

(e)   *Divides*

$$
\begin{array}{l}
\textit{(for all integer } x) \\
\textit{(for all integer } y)
\end{array}
\begin{bmatrix}
x \preceq_{div} y \\
\textit{if and only if} \\
(\textit{for some integer } z)[x \cdot z = y]
\end{bmatrix} .
$$

Problem 6.10 (greatest common divisor)   page 351

Establish that the greatest common divisor $gcd(x, y)$ is indeed the "greatest" of the common divisors of x and y, with respect to the divides relation $\preceq_{div}$; in other words, in the augmented theory of the nonnegative integers, establish the validity of the sentence

$$
\begin{array}{l}
(\textit{for all integer } x) \\
(\textit{for all integer } y) \\
(\textit{for all integer } z)
\end{array}
\left[
\begin{array}{l}
\textit{if } z \preceq_{div} x \textit{ and } z \preceq_{div} y \\
\textit{then } z \preceq_{div} gcd(x, y)
\end{array}
\right].
$$

Problem 6.11 (fallacious induction principle)   page 288

One would expect that, for each sentence $\mathcal{F}[x]$ in the theory of the nonnegative integers, the universal closure of the following sentence would be valid:

$$
\textit{if }
\left[
\begin{array}{l}
\mathcal{F}[0] \\
\quad \textit{and} \\
(\textit{for all integer } y)
\left[
\begin{array}{l}
\textit{if } \mathcal{F}[y] \\
\textit{then } \mathcal{F}[y^+]
\end{array}
\right]
\end{array}
\right]
$$
$$
\textit{then } (\textit{for all integer } x)\mathcal{F}[x].
$$

After all, the above sentence is obtained from the original induction principle by renaming the bound variable x of the inductive step to y.

In fact, if y occurs free in $\mathcal{F}[x]$, the sentence is not always true. Find a sentence $\mathcal{F}[x]$ in the theory for which the universal closure of the above implication is not valid.

Problem 6.12 (altered theories)   pages 291, 320

(a) Consider the theory obtained by omitting the induction principle from the basic theory of the nonnegative integers. Construct a model for this theory under which both the induction principle and the *decomposition property*,

$$
(\textit{for all integer } x)
\left[
\begin{array}{l}
\textit{if } not\ (x = 0) \\
\textit{then } (\textit{for some integer } y)[x = y^+]
\end{array}
\right],
$$

are false.

(b) Consider the theory obtained from the basic theory of the nonnegative integers as follows:

  • Add the definition of the predecessor function,

$$
(\textit{for all integer } x)\big[(x + 1) - 1 \ = \ x\big],
$$

and the definition of the *positive* relation,

$$(\textit{for all } x) \begin{bmatrix} positive(x) \\ \textit{if and only if} \\ integer(x) \;\; and \;\; not \; (x = 0) \end{bmatrix},$$

as axioms.

- Replace the original, generator version of the stepwise induction principle with the following *decomposition* version:

For each sentence $\mathcal{F}[x]$, the universal closure of the sentence

$$if \begin{bmatrix} \mathcal{F}[0] \\ \textit{and} \\ (\textit{for all positive } x) \begin{bmatrix} if \;\; \mathcal{F}[x-1] \\ then \;\; \mathcal{F}[x] \end{bmatrix} \end{bmatrix}$$
$$then \;\; (\textit{for all integer } x)\mathcal{F}[x]$$

is an axiom.

Construct a model for this theory under which both the *decomposition* property of the predecessor function,

$$(\textit{for all positive } x)\Big[x \;=\; (x-1)+1\Big],$$

and the generator version of the induction principle are false.

7

Strings

In this section we present *strings* as a theory with induction. Intuitively speaking, we are given a set (called the *alphabet*) of elements (called *characters*); strings are formed by "concatenating" characters from the alphabet. For example, if the alphabet is the set $\{A, B, C\}$, then

ABBC,   CCBCA,   and   A

are all strings. Note that single characters are also regarded as strings. We include among the strings the empty string, which has no characters at all. The alphabet may be either finite or infinite, but each string must be finite, i.e., must contain only finitely many characters.

7.1   BASIC PROPERTIES

The vocabulary of the theory of strings consists of

- A constant symbol Λ, denoting the *empty string*

- A binary function symbol $u \bullet x$, denoting the *prefix* function

- A unary predicate symbol $char(x)$, denoting the *character* relation

- A unary predicate symbol $string(x)$.

The reader should remember that these notations are our private pseudonyms for standard constant, predicate, and function symbols such as a_{17}, $f_{101}(u, x)$, and $p_{22}(x)$.

Under the intended models for the theory, the character relation $char(x)$ is true if x is a character in the alphabet, and false otherwise. The string relation $string(x)$ is true for all strings. Also the value of the prefix function $u \bullet x$ is the string obtained by inserting the character u at the beginning of the string x. Thus if u is the character A and x is the string AB, then $u \bullet x$ is the string AAB. The axioms will not specify the result $y \bullet x$ of prefixing a string y to a string x if y is not a character.

Thus the terms of the theory include Λ, $u \bullet \Lambda$, $u \bullet (v \bullet \Lambda)$, and so forth. Notations such as ABBC and A are informal and are not part of the language of the theory. Under a particular model for the theory, if u is A, v is B, and w is C, the value of the term $u \bullet (v \bullet (v \bullet (w \bullet \Lambda)))$ is the string ABBC in the domain of the model.

The theory of strings is a theory with equality having the following special axioms:

- The *generation* axioms

$$string(\Lambda) \qquad\qquad\qquad\qquad\qquad\qquad (empty)$$

$$(for\ all\ char\ u)\big[string(u)\big] \qquad\qquad\qquad (character)$$

$$\begin{matrix}(for\ all\ char\ u)\\ (for\ all\ string\ x)\end{matrix}\big[string(u \bullet x)\big] \qquad\qquad (prefix)$$

(We shall actually be able to prove the *character* axiom from the other axioms.)

- The *uniqueness* axioms

$$\begin{matrix}(for\ all\ char\ u)\\ (for\ all\ string\ x)\end{matrix}\big[not\ (u \bullet x = \Lambda)\big] \qquad\qquad (empty)$$

$$\begin{matrix}(for\ all\ char\ u)(for\ all\ string\ x)\\ (for\ all\ char\ v)(for\ all\ string\ y)\end{matrix}\begin{bmatrix}if\ u \bullet x = v \bullet y\\ then\ u = v\ \ and\ \ x = y\end{bmatrix} (prefix)$$

- The special *character* equality axiom

$$(for\ all\ char\ u)\big[u \bullet \Lambda = u\big] \qquad\qquad\qquad (character)$$

• The *induction* principle

For each sentence $\mathcal{F}[x]$ in the theory, the universal closure of the sentence

$$\textit{if}\begin{bmatrix}\mathcal{F}[\Lambda]\\ \textit{and}\\ (\textit{for all char } u)\begin{bmatrix}\textit{if}\ \mathcal{F}[x]\\ \textit{then}\ \ \mathcal{F}[u \bullet x]\end{bmatrix}\\ (\textit{for all string } x)\end{bmatrix} \qquad (\textit{induction})$$

$$\textit{then}\ \ (\textit{for all string } x)\mathcal{F}[x],$$

where u does not occur free in $\mathcal{F}[x]$, is an axiom.

The three generation axioms have the intuitive meaning that any element that can be constructed from the empty string Λ, the characters of the alphabet, and the prefix function $u \bullet x$ is a string. The two uniqueness axioms have the intuitive meaning that a string can be constructed in at most one way from the empty string Λ, the characters of the alphabet, and the prefix function $u \bullet x$. The one exception, given by the *character* equality axiom, is that we identify strings of form $u \bullet \Lambda$, where u is a character, with u itself. Thus under a model for the theory, if u is assigned the string B, then the values of u, $u \bullet \Lambda$, $(u \bullet \Lambda) \bullet \Lambda$, and so forth are all the string B. Informally speaking, B, B$\bullet\Lambda$, and $(\text{B} \bullet \Lambda) \bullet \Lambda$ are the same.

DISCUSSION OF INDUCTION

In the induction principle, the sentence $\mathcal{F}[x]$ is called the *inductive sentence*. The subsentence

$$\mathcal{F}[\Lambda]$$

is called the *base case* of the induction. The subsentence

$$(\textit{for all char } u)\begin{bmatrix}\textit{if}\ \mathcal{F}[x]\\ \textit{then}\ \ \mathcal{F}[u \bullet x]\end{bmatrix}$$
$$(\textit{for all string } x)$$

is called the *inductive step*; the subsentences $\mathcal{F}[x]$ and $\mathcal{F}[u \bullet x]$ of the inductive step are called the *induction hypothesis* and the *desired conclusion*, respectively. The variable x is called the *inductive variable*.

The induction principle may be paraphrased intuitively as follows:

To prove that a sentence $\mathcal{F}[x]$ is true for every string x, it suffices to prove the base case

$\mathcal{F}[\Lambda]$ is true

and the inductive step

for an arbitrary character u (where u does not occur free in $\mathcal{F}[x]$)
and string x,
if $\mathcal{F}[x]$ is true
then $\mathcal{F}[u \bullet x]$ is also true.

The constraint on the induction principle that the variable u does not occur free in the sentence $\mathcal{F}[x]$ is essential. In **Problem 7.16**, the reader is requested to show that the induction principle is not valid for a sentence $\mathcal{F}[x]$ that violates the constraint. (This exercise is left until last because of its theoretical nature.) The constraint on the complete induction principles that x' not occur free in $\mathcal{F}[x]$ is imposed for the same reason.

If we want to use the induction principle with an inductive sentence $\mathcal{F}[x]$ that violates the constraint, we can simply rename the variable u in the inductive step of the principle to a new variable.

DISCUSSION OF EQUALITY

Since the theory of strings is a theory with equality, we include among our axioms the *transitivity, symmetry,* and *reflexivity* axioms for equality. Because the only function symbol in the theory is the binary prefix function $u \bullet x$, we include only the two instances of the *functional-substitutivity* axiom schema for the prefix function,

$$\begin{array}{l}(\textit{for all } x) \\ (\textit{for all } y) \\ (\textit{for all } z)\end{array} \left[\begin{array}{l}\textit{if } x = y \\ \textit{then } x \bullet z = y \bullet z\end{array}\right] \qquad (\textit{left functional substitutivity})$$

$$\begin{array}{l}(\textit{for all } x) \\ (\textit{for all } y) \\ (\textit{for all } z)\end{array} \left[\begin{array}{l}\textit{if } x = y \\ \textit{then } z \bullet x = z \bullet y\end{array}\right] \qquad (\textit{right functional substitutivity})$$

Because the only predicate symbols, other than $=$, in the vocabulary are the unary character predicate $char(x)$ and the unary string predicate $string(x)$, we include only the corresponding instances of the *predicate-substitutivity* axiom schema for the character relation,

$$\begin{array}{l}(\textit{for all } x) \\ (\textit{for all } y)\end{array} \left[\begin{array}{l}\textit{if } x = y \\ \textit{then } char(x) \\ \qquad \textit{if and only if} \\ \qquad char(y)\end{array}\right] \qquad (\textit{predicate substitutivity})$$

and for the *string* relation,

$$
(for\ all\ x)\ (for\ all\ y)\ \begin{bmatrix} if\ x = y \\ then\ \ string(x) \\ \qquad if\ and\ only\ if \\ \qquad string(y) \end{bmatrix} \qquad (predicate\ substitutivity)
$$

Note that the *left functional-substitutivity* axiom for the prefix function discusses the terms $x \bullet z$ and $y \bullet z$ when x and y are any strings, even when they are not characters. Although the axioms for the strings do not specify the values of $x \bullet z$ and $y \bullet z$ in this case, the axioms for equality tell us that these terms must be equal if x and y are equal. A similar remark applies to the *right functional-substitutivity* axiom for this function.

The converse of the *prefix* uniqueness axiom,

$$
(for\ all\ char\ u)(for\ all\ string\ x)\ (for\ all\ char\ v)(for\ all\ string\ y)\ \begin{bmatrix} if\ u = v\ \ and\ \ x = y \\ then\ \ u \bullet x = v \bullet y \end{bmatrix},
$$

follows from the *left-* and *right-functional substitutivity* axioms for the prefix function. It also follows from the equality axioms that the empty string Λ is not itself a character; the proof, which is straightforward, is requested in **Problem 7.1**.

DECOMPOSITION

In this chapter, when we refer to the validity of a sentence, we shall always mean validity in the theory of the strings. Let us show the validity of a sentence in this theory.

Proposition (decomposition)

The sentence

$$
(for\ all\ string\ x)\ \begin{bmatrix} if\ \ not\ (x = \Lambda) \\ then\ \ \ (for\ some\ char\ v) \\ \qquad (for\ some\ string\ y) \end{bmatrix}[x = v \bullet y] \end{bmatrix}
$$

is valid (in the theory of strings). ⌟

This proposition is analogous to the *decomposition* proposition for the nonnegative integers, which established that

$$
(for\ all\ integer\ x)\ \begin{bmatrix} if\ \ not\ (x = 0) \\ then\ (for\ some\ integer\ y)[x = y^{+}] \end{bmatrix}.
$$

Proof

The proof is by induction on x; taking the inductive sentence to be

$$\mathcal{F}[x] : \quad \begin{array}{l} \textit{if } not\,(x = \Lambda) \\ \textit{then } \begin{array}{l} (\textit{for some char } v) \\ (\textit{for some string } y) \end{array}\Big[x = v \bullet y\Big]. \end{array}$$

To prove

$$(\textit{for all string } x)\,\mathcal{F}[x],$$

it suffices to establish the base case,

$$\mathcal{F}[\Lambda],$$

and the inductive step,

$$\begin{array}{l} (\textit{for all char } u) \\ (\textit{for all string } x) \end{array} \left[\begin{array}{l} \textit{if } \mathcal{F}[x] \\ \textit{then } \mathcal{F}[u \bullet x] \end{array}\right].$$

(Note that u does not occur free in $\mathcal{F}[x]$; therefore we do not need to rename the variable u in the inductive step.)

Base Case

We want to prove

$$\mathcal{F}[\Lambda] : \quad \begin{array}{l} \textit{if } not\,(\Lambda = \Lambda) \\ \textit{then } \begin{array}{l} (\textit{for some char } v) \\ (\textit{for some string } y) \end{array}\Big[\Lambda = v \bullet y\Big]. \end{array}$$

Because (by the *reflexivity* axiom for equality) $\Lambda = \Lambda$, the antecedent

$$not\,(\Lambda = \Lambda)$$

of this implication is false and the entire sentence is true.

Inductive Step

We want to prove

$$\begin{array}{l} (\textit{for all char } u) \\ (\textit{for all string } x) \end{array} \left[\begin{array}{l} \textit{if } \mathcal{F}[x] \\ \textit{then } \mathcal{F}[u \bullet x] \end{array}\right].$$

Consider an arbitrary character u and string x, that is, elements u and x such that

$$char(u) \quad \text{and} \quad string(x).$$

We assume the induction hypothesis

$$\mathcal{F}[x]: \quad \begin{array}{l} \textit{if not } (x = \Lambda) \\ \textit{then} \quad \begin{array}{l} \textit{(for some char } v) \\ \textit{(for some string } y) \end{array} \Big[x = v \bullet y \Big] \end{array}$$

and would like to show the desired conclusion

$$\mathcal{F}[u \bullet x]: \quad \begin{array}{l} \textit{if not } (u \bullet x = \Lambda) \\ \textit{then} \quad \begin{array}{l} \textit{(for some char } v) \\ \textit{(for some string } y) \end{array} \Big[u \bullet x = v \bullet y \Big]. \end{array}$$

It suffices to show the consequent,

$$\begin{array}{l} \textit{(for some char } v) \\ \textit{(for some string } y) \end{array} \Big[u \bullet x = v \bullet y \Big],$$

of the desired conclusion.

Because we have supposed $char(u)$ and $string(x)$ and because we know (by the *reflexivity* axiom for equality) $u \bullet x = u \bullet x$, we have

$$char(u) \textit{ and } string(x)$$
$$\textit{and}$$
$$u \bullet x = u \bullet x.$$

The desired result then follows from the *existential quantifier-instantiation* proposition, taking v to be u and y to be x.

Since we have established both the base case and the inductive step, the proof is complete. ⌐

Like the proof of the *decomposition* property in the theory of nonnegative integers, the above proof has the unusual feature that it requires the induction principle but makes no use of the induction hypothesis in the inductive step. Nevertheless, the principle is essential in this proof.

7.2 THE HEAD AND TAIL FUNCTIONS

We would now like to augment our theory of strings by defining two unary function symbols, $head(x)$ and $tail(x)$. Under the intended models for the augmented theory, $head(x)$ denotes the first character of a nonempty string x, and $tail(x)$ denotes the string of all but the first character of x; for example, $head(\text{BAABA}) = \text{B}$ and $tail(\text{BAABA}) = \text{AABA}$.

The axioms that define the *head* and *tail* functions are

$$\begin{array}{ll} \begin{array}{l}(for\ all\ char\ u)\\(for\ all\ string\ x)\end{array}\left[head(u \bullet x) = u\right] & (head) \end{array}$$

$$\begin{array}{ll} \begin{array}{l}(for\ all\ char\ u)\\(for\ all\ string\ x)\end{array}\left[tail(u \bullet x) = x\right] & (tail) \end{array}$$

Note that these axioms do not specify the values of the terms $head(\Lambda)$ and $tail(\Lambda)$. Although these terms are legal in the language of the theory, the axioms do not force them to have any particular values.

As usual, since we introduce new unary function symbols into a theory with equality, we automatically add the two instances of the *functional-substitutivity* axiom schema for *head* and *tail*.

From these axioms we can prove the following properties of *head* and *tail*:

$$(for\ all\ string\ x)\left[\begin{array}{l}if\ not\ (x = \Lambda)\\then\ char\big(head(x)\big)\end{array}\right] \qquad (sort\ of\ head)$$

$$(for\ all\ string\ x)\left[\begin{array}{l}if\ not\ (x = \Lambda)\\then\ string\big(tail(x)\big)\end{array}\right] \qquad (sort\ of\ tail)$$

In other words, the head of a nonempty string is a character, and the tail of a nonempty string is also a string.

$$(for\ all\ string\ x)\left[\begin{array}{l}if\ not\ (x = \Lambda)\\then\ x = head(x) \bullet tail(x)\end{array}\right] \qquad (decomposition)$$

In other words, every nonempty string is the result of prefixing its head to its tail.

$$(for\ all\ char\ u)\left[head(u) = u\right] \qquad (character\ of\ head)$$

$$(for\ all\ char\ u)\left[tail(u) = \Lambda\right] \qquad (character\ of\ tail)$$

In other words, the head of a string consisting of a single character is the character itself, and its tail is the empty string. The proofs of these properties are left as an exercise (**Problem 7.2**).

7.3   THE CONCATENATION FUNCTION

Let us further augment our theory by defining a binary function symbol $x * y$. Under the intended models, $x * y$ denotes the *concatenation* function, whose value

is the string composed of the characters of the string x followed by the characters of the string y; for example,

$$AB * CCA = ABCCA.$$

The axioms that define the concatenation function are

> (*for all string y*)$[\Lambda * y = y]$ (*left empty*)
>
> (*for all char u*)
> (*for all string x*)$\Big[(u \bullet x) * y = u \bullet (x * y)\Big]$ (*left prefix*)
> (*for all string y*)

As usual, we automatically introduce the corresponding two instances of the *functional-substitutivity* equality axiom schema for concatenation.

The axioms for the concatenation function suggest a way to compute it.

Example (computation of concatenation)

Suppose we would like to compute $A * CB$, that is, $(A \bullet \Lambda) * \big(C \bullet (B \bullet \Lambda)\big)$. Then we have

$$(A \bullet \Lambda) * \big(C \bullet (B \bullet \Lambda)\big) = A \bullet \big(\Lambda * \big(C \bullet (B \bullet \Lambda)\big)\big)$$
$$\text{(by the \textit{left-prefix} axiom)}$$
$$= A \bullet \big(C \bullet (B \bullet \Lambda)\big)$$
$$\text{(by the \textit{left-empty} axiom)}.$$

In other words,

$$A * CB = ACB.\quad \lrcorner$$

From the axioms for concatenation, we can establish the validity of the following basic properties:

> (*for all string x*)
> (*for all string y*)$\Big[string(x * y)\Big]$ (*sort*)

> (*for all char u*)
> (*for all string y*)$\Big[u * y = u \bullet y\Big]$ (*character*)

> (*for all string x*)$\Big[x * \Lambda = x\Big]$ (*right empty*)

$$\begin{array}{l} (\textit{for all string } x) \\ (\textit{for all string } y) \\ (\textit{for all string } z) \end{array} \left[(x * y) * z \ = \ x * (y * z) \right] \qquad (\textit{associativity})$$

We can also establish the following properties:

$$\begin{array}{l} (\textit{for all string } x) \\ (\textit{for all string } y) \end{array} \left[\begin{array}{l} \textit{if } x * y = \Lambda \\ \textit{then } x = \Lambda \ \textit{ and } \ y = \Lambda \end{array} \right] \qquad (\textit{annihilation})$$

In other words, if the result of concatenating two strings is empty, both strings must themselves be empty.

$$\begin{array}{l} (\textit{for all string } x) \\ (\textit{for all string } y) \end{array} \left[\begin{array}{l} \textit{if } \ not \ (x = \Lambda) \\ \textit{then } \ head(x * y) = head(x) \end{array} \right] \qquad (\textit{head})$$

$$\begin{array}{l} (\textit{for all string } x) \\ (\textit{for all string } y) \end{array} \left[\begin{array}{l} \textit{if } \ not \ (x = \Lambda) \\ \textit{then } \ tail(x * y) = tail(x) * y \end{array} \right] \qquad (\textit{tail})$$

The following properties concern the result of "suffixing," i.e., of inserting a character at the end of a string:

$$(\textit{for all string } x) \left[\begin{array}{l} \textit{if } \ not \ (x = \Lambda) \\ \textit{then } \ \begin{array}{l}(\textit{for some char } u) \\ (\textit{for some string } y)\end{array} \left[x = y * u \right] \end{array} \right]$$
$$(\textit{suffix decomposition})$$

$$\begin{array}{l} (\textit{for all char } u)(\textit{for all string } x) \\ (\textit{for all char } v)(\textit{for all string } y) \end{array} \left[\begin{array}{l} \textit{if } x * u = y * v \\ \textit{then } x = y \ \textit{ and } \ u = v \end{array} \right]$$
$$(\textit{suffix uniqueness})$$

Let us prove the *annihilation* property; the proofs of the others are left as exercises (**Problem 7.3**).

Proposition (annihilation)

The sentence

$$\begin{array}{l} (\textit{for all string } x) \\ (\textit{for all string } y) \end{array} \left[\begin{array}{l} \textit{if } x * y = \Lambda \\ \textit{then } x = \Lambda \ \textit{ and } \ y = \Lambda \end{array} \right]$$

is valid. ⌐

The proof does not require induction.

Proof

The proof is by contradiction. We consider arbitrary strings x and y and suppose that

(†) $x * y = \Lambda$

but that, contrary to the proposition,

$$not\ (x = \Lambda\ \ and\ \ y = \Lambda),$$

that is,

(‡) $not\ (x = \Lambda)\ \ or\ \ not\ (y = \Lambda).$

We distinguish between two cases, depending on whether or not $x = \Lambda$, and derive a contradiction in each case.

Case: $x = \Lambda$

Then we have, by (‡), that

$$not\ (y = \Lambda).$$

We know

$$x * y\ =\ \Lambda * y$$
$$\text{(by our case assumption)}$$

$$=\ y$$
$$\text{(by the \textit{left-empty} axiom for concatenation).}$$

Therefore, because $not\ (y = \Lambda)$ and $x * y = y$, we have

$$not\ (x * y = \Lambda),$$

contradicting our supposition (†).

Case: $not\ (x = \Lambda)$

Then (by the *decomposition* proposition) there exists a character u and a string x' such that

$$x = u \bullet x'.$$

Thus

$$x * y\ =\ (u \bullet x') * y$$

$$=\ u \bullet (x' * y)$$
$$\text{(by the \textit{left-prefix} axiom for concatenation).}$$

Because (by the *empty* uniqueness axiom for strings)

$$not \left(u \bullet (x' * y) = \Lambda \right)$$

and because $x * y = u \bullet (x' * y)$, it follows that

$$not \left(x * y = \Lambda \right),$$

again contradicting our supposition (†). ⌐

7.4   THE REVERSE FUNCTION

We now define a unary function symbol *reverse*(x). Under the intended models, *reverse*(x) denotes the string obtained by reversing the order of the characters of the string x; for example, *reverse*(AABC) = CBAA.

The axioms that define the *reverse* function are

$$reverse(\Lambda) = \Lambda \qquad\qquad\qquad\qquad\qquad (empty)$$

$$\begin{array}{l}(for\ all\ char\ u)\\(for\ all\ string\ x)\end{array}\left[reverse(u \bullet x) \ = \ reverse(x) * u \right] \qquad (prefix)$$

As usual, we introduce the corresponding instance of the *functional-substitutivity* equality axiom schema for *reverse*.

The axioms for *reverse* suggest a method for computing it.

Example (computation of *reverse*)

Suppose we would like to reverse the string AB, that is, A $\bullet$ (B $\bullet$ Λ). Then we have

$$\begin{aligned}reverse\left(A \bullet (B \bullet \Lambda) \right) &= reverse(B \bullet \Lambda) * A\\&\qquad \text{(by the } prefix \text{ axiom for } reverse)\\[4pt]&= \left(reverse(\Lambda) * B \right) * A\\&\qquad \text{(by the } prefix \text{ axiom for } reverse \text{ again)}\\[4pt]&= (\Lambda * B) * A\\&\qquad \text{(by the } empty \text{ axiom for } reverse)\\[4pt]&= B \bullet (A \bullet \Lambda)\\&\qquad \text{(by properties of strings).}\end{aligned}$$

In other words,

$$reverse(\text{AB}) \;=\; \text{BA}. \quad \lrcorner$$

From the axioms for *reverse* we can establish the validity of the following properties:

$$(\textit{for all string } x)\big[string\,(reverse(x))\big] \tag{\textit{sort}}$$

$$(\textit{for all char } u)\big[reverse(u) = u\big] \tag{\textit{character}}$$

$$\begin{matrix}(\textit{for all string } x)\\ (\textit{for all string } y)\end{matrix}\Big[reverse(x * y) \;=\; reverse(y) * reverse(x)\Big]$$
$$\tag{\textit{concatenation}}$$

$$(\textit{for all string } x)\big[reverse\,(reverse(x)) \;=\; x\big] \tag{\textit{reverse}}$$

$$\begin{matrix}(\textit{for all char } u)\\ (\textit{for all string } x)\end{matrix}\Big[reverse(x * u) \;=\; u \bullet reverse(x)\Big] \tag{\textit{suffix}}$$

The *character* and *suffix* properties can be established directly without the use of the induction principle. We give the proof of the *concatenation* property here. The proof of the *reverse* property is left as an exercise (**Problem 7.4**). The proof of the *sort* property is omitted.

Proposition (concatenation)

The sentence

$$\begin{matrix}(\textit{for all string } x)\\ (\textit{for all string } y)\end{matrix}\Big[reverse(x * y) \;=\; reverse(y) * reverse(x)\Big]$$

is valid. $\quad \lrcorner$

Proof

We reverse the quantifiers and prove

$$\begin{matrix}(\textit{for all string } y)\\ (\textit{for all string } x)\end{matrix}\Big[reverse(x * y) \;=\; reverse(y) * reverse(x)\Big].$$

Consider an arbitrary string y; we attempt to show

$$(for\ all\ string\ x)\big[reverse(x * y)\ =\ reverse(y) * reverse(x)\big].$$

The proof is by induction on x, taking the inductive sentence to be

$$\mathcal{F}[x]:\quad reverse(x * y)\ =\ reverse(y) * reverse(x).$$

Base Case

We would like to prove

$$\mathcal{F}[\Lambda]:\quad reverse(\Lambda * y)\ =\ reverse(y) * reverse(\Lambda).$$

We have

$$reverse(\Lambda * y)\ =\ reverse(y)$$
$$\text{(by the } left\text{-}empty \text{ axiom for concatenation).}$$

But on the other hand,

$$reverse(y) * reverse(\Lambda)\ =\ reverse(y) * \Lambda$$
$$\text{(by the } empty \text{ axiom for } reverse\text{)}$$

$$=\ reverse(y)$$
$$\text{(by the } right\text{-}empty \text{ property of}$$
$$\text{concatenation).}$$

Inductive Step

For an arbitrary character u and string x, we assume the induction hypothesis

$$\mathcal{F}[x]:\quad reverse(x * y)\ =\ reverse(y) * reverse(x)$$

and attempt to show the desired conclusion

$$\mathcal{F}[u \bullet x]:\quad reverse\big((u \bullet x) * y\big)\ =\ reverse(y) * reverse(u \bullet x).$$

Because we have supposed that u is a character, we have

$$reverse\big((u \bullet x) * y\big)\ =\ reverse\big(u \bullet (x * y)\big)$$
$$\text{(by the } left\text{-}prefix \text{ axiom for concatenation)}$$

$$=\ reverse(x * y) * u$$
$$\text{(by the } prefix \text{ axiom for } reverse\text{)}$$

$$=\ \big(reverse(y) * reverse(x)\big) * u$$
$$\text{(by our induction hypothesis).}$$

But on the other hand,

$$reverse(y) * reverse(u \bullet x) = reverse(y) * \big(reverse(x) * u\big)$$
$$\text{(by the } prefix \text{ axiom for } reverse\text{)}$$

$$= \big(reverse(y) * reverse(x)\big) * u$$
$$\text{(by the } associativity \text{ property of}$$
$$\text{concatenation).} \quad \lrcorner$$

Remark (treatment of quantifiers)

The property we established in the *concatenation* proposition was of form

$$\begin{array}{l}(for\ all\ string\ x)\\(for\ all\ string\ y)\end{array} \mathcal{G}[x,\ y].$$

In the above proof we reversed the quantifiers, considered an arbitrary string y, and established the subsentence

$$(for\ all\ string\ x)\mathcal{G}[x,\ y]$$

by induction on x, taking the inductive sentence to be

$$\mathcal{F}[x]: \quad \mathcal{G}[x,\ y].$$

Alternatively, we could have proved the original property

$$\begin{array}{l}(for\ all\ string\ x)\\(for\ all\ string\ y)\end{array} \mathcal{G}[x,\ y]$$

directly by induction on x, taking the inductive sentence to be

$$\mathcal{F}[x]: \quad (for\ all\ string\ y)\mathcal{G}[x,\ y].$$

The resulting proof, however, would have been slightly more complex, because we would have had to dispose of the quantifier (*for all string y*) twice, once in the base case and once in the inductive step. Later in this section, in the *rev2* proposition, we shall see a proof in which we must adopt the alternative, more complex approach. $\quad \lrcorner$

ALTERNATIVE DEFINITION

Let us give an alternative definition for the *reverse* function. Suppose we define a new binary function symbol $rev2(x,\ y)$ by the following two axioms:

$$(for\ all\ string\ y)\big[rev2(\Lambda,\ y) = y\big] \qquad\qquad (left\ empty)$$

$$\begin{array}{l}(\textit{for all char } u)\\(\textit{for all string } x)\\(\textit{for all string } y)\end{array}\left[rev2(u \bullet x,\ y)\ =\ rev2(x,\ u \bullet y)\right] \qquad (\textit{left prefix})$$

Intuitively speaking, $rev2(x,\ y)$ is the function that reverses the string x and concatenates the result with the string y; for example, $rev2(\text{AAB},\ \text{CD}) = \text{BAACD}$.

That the function $rev2$ gives us an alternative definition of the *reverse* function is expressed more precisely in the following proposition.

Proposition (alternative reverse)

The sentence

$$(\textit{for all string } x)\left[reverse(x)\ =\ rev2(x,\ \Lambda)\right]$$

is valid. ⌐

Before proving the proposition, let us see how it suggests an alternative method for reversing a string.

Example (computation of $rev2$)

Assuming the proposition is true, suppose we would like to reverse the string AB, that is, $\text{A} \bullet (\text{B} \bullet \Lambda)$. Then we have

$$\begin{aligned}reverse\big(\text{A} \bullet (\text{B} \bullet \Lambda))\big)\ &=\ rev2\big(\text{A} \bullet (\text{B} \bullet \Lambda),\ \Lambda\big)\\&\qquad \text{(by the proposition)}\\[4pt]&=\ rev2(\text{B} \bullet \Lambda,\ \text{A} \bullet \Lambda)\\&\qquad \text{(by the \textit{left-prefix} axiom for } rev2)\\[4pt]&=\ rev2\big(\Lambda,\ \text{B} \bullet (\text{A} \bullet \Lambda)\big)\\&\qquad \text{(by the \textit{left-prefix} axiom for } rev2 \text{ again)}\\[4pt]&=\ \text{B} \bullet (\text{A} \bullet \Lambda)\\&\qquad \text{(by the \textit{left-empty} axiom for } rev2).\end{aligned}$$

In other words,

$$reverse(\text{AB})\ =\ \text{BA}.$$

Note that the computation method suggested by the axioms for $rev2$ is more "efficient" than that suggested by the axioms for the *reverse* function itself, because we are not required to apply properties of the concatenation function $*$ during the computation. ⌐

Proof (alternative reverse)

We actually prove the more general sentence

$$\begin{matrix} (for\ all\ string\ x) \\ (for\ all\ string\ y) \end{matrix} \Big[rev2(x,\ y) \ = \ reverse(x) * y \Big],$$

which fully describes the behavior of the function *rev2*. Once we have proved this sentence, we can infer the sentence we really want to prove,

$$(for\ all\ string\ x) \big[reverse(x) \ = \ rev2(x,\ \Lambda) \big].$$

For in the more general sentence, considering an arbitrary string x and taking y to be Λ, we obtain

$$rev2(x,\ \Lambda) \ = \ reverse(x) * \Lambda.$$

It follows (by the *right-empty* property of concatenation) that

$$rev2(x,\ \Lambda) = reverse(x).$$

The proof of the more general sentence

$$\begin{matrix} (for\ all\ string\ x) \\ (for\ all\ string\ y) \end{matrix} \Big[rev2(x,\ y) \ = \ reverse(x) * y \Big]$$

is by induction on x, taking the inductive sentence to be

$$\mathcal{F}[x]: \quad (for\ all\ string\ y) \big[rev2(x,\ y) \ = \ reverse(x) * y \big].$$

Base Case

We would like to show

$$\mathcal{F}[\Lambda]: \quad (for\ all\ string\ y) \big[rev2(\Lambda,\ y) \ = \ reverse(\Lambda) * y \big].$$

For an arbitrary string y, we have

$$rev2(\Lambda,\ y) \ = \ y$$
$$\text{(by the \textit{left-empty} axiom for \textit{rev2})}.$$

But on the other hand,

$$reverse(\Lambda) * y \ = \ \Lambda * y$$
$$\text{(by the \textit{empty} axiom for \textit{reverse})}$$

$$= \ y$$
$$\text{(by the \textit{left-empty} axiom for concatenation)}.$$

Inductive Step

   For arbitrary character u and string x, we assume the induction hypothesis

$$\mathcal{F}[x]: \quad (for\ all\ string\ y)\big[rev2(x,\ y)\ =\ reverse(x) * y\big]$$

and would like to show the desired conclusion

$$\mathcal{F}[u \bullet x]: \quad (for\ all\ string\ y')\big[rev2(u \bullet x,\ y')\ =\ reverse(u \bullet x) * y'\big].$$

(Here we have renamed the bound variable y of the desired conclusion to y', to avoid confusion with the variable y in the induction hypothesis.)

   Recall we have supposed that u is a character. Then for an arbitrary string y', we have

$$rev2(u \bullet x,\ y')\ =\ rev2(x,\ u \bullet y')$$
$$(by\ the\ \textit{left-prefix}\ axiom\ for\ rev2).$$

But on the other hand,

$$reverse(u \bullet x) * y'$$

$$= \big(reverse(x) * u\big) * y'$$
$$(by\ the\ \textit{prefix}\ axiom\ for\ reverse)$$

$$= reverse(x) * (u * y')$$
$$(by\ the\ \textit{associativity}\ property\ of\ concatenation)$$

$$= reverse(x) * (u \bullet y')$$
$$(by\ the\ \textit{character}\ property\ of\ concatenation).$$

   Therefore it suffices to establish that

$$rev2(x,\ u \bullet y')\ =\ reverse(x) * (u \bullet y').$$

But this follows from our induction hypothesis,

$$(for\ all\ string\ y)\big[rev2(x,\ y)\ =\ reverse(x) * y\big],$$

taking y to be $u \bullet y'$. ◢

   Note that we were forced to generalize the original property,

$$(for\ all\ string\ x)\big[reverse(x)\ =\ rev2(x,\ \Lambda)\big]\ .$$

The stronger property we used as our inductive sentence was

$$\begin{matrix}(for\ all\ string\ x)\\(for\ all\ string\ y)\end{matrix}\big[rev2(x,\ y)\ =\ reverse(x) * y\big].$$

Had we taken the inductive sentence to be the original property, without first generalizing, we would not have been able to establish the inductive step.

This proposition illustrates another strategic aspect of an inductive proof, discussed in the following remark:

Remark (treatment of quantifiers)

Let us recapitulate the above proof of the *alternative reverse* proposition. We established the property

$$(\textit{for all string } x) \atop (\textit{for all string } y) \Big[rev2(x,\ y)\ =\ reverse(x) * y \Big],$$

which is of the form

$$(\textit{for all string } x) \atop (\textit{for all string } y)\ \mathcal{G}[x,\ y].$$

The proof was by induction on x, taking the inductive sentence to be

$$\mathcal{F}[x]:\quad (\textit{for all string } y)\mathcal{G}[x,\ y].$$

In proving the inductive step, we considered an arbitrary character u and string x and assumed the induction hypothesis

$$\mathcal{F}[x]:\quad (\textit{for all string } y)\big[rev2(x,\ y)\ =\ reverse(x) * y\big],$$

that is,

$$(\textit{for all string } y)\mathcal{G}[x,\ y],$$

and attempted to show the desired conclusion

$$\mathcal{F}[u \bullet x]:\quad (\textit{for all string } y')\big[rev2(u \bullet x,\ y')\ =\ reverse(u \bullet x) * y'\big].$$

For an arbitrary string y', we found that it suffices to establish that

$$rev2(x,\ u \bullet y')\ =\ reverse(x) * (u \bullet y'),$$

that is,

$$\mathcal{G}[x,\ u \bullet y'].$$

This followed from the induction hypothesis, taking y to be $u \bullet y'$.

In proving certain properties of form

$$(\textit{for all string } x) \atop (\textit{for all string } y)\ \mathcal{G}[x,\ y]$$

previously (e.g., in the proof of the *concatenation* proposition for *reverse*), we were able to reverse the quantifiers, obtaining the equivalent sentence of form

$$\begin{array}{l} (\textit{for all string } y) \\ (\textit{for all string } x) \end{array} \mathcal{G}[x,\, y],$$

consider an arbitrary string y, and establish the subsentence

$$(\textit{for all string } x)\mathcal{G}[x,\, y]$$

by induction on x, taking the inductive sentence to be

$$\mathcal{F}[x]: \quad \mathcal{G}[x,\, y].$$

In other words, we removed the quantifier (*for all string y*) before applying the induction principle. By disposing of the quantifier, we simplified both the base case and the inductive step.

This approach, however, does not work in establishing the *alternative-reverse* proposition. For according to this approach, in proving the inductive step we would consider an arbitrary character u and string x and assume the induction hypothesis

$$\mathcal{F}[x]: \quad rev2(x,\, y) \; = \; reverse(x) * y,$$

which is of the form

$$\mathcal{G}[x,\, y],$$

and attempt to show the desired conclusion

$$\mathcal{F}[u \bullet x]: \quad rev2(u \bullet x,\, y) \; = \; reverse(u \bullet x) * y.$$

As in the above proof, we find it suffices to establish that

$$rev2(x,\, u \bullet y) \; = \; reverse(x) * (u \bullet y),$$

that is,

$$\mathcal{G}[x,\, u \bullet y].$$

But the desired result $\mathcal{G}[x,\, u \bullet y]$ does not follow from the induction hypothesis $\mathcal{G}[x,\, y]$, because y is a particular arbitrary string; our induction hypothesis no longer contains the universal quantifier (*for all string y*), so we cannot instantiate y to the required value. ⌋

Some additional functions over the strings are defined in **Problem 7.5**. An alternative induction principle over the strings, based on suffixing rather than prefixing, is introduced in **Problem 7.6**. Using this induction principle, the reader is asked to establish an alternative definition of the concatenation function in **Problem 7.7**.

7.5 THE DECOMPOSITION INDUCTION PRINCIPLE

In the theory of the nonnegative integers, we established a decomposition induction principle. This principle is expressed in terms of the predecessor function x^-, just as the generator induction principle is expressed in terms of the successor function x^+. The two induction principles were shown to be interchangeable in a certain sense.

In the theory of strings, the generator induction principle is expressed in terms of the prefix function $u \bullet x$; we now introduce a corresponding decomposition induction principle expressed in terms of the tail function $tail(x)$.

Proposition (decomposition induction principle)

For each sentence $\mathcal{F}[x]$, the universal closure of the sentence

$$
if \begin{bmatrix} \mathcal{F}[\Lambda] \\ and \\ (for\ all\ string\ x) \begin{bmatrix} if\ not\ (x = \Lambda) \\ then\ if\ \mathcal{F}[tail(x)] \\ then\ \mathcal{F}[x] \end{bmatrix} \end{bmatrix} \qquad \begin{array}{c} (decomposition \\ induction) \end{array}
$$
$$
then\ (for\ all\ string\ x)\mathcal{F}[x]
$$

is valid. ◢

As before, the sentence

$$\mathcal{F}[x]$$

is called the *inductive sentence* of the decomposition induction principle. The subsentence

$$\mathcal{F}[\Lambda]$$

is called the *base case*. The subsentence

$$
(for\ all\ string\ x) \begin{bmatrix} if\ not\ (x = \Lambda) \\ then\ if\ \mathcal{F}[tail(x)] \\ then\ \mathcal{F}[x] \end{bmatrix}
$$

is called the *inductive step*; the subsentences $\mathcal{F}[tail(x)]$ and $\mathcal{F}[x]$ of the inductive step are called the *induction hypothesis* and the *desired conclusion*, respectively.

Together the generator and decomposition induction principles for the strings will be referred to as *stepwise* induction principles.

As in the theory of the nonnegative integers, the decomposition induction principle is interchangeable with the generator induction principle. We are content, however, to show simply that the decomposition induction principle is valid.

Proof

For an arbitrary sentence $\mathcal{F}[x]$, suppose that the base case of the decomposition induction principle,

$$(\dagger) \qquad \mathcal{F}[\Lambda],$$

and the inductive step of the decomposition induction principle,

$$(\ddagger) \qquad (\textit{for all string } x) \begin{bmatrix} \textit{if } \textit{not } (x = \Lambda) \\ \textit{then } \textit{if } \mathcal{F}[tail(x)] \\ \textit{then } \mathcal{F}[x] \end{bmatrix},$$

are true; we would like to show that then the consequent,

$$(\textit{for all string } x)\,\mathcal{F}[x],$$

is also true.

The proof is by the generator version of the induction principle over the strings. We take the inductive sentence to be $\mathcal{F}[x]$ itself.

Base Case

We would like to show $\mathcal{F}[\Lambda]$; but this is our supposition $(\dagger)$.

Inductive Step

For arbitrary character u and string x', we assume the (generator) induction hypothesis,

$$\mathcal{F}[x'],$$

and establish the (generator) desired conclusion,

$$\mathcal{F}[u \bullet x'].$$

(To avoid confusion with the variable x in our supposition $(\ddagger)$, we have renamed the inductive variable x here to a new variable x'.)

By our supposition $(\ddagger)$, taking x to be $u \bullet x'$, we have

$$(*) \qquad \begin{array}{l} \textit{if } \textit{not } (u \bullet x' = \Lambda) \\ \textit{then } \textit{if } \mathcal{F}[tail(u \bullet x')] \\ \qquad \textit{then } \mathcal{F}[u \bullet x']. \end{array}$$

We know (by the *empty* uniqueness axiom) that

$$not\ (u \bullet x' = \Lambda).$$

Since we supposed u to be a character, we have (by the definition of the *tail* function) $tail(u \bullet x') = x'$ and hence (by our (generator) induction hypothesis $\mathcal{F}[x']$)

$$\mathcal{F}[tail(u \bullet x')].$$

Therefore by $(*)$ above, we obtain our (generator) desired conclusion

$$\mathcal{F}[u \bullet x'].$$

Because we have established both the base case and the inductive step, we may conclude (by the generator version of the induction principle) that

$$(for\ all\ string\ x)\mathcal{F}[x]$$

is true. This concludes the proof of the validity of the decomposition induction principle. ⌐

The decomposition version of the induction principle is more convenient to use when we are dealing with axioms and properties that are expressed in terms of the tail function $tail(x)$ rather than the prefix function $u \bullet x$. In this book, we typically use the prefix function; therefore the generator version is usually easier to use. To illustrate the use of the decomposition induction principle, however, we define below a new relation in terms of the *tail* function rather than the prefix function, and we prove one of its properties by decomposition induction rather than by generator induction.

THE END RELATION

Let us introduce a binary predicate symbol $x \preceq_{end} y$ to denote the *end* relation; this relation is true if the string x is at the end of the string y, that is, x can be obtained from y by dropping some (perhaps none) of the initial characters of y. For instance,

$$\text{AT} \preceq_{end} \text{CAT}, \quad \text{T} \preceq_{end} \text{CAT}, \quad \Lambda \preceq_{end} \text{CAT}, \quad \text{CAT} \preceq_{end} \text{CAT}.$$

If $x \preceq_{end} y$, we shall say in words that x is an *end* of y.

Formally we define the end relation by the following two axioms:

$$(for\ all\ string\ x) \begin{bmatrix} x \preceq_{end} \Lambda \\ if\ and\ only\ if \\ x = \Lambda \end{bmatrix} \qquad (empty)$$

$$\begin{matrix} (for\ all\ string\ x) \\ (for\ all\ string\ y) \end{matrix} \begin{bmatrix} if\ not\ (y = \Lambda) \\ then \begin{bmatrix} x \preceq_{end} y \\ if\ and\ only\ if \\ x = y\ \ or\ \ x \preceq_{end} tail(y) \end{bmatrix} \end{bmatrix} \qquad (tail)$$

From these axioms we establish the following property.

Proposition (end concatenation)

The sentence

$$\begin{matrix} (for\ all\ string\ x) \\ (for\ all\ string\ y) \end{matrix} \begin{bmatrix} x \preceq_{end} y \\ if\ and\ only\ if \\ (for\ some\ string\ z)[z * x = y] \end{bmatrix} \qquad (concatenation)$$

is valid.   ⌟

In other words, x is an end of y precisely when y can be obtained by concatenating some string z to x.

To facilitate the use of the decomposition version of the induction principle in the proof, we suppose that we have established the validity of the following property of concatenation, which paraphrases the *left-prefix* axiom for concatenation in terms of the *head* and *tail* function:

$$\begin{matrix} (for\ all\ string\ x) \\ (for\ all\ string\ y) \end{matrix} \begin{bmatrix} if\ not\ (x = \Lambda) \\ then\ \ x * y\ =\ head(x) \bullet (tail(x) * y) \end{bmatrix} \qquad (head\text{-}tail)$$

Let us prove the *end-concatenation* proposition.

Proof

By predicate logic, it suffices to establish the validity of the two sentences:

$$(\Rightarrow) \qquad \begin{matrix} (for\ all\ string\ x) \\ (for\ all\ string\ y) \end{matrix} \begin{bmatrix} if\ x \preceq_{end} y \\ then\ (for\ some\ string\ z)[z * x = y] \end{bmatrix}$$

and

$$(\Leftarrow) \qquad \begin{array}{l} \text{(for all string } x) \\ \text{(for all string } y) \end{array} \left[\begin{array}{l} \text{if (for some string } z)[z * x = y] \\ \text{then } x \preceq_{end} y \end{array} \right].$$

We prove only the ($\Leftarrow$) part here; the proof of the ($\Rightarrow$) part is left as an exercise (**Problem 7.8**).

To prove the ($\Leftarrow$) part, consider an arbitrary string x; we would like to show

$$(\text{for all string } y) \left[\begin{array}{l} \text{if (for some string } z)[z * x = y] \\ \text{then } x \preceq_{end} y \end{array} \right].$$

The proof is by decomposition induction on y, taking the inductive sentence to be

$$\mathcal{F}[y]: \quad \begin{array}{l} \text{if (for some string } z)[z * x = y] \\ \text{then } x \preceq_{end} y. \end{array}$$

Base Case

We would like to show

$$\mathcal{F}[\Lambda]: \quad \begin{array}{l} \text{if (for some string } z)[z * x = \Lambda] \\ \text{then } x \preceq_{end} \Lambda. \end{array}$$

Suppose that, for some string z,

$$z * x = \Lambda;$$

then (by the *annihilation* property of concatenation)

$$z = \Lambda \quad \text{and} \quad x = \Lambda.$$

Therefore (by the *empty* axiom for the *end* relation $\preceq_{end}$, because $x = \Lambda$)

$$x \preceq_{end} \Lambda,$$

which is the consequent of our base case $\mathcal{F}[\Lambda]$.

Inductive Step

For an arbitrary string y, suppose

$$not \ (y = \Lambda)$$

and assume the induction hypothesis

$$\mathcal{F}[tail(y)]: \quad \begin{array}{l} \text{if (for some string } z)[z * x = tail(y)] \\ \text{then } x \preceq_{end} tail(y). \end{array}$$

We would like to establish the desired conclusion

$$\mathcal{F}[y]: \quad \begin{array}{l} \textit{if (for some string } z')\,[z' * x \;=\; y] \\ \textit{then } x \preceq_{end} y. \end{array}$$

(Here we have renamed the bound variable z of the desired conclusion to z', to avoid confusion with the bound variable z of the induction hypothesis.)

Suppose that, for some string z',

$$z' * x = y;$$

we would like to show that

$$x \preceq_{end} y.$$

The proof distinguishes between two cases, depending on whether or not z' is empty.

Case: $z' = \Lambda$

Then (by the supposition above)

$$\Lambda * x = y,$$

and hence (by the *left-empty* axiom for concatenation)

$$x = y.$$

Therefore (by the *tail* axiom for the $\preceq_{end}$ relation, because *not* $(y = \Lambda)$)

$$x \preceq_{end} y,$$

which is the desired result.

Case: *not* $(z' = \Lambda)$

Then (by the *head-tail* property of concatenation, because *not* $(z' = \Lambda)$) we can rewrite our supposition $z' * x = y$ as

$$head(z') \bullet (tail(z') * x) \;=\; y.$$

Therefore

$$tail\big(head(z') \bullet (tail(z') * x)\big) \;=\; tail(y)$$

and hence (by the definition of the *tail* function)

$$tail(z') * x \;=\; tail(y).$$

It follows (by the *existential quantifier-instantiation* proposition, taking z to be $tail(z')$) that

$$(for\ some\ string\ z)\big[z * x \ = \ tail(y)\big].$$

Hence (by our induction hypothesis)

$$x \preceq_{end} tail(y)$$

and (by the *tail* axiom for the $\preceq_{end}$ relation, because *not* $(y = \Lambda)$)

$$x \preceq_{end} y,$$

which is the desired result.   ⏌

7.6   THE SUBSTRING RELATION

A string x is said to be a "substring" of another string y if the characters of x occur consecutively in y. For example, BBC is a substring of ABBCD but not of ABCD or of BABC. A string is regarded as a substring of itself.

Let us augment our theory by defining a binary predicate symbol $x \preceq_{string} y$ to denote the *substring* relation; thus

$$BBC \preceq_{string} ABBCD \quad and \quad BBC \preceq_{string} BBC.$$

The sole axiom for the substring relation is

$$\begin{array}{l}(for\ all\ string\ x)\\(for\ all\ string\ y)\end{array}\left[\begin{array}{l}x \preceq_{string} y\\ \quad if\ and\ only\ if\\(for\ some\ string\ z_1)\\(for\ some\ string\ z_2)\end{array}\Big[z_1 * x * z_2 \ = \ y\Big]\right] \quad (substring)$$

Note that we can write $z_1 * x * z_2$ without parentheses because the concatenation function $*$ is associative.

The definition of the substring relation $\preceq_{string}$ does not immediately suggest a method to compute it, because of the existential quantifiers (*for some string* z_1) and (*for some string* z_2). An alternative definition of the substring relation that does suggest a computational method is given in **Problem 7.9**.

From the *substring* axiom we may establish that the substring relation is a weak partial ordering, that is,

$$(for\ all\ string\ x) \atop (for\ all\ string\ y) \atop (for\ all\ string\ z) \left[if\ x \preceq_{string} y\ and\ y \preceq_{string} z \atop then\ x \preceq_{string} z \right] \qquad (transitivity)$$

$$(for\ all\ string\ x) \atop (for\ all\ string\ y) \left[if\ x \preceq_{string} y\ and\ y \preceq_{string} x \atop then\ x = y \right] \qquad (antisymmetry)$$

$$(for\ all\ string\ x) \left[x \preceq_{string} x \right] \qquad (reflexivity)$$

One can also establish the following properties:

$$(for\ all\ string\ x) \left[\Lambda \preceq_{string} x \right] \qquad (left\ empty)$$

$$(for\ all\ string\ x) \atop (for\ all\ string\ y) \left[x \preceq_{string} x * y \right] \qquad (left\ concatenation)$$

$$(for\ all\ string\ x) \atop (for\ all\ string\ y) \left[y \preceq_{string} x * y \right] \qquad (right\ concatenation)$$

We define the *proper substring* relation, denoted by $x \prec_{string} y$, to be the irreflexive restriction of the substring relation $\preceq_{string}$; this is expressed by the axiom

$$(for\ all\ string\ x) \atop (for\ all\ string\ y) \left[\begin{matrix} x \prec_{string} y \\ if\ and\ only\ if \\ x \preceq_{string} y\ and\ not\ (x = y) \end{matrix} \right] \qquad (proper\ substring)$$

Because the substring relation $\preceq_{string}$ has been shown to be a weak partial ordering, we know (by the *strict partial-ordering* proposition of the theory of associated relations) that its irreflexive restriction $\prec_{string}$ is a strict partial ordering. Thus the proper substring relation $\prec_{string}$ has the following properties:

$$(for\ all\ string\ x) \atop (for\ all\ string\ y) \atop (for\ all\ string\ z) \left[if\ x \prec_{string} y\ and\ y \prec_{string} z \atop then\ x \prec_{string} z \right] \qquad (transitivity)$$

$$(for\ all\ string\ x) \left[not\ (x \prec_{string} x) \right] \qquad (irreflexivity)$$

$$(for\ all\ string\ x) \atop (for\ all\ string\ y) \left[if\ x \prec_{string} y \atop then\ not\ (y \prec_{string} x) \right] \qquad (asymmetry)$$

By the *mixed-transitivity* proposition of the theory of associated relations, we can also conclude that

$$\begin{array}{l}(\textit{for all string } x)\\(\textit{for all string } y)\\(\textit{for all string } z)\end{array}\left[\begin{array}{l}\textit{if } x \preceq_{string} y \textit{ and } y \prec_{string} z\\\textit{then } x \prec_{string} z\end{array}\right]$$

(left mixed transitivity)

$$\begin{array}{l}(\textit{for all string } x)\\(\textit{for all string } y)\\(\textit{for all string } z)\end{array}\left[\begin{array}{l}\textit{if } x \prec_{string} y \textit{ and } y \preceq_{string} z\\\textit{then } x \prec_{string} z\end{array}\right]$$

(right mixed transitivity)

Using properties of strings, we can also establish the following properties

$$(\textit{for all string } x)\left[not\,(x \prec_{string} \Lambda)\right] \qquad (\textit{right empty})$$

$$\begin{array}{l}(\textit{for all char } u)\\(\textit{for all string } x)\end{array}\left[x \prec_{string} u \bullet x\right] \qquad (\textit{prefix adjacent})$$

$$\begin{array}{l}(\textit{for all char } u)\\(\textit{for all string } x)\end{array}\left[x \prec_{string} x * u\right] \qquad (\textit{suffix adjacent})$$

7.7   THE COMPLETE INDUCTION PRINCIPLE

Using the proper substring relation $\prec_{string}$, we can state and prove an alternative version of the induction principle. This principle is called the *complete induction principle* for the strings; it is analogous to that principle for the nonnegative integers.

Proposition (complete induction principle)

For each sentence $\mathcal{F}[x]$, the universal closure of the sentence

$$\textit{if } (\textit{for all string } x)\left[\begin{array}{l}\textit{if } (\textit{for all string } x')\left[\begin{array}{l}\textit{if } x' \prec_{string} x\\\textit{then } \mathcal{F}[x']\end{array}\right]\\\textit{then } \mathcal{F}[x]\end{array}\right]$$
$$\textit{then } (\textit{for all string } x)\mathcal{F}[x]$$

(complete induction)

where x' does not occur free in $\mathcal{F}[x]$, is valid.   ⌐

The proof of the proposition will be given in a later chapter (on well-founded relations) in Volume II. Let us illustrate its application here.

PALINDROMES

We first introduce the notion of a "palindrome," a symmetric string, which reads the same left to right as right to left. For example, CAAC and CABAC are palindromes; the empty string Λ is regarded as a palindrome.

Formally we introduce a unary predicate symbol $palin(x)$ to denote that the string x is a palindrome. It is defined by the following axiom:

$$(for\ all\ string\ x)\begin{bmatrix} palin(x) \\ if\ and\ only\ if \\ x = reverse(x) \end{bmatrix} \qquad (palindrome)$$

From this axiom we establish the following property of palindromes.

Proposition (palindrome)

The sentence

$$(for\ all\ string\ x)\begin{bmatrix} palin(x) \\ if\ and\ only\ if \\ \begin{bmatrix} (for\ some\ string\ y)[x\ =\ y * reverse(y)] \\ or \\ (for\ some\ char\ u) \\ (for\ some\ string\ y) \end{bmatrix} [x\ =\ y * u * reverse(y)] \end{bmatrix}$$

is valid. ◢

Note again that, in stating the proposition, we may write $y * u * reverse(y)$ without parentheses because the concatenation function $*$ is associative.

Intuitively speaking, the proposition states that a palindrome is built up in one of two ways: Either it has an even number of characters and is of the form $y * reverse(y)$, or it has an odd number of characters and is of the form $y * u * reverse(y)$, for some character u and string y. For example,

$$CAAC\quad =\quad CA * reverse(CA)$$

$$CABAC\quad =\quad CA * B * reverse(CA).$$

The proof of this proposition, which uses the complete induction principle for the strings, is more complex than those we have seen previously. It relies on the following property of the concatenation function:

$$(\textit{for all string } x) \begin{bmatrix} x = \Lambda \ \ or \ \ char(x) \\ or \\ (\textit{for some char } u) \\ (\textit{for some char } v) \begin{bmatrix} x = u * y * v \end{bmatrix} \\ (\textit{for some string } y) \end{bmatrix}$$

$$(\textit{prefix-suffix decomposition})$$

In other words, a string is either empty or a character, or (if it has at least two characters) it may be obtained by affixing characters to the beginning and end of some other string. The proof of this property is left as an exercise (**Problem 7.3(i)**).

Proof (palindrome)

By predicate logic it suffices to prove the two sentences

$$(\Rightarrow) \quad (\textit{for all string } x) \begin{bmatrix} \textit{if } palin(x) \\ \textit{then} \begin{bmatrix} (\textit{for some string } y)\begin{bmatrix} x = y * reverse(y) \end{bmatrix} \\ or \\ (\textit{for some char } u) \\ (\textit{for some string } y) \begin{bmatrix} x = y * u * reverse(y) \end{bmatrix} \end{bmatrix} \end{bmatrix}$$

and

$$(\Leftarrow) \quad (\textit{for all string } x) \begin{bmatrix} \textit{if} \begin{bmatrix} (\textit{for some string } y)\begin{bmatrix} x = y * reverse(y) \\ or \\ (\textit{for some char } u) \\ (\textit{for some string } y) \begin{bmatrix} x = y * u * reverse(y) \end{bmatrix} \end{bmatrix} \\ \textit{then } palin(x) \end{bmatrix}$$

We prove only the ($\Rightarrow$) part here; the proof of the ($\Leftarrow$) part is left as an exercise (**Problem 7.10**).

The proof of the ($\Rightarrow$) part is by complete induction on x, taking the inductive sentence to be

$$\mathcal{F}[x]: \quad \begin{matrix} \textit{if } palin(x) \\ \textit{then} \end{matrix} \begin{bmatrix} (\textit{for some string } y)\begin{bmatrix} x = y * reverse(y) \end{bmatrix} \\ or \\ (\textit{for some char } u) \\ (\textit{for some string } y) \begin{bmatrix} x = y * u * reverse(y) \end{bmatrix} \end{bmatrix}$$

To prove

$$(for\ all\ string\ x)\mathcal{F}[x],$$

it suffices to establish a single inductive step.

Inductive Step

We would like to show

$$(for\ all\ string\ x)\left[\begin{array}{l} if\ (for\ all\ string\ x')\begin{bmatrix} if\ x' \prec_{string} x \\ then\ \mathcal{F}[x'] \end{bmatrix} \\ then\ \ \mathcal{F}[x] \end{array}\right].$$

For an arbitrary string x, we assume the induction hypothesis

$$(for\ all\ string\ x')\begin{bmatrix} if\ x' \prec_{string} x \\ then\ \mathcal{F}[x'] \end{bmatrix}$$

and attempt to show the desired conclusion

$$\mathcal{F}[x],$$

that is,

$$if\ palin(x)$$
$$then\ \left[\begin{array}{l} (for\ some\ string\ y)\bigl[x\ =\ y * reverse(y)\bigr] \\ or \\ (for\ some\ char\ u) \\ (for\ some\ string\ y)\bigl[x\ =\ y * u * reverse(y)\bigr] \end{array}\right].$$

Suppose that x is a palindrome, that is,

$$palin(x);$$

then we want to show

(†)
$$\begin{array}{l} (for\ some\ string\ y)\bigl[x\ =\ y * reverse(y)\bigr] \\ or \\ (for\ some\ char\ u) \\ (for\ some\ string\ y)\bigl[x\ =\ y * u * reverse(y)\bigr]. \end{array}$$

We distinguish among three cases, according to whether x is empty, a character, or a longer string.

Case: $x = \Lambda$

Then we have

$$x\ =\ \Lambda * \Lambda$$
(by the *left-empty* axiom for concatenation)

$$= \Lambda * reverse(\Lambda)$$

(by the *empty* axiom for *reverse*).

Hence (by the *existential quantifier-instantiation* proposition, taking y to be Λ),

$$(for\ some\ string\ y)\big[x\ =\ y * reverse(y)\big].$$

This is one disjunct of the desired result (†).

Case: $char(x)$

Then we have

$$x\ =\ \Lambda * x * \Lambda$$

(by the *left-empty* axiom and the *right-empty* property
of concatenation)

$$=\ \Lambda * x * reverse(\Lambda)$$

(by the *empty* axiom for *reverse*).

Hence (by the *existential quantifier-instantiation* proposition, taking u to be x and y to be Λ, because x is a character) we have

$$\begin{matrix}(for\ some\ char\ u)\\(for\ some\ string\ y)\end{matrix}\big[x\ =\ y * u * reverse(y)\big].$$

This is one disjunct of the desired result (†).

Case: $not\ (x = \Lambda)$ *and* $not\ (char(x))$

Then (by the *prefix-suffix decomposition* property of concatenation mentioned above) we have

$$\begin{matrix}(for\ some\ char\ v)\\(for\ some\ char\ w)\\(for\ some\ string\ x')\end{matrix}\Big[x\ =\ v * x' * w\Big].$$

Let v and w be characters and x' be a string such that

$$x\ =\ v * x' * w.$$

We shall first show that x' is a proper substring of x, so that we can apply the induction hypothesis to x'.

Proof that $x' \prec_{string} x$

We know (by the *left-concatenation* property of $\preceq_{string}$) that

$$x'\ \preceq_{string}\ x' * w.$$

Also (by the *prefix-adjacent* property of $\prec_{string}$, because v is a character) we have $x' * w \prec_{string} v \bullet (x' * w)$; that is (by the *character* property for concatenation, because v is a character),

$$x' * w \;\prec_{string}\; v * x' * w.$$

Hence (by the *left mixed-transitivity* property of the substring relation)

$$x' \;\prec_{string}\; v * x' * w,$$

that is (because $x = v * x' * w$),

$$x' \prec_{string} x.$$

Thus x' is a proper substring of x, and we can apply the induction hypothesis to x'.

The induction hypothesis now tells us that $\mathcal{F}[x']$, that is,

(‡) $\quad$ *if palin*(x')
$\quad\quad$ *then* $\left[\begin{array}{l} (for\ some\ string\ y')\big[x' = y' * reverse(y')\big] \\ or \\ (for\ some\ char\ u') \\ (for\ some\ string\ y')\big[x' = y' * u' * reverse(y')\big] \end{array}\right]$

Note that we have renamed the bound variables y and u to y' and u', respectively, to avoid future confusion.

Let us now show that x' is a palindrome, so that we may deduce the consequent of (‡).

Proof of palin(x')

We have (recalling that v and w are characters)

$$v \bullet (x' * w) \;=\; v * x' * w$$
$$\text{(by the \textit{character} property of concatenation)}$$

$$= \; x$$

$$= \; reverse(x)$$
$$\text{(by the definition of palindrome}$$
$$\text{and our supposition that } palin(x))$$

$$= \; reverse(v * x' * w)$$

$$= \; reverse(x' * w) * reverse(v)$$
$$\text{(by the \textit{concatenation} property of \textit{reverse})}$$

$$= \ reverse(x' * w) * v$$
$$\text{(by the } \textit{character} \text{ property of } \textit{reverse})$$

$$= \ \bigl(w \bullet reverse(x')\bigr) * v$$
$$\text{(by the } \textit{suffix} \text{ property of } \textit{reverse})$$

$$= \ w \bullet \bigl(reverse(x') * v\bigr)$$
$$\text{(by the } \textit{left-prefix} \text{ axiom for concatenation)}.$$

In short,

$$v \bullet (x' * w) \ = \ w \bullet \bigl(reverse(x') * v\bigr).$$

Hence (by the *prefix* uniqueness axiom for the strings)

$$v = w \qquad \text{and} \qquad x' * w \ = \ reverse(x') * v.$$

Consequently (by the *suffix-uniqueness* property for concatenation, because w and v are characters),

$$x' \ = \ reverse(x')$$

and hence (by the definition of palindrome)

$$palin(x').$$

We therefore can conclude from (‡) that

$$(\textit{for some string } y')\,\bigl[x' \ = \ y' * reverse(y')\bigr]$$
$$\quad \textit{or}$$
$$(\textit{for some char } u')$$
$$(\textit{for some string } y')\Bigl[x' \ = \ y' * u' * reverse(y')\Bigr].$$

It remains to show the desired result (†).

Proof of (†)

Let y' be a string and u' a character such that

$$x' \ = \ y' * reverse(y')$$
$$\quad \textit{or}$$
$$x' \ = \ y' * u' * reverse(y').$$

Therefore (concatenating the character v on the left and right)

$$v * x' * v = v * y' * reverse(y') * v$$
$$\quad \textit{or}$$
$$v * x' * v = v * y' * u' * reverse(y') * v.$$

Then, because $v * x' * w = x$ and $w = v$, we have

$$x = v * y' * reverse(y') * v$$
$$or$$
$$x = v * y' * u' * reverse(y') * v.$$

Hence (by the *character* property of concatenation applied to $v * y'$ and the *prefix* axiom for *reverse* applied to $reverse(y') * v$, because v is a character) we have

$$x = (v \bullet y') * reverse(v \bullet y')$$
$$or$$
$$x = (v \bullet y') * u' * reverse(v \bullet y').$$

Therefore (by two applications of the *existential quantifier-instantiation* property, taking y to be $v \bullet y'$ and u to be u', because u' is a character) we have

$$(for\ some\ string\ y)\big[x = y * reverse(y)\big]$$
$$or$$
$$\begin{matrix}(for\ some\ char\ u)\\(for\ some\ string\ y)\end{matrix}\Big[x = y * u * reverse(y)\Big],$$

which is our desired result (†).   ◢

The *palindrome* proposition would have been less convenient to prove by stepwise induction. In the inductive step of, say, a decomposition induction proof, we consider an arbitrary nonempty string x, assume the induction hypothesis $\mathcal{F}[tail(x)]$, and attempt to establish the desired conclusion $\mathcal{F}[x]$. But this induction hypothesis would be of little use in the above proof, because if x is a palindrome, $tail(x)$ generally is not. To find a substring x' that is a palindrome, to which the (complete) induction hypothesis could be applied, it was necessary to chop off both the first character v and the last character w of x, not just the first character.

7.8   NONNEGATIVE INTEGERS AND STRINGS

Under the intended models for the theory of the nonnegative integers, every term denotes a nonnegative integer. Under the intended models for the theory of strings, every term denotes a string. But how do we formulate a theory whose sentences may discuss both nonnegative integers and strings? For example, we might wish to define a function $length(x)$, denoting the number of characters in a given string x, and to establish that, for all strings x and y,

$$length(x * y) = length(x) + length(y).$$

We cannot define the *length* function and establish the above property in either theory alone. In this section we show how to combine the theories of the nonnegative integers and the strings into a single theory in which we can establish properties that discuss objects from both theories.

The vocabulary for the combined theory consists of the combined vocabularies of the two constituent theories, the nonnegative integers and the strings. The axioms for the combined theory include all the axioms for the constituent theories. In the combined theory we have a single binary equality predicate symbol =, satisfying the usual axioms for equality.

Because the axioms for the combined theory include the axioms for the constituent theories, any sentence we can prove valid in the theory of the nonnegative integers or the theory of strings is also valid in the combined theory. We also include the special axioms that define new functions and relations, such as the addition function and the substring relation.

Note that the axioms for the combined theory do not specify the relationship between the nonnegative integers and the strings. In some augmentations of the combined theory we will assume that the two classes are disjoint; this will be expressed by adding the special axiom

$$(\textit{for all } x)\bigl[\textit{not } (\textit{integer}(x) \ \textit{and} \ \textit{string}(x))\bigr] \qquad (\textit{disjoint})$$

Under the models for a combined theory that includes this axiom, no domain element can be both a nonnegative integer and a string.

On the other hand, we shall see another augmentation of the combined theory, which does not include the *disjoint* axiom, in which some elements are regarded as both nonnegative integers and strings. But first let us establish some results in a combined theory (without the *disjoint* axiom) in which we know nothing about the relationship between nonnegative integers and strings.

THE LENGTH FUNCTION

Let us define a unary function symbol $length(x)$ in the combined theory of the nonnegative integers and strings. Under the intended model for the combined theory, $length(x)$ denotes the number of characters in the string x; for example, $length(\text{AAB}) = 3$. As we have remarked, this function can only be defined in the combined theory, because its argument is a string and its value is a nonnegative integer.

The special axioms that define the *length* function are

$$length(\Lambda) = 0 \qquad\qquad\qquad\qquad\qquad\qquad (empty)$$

$$\begin{array}{l}(for\ all\ char\ u) \\ (for\ all\ string\ x)\end{array}\Big[length(u \bullet x)\ =\ length(x)+1\Big] \qquad (prefix)$$

From these axioms we can establish the validity of the following properties in the combined theory:

$$(for\ all\ string\ x)\big[integer\,(length(x))\big] \qquad\qquad\qquad (sort)$$

$$(for\ all\ string\ x) \begin{bmatrix} if\ length(x) = 0 \\ then\ \ x = \Lambda \end{bmatrix} \qquad\qquad\qquad (zero)$$

$$(for\ all\ char\ u)\big[length(u) = 1\big] \qquad\qquad\qquad (character)$$

$$\begin{array}{l}(for\ all\ string\ x) \\ (for\ all\ string\ y)\end{array}\Big[length(x * y)\ =\ length(x) + length(y)\Big]$$

$$(concatenation)$$

$$(for\ all\ string\ x)\big[length\,(reverse(x))\ =\ length(x)\big] \qquad (reverse)$$

$$\begin{array}{l}(for\ all\ string\ x) \\ (for\ all\ string\ y)\end{array}\begin{bmatrix} if\ x \prec_{string} y \\ then\ \ length(x) < length(y) \end{bmatrix} \ \ (proper\ substring)$$

We establish the *concatenation* property here; the proofs of the other properties are left as an exercise (**Problem 7.11**).

Proposition (concatenation)

The sentence

$$\begin{array}{l}(for\ all\ string\ x) \\ (for\ all\ string\ y)\end{array}\Big[length(x * y)\ =\ length(x) + length(y)\Big]$$

is valid (in the combined theory).   ⌐

Proof

We actually prove the equivalent sentence

$$\begin{matrix} (\textit{for all string } y) \\ (\textit{for all string } x) \end{matrix} \Big[length(x * y) \ = \ length(x) + length(y) \Big],$$

obtained by reversing the quantifiers. Consider an arbitrary string y; we would like to show

$$(\textit{for all string } x) \big[length(x * y) \ = \ length(x) + length(y) \big].$$

The proof is by stepwise induction over the strings, taking the inductive sentence to be

$$\mathcal{F}[x]: \quad length(x * y) \ = \ length(x) + length(y).$$

Base Case

We want to prove

$$\mathcal{F}[\Lambda]: \quad length(\Lambda * y) \ = \ length(\Lambda) + length(y).$$

We have

$$length(\Lambda) + length(y)$$

$$= \ 0 + length(y)$$
$$\text{(by the } \textit{empty} \text{ axiom for the } \textit{length} \text{ function)}$$

$$= \ length(y)$$
$$\text{(by the } \textit{left-zero} \text{ property of addition)}$$

$$= \ length(\Lambda * y)$$
$$\text{(by the } \textit{left-empty} \text{ axiom for concatenation)}.$$

Inductive Step

For an arbitrary character u and string x, assume the induction hypothesis

$$\mathcal{F}[x]: \quad length(x * y) \ = \ length(x) + length(y).$$

We would like to show the desired conclusion

$$\mathcal{F}[u \bullet x]: \quad length\big((u \bullet x) * y\big) \ = \ length(u \bullet x) + length(y).$$

Because u is a character, we have

$$length\big((u \bullet x) * y\big) \ = \ length\big(u \bullet (x * y)\big)$$
$$\text{(by the } \textit{left-prefix} \text{ axiom for concatenation)}$$

$$= \ length(x * y) + 1$$
$$\text{(by the } \textit{prefix} \text{ axiom for the } \textit{length} \text{ function)}$$

$$= \big(length(x) + length(y)\big) + 1$$
$$\text{(by our induction hypothesis)}.$$

But on the other hand,

$$length(u \bullet x) + length(y)$$

$$= \big(length(x) + 1\big) + length(y)$$
$$\text{(by the \textit{prefix} axiom for the \textit{length} function again)}$$

$$= \big(length(x) + length(y)\big) + 1$$
$$\text{(by the \textit{left-successor} property of addition)}. \quad \lrcorner$$

7.9   STRING REPRESENTATION OF INTEGERS

In our combined theory of the nonnegative integers and the strings, we have not yet specified whether a single domain element can be both a nonnegative integer and a string. In this section we shall introduce a special augmentation of the combined theory, called *the string representation of the (nonnegative) integers*, in which the digits 0, 1, ..., 9 are identified with the characters of the strings and each nonnegative integer is identified with the string of digits that constitutes its decimal representation. For example, the nonnegative integer 503 will be identified with the string of three characters 5, 0, and 3.

The domain of the intended model of this combined theory consists of strings of the digits 0 through 9; thus the strings 1, 305, and 0027 are all elements of the domain. Not all of these strings, however, are regarded as nonnegative integers; the empty string and strings with "leading zeroes," such as 0027, are not nonnegative integers.

We provide the following special axioms for the string representation of the integers, indicating how nonnegative integers are to be viewed as strings of digits.

$$
(\textit{for all } x) \left[
\begin{array}{l}
char(x) \\
\quad \textit{if and only if} \\
integer(x) \ \textit{and} \ x \le 9
\end{array}
\right]
\qquad (\textit{character})
$$

$$
\begin{array}{l}
(\textit{for all positive } x) \\
(\textit{for all char } u)
\end{array}
\Big[x * u \ = \ 10 \cdot x + u \Big]
\qquad (\textit{suffix})
$$

According to the above axioms, the characters of the theory are precisely the integers 0, 1, ..., 9. The result of "suffixing" a digit (character) u at the end of a positive integer (string) x is equal to $10 \cdot x + u$; for example, $56 * 3$, that is, 563, is equal to $10 \cdot 56 + 3$.

As a consequence of these axioms, we have that every nonnegative integer is a string; that is,

$$(\textit{for all } x) \begin{bmatrix} \textit{if integer}(x) \\ \textit{then string}(x) \end{bmatrix} \qquad (\textit{integer string})$$

The fact that the empty string Λ and strings with "leading zeroes," such as 001, do not represent nonnegative integers is expressed by the following properties:

$$\textit{not } \big(\textit{integer}(\Lambda)\big) \qquad (\textit{empty})$$

$$(\textit{for all integer } x) \begin{bmatrix} \textit{if } \textit{head}(x) = 0 \\ \textit{then } \textit{tail}(x) = \Lambda \end{bmatrix} \qquad (\textit{leading zeroes})$$

The proofs are left as an exercise (**Problem 7.12**).

We would like to use this special combined theory to express and prove a useful property of the nonnegative integers that is difficult to formulate in the theory of the nonnegative integers alone: that a nonnegative integer is divisible by 9 if and only if the sum of its digits is divisible by 9. For this purpose we define a new unary function symbol $sum(x)$, to denote the sum of the digits of the nonnegative integer x. Formally the sum function is defined by the axioms

$$\boxed{\begin{array}{l} (\textit{for all char } u) \big[sum(u) = u \big] \qquad\qquad\qquad\quad (\textit{character}) \\[2ex] \begin{array}{l} (\textit{for all positive } x) \\ (\textit{for all char } u) \end{array} \Big[sum(x * u) = sum(x) + u \Big] \qquad (\textit{suffix}) \end{array}}$$

We can now state the above property in our theory.

Proposition (casting out nines)

The sentence

$$(\textit{for all integer } x) \begin{bmatrix} 9 \preceq_{div} x \\ \textit{if and only if} \\ 9 \preceq_{div} sum(x) \end{bmatrix}$$

is valid. ∎

Proof

The sentence is equivalent (by the *remainder* property of the divides relation $\preceq_{div}$) to

$$(\textit{for all integer } x)\left[\begin{array}{c} rem(x,\,9) = 0 \\ \textit{if and only if} \\ rem\big(sum(x),\,9\big) = 0 \end{array}\right],$$

where we recall that $rem(y,\,z)$ is the remainder of dividing y by z. We actually prove the more general sentence

$$(\textit{for all integer } x)\Big[rem(x,\,9) \;=\; rem\big(sum(x),\,9\big)\Big].$$

The original sentence then follows by the substitutivity of equality.

The proof of the more general property relies on the following properties of the quotient and the remainder functions, which are given here without proof.

$$\begin{array}{l} (\textit{for all positive } x) \\ (\textit{for all integer } y) \end{array}\left[\begin{array}{l} \textit{if } 1 < y \\ \textit{then } quot(x,\,y) < x \end{array}\right] \qquad (\textit{smaller-than})$$

$$rem(10,\,9) = 1$$

$$\begin{array}{l} (\textit{for all integer } x) \\ (\textit{for all integer } y) \\ (\textit{for all positive } z) \end{array}\left[\begin{array}{c} rem(x+y,\,z) \\ = \\ rem\big(rem(x,z) + rem(y,z),\; z\big) \end{array}\right] \qquad (\textit{addition})$$

$$\begin{array}{l} (\textit{for all integer } x) \\ (\textit{for all integer } y) \\ (\textit{for all positive } z) \end{array}\left[\begin{array}{c} rem(x \cdot y,\,z) \\ = \\ rem\big(rem(x,z) \cdot rem(y,z),\; z\big) \end{array}\right] \qquad (\textit{multiplication})$$

$$\begin{array}{l} (\textit{for all integer } x) \\ (\textit{for all positive } z) \end{array}\Big[rem\big(rem(x,z),\,z\big) \;=\; rem(x,z)\Big] \qquad (\textit{remainder})$$

We also use without proof simple properties of the nonnegative integers, such as $not\,(9 = 0)$, $not\,(10 = 0)$, and $1 < 10$.

We prove the more general sentence,

$$(\textit{for all integer } x)\big[rem(x,\,9) \;=\; rem\big(sum(x),\,9\big)\big].$$

The proof is by complete induction over the nonnegative integers, taking the inductive sentence to be

$$\mathcal{F}[x]: \quad rem(x,\,9) \;=\; rem\big(sum(x),\,9\big).$$

Inductive Step

For an arbitrary nonnegative integer x, we assume the induction hypothesis

$$(\textit{for all integer } x') \begin{bmatrix} \textit{if } x' < x \\ \textit{then } \mathcal{F}[x'] \end{bmatrix}$$

and attempt to show the desired conclusion

$$\mathcal{F}[x],$$

which is

$$rem(x, 9) \;=\; rem\big(sum(x), 9\big).$$

The proof distinguishes between two cases, according to whether or not $x \leq 9$.

Case: $x \leq 9$

Then (by the *character* axiom for the string representation)

$$char(x)$$

and hence (by the *character* axiom for the *sum* function)

$$sum(x) \;=\; x.$$

Therefore

$$rem(x, 9) \;=\; rem\big(sum(x), 9\big),$$

as we wanted to show.

Case: *not* $(x \leq 9)$

Then

$$not \; (x = 0).$$

For otherwise, if $x = 0$, we would have *not* $(0 \leq 9)$.

We have (by the *quotient-remainder* property of the nonnegative integers, because *not* $(10 = 0)$)

$$x \;=\; 10 \cdot quot(x, 10) + rem(x, 10)$$
$$and$$
$$rem(x, 10) < 10$$

and (by the aforementioned *smaller-than* property of the quotient function, because *not* $(x = 0)$ and $1 < 10$)

$$quot(x, 10) < x.$$

Also (by the *sort* properties of *quot* and *rem*) $quot(x, 10)$ and $rem(x, 10)$ are nonnegative integers.

Let us abbreviate $quot(x, 10)$ as x' and $rem(x, 10)$ as u. Then we have

$$x = 10 \cdot x' + u, \qquad u < 10, \qquad x' < x,$$

and that x' and u are nonnegative integers.

From these conditions we may derive several consequences

Because $u < 10$, we have (by the *right-successor* property of the less-than relation) that

$$u \leq 9.$$

From this we can also deduce that

$$not\ (x' = 0).$$

For suppose, to the contrary, that $x' = 0$. Then (by the *right-zero* axiom for multiplication and the *left-zero* property of addition, because $x = 10 \cdot x' + u$) we have $x = u$. But then, because $u \leq 9$, we have that $x \leq 9$, contradicting our case assumption.

Because u is a nonnegative integer and $u \leq 9$, we have (by the *character* axiom for the string representation)

$$char(u)$$

and hence (by the *suffix* axiom for the string representation, because x' is positive) $x' * u = 10 \cdot x' + u$. Therefore, because $x = 10 \cdot x' + u$, we have

$$x = x' * u.$$

Furthermore, because $x' < x$, we can apply our induction hypothesis to conclude that $\mathcal{F}[x']$, that is,

(†) $\qquad rem(x', 9) = rem\big(sum(x'), 9\big).$

We are now ready to show the desired result, that

$$rem(x, 9) = rem\big(sum(x), 9\big).$$

We use throughout the fact that $not\ (9 = 0)$.

We have

$$rem(x, 9) = rem(10 \cdot x' + u, 9)$$
$$(\text{because } x = 10 \cdot x' + u)$$

$$= rem\left(\begin{bmatrix} rem(10 \cdot x', \, 9) \\ + \\ rem(u, \, 9) \end{bmatrix}, \; 9\right)$$

(by the *addition* property of the remainder)

$$= rem\left(\begin{bmatrix} rem\big(rem(10, 9) \cdot rem(x', 9), \, 9\big) \\ + \\ rem(u, \, 9) \end{bmatrix}, \; 9\right)$$

(by the *multiplication* property of the remainder)

$$= rem\left(\begin{bmatrix} rem\big(rem(x', 9), \, 9\big) \\ + \\ rem(u, \, 9) \end{bmatrix}, \; 9\right)$$

(by the *left-one* property of multiplication,
because $rem(10, 9) = 1$)

$$= rem\left(\begin{bmatrix} rem(x', \, 9) \\ + \\ rem(u, \, 9) \end{bmatrix}, \; 9\right)$$

(by the *remainder* property of the remainder).

But on the other hand,

$$rem\big(sum(x), \, 9\big) = rem\big(sum(x' * u), \, 9\big)$$
(because $x = x' * u$)

$$= rem\big(sum(x') + u, \; 9\big)$$

(by the *suffix* axiom for the *sum* function,
because x' is positive)

$$= rem\left(\begin{bmatrix} rem\big(sum(x'), \, 9\big) \\ + \\ rem(u, \, 9) \end{bmatrix}, \; 9\right)$$

(by the *addition* property of the remainder)

$$= rem\left(\begin{bmatrix} rem(x', \, 9) \\ + \\ rem(u, \, 9) \end{bmatrix}, \; 9\right)$$

(by the condition (†) we concluded from the
induction hypothesis).

Because the left- and right-hand sides of the desired conclusion are equal, this establishes the inductive step in this case. ◢

Remark (generalization)

The above proof illustrates that a certain amount of ingenuity may be required in finding an appropriate generalization. To prove the sentence

$$(for\ all\ integer\ x) \begin{bmatrix} 9 \preceq_{div} x \\ if\ and\ only\ if \\ 9 \preceq_{div} sum(x) \end{bmatrix},$$

we were actually forced to prove the superficially dissimilar sentence

$$(for\ all\ integer\ x)\left[rem(x,\ 9)\ =\ rem\big(sum(x),\ 9\big)\right]. \quad ◢$$

The above result is the basis for a practical test for determining whether a given positive integer is divisible by 9:

Take the sum of the digits of the given positive integer x, and then take the sum of the digits of the result, and so forth, until the result is itself a digit. Then the given integer x is divisible by 9 precisely when the ultimate digit is itself 9.

To establish the correctness of this test, we define a new unary function symbol $reduce(x)$ by the following axioms:

$$(for\ all\ positive\ x) \begin{bmatrix} if\ x \leq 9 \\ then\ reduce(x) = x \end{bmatrix} \qquad (digit)$$

$$(for\ all\ positive\ x)\left[reduce(x)\ =\ reduce\big(sum(x)\big)\right] \qquad (sum)$$

Then the technique for testing a positive integer for divisibility by 9 is based on the following property:

$$(for\ all\ positive\ x) \begin{bmatrix} 9 \preceq_{div} x \\ if\ and\ only\ if \\ reduce(x) = 9 \end{bmatrix} \qquad (nine\ test)$$

Example (nine test)

Suppose we would like to determine whether the integer 9243 is divisible by

9. We have

$$reduce(9243) \;=\; reduce\big(sum(9243)\big)$$
$$\text{(by the } sum \text{ axiom for } reduce)$$

$$=\; reduce(18)$$
$$\text{(by the axioms for the } sum \text{ function)}$$

$$=\; reduce\big(sum(18)\big)$$
$$\text{(by the } sum \text{ axiom for } reduce \text{ again)}$$

$$=\; reduce(9)$$
$$\text{(by the axioms for the } sum \text{ function again)}$$

$$=\; 9$$
$$\text{(by the } digit \text{ axiom for } reduce).$$

In short,

$$reduce(9243) = 9.$$

Therefore, according to the *nine-test* property, the integer 9243 is divisible by 9. ⌐

The proof of the *nine-test* property is left as an exercise (**Problem 7.13**).

In **Problems 7.14** and **7.15**, the reader is requested to devise axioms and prove some properties of a new *intersperse* relation $\preceq_{inter}$ and functions *left* and *right*.

PROBLEMS

Problem 7.1 (empty string)   page 367

Show that the empty string is not a character, i.e., that the sentence

$$not\,\big(char(\Lambda)\big)$$

is valid.

Problem 7.2 (head and tail)   page 370

Without using the induction principle, establish the following properties of the *head* and *tail* functions:

(a)   *Sort of head*

$$(\textit{for all string } x) \begin{bmatrix} \textit{if not } (x = \Lambda) \\ \textit{then char}(head(x)) \end{bmatrix}$$

(b)   *Sort of tail*

$$(\textit{for all string } x) \begin{bmatrix} \textit{if not } (x = \Lambda) \\ \textit{then string}(tail(x)) \end{bmatrix}$$

(c)   *Decomposition*

$$(\textit{for all string } x) \begin{bmatrix} \textit{if not } (x = \Lambda) \\ \textit{then } x = head(x) \bullet tail(x) \end{bmatrix}$$

(d)   *Character of head*

$$(\textit{for all char } u) \begin{bmatrix} head(u) = u \end{bmatrix}$$

(e)   *Character of tail*

$$(\textit{for all char } u) \begin{bmatrix} tail(u) = \Lambda \end{bmatrix}.$$

Problem 7.3 (concatenation)   pages 372, 393

Establish the following properties of concatenation:

(a)   *Sort*

$$\begin{matrix} (\textit{for all string } x) \\ (\textit{for all string } y) \end{matrix} \begin{bmatrix} string(x * y) \end{bmatrix}$$

(b)   *Character*

$$\begin{matrix} (\textit{for all char } u) \\ (\textit{for all string } y) \end{matrix} \begin{bmatrix} u * y = u \bullet y \end{bmatrix}$$

(c)   *Right empty*

$$(\textit{for all string } x) \begin{bmatrix} x * \Lambda = x \end{bmatrix}$$

(d)   *Associativity*

$$\begin{matrix} (\textit{for all string } x) \\ (\textit{for all string } y) \\ (\textit{for all string } z) \end{matrix} \begin{bmatrix} (x * y) * z = x * (y * z) \end{bmatrix}$$

(e)   *Head*

$$\begin{matrix} (\textit{for all string } x) \\ (\textit{for all string } y) \end{matrix} \begin{bmatrix} \textit{if not } (x = \Lambda) \\ \textit{then head}(x * y) = head(x) \end{bmatrix}$$

(f) *Tail*

$$
\begin{array}{l}
(\textit{for all string } x) \\
(\textit{for all string } y)
\end{array}
\left[
\begin{array}{l}
\textit{if } \textit{not } (x = \Lambda) \\
\textit{then } tail(x * y) = tail(x) * y
\end{array}
\right]
$$

(g) *Suffix decomposition*

$$
(\textit{for all string } x)
\left[
\begin{array}{l}
\textit{if } \textit{not } (x = \Lambda) \\
\textit{then } \begin{array}{l} (\textit{for some char } u) \\ (\textit{for some string } y) \end{array} \left[x = y * u \right]
\end{array}
\right]
$$

(h) *Suffix uniqueness*

$$
\begin{array}{l}
(\textit{for all char } u)(\textit{for all string } x) \\
(\textit{for all char } v)(\textit{for all string } y)
\end{array}
\left[
\begin{array}{l}
\textit{if } x * u = y * v \\
\textit{then } x = y \textit{ and } u = v
\end{array}
\right]
$$

(i) *Prefix-suffix decomposition*

$$
(\textit{for all string } x)
\left[
\begin{array}{l}
x = \Lambda \textit{ or } char(x) \\[4pt]
\textit{or} \\[4pt]
(\textit{for some char } u) \\
(\textit{for some char } v) \\
(\textit{for some string } y)
\end{array}
\left[x = u * y * v \right]
\right].
$$

Problem 7.4 (**reverse**) page 375

Establish the *reverse* property of *reverse*, that is,

$$(\textit{for all string } x)\left[reverse\big(reverse(x)\big) = x\right].$$

Problem 7.5 (**front and last**) page 382

Suppose we augment our theory by defining two unary function symbols $front(x)$ and $last(x)$. Under the intended model, $last(x)$ is the last character of a nonempty string x, and $front(x)$ is the string of all but the last character of x; for example, $front(\text{BAABC}) = \text{BAAB}$ and $last(\text{BAABC}) = \text{C}$. The axioms are

$$
\begin{array}{l}
(\textit{for all char } u) \\
(\textit{for all string } x)
\end{array}
\left[front(x * u) = x \right]
\qquad\qquad (\textit{front})
$$

$$
\begin{array}{l}
(\textit{for all char } u) \\
(\textit{for all string } x)
\end{array}
\left[last(x * u) = u \right]
\qquad\qquad (\textit{last})
$$

Without using the induction principle, establish the following properties of *front* and *last*:

(a) *Sort of front*

$$(\textit{for all string } x) \begin{bmatrix} \textit{if } not\,(x = \Lambda) \\ \textit{then } string\,(front(x)) \end{bmatrix}$$

(b) *Sort of last*

$$(\textit{for all string } x) \begin{bmatrix} \textit{if } not\,(x = \Lambda) \\ \textit{then } char\,(last(x)) \end{bmatrix}$$

(c) *Decomposition*

$$(\textit{for all string } x) \begin{bmatrix} \textit{if } not\,(x = \Lambda) \\ \textit{then } x = front(x) * last(x) \end{bmatrix}$$

(d) *Tail-reverse*

$$(\textit{for all string } x) \begin{bmatrix} \textit{if } not\,(x = \Lambda) \\ \textit{then } front(x) = reverse\,(tail\,(reverse(x))) \end{bmatrix}$$

(e) *Head-reverse*

$$(\textit{for all string } x) \begin{bmatrix} \textit{if } not\,(x = \Lambda) \\ \textit{then } last(x) = head\,(reverse(x)) \end{bmatrix}.$$

[*Hint*: Use the *suffix-decomposition* property of concatenation.]

Problem 7.6 (suffix induction principle)   page 382

Establish the following *suffix induction principle*:

For each sentence $\mathcal{F}[x]$ in the theory, the universal closure of the sentence

$$if \begin{bmatrix} \mathcal{F}[\Lambda] \\ and \\ (\textit{for all char } u) \begin{bmatrix} \textit{if } \mathcal{F}[x] \\ \textit{then } \mathcal{F}[x * u] \end{bmatrix} \\ (\textit{for all string } x) \end{bmatrix} \qquad (\textit{suffix induction})$$
$$then \ (\textit{for all string } x)\mathcal{F}[x],$$

where u does not occur free in $\mathcal{F}[x]$, is valid. [*Hint*: Use the *reverse* function.]

Problem 7.7 (suffix concatenation)   page 382

Suppose we define a new binary function symbol $conc2(x, y)$ by the following two axioms:

$$(\textit{for all string } y)\big[conc2(\Lambda, \, y) \, = \, y\big] \qquad\qquad (\textit{left empty})$$

$$\begin{array}{l}(\textit{for all char } u) \\ (\textit{for all string } x) \\ (\textit{for all string } y)\end{array}\Big[conc2(x * u, \, y) \, = \, conc2(x, \, u \bullet y)\Big] \quad (\textit{left suffix})$$

Show that these axioms provide an alternative definition for the concatenation function, in the sense that the sentence

$$\begin{array}{l}(\textit{for all string } x) \\ (\textit{for all string } y)\end{array}\Big[x * y \, = \, conc2(x, \, y)\Big]$$

is valid. [*Hint*: You may use the above suffix induction principle.]

Problem 7.8 (end concatenation)   page 387

Establish the validity of the ($\Rightarrow$) part of the *end-concatenation* proposition, that is,

$$\begin{array}{l}(\textit{for all string } x) \\ (\textit{for all string } y)\end{array}\left[\begin{array}{l}\textit{if } x \preceq_{end} y \\ \textit{then } (\textit{for some string } z)\big[z * x \, = \, y\big]\end{array}\right].$$

Problem 7.9 (substring)   page 389

(a) Suppose we define a new binary predicate symbol $x \preceq_{init} y$ by the following four axioms:

$$(\textit{for all string } y)\big[\Lambda \preceq_{init} y\big] \qquad\qquad (\textit{left empty})$$

$$\begin{array}{l}(\textit{for all char } u) \\ (\textit{for all string } x)\end{array}\Big[not \, (u \bullet x \preceq_{init} \Lambda)\Big] \qquad\qquad (\textit{right empty})$$

$$\begin{array}{l}(\textit{for all char } u) \\ (\textit{for all string } x) \\ (\textit{for all string } y)\end{array}\left[\begin{array}{c}u \bullet x \preceq_{init} u \bullet y \\ \textit{if and only if} \\ x \preceq_{init} y\end{array}\right] \qquad (\textit{equal prefix})$$

$$\begin{array}{l}(\textit{for all char } u)(\textit{for all string } x) \\ (\textit{for all char } v)(\textit{for all string } y)\end{array}\left[\begin{array}{l}\textit{if } not \, (u = v) \\ \textit{then } not \, (u \bullet x \preceq_{init} v \bullet y)\end{array}\right]$$
$$(\textit{nonequal prefix})$$

Show that these axioms define a relation $x \preceq_{init} y$ that holds if x is an initial substring of y; that is

$$\begin{array}{l}(\textit{for all string } x) \\ (\textit{for all string } y)\end{array}\left[\begin{array}{l}x \preceq_{init} y \\ \textit{if and only if} \\ (\textit{for some string } z)\big[x * z = y\big]\end{array}\right]$$

is valid.

(b) Suppose we define a new binary predicate symbol $x \preceq_{string2} y$ by the following two axioms:

$$\begin{array}{l} (for\ all\ char\ u) \\ (for\ all\ string\ x) \end{array} \Big[not\ (u \bullet x \preceq_{string2} \Lambda) \Big] \qquad\qquad (right\ empty)$$

$$\begin{array}{l} (for\ all\ string\ x) \\ (for\ all\ char\ u) \\ (for\ all\ string\ y) \end{array} \left[\begin{array}{l} x \preceq_{string2} u \bullet y \\ \quad if\ and\ only\ if \\ x \preceq_{init} u \bullet y \ \ or\ \ x \preceq_{string2} y \end{array} \right] \qquad (right\ prefix)$$

Show that these axioms provide an alternative definition for the substring relation $\preceq_{string}$, in the sense that

$$\begin{array}{l} (for\ all\ string\ x) \\ (for\ all\ string\ y) \end{array} \left[\begin{array}{l} x \preceq_{string} y \\ \quad if\ and\ only\ if \\ x \preceq_{string2} y \end{array} \right]$$

is valid.

(c) Use these axioms to determine whether BC is a substring of ABCA and whether A is a substring of B.

Problem 7.10 (palindrome)   page 393

Without the use of the induction principle, establish the ($\Leftarrow$) part of the *palindrome* proposition, that is,

$$(for\ all\ string\ x) \left[\begin{array}{l} if \left[\begin{array}{l} (for\ some\ string\ y)[x = y * reverse(y)] \\ or \\ (for\ some\ char\ u) \\ (for\ some\ string\ y) \end{array} [x = y * u * reverse(y)] \right] \\ then\ palin(x) \end{array} \right].$$

Problem 7.11 (length)   page 400

In the combined theory of nonnegative integers and strings, establish the following properties of the *length* function:

(a) *Sort*

$$(for\ all\ string\ x)[integer\,(length(x))]$$

(b) *Zero*

$$(\textit{for all string } x) \left[\begin{array}{l} \textit{if } length(x) = 0 \\ \textit{then } x = \Lambda \end{array} \right]$$

(c) *Character*

$$(\textit{for all char } u) \left[length(u) = 1 \right]$$

(d) *Reverse*

$$(\textit{for all string } x) \left[length\big(reverse(x)\big) = length(x) \right]$$

(e) *Proper substring*

$$(\textit{for all string } x) \atop (\textit{for all string } y) \left[\begin{array}{l} \textit{if } x \prec_{string} y \\ \textit{then } length(x) < length(y) \end{array} \right]$$

Make a list of any "new" properties of the nonnegative integers, i.e., properties you use that have not been mentioned previously; you need not prove them. You should prove any new properties of the strings.

Problem 7.12 (string representation of the integers)   page 403

In the theory for the string representation of the nonnegative integers, establish the following properties:

(a) *Integer-string*

$$(\textit{for all } x) \left[\begin{array}{l} \textit{if } integer(x) \\ \textit{then } string(x) \end{array} \right]$$

(b) *Empty*

$$not \big(integer(\Lambda) \big)$$

(c) *Leading zeros*

$$(\textit{for all integer } x) \left[\begin{array}{l} \textit{if } head(x) = 0 \\ \textit{then } tail(x) = \Lambda \end{array} \right].$$

Problem 7.13 (test for divisibility by 9)   page 409

Show the correctness of the test for divisibility by 9 described in the text; in other words, establish the *nine-test* property

$$(\textit{for all positive } x) \left[\begin{array}{l} 9 \preceq_{div} x \\ \quad \textit{if and only if} \\ reduce(x) = 9 \end{array} \right]$$

in the theory for the string representation of the integers. List without proof any new properties of the nonnegative integers you require.

Problem 7.14 (intersperse relation)   page 409

We have defined the substring relation $x \preceq_{string} y$ so that the characters of the substring x must occur consecutively in the larger string y.

(a) Give axioms for an *intersperse* relation $x \preceq_{inter} y$, which holds if the elements of x occur in y in the same order but not necessarily consecutively. For example,

$$\text{AAB} \preceq_{inter} \text{CACAB}$$

but

$$not\,(\text{AAB} \preceq_{inter} \text{CBCAA}) \qquad and \qquad not\,(\text{AAB} \preceq_{inter} \text{CAB}).$$

Using your axioms, prove the following properties:

(b) *Substring*

$$(for\ all\ string\ x) \begin{bmatrix} if\ x \preceq_{string} y \\ then\ x \preceq_{inter} y \end{bmatrix}$$
$$(for\ all\ string\ y)$$

(c) *Concatenation*

$$(for\ all\ string\ x)$$
$$(for\ all\ string\ y) \Big[x * y \preceq_{inter} x * z * y \Big].$$
$$(for\ all\ string\ z)$$

Problem 7.15 (left and right)   page 409

In the theory of strings, we would like to define two unary function symbols $left(x)$ and $right(x)$ to denote functions that divide the string x into two roughly equal parts. Thus

$$left(\text{ABCD}) = \text{AB} \qquad right(\text{ABCD}) = \text{CD}$$

$$left(\text{ABC}) = \text{AB} \qquad right(\text{ABC}) = \text{C}.$$

(a) Give axioms that define these functions in the theory of strings (not in the combined theory of nonnegative integers and strings). Make sure that your axioms suggest a method for computing the functions.

(b) Using your axioms, establish the following *concatenation* property of *left* and *right*:

$$(\textit{for all string } x)\big[\textit{left}(x) * \textit{right}(x) = x\big].$$

(c) In the combined theory of nonnegative integers and strings, using your axioms, establish the following *length* property of *left* and *right*:

$$(\textit{for all string } x) \left[\begin{array}{l} \textit{length}\big(\textit{left}(x)\big) = \textit{length}\big(\textit{right}(x)\big) \\ \textit{or} \\ \textit{length}\big(\textit{left}(x)\big) = \textit{length}\big(\textit{right}(x)\big) + 1 \end{array} \right].$$

As usual, you may use the appropriate *sort* properties of *left* and *right* without proof.

Problem 7.16 (constraint on induction principle)   page 366

Show that the constraint on the induction principle, that the variable u not occur free in the sentence $\mathcal{F}[x]$, is essential. In other words, show that the induction principle is false (under some interpretation) for a particular inductive sentence that violates this constraint. [*Hint:* Take the inductive sentence to be $\mathcal{F}[x] : x = \Lambda \ \ \textit{or} \ \ \textit{head}(x) = u$, which contains a free occurrence of u.]

8

Trees

In this section we present another theory with induction, the theory of trees. The development of the theory is analogous to that of the theory of strings. Intuitively speaking, we are given a set of elements (called the *atoms*) and consider trees whose leaves are atoms. For example, if the set of atoms is $\{A, B, C\}$, then

A
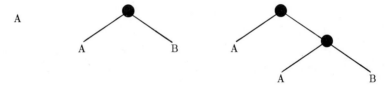

are all trees.

The set of atoms may be either finite or infinite, but each tree must be finite, i.e., must contain only finitely many atoms and nodes. Our trees are binary; in other words, each node ● has precisely two arcs leading from it.

8.1   BASIC PROPERTIES

The vocabulary of the theory consists of

- A unary predicate symbol $atom(x)$

- A unary predicate symbol $tree(x)$

- A binary function symbol $x \bullet y$, denoting the *construction* function.

Under the intended models for the theory, the relation $atom(x)$ is true if x is an atom and false otherwise. Also, if x and y denote two trees, $x \bullet y$ denotes the tree

Thus if under a particular interpretation x denotes the atom A and y denotes the atom B, then $x \bullet (x \bullet y)$ denotes the tree

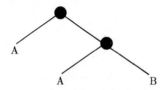

We shall also use A $\bullet$ (A $\bullet$ B) as an informal notation for the above tree.

The theory of trees is a theory with equality having the following special axioms:

- The *generation* axioms

$$(\text{for all atom } x)[tree(x)] \qquad\qquad (\text{atom})$$

$$\begin{array}{l}(\text{for all tree } x) \\ (\text{for all tree } y)\end{array}\Big[tree(x \bullet y)\Big] \qquad\qquad (\text{construction})$$

- The *uniqueness* axioms

$$\begin{array}{l}(\text{for all tree } x) \\ (\text{for all tree } y)\end{array}\Big[not \,\big(atom(x \bullet y)\big)\Big] \qquad\qquad (\text{atom})$$

$$\begin{array}{l}(\text{for all tree } x_1)(\text{for all tree } y_1) \\ (\text{for all tree } x_2)(\text{for all tree } y_2)\end{array}\left[\begin{array}{l} \text{if } x_1 \bullet x_2 = y_1 \bullet y_2 \\ \text{then } x_1 = y_1 \ \text{ and } \ x_2 = y_2 \end{array}\right]$$
$$(\text{construction})$$

● The *induction* principle

For each sentence $\mathcal{F}[x]$ in the theory, the universal closure of the sentence

$$
if \left[\begin{array}{l} (for\ all\ atom\ u)\,\mathcal{F}[u] \\ \quad and \\ \begin{array}{l} (for\ all\ tree\ x_1) \\ (for\ all\ tree\ x_2) \end{array} \left[\begin{array}{l} if\ \mathcal{F}[x_1]\ \ and\ \ \mathcal{F}[x_2] \\ then\ \ \mathcal{F}[x_1 \bullet x_2] \end{array} \right] \end{array} \right] \quad (induction)
$$

$$ then\ (for\ all\ tree\ x)\,\mathcal{F}[x], $$

where u, x_1, and x_2 do not occur free in $\mathcal{F}[x]$, is an axiom.

The two generation axioms have the intuitive meaning that every atom is a tree and the result of applying the construction function to two trees is also a tree. The two uniqueness axioms have the intuitive meaning that a tree can be constructed in at most one way from the atoms and the construction function $x \bullet y$.

For the induction principle, the sentence $\mathcal{F}[x]$ is called the *inductive* sentence. The subsentence

$$(for\ all\ atom\ u)\,\mathcal{F}[u]$$

is called the *base case*. The subsentence

$$
\begin{array}{l} (for\ all\ tree\ x_1) \\ (for\ all\ tree\ x_2) \end{array} \left[\begin{array}{l} if\ \mathcal{F}[x_1]\ \ and\ \ \mathcal{F}[x_2] \\ then\ \ \mathcal{F}[x_1 \bullet x_2] \end{array} \right]
$$

is called the *inductive step*; the subsentences $\mathcal{F}[x_1]$ and $\mathcal{F}[x_2]$ of the inductive step are called the *induction hypotheses*, and the subsentence $\mathcal{F}[x_1 \bullet x_2]$ is called the *desired conclusion*.

Since the theory of trees is a theory with equality, we include among our axioms the *transitivity*, *symmetry*, and *reflexivity* axioms for equality, as well as the instances of the *functional-substitutivity* axiom schema for the construction function and the instances of the *predicate-substitutivity* axiom schema for the *atom* and *tree* relations.

In this theory we can establish the following decomposition property:

$$
(for\ all\ tree\ x) \left[\begin{array}{l} if\ not\ \big(atom(x)\big) \\ then\ \begin{array}{l} (for\ some\ tree\ x_1) \\ (for\ some\ tree\ x_2) \end{array} \big[x = x_1 \bullet x_2 \big] \end{array} \right] \quad (decomposition)
$$

The proof is analogous to that of the *decomposition* properties of earlier theories.

There is some similarity between the theory of strings and the theory of trees. Roughly speaking, the *atom* predicate for the trees is analogous to the *char* predicate for the strings, and the construction function $x \bullet y$ for the trees is analogous to the prefix function $u \bullet x$ for the strings. This analogy is not precise, however, because the axioms for the prefix function $u \bullet x$ presuppose that the first argument u is a character, while the axioms for the construction function $x \bullet y$ admit the possibility that the first argument x is any tree, not necessarily an atom. Also there is an empty string Λ but no empty tree. These are the basic differences between the two theories.

8.2   THE LEFT AND RIGHT FUNCTIONS

We may augment our theory of trees by defining two unary function symbols $left(x)$ and $right(x)$, denoting the *left subtree* and *right subtree*, respectively, of x. These functions are analogous to the *head* and *tail* functions over the strings; they are defined by the following axioms:

$$\begin{array}{ll} (\textit{for all tree } x) \\ (\textit{for all tree } y) \end{array} \left[left(x \bullet y) = x \right] \qquad\qquad (\textit{left})$$

$$\begin{array}{ll} (\textit{for all tree } x) \\ (\textit{for all tree } y) \end{array} \left[right(x \bullet y) = y \right] \qquad\qquad (\textit{right})$$

For example, the *left* and *right* functions applied to the tree $(C \bullet A) \bullet ((B \bullet A) \bullet C)$, that is,

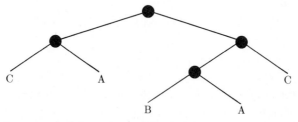

yield the trees $C \bullet A$ and $(B \bullet A) \bullet C$, that is,

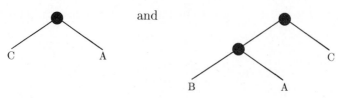

and

respectively.

Note that these axioms do not specify the values of the terms $left(u)$ and $right(u)$ if u denotes an atom, because, by the *atom* uniqueness axiom, $x \bullet y$ is not an atom. Although such terms are legal in the language, our axioms do not force them to have any particular value.

As usual when we introduce new function symbols into a theory with equality, we automatically add the corresponding instances of the *functional-substitutivity* axiom schema.

From the axioms for *left* and *right* we can establish the following properties:

$$(\textit{for all tree } x) \left[\begin{array}{l} \textit{if not } (atom(x)) \\ \textit{then } tree(left(x)) \end{array} \right] \qquad (\textit{sort of left})$$

$$(\textit{for all tree } x) \left[\begin{array}{l} \textit{if not } (atom(x)) \\ \textit{then } tree(right(x)) \end{array} \right] \qquad (\textit{sort of right})$$

$$(\textit{for all tree } x) \left[\begin{array}{l} \textit{if not } (atom(x)) \\ \textit{then } x = left(x) \bullet right(x) \end{array} \right] \qquad (\textit{decomposition})$$

The proofs, which are straightforward, are left as an exercise (**Problem 8.1**).

The *left* and *right* functions may be used to express a *decomposition version* of the induction principle for the trees.

Proposition (decomposition induction principle)

For each sentence $\mathcal{F}[x]$, the universal closure of the sentence

$$\textit{if} \left[\begin{array}{l} (\textit{for all atom } u)\mathcal{F}[u] \\ \quad \textit{and} \\ (\textit{for all tree } x) \left[\begin{array}{l} \textit{if not } (atom(x)) \\ \textit{then if } \mathcal{F}[left(x)] \ \textit{and} \ \mathcal{F}[right(x)] \\ \qquad \quad \textit{then } \mathcal{F}[x] \end{array} \right] \end{array} \right]$$

$$\textit{then } (\textit{for all tree } x)\mathcal{F}[x],$$

$$(\textit{decomposition induction})$$

where u does not occur free in $\mathcal{F}[x]$, is valid. ◢

The proof is left as an exercise (**Problem 8.2**).

The decomposition induction principle is most convenient to use when dealing with axioms and properties expressed in terms of the *left* and *right* functions. Because in this book we typically express our properties in terms of the construction function $x \bullet y$ instead, we find the original generator version of the induction principle more useful.

8.3   THE SUBTREE RELATION

The *subtrees* of a given tree x are the tree itself, the left and right subtrees of x (if x is not an atom), the left and right subtrees of *left*(x) and *right*(x) (if they are not atoms), and so forth. For example, the subtrees of the tree A $\bullet$ (B $\bullet$ C), that is,

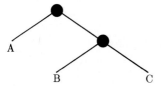

are A $\bullet$ (B $\bullet$ C) itself, the left subtree A, the right subtree B $\bullet$ C, and its subtrees B and C. That is,

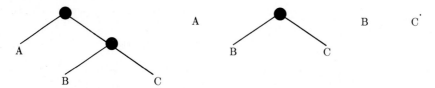

The *proper subtrees* of a given tree x are the subtrees of x other than x itself.

Formally, we augment our theory by defining at the same time two binary predicate symbols, $x \preceq_{tree} y$ and $x \prec_{tree} y$, denoting that x is a *subtree* and a *proper subtree*, respectively, of y. The subtree relation $\preceq_{tree}$ is defined to be the reflexive closure of the proper subtree relation $\prec_{tree}$, that is,

$$
\begin{array}{l}
(\textit{for all tree } x) \\
(\textit{for all tree } y)
\end{array}
\left[
\begin{array}{l}
x \preceq_{tree} y \\
\quad \textit{if and only if} \\
x \prec_{tree} y \ \ \textit{or} \ \ x = y
\end{array}
\right]
\qquad (\textit{subtree})
$$

where the proper subtree relation $\prec_{tree}$ is defined by the two axioms

$$\begin{matrix}(\textit{for all atom } u) \\ (\textit{for all tree } x)\end{matrix}\left[not\ (x \prec_{tree} u)\right] \qquad\qquad (\textit{atom})$$

$$\begin{matrix}(\textit{for all tree } x) \\ (\textit{for all tree } y) \\ (\textit{for all tree } z)\end{matrix}\left[\begin{matrix}x \prec_{tree} y \bullet z \\ \textit{if and only if} \\ x \preceq_{tree} y \ \textit{or} \ x \preceq_{tree} z\end{matrix}\right] \qquad (\textit{construction})$$

Note that these definitions depend on each other: The definition of the subtree relation $\preceq_{tree}$ refers to the proper subtree relation $\prec_{tree}$, and the definition of the proper subtree relation $\prec_{tree}$ refers to the subtree relation $\preceq_{tree}$. Such definitions are said to be "mutually recursive."

We can establish the following properties of the two relations:

$$\begin{matrix}(\textit{for all atom } u) \\ (\textit{for all tree } x)\end{matrix}\left[\begin{matrix}\textit{if } x \preceq_{tree} u \\ \textit{then } x = u\end{matrix}\right] \qquad\qquad (\textit{atom})$$

$$\begin{matrix}(\textit{for all tree } x) \\ (\textit{for all tree } y)\end{matrix}\left[x \prec_{tree} x \bullet y\right] \qquad\qquad (\textit{left construction})$$

$$\begin{matrix}(\textit{for all tree } x) \\ (\textit{for all tree } y)\end{matrix}\left[y \prec_{tree} x \bullet y\right] \qquad\qquad (\textit{right construction})$$

$$(\textit{for all tree } x)\left[\begin{matrix}\textit{if } not\ (atom(x)) \\ \textit{then } \ left(x) \prec_{tree} x\end{matrix}\right] \qquad (\textit{left subtree})$$

$$(\textit{for all tree } x)\left[\begin{matrix}\textit{if } not\ (atom(x)) \\ \textit{then } \ right(x) \prec_{tree} x\end{matrix}\right] \qquad (\textit{right subtree})$$

The proofs are straightforward.

We would like to establish that the proper subtree relation $\prec_{tree}$ is a strict partial ordering, i.e., that it is transitive and irreflexive. It is convenient to establish first the right mixed transitivity of $\preceq_{tree}$.

Proposition (right mixed transitivity)

The sentence

$$\begin{matrix}(\textit{for all tree } x) \\ (\textit{for all tree } y) \\ (\textit{for all tree } z)\end{matrix}\left[\begin{matrix}\textit{if } x \prec_{tree} y \ \textit{and} \ y \preceq_{tree} z \\ \textit{then } x \prec_{tree} z\end{matrix}\right] \qquad (\textit{right mixed transitivity})$$

is valid. ◢

Proof

We shall actually show the equivalent (by predicate logic, pushing in the quantifier (*for all tree z*)) sentence

$$(\textit{for all tree } x) \begin{bmatrix} \textit{if } x \prec_{tree} y \\ \textit{then } (\textit{for all tree } z) \begin{bmatrix} \textit{if } y \preceq_{tree} z \\ \textit{then } x \prec_{tree} z \end{bmatrix} \end{bmatrix}.$$
$$(\textit{for all tree } y)$$

Consider arbitrary trees x and y such that

$$x \prec_{tree} y.$$

It suffices to show that

$$(\textit{for all tree } z) \begin{bmatrix} \textit{if } y \preceq_{tree} z \\ \textit{then } x \prec_{tree} z \end{bmatrix}.$$

The proof is by induction on z, taking the inductive sentence to be

$$\mathcal{F}[z] : \quad \begin{array}{l} \textit{if } y \preceq_{tree} z \\ \textit{then } x \prec_{tree} z. \end{array}$$

Base Case

We would like to show

$$(\textit{for all atom } u)\mathcal{F}[u],$$

that is,

$$(\textit{for all atom } u) \begin{bmatrix} \textit{if } y \preceq_{tree} u \\ \textit{then } x \prec_{tree} u \end{bmatrix}.$$

For an arbitrary atom u, suppose that

$$y \preceq_{tree} u;$$

then (by the *atom* property of the subtree relation)

$$y = u$$

and hence (by our initial supposition that $x \prec_{tree} y$)

$$x \prec_{tree} u.$$

Inductive Step

We would like to show

$$(\text{for all tree } z_1) \begin{bmatrix} \text{if } \mathcal{F}[z_1] \text{ and } \mathcal{F}[z_2] \\ (\text{for all tree } z_2) \begin{bmatrix} \text{then } \mathcal{F}[z_1 \bullet z_2] \end{bmatrix} \end{bmatrix}.$$

For arbitrary trees z_1 and z_2, assume the two induction hypotheses

$$\mathcal{F}[z_1]: \quad \begin{array}{l} \text{if } y \preceq_{tree} z_1 \\ \text{then } x \prec_{tree} z_1 \end{array}$$

and

$$\mathcal{F}[z_2]: \quad \begin{array}{l} \text{if } y \preceq_{tree} z_2 \\ \text{then } x \prec_{tree} z_2. \end{array}$$

We would like to establish the desired conclusion

$$\mathcal{F}[z_1 \bullet z_2]: \quad \begin{array}{l} \text{if } y \preceq_{tree} z_1 \bullet z_2 \\ \text{then } x \prec_{tree} z_1 \bullet z_2. \end{array}$$

Suppose that

$$y \preceq_{tree} z_1 \bullet z_2;$$

we would like to show that

$$x \prec_{tree} z_1 \bullet z_2.$$

Because $y \preceq_{tree} z_1 \bullet z_2$, we have (by the definition of the subtree relation $\preceq_{tree}$) that

$$y \prec_{tree} z_1 \bullet z_2 \quad \text{or} \quad y = z_1 \bullet z_2.$$

We treat each case separately.

Case: $y = z_1 \bullet z_2$

By our initial supposition that $x \prec_{tree} y$, we have

$$x \prec_{tree} z_1 \bullet z_2.$$

Case: $y \prec_{tree} z_1 \bullet z_2$

Then (by the *construction* axiom for the proper subtree relation $\prec_{tree}$) we have

$$y \preceq_{tree} z_1 \quad \text{or} \quad y \preceq_{tree} z_2.$$

By our two induction hypotheses $\mathcal{F}[z_1]$ and $\mathcal{F}[z_2]$, therefore, we have

$$x \prec_{tree} z_1 \quad \text{or} \quad x \prec_{tree} z_2$$

and hence (by the definition of the subtree relation $\preceq_{tree}$)

$$x \preceq_{tree} z_1 \quad or \quad x \preceq_{tree} z_2.$$

It follows (by the *construction* axiom for the proper subtree relation $\prec_{tree}$ again) that

$$x \prec_{tree} z_1 \bullet z_2,$$

as we wanted to show.   ⌐

PARTIAL ORDERING

We have established the right mixed-transitivity property of $\preceq_{tree}$. Also we know (by definition) that $\preceq_{tree}$ is the reflexive closure of $\prec_{tree}$. It follows (by the *mixed-transitivity* proposition of the theory of associated relations) that $\prec_{tree}$ is itself transitive, that is,

$$\begin{array}{l} (\textit{for all tree } x) \\ (\textit{for all tree } y) \\ (\textit{for all tree } z) \end{array} \left[\begin{array}{l} \textit{if } x \prec_{tree} y \textit{ and } y \prec_{tree} z \\ \textit{then } x \prec_{tree} z \end{array} \right]. \qquad (\textit{transitivity})$$

The right mixed-transitivity property of $\preceq_{tree}$ is also used to establish the irreflexivity of $\prec_{tree}$.

Proposition (irreflexivity)

The sentence

$$(\textit{for all tree } x) \left[\textit{not } (x \prec_{tree} x) \right] \qquad\qquad (\textit{irreflexivity})$$

is valid.   ⌐

Proof

The proof is by induction on x, taking the inductive sentence to be

$$\mathcal{F}[x]: \quad not \ (x \prec_{tree} x).$$

Base Case

We would like to show

$$(\textit{for all atom } u) \left[\textit{not } (u \prec_{tree} u) \right],$$

but this follows from the *atom* axiom for $\prec_{tree}$, taking x to be u.

Inductive Step

For arbitrary trees x_1 and x_2, assume the two induction hypotheses

$$\mathcal{F}[x_1]: \quad not\,(x_1 \prec_{tree} x_1)$$

and

$$\mathcal{F}[x_2]: \quad not\,(x_2 \prec_{tree} x_2);$$

we would like to establish the desired conclusion

$$\mathcal{F}[x_1 \bullet x_2]: \quad not\,(x_1 \bullet x_2 \prec_{tree} x_1 \bullet x_2).$$

Suppose, contrary to our desired conclusion,

$$x_1 \bullet x_2 \prec_{tree} x_1 \bullet x_2.$$

Then (by the *construction* axiom for the proper subtree relation $\prec_{tree}$)

$$x_1 \bullet x_2 \preceq_{tree} x_1 \quad or \quad x_1 \bullet x_2 \preceq_{tree} x_2.$$

We know (by the *left-* and *right-construction* properties of the proper subtree relation $\prec_{tree}$) that

$$x_1 \prec_{tree} x_1 \bullet x_2 \quad and \quad x_2 \prec_{tree} x_1 \bullet x_2.$$

Therefore (by the *right mixed-transitivity* property of the subtree relation $\preceq_{tree}$)

$$x_1 \prec_{tree} x_1 \quad or \quad x_2 \prec_{tree} x_2.$$

But each of these conditions contradicts one of our induction hypotheses $\mathcal{F}[x_1]$ and $\mathcal{F}[x_2]$. ◢

We have established that $\prec_{tree}$ is transitive and irreflexive; in other words, it is a strict partial ordering. We know (by definition) that $\preceq_{tree}$ is the reflexive closure of $\prec_{tree}$; therefore (by the *weak partial-ordering* proposition of the theory of associated relations) we can conclude that $\preceq_{tree}$ is a weak partial ordering, that is,

$$\begin{array}{l} (\textit{for all tree } x) \\ (\textit{for all tree } y) \\ (\textit{for all tree } z) \end{array} \left[\begin{array}{l} \textit{if } x \preceq_{tree} y \ \textit{ and } \ y \preceq_{tree} z \\ \textit{then } x \preceq_{tree} z \end{array} \right] \qquad (\textit{transitivity})$$

$$\begin{array}{l} (\textit{for all tree } x) \\ (\textit{for all tree } y) \end{array} \left[\begin{array}{l} \textit{if } x \preceq_{tree} y \ \textit{ and } \ y \preceq_{tree} x \\ \textit{then } x = y \end{array} \right] \qquad (\textit{antisymmetry})$$

$$(\textit{for all tree } x)\left[x \preceq_{tree} x \right] \qquad (\textit{reflexivity})$$

8.4   STRINGS AND TREES

We have seen in the previous chapter that the theory of the strings can be combined with the theory of the nonnegative integers. We now introduce a theory that combines the theories of the strings and the trees.

In the combined theory we shall identify the characters of the strings with the atoms of the trees; this is expressed by the axiom

$$(\textit{for all } x)\big[\textit{char}(x) \ \textit{if and only if } \textit{atom}(x)\big] \qquad (\textit{character atom})$$

Let us augment our combined theory by defining a unary function symbol $\textit{flattree}(x)$. Under the intended models, for any tree x the value of $\textit{flattree}(x)$ is the string whose characters are the atoms of x, in left-to-right order. For example, if x is the tree $A \bullet \big((B \bullet C) \bullet B\big)$, that is,

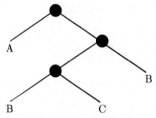

then $\textit{flattree}(x)$ is the string ABCB.

The function is defined by the axioms

$$(\textit{for all atom } x)\Big[\textit{flattree}(x) = x\Big] \qquad (\textit{atom})$$

$$(\textit{for all tree } x)\ \begin{bmatrix}\textit{flattree}(x \bullet y) \ = \\ \textit{flattree}(x) * \textit{flattree}(y)\end{bmatrix} \qquad (\textit{construction})$$
$$(\textit{for all tree } y)$$

Here $*$ is the concatenation function for strings.

From these axioms we can establish the appropriate *sort* property of *flattree*, namely,

$$(\textit{for all tree } x)\big[\textit{string}\,(\textit{flattree}(x))\big] \qquad (\textit{sort})$$

Now let us introduce an alternative method of flattening a tree. We define a new binary function symbol $\textit{flattree2}(x, z)$; intuitively speaking, for a given tree x and string z, $\textit{flattree2}(x, z)$ flattens x and concatenates the resulting string with the string z. The function is defined by the following axioms:

$$\begin{array}{l}(\textit{for all atom } u)\\(\textit{for all string } z)\end{array}\left[\textit{flattree2}(u,\ z)\ =\ u\bullet z\right] \qquad\qquad (\textit{atom})$$

$$\begin{array}{l}(\textit{for all tree } x)\\(\textit{for all tree } y)\\(\textit{for all string } z)\end{array}\left[\begin{array}{l}\textit{flattree2}(x\bullet y,\ z)\ =\\\textit{flattree2}\big(x,\ \textit{flattree2}(y,\ z)\big)\end{array}\right]\qquad (\textit{construction})$$

Note that, in the above *atom* axiom, $u \bullet z$ is the string prefix function applied to the atom (i.e., character) u and string z; in the *construction* axiom, $x \bullet y$ is the tree construction function applied to the trees x and y.

As before, we can establish the appropriate *sort* property,

$$\begin{array}{l}(\textit{for all tree } x)\\(\textit{for all string } z)\end{array}\left[\textit{string}\big(\textit{flattree2}(x,\ z)\big)\right] \qquad\qquad (\textit{sort})$$

That *flattree2* provides an alternative definition for the *flattree* function is expressed in the following proposition.

Proposition (flattree2)

The sentence

$$(\textit{for all tree } x)\left[\textit{flattree}(x)\ =\ \textit{flattree2}(x,\ \Lambda)\right]$$

is valid.   ◢

The proof provides another example of the need for generalization.

Proof

We actually establish the more general sentence

(†) $\qquad\begin{array}{l}(\textit{for all tree } x)\\(\textit{for all string } z)\end{array}\left[\textit{flattree2}(x,\ z)\ =\ \textit{flattree}(x)*z\right],$

which expresses the relationship between the two functions. This implies the original sentence, taking z to be Λ (by the *right-empty* property of the concatenation function $*$).

The proof of the more general sentence (†) is by induction on x, over the trees, taking the inductive sentence to be

$$\mathcal{F}[x]:\quad(\textit{for all string } z)\left[\textit{flattree2}(x,\ z)\ =\ \textit{flattree}(x)*z\right].$$

Base Case

We would like to show

$$(\textit{for all atom } u)\mathcal{F}[u],$$

that is,

$$(\textit{for all atom } u) \atop (\textit{for all string } z)\left[\textit{flattree2}(u,\ z)\ =\ \textit{flattree}(u) * z\right].$$

Consider an arbitrary atom (i.e., character) u and string z; then we have

$$\textit{flattree2}(u,\ z)\ =\ u \bullet z$$
$$\text{(by the } \textit{atom} \text{ axiom for } \textit{flattree2}).$$

But on the other hand,

$$\textit{flattree}(u) * z\ =\ u * z$$
$$\text{(by the } \textit{atom} \text{ axiom for } \textit{flattree})$$

$$=\ u \bullet z$$
$$\text{(by the } \textit{character} \text{ property of concatenation,}$$
$$\text{because } u \text{ is a character).}$$

Inductive Step

We would like to show

$$(\textit{for all tree } x_1) \atop (\textit{for all tree } x_2)\left[\begin{matrix} \textit{if } \mathcal{F}[x_1] \ \textit{and} \ \mathcal{F}[x_2] \\ \textit{then} \ \mathcal{F}[x_1 \bullet x_2] \end{matrix}\right].$$

For arbitrary trees x_1 and x_2, assume the two induction hypotheses,

$$\mathcal{F}[x_1]: \quad (\textit{for all string } z_1)\left[\textit{flattree2}(x_1,\ z_1)\ =\ \textit{flattree}(x_1) * z_1\right]$$

and

$$\mathcal{F}[x_2]: \quad (\textit{for all string } z_2)\left[\textit{flattree2}(x_2,\ z_2)\ =\ \textit{flattree}(x_2) * z_2\right].$$

(Note that to avoid confusion we have renamed the bound variables of the two induction hypotheses.)

We would like to establish the desired conclusion

$$\mathcal{F}[x_1 \bullet x_2]: \quad (\textit{for all string } z)\left[\textit{flattree2}(x_1 \bullet x_2,\ z)\ =\ \textit{flattree}(x_1 \bullet x_2) * z\right].$$

For an arbitrary string z, we have

$$\textit{flattree2}(x_1 \bullet x_2,\ z)\ =\ \textit{flattree2}\big(x_1,\ \textit{flattree2}(x_2,\ z)\big)$$
$$\text{(by the } \textit{construction} \text{ axiom for } \textit{flattree2})$$

$$= flattree(x_1) * flattree2(x_2, \ z)$$
(by our first induction hypothesis $\mathcal{F}[x_1]$,
taking z_1 to be $flattree2(x_2, z)$)

$$= flattree(x_1) * \big(flattree(x_2) * z\big)$$
(by our second induction hypothesis $\mathcal{F}[x_2]$,
taking z_2 to be z).

But on the other hand,

$$flattree(x_1 \bullet x_2) * z \ = \ \big(flattree(x_1) * flattree(x_2)\big) * z$$
(by the *construction* axiom for *flattree*)

$$= flattree(x_1) * \big(flattree(x_2) * z\big)$$
(by the associativity of concatenation). ◢

Another alternative definition for *flattree* is given in **Problem 8.3**. In **Problem 8.4**, some relationships between the number of nodes, the number of atoms, and the depth of a tree are formulated in a combined theory of trees and nonnegative integers.

PROBLEMS

Problem 8.1 (left and right)   page 423

Establish the following properties:

(a) *Sort of left*

$$(for\ all\ tree\ x) \begin{bmatrix} if\ not\ (atom(x)) \\ then\ tree(left(x)) \end{bmatrix}$$

(b) *Sort of right*

$$(for\ all\ tree\ x) \begin{bmatrix} if\ not\ (atom(x)) \\ then\ tree(right(x)) \end{bmatrix}$$

(c) *Decomposition*

$$(for\ all\ tree\ x) \begin{bmatrix} if\ not\ (atom(x)) \\ then\ x\ =\ left(x) \bullet right(x) \end{bmatrix}.$$

Problem 8.2 (Decomposition induction principle)   page 423

Establish the decomposition induction principle, that is,

for each sentence $\mathcal{F}[x]$, the universal closure of the sentence

$$if \left[\begin{array}{l} (for\ all\ atom\ u)\mathcal{F}[u] \\ \quad and \\ (for\ all\ tree\ x) \left[\begin{array}{l} if\ not\ (atom(x)) \\ then\ if\ \mathcal{F}[left(x)]\ \ and\ \ \mathcal{F}[right(x)] \\ \quad\quad then\ \ \mathcal{F}[x] \end{array} \right] \end{array} \right]$$

then $(for\ all\ tree\ x)\mathcal{F}[x],$

where u does not occur free in $\mathcal{F}[x]$, is valid.

Problem 8.3 (alternative definition for flattree)   page 433

In the combined theory of strings and trees, suppose we define a new unary function symbol $flattree1(x)$ by the following axioms:

$$(for\ all\ atom\ u)\left[flattree1(u)\ =\ u\right] \qquad\qquad\qquad (atom)$$

$$\begin{array}{l}(for\ all\ atom\ u) \\ (for\ all\ tree\ y)\end{array}\left[flattree1(u \bullet y)\ =\ u \bullet flattree1(y)\right]$$

$$(atom\ construction)$$

$$\begin{array}{l}(for\ all\ tree\ x_1) \\ (for\ all\ tree\ x_2) \\ (for\ all\ tree\ y)\end{array}\left[flattree1((x_1 \bullet x_2) \bullet y)\ =\ flattree1(x_1 \bullet (x_2 \bullet y))\right]$$

$$(construction)$$

(a) Establish that

$$(for\ all\ tree\ x)\left[string(flattree1(x))\right].$$

Hint: First show that

$$\begin{array}{l}(for\ all\ tree\ x) \\ (for\ all\ tree\ y)\end{array}\left[\begin{array}{l} if\ string(flattree1(y)) \\ then\ string(flattree1(x \bullet y)) \end{array} \right].$$

(b) Establish that

$$\begin{array}{l}(for\ all\ tree\ x) \\ (for\ all\ tree\ y)\end{array}\left[flattree1(x \bullet y)\ =\ flattree(x) * flattree1(y)\right].$$

(c) Show that *flattree*1 provides an alternative definition for the *flattree* function, in the sense that

$$(\textit{for all tree } x)\big[\textit{flattree}(x) \ = \textit{flattree}1(x)\big].$$

Problem 8.4 (size, tips, and depth)   page 433

In a combined theory of trees and nonnegative integers, we define three unary functions:

- *size*(x), the number of nodes and atoms in a tree x, by the axioms

$$(\textit{for all atom } u)\big[\textit{size}(u) = 1\big] \qquad\qquad\qquad\qquad (\textit{atom})$$

$$(\textit{for all tree } x)\atop(\textit{for all tree } y)\Big[\textit{size}(x \bullet y) \ = \ \textit{size}(x) + \textit{size}(y) + 1\Big] \qquad (\textit{construction})$$

- *tips*(x), the number of atoms in a tree x, by the axioms

$$(\textit{for all atom } u)\big[\textit{tips}(u) = 1\big] \qquad\qquad\qquad\qquad (\textit{atom})$$

$$(\textit{for all tree } x)\atop(\textit{for all tree } y)\Big[\textit{tips}(x \bullet y) \ = \ \textit{tips}(x) + \textit{tips}(y)\Big] \qquad (\textit{construction})$$

- *depth*(x), the number of nodes and atoms in the longest path of a tree x, by the axioms

$$(\textit{for all atom } u)\big[\textit{depth}(u) = 1\big] \qquad\qquad\qquad\qquad (\textit{atom})$$

$$(\textit{for all tree } x)\atop(\textit{for all tree } y)\left[\begin{matrix}\textit{depth}(x \bullet y) \\ = \\ \textit{max}\big(\textit{depth}(x), \ \textit{depth}(y)\big) + 1\end{matrix}\right] \qquad (\textit{construction})$$

For example, if x is the tree

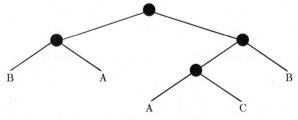

then $\textit{size}(x) = 9$, $\textit{tips}(x) = 5$, and $\textit{depth}(x) = 4$.

Establish the validity of the following properties:

(a) $(\textit{for all } x)\big[size(x) \ = \ 2 \cdot tips(x) - 1\big]$

(b) $(\textit{for all } x)\big[size(x) \ \leq \ 2^{depth(x)} - 1\big].$

You may use whatever properties of the nonnegative integers you wish without proof, but provide a list of the properties you use. Be sure to prove any properties of the trees you use, if they have not been mentioned earlier.

9

Lists

The theory of lists, which we are abcut to introduce, is closely related to the theory of trees. Intuitively speaking, we are given a set of elements (called *atoms*) and consider lists whose elements are either atoms or themselves lists. For example, if the set of atoms is $\{A, B, C\}$, then

$$[A, B], \qquad [A, A, [A, B], C], \qquad \text{and} \qquad [\,]$$

are all lists.

In contrast with the trees, we do not include the atoms themselves among the lists, but we do include the empty list $[\,]$, which has no elements. In contrast with the strings, our lists are nested: A list may be an element of another list. As for trees, the set of atoms may be either finite or infinite, but each list must be finite.

9.1   BASIC PROPERTIES

The vocabulary of the theory of lists consists of

- A constant symbol $[\,]$, denoting the *empty list*

- A unary predicate symbol $atom(x)$

- A unary predicate symbol $list(x)$

- A unary predicate symbol $atlist(x)$

- A binary function symbol $x \circ y$, denoting the *insertion* function.

Under the intended models for the theory, the relation $atom(x)$ is true if x is an atom, the relation $list(x)$ is true if x is a list, and the relation $atlist(x)$, included for our convenience, is true if x is an atom or a list. Also, the value of the insertion function $x \circ y$ is the result of inserting the atom or list x at the beginning of the list y; for example, under the intended model

$$A \circ [B,\ C] \qquad\quad \text{is} \quad\ [A,\ B,\ C]$$

$$[A,\ B] \circ [B,\ C] \quad \text{is} \quad \big[[A,\ B],\ B,\ C\big]$$

$$A \circ [\ ] \qquad\qquad \text{is} \quad\ [A]$$

$$[A] \circ [\ ] \qquad\quad\ \text{is} \quad\ \big[[A]\big].$$

Note that notations such as $[A,\ B,\ C]$ are informal and are not part of the language of the theory.

The theory of lists is a theory with equality having the following special axioms:

- The *generation* axioms

$$list([\ ]) \hspace{9cm} (empty)$$

$$\begin{array}{l}(\textit{for all atlist }x) \\ \quad(\textit{for all list }y)\end{array}\Big[list(x \circ y)\Big] \hspace{5.2cm} (insertion)$$

where *atlist* is defined by the axiom

$$(\textit{for all }x)\ \begin{bmatrix} atlist(x) \\ \quad \textit{if and only if} \\ atom(x)\quad or\quad list(x) \end{bmatrix} \hspace{3.5cm} (atlist)$$

- The *uniqueness* axioms

$$\begin{array}{l}(\textit{for all atlist }x) \\ \quad(\textit{for all list }y)\end{array}\Big[not\ (x \circ y = [\ ])\Big] \hspace{4.2cm} (empty)$$

$$\begin{array}{l}(\textit{for all atlist }x) \\ \quad(\textit{for all list }y)\end{array}\Big[not\ (atom(x \circ y))\Big] \hspace{4.4cm} (atom)$$

$$\begin{array}{l}(\textit{for all atlist }x_1)(\textit{for all list }x_2) \\ (\textit{for all atlist }y_1)(\textit{for all list }y_2)\end{array}\begin{bmatrix} \textit{if }x_1 \circ x_2 = y_1 \circ y_2 \\ \textit{then }x_1 = y_1\quad and\quad x_2 = y_2 \end{bmatrix}$$
$$(insertion)$$

- The *induction* principle

> For each sentence $\mathcal{F}[x]$ in the theory, the universal closure of the sentence
>
> $$if \begin{bmatrix} \mathcal{F}[[\,]] \\ \quad and \\ (for\ all\ atom\ u) \begin{bmatrix} if\ \ \mathcal{F}[x] \\ then\ \ \mathcal{F}[u \circ x] \end{bmatrix} \\ (for\ all\ list\ x) \\ \quad and \\ (for\ all\ list\ x') \begin{bmatrix} if\ \mathcal{F}[x']\ \ and\ \ \mathcal{F}[x] \\ then\ \ \mathcal{F}[x' \circ x] \end{bmatrix} \\ (for\ all\ list\ x) \end{bmatrix} \qquad (induction)$$
>
> $then\ \ (for\ all\ list\ x)\mathcal{F}[x],$
>
> where u and x' do not occur free in $\mathcal{F}[x]$, is an axiom.

The generation axioms have the intuitive meaning that the empty list is a list, and the result of inserting an atom or list at the beginning of a list is also a list. The axioms do not specify the result $x \circ u$ of inserting an atom or list x at the beginning of an atom u.

The uniqueness axioms have the intuitive meaning that a list can be constructed in at most one way from the empty list, the atoms, and the insertion function. Note that the axioms do not specify whether or not the empty list [ ] is an atom.

For the induction principle:

- The sentence

$$\mathcal{F}[x]$$

is the *inductive sentence*.

- The subsentence

$$\mathcal{F}[[\,]]$$

is the *base case*.

- The subsentence

$$(for\ all\ atom\ u) \begin{bmatrix} if\ \ \mathcal{F}[x] \\ then\ \ \mathcal{F}[u \circ x] \end{bmatrix}$$
$$(for\ all\ list\ x)$$

is the *atom inductive step*; the subsentence $\mathcal{F}[x]$ is the *induction hypothesis*, and the subsentence $\mathcal{F}[u \circ x]$ is the *desired conclusion*, for this inductive step.

- The subsentence

$$(\textit{for all list } x') \begin{bmatrix} \textit{if } \mathcal{F}[x'] \textit{ and } \mathcal{F}[x] \\ \textit{then } \mathcal{F}[x' \circ x] \end{bmatrix}$$
$$(\textit{for all list } x)$$

is the *list inductive step*; the subsentences $\mathcal{F}[x']$ and $\mathcal{F}[x]$ are the two *induction hypotheses*, and the subsentence $\mathcal{F}[x' \circ x]$ is the *desired conclusion*, for this inductive step.

Note that the induction principle has two separate inductive steps. This reflects the fact that a nonempty list may be either of form $u \circ x$, where u is an atom, or of form $x' \circ x$, where x' is another list.

Since the theory of lists is a theory with equality, we include among our axioms the *transitivity, symmetry,* and *reflexivity* axioms, as well as the instances of the *functional-substitutivity* axiom schema for the insertion function and the instances of the *predicate-substitutivity* axiom schema for the *atom, list,* and *atlist* predicate symbols.

In this theory we may establish the familiar decomposition property,

$$(\textit{for all list } x) \begin{bmatrix} \textit{if } not \ (x = [\ ]) \\ \textit{then } \begin{array}{l} (\textit{for some atlist } x_1) \\ (\textit{for some list } x_2) \end{array} [x = x_1 \circ x_2] \end{bmatrix}$$

$$(\textit{decomposition})$$

In other words, every nonempty list is the result of inserting an atom or list into a list.

From this and from the *atom* uniqueness axiom, we may conclude the uniqueness property

$$(\textit{for all } x) \begin{bmatrix} \textit{if } list(x) \textit{ and } atom(x) \\ \textit{then } x = [\ ] \end{bmatrix} \qquad (\textit{atom list})$$

In other words, the only domain element that can be both a list and an atom is the empty list $[\ ]$. (This does not imply that $[\ ]$ is an atom.)

The reader is requested to prove (in **Problem 9.1**) some properties of the insertion function.

9.2   THE HEAD AND TAIL FUNCTIONS

We may augment our theory of lists by defining two unary function symbols, $head(x)$ and $tail(x)$, to be analogous to the same functions over the strings. The head of a nonempty list is the first element, and its tail is the list of all but the first element. For example, for the list $[[\text{A, C}], \text{C}]$, that is, $[\text{A, C}] \circ [\text{C}]$, we have

$$head\big([[\text{A, C}], \text{C}]\big) \;=\; head\big([\text{A, C}] \circ [\text{C}]\big) \;=\; [\text{A, C}]$$

$$tail\big([[\text{A, C}], \text{C}]\big) \;=\; tail\big([\text{A, C}] \circ [\text{C}]\big) \;=\; [\text{C}],$$

and for the list $[\text{A}]$, that is, $\text{A} \circ [\,]$, we have

$$head\big([\text{A}]\big) \;=\; head\big(\text{A} \circ [\,]\big) \;=\; \text{A}$$

$$tail\big([\text{A}]\big) \;=\; tail\big(\text{A} \circ [\,]\big) \;=\; [\,].$$

The *head* and *tail* functions are defined by the following axioms:

$$\begin{matrix} (\textit{for all atlist } x) \\ (\textit{for all list } y) \end{matrix} \Big[head(x \circ y) \;=\; x \Big] \qquad\qquad (head)$$

$$\begin{matrix} (\textit{for all atlist } x) \\ (\textit{for all list } y) \end{matrix} \Big[tail(x \circ y) \;=\; y \Big] \qquad\qquad (tail)$$

Note that these axioms do not specify the results of applying the *head* and *tail* functions to the empty list $[\,]$ or to the atoms; by the *empty* and *atom* uniqueness axioms, $x \circ y$ is neither the empty list nor an atom.

As usual, we automatically introduce the instances of the *functional-substitutivity* equality axiom schema for the *head* and *tail* functions. Also, we can establish the following properties of the *head* and *tail* functions:

$$(\textit{for all list } x) \begin{bmatrix} \textit{if } not\,(x = [\,]) \\ \textit{then } atlist(head(x)) \end{bmatrix} \qquad\qquad (\textit{sort of head})$$

$$(\textit{for all list } x) \begin{bmatrix} \textit{if } not\,(x = [\,]) \\ \textit{then } list(tail(x)) \end{bmatrix} \qquad\qquad (\textit{sort of tail})$$

$$(\textit{for all list } x) \begin{bmatrix} \textit{if } not\,(x = [\,]) \\ \textit{then } x = head(x) \circ tail(x) \end{bmatrix} \qquad\qquad (\textit{decomposition})$$

Note that the *tail* of any nonempty list must be a list, but its *head* may be either an atom or a list.

The *head* and *tail* functions may be used to express a *decomposition version* of the induction principle for the lists.

Proposition (decomposition induction principle)

For each sentence $\mathcal{F}[x]$, the universal closure of the sentence

$$
if \begin{bmatrix} \mathcal{F}[[\,]] \\ \quad and \\ (for\ all\ list\ x) \begin{bmatrix} if\ not\,(x = [\,])\ \ and\ \ atom(head(x)) \\ then\ \ if\ \mathcal{F}[tail(x)] \\ \qquad then\ \ \mathcal{F}[x] \end{bmatrix} \\ \quad and \\ (for\ all\ list\ x) \begin{bmatrix} if\ not\,(x = [\,])\ \ and\ \ list(head(x)) \\ then\ \ if\ \mathcal{F}[head(x)]\ \ and\ \ \mathcal{F}[tail(x)] \\ \qquad then\ \ \mathcal{F}[x] \end{bmatrix} \end{bmatrix}
$$
$$
then\ (for\ all\ list\ x)\,\mathcal{F}[x]
$$

(*decomposition induction*)

is valid. ⌐

The proof is analogous to that of the decomposition version of the induction principle for strings.

9.3   APPEND AND MEMBER

We now define a basic function and relation for the lists.

APPEND FUNCTION

Let us further augment our theory by defining a binary function symbol $x \,\square\, y$, denoting the *append* function. The value of $x \,\square\, y$ is to be the list whose elements are the elements of the list x followed by the elements of the list y. For example,

$$[A, B] \,\square\, [B, C] \qquad is \qquad [A, B, B, C]$$

$$[[A]] \,\square\, [[B], C] \qquad is \qquad [[A], [B], C].$$

In contrast, for the insertion function ∘

$$[A, B] \circ [B, C] \qquad is \qquad [[A, B], B, C]$$

$$[[A]] \circ [[B], C] \qquad is \qquad [[[A]], [B], C].$$

The append function is defined by the following axioms:

$$(\textit{for all list } y)\big[[\,] \,\square\, y \;=\; y\big] \qquad\qquad (\textit{left empty})$$

$$\begin{array}{l}(\textit{for all atlist } u)\\ \quad (\textit{for all list } x)\\ \quad (\textit{for all list } y)\end{array}\big[(u \circ x) \,\square\, y \;=\; u \circ (x \,\square\, y)\big] \qquad (\textit{left insertion})$$

Note that the value of $x \,\square\, y$ is not specified by these axioms if x or y is an atom. As usual, we introduce the corresponding two instances of the *functional-substitutivity* equality axiom schema for the append function.

From the axioms we can prove the following properties of the append function:

$$\begin{array}{l}(\textit{for all list } x)\\ (\textit{for all list } y)\end{array}\Big[list(x \,\square\, y)\Big] \qquad\qquad (\textit{sort})$$

$$(\textit{for all list } x)\big[x \,\square\, [\,] \;=\; x\big] \qquad\qquad (\textit{right empty})$$

$$\begin{array}{l}(\textit{for all list } x)\\ (\textit{for all list } y)\\ (\textit{for all list } z)\end{array}\big[(x \,\square\, y) \,\square\, z \;=\; x \,\square\, (y \,\square\, z)\big] \qquad (\textit{associativity})$$

$$\begin{array}{l}(\textit{for all list } x)\\ (\textit{for all list } y)\end{array}\left[\begin{array}{l}\textit{if } \, not \, (x = [\,])\\ \textit{then } \, head(x \,\square\, y) \;=\; head(x)\end{array}\right] \qquad (\textit{head})$$

$$\begin{array}{l}(\textit{for all list } x)\\ (\textit{for all list } y)\end{array}\left[\begin{array}{l}\textit{if } \, not \, (x = [\,])\\ \textit{then } \, tail(x \,\square\, y) \;=\; tail(x) \,\square\, y\end{array}\right] \qquad (\textit{tail})$$

The proofs, which are routine, are left as an exercise (**Problem 9.2**). Some other functions of the theory of lists are defined in **Problems 9.3** and **9.4**.

MEMBER RELATION

We say that an atom or list u is a *member* of a list x if u is one of the "top level" elements of x; for example, the members of

$$[\text{A}, \; [\text{B}, \; \text{C}], \; [[\text{C}]]]$$

are

$$\textsc{a}, \quad [\textsc{b}, \textsc{c}], \quad \text{and} \quad [[\textsc{c}]]$$

but not $\textsc{b}, \textsc{c},$ or $[\textsc{c}]$.

We augment our theory by defining a binary predicate symbol $u \in x$, denoting the *member* relation, which is true if u is a member of x. The relation is defined by the following axioms:

$$
\begin{array}{ll}
(\textit{for all atlist } u)\left[\textit{not }(u \in [\,])\right] & (\textit{empty})
\end{array}
$$

$$
\begin{array}{ll}
\begin{array}{l}
(\textit{for all atlist } u) \\
(\textit{for all atlist } v) \\
\quad(\textit{for all list } x)
\end{array}
\left[
\begin{array}{l}
u \in v \circ x \\
\quad\textit{if and only if} \\
u = v \ \textit{ or } \ u \in x
\end{array}
\right] & (\textit{insertion})
\end{array}
$$

Note that these axioms do not specify the value of $u \in v$ if v is an atom.

From these axioms we can establish the following properties:

$$
(\textit{for all list } x)
\left[
\begin{array}{l}
\textit{if } \ \textit{not } (x = [\,]) \\
\textit{then } \ \textit{head}(x) \in x
\end{array}
\right]
\qquad (\textit{head})
$$

$$
\begin{array}{ll}
\begin{array}{l}
(\textit{for all atlist } u) \\
\quad(\textit{for all list } x) \\
\quad(\textit{for all list } y)
\end{array}
\left[
\begin{array}{l}
u \in x \,\square\, y \\
\quad\textit{if and only if} \\
u \in x \ \textit{ or } \ u \in y
\end{array}
\right] & (\textit{append})
\end{array}
$$

The proofs, which are straightforward, are omitted. Note that the member relation $\in$ is not transitive; for example, we have $\textsc{a} \in [\textsc{a}]$ and $[\textsc{a}] \in [\textsc{b}, [\textsc{a}]]$ but not $\textsc{a} \in [\textsc{b}, [\textsc{a}]]$ (because $\textsc{a}$ is not a top-level element of the list $[\textsc{b}, [\textsc{a}]]$).

9.4   EXAMPLE: FLATLIST

This example illustrates a relationship between the theories of strings and lists. We combine these two theories by identifying the characters of the strings with the atoms of the lists; this is expressed by the axiom

$$
(\textit{for all } x)
\left[
\begin{array}{l}
\textit{char}(x) \\
\quad\textit{if and only if} \\
\textit{atom}(x)
\end{array}
\right]
\qquad (\textit{character atom})
$$

In the combined theory we define a unary function symbol *flatlist(x)*, which is analogous to *flattree(x)* for the trees. The value of *flatlist(x)* is to be the string whose characters are the atoms that occur at any level in the list *x*, in left-to-right order. For example,

$$\textit{flatlist}\big([\text{A},\ [[\text{B}],\ \text{B},\ [\text{A}]]]\big)\ =\ \text{ABBA}.$$

In other words, the list is flattened by deleting its brackets and commas.

The *flatlist* function is defined by the following axioms:

$$\textit{flatlist}([\,]) \ = \ \Lambda \qquad\qquad\qquad\qquad\qquad\qquad\qquad (\textit{empty})$$

$$\begin{array}{l}(\textit{for all atom } u)\\ \ \ (\textit{for all list } y)\end{array}\Big[\textit{flatlist}(u \circ y) \ = \ u \bullet \textit{flatlist}(y)\Big]\quad (\textit{atom insertion})$$

$$\begin{array}{l}(\textit{for all list } x)\\ (\textit{for all list } y)\end{array}\Big[\textit{flatlist}(x \circ y) \ = \ \textit{flatlist}(x) * \textit{flatlist}(y)\Big]\ (\textit{list insertion})$$

Recall that $u \bullet \textit{flatlist}(y)$ is the result of prefixing the atom (i.e., character) u to the string $\textit{flatlist}(y)$, and $\textit{flatlist}(x) * \textit{flatlist}(y)$ is the result of concatenating the two strings $\textit{flatlist}(x)$ and $\textit{flatlist}(y)$.

We can establish the *sort* property of *flatlist*,

$$(\textit{for all list } x)\big[\textit{string}\big(\textit{flatlist}(x)\big)\big] \qquad\qquad\qquad\qquad (\textit{sort})$$

In other words, the result of flattening a list is always a string; the proof is omitted.

We now establish a property relating the *flatlist*, append, and concatenation functions.

Proposition (flatlist-append)

The sentence

$$\begin{array}{l}(\textit{for all list } x)\\ (\textit{for all list } y)\end{array}\Big[\textit{flatlist}(x \mathbin{\square} y) \ = \ \textit{flatlist}(x) * \textit{flatlist}(y)\Big] \qquad (\textit{append})$$

is valid.   ⌐

The proof is relatively straightforward.

Proof

We reverse the quantifiers and consider an arbitrary list y; we attempt to show that

$$(\textit{for all list } x)\big[\textit{flatlist}(x \,\square\, y) \;=\; \textit{flatlist}(x) * \textit{flatlist}(y)\big].$$

The proof is by induction on x over the lists, taking the inductive sentence to be

$$\mathcal{F}[x]: \quad \textit{flatlist}(x \,\square\, y) \;=\; \textit{flatlist}(x) * \textit{flatlist}(y).$$

Base Case

We would like to show

$$\mathcal{F}\big[[\,]\big]: \quad \textit{flatlist}\big([\,] \,\square\, y\big) \;=\; \textit{flatlist}\big([\,]\big) * \textit{flatlist}(y).$$

We have

$$\textit{flatlist}\big([\,] \,\square\, y\big) \;=\; \textit{flatlist}(y)$$

$$\text{(by the \textit{left-empty} axiom for append).}$$

But on the other hand,

$$\textit{flatlist}\big([\,]\big) * \textit{flatlist}(y)$$

$$= \; \Lambda * \textit{flatlist}(y)$$

$$\text{(by the \textit{empty} axiom for \textit{flatlist})}$$

$$= \; \textit{flatlist}(y)$$

$$\text{(by the \textit{left-empty} axiom for concatenation).}$$

We must prove two inductive steps.

Atom Inductive Step

We would like to show

$$\begin{array}{l}(\textit{for all atom } u) \\ (\textit{for all list } x)\end{array}\left[\begin{array}{l}\textit{if } \;\mathcal{F}[x] \\ \textit{then } \;\mathcal{F}[u \circ x]\end{array}\right].$$

For an arbitrary atom u and list x, assume the induction hypothesis

$$\mathcal{F}[x]: \quad \textit{flatlist}(x \,\square\, y) \;=\; \textit{flatlist}(x) * \textit{flatlist}(y).$$

We would like to establish the desired conclusion

$$\mathcal{F}[u \circ x]: \quad \textit{flatlist}\big((u \circ x) \,\square\, y\big) \;=\; \textit{flatlist}(u \circ x) * \textit{flatlist}(y).$$

Recalling that u is an atom (i.e., a character), we have

$$\textit{flatlist}\big((u \circ x) \,\square\, y\big) \;=\; \textit{flatlist}\big(u \circ (x \,\square\, y)\big)$$

$$\text{(by the \textit{left-insertion} axiom for append)}$$

$$= u \bullet \textit{flatlist}(x \,\square\, y)$$
$$\quad\text{(by the \textit{atom-insertion} axiom for \textit{flatlist})}$$

$$= u \bullet \big(\textit{flatlist}(x) * \textit{flatlist}(y)\big)$$
$$\quad\text{(by our induction hypothesis } \mathcal{F}[x]).$$

But on the other hand,

$$\textit{flatlist}(u \circ x) * \textit{flatlist}(y)$$

$$= \big(u \bullet \textit{flatlist}(x)\big) * \textit{flatlist}(y)$$
$$\quad\text{(by the \textit{atom-insertion} axiom for \textit{flatlist} again)}$$

$$= u \bullet \big(\textit{flatlist}(x) * \textit{flatlist}(y)\big)$$
$$\quad\text{(by the \textit{left-prefix} axiom for concatenation).}$$

List Inductive Step

We would like to show

$$\begin{array}{l}(\textit{for all list } x') \\ (\textit{for all list } x)\end{array} \left[\begin{array}{l} \textit{if } \mathcal{F}[x'] \ \textit{and} \ \mathcal{F}[x] \\ \textit{then} \ \mathcal{F}[x' \circ x]\end{array}\right].$$

For arbitrary lists x' and x, assume the two induction hypotheses

$$\mathcal{F}[x'] : \quad \textit{flatlist}(x' \,\square\, y) \;=\; \textit{flatlist}(x') * \textit{flatlist}(y)$$

and

$$\mathcal{F}[x] : \quad \textit{flatlist}(x \,\square\, y) \;=\; \textit{flatlist}(x) * \textit{flatlist}(y).$$

We would like to show the desired conclusion

$$\mathcal{F}[x' \circ x] : \quad \textit{flatlist}\big((x' \circ x) \,\square\, y\big) \;=\; \textit{flatlist}(x' \circ x) * \textit{flatlist}(y).$$

Recalling that x', x, and y are lists, we have

$$\textit{flatlist}\big((x' \circ x) \,\square\, y\big) \;=\; \textit{flatlist}\big(x' \circ (x \,\square\, y)\big)$$
$$\quad\text{(by the \textit{left-insertion} axiom for append)}$$

$$= \textit{flatlist}(x') * \textit{flatlist}(x \,\square\, y)$$
$$\quad\text{(by the \textit{list-insertion} axiom for \textit{flatlist})}$$

$$= \textit{flatlist}(x') * \big(\textit{flatlist}(x) * \textit{flatlist}(y)\big)$$
$$\quad\text{(by the second induction hypothesis } \mathcal{F}[x]).$$

But on the other hand,

$$\textit{flatlist}(x' \circ x) * \textit{flatlist}(y)$$

$$= \big(\textit{flatlist}(x') * \textit{flatlist}(x)\big) * \textit{flatlist}(y)$$
$$\text{(by the \textit{list-insertion} axiom for \textit{flatlist} again)}$$

$$= \textit{flatlist}(x') * \big(\textit{flatlist}(x) * \textit{flatlist}(y)\big)$$
$$\text{(by the \textit{associativity} property of concatenation).}$$

Note that we did not use the first induction hypothesis $\mathcal{F}[x']$ in the proof of the list inductive step. ◢

An alternative definition of the *flatlist* function is given in **Problem 9.5**.

9.5   TREE REPRESENTATION OF LISTS

In this section we explore the relationship between the theories of lists and trees (over the same set of atoms). We represent each list as a tree in such a way that distinct lists are represented as distinct trees.

In the combined theory of nonnegative integers and strings, we formulated a string representation of nonnegative integers by actually identifying each nonnegative integer with a different string; in other words, we did not distinguish between the integer and the string that represented it. For this section we construct a combined theory of lists and trees in which we preserve the distinction between lists and trees. We relate lists and trees by defining a representation function *treelist* that "maps" the lists into the trees, in the sense that, for each list x, $treelist(x)$ is a distinct tree.

Recall that our axioms for the theory of lists do not specify whether or not the empty list [ ] is an atom. For the tree representation of lists, it is convenient to assume that [ ] is indeed an atom.

The *treelist* function "replaces" the list insertion function with the tree construction function. Suppose, for example, that x is the list

$$[[A,\ B],\ C],$$

that is,

$$\big(A \circ (B \circ [\,])\big) \circ (C \circ [\,]).$$

Then the value of *treelist*(x) is the tree

$$\big(A \bullet (B \bullet [\,])\big) \bullet (C \bullet [\,]),$$

that is,

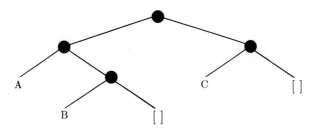

Let us now develop the combined theory of lists and trees in which we may describe this representation precisely.

Because we identify the atoms of the lists with the atoms of the trees, we use a single unary predicate symbol $atom(x)$ to characterize the atoms of the two theories. Because we assume that the empty list is an atom, we include in our combined theory the new generation axiom

$$atom([\,]) \qquad\qquad\qquad\qquad\qquad\qquad\qquad\qquad (empty\ atom)$$

Thus the empty list $[\,]$ is regarded both as a list (by the *empty* generation axiom) and as an atom (by this axiom).

TREELIST

The representation function symbol $treelist(x)$ may then be defined by the following axioms:

$$treelist([\,]) = [\,] \qquad\qquad\qquad\qquad\qquad\qquad\qquad (empty)$$

$$\begin{array}{l}(for\ all\ atom\ x)\\(for\ all\ list\ y)\end{array}\Big[treelist(x \circ y) \ = \ x \bullet treelist(y)\Big] \quad (atom\ insertion)$$

$$\begin{array}{l}(for\ all\ list\ x)\\(for\ all\ list\ y)\end{array}\Big[treelist(x \circ y) = treelist(x) \bullet treelist(y)\Big] \quad (list\ insertion)$$

Note that these axioms do not specify the value of $treelist(u)$ on atoms u other than the empty list $[\,]$.

From these axioms we may establish the following properties of the *treelist* function:

$$(\textit{for all list } x)\,\big[\textit{tree}\,(\textit{treelist}(x))\big] \qquad\qquad (\textit{sort})$$

$$(\textit{for all list } x)\,\begin{bmatrix}\textit{if}\ \ \textit{not}\,(x = [\,]) \\ \textit{then}\ \ \textit{not}(\textit{atom}\,(\textit{treelist}(x)))\end{bmatrix} \qquad (\textit{nonatom})$$

The proofs are omitted.

LISTTREE

To express and establish the properties of the *treelist* function, it is convenient to define an inverse function *listtree*, which maps the trees back into the lists. Suppose, for example, that x is the tree

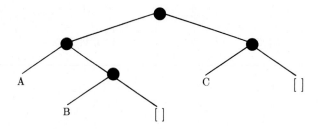

that is,

$$\big(\text{A} \bullet (\text{B} \bullet [\,])\big) \bullet (\text{C} \bullet [\,]).$$

Then *listtree*(x) is the list

$$\big(\text{A} \circ (\text{B} \circ [\,])\big) \circ (\text{C} \circ [\,]),$$

that is,

$$\big[[\text{A, B}], \text{C}\big].$$

The reader may remember the names "treelist" and "listtree" by recalling that the *treelist* function "trees" a list, i.e., produces a tree from a list, while the *listtree* function "lists" a tree, i.e., produces a list from a tree.

The *listtree* function is defined by the axioms

$$listtree([\,]) = [\,] \qquad\qquad (empty)$$

$$(for\ all\ tree\ x)\ \begin{bmatrix} if\ atom(x) \\ then\ listtree(x \bullet y)\ =\ x \circ listtree(y) \end{bmatrix}$$
$$(for\ all\ tree\ y)$$
$$(atom\ construction)$$

$$(for\ all\ tree\ x)\ \begin{bmatrix} if\ not\ \big(atom(x)\big) \\ then\ listtree(x \bullet y)\ =\ listtree(x) \circ listtree(y) \end{bmatrix}$$
$$(for\ all\ tree\ y)$$
$$(nonatom\ construction)$$

PROPER TREES

Note that the axioms do not specify the value of $listtree(x)$ for every tree x. For example, they do not specify any properties of $listtree(x)$ if x is an atom other than $[\,]$ or if x is of form $y \bullet z$, where z is an atom other than $[\,]$, and so forth.

Let us introduce a unary predicate symbol $proper(x)$ to characterize the "proper" trees x, for which the value $listtree(x)$ is specified by the above axioms. Intuitively speaking, a tree is proper if it is not an atom u other than the empty list $[\,]$ and if it has no subtrees of form $x \bullet u$, where u is an atom other than the empty list $[\,]$. For example, $[\,]$ and $(A \bullet [\,]) \bullet [\,]$ are proper trees, while B and $(A \bullet B) \bullet [\,]$ are nonproper trees.

The *proper* relation is defined by the following axiom:

$$(for\ all\ atom\ x)\ \begin{bmatrix} proper(x) \\ \quad if\ and\ only\ if \\ x = [\,] \end{bmatrix} \qquad (atom)$$

$$(for\ all\ tree\ x)\ \begin{bmatrix} if\ atom(x) \\ then\ \begin{bmatrix} proper(x \bullet y) \\ \quad if\ and\ only\ if \\ proper(y) \end{bmatrix} \end{bmatrix} \qquad (atom\ construction)$$
$$(for\ all\ tree\ y)$$

$$(for\ all\ tree\ x)\ \begin{bmatrix} if\ not\ \big(atom(x)\big) \\ then\ \begin{bmatrix} proper(x \bullet y) \\ \quad if\ and\ only\ if \\ proper(x)\ and\ proper(y) \end{bmatrix} \end{bmatrix}$$
$$(for\ all\ tree\ y)$$
$$(nonatom\ construction)$$

From these axioms we can establish the *sort* property of the *listtree* function:

$$(\textit{for all tree } x) \left[\begin{array}{l} \textit{if } \ proper(x) \\ \textit{then } \ list(listtree(x)) \end{array} \right] \qquad (\textit{sort})$$

In other words, the result of applying the *listtree* function to a proper tree is a list.

TREE REPRESENTATION

We are finally ready to describe the properties of the tree representation of lists.

Proposition (tree representation of lists)

The sentences

$$(\textit{for all list } x) \big[listtree(treelist(x)) = x \big] \qquad (\textit{list-tree-list})$$

$$(\textit{for all tree } y) \left[\begin{array}{l} \textit{if } \ proper(y) \\ \textit{then } \ treelist(listtree(y)) = y \end{array} \right] \qquad (\textit{tree-list-tree})$$

are valid.   ◢

The proof of the first property is by induction over the lists; the proof of the second, by induction over the trees. We show the first part of the proposition.

Proof (list-tree-list part)

We want to prove

$$(\textit{for all list } x) \big[listtree(treelist(x)) = x \big].$$

The proof is by induction over the lists, taking the inductive sentence to be

$$\mathcal{F}[x]: \quad listtree(treelist(x)) = x.$$

Base Case

We want to show that

$$\mathcal{F}\big[[\,]\big]: \quad listtree(treelist([\,])) = [\,].$$

But we have

$$listtree(treelist([\,])) \;=\; listtree([\,])$$
$$\text{(by the } empty \text{ axiom for } treelist)$$

$$=\; [\,]$$
$$\text{(by the } empty \text{ axiom for } listtree).$$

Atom Inductive Step

For an arbitrary atom u and list x, assume the induction hypothesis

$$\mathcal{F}[x]: \quad listtree(treelist(x)) = x.$$

We would like to establish the desired conclusion

$$\mathcal{F}[u \circ x]: \quad listtree(treelist(u \circ x)) = u \circ x.$$

Because u is an atom, we have

$$listtree(treelist(u \circ x))$$

$$=\; listtree(u \bullet treelist(x))$$
$$\text{(by the } atom\ insertion \text{ axiom for } treelist)$$

$$=\; u \circ listtree(treelist(x))$$
$$\text{(by the } atom\ construction \text{ axiom for } listtree)$$

$$=\; u \circ x$$
$$\text{(by our induction hypothesis } \mathcal{F}[x]).$$

List Inductive Step

For arbitrary lists x' and x, assume the two induction hypotheses

$$\mathcal{F}[x']: \quad listtree(treelist(x')) = x'$$

and

$$\mathcal{F}[x]: \quad listtree(treelist(x)) = x.$$

We would like to show the desired conclusion

$$\mathcal{F}[x' \circ x]: \quad listtree(treelist(x' \circ x)) \;=\; x' \circ x.$$

We distinguish between two subcases, depending on whether or not $x' = [\,]$.

Case: $x' = [\,]$

Then (by the new *empty-atom* generation axiom of the combined theory) we know x' is an atom; therefore the desired conclusion can be established as in the atom inductive step.

Case: $not\ (x' = [\ ])$

Then (by the *nonatom* property of the *treelist* function) $treelist(x')$ is not an atom, that is,

$$not\ \big(atom\big(treelist(x')\big)\big).$$

We have

$$listtree\big(treelist(x' \circ x)\big)$$

$$= listtree\big(treelist(x') \bullet treelist(x)\big)$$
$$\text{(by the } \textit{list-insertion} \text{ axiom for } \textit{treelist},$$
$$\text{because } x' \text{ is a list)}$$

$$= listtree\big(treelist(x')\big) \circ listtree\big(treelist(x)\big)$$
$$\text{(by the } \textit{nonatom-construction} \text{ axiom for } \textit{listtree},$$
$$\text{because } treelist(x') \text{ is not an atom)}$$

$$= x' \circ x$$
$$\text{(by our two induction hypotheses } \mathcal{F}[x'] \text{ and } \mathcal{F}[x]),$$

as we wanted to show.

Note that we have used both induction hypotheses for the list inductive step. ◢

Now let us prove the second part of the proposition.

Proof (tree-list-tree part)

We want to prove

$$(\textit{for all tree } y) \begin{bmatrix} \textit{if } proper(y) \\ \textit{then } treelist\big(listtree(y)\big) = y \end{bmatrix}.$$

The proof is by induction on y over the trees (not the lists), taking the inductive sentence to be

$$\mathcal{F}[y]: \quad \begin{aligned} &\textit{if } proper(y) \\ &\textit{then } treelist\big(listtree(y)\big) = y. \end{aligned}$$

Base Case

We want to show that

$$(\textit{for all atom } u)\,\mathcal{F}[u].$$

Consider an arbitrary atom u; we would like to show

$$\mathcal{F}[u]: \quad \begin{array}{l} \textit{if } proper(u) \\ \textit{then } treelist(listtree(u)) = u. \end{array}$$

Suppose that u is proper, that is,

$$proper(u);$$

then (by the *atom* axiom for *proper*)

$$u = [\,].$$

We would like to show that then

$$treelist(listtree(u)) = u,$$

that is,

$$treelist(listtree([\,])) = [\,].$$

But we have

$$\begin{aligned} treelist(listtree([\,])) &= treelist([\,]) \\ &\qquad \text{(by the } \textit{empty} \text{ axiom for } listtree) \\[2mm] &= [\,] \\ &\qquad \text{(by the } \textit{empty} \text{ axiom for } treelist). \end{aligned}$$

Inductive Step

We want to show that

$$\begin{array}{l} (\textit{for all tree } y_1) \\ (\textit{for all tree } y_2) \end{array} \left[\begin{array}{l} \textit{if } \mathcal{F}[y_1] \textit{ and } \mathcal{F}[y_2] \\ \textit{then } \mathcal{F}[y_1 \bullet y_2] \end{array} \right]$$

For arbitrary trees y_1 and y_2, assume the two induction hypotheses

$$\mathcal{F}[y_1]: \quad \begin{array}{l} \textit{if } proper(y_1) \\ \textit{then } treelist(listtree(y_1)) = y_1 \end{array}$$

and

$$\mathcal{F}[y_2]: \quad \begin{array}{l} \textit{if } proper(y_2) \\ \textit{then } treelist(listtree(y_2)) = y_2. \end{array}$$

We would like to establish the desired conclusion

$$\mathcal{F}[y_1 \bullet y_2]: \quad \begin{array}{l} \textit{if } proper(y_1 \bullet y_2) \\ \textit{then } treelist(listtree(y_1 \bullet y_2)) = y_1 \bullet y_2. \end{array}$$

We suppose that

$$proper(y_1 \bullet y_2)$$

and show that then

$$treelist\big(listtree(y_1 \bullet y_2)\big) = y_1 \bullet y_2.$$

We distinguish between two subcases, depending on whether or not y_1 is an atom.

Case: $atom(y_1)$

Then (by the *atom-construction* axiom for *proper*, because $proper(y_1 \bullet y_2)$) we know

$$proper(y_2),$$

and therefore (by the second induction hypothesis $\mathcal{F}[y_2]$)

(†) $treelist\big(listtree(y_2)\big) = y_2.$

Then we have

$$treelist\big(listtree(y_1 \bullet y_2)\big)$$

$= treelist\big(y_1 \circ listtree(y_2)\big)$
  (by the *atom-construction* axiom for *listtree*,
  because y_1 is an atom)

$= y_1 \bullet treelist\big(listtree(y_2)\big)$
  (by the *atom-insertion* axiom for *treelist*,
  because y_1 is an atom)

$= y_1 \bullet y_2$
  (by the above consequence (†) of our induction hypothesis).

Case: $not\,\big(atom(y_1)\big)$

Then, because $proper(y_1 \bullet y_2)$, we know (by the *nonatom-construction* axiom for *proper*)

$$proper(y_1) \quad and \quad proper(y_2),$$

and therefore (by the two induction hypotheses $\mathcal{F}[y_1]$ and $\mathcal{F}[y_2]$)

(‡) $treelist\big(listtree(y_1)\big) = y_1 \quad and \quad treelist\big(listtree(y_2)\big) = y_2.$

Also, because y_1 is a proper tree, we know (by the *sort* property for *listtree*) that $listtree(y_1)$ is a list. Then we have

$$treelist\big(listtree(y_1 \bullet y_2)\big)$$

$$= \; treelist\bigl(listtree(y_1) \circ listtree(y_2)\bigr)$$
(by the *nonatom-construction* axiom for *listtree*,
because y_1 is not an atom)

$$= \; treelist\bigl(listtree(y_1)\bigr) \bullet treelist\bigl(listtree(y_2)\bigr)$$
(by the *list-insertion* axiom for *treelist*,
because *listtree*(y_1) is a list)

$$= \; y_1 \bullet y_2$$
(by the above consequence (‡)
of our two induction hypotheses),

as we wanted to show.   ◢

Remark (**uniqueness of representation**)

The *list-tree-list* part of the proposition implies that the tree representation of lists is unique, in the sense that the *treelist* function maps distinct lists into distinct trees; that is,

$$(for\ all\ list\ x) \begin{bmatrix} if\ not\ (x = x') \\ then\ not\ \bigl(treelist(x) = treelist(x')\bigr) \end{bmatrix} \quad (one\ to\ one)$$
$$(for\ all\ list\ x')$$

For suppose, for arbitrary lists x and x', that

$$treelist(x) = treelist(x');$$

then

$$listtree\bigl(treelist(x)\bigr) = listtree\bigl(treelist(x')\bigr)$$

and hence (by the *list-tree-list* part of the proposition)

$$x = x'.$$

Also, the *tree-list-tree* part of the proposition implies that every proper tree is the representation of some list; that is,

$$(for\ all\ tree\ y) \begin{bmatrix} if\ proper(y) \\ then\ (for\ some\ list\ x)\bigl[treelist(x) = y\bigr] \end{bmatrix} \quad (onto)$$

For suppose, for an arbitrary tree y, that

$$proper(y).$$

Then (by the *tree-list-tree* part of the proposition)

$$treelist\big(listtree(y)\big) = y.$$

Therefore (taking x to be $listtree(y)$)

$$(for\ some\ list\ x)\big[treelist(x) = y\big]. \quad \rfloor$$

Some relationships between the theories of strings, trees, and lists are explored in **Problem 9.6**.

We can also establish the following property of the *treelist* function, that is,

$$(for\ all\ list\ x)\ \left[\begin{matrix} if\ x \in y \\ (for\ all\ list\ y) \end{matrix}\ \begin{matrix} \\ then\ \ treelist(x) \prec_{tree} treelist(y) \end{matrix}\right] \quad (monotonicity)$$

The proof is requested in **Problem 9.7**.

Some functions in a combined theory of nonnegative integers and lists are given in **Problem 9.8**.

9.6   EXAMPLE: PARSING

In this section we use a combined theory of strings, trees, and lists. We consider how a tree might be represented as a string of symbols and how we might determine which tree a given string represents.

We begin with the theory of trees. Let us augment this theory by introducing a theory of strings in which the characters of the strings are the atoms of the trees and three special characters, denoted by the constant symbols $\widehat{(}$, called *left parenthesis*, $\widehat{)}$, called *right parenthesis*, and $\widehat{\bullet}$, called *constructor*. Thus we have, as an axiom of the augmented theory,

$$(for\ all\ x)\ \left[\begin{matrix} char(x) \\ if\ and\ only\ if \\ atom(x)\ \ or\ \ x = \widehat{(}\ \ or\ \ x = \widehat{)}\ \ or\ \ x = \widehat{\bullet} \end{matrix}\right] \quad (character)$$

Here the symbols $\widehat{(}$, $\widehat{)}$, and $\widehat{\bullet}$ are our private notations for standard constant symbols, such as a_5, b_{13}, or c_{147}. Under the intended model for the theory, the constant symbols $\widehat{(}$, $\widehat{)}$, and $\widehat{\bullet}$ will denote three characters from the strings' alphabet: the left parenthesis (, the right parenthesis), and the constructor character $\bullet$, respectively.

As in the theory of trees, we shall use informal notations such as (A • B) to indicate the tree

To distinguish this tree from the string (A • B), which has five characters (, A, •, B, and), we shall use the informal notation "(A • B)", with quotation marks, to indicate the string. (Otherwise, we would be using the same informal notation (A • B) to indicate two distinct domain elements, a tree and a string.)

Let us augment our theory further by introducing a theory of lists in which the atoms of the lists, characterized by the predicate *atomℓ*, are precisely the trees of our given theory. Thus we have, as an axiom of the augmented theory,

$$
(\textit{for all } x) \begin{bmatrix} atom\ell(x) \\ \textit{if and only if} \\ tree(x) \end{bmatrix} \qquad (atom\ell)
$$

Under the intended model for this theory, the list $[A, [A \bullet B, C]]$, for example, is a domain element. (Note that we denote the relation by *atomℓ*, rather than by our customary *atom*, because we do not wish to identify the atoms of the lists, which are denoted by *atomℓ*, with the given atoms of the trees, which are denoted by *atom*.)

The unary function symbol $generate(x)$ denotes the function that maps a tree x into its informal notation as a string. For example, if x is the tree

then $generate(x)$ is the string "(B • C)" of five characters.

The axioms for the *generate* function are

$$
(\textit{for all atom } u)\big[generate(u) = u\big] \qquad (atom)
$$

$$
\begin{array}{l} (\textit{for all tree } x) \\ (\textit{for all tree } y) \end{array} \begin{bmatrix} generate(x \bullet y) \\ = \\ \widehat{(}\ *\ generate(x)\ *\ \widehat{\bullet}\ *\ generate(y)\ *\ \widehat{)} \end{bmatrix}
$$
$$(constructor)$$

Note that we have taken advantage of the associativity of the concatenation function $*$ to omit parentheses from the *constructor* axiom.

We now define a unary function symbol $parse(x)$ to denote an inverse of the generate function. In other words, *parse* maps strings back into the trees they represent. For example, if x is the string "$(B \bullet C)$", then $parse(x)$ is the tree

We define the function symbol $parse(x)$ in terms of a binary function symbol $parse2(x, y)$, where x is a string and y is a list of trees.

The single axiom for *parse* is as follows:

$$\boxed{(for\ all\ string\ x)\big[parse(x)\ =\ parse2(x,\ [\,])\big]} \qquad (parse)$$

The axioms for *parse2* are as follows:

$$\begin{array}{l}(for\ all\ atom\ u)\\(for\ all\ string\ x)\\(for\ all\ list\ y)\end{array}\Big[parse2(u * x,\ y)\ =\ parse2(x,\ u \circ y)\Big] \qquad (atom)$$

$$\begin{array}{l}(for\ all\ string\ x)\\(for\ all\ list\ y)\end{array}\Big[parse2\big(\widehat{(}* x,\ y\big)\ =\ parse2(x,\ y)\Big] \qquad (left\ paren)$$

$$\begin{array}{l}(for\ all\ string\ x)\\(for\ all\ list\ y)\end{array}\Big[parse2(\widehat{\bullet} * x,\ y)\ =\ parse2(x,\ y)\Big] \qquad (constructor)$$

$$\begin{array}{l}(for\ all\ tree\ u)\\(for\ all\ tree\ v)\\(for\ all\ string\ x)\\(for\ all\ list\ y)\end{array}\left[\begin{array}{l}parse2\big(\widehat{)} * x,\ v \circ (u \circ y)\big)\\=\\parse2\big(x,\ (u \bullet v) \circ y\big)\end{array}\right] \qquad (right\ paren)$$

$$(for\ all\ tree\ z)\big[parse2(\Lambda,\ z \circ [\,])\ =\ z\big] \qquad (empty)$$

We establish that *parse* is an inverse of *generate*, as expressed in the following property.

Proposition (parse)

In the combined theory of strings, trees, and lists, the sentence

$$(for\ all\ tree\ z)\big[parse\big(generate(z)\big)\ =\ z\big]$$

is valid. ⌐

We do not explain the function *parse2*; the principal property of *parse2* we need is expressed in the following result.

Lemma (parse2)

In the combined theory of strings, trees, and lists, the sentence

$$(\textit{for all tree } z) \\ (\textit{for all string } x) \\ (\textit{for all list } y) \left[\begin{array}{c} parse2\big(generate(z) * x, \ y\big) \\ = \\ parse2(x, \ z \circ y) \end{array} \right]$$

is valid. ⌐

In other words, the value of *parse2* applied to a string of form "z" $*$ x and a list y (where "z" is the informal string notation for the tree z) is the same as the value of *parse2* applied to the string x and the list $z \circ y$. For example,

$$parse2\big(\text{``(B} \bullet \text{C)''} * \text{``)''}, \ [\text{A}]\big) \ = \ parse2\big(\text{``)''}, \ [(\text{B} \bullet \text{C}), \ \text{A}]\big).$$

The definitions of *parse* and *parse2* suggest a method of computing them. Before proving the proposition, we present a sample computation.

Example (computation of parse)

Suppose x is the string "(A $\bullet$ (B $\bullet$ C))" of nine characters, which could also be written as "(" $*$ A $*$ "$\bullet$" $*$ "(" $*$ B $*$ "$\bullet$" $*$ C $*$ ")" $*$ ")". Then *parse(x)* is the tree

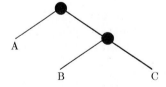

that is, A $\bullet$ (B $\bullet$ C).

For

$$parse(x) \ = \ parse\big(\text{``(A} \bullet \text{(B} \bullet \text{C))''}\big)$$

$$= \ parse2\big(\text{``(A} \bullet \text{(B} \bullet \text{C))''}, \ [\,]\big)$$
$$\text{(by the definition of } parse\text{)}$$

$$= parse2\big(\text{``A} \bullet (\text{B} \bullet \text{C}))\text{''},\ [\,]\big)$$
    (by the *left-paren* axiom for *parse2*)

$$= parse2\big(\text{``}\bullet(\text{B} \bullet \text{C}))\text{''},\ \text{A} \circ [\,]\big)$$
    (by the *atom* axiom for *parse2*)

$$= parse2\big(\text{``(B} \bullet \text{C}))\text{''},\ \text{A} \circ [\,]\big)$$
    (by the *constructor* axiom for *parse2*)

$$= parse2\big(\text{``))''},\ \text{C} \circ \big(\text{B} \circ (\text{A} \circ [\,])\big)\big)$$
    (by repeated application of the axioms for *parse2*)

$$= parse2\big(\text{``)''} * \Lambda,\ (\text{B} \bullet \text{C}) \circ (\text{A} \circ [\,])\big)$$
    (by the *right-paren* axiom for *parse2*)

$$= parse2\big(\Lambda,\ \big(\text{A} \bullet (\text{B} \bullet \text{C})\big) \circ [\,]\big)$$
    (by the *right-paren* axiom for *parse2* again)

$$= \text{A} \bullet (\text{B} \bullet \text{C})$$
    (by the *empty* axiom for *parse2*). ◢

We first show that the *parse2* lemma implies the *parse* proposition.

Proof (parse)

For an arbitrary tree z, we would like to show

$$parse\big(generate(z)\big)\ =\ z.$$

But we have

$$parse\big(generate(z)\big)\ =\ parse2\big(generate(z),\ [\,]\big)$$
    (by the definition of *parse*)

$$= parse2\big(generate(z) * \Lambda,\ [\,]\big)$$
    (by *right-empty* property of the
    concatenation function)

$$= parse2\big(\Lambda,\ z \circ [\,]\big)$$
    (by the *parse2* lemma)

$$= z$$
    (by the *empty* axiom for *parse2*),

as we wanted to show. ◢

It remains to establish the *parse2* lemma.

Proof (parse2)

The proof is by induction over the trees, on z. We take the inductive sentence to be

$$\mathcal{F}[z]: \quad \begin{array}{l} \textit{(for all string } x) \\ \textit{(for all list } y) \end{array} \left[\begin{array}{l} parse2\big(generate(z) * x, \ y\big) \\ = \\ parse2(x, \ z \circ y) \end{array} \right].$$

Base Case

We would like to show *(for all atom* u*)* $\mathcal{F}[u]$, that is,

$$\textit{(for all atom } u) \begin{array}{l} \textit{(for all string } x) \\ \textit{(for all list } y) \end{array} \left[\begin{array}{l} parse2\big(generate(u) * x, \ y\big) \\ = \\ parse2(x, \ u \circ y) \end{array} \right].$$

But for an arbitrary atom u, string x, and list y, we have

$$parse2\big(generate(u) * x, \ y\big) \ = \ parse2(u * x, \ y)$$
$$\text{(by the } atom \text{ axiom for } generate\text{)}$$

$$= \ parse2(x, \ u \circ y)$$
$$\text{(by the } atom \text{ axiom for } parse2\text{)},$$

as we wanted to show.

Inductive Step

For arbitrary trees z_1 and z_2, suppose as our two induction hypotheses that

$$\mathcal{F}[z_1]: \quad \begin{array}{l} \textit{(for all string } x_1) \\ \textit{(for all list } y_1) \end{array} \left[\begin{array}{l} parse2\big(generate(z_1) * x_1, \ y_1\big) \\ = \\ parse2(x_1, \ z_1 \circ y_1) \end{array} \right]$$

and

$$\mathcal{F}[z_2]: \quad \begin{array}{l} \textit{(for all string } x_2) \\ \textit{(for all list } y_2) \end{array} \left[\begin{array}{l} parse2\big(generate(z_2) * x_2, \ y_2\big) \\ = \\ parse2(x_2, \ z_2 \circ y_2) \end{array} \right].$$

We would like to establish the desired conclusion that

$$\mathcal{F}[z_1 \bullet z_2]: \quad \begin{array}{l} \textit{(for all string } x) \\ \textit{(for all list } y) \end{array} \left[\begin{array}{l} parse2\big(generate(z_1 \bullet z_2) * x, \ y\big) \\ = \\ parse2\big(x, \ (z_1 \bullet z_2) \circ y\big) \end{array} \right].$$

But for an arbitrary string x and list y, we have

$$parse2\big(generate(z_1 \bullet z_2) * x, \ y\big)$$

$$= parse2\big(\widehat{(} * generate(z_1) * \widehat{\bullet} * generate(z_2) * \widehat{)} * x, \ y\big)$$
(by the *constructor* axiom for *generate*)

$$= parse2\big(generate(z_1) * \widehat{\bullet} * generate(z_2) * \widehat{)} * x, \ y\big)$$
(by the *left-paren* axiom for *parse2*)

$$= parse2\big(\widehat{\bullet} * generate(z_2) * \widehat{)} * x, \ z_1 \circ y\big)$$
(by our first induction hypothesis $\mathcal{F}[z_1]$,
taking x_1 to be $\widehat{\bullet} * generate(z_2) * \widehat{)} * x$ and y_1 to be y)

$$= parse2\big(generate(z_2) * \widehat{)} * x, \ z_1 \circ y\big)$$
(by the *constructor* axiom for *parse2*)

$$= parse2\big(\widehat{)} * x, \ z_2 \circ (z_1 \circ y)\big)$$
(by our second induction hypothesis $\mathcal{F}[z_2]$,
taking x_2 to be $\widehat{)} * x$ and y_2 to be $z_1 \circ y$)

$$= parse2\big(x, \ (z_1 \bullet z_2) \circ y\big)$$
(by the *right-paren* axiom for *parse2*),

as we wanted to show. ⌐

This concludes our discussion of lists.

PROBLEMS

Problem 9.1 (insertion)   page 440

Establish the validity of the following properties of the insertion function:

(a) *Left nonidentity*

$$\begin{array}{l}(\textit{for all atlist } x) \\ (\textit{for all list } y)\end{array}\Big[not\ (x = x \circ y)\Big]$$

(b) *Right nonidentity*

$$\begin{array}{l}(\textit{for all atlist } x) \\ (\textit{for all list } y)\end{array}\Big[not\ (y = x \circ y)\Big]$$

[*Hint*: You may need to prove a more general property.]

Problem 9.2 (append)   page 443

Establish the following properties of the append function:

(a) *Sort*

$$\begin{pmatrix} \textit{for all list } x) \\ (\textit{for all list } y) \end{pmatrix} \Big[list(x \mathbin{\square} y) \Big]$$

(b) *Right empty*

$$(\textit{for all list } x) \Big[x \mathbin{\square} [\,] \ = \ x \Big]$$

(c) *Associativity*

$$\begin{pmatrix} \textit{for all list } x) \\ (\textit{for all list } y) \\ (\textit{for all list } z) \end{pmatrix} \Big[(x \mathbin{\square} y) \mathbin{\square} z \ = \ x \mathbin{\square} (y \mathbin{\square} z) \Big]$$

(d) *Head*

$$\begin{pmatrix} \textit{for all list } x) \\ (\textit{for all list } y) \end{pmatrix} \begin{bmatrix} \textit{if } \ not \ (x = [\,]) \\ \textit{then } \ head(x \mathbin{\square} y) \ = \ head(x) \end{bmatrix}$$

(e) *Tail*

$$\begin{pmatrix} \textit{for all list } x) \\ (\textit{for all list } y) \end{pmatrix} \begin{bmatrix} \textit{if } \ not \ (x = [\,]) \\ \textit{then } \ tail(x \mathbin{\square} y) \ = \ tail(x) \mathbin{\square} y \end{bmatrix}.$$

Problem 9.3 (affix, front, and last)   page 443

Suppose we augment our theory of lists by introducing a binary function symbol $affix(x, u)$ and two unary function symbols $front(x)$ and $last(x)$, with the intended meaning that $affix(x, u)$ is the list obtained by inserting the atom or list u at the end of the list x, $last(x)$ is the last element of the nonempty list x, and $front(x)$ is the list of all but the last element of the nonempty list x. Thus

$$affix([\text{A, B}], [\text{C}]) \ = \ [\text{A, B, } [\text{C}]]$$

$$last([\text{A, B, } [\text{C}]]) \ = \ [\text{C}]$$

$$front([\text{A, B, } [\text{C}]]) \ = \ [\text{A, B}].$$

• The *affix* function is defined by the axioms

$$(\textit{for all atlist } u) \Big[affix([\,], u) \ = \ u \circ [\,] \Big] \qquad\qquad (\textit{empty})$$

$$\begin{pmatrix} \textit{for all atlist } u) \\ (\textit{for all atlist } v) \\ (\textit{for all list } x) \end{pmatrix} \Big[affix(v \circ x, u) \ = \ v \circ affix(x, u) \Big] \qquad (\textit{insertion})$$

- The *front* function is defined by the axioms

$$(for\ all\ atlist\ u)\big[front(u \circ [\,]) = [\,]\big] \qquad (empty)$$

$$(for\ all\ atlist\ u)\ \begin{bmatrix} if\ \ not\ (x = [\,]) \\ (for\ all\ list\ x)\ \begin{bmatrix} then\ \ front(u \circ x) = u \circ front(x) \end{bmatrix} \end{bmatrix} \qquad (nonempty)$$

- The *last* function is defined by the axioms

$$(for\ all\ atlist\ u)\big[last(u \circ [\,]) = u\big] \qquad (empty)$$

$$\begin{matrix} (for\ all\ atlist\ u) \\ (for\ all\ atlist\ v) \\ (for\ all\ list\ x) \end{matrix} \Big[last(u \circ (v \circ x)) = last(v \circ x)\Big] \qquad (insertion)$$

Establish the following properties of the *affix* function:

(a) *Decomposition*

$$(for\ all\ list\ x)\ \begin{bmatrix} if\ \ not\ (x = [\,]) \\ then\ \ x = affix(front(x),\ last(x)) \end{bmatrix}$$

(b) *Front*

$$\begin{matrix} (for\ all\ atlist\ u) \\ (for\ all\ list\ x) \end{matrix} \Big[front(affix(x,\ u)) = x\Big]$$

(c) *Last*

$$\begin{matrix} (for\ all\ atlist\ u) \\ (for\ all\ list\ x) \end{matrix} \Big[last(affix(x,\ u)) = u\Big].$$

Be sure to state and prove any properties you use that have not been previously mentioned.

Problem 9.4 (revall)   page 443

Suppose we augment our theory of lists by introducing a unary function symbol $revall(x)$ to denote the function that reverses the elements of a list at every level; thus

$$revall(\big[B,\ [C,\ D],\ [E,\ [C,\ F]]\big]) = \big[[[F,\ C],\ E],\ [D,\ C],\ B\big].$$

The *revall* function is defined by the following axioms:

$$revall([\,]) = [\,] \qquad\qquad\qquad (empty)$$

$$\begin{array}{l} (for\ all\ atom\ u) \\ (for\ all\ list\ y) \end{array} \Big[revall(u \circ y) = affix(revall(y),\ u) \Big] \qquad (atom\ insertion)$$

$$\begin{array}{l} (for\ all\ list\ x) \\ (for\ all\ list\ y) \end{array} \Big[revall(x \circ y) = affix(revall(y),\ revall(x)) \Big] \qquad (list\ insertion)$$

where *affix* is defined in the previous problem.

Establish the following properties of the *revall* function:

(a)   *Atom affixation*

$$\begin{array}{l} (for\ all\ list\ x) \\ (for\ all\ atom\ u) \end{array} \Big[revall(affix(x,\ u)) = u \circ revall(x) \Big]$$

(b)   *List affixation*

$$\begin{array}{l} (for\ all\ list\ x) \\ (for\ all\ list\ y) \end{array} \Big[revall(affix(x,\ y)) = revall(y) \circ revall(x) \Big]$$

(c)   *Revall*

$$(for\ all\ list\ x) \Big[revall(revall(x)) = x \Big].$$

Problem 9.5 (alternative definition for flatlist)   page 448

Consider the following alternative definition of the *flatlist* function, expressed in terms of the new binary function symbol *flatlist2*$(x,\ w)$, where x is a list and w is a string. The function *flatlist2* is defined by the following axioms:

$$(for\ all\ string\ w) \Big[flatlist2([\,],\ w) = w \Big] \qquad\qquad (empty)$$

$$\begin{array}{l} (for\ all\ atom\ u) \\ (for\ all\ list\ y) \\ (for\ all\ string\ w) \end{array} \Big[flatlist2(u \circ y,\ w) = u \bullet flatlist2(y,\ w) \Big]$$

$$(atom\ insertion)$$

$$\begin{array}{l} (for\ all\ list\ x) \\ (for\ all\ list\ y) \\ (for\ all\ string\ w) \end{array} \Big[flatlist2(x \circ y,\ w) = flatlist2(x,\ flatlist2(y,\ w)) \Big]$$

$$(list\ insertion)$$

Prove that *flatlist2* does indeed provide an alternative definition of the *flatlist* function, in the sense that

$$(for\ all\ list\ x)\big[flatlist(x)\ =\ flatlist2(x,\ \Lambda)\big].$$

[*Hint*: Prove a more general property.]

Problem 9.6 (flatlist and flattree)   page 458

Consider a combined theory of strings, trees, and lists in which the characters of the strings, the atoms of the trees, and the atoms of the lists are all identified; thus we have the axiom

$$(for\ all\ x)\big[char(x)\ if\ and\ only\ if\ atom(x)\big] \qquad (character\ atom)$$

Assume also that the empty list is regarded as an atom; thus we have the axiom

$$atom([\,]) \qquad\qquad (empty\ atom)$$

Recall that the *flattree* function (defined in the previous chapter) maps trees into strings. Let us revise the definition of *flattree* so that it maps the atom [ ] into the empty string Λ; thus we have the axioms for *flattree*:

$$flattree([\,]) = \Lambda \qquad\qquad (empty\ atom)$$

$$(for\ all\ atom\ u)\ \begin{bmatrix} if\ not\ (u = [\,]) \\ then\ flattree(u) = u \end{bmatrix} \qquad (nonempty\ atom)$$

$$\begin{matrix}(for\ all\ tree\ x)\\(for\ all\ tree\ y)\end{matrix}\Big[flattree(x \bullet y)\ =\ flattree(x) * flattree(y)\Big]$$

$$(construction)$$

Here the *empty-atom* and *nonempty-atom* axioms for *flattree* replace the *atom* axiom for *flattree* from the previous chapter.

Suppose that *flatlist* and *treelist* are defined as in the text. Then establish that

$$(for\ all\ list\ x)\big[flattree\big(treelist(x)\big) = flatlist(x)\big].$$

Problem 9.7 (monotonicity of treelist)   page 458

In the combined theory of trees and lists, establish the *monotonicity* property of the *treelist* function, that is,

$$\begin{matrix}(for\ all\ list\ x)\\(for\ all\ list\ y)\end{matrix}\begin{bmatrix} if\ x \in y \\ then\ treelist(x) \prec_{tree} treelist(y) \end{bmatrix}.$$

Problem 9.8 (atoms)   page 458

In a combined theory of nonnegative integers and lists, let the unary function symbol $atoms(x)$ denote the number of occurrences of atoms (other than [ ]) in the list (or atom) x; thus $atoms([A, [A, B]]) = 3$ and $atoms([A, [[ ], B]]) = 2$. The *atoms* function is defined by the axioms

$$atoms([\ ]) = 0 \qquad\qquad (empty)$$

$$(for\ all\ atom\ u) \begin{bmatrix} if\ not\ (u = [\ ]) \\ then\ \ atoms(u) = 1 \end{bmatrix} \qquad\qquad (atom)$$

$$\begin{matrix} (for\ all\ atlist\ x) \\ (for\ all\ list\ y) \end{matrix} \Big[atoms(x \circ y) = atoms(x) + atoms(y) \Big] \quad (insertion)$$

Consider the following alternative definition of *atoms*, expressed in terms of the unary function symbol $atoms1(x)$, whose axioms are

$$atoms1([\ ]) = 0 \qquad\qquad (empty)$$

$$(for\ all\ atom\ u) \begin{bmatrix} if\ not\ (u = [\ ]) \\ then\ \ atoms1(u) = 1 \end{bmatrix} \qquad\qquad (atom)$$

$$(for\ all\ list\ x) \big[atoms1([\ ] \circ x) = atoms1(x) \big] \qquad (empty\ insertion)$$

$$\begin{matrix} (for\ all\ atom\ u) \\ (for\ all\ list\ x) \end{matrix} \begin{bmatrix} if\ not\ (u = [\ ]) \\ then\ \ atoms1(u \circ x) = 1 + atoms1(x) \end{bmatrix}$$
$$(atom\ insertion)$$

$$\begin{matrix} (for\ all\ atlist\ x) \\ (for\ all\ list\ y) \\ (for\ all\ list\ z) \end{matrix} \Big[atoms1\big((x \circ y) \circ z\big) = atoms1\big(x \circ (y \circ z)\big) \Big]$$
$$(insertion\ insertion)$$

Show that *atoms1* does indeed provide an alternative definition for *atoms*, that is,

$$(for\ all\ atlist\ x) \big[atoms(x) = atoms1(x) \big].$$

10

Sets

We now present a theory of finite sets analogous to our previous theories with induction. Intuitively speaking, a set is a finite collection of elements, called *atoms*, in which we disregard the order of occurrence of the elements and their multiplicity (i.e., the number of occurrences). Thus if the atoms are A, B, and C, we regard the sets

$$\{A, A, B\}, \qquad \{B, A, A\}, \qquad \text{and} \qquad \{A, B\}$$

as identical. We do not consider infinite sets, and we do not specify whether sets may be nested, i.e., whether the atoms may themselves be sets. There are versions of this theory that explicitly include infinite sets and nested sets, but we shall not require such a theory in this book.

10.1   BASIC PROPERTIES

The vocabulary of the theory of sets consists of

- A constant symbol { }, denoting the *empty set*

- A unary predicate symbol $atom(x)$

- A unary predicate symbol $set(x)$

- A binary function symbol $u \circ x$, denoting the *insertion* function

- A binary predicate symbol $u \in x$, denoting the *member* relation.

Under the intended models for the theory, the insertion function $u \circ x$ is the result of inserting the atom u among the elements of the set x; thus

$$\text{A} \circ \{\text{B, C}\} \quad \text{is} \quad \{\text{A, B, C}\}$$

and

$$\text{A} \circ \{\text{A, B, C}\} \quad \text{is also} \quad \{\text{A, B, C}\}.$$

The member relation $u \in x$ is true if the atom u is one of the elements of the set x; thus

$$\text{A} \in \{\text{A, B, C}\} \quad \text{but} \quad \text{not} \quad \text{A} \in \{\text{B, C}\}.$$

Notations such as $\{\text{A}\}$ and $\{\text{A, B}\}$ are informal and are not part of the language of the theory. Under a particular model for the theory, if the terms s and t denote the atoms A and B, respectively, then $s \circ \{\ \}$ denotes the set we express informally as $\{\text{A}\}$, and $s \circ (t \circ \{\ \})$ denotes the set we express informally as $\{\text{A, B}\}$.

The theory of sets is a theory with equality and the following axioms:

- The *generation* axioms

$$\boxed{\begin{array}{ll} set(\{\ \}) & (empty) \\[2em] (for\ all\ atom\ u) \\ (for\ all\ set\ x) \end{array}\Big[set(u \circ x)\Big] \qquad\qquad (insertion)}$$

- The *member* axioms

The member relation $u \in x$ is defined by

$$\boxed{\begin{array}{l} (for\ all\ atom\ u)\big[not\ (u \in \{\ \})\big] \hfill (empty) \\[2em] \begin{array}{l}(for\ all\ atom\ u) \\ (for\ all\ atom\ v) \\ (for\ all\ set\ x)\end{array}\left[\begin{array}{l} u \in (v \circ x) \\ \quad if\ and\ only\ if \\ u = v\ \ or\ \ u \in x\end{array}\right] \hfill (insertion) \end{array}}$$

Because a nonempty set can be constructed in more than one way, we do not have the usual uniqueness axioms. Instead, we include axioms for the equality relation that indicate which terms in our theory denote the same set.

- The special *equality* axioms

In addition to the usual equality axioms, we assume that the equality relation satisfies the following additional axioms:

$$
\begin{array}{l}
\textit{(for all atom u)} \\
\textit{(for all set x)}
\end{array}
\left[u \circ (u \circ x) \;=\; u \circ x \right]
\qquad\qquad (\textit{multiplicity})
$$

$$
\begin{array}{l}
\textit{(for all atom u)} \\
\textit{(for all atom v)} \\
\textit{(for all set x)}
\end{array}
\left[u \circ (v \circ x) \;=\; v \circ (u \circ x) \right]
\qquad (\textit{exchange})
$$

The first axiom expresses that the multiplicity of the elements in a set is irrelevant, and the second expresses that their order is also irrelevant. According to these axioms, the sets

$$
\mathrm{A} \circ (\mathrm{B} \circ \{\,\}), \quad \mathrm{A} \circ \big(\mathrm{A} \circ (\mathrm{B} \circ \{\,\})\big), \quad \text{and} \quad \mathrm{B} \circ (\mathrm{A} \circ \{\,\})
$$

are all equal.

- The *induction* principle

> For each sentence $\mathcal{F}[x]$ in the theory, the universal closure of the sentence
>
> $$
> if \left[\begin{array}{l}
> \mathcal{F}[\{\,\}] \\
> \quad and \\
> \textit{(for all atom u)} \left[\begin{array}{l} if \;\; \mathcal{F}[x] \\ then \;\; \mathcal{F}[u \circ x] \end{array}\right] \\
> \textit{(for all set x)}
> \end{array}\right]
> \qquad (\textit{induction})
> $$
>
> $then$ $(\textit{for all set } x)\mathcal{F}[x]$,
>
> where u does not occur free in $\mathcal{F}[x]$, is an axiom.

Note that the axioms do not specify whether or not the atoms may themselves be sets. If we want to forbid atoms to be sets, we must add appropriate uniqueness axioms. On the other hand, if we want to consider nested sets, which have other sets as elements, we must add the appropriate generation axioms.

The *insertion* axiom for the member relation immediately implies the property

$$
\begin{array}{l}
\textit{(for all atom u)} \\
\textit{(for all set x)}
\end{array}
\left[u \in u \circ x \right]
\qquad\qquad (\textit{component})
$$

Although we have no uniqueness axioms for sets, they do have the following uniqueness property, which can be established from the other axioms.

Proposition (empty uniqueness)

The sentence

$$\begin{array}{l} \textit{(for all atom u)} \\ \textit{(for all set x)} \end{array} \Big[\textit{not} \, (u \circ x = \{ \, \}) \Big] \qquad (\textit{empty uniqueness})$$

is valid. ◢

Proof

For an arbitrary atom u and set x, we know (by the *component* property of the member relation) that

$$u \in u \circ x.$$

On the other hand, we know (by the *empty* axiom for the member relation) that

$$\textit{not} \, (u \in \{ \, \}).$$

Therefore (by the *predicate-substitutivity* equality axiom for the member relation)

$$\textit{not} \, (u \circ x = \{ \, \}),$$

as we wanted to prove. ◢

Remark (member)

Note that the proof of the *empty-uniqueness* property uses properties of the member relation. The reader may have wondered why we included this relation as part of the basic theory. In fact, had we not, there would have been unintended models for the theory, under which the *empty-uniqueness* property and other familiar properties of sets would be false. In particular, the interpretation under which the equality predicate symbol is true for any two sets would have been one of these unintended models. ◢

The insertion function ∘ may be shown to satisfy the following property:

Proposition (absorption)

The sentence

$$\begin{array}{l} \textit{(for all atom u)} \\ \textit{(for all set x)} \end{array} \left[\begin{array}{l} \textit{if} \; u \in x \\ \textit{then} \; u \circ x = x \end{array} \right] \qquad (\textit{absorption})$$

is valid. ⌐

Proof

For an arbitrary atom u, we prove

$$\text{(for all set } x) \left[\begin{array}{l} \textit{if } u \in x \\ \textit{then } u \circ x = x \end{array} \right].$$

The proof is by induction over the sets, taking the inductive sentence to be

$$\mathcal{F}[x]: \quad \begin{array}{l} \textit{if } u \in x \\ \textit{then } u \circ x = x. \end{array}$$

Base Case

We would like to show

$$\mathcal{F}[\{\,\}]: \quad \begin{array}{l} \textit{if } u \in \{\,\} \\ \textit{then } u \circ \{\,\} = \{\,\}. \end{array}$$

But we have (by the *empty* axiom for the member relation)

$$\textit{not } (u \in \{\,\}).$$

Because its antecedent is false, the entire implication $\mathcal{F}[\{\,\}]$ is true.

Inductive Step

We would like to show

$$\begin{array}{l} \text{(for all atom } v) \\ \text{(for all set } x) \end{array} \left[\begin{array}{l} \textit{if } \mathcal{F}[x] \\ \textit{then } \mathcal{F}[v \circ x] \end{array} \right].$$

Note that we have taken the bound variable in the inductive step to be v rather than u, because u occurs free in $\mathcal{F}[x]$.

For an arbitrary atom v and set x, we assume the induction hypothesis

$$\mathcal{F}[x]: \quad \begin{array}{l} \textit{if } u \in x \\ \textit{then } u \circ x = x \end{array}$$

and would like to show the desired conclusion

$$\mathcal{F}[v \circ x]: \quad \begin{array}{l} \textit{if } u \in v \circ x \\ \textit{then } u \circ (v \circ x) = v \circ x. \end{array}$$

We suppose that

$$u \in v \circ x$$

and show that

$$u \circ (v \circ x) = v \circ x.$$

The proof distinguishes between two subcases, depending whether or not $u = v$.

Case: $u = v$

Then we have

$$u \circ (v \circ x) = v \circ (v \circ x)$$

$$= v \circ x$$
$$\text{(by the } \textit{multiplicity} \text{ equality axiom),}$$

as we wanted to show.

Case: $\textit{not } (u = v)$

Because, by our supposition, $u \in v \circ x$, we have (by the *insertion* axiom for the member relation)

$$u = v \;\; \textit{or} \;\; u \in x.$$

Because in this case $\textit{not } (u = v)$, this implies that

$$u \in x.$$

Hence (by our induction hypothesis $\mathcal{F}[x]$)

$$u \circ x = x.$$

Therefore we have

$$u \circ (v \circ x) = v \circ (u \circ x)$$
$$\text{(by the } \textit{exchange} \text{ equality axiom)}$$

$$= v \circ x,$$

as we wanted to show. ⌐

THE MODIFIED INDUCTION PRINCIPLE

We can now establish the following version of the induction principle, which is often more convenient to apply than the original.

Proposition (modified induction principle)

For each sentence $\mathcal{F}[x]$ in the theory, the universal closure of the sentence

$$
if\ \begin{bmatrix} \mathcal{F}[\{\ \}] \\ and \\ (for\ all\ atom\ u) \\ (for\ all\ set\ x) \end{bmatrix}\begin{bmatrix} if\ not\ (u \in x) \\ then\ if\ \mathcal{F}[x] \\ \qquad then\ \ \mathcal{F}[u \circ x] \end{bmatrix}\qquad \begin{matrix}(modified \\ induction)\end{matrix}
$$

$then\ (for\ all\ set\ x)\mathcal{F}[x],$

where u does not occur free in $\mathcal{F}[x]$, is valid. ⌟

This principle differs from the original induction principle in that, in the inductive step, it requires us to establish the desired conclusion $\mathcal{F}[u \circ x]$ from the induction hypothesis $\mathcal{F}[x]$ only in the case in which *not* $(u \in x)$. Otherwise, in the case in which $u \in x$, we know (by the *absorption* property of the member relation) that $u \circ x = x$ and hence the induction hypothesis and the desired conclusion are identical. The detailed proof of the modified induction principle is omitted.

The additional condition *not* $(u \in x)$ often makes the inductive step easier to prove. Henceforth, we shall always use the modified induction principle in place of the original induction principle for sets.

10.2 THE EQUALITY PROPOSITION

A fundamental property of the equality relation between sets is that two sets are equal when they have the same members. This property is established in the following result.

Proposition (equality)

The sentence

$$
\begin{matrix}(for\ all\ set\ x) \\ (for\ all\ set\ y)\end{matrix}\begin{bmatrix} x = y \\ if\ and\ only\ if \\ (for\ all\ atom\ u) \begin{bmatrix} u \in x \\ if\ and\ only\ if \\ u \in y \end{bmatrix} \end{bmatrix}\qquad (equality)
$$

is valid. ⌐

The proof depends on the following two properties of sets:

$$(\textit{for all atom } w)\ (\textit{for all set } x)\ \left[\begin{array}{l} \textit{if } w \in x \\ \textit{then } (\textit{for some set } z)\ \left[\begin{array}{c} x = w \circ z \\ \textit{and} \\ \textit{not } (w \in z) \end{array}\right] \end{array}\right]\quad \begin{array}{l}(\textit{member} \\ \quad\textit{decomposition})\end{array}$$

$$(\textit{for all set } x)\ \left[\begin{array}{l} \textit{not } (x = \{\,\}) \\ \quad\textit{if and only if} \\ (\textit{for some atom } u)[u \in x] \end{array}\right]\quad (\textit{nonempty member})$$

The proofs of these properties are left as an exercise (**Problem 10.1**). We proceed with the proof of the proposition.

Proof (equality)

By the substitutivity of equality, we have one direction of the equivalence, that is,

$$\begin{array}{l}(\textit{for all set } x)\\(\textit{for all set } y)\end{array}\ \left[\begin{array}{l} \textit{if } x = y \\ \textit{then } (\textit{for all atom } u)\ \left[\begin{array}{l} u \in x \\ \quad\textit{if and only if} \\ u \in y \end{array}\right] \end{array}\right].$$

We show the other direction, that is,

$$\begin{array}{l}(\textit{for all set } x)\\(\textit{for all set } y)\end{array}\ \left[\begin{array}{l} \textit{if } (\textit{for all atom } u)\ \left[\begin{array}{l} u \in x \\ \quad\textit{if and only if} \\ u \in y \end{array}\right] \\ \textit{then } x = y \end{array}\right].$$

The proof is by the modified induction principle over the sets, on y, taking the inductive sentence to be

$$\mathcal{F}[y]:\quad (\textit{for all set } x)\ \left[\begin{array}{l} \textit{if } (\textit{for all atom } u)\ \left[\begin{array}{l} u \in x \\ \quad\textit{if and only if} \\ u \in y \end{array}\right] \\ \textit{then } x = y \end{array}\right].$$

Base Case

We would like to show

$$\mathcal{F}[\{\,\}]: \quad (for\ all\ set\ x) \left[if\ (for\ all\ atom\ u) \begin{bmatrix} u \in x \\ \quad if\ and\ only\ if \\ u \in \{\,\} \end{bmatrix} \\ then\ x = \{\,\} \right].$$

We know (by the *empty* axiom for the member relation) that

$$not\ (u \in \{\,\})$$

for every atom u. Therefore (by propositional logic) the sentence $\mathcal{F}[\{\,\}]$ reduces to

$$(for\ all\ set\ x) \left[\begin{matrix} if\ (for\ all\ atom\ u) \big[not\ (u \in x) \big] \\ then\ x = \{\,\} \end{matrix} \right].$$

But this follows directly (by the *nonempty-member* property and the duality between the quantifiers).

Inductive Step

According to the modified induction principle, we must show

$$\begin{matrix} (for\ all\ atom\ v) \\ (for\ all\ set\ y) \end{matrix} \left[\begin{matrix} if\ not\ (v \in y) \\ then\ if\ \mathcal{F}[y] \\ \quad then\ \mathcal{F}[v \circ y] \end{matrix} \right].$$

For an arbitrary atom v and set y, suppose that

$$not\ (v \in y)$$

and assume as our induction hypothesis that

$$\mathcal{F}[y]: \quad (for\ all\ set\ x) \left[if\ (for\ all\ atom\ u) \begin{bmatrix} u \in x \\ \quad if\ and\ only\ if \\ u \in y \end{bmatrix} \\ then\ x = y \right].$$

We would like to show the desired conclusion that

$$\mathcal{F}[v \circ y]: \quad (for\ all\ set\ x') \left[if\ (for\ all\ atom\ u') \begin{bmatrix} u' \in x' \\ \quad if\ and\ only\ if \\ u' \in v \circ y \end{bmatrix} \\ then\ x' = v \circ y \right].$$

For an arbitrary set x', we suppose that

$$(\dagger) \qquad (for\ all\ atom\ u') \begin{bmatrix} u' \in x' \\ \quad if\ and\ only\ if \\ u' \in v \circ y \end{bmatrix}$$

and show that then

$$x' = v \circ y.$$

We know (by the *component* property of the member relation) that

$$v \in v \circ y.$$

Therefore by our supposition (†), taking u' to be v, we have

$$v \in x'.$$

It follows (by the *member-decomposition* property) that there exists a set z such that

$$x' = v \circ z$$
$$and$$
$$not \ (v \in z).$$

Therefore to show the desired result $x' = v \circ y$, we are required only to show

$$z = y.$$

By our induction hypothesis $\mathcal{F}[y]$, taking x to be z, it suffices to show that z and y have the same members, that is,

(‡)   (*for all atom u*) $\begin{bmatrix} u \in z \\ \ \ \textit{if and only if} \\ u \in y \end{bmatrix}.$

Because $x' = v \circ z$, we have (by our supposition (†) again, replacing x' with $v \circ z$)

(*for all atom u'*) $\begin{bmatrix} u' \in v \circ z \\ \ \ \textit{if and only if} \\ u' \in v \circ y \end{bmatrix}$

or, equivalently (by the *insertion* axiom for the member relation),

(‡‡)   (*for all atom u'*) $\begin{bmatrix} u' = v \ \ or \ \ u' \in z \\ \ \ \textit{if and only if} \\ u' = v \ \ or \ \ u' \in y \end{bmatrix}.$

We show that this implies the desired result (‡). Consider an arbitrary atom u; we show each direction of (‡) separately.

Suppose that

$$u \in z.$$

Then, (by (‡‡), taking u' to be u) we have

$$u = v \ \ or \ \ u \in y.$$

Because (by our supposition) $u \in z$ and (by the way z was chosen) *not* $(v \in z)$, we have

$$not \ (u = v),$$

and therefore

$$u \in y,$$

as we wanted to show. The proof for the other direction of (‡) is similar. ⌐

In **Problem 10.1(c)**, the reader is requested to prove the *decomposition* property for sets:

$$(\textit{for all set } x) \left[\begin{array}{l} \textit{if } \ not \ (x = \{\,\}) \\ \\ \textit{then} \quad \begin{array}{l} (\textit{for some atom } w) \\ (\textit{for some set } z) \end{array} \left[\begin{array}{l} x = w \circ z \\ \textit{and} \\ not \ (w \in z) \end{array} \right] \end{array} \right] \qquad (\textit{decomposition})$$

10.3 THE CHOICE AND REST FUNCTIONS

Intuitively speaking, for a nonempty set x, the atom $choice(x)$ is an arbitrary member of x, and $rest(x)$ is the set of all the other members of x. The *choice* and *rest* functions are defined by the axioms

$$(\textit{for all set } x) \left[\begin{array}{l} \textit{if } \ not \ (x = \{\,\}) \\ \textit{then} \ \ x = choice(x) \circ rest(x) \end{array} \right] \qquad (\textit{decomposition})$$

$$(\textit{for all set } x) \left[\begin{array}{l} \textit{if } \ not \ (x = \{\,\}) \\ \textit{then} \ \ not \ (choice(x) \in rest(x)) \end{array} \right] \qquad (\textit{nonmember})$$

$$(\textit{for all set } x) \left[\begin{array}{l} \textit{if } \ not \ (x = \{\,\}) \\ \\ \textit{then} \quad \left[\begin{array}{l} atom(choice(x)) \\ \textit{and} \\ set(rest(x)) \end{array} \right] \end{array} \right] \qquad (\textit{sort})$$

From the *decomposition* axiom we can establish the property

$$(\textit{for all set } x) \begin{bmatrix} \textit{if } not\,(x = \{\,\}) \\ \textit{then } choice(x) \in x \end{bmatrix} \qquad\qquad (\textit{member})$$

Note that these axioms do not specify the precise value of *choice*(*x*); they only indicate that it is one of the elements of the set *x*. The *choice* function applied to a given set may yield different elements of the set under different models for the theory. For example, under one model

$$choice(\{\text{A, B}\}) = \text{A} \quad \text{and} \quad rest(\{\text{A, B}\}) = \{\text{B}\},$$

whereas under another model

$$choice(\{\text{A, B}\}) = \text{B} \quad \text{and} \quad rest(\{\text{A, B}\}) = \{\text{A}\}.$$

In other words, there are many functions satisfying the above axioms.

Nevertheless, we include in our theory the *functional-substitutivity* equality axiom schema for *choice* and *rest*, that is,

$$\begin{matrix} (\textit{for all set } x) \\ (\textit{for all set } y) \end{matrix} \begin{bmatrix} \textit{if } x = y \\ \textit{then } choice(x) = choice(y) \end{bmatrix}$$

$$\begin{matrix} (\textit{for all set } x) \\ (\textit{for all set } y) \end{matrix} \begin{bmatrix} \textit{if } x = y \\ \textit{then } rest(x) = rest(y) \end{bmatrix}.$$

In other words, under a given model, if *x* and *y* are equal sets, then *choice*(*x*) and *choice*(*y*) must be equal elements of those sets. For example, under a given model, because {A, B} = {B, A}, we have

$$choice(\{\text{A, B}\}) = choice(\{\text{B, A}\})$$

$$rest(\{\text{A, B}\}) = rest(\{\text{B, A}\}).$$

Remark (independence of axioms)

Some readers may wonder why the *decomposition* axiom above does not suffice to define the *choice* and *rest* functions.

The *nonmember* axiom is essential, for without it we could have models for the theory under which, say, *choice*({A, B}) = A and *rest*({A, B}) = {A, B}. In other words, *rest*(*x*) could be the entire set.

Also, the *sort* axiom is not implied by the *decomposition* axiom. Our axioms for sets do not specify the value of the insertion function *v* ∘ *y* unless *v* is an atom and *y* is a set. In other words, there are bizarre models for the theory under which $v \circ y$ is a set even though v is not an atom or y is not a set. Without the *sort* axiom for *choice* and *rest*, we could have

$$choice(v \circ y) = v \quad \text{and} \quad rest(v \circ y) = y$$

under such a model. ◢

10.4   THE UNION AND INTERSECTION FUNCTIONS

We now define some familiar functions over the sets.

UNION

The binary function symbol $x \cup y$ denotes the *union* of two sets x and y, i.e., the set of atoms belonging to either set; thus

$$\{\text{A, B}\} \cup \{\text{B, C}\} = \{\text{A, B, C}\}.$$

The *union* function is defined by the two axioms

(for all set y) $\left[\{ \} \cup y = y \right]$ *(empty)*

(for all atom u)
  (for all set x) $\left[(u \circ x) \cup y = u \circ (x \cup y) \right]$ *(insertion)*
  (for all set y)

From these axioms we can establish the properties

$$
\begin{array}{l}
\textit{(for all atom u)} \\
\quad \textit{(for all set x)} \\
\quad \textit{(for all set y)}
\end{array}
\left[
\begin{array}{c}
u \in (x \cup y) \\
\textit{if and only if} \\
u \in x \ \textit{or} \ u \in y
\end{array}
\right]
\qquad (\textit{member})
$$

$$
\begin{array}{l}
\textit{(for all set x)} \\
\textit{(for all set y)}
\end{array}
\left[x \cup y = y \cup x \right]
\qquad (\textit{commutativity})
$$

$$
\begin{array}{l}
\textit{(for all set x)} \\
\textit{(for all set y)} \\
\textit{(for all set z)}
\end{array}
\left[(x \cup y) \cup z = x \cup (y \cup z) \right]
\qquad (\textit{associativity})
$$

The proof of the *member* property is left as an exercise (**Problem 10.2**); the *commutativity* and *associativity* of the union function follow directly from this property.

INTERSECTION

The binary function symbol $x \cap y$ denotes the *intersection* of two sets x and y, that is, the set of atoms belonging to both sets; thus

$$\{A,\ B\} \cap \{B,\ C\} \ = \ \{B\}$$

$$\{A,\ B\} \cap \{C\} \ = \ \{\ \}.$$

The intersection function is defined by the axioms

$$(\textit{for all set } y)\big[\{\ \} \cap y \ = \ \{\ \}\big] \qquad\qquad (\textit{empty})$$

$$
(\textit{for all atom } u) \\
\quad (\textit{for all set } x) \\
\quad (\textit{for all set } y)
\left[(u \circ x) \cap y \ = \
\begin{matrix}
\textit{if } u \in y \\
\textit{then } u \circ (x \cap y) \\
\textit{else } x \cap y
\end{matrix}
\right] \qquad (\textit{insertion})
$$

From these axioms we can establish the properties

$$
(\textit{for all atom } u) \\
\quad (\textit{for all set } x) \\
\quad (\textit{for all set } y)
\left[
\begin{matrix}
u \in (x \cap y) \\
\textit{if and only if} \\
u \in x \ \textit{ and } \ u \in y
\end{matrix}
\right] \qquad (\textit{member})
$$

$$
(\textit{for all set } x) \\
(\textit{for all set } y)
\big[x \cap y \ = \ y \cap x \big] \qquad\qquad (\textit{commutativity})
$$

$$
(\textit{for all set } x) \\
(\textit{for all set } y) \\
(\textit{for all set } z)
\big[(x \cap y) \cap z \ = \ x \cap (y \cap z) \big] \qquad (\textit{associativity})
$$

The relationship between the union and intersection functions is given by the following *distributivity* properties:

$$(\textit{for all set } x) \atop (\textit{for all set } y) \atop (\textit{for all set } z) \left[x \cup (y \cap z) \;=\; (x \cup y) \cap (x \cup z) \right]$$

(union over intersection)

$$(\textit{for all set } x) \atop (\textit{for all set } y) \atop (\textit{for all set } z) \left[x \cap (y \cup z) \;=\; (x \cap y) \cup (x \cap z) \right]$$

(intersection over union)

We prove the *member* property for intersection below; the other properties follow directly.

Proposition (member)

The sentence

$$\begin{array}{r} (\textit{for all atom } u) \\ (\textit{for all set } x) \\ (\textit{for all set } y) \end{array} \left[\begin{array}{c} u \in (x \cap y) \\ \textit{if and only if} \\ u \in x \ \textit{ and } \ u \in y \end{array} \right]$$

is valid. ⌟

Proof

For an arbitrary atom u and set y, we prove

$$(\textit{for all set } x) \left[\begin{array}{c} u \in (x \cap y) \\ \textit{if and only if} \\ u \in x \ \textit{ and } \ u \in y \end{array} \right].$$

The proof is by the (modified) induction principle over the sets, taking the inductive sentence to be

$$\mathcal{F}[x]: \quad \begin{array}{c} u \in (x \cap y) \\ \textit{if and only if} \\ u \in x \ \textit{ and } \ u \in y. \end{array}$$

Base Case

We would like to show

$$\mathcal{F}[\{\,\}]: \quad \begin{array}{c} u \in (\{\,\} \cap y) \\ \textit{if and only if} \\ u \in \{\,\} \ \textit{ and } \ u \in y. \end{array}$$

We have

$$u \in (\{\,\} \cap y)$$

precisely when (by the *empty* axiom for intersection)

$$u \in \{\,\}$$

precisely when (by the *empty* axiom for the member relation)

false.

But on the other hand,

$$u \in \{\,\} \quad and \quad u \in y$$

precisely when (by the *empty* axiom for the member relation again)

false and $u \in y$

precisely when (by propositional logic)

false.

Inductive Step

We would like to show

$$(\textit{for all atom } v) \\ (\textit{for all set } x) \left[\begin{array}{l} \textit{if } \ \textit{not } (v \in x) \\ \textit{then } \textit{if } \mathcal{F}[x] \\ \qquad \textit{then } \ \mathcal{F}[v \circ x] \end{array} \right].$$

For an arbitrary atom v and set x, suppose that

$$\textit{not } (v \in x)$$

and assume the induction hypothesis

$$\mathcal{F}[x]: \quad \begin{array}{c} u \in (x \cap y) \\ \textit{if and only if} \\ u \in x \ \ \textit{and} \ \ u \in y. \end{array}$$

We would like to show the desired conclusion

$$\mathcal{F}[v \circ x]: \quad \begin{array}{c} u \in \big((v \circ x) \cap y\big) \\ \textit{if and only if} \\ u \in (v \circ x) \ \ \textit{and} \ \ u \in y. \end{array}$$

The proof distinguishes between two subcases, depending on whether or not $v \in y$.

Case: $v \in y$

Then we have

$$u \in \big((v \circ x) \cap y \big)$$

precisely when (by the *insertion* axiom for intersection, because $v \in y$)

$$u \in \big(v \circ (x \cap y) \big)$$

precisely when (by the *insertion* axiom for the member relation)

$$u = v \ \ or \ \ u \in (x \cap y)$$

precisely when (by our induction hypothesis $\mathcal{F}[x]$)

$$
\begin{array}{l}
u = v \\
\quad or \\
u \in x \ \ and \ \ u \in y.
\end{array}
$$
(†)

But on the other hand,

$$u \in (v \circ x) \ \ and \ \ u \in y$$

precisely when (by the *insertion* axiom for the member relation again)

$$
\begin{array}{l}
u = v \ \ or \ \ u \in x \\
\quad and \\
u \in y
\end{array}
$$

precisely when (by propositional logic)

$$
\begin{array}{l}
u = v \ \ and \ \ u \in y \\
\quad or \\
u \in x \ \ and \ \ u \in y
\end{array}
$$

precisely when (by the substitutivity of equality)

$$
\begin{array}{l}
u = v \ \ and \ \ v \in y \\
\quad or \\
u \in x \ \ and \ \ u \in y
\end{array}
$$

precisely when (since, in this case, $v \in y$)

$$
\begin{array}{l}
u = v \\
\quad or \\
u \in x \ \ and \ \ u \in y,
\end{array}
$$

which is (†).

Case: not $(v \in y)$

Then we have

$$u \in \big((v \circ x) \cap y\big)$$

precisely when (by the *insertion* axiom for intersection, because *not* $(v \in y)$)

$$u \in (x \cap y)$$

precisely when (by our induction hypothesis $\mathcal{F}[x]$)

(‡) $u \in x$ *and* $u \in y$.

But on the other hand,

$$u \in (v \circ x) \ \textit{and} \ u \in y$$

precisely when (by the *insertion* axiom for the member relation)

$$u = v \ \textit{or} \ u \in x$$
$$\textit{and}$$
$$u \in y$$

precisely when (by propositional logic)

$$u = v \ \textit{and} \ u \in y$$
$$\textit{or}$$
$$u \in x \ \textit{and} \ u \in y$$

precisely when (by the substitutivity of equality)

$$u = v \ \textit{and} \ v \in y$$
$$\textit{or}$$
$$u \in x \ \textit{and} \ u \in y$$

precisely when (since, in this case, *not* $(v \in y)$)

$$\textit{false}$$
$$\textit{or}$$
$$u \in x \ \textit{and} \ u \in y$$

precisely when

$$u \in x \ \textit{and} \ u \in y,$$

which is (‡).   ⌟

DISJOINT SETS

Two sets are said to be *disjoint* if their intersection is empty; thus

$\{A, B\}$ and $\{C, D\}$ are disjoint

$\{A, B\}$ and $\{B, C\}$ are not disjoint.

The binary predicate symbol *disjoint*(x, y) is defined accordingly by the axiom

$$(\textit{for all set } x) \atop (\textit{for all set } y) \left[\begin{array}{l} \textit{disjoint}(x, y) \\ \quad \textit{if and only if} \\ (x \cap y) = \{\,\} \end{array} \right] \qquad (\textit{disjoint})$$

From this axiom it is straightforward to prove the property

$$(\textit{for all set } x) \atop (\textit{for all set } y) \left[\begin{array}{l} \textit{disjoint}(x, y) \\ \quad \textit{if and only if} \\ \textit{not (for some atom } u)\left[u \in x \;\; \textit{and} \;\; u \in y\right] \end{array} \right] \qquad (\textit{member})$$

10.5   THE DELETION AND DIFFERENCE FUNCTIONS

We continue to define conventional functions over the sets.

DELETION

The binary function symbol $x - u$ denotes the set obtained by *deleting* the atom u from the set x. If u is not an element of x, then $x - u$ is x itself. For example,

$\{A, B\} \; - \; B \; = \; \{A\}$

$\{A, A, B\} \; - \; A = \{B\}$

$\{A, B\} \; - \; C \; = \; \{A, B\}.$

The deletion function is defined by the axioms

$$(\textit{for all atom } u)\left[\{\,\} - u \; = \; \{\,\}\right] \qquad (\textit{empty})$$

$$\left|\begin{array}{l} \textit{(for all atom } u) \\ \textit{(for all atom } v) \\ \quad \textit{(for all set } x) \end{array}\left[(u \circ x) - v = \begin{array}{l} \textit{if } u = v \\ \textit{then } x - v \\ \textit{else } u \circ (x - v) \end{array}\right]\right| \quad \textit{(insertion)}$$

These axioms suggest a method for computing the deletion function, but it may not be immediately clear that they define the function we have in mind. However, from these axioms we can establish the property

$$\begin{array}{l} \textit{(for all atom } u) \\ \textit{(for all atom } v) \\ \quad \textit{(for all set } x) \end{array}\left[\begin{array}{l} u \in (x - v) \\ \quad \textit{if and only if} \\ u \in x \;\; \textit{and} \;\; \textit{not}\,(u = v) \end{array}\right] \quad \textit{(member)}$$

This property establishes that the function defined by the *empty* and *insertion* axioms actually exhibits the behavior we expect of the deletion function.

We can also establish the following properties of the deletion function:

$$\begin{array}{l} \textit{(for all atom } u) \\ \quad \textit{(for all set } x) \end{array}\left[\begin{array}{l} \textit{if } u \in x \\ \textit{then } x = u \circ (x - u) \end{array}\right] \quad \textit{(decomposition)}$$

$$\begin{array}{l} \textit{(for all atom } u) \\ \quad \textit{(for all set } x) \end{array}\left[\begin{array}{l} \textit{if } \textit{not}\,(u \in x) \\ \textit{then } x = x - u \end{array}\right] \quad \textit{(absorption)}$$

The following property uses the deletion function to relate the *choice* and *rest* functions:

$$\textit{(for all set } x)\left[\begin{array}{l} \textit{if } \textit{not}\,(x = \{\,\}) \\ \textit{then } rest(x) = x - choice(x) \end{array}\right] \quad \textit{(choice rest)}$$

The proofs of the *member* and *choice-rest* properties are left as an exercise (**Problem 10.3**); the other properties follow directly from the *member* property.

DIFFERENCE

Now let us define the binary function symbol $x \sim y$ to denote the set of all elements of the set x that are not members of the set y; thus

$$\{A,\ B\} \sim \{B,\ C\} = \{A\}$$

$$\{A\} \sim \{A,\ B\} = \{\,\}$$

$$\{A,\ B\} \sim \{C,\ D\} = \{A,\ B\}.$$

The difference function is defined by the axioms

$$(\textit{for all set } x)\big[x \sim \{\,\} \;=\; x\big] \qquad\qquad (\textit{right empty})$$

$$(\textit{for all atom } u)$$
$$(\textit{for all set } x)\big[x \sim (u \circ y) \;=\; (x - u) \sim y\big] \qquad (\textit{right insertion})$$
$$(\textit{for all set } y)$$

From these axioms we can establish the property

$$(\textit{for all atom } u) \begin{bmatrix} u \in (x \sim y) \\ \quad \textit{if and only if} \\ u \in x \;\; \textit{and} \;\; \textit{not}\,(u \in y) \end{bmatrix} \qquad (\textit{member})$$
$$(\textit{for all set } x)$$
$$(\textit{for all set } y)$$

This property demonstrates that the function defined by the two axioms actually does exhibit the behavior we expect of the difference function.

10.6   THE SUBSET RELATION

The binary predicate symbol $x \subseteq y$ denotes the subset relation, which is true if every element of the set x is also an element of the set y; thus $\{A,\,B\}$ is a subset of $\{A,\,B,\,C\}$ but not of $\{B,\,C\}$, that is,

$$\{A,\,B\} \subseteq \{A,\,B,\,C\}$$

but

$$\text{not} \quad \{A,\,B\} \subseteq \{B,\,C\}.$$

The subset relation is defined by the axioms

$$(\textit{for all set } y)\big[\{\,\} \subseteq y\big] \qquad\qquad (\textit{left empty})$$

$$(\textit{for all atom } u) \begin{bmatrix} (u \circ x) \subseteq y \\ \quad \textit{if and only if} \\ u \in y \;\; \textit{and} \;\; x \subseteq y \end{bmatrix} \qquad (\textit{left insertion})$$
$$(\textit{for all set } x)$$
$$(\textit{for all set } y)$$

From these axioms we can establish the following property of the subset relation:

$$(\textit{for all set } x) \begin{bmatrix} x \subseteq y \\ \quad \textit{if and only if} \\ (\textit{for all atom } u) \begin{bmatrix} \textit{if } u \in x \\ \textit{then } u \in y \end{bmatrix} \end{bmatrix} \qquad (\textit{member})$$
$$(\textit{for all set } y)$$

This property could be used as an alternative definition of the subset relation. The proof is requested as an exercise (**Problem 10.4**).

Some relationships between the subset relation and the union and intersection functions are expressed in the following properties:

$$(\textit{for all set } x) \left[\begin{array}{c} x \subseteq (x \cup y) \\ \textit{and} \\ y \subseteq (x \cup y) \end{array} \right] \qquad (\textit{union})$$

$$(\textit{for all set } x) \left[\begin{array}{c} (x \cap y) \subseteq x \\ \textit{and} \\ (x \cap y) \subseteq y \end{array} \right] \qquad (\textit{intersection})$$

$$(\textit{for all set } x) \left[\begin{array}{c} x \subseteq y \\ \textit{if and only if} \\ x \cup y \ = \ y \end{array} \right] \qquad (\textit{union absorption})$$

$$(\textit{for all set } x) \left[\begin{array}{c} x \subseteq y \\ \textit{if and only if} \\ x \cap y \ = \ x \end{array} \right] \qquad (\textit{intersection absorption})$$

We can show that the subset relation is a weak partial ordering over the sets; that is,

$$\begin{array}{l} (\textit{for all set } x) \\ (\textit{for all set } y) \\ (\textit{for all set } z) \end{array} \left[\begin{array}{l} \textit{if } x \subseteq y \ \textit{and} \ y \subseteq z \\ \textit{then} \ x \subseteq z \end{array} \right] \qquad (\textit{transitivity})$$

$$\begin{array}{l} (\textit{for all set } x) \\ (\textit{for all set } y) \end{array} \left[\begin{array}{l} \textit{if } x \subseteq y \ \textit{and} \ y \subseteq x \\ \textit{then} \ x = y \end{array} \right] \qquad (\textit{antisymmetry})$$

$$(\textit{for all set } x) \left[x \subseteq x \right] \qquad (\textit{reflexivity})$$

The *proper-subset* relation $x \subset y$ is the irreflexive restriction of the subset relation $x \subseteq y$; that is,

$$\begin{array}{l} (\textit{for all set } x) \\ (\textit{for all set } y) \end{array} \left[\begin{array}{l} x \subset y \\ \textit{if and only if} \\ x \subseteq y \ \textit{and} \ \textit{not} \ (x = y) \end{array} \right] \qquad (\textit{proper subset})$$

It follows that

$$
(\textit{for all set } x) \atop (\textit{for all set } y)
\left[
\begin{array}{l}
x \subset y \\
\quad \textit{if and only if} \\
\left[
\begin{array}{l}
(\textit{for all atom } u)[\textit{if } u \in x \;\; \textit{then } u \in y] \\
\quad \textit{and} \\
(\textit{for some atom } v)\big[v \in y \;\; \textit{and} \;\; \textit{not } (v \in x)\big]
\end{array}
\right]
\end{array}
\right]
\qquad (\textit{member})
$$

In other words, x is a proper subset of y if every member of x is also a member of y but some member of y is not a member of x.

We have remarked that the subset relation $\subseteq$ is a weak partial ordering, and we have defined the proper-subset relation $\subset$ to be the irreflexive restriction of $\subseteq$. Therefore (by the *strict-partial-ordering* proposition of the theory of associated relations) we can conclude that $\subset$ is a strict partial ordering, that is,

$$
(\textit{for all set } x) \atop {(\textit{for all set } y) \atop (\textit{for all set } z)}
\left[
\begin{array}{l}
\textit{if } x \subset y \;\; \textit{and} \;\; y \subset z \\
\textit{then } x \subset z
\end{array}
\right]
\qquad (\textit{transitivity})
$$

$$
(\textit{for all set } x)\big[\textit{not } (x \subset x)\big]
\qquad (\textit{irreflexivity})
$$

Note that the proper-subset relation is not a total relation, i.e., it is possible that, for some sets x and y, neither $x \subset y$ nor $y \subset x$ nor $x = y$. For example, neither $\{A, B\} \subset \{B, C\}$ nor $\{B, C\} \subset \{A, B\}$ nor $\{A, B\} = \{B, C\}$.

For any nonempty set x, the set $rest(x)$ may be shown to be a proper subset of x, that is,

$$
(\textit{for all set } x)
\left[
\begin{array}{l}
\textit{if not } (x = \{\ \}) \\
\textit{then } rest(x) \subset x
\end{array}
\right]
\qquad (\textit{rest})
$$

The proofs of all these properties follow directly from the *member* property of the subset relation.

10.7   THE SET CONSTRUCTOR

For each sentence $\mathcal{F}[u]$ in the theory of sets, we define a unary function symbol

$$
\{u : \; u \in x \;\; \textit{and} \;\; \mathcal{F}[u]\}
$$

to denote the *set-constructor* function, which, for any set x, yields the set of all elements u of x such that $\mathcal{F}[u]$ is true. For example, if our elements are the nonnegative integers and $\mathcal{F}[u]$ is $2 \preceq_{div} u$ ("2 divides u"), then the corresponding set-constructor function is

$$\{u : \ u \in x \ \ and \ \ 2 \preceq_{div} u\},$$

that is, the set of all nonnegative integers in x which are divisible by 2. In particular, if x is the set $\{1, 2, 3, 4\}$, the constructor function yields the set $\{2, 4\}$.

The set-constructor function is defined by the following two axiom schemata:

For each sentence $\mathcal{F}[u]$, the universal closure of the sentence

$$\{u : \ u \in \{\,\} \ \ and \ \ \mathcal{F}[u]\} \ = \ \{\,\} \qquad (empty)$$

is an axiom.

For each sentence $\mathcal{F}[u]$, the universal closure of the sentence

$$(for\ all\ atom\ v) \atop (for\ all\ set\ x)} \left[\begin{array}{l} \{u : \ u \in (v \circ x) \ \ and \ \ \mathcal{F}[u]\} \\[2mm] = \left[\begin{array}{l} if\ \mathcal{F}[v] \\ then\ v \circ \{u : \ u \in x \ \ and \ \ \mathcal{F}[u]\} \\ else\ \{u : \ u \in x \ \ and \ \ \mathcal{F}[u]\} \end{array} \right] \\ \hfill (insertion) \end{array} \right]$$

is an axiom.

In giving the definition of the set constructor, we are not introducing the new construct $\{u : \ \dots \}$ into our language. Actually, for a given sentence $\mathcal{F}[u]$, the set constructor $\{u : \ u \in x \ \ and \ \ \mathcal{F}[u]\}$ is a conventional notation for a unary function symbol of predicate logic, such as $f_{17}(x)$; for a different sentence $\mathcal{F}[u]$, there will correspond a different function symbol, say, $f_{21}(x)$. Thus for each sentence $\mathcal{F}[u]$, there is a different unary function symbol $f_i(x)$ in the corresponding instance of the axiom schemata.

Because x is a finite set in the theory of sets, the condition $u \in x$ in the set constructor $\{u : \ u \in x \ \ and \ \ \mathcal{F}[u]\}$ ensures that the collection of elements it describes is also a finite set in our theory. Otherwise, one could write $\{u : true\}$, for example, which describes the set of all the atoms in our domain, which is not necessarily a finite set.

We can establish the following property of the set constructor:

For each sentence $\mathcal{F}[u]$, the universal closure of the sentence

$$(for\ all\ atom\ v) \atop (for\ all\ set\ x)} \left[\begin{array}{c} v \in \{u : \ u \in x \ \ and \ \ \mathcal{F}[u]\} \\ if\ and\ only\ if \\ v \in x \ \ and \ \ \mathcal{F}[v] \end{array} \right] \qquad (member)$$

is valid. For example, if $\mathcal{F}[u]$ is taken to be the sentence $u = w$, the property tells us that

$$\begin{array}{l}(\textit{for all } w) \\ (\textit{for all atom } v) \\ (\textit{for all set } x)\end{array} \left[\begin{array}{l} v \in \{u : u \in x \ \textit{ and } \ u = w\} \\ \quad \textit{if and only if} \\ v \in x \ \textit{ and } \ v = w \end{array}\right].$$

The quantifier (*for all w*) appears because the property refers to the universal closure of the sentence.

The *member* property can actually be taken as an alternative definition of the set constructor (**Problem 10.5**).

We can immediately establish the following simple properties of the set constructor:

$$(\textit{for all set } x)\left[\{u : u \in x \ \textit{ and } \ true\} \ = \ x\right] \qquad (\textit{true})$$

$$(\textit{for all set } x)\left[\{u : u \in x \ \textit{ and } \ false\} \ = \ \{\,\}\right] \qquad (\textit{false})$$

Alternative definitions for some of the functions of set theory can be given in terms of the set constructor:

$$\begin{array}{l}(\textit{for all set } x) \\ (\textit{for all set } y)\end{array}\left[x \cap y \ = \ \{u : u \in x \ \textit{ and } \ u \in y\}\right] \qquad (\textit{intersection})$$

$$\begin{array}{l}(\textit{for all set } x) \\ (\textit{for all atom } v)\end{array}\left[x - v \ = \ \{u : u \in x \ \textit{ and } \ not \ (u = v)\}\right] \qquad (\textit{deletion})$$

$$\begin{array}{l}(\textit{for all set } x) \\ (\textit{for all set } y)\end{array}\left[x \sim y \ = \ \{u : u \in x \ \textit{ and } \ not \ (u \in y)\}\right] \qquad (\textit{difference})$$

We can also establish the following properties of the set constructor:

$$(\textit{for all set } x) \left[\begin{array}{l} \{u : u \in x \ \textit{ and } \ (\mathcal{F}[u] \ \textit{ or } \ \mathcal{G}[u])\} \\ \\ = \begin{array}{l} \{u : u \in x \ \textit{ and } \ \mathcal{F}[u]\} \\ \cup \\ \{u : u \in x \ \textit{ and } \ \mathcal{G}[u]\} \end{array} \end{array}\right] \qquad (\textit{or})$$

$$(\textit{for all set } x) \left[\begin{array}{l} \{u : u \in x \ \textit{ and } \ (\mathcal{F}[u] \ \textit{ and } \ \mathcal{G}[u])\} \\ \\ = \begin{array}{l} \{u : u \in x \ \textit{ and } \ \mathcal{F}[u]\} \\ \cap \\ \{u : u \in x \ \textit{ and } \ \mathcal{G}[u]\} \end{array} \end{array}\right] \qquad (\textit{and})$$

The proofs are omitted.

10.8 CARDINALITY

In a combined theory of nonnegative integers and sets, we introduce the unary function symbol $card(x)$ to denote the *cardinality* of a set x, that is, the number of (distinct) elements it contains. For example, $card(\{A, B\}) = card(\{A, A, B\}) = 2$.

The cardinality function is defined by the following axioms:

$$card(\{\,\}) = 0 \qquad\qquad (empty)$$

$$(for\ all\ atom\ u)\ \begin{bmatrix} if\ not\ (u \in x) \\ (for\ all\ set\ x)\ \end{bmatrix} \begin{bmatrix} \\ then\ card(u \circ x) = card(x) + 1 \end{bmatrix} \qquad (insertion)$$

Note that the *insertion* axiom specifies the value of $card(u \circ x)$ only for the case in which $not\ (u \in x)$. No axiom is required for the alternate case, in which $u \in x$, because we can establish the property

$$(for\ all\ atom\ u)\ \begin{bmatrix} if\ u \in x \\ (for\ all\ set\ x)\ \end{bmatrix}\begin{bmatrix} \\ then\ card(u \circ x) = card(x) \end{bmatrix} \qquad (absorption)$$

This is because, in the case in which $u \in x$, we have (by the *absorption* property of the insertion function) $u \circ x = x$.

We can also establish the following properties of the cardinality function:

$$(for\ all\ set\ x)\big[integer(card(x))\big] \qquad\qquad (sort)$$

$$(for\ all\ set\ x)\ \begin{bmatrix} card(x \cap y) \le card(x) \\ (for\ all\ set\ y)\ \end{bmatrix}\begin{bmatrix} and \\ card(x \cap y) \le card(y) \end{bmatrix} \qquad (intersection)$$

$$\begin{matrix}(for\ all\ set\ x) \\ (for\ all\ set\ y)\end{matrix}\big[card(x \cup y) + card(x \cap y)\ =\ card(x) + card(y)\big]$$

$$(union)$$

$$(for\ all\ set\ x)\ \begin{bmatrix} if\ x \subset y \\ (for\ all\ set\ y)\ \end{bmatrix}\begin{bmatrix} \\ then\ card(x) < card(y) \end{bmatrix} \qquad (proper\ subset)$$

The proof of the *sort* property is straightforward. The proofs of the *intersection* and *proper-subset* properties we leave as an exercise (**Problem 10.6**); let us prove the *union* property here.

Proposition (union)

The sentence

$$\begin{matrix}(for\ all\ set\ x)\\(for\ all\ set\ y)\end{matrix}\Big[card(x \cup y) + card(x \cap y) \;=\; card(x) + card(y)\Big]$$

is valid.   ⌟

Proof

For an arbitrary set y, we prove

$$(for\ all\ set\ x)\Big[card(x \cup y) + card(x \cap y) \;=\; card(x) + card(y)\Big]$$

by the (modified) induction principle over the sets, on x. We take the inductive sentence to be

$$\mathcal{F}[x]: \quad card(x \cup y) + card(x \cap y) \;=\; card(x) + card(y).$$

Base Case

We would like to show

$$\mathcal{F}[\{\ \}]: \quad card(\{\ \} \cup y) + card(\{\ \} \cap y) \;=\; card(\{\ \}) + card(y).$$

But this follows from the *empty* axioms for union and intersection and the commutativity of addition.

Inductive Step

We would like to show

$$\begin{matrix}(for\ all\ atom\ u)\\(for\ all\ set\ x)\end{matrix}\begin{bmatrix}if\ \ not\ (u \in x)\\then\ \ if\ \mathcal{F}[x]\\\qquad then\ \ \mathcal{F}[u \circ x]\end{bmatrix}.$$

Consider an arbitrary atom u and set x such that

$$not\ (u \in x),$$

and assume as our induction hypothesis that

$$\mathcal{F}[x]: \quad card(x \cup y) + card(x \cap y) \;=\; card(x) + card(y).$$

We would like to establish the desired conclusion that

$$\mathcal{F}[u \circ x]: \quad \begin{matrix}card\big((u \circ x) \cup y\big) + card\big((u \circ x) \cap y\big) \;=\;\\ card(u \circ x) + card(y).\end{matrix}$$

We know (by the *insertion* property for union) that

$$card\big((u \circ x) \cup y\big) \;=\; card\big(u \circ (x \cup y)\big).$$

Also (by the *insertion* property for cardinality, because $not(u \in x)$) we have $card(u \circ x) = card(x) + 1$. Therefore to establish $\mathcal{F}[u \circ x]$, it suffices to show that

$$(*) \qquad card\big(u \circ (x \cup y)\big) + card\big((u \circ x) \cap y\big) \;=\; card(x) + card(y) + 1.$$

Our proof distinguishes between two subcases, depending on whether or not $u \in y$.

Case: $u \in y$

Then (by the *member* property of the union function)

$$u \in (x \cup y)$$

and hence (by the *absorption* property of the insertion function)

$$u \circ (x \cup y) \;=\; x \cup y.$$

Note also that (by the *member* property of the intersection function, because $not\,(u \in x)$)

$$not\,\big(u \in (x \cap y)\big).$$

To show $(*)$, we have

$$card\big(u \circ (x \cup y)\big) \;+\; card\big((u \circ x) \cap y\big)$$

$$\begin{aligned}
&= \; card(x \cup y) \;+\; card\big((u \circ x) \cap y\big) \\
&\qquad \text{(because } u \circ (x \cup y) = x \cup y) \\[4pt]
&= \; card(x \cup y) \;+\; card\big(u \circ (x \cap y)\big) \\
&\qquad \text{(by the \textit{insertion} property of intersection,} \\
&\qquad \text{because } u \in y) \\[4pt]
&= \; card(x \cup y) \;+\; card(x \cap y) \;+\; 1 \\
&\qquad \text{(by the \textit{insertion} property of cardinality,} \\
&\qquad \text{because } not\,\big(u \in (x \cap y)\big)) \\[4pt]
&= \; card(x) \;+\; card(y) \;+\; 1 \\
&\qquad \text{(by our induction hypothesis } \mathcal{F}[x]),
\end{aligned}$$

as we wanted to show.

Case: $not\,(u \in y)$

Then (by the *member* property of union, because also $not\,(u \in x)$) we have

$$not\,\big(u \in (x \cup y)\big).$$

To show $(*)$, we have

$$card\big(u \circ (x \cup y)\big) + card\big((u \circ x) \cap y\big)$$

$$= card(x \cup y) + card\big((u \circ x) \cap y\big) + 1$$
(by the *insertion* axiom for cardinality,
because *not* $\big(u \in (x \cup y)\big)$)

$$= card(x \cup y) + card(x \cap y) + 1$$
(by the *insertion* axiom for intersection,
because *not* $(u \in y)$)

$$= card(x) + card(y) + 1$$
(by our induction hypothesis $\mathcal{F}[x]$),

as we wanted to show. ⌐

10.9   SINGLETON SETS

A set with precisely one element is called a *singleton*; thus $\{A\}$ is a singleton but
$\{\,\}$ and $\{A, B\}$ are not.

We introduce a unary predicate symbol $sing(x)$, to denote the relation that
is true if the set x is a singleton. This singleton relation is defined by the axiom

$$(for\ all\ set\ x) \left[\begin{array}{l} sing(x) \\ \quad if\ and\ only\ if \\ (for\ some\ atom\ u)\big[x = u \circ \{\,\}\big] \end{array} \right] \qquad (singleton)$$

From this axiom we can establish the following property of the singleton
relation:

$$(for\ all\ set\ x) \left[\begin{array}{l} sing(x) \\ \quad if\ and\ only\ if \\ not\ (x = \{\,\})\ \ and\ \ rest(x) = \{\,\} \end{array} \right] \qquad (rest)$$

In the combined theory of nonnegative integers and sets, we can also establish
the property

$$(for\ all\ set\ x) \left[\begin{array}{l} sing(x) \\ \quad if\ and\ only\ if \\ card(x) = 1 \end{array} \right] \qquad (cardinality)$$

The proofs of the *rest* and *cardinality* properties are left as an exercise (**Problem 10.7**).

PROBLEMS

Problem 10.1 (decomposition)   pages 478, 481

Prove the following properties of the sets:

(a) *Member decomposition*

$$(for\ all\ atom\ w)\ (for\ all\ set\ x)\ \begin{bmatrix} if\ w \in x \\ then\ (for\ some\ set\ z) \begin{bmatrix} x = w \circ z \\ and \\ not\ (w \in z) \end{bmatrix} \end{bmatrix}$$

(b) *Nonempty member*

$$(for\ all\ set\ x)\ \begin{bmatrix} not\ (x = \{\ \}) \\ if\ and\ only\ if \\ (for\ some\ atom\ u)[u \in x] \end{bmatrix}$$

(c) *Decomposition*

$$(for\ all\ set\ x)\ \begin{bmatrix} if\ not\ (x = \{\ \}) \\ then\ \begin{matrix} (for\ some\ atom\ w) \\ (for\ some\ set\ z) \end{matrix} \begin{bmatrix} x = w \circ z \\ and \\ not\ (w \in z) \end{bmatrix} \end{bmatrix}.$$

Problem 10.2 (union)   page 484

Establish the *member* property of the union function, that is,

$$(for\ all\ atom\ u)\ (for\ all\ set\ x)\ (for\ all\ set\ y)\ \begin{bmatrix} u \in (x \cup y) \\ if\ and\ only\ if \\ u \in x\ \ or\ \ u \in y \end{bmatrix}.$$

Problem 10.3 (deletion)   page 490

Establish the following properties of the deletion function:

(a) *Member*

$$(for\ all\ atom\ u) \begin{bmatrix} u \in (x - v) \\ \quad if\ and\ only\ if \\ u \in x\ \ and\ \ not\ (u = v) \end{bmatrix}$$
$$(for\ all\ atom\ v)$$
$$(for\ all\ set\ x)$$

(b) *Choice rest*

$$(for\ all\ set\ x) \begin{bmatrix} if\ not\ (x\ =\ \{\ \}) \\ then\ \ rest(x)\ =\ x - choice(x) \end{bmatrix}.$$

Problem 10.4 (subset relation)   page 492

Establish the following property of the subset relation:

(a) *Member*

$$(for\ all\ set\ x) \begin{bmatrix} x \subseteq y \\ \quad if\ and\ only\ if \\ (for\ all\ atom\ u) \begin{bmatrix} if\ u \in x \\ then\ \ u \in y \end{bmatrix} \end{bmatrix}.$$
$$(for\ all\ set\ y)$$

Show that the above *member* property could be taken as an alternative definition of the subset relation. In other words, taking this property as the axiom, establish the validity of the following properties of the subset relation:

(b) *Left empty*

$$(for\ all\ set\ y) \begin{bmatrix} \{\ \} \subseteq y \end{bmatrix}$$

(c) *Left insertion*

$$(for\ all\ atom\ u) \begin{bmatrix} (u \circ x) \subseteq y \\ \quad if\ and\ only\ if \\ u \in y\ \ and\ \ x \subseteq y \end{bmatrix}.$$
$$(for\ all\ set\ x)$$
$$(for\ all\ set\ y)$$

Problem 10.5 (set constructor)   page 495

Establish the following property of the set constructor:

(a) *Member*

For each sentence $\mathcal{F}[u]$, the universal closure of the sentence

$$(for\ all\ atom\ v) \begin{bmatrix} v \in \{u:\ \ u \in x\ \ and\ \ \mathcal{F}[u]\} \\ \quad if\ and\ only\ if \\ v \in x\ \ and\ \ \mathcal{F}[v] \end{bmatrix}$$
$$(for\ all\ set\ x)$$

is valid.

Show that the *member* property could be taken as an alternative definition of the set constructor. In other words, taking this property as the axiom, establish the following properties of the set constructor:

(b) *Empty*

For each sentence $\mathcal{F}[u]$, the universal closure of the sentence

$$\{u: \ u \in \{\} \ and \ \mathcal{F}[u]\} \ = \ \{\}$$

is valid.

(c) *Insertion*

For each sentence $\mathcal{F}[u]$, the universal closure of the sentence

$$(for\ all\ atom\ v) \\ (for\ all\ set\ x) \left[\begin{array}{l} \{u: \ u \in (v \circ x) \ and \ \mathcal{F}[u]\} \\ = \left[\begin{array}{l} if\ \mathcal{F}[v] \\ then\ v \circ \{u: \ u \in x \ and \ \mathcal{F}[u]\} \\ else\ \{u: \ u \in x \ and \ \mathcal{F}[u]\} \end{array} \right] \end{array} \right]$$

is valid.

Problem 10.6 (cardinality)   page 496

Establish the following properties of the cardinality function:

(a) *Intersection*

$$(for\ all\ set\ x) \\ (for\ all\ set\ y) \left[\begin{array}{l} card(x \cap y) \le card(x) \\ and \\ card(x \cap y) \le card(y) \end{array} \right]$$

(b) *Proper subset*

$$(for\ all\ set\ x) \\ (for\ all\ set\ y) \left[\begin{array}{l} if\ x \subset y \\ then\ .card(x) < card(y) \end{array} \right]_{.}$$

List whatever properties of the nonnegative integers you require; you need not prove them. Of course, you should state and prove whatever new properties of the sets you use.

Problem 10.7 (singleton)   page 500

Establish the following properties of the singleton relation:

(a) *Rest*

$$(for\ all\ set\ x) \left[\begin{array}{l} sing(x) \\ \quad if\ and\ only\ if \\ not\ (x = \{\ \}) \ \ and\ \ rest(x) = \{\ \} \end{array} \right]$$

(b) *Cardinality*

$$(for\ all\ set\ x) \left[\begin{array}{l} sing(x) \\ \quad if\ and\ only\ if \\ card(x) = 1 \end{array} \right].$$

11

Bags

In the theory of sets we consider two sets to be equal if they contain the same elements, regardless of their order and multiplicity. We are about to introduce a theory of (finite) bags, which is analogous to the theory of sets.

A bag is a finite collection of elements, called *atoms*, in which we disregard the order of occurrence of the elements, but regard the multiplicity (i.e., the number of occurrences) of each element as significant. In other words, we consider two bags to be equal if they contain the same elements, regardless of their order, but we insist that all elements have the same multiplicity in each bag.

Thus while the bag [[A, A, B]] is considered to be equal to the bag [[B, A, A]], we distinguish between the bag [[A, B, B]], in which B occurs twice, and the bag [[A, B]], in which B occurs only once. This is the only difference between sets and bags; bags are therefore sometimes called *multisets*.

As in the theory of sets, the collection of atoms may be finite or infinite, but we consider only finite bags. Because the theory of bags so closely resembles the theory of sets, we shall be rather brisk in our presentation, emphasizing the differences between the two theories.

11.1 BASIC PROPERTIES

The vocabulary of the theory of bags consists of

- A constant symbol [[ ]], denoting the *empty bag*

- A unary predicate symbol $atom(x)$

- A unary predicate symbol $bag(x)$

- A binary function symbol $u \circ x$, denoting the *insertion* function

- A binary predicate symbol $u \in x$, denoting the *member* relation.

These symbols are analogous to their set-theoretic counterparts.

Notations such as $[\![A]\!]$ and $[\![A, B]\!]$ are informal and are not part of the language of the theory. Under a particular model for the theory, if the terms s and t denote the atoms A and B, respectively, then $s \circ [\![\ ]\!]$ denotes the bag we express informally as $[\![A]\!]$, and $s \circ (t \circ [\![\ ]\!])$ denotes the bag we express informally as $[\![A, B]\!]$.

The theory of bags is a theory with equality and the following axioms:

- The *generation* axioms

$$bag([\![\ ]\!]) \qquad\qquad\qquad\qquad\qquad\qquad\qquad (empty)$$

$$(for\ all\ atom\ u) \atop (for\ all\ bag\ x) \Big[bag(u \circ x) \Big] \qquad\qquad\qquad (insertion)$$

- The *member* axioms

$$(for\ all\ atom\ u) \Big[not\ \big(u \in [\![\ ]\!]\big) \Big] \qquad\qquad\qquad (empty)$$

$$\begin{matrix} (for\ all\ atom\ u) \\ (for\ all\ atom\ v) \\ (for\ all\ bag\ x) \end{matrix} \begin{bmatrix} u \in (v \circ x) \\ \quad if\ and\ only\ if \\ u = v\ \ or\ \ u \in x \end{bmatrix} \qquad (insertion)$$

- The *uniqueness* axiom

For bags, in contrast with sets, we do have a uniqueness axiom:

$$\begin{matrix} (for\ all\ atom\ u) \\ (for\ all\ bag\ x) \\ (for\ all\ bag\ y) \end{matrix} \begin{bmatrix} if\ u \circ x = u \circ y \\ then\ \ x = y \end{bmatrix} \qquad (insertion)$$

- The *equality* axiom

The equality relation $=$ is assumed to satisfy an additional axiom

$$\begin{matrix} (for\ all\ atom\ u) \\ (for\ all\ atom\ v) \\ (for\ all\ bag\ x) \end{matrix} \Big[u \circ (v \circ x)\ =\ v \circ (u \circ x) \Big] \qquad (exchange)$$

This axiom expresses that the order of the elements in a bag is irrelevant. In contrast with sets, we do not have a *multiplicity* equality axiom for bags.

- The *induction* principle

For each sentence $\mathcal{F}[x]$ in the theory, the universal closure of the sentence

$$
if \left[\begin{array}{l} \mathcal{F}[\![\,]\!] \\ \quad and \\ (for\ all\ atom\ u) \left[\begin{array}{l} if\ \ \mathcal{F}[x] \\ then\ \ \mathcal{F}[u \odot x] \end{array}\right] \\ then\ (for\ all\ bag\ x)\mathcal{F}[x], \end{array}\right. \qquad (induction)
$$

where u does not occur free in $\mathcal{F}[x]$, is an axiom.

From these axioms, we can establish the familiar *decomposition* property,

$$
(for\ all\ bag\ x) \left[\begin{array}{l} if\ not\ (x = [\![\,]\!]) \\ then \quad \begin{array}{l}(for\ some\ atom\ u) \\ (for\ some\ bag\ y)\end{array} [x\ =\ u \odot y] \end{array}\right] \qquad (decomposition)
$$

We can also establish the same uniqueness property we had for sets:

$$
\begin{array}{l}(for\ all\ atom\ u) \\ (for\ all\ bag\ x)\end{array} \left[not\ (u \odot x = [\![\,]\!])\right] \qquad (empty\ uniqueness)
$$

Finally, we can establish a basic property:

$$
\begin{array}{l}(for\ all\ atom\ u) \\ (for\ all\ bag\ x)\end{array} \left[\begin{array}{l} if\ u \in x \\ then\ (for\ some\ bag\ y)[x\ =\ u \odot y] \end{array}\right]
$$
$$
(member\ decomposition)
$$

The proofs are the same as the corresponding proofs for sets.

Now let us augment the theory of bags by defining some additional relations and functions.

11.2   THE EQUAL-MULTIPLICITY RELATION

The ternary predicate symbol *eqmult*(u, x, y) denotes the *equal-multiplicity* relation, which holds if the atom u has the same number of occurrences in the bag x

and in the bag y. Thus

$$eqmult\big(\text{A}, [\![\text{A, B}]\!], [\![\text{A, B, B}]\!]\big) \quad \text{is true,}$$

because there is one occurrence of A in $[\![\text{A, B}]\!]$ and one in $[\![\text{A, B, B}]\!]$; on the other hand,

$$eqmult\big(\text{B}, [\![\text{A, B}]\!], [\![\text{A, B, B}]\!]\big) \quad \text{is false,}$$

because there is one occurrence of B in $[\![\text{A, B}]\!]$, but two in $[\![\text{A, B, B}]\!]$.

The *eqmult* relation is defined by the following six axioms:

$$\boxed{(\textit{for all atom } u)\big[eqmult(u, [\![\,]\!], [\![\,]\!])\big] \qquad\qquad (\textit{empty})}$$

In other words, any atom has the same multiplicity in two empty bags.

$$\boxed{\begin{array}{l}(\textit{for all atom } u)\\ (\textit{for all bag } y)\end{array}\big[not\ (eqmult(u, [\![\,]\!], u \odot y))\big] \quad (\textit{empty insertion})}$$

$$\boxed{\begin{array}{l}(\textit{for all atom } u)\\ (\textit{for all bag } x)\end{array}\big[not\ (eqmult(u, u \odot x, [\![\,]\!]))\big] \quad (\textit{insertion empty})}$$

In other words, no atom u has the same multiplicity in the empty bag $[\![\,]\!]$ and a bag $[\![u, \dots]\!]$ containing u itself.

$$\boxed{\begin{array}{l}(\textit{for all atom } u)\\ (\textit{for all atom } v)\\ (\textit{for all bag } x)\\ (\textit{for all bag } y)\end{array}\left[\begin{array}{c}eqmult(u,\ v \odot x,\ v \odot y)\\ \textit{if and only if}\\ eqmult(u,\ x,\ y)\end{array}\right] \qquad (\textit{equal insertion})}$$

In other words, an atom u has the same multiplicity in two bags $v \odot x$ and $v \odot y$ precisely when u has the same multiplicity in x and y.

$$\boxed{\begin{array}{l}(\textit{for all atom } u)\\ (\textit{for all atom } v)\\ (\textit{for all bag } x)\\ (\textit{for all bag } y)\end{array}\left[\begin{array}{l}\textit{if not } (u = v)\\ \quad\left[\begin{array}{c}eqmult(u,\ v \odot x,\ y)\\ \textit{if and only if}\\ eqmult(u,\ x,\ y)\end{array}\right]\\ \textit{then}\end{array}\right] \qquad (\textit{left insertion})}$$

$$\boxed{\begin{array}{l}(\textit{for all atom } u)\\ (\textit{for all atom } v)\\ (\textit{for all bag } x)\\ (\textit{for all bag } y)\end{array}\left[\begin{array}{l}\textit{if not } (u = v)\\ \quad\left[\begin{array}{c}eqmult(u,\ x,\ v \odot y)\\ \textit{if and only if}\\ eqmult(u,\ x,\ y)\end{array}\right]\\ \textit{then}\end{array}\right] \qquad (\textit{right insertion})}$$

In other words, in comparing the multiplicity of an atom u in two bags we can disregard any elements of the bags that are distinct from u.

These axioms suggest a method for computing the *eqmult* relation; we illustrate this with an example.

Example (computation of eqmult)

Suppose we would like to determine whether the element A has the same multiplicity in the bags $[\![$B, A, A, C$]\!]$ and $[\![$A, B, A$]\!]$. Then we have

$$eqmult\big(\text{A},\ [\![\text{B, A, A, C}]\!],\ [\![\text{A, B, A}]\!]\big),$$

that is,

$$eqmult\big(\text{A},\ \text{B} \odot (\text{A} \odot (\text{A} \odot (\text{C} \odot [\![\ ]\!]))),\ \text{A} \odot (\text{B} \odot (\text{A} \odot [\![\ ]\!])))\big)$$

precisely when (by the *left-insertion* axiom, because *not* (A = B))

$$eqmult\big(\text{A},\ \text{A} \odot (\text{A} \odot (\text{C} \odot [\![\ ]\!])),\ \text{A} \odot (\text{B} \odot (\text{A} \odot [\![\ ]\!])))\big)$$

precisely when (by the *equal-insertion* axiom)

$$eqmult\big(\text{A},\ \text{A} \odot (\text{C} \odot [\![\ ]\!]),\ \text{B} \odot (\text{A} \odot [\![\ ]\!]))\big)$$

precisely when (by the *right-insertion* axiom, because *not*(A = B))

$$eqmult\big(\text{A},\ \text{A} \odot (\text{C} \odot [\![\ ]\!]),\ \text{A} \odot [\![\ ]\!])\big)$$

precisely when (by the *equal-insertion* axiom again)

$$eqmult\big(\text{A},\ \text{C} \odot [\![\ ]\!],\ [\![\ ]\!]\big)$$

precisely when (by the *left-insertion* axiom, because *not*(A = C))

$$eqmult\big(\text{A},\ [\![\ ]\!],\ [\![\ ]\!]\big),$$

which is true (by the *empty* axiom). ⌐

From the axioms for the *eqmult* relation we can establish the following properties:

$$\begin{array}{l}(\textit{for all atom } u)\\ (\textit{for all bag } x)\\ (\textit{for all bag } y)\end{array}\begin{bmatrix}\textit{eqmult}(u,\ x,\ y)\\ \quad \textit{if and only if}\\ \textit{eqmult}(u,\ y,\ x)\end{bmatrix} \qquad (\textit{symmetry})$$

$$\begin{array}{l}(\textit{for all atom } u)\\ (\textit{for all bag } x)\end{array}\big[\textit{eqmult}(u,\ x,\ x)\big] \qquad (\textit{reflexivity})$$

$$\begin{array}{l}(\textit{for all atom } u)\\ (\textit{for all bag } x)\\ (\textit{for all bag } y)\end{array}\begin{bmatrix}\textit{if } \textit{eqmult}(u,\ x,\ y)\\ \textit{then} \begin{bmatrix}u \in x\\ \quad \textit{if and only if}\\ u \in y\end{bmatrix}\end{bmatrix} \qquad (\textit{member})$$

$$\begin{array}{l}(\textit{for all atom } u)\\ (\textit{for all bag } x)\\ (\textit{for all bag } y)\end{array}\begin{bmatrix}\textit{if not } (u \in x)\\ \textit{then} \begin{bmatrix}\textit{eqmult}(u,\ x,\ y)\\ \quad \textit{if and only if}\\ \textit{not } (u \in y)\end{bmatrix}\end{bmatrix} \qquad (\textit{nonmember})$$

We show the *symmetry* property below; the proofs of the other three properties are left as an exercise (**Problem 11.1**).

Proposition (**symmetry**)

The sentence

$$\begin{array}{l}(\textit{for all atom } u)\\ (\textit{for all bag } x)\\ (\textit{for all bag } y)\end{array}\begin{bmatrix}\textit{eqmult}(u,\ x,\ y)\\ \quad \textit{if and only if}\\ \textit{eqmult}(u,\ y,\ x)\end{bmatrix} \qquad (\textit{symmetry})$$

is valid. ┘

The proof illustrates "double induction": an induction within an induction.

Proof

Consider an arbitrary atom u; we would like to show

$$\begin{array}{l}(\textit{for all bag } x)\\ (\textit{for all bag } y)\end{array}\begin{bmatrix}\textit{eqmult}(u,\ x,\ y)\\ \quad \textit{if and only if}\\ \textit{eqmult}(u,\ y,\ x)\end{bmatrix}.$$

The proof is by induction on x, taking the inductive sentence to be

$$\mathcal{F}[x]: \quad (\text{for all bag } y) \left[\begin{array}{c} eqmult(u, \ x, \ y) \\ \textit{if and only if} \\ eqmult(u, \ y, \ x) \end{array} \right].$$

Base Case for $\mathcal{F}[x]$

We would like to show

$$\mathcal{F}[\![\ ]\!]: \quad (\text{for all bag } y) \left[\begin{array}{c} eqmult\big(u, \ [\![\ ]\!], \ y\big) \\ \textit{if and only if} \\ eqmult\big(u, \ y, \ [\![\ ]\!]\big) \end{array} \right].$$

The proof of $\mathcal{F}[\![\ ]\!]$ is itself by induction on y, taking the inductive sentence to be

$$\mathcal{G}[y]: \quad \begin{array}{c} eqmult\big(u, \ [\![\ ]\!], \ y\big) \\ \textit{if and only if} \\ eqmult\big(u, \ y, \ [\![\ ]\!]\big). \end{array}$$

Base Subcase for $\mathcal{G}[y]$

We would like to show

$$\mathcal{G}[\![\ ]\!]: \quad \begin{array}{c} eqmult\big(u, \ [\![\ ]\!], \ [\![\ ]\!]\big) \\ \textit{if and only if} \\ eqmult\big(u, \ [\![\ ]\!], \ [\![\ ]\!]\big), \end{array}$$

which is true by propositional logic.

Inductive Substep for $\mathcal{G}[y]$

Consider an arbitrary atom v and bag y, and assume the induction hypothesis

$$\mathcal{G}[y]: \quad \begin{array}{c} eqmult\big(u, \ [\![\ ]\!], \ y\big) \\ \textit{if and only if} \\ eqmult\big(u, \ y, \ [\![\ ]\!]\big). \end{array}$$

We would like to establish the desired conclusion

$$\mathcal{G}[v \odot y]: \quad \begin{array}{c} eqmult\big(u, \ [\![\ ]\!], \ v \odot y\big) \\ \textit{if and only if} \\ eqmult\big(u, \ v \odot y, \ [\![\ ]\!]\big). \end{array}$$

In the case in which $u = v$, the left- and right-hand sides of the above equivalence are both false (by the *empty-insertion* and *insertion-empty* axioms for *eqmult*); therefore the entire equivalence is true.

In the case in which *not* $(u = v)$, the desired conclusion $\mathcal{G}[v \circ y]$ holds precisely when (by the *right*- and *left-insertion* axioms for *eqmult*)

$$eqmult(u, \; [\![\;]\!], \; y)$$
$$\textit{if and only if}$$
$$eqmult(u, \; y, \; [\![\;]\!]),$$

which is exactly our induction hypothesis $\mathcal{G}[y]$.

Inductive Step for $\mathcal{F}[x]$

Consider an arbitrary atom w and bag x, and assume the induction hypothesis

$$\mathcal{F}[x]: \quad (\textit{for all bag } y) \begin{bmatrix} eqmult(u, \; x, \; y) \\ \textit{if and only if} \\ eqmult(u, \; y, \; x) \end{bmatrix}.$$

We would like to establish the desired conclusion that

$$\mathcal{F}[w \circ x]: \quad (\textit{for all bag } z) \begin{bmatrix} eqmult(u, \; w \circ x, \; z) \\ \textit{if and only if} \\ eqmult(u, \; z, \; w \circ x) \end{bmatrix}.$$

The proof of $\mathcal{F}[w \circ x]$ is itself by induction on z, taking the inductive sentence to be

$$\mathcal{H}[z]: \quad \begin{array}{c} eqmult(u, \; w \circ x, \; z) \\ \textit{if and only if} \\ eqmult(u, \; z, \; w \circ x) \end{array}.$$

Base Subcase for $\mathcal{H}[z]$

We would like to show

$$\mathcal{H}[[\![\;]\!]]: \quad \begin{array}{c} eqmult(u, \; w \circ x, \; [\![\;]\!]) \\ \textit{if and only if} \\ eqmult(u, \; [\![\;]\!], \; w \circ x) \end{array}.$$

In the case in which $u = w$, the left- and right-hand side of the above equivalence are both false (by the *insertion-empty* and the *empty-insertion* axioms for *eqmult*); therefore the entire equivalence is true.

In the case in which *not* $(u = w)$, the desired conclusion $\mathcal{H}[[\![\;]\!]]$ holds precisely when (by the *left*- and *right-insertion* axioms for *eqmult*)

$$eqmult(u, \; x, \; [\![\;]\!])$$
$$\textit{if and only if}$$
$$eqmult(u, \; [\![\;]\!], \; x),$$

which is true by our induction hypothesis $\mathcal{F}[x]$ (taking y to be $[\![\,]\!]$).

Inductive Substep for $\mathcal{H}[z]$

Consider an arbitrary atom t and bag z and assume the induction hypothesis

$$\mathcal{H}[z]: \qquad \begin{array}{c} eqmult(u,\ w \circ x,\ z) \\ \textit{if and only if} \\ eqmult(u,\ z,\ w \circ x) \end{array}$$

We would like to show the desired conclusion

$$\mathcal{H}[t \circ z]: \qquad \begin{array}{c} eqmult(u,\ w \circ x,\ t \circ z) \\ \textit{if and only if} \\ eqmult(u,\ t \circ z,\ w \circ x) \end{array}$$

The proof distinguishes among three cases, depending on whether

$$not\ (u = w),$$

$$not\ (u = t),$$

or

$$u = w \ \textit{and} \ u = t.$$

Subcase: $not\ (u = w)$

Then our desired conclusion $\mathcal{H}[t \circ z]$ is true precisely when (by the *left-* and *right-insertion* axioms for *eqmult*)

$$\begin{array}{c} eqmult(u,\ x,\ t \circ z) \\ \textit{if and only if} \\ eqmult(u,\ t \circ z,\ x), \end{array}$$

which follows from our main induction hypothesis $\mathcal{F}[x]$ (taking y to be $t \circ z$).

Subcase: $not\ (u = t)$

Then our desired conclusion $\mathcal{H}[t \circ z]$ is true precisely when (by the *right-* and *left-insertion* axioms for *eqmult*)

$$\begin{array}{c} eqmult(u,\ w \circ x,\ z) \\ \textit{if and only if} \\ eqmult(u,\ z,\ w \circ x), \end{array}$$

which is exactly our induction hypothesis $\mathcal{H}[z]$.

Subcase: $u = w$ *and* $u = t$

Then our desired conclusion $\mathcal{H}[t \circ z]$, that is (in this case),

> $eqmult(u, \ u \circ x, \ u \circ z)$
>   *if and only if*
> $eqmult(u, \ u \circ z, \ u \circ x)$,

is true precisely when (by the *equal-insertion* axiom for *eqmult*)

> $eqmult(u, \ x, \ z)$
>   *if and only if*
> $eqmult(u, \ z, \ x)$,

which follows from our main induction hypothesis $\mathcal{F}[x]$ (taking y to be z).

Remark (double induction)

The above proof illustrates the use of a "double induction": In establishing both the base case and the inductive step of the main induction proof, we are required to invoke two subsidiary applications of the induction principle. Let us recapitulate the proof schematically.

We first attempted to prove a sentence of form

$$\genfrac{}{}{0pt}{}{(for\ all\ bag\ x)}{(for\ all\ bag\ y)}\mathcal{E}[x, \ y]$$

by induction on x.

The proof of the base case

$$(for\ all\ bag\ y)\mathcal{E}\left[[\![\ ]\!], \ y\right]$$

was itself by induction on y.

In proving the inductive step we considered an arbitrary atom w and bag x, assumed the induction hypothesis

$$(for\ all\ bag\ y)\mathcal{E}[x, \ y],$$

and attempted to prove the desired conclusion

$$(for\ all\ bag\ z)\mathcal{E}[w \circ x, \ z].$$

The proof of the desired conclusion was itself by induction on z. In the inductive step of this proof we could take advantage of both the induction hypothesis $(for\ all\ bag\ y)\mathcal{E}[x, \ y]$ of the main inductive step and the induction hypothesis $\mathcal{E}[w \circ x, \ z]$ of the subsidiary induction step.

11.3   MULTIPLICITY AND EQUALITY

The equality relation between bags may be characterized in terms of the equal-multiplicity relation as follows:

Proposition (equal-multiplicity)

The sentence

$$(\textit{for all bag } x)\ (\textit{for all bag } y)\ \begin{bmatrix} x = y \\ \textit{if and only if} \\ (\textit{for all atom } u)\,[\textit{eqmult}(u,\ x,\ y)] \end{bmatrix}\quad (\textit{equal-multiplicity})$$

is valid. ⌐

In other words, two bags are equal precisely when they have the same members, each with the same multiplicity. This is the fundamental property of bag equality.

Proof

The proof is by induction on x (over the bags), taking the inductive sentence to be

$$\mathcal{F}[x]:\quad (\textit{for all bag } y)\ \begin{bmatrix} x = y \\ \textit{if and only if} \\ (\textit{for all atom } u)\,[\textit{eqmult}(u,\ x,\ y)] \end{bmatrix}.$$

Base Case

We would like to show

$$\mathcal{F}[\![\,]\!]:\quad (\textit{for all bag } y)\ \begin{bmatrix} [\![\,]\!] = y \\ \textit{if and only if} \\ (\textit{for all atom } u)\,[\textit{eqmult}(u,\ [\![\,]\!],\ y)] \end{bmatrix}.$$

Consider an arbitrary bag y. We show separately

(†) $\textit{if } [\![\,]\!] = y$
         $\textit{then } (\textit{for all atom } u)\,[\textit{eqmult}(u,\ [\![\,]\!],\ y)]$

and

(‡) $\textit{if not } ([\![\,]\!] = y)$
         $\textit{then not } (\textit{for all atom } u)\,[\textit{eqmult}(u,\ [\![\,]\!],\ y)].$

To show (†), suppose

$$[\![\,]\!] = y.$$

Then (by the *empty* axiom for *eqmult*)

$$(\textit{for all atom } u)[\textit{eqmult}(u, \; [\![\,]\!], \; y)],$$

as we wanted to show.

To show (‡), suppose

$$\textit{not} \; ([\![\,]\!] = y);$$

then (by the *decomposition* property) there is an atom v and a bag z such that

$$y \; = \; v \odot z.$$

We have (by the *empty-insertion* axiom for *eqmult*)

$$\textit{not} \; \big(\textit{eqmult}(v, \; [\![\,]\!], \; v \odot z)\big)$$

and hence

$$\textit{not}\big(\textit{eqmult}(v, \; [\![\,]\!], \; y)\big).$$

We therefore obtain

$$(\textit{for some atom } u)\big[\textit{not} \; (\textit{eqmult}(u, \; [\![\,]\!], \; y))\big],$$

taking u to be v, and (by the duality between the quantifiers)

$$\textit{not} \; (\textit{for all atom } u)\big[\textit{eqmult}(u, \; [\![\,]\!], \; y)\big],$$

as we wanted to show.

Inductive Step

We would like to show

$$(\textit{for all atom } v) \; \begin{bmatrix} \textit{if} \;\; \mathcal{F}[x] \\ (\textit{for all bag } x) \begin{bmatrix} \textit{then} \;\; \mathcal{F}[v \odot x] \end{bmatrix} \end{bmatrix}.$$

Consider an arbitrary atom v and bag x and assume the induction hypothesis

$$\mathcal{F}[x]: \quad (\textit{for all bag } y) \begin{bmatrix} x = y \\ \textit{if and only if} \\ (\textit{for all atom } u)[\textit{eqmult}(u, \; x, \; y)] \end{bmatrix}.$$

We would like to establish the desired conclusion

$$\mathcal{F}[v \odot x]: \quad (\textit{for all bag } y') \begin{bmatrix} v \odot x = y' \\ \textit{if and only if} \\ (\textit{for all atom } u)[\textit{eqmult}(u, \; v \odot x, \; y')] \end{bmatrix}.$$

Consider an arbitrary bag y'. We establish separately the two conditions

(††)   *if* $v \circ x = y'$
          then $(for\ all\ atom\ u)[eqmult(u,\ v \circ x,\ y')]$

and

(‡‡)   *if* $(for\ all\ atom\ u)[eqmult(u,\ v \circ x,\ y')]$
          then $v \circ x = y'$.

To show (††), suppose that

$$v \circ x = y'.$$

Then (by the *reflexivity* property of *eqmult*)

$$(for\ all\ atom\ u)[eqmult(u,\ v \circ x,\ v \circ x)],$$

that is,

$$(for\ all\ atom\ u)[eqmult(u,\ v \circ x,\ y')],$$

as we wanted to show.

To show (‡‡), suppose

(∗) $(for\ all\ atom\ u)[eqmult(u,\ v \circ x,\ y')].$

We would like to show

$$v \circ x \ = \ y'.$$

By our supposition (∗) we have (taking u to be v)

$$eqmult(v,\ v \circ x,\ y').$$

Therefore (by the *member* property of *eqmult*)

$$v \in v \circ x \ \ if\ and\ only\ if\ \ v \in y'.$$

Because (by the *insertion* axiom for the member relation)

$$v \in v \circ x,$$

we may conclude that

$$v \in y'.$$

Then (by the *member-decomposition* property) there exists a bag y such that

$$y' \ = \ v \circ y.$$

By our supposition $(*)$ we have

$$(\textit{for all atom } u)\big[eqmult(u, \ v \circ x, \ v \circ y)\big].$$

Therefore (by the *equal-insertion* axiom for *eqmult*)

$$(\textit{for all atom } u)\big[eqmult(u, \ x, \ y)\big].$$

Hence (by our induction hypothesis $\mathcal{F}[x]$)

$$x = y$$

and, consequently,

$$v \circ x = v \circ y.$$

In other words (because $y' = v \circ y$),

$$v \circ x = y',$$

as we wanted to show. ⌐

We have characterized the equality relation between bags in terms of the equal-multiplicity relation. In **Problem 11.2**, we characterize the equality relation in terms of a new function.

11.4   THE COUNT FUNCTION

It is now convenient to combine the theory of bags with the theory of nonnegative integers and define a binary function symbol $count(u, x)$, denoting the *multiplicity* (i.e., the number of occurrences) of the atom u in the bag x; thus

$$count\big(\text{A}, \ [\![\text{A}, \ \text{A}, \ \text{B}]\!]\big) = 2 \quad \text{and} \quad count\big(\text{C}, \ [\![\text{A}, \ \text{A}, \ \text{B}]\!]\big) = 0.$$

Many properties of the other functions and relations of bag theory can be expressed in terms of this multiplicity function.

The multiplicity function *count* is defined in a combined theory of nonnegative integers and bags by the following axioms:

$$(for\ all\ atom\ u)\big[count(u,\ [\![\,]\!]) \,=\, 0\big] \qquad\qquad (empty)$$

$$\begin{array}{l}(for\ all\ atom\ u)\\ \quad(for\ all\ bag\ x)\end{array}\Big[count(u,\ u{\circ}x) \;=\; count(u, x){+}1\Big] \ (equal\ insertion)$$

$$\begin{array}{l}(for\ all\ atom\ u)\\ \quad(for\ all\ atom\ v)\\ \quad\quad(for\ all\ bag\ x)\end{array}\left[\begin{array}{l}if\ not\ (u = v)\\ then\ \ count(u,\ v \circ x) \;=\; count(u,\ x)\end{array}\right]$$

$$(nonequal\ insertion)$$

From these axioms, we can establish the usual *sort* property for the multiplicity function *count*, that is,

$$\begin{array}{l}(for\ all\ atom\ u)\\ \quad(for\ all\ bag\ x)\end{array}\Big[integer\big(count(u,\ x)\big)\Big] \qquad\qquad (sort)$$

We may characterize other bag relations in terms of the multiplicity function *count*:

• The member relation

$$\begin{array}{l}(for\ all\ atom\ u)\\ \quad(for\ all\ bag\ x)\end{array}\left[\begin{array}{l}u \in x\\ \quad if\ and\ only\ if\\ not\big(count(u,\ x) = 0\big)\end{array}\right] \qquad (count\ of\ member)$$

• The equal-multiplicity relation

$$\begin{array}{l}(for\ all\ atom\ u)\\ \quad(for\ all\ bag\ x)\\ \quad\quad(for\ all\ bag\ y)\end{array}\left[\begin{array}{l}eqmult(u,\ x,\ y)\\ \quad if\ and\ only\ if\\ count(u,\ x) = count(u,\ y)\end{array}\right] \qquad (count\ of\ eqmult)$$

• The equality relation

$$\begin{array}{l}(for\ all\ bag\ x)\\ \quad(for\ all\ bag\ y)\end{array}\left[\begin{array}{l}x = y\\ \quad if\ and\ only\ if\\ (for\ all\ atom\ u)\big[count(u,\ x) \;=\; count(u,\ y)\big]\end{array}\right]$$

$$(count\ of\ equality)$$

The proof of the *count* property of the equal-multiplicity relation *eqmult* is requested in **Problem 11.3**.

11.5   ADDITIONAL FUNCTIONS AND RELATIONS

In this section we augment the theory of bags by defining new functions and relations analogous to those we have introduced for sets.

THE CHOICE AND REST FUNCTIONS

For a nonempty bag x, $choice(x)$ is an arbitrary element of x, and $rest(x)$ is the bag of all occurrences of remaining elements of x. They are defined by the axioms

$$
(\textit{for all bag } x) \begin{bmatrix} \textit{if } \textit{not } (x = [\![\,]\!]) \\ \textit{then } x \ = \ choice(x) \circ rest(x) \end{bmatrix} \qquad (\textit{decomposition})
$$

$$
(\textit{for all bag } x) \begin{bmatrix} \textit{if } \textit{not } (x = [\![\,]\!]) \\ \textit{then } atom\big(choice(x)\big) \\ \textit{and} \\ bag\big(rest(x)\big) \end{bmatrix} \qquad (\textit{sort})
$$

Recall that in the theory of sets we had an additional *nonmember* axiom for *choice* and *rest*, stating that, for every nonempty set x, $not\,\big(choice(x) \in rest(x)\big)$. This is not true for bags; for example, if $x = [\![A, A, B]\!]$ and $choice(x) = A$, then $rest(x) = [\![A, B]\!]$.

From these axioms we can establish the property

$$
(\textit{for all bag } x) \begin{bmatrix} \textit{if } \textit{not } (x = [\![\,]\!]) \\ \textit{then } choice(x) \in x \end{bmatrix} \qquad (\textit{member})
$$

THE SUBBAG RELATION

The binary predicate symbol $x \subseteq y$ denotes the *subbag* relation, which holds if, for each occurrence of an element in the bag x, there corresponds a distinct occurrence of the same element in the bag y. Thus

$$[\![A, B]\!] \ \subseteq \ [\![A, A, B, C]\!]$$

but

$$not \quad [\![A, B, B]\!] \ \subseteq \ [\![A, A, B, C]\!].$$

The subbag relation is defined by the following axioms:

$$(\textit{for all bag } y)\Big[\![\,]\!] \subseteq y\Big] \qquad\qquad (\textit{empty})$$

$$\begin{array}{l}(\textit{for all atom } u)\\(\textit{for all bag } x)\\(\textit{for all bag } y)\end{array}\left[\begin{array}{l}(u \circ x) \subseteq (u \circ y)\\ \quad \textit{if and only if}\\ x \subseteq y\end{array}\right] \qquad (\textit{equal insertion})$$

$$\begin{array}{l}(\textit{for all atom } u)\\(\textit{for all bag } x)\\(\textit{for all bag } y)\end{array}\left[\begin{array}{l}\textit{if } (u \circ x) \subseteq y\\ \textit{then } u \in y\end{array}\right] \qquad\qquad (\textit{member})$$

We can characterize the subbag relation in terms of the multiplicity function *count* by the property (**Problem 11.4**):

$$\begin{array}{l}(\textit{for all bag } x)\\(\textit{for all bag } y)\end{array}\left[\begin{array}{l}x \subseteq y\\ \quad \textit{if and only if}\\ (\textit{for all atom } u)\big[count(u,\, x) \leq count(u,\, y)\big]\end{array}\right] \quad (\textit{count})$$

Therefore we may characterize the equality relation in terms of the subbag relation as follows:

$$\begin{array}{l}(\textit{for all bag } x)\\(\textit{for all bag } y)\end{array}\left[\begin{array}{l}x = y\\ \quad \textit{if and only if}\\ x \subseteq y \ \textit{ and } \ y \subseteq x\end{array}\right] \qquad\qquad (\textit{subbag})$$

The subbag relation can be shown to be a weak partial ordering. Its irreflexive restriction, the *proper-subbag* relation $x \subset y$, defined by the axiom

$$\begin{array}{l}(\textit{for all bag } x)\\(\textit{for all bag } y)\end{array}\left[\begin{array}{l}x \subset y\\ \quad \textit{if and only if}\\ x \subseteq y \ \textit{ and } \ \textit{not } (x = y)\end{array}\right] \qquad (\textit{proper subbag})$$

is then a strict partial ordering.

For any nonempty bag x, the bag $rest(x)$ may be shown to be a proper subbag of x; that is,

$$(\textit{for all bag } x)\left[\begin{array}{l}\textit{if } \textit{not } (x = [\![\,]\!])\\ \textit{then } \ rest(x) \subset x\end{array}\right] \qquad\qquad (\textit{rest})$$

11.6   SUM, UNION, AND INTERSECTION

We now define some functions over the bags.

THE SUM FUNCTION

The binary function symbol $x \oplus y$ denotes the *sum* of the two bags x and y. The number of occurrences of an atom u in $x \oplus y$ is the numerical sum of the number of occurrences of u in x and the number of occurrences of u in y; thus

$$[\![A, B, B]\!] \oplus [\![A, C]\!] \;=\; [\![A, A, B, B, C]\!].$$

The sum function is defined by the two axioms

$$(\textit{for all bag } y)\Big[[\![\;]\!] \oplus y \;=\; y\Big] \qquad\qquad\qquad (\textit{left empty})$$

$$\begin{array}{l}(\textit{for all atom } u)\\\quad(\textit{for all bag } x)\\\quad(\textit{for all bag } y)\end{array}\Big[(u \circ x) \oplus y \;=\; u \circ (x \oplus y)\Big] \qquad (\textit{left insertion})$$

We can characterize the sum function in terms of the multiplicity function *count* by the property

$$\begin{array}{l}(\textit{for all atom } u)\\\quad(\textit{for all bag } x)\\\quad(\textit{for all bag } y)\end{array}\Big[count(u, \, x \oplus y) \;=\; count(u, \, x) + count(u, \, y)\Big] \quad (\textit{count})$$

The proof is requested in **Problem 11.5(a)**.

THE UNION FUNCTION

The binary function symbol $x \cup y$ denotes the *union* of the two bags x and y. The number of occurrences of an atom u in the union $x \cup y$ is the maximum of the number of occurrences of u in x and the number of occurrences of u in y. For example,

$$[\![A, A, B, B]\!] \cup [\![A, B, C]\!] \;=\; [\![A, A, B, B, C]\!].$$

In contrast, for the sum function,

$$[\![A, A, B, B]\!] \oplus [\![A, B, C]\!] \;=\; [\![A, A, A, B, B, B, C]\!].$$

The union function is defined by the axioms

$$(\textit{for all bag } y)\left[\llbracket \; \rrbracket \cup y \; = \; y\right] \qquad\qquad (\textit{left empty})$$

$$\begin{array}{l}(\textit{for all atom } u)\\ \quad (\textit{for all bag } x)\\ \quad (\textit{for all bag } y)\end{array}\left[\begin{array}{l}(u \circ x) \; \cup \; (u \circ y) \; =\\ u \circ (x \cup y)\end{array}\right] \qquad (\textit{member insertion})$$

$$\begin{array}{l}(\textit{for all atom } u)\\ \quad (\textit{for all bag } x)\\ \quad (\textit{for all bag } y)\end{array}\left[\begin{array}{l}\textit{if } \; not \, (u \in y)\\ \textit{then } \, (u \circ x) \; \cup \; y \; =\\ \qquad u \circ (x \cup y)\end{array}\right] \qquad (\textit{nonmember insertion})$$

We can characterize the union function in terms of the multiplicity function *count* by the property

$$\begin{array}{l}(\textit{for all atom } u)\\ \quad (\textit{for all bag } x)\\ \quad (\textit{for all bag } y)\end{array}\left[\begin{array}{l}count(u, \; x \cup y)\\ =\\ max\big(count(u, \; x), \; count(u, \; y)\big)\end{array}\right] \qquad (\textit{count})$$

The proof is requested in **Problem 11.5(b)**.

THE INTERSECTION FUNCTION

The binary function symbol $x \cap y$ denotes the *intersection* of the two bags x and y. The number of occurrences of an atom u in the intersection $x \cap y$ is the minimum of the number of occurrences of u in x and the number of occurrences of u in y. For example,

$$\llbracket A, \; A, \; B, \; B \rrbracket \cap \llbracket A, \; B, \; C \rrbracket \; = \; \llbracket A, \; B \rrbracket.$$

The intersection function is defined by the axioms

$$(\textit{for all bag } y)\left[\llbracket \; \rrbracket \cap y \; = \; \llbracket \; \rrbracket\right] \qquad\qquad (\textit{left empty})$$

$$\begin{array}{l}(\textit{for all atom } u)\\ \quad (\textit{for all bag } x)\\ \quad (\textit{for all bag } y)\end{array}\left[(u \circ x) \cap (u \circ y) \; = \; u \circ (x \cap y)\right] \; (\textit{member insertion})$$

$$\begin{array}{l}(\textit{for all atom } u)\\ \quad (\textit{for all bag } x)\\ \quad (\textit{for all bag } y)\end{array}\left[\begin{array}{l}\textit{if } \; not \, (u \in y)\\ \textit{then } \, (u \circ x) \cap y \; = \; x \cap y\end{array}\right] \; (\textit{nonmember insertion})$$

We can characterize the intersection function in terms of the multiplicity function by the property

$$
\begin{array}{l}
(\textit{for all atom } u) \\
\quad (\textit{for all bag } x) \\
\quad (\textit{for all bag } y)
\end{array}
\Big[count(u,\ x \cap y)\ =\ min\big(count(u,\ x),\ count(u,\ y)\big)\Big]
$$

$$(\textit{count})$$

The proof is requested in **Problem 11.5(c)**.

Many of the properties of the set-theoretic union and intersection functions also hold for their bag-theoretic counterparts. The characterization of these functions in terms of the multiplicity function *count* is instrumental in many of these proofs. We illustrate one such proof.

Proposition (distributivity)

The sentence

$$
\begin{array}{l}
(\textit{for all bag } x) \\
(\textit{for all bag } y) \\
(\textit{for all bag } z)
\end{array}
\left[
\begin{array}{c}
x \cap (y \cup z) \\
= \\
(x \cap y) \cup (x \cap z)
\end{array}
\right]
\qquad (\textit{intersection over union})
$$

is valid. ⏌

Proof

The proof requires no induction. Consider arbitrary bags x, y, and z; we would like to show that

$$x \cap (y \cup z)\ =\ (x \cap y) \cup (x \cap z).$$

It suffices (by the *count* characterization of the equality relation) to prove

$$(\textit{for all atom } u)\ \Big[count\big(u,\ x \cap (y \cup z)\big)\ =\ count\big(u,\ (x \cap y) \cup (x \cap z)\big)\Big].$$

Consider an arbitrary atom u. Then we have

$$count\big(u,\ x \cap (y \cup z)\big)$$

$$= min\big(count(u,\ x),\ count(u,\ y \cup z)\big)$$
(by the *count* characterization of the intersection function)

$$= min\Big(count(u,\ x),\ max\big(count(u,\ y),\ count(u,\ z)\big)\Big)$$
(by the *count* characterization of the union function).

But on the other hand,

$$count(u, \ (x \cap y) \cup (x \cap z))$$

$$= max(count(u, \ x \cap y), \ count(u, \ x \cap z))$$
(by the *count* characterization of the union function)

$$= max \begin{pmatrix} min(count(u, \ x), \ count(u, \ y)), \\ min(count(u, \ x), \ count(u, \ z)) \end{pmatrix}$$
(by the *count* characterization of the intersection function)

$$= min\Big(count(u, \ x), \ max(count(u, \ y), \ count(u, \ z))\Big)$$
(by the *minimax* property of the maximum and minimum functions). ◢

PROBLEMS

Problem 11.1 (equal multiplicity)   page 510

Establish the validity of the following properties of the equal-multiplicity relation *eqmult*:

(a)   *Reflexivity*

$$\begin{matrix} (for \ all \ atom \ u) \\ (for \ all \ bag \ x) \end{matrix} \Big[eqmult(u, \ x, \ x) \Big]$$

(b)   *Member*

$$\begin{matrix} (for \ all \ atom \ u) \\ (for \ all \ bag \ x) \\ (for \ all \ bag \ y) \end{matrix} \begin{bmatrix} if \ eqmult(u, \ x, \ y) \\ then \quad \begin{bmatrix} u \in x \\ \quad if \ and \ only \ if \\ u \in y \end{bmatrix} \end{bmatrix}$$

(c)   *Nonmember*

$$\begin{matrix} (for \ all \ atom \ u) \\ (for \ all \ bag \ x) \\ (for \ all \ bag \ y) \end{matrix} \begin{bmatrix} if \ not \ (u \in x) \\ then \quad \begin{bmatrix} eqmult(u, \ x, \ y) \\ \quad if \ and \ only \ if \\ not \ (u \in y) \end{bmatrix} \end{bmatrix}.$$

Problem 11.2 (extract)   page 518

Suppose we augment our theory of bags by introducing a binary function symbol *extract*(*u*, *x*) to denote the function which, for any atom *u* and bag *x*, extracts from *x* the subbag consisting of all occurrences of *u* in *x*. Thus

$$extract(\text{A}, \ [\![\text{A}, \text{B}, \text{A}, \text{C}]\!]) \ = \ [\![\text{A}, \text{A}]\!].$$

The *extract* function is defined by the following axioms:

$$(for\ all\ atom\ u)\big[extract(u,\ [\![\ ]\!]) = [\![\ ]\!]\big] \qquad\qquad (empty)$$

$$\begin{array}{l}(for\ all\ atom\ u)\\ (for\ all\ bag\ x)\end{array}\Big[extract(u,\ u \circ x) = u \circ extract(u,\ x)\Big] \qquad (same)$$

$$\begin{array}{l}(for\ all\ atom\ u)\\ (for\ all\ atom\ v)\\ (for\ all\ bag\ x)\end{array}\left[\begin{array}{l}if\ not\ (u = v)\\ then\ extract(u,\ v \circ x) = extract(u,\ x)\end{array}\right] \quad (distinct)$$

(a) Establish the following *member* property of the *extract* function:

$$\begin{array}{l}(for\ all\ atom\ u)\\ (for\ all\ bag\ x)\end{array}\left[\begin{array}{l}if\ not\ (u \in x)\\ then\ extract(u,\ x) = [\![\ ]\!]\end{array}\right].$$

(b) Show that the equality relation between bags can be characterized in terms of the *extract* function. In other words, establish the following *extract* property of the equality relation:

$$\begin{array}{l}(for\ all\ bag\ x)\\ (for\ all\ bag\ y)\end{array}\left[\begin{array}{l}x = y\\ \quad if\ and\ only\ if\\ (for\ all\ atom\ u)\big[extract(u,\ x) = extract(u,\ y)\big]\end{array}\right].$$

As usual, you may use the appropriate *sort* property of the *extract* function without proof.

Problem 11.3 (equal multiplicity and count)   page 519

Prove the property that characterizes the equal-multiplicity relation *eqmult* in terms of the multiplicity function *count*, that is,

$$\begin{array}{l}(for\ all\ atom\ u)\\ (for\ all\ bag\ x)\\ (for\ all\ bag\ y)\end{array}\left[\begin{array}{l}eqmult(u,\ x,\ y)\\ \quad if\ and\ only\ if\\ count(u,\ x) \ = \ count(u,\ y)\end{array}\right].$$

Problem 11.4 (subbag) page 521

Prove the property that characterizes the subbag relation $\subseteq$ in terms of the multiplicity function *count*, that is,

$$\begin{array}{l} (\textit{for all bag } x) \\ (\textit{for all bag } y) \end{array} \left[\begin{array}{l} x \subseteq y \\ \quad \textit{if and only if} \\ (\textit{for all atom } u)\,[count(u,\ x) \leq count(u,\ y)] \end{array} \right].$$

Problem 11.5 (sum, union, and intersection) pages 522–524

Prove the properties that characterize the sum function $\oplus$, the union function $\cup$, and the intersection functions $\cap$ in terms of the multiplicity function *count*, that is,

(a) *Sum*

$$\begin{array}{l} (\textit{for all atom } u) \\ \quad (\textit{for all bag } x) \\ \quad (\textit{for all bag } y) \end{array} \Big[count(u,\ x \oplus y) \ = \ count(u,\ x) + count(u,\ y) \Big]$$

(b) *Union*

$$\begin{array}{l} (\textit{for all atom } u) \\ \quad (\textit{for all bag } x) \\ \quad (\textit{for all bag } y) \end{array} \Big[count(u,\ x \cup y) \ = \ max\big(count(u,\ x),\ count(u,\ y)\big) \Big]$$

(c) *Intersection*

$$\begin{array}{l} (\textit{for all atom } u) \\ \quad (\textit{for all bag } x) \\ \quad (\textit{for all bag } y) \end{array} \Big[count(u,\ x \cap y) \ = \ min\big(count(u,\ x),\ count(u,\ y)\big) \Big].$$

You may use whatever properties of the nonnegative integers you need without proof.

12

Tuples

In this chapter we introduce a very simple and fundamental theory, the theory of tuples. Intuitively speaking, a tuple is a finite collection of elements, called *atoms*, in which we regard both the order of the elements and their multiplicity as significant. Thus we regard

$$\langle A, B \rangle, \quad \langle B, A \rangle \quad \text{and} \quad \langle A, A, B \rangle$$

as distinct tuples. As usual, the set of atoms may be either finite or infinite, but each tuple must be finite.

We can consider bags to be tuples in which we disregard the order of the elements; similarly, we can consider sets to be tuples in which we disregard the order and the multiplicity of the elements.

The theory of tuples is simpler than the theory of lists, in that the elements of a tuple must all be atoms, while the elements of a list may be either atoms or other lists; thus $\langle \langle A \rangle, B \rangle$ is not a tuple. The theory of tuples is similar to the theory of strings, except that we do not identify a tuple of a single element with the element itself; thus the tuple $\langle A \rangle$ is distinct from the atom A.

Sections 12.1 through 12.6 describe fundamental properties and applications of the theory; Section 12.7 describes a more advanced and theoretical topic, which may be omitted on first reading.

12.1 BASIC PROPERTIES

Let us give a brisk outline of the theory here. The vocabulary of the theory of tuples consists of

- A constant symbol $\langle\ \rangle$, denoting the *empty tuple*

- A unary predicate symbol $atom(x)$

- A unary predicate symbol $tuple(x)$

- A binary function symbol $u \diamond x$, denoting the *insertion* function.

These notions are analogous to their counterparts in the theories of sets and bags. Again notations such as $\langle A, B \rangle$ are informal and are not part of the language.

The theory of tuples is a theory with equality having the following special axioms:

- The *generation* axioms

$$tuple(\langle\ \rangle) \qquad\qquad (empty)$$

$$(\textit{for all atom } u)(\textit{for all tuple } x)\Big[tuple(u \diamond x)\Big] \qquad (insertion)$$

- The *uniqueness* axioms

$$\begin{matrix}(\textit{for all atom } u)\\(\textit{for all tuple } x)\end{matrix}\Big[not\ (u \diamond x = \langle\ \rangle)\Big] \qquad\qquad (empty)$$

$$\begin{matrix}(\textit{for all atom } u)(\textit{for all tuple } x)\\(\textit{for all atom } v)(\textit{for all tuple } y)\end{matrix}\begin{bmatrix}\textit{if } u \diamond x = v \diamond y\\\textit{then } u = v \ \ \textit{and} \ \ x = y\end{bmatrix}(insertion)$$

- The *induction* principle

For each sentence $\mathcal{F}[x]$ in the theory, the universal closure of the sentence

$$if\ \begin{bmatrix}\mathcal{F}[\langle\ \rangle]\\ \quad and\\(\textit{for all atom } u)\begin{bmatrix}\textit{if } \mathcal{F}[x]\\\textit{then } \mathcal{F}[u \diamond x]\end{bmatrix}\\ \quad \quad (\textit{for all tuple } x)\end{bmatrix} \qquad (induction)$$

$$then\ (\textit{for all tuple } x)\mathcal{F}[x],$$

where u does not occur free in $\mathcal{F}[x]$, is an axiom.

Note that the axioms for tuples are the same as the axioms for the strings, except for changes in notation and the absence of an analog to the *character* axioms for strings.

From the basic axioms for tuples, we can establish the familiar property,

$$(for\ all\ tuple\ x) \left[\begin{array}{l} if\ not\ (x = \langle\,\rangle) \\ then\ \begin{array}{l} (for\ some\ atom\ u) \\ (for\ some\ tuple\ y) \end{array} \left[x = u \diamond y \right] \end{array} \right] \qquad (decomposition)$$

We can augment our theory by introducing additional relations and functions.

THE MEMBER RELATION

The binary predicate symbol $u \in x$ denotes the *member* relation, which indicates that the atom u is one of the elements of the tuple x; it is defined by the axioms

$$(for\ all\ atom\ u) \left[not\ (u \in \langle\,\rangle) \right] \qquad (empty)$$

$$\begin{array}{l} (for\ all\ atom\ u) \\ (for\ all\ atom\ v) \\ (for\ all\ tuple\ x) \end{array} \left[\begin{array}{l} u \in (v \diamond x) \\ \quad if\ and\ only\ if \\ u = v\ \ or\ \ u \in x \end{array} \right] \qquad (insertion)$$

THE APPEND FUNCTION

The binary function symbol $x \diamond y$ denotes the *append* function, which yields the tuple whose elements are the elements of the tuple x followed by the elements of the tuple y; thus

$$\langle A,\ B \rangle \diamond \langle B,\ C \rangle \ = \ \langle A,\ B,\ B,\ C \rangle.$$

The append function is defined by the axioms

$$(for\ all\ tuple\ y) \left[\langle\,\rangle \diamond y \ = \ y \right] \qquad (left\ empty)$$

$$\begin{array}{l} (for\ all\ atom\ u) \\ (for\ all\ tuple\ x) \\ (for\ all\ tuple\ y) \end{array} \left[(u \diamond x) \diamond y \ = \ u \diamond (x \diamond y) \right] \qquad (left\ insertion)$$

From these axioms we can establish the following properties:

$$(for\ all\ tuple\ x)\big[x \diamond \langle\ \rangle\ =\ x\big] \qquad\qquad (right\ empty)$$

$$\begin{array}{l}(for\ all\ tuple\ x)\\(for\ all\ tuple\ y)\\(for\ all\ tuple\ z)\end{array}\big[(x \diamond y) \diamond z\ =\ x \diamond (y \diamond z)\big] \qquad (associativity)$$

$$\begin{array}{l}(for\ all\ atom\ u)\\(for\ all\ tuple\ x)\\(for\ all\ tuple\ y)\end{array}\left[\begin{array}{l}u \in (x \diamond y)\\ \quad if\ and\ only\ if\\ u \in x\ \ or\ \ u \in y\end{array}\right] \qquad (member)$$

THE SAME RELATION

The unary predicate symbol $same(x)$ denotes the relation that is true if all the elements of the tuple x are identical; thus $same(\langle A,\ A,\ A\rangle)$ is true, but $same(\langle A,\ A,\ B\rangle)$ is false.

The *same* relation is defined by the axioms

$$\begin{array}{ll} same(\langle\ \rangle) & (empty)\\[1.5em] (for\ all\ atom\ u)\big[same(u \diamond \langle\ \rangle)\big] & (singleton)\\[1.5em] \begin{array}{l}(for\ all\ atom\ u)\\(for\ all\ atom\ v)\\(for\ all\ tuple\ x)\end{array}\left[\begin{array}{l}same(u \diamond (v \diamond x))\\ \quad if\ and\ only\ if\\ u = v\ \ and\ \ same(v \diamond x)\end{array}\right] & (double\ insertion)\end{array}$$

The *same* relation is characterized by the property

$$(for\ all\ tuple\ x)\left[\begin{array}{l}same(x)\\ \quad if\ and\ only\ if\\ (for\ all\ atom\ u)\\ (for\ all\ atom\ v)\end{array}\left[\begin{array}{l}if\ \ u \in x\ \ and\ \ v \in x\\ then\ \ u = v\end{array}\right]\right] \qquad (equality)$$

The reader is requested (in **Problem 12.1**) to show that this property constitutes an alternative definition of the *same* relation.

THE SINGLETON FUNCTION

The unary function symbol $\langle u\rangle$ denotes the *singleton* function, which yields the tuple whose sole element is the atom u. It is defined by the axiom

$$(for\ all\ atom\ u)\left[\langle u\rangle\ =\ u\diamond\langle\ \rangle\right] \qquad\qquad (singleton)$$

We can immediately establish the property of the append function

$$\begin{array}{l}(for\ all\ atom\ u)\\(for\ all\ tuple\ x)\end{array}\left[\langle u\rangle\diamond x\ =\ u\diamond x\right] \qquad\qquad (singleton)$$

The member relation can be characterized in terms of the append and singleton functions by the property

$$\begin{array}{l}(for\ all\ atom\ u)\\(for\ all\ tuple\ x)\end{array}\left[\begin{array}{l}u\in x\\\quad if\ and\ only\ if\\(for\ some\ tuple\ y_1)\\(for\ some\ tuple\ y_2)\end{array}\left[x=y_1\diamond\langle u\rangle\diamond y_2\right]\right]$$

$$(append\ singleton)$$

THE EQUAL-MULTIPLICITY RELATION

The ternary predicate symbol $eqmult(u,\ x,\ y)$, denoting the *equal-multiplicity* relation for tuples, is analogous to that for bags. The relation holds if the atom u has the same multiplicity, i.e., number of occurrences, in each of the tuples x and y.

The multiplicity relation $eqmult$ is defined by the following axioms:

$$(for\ all\ atom\ u)\left[eqmult(u,\ \langle\ \rangle,\ \langle\ \rangle)\right] \qquad\qquad (empty)$$

$$\begin{array}{l}(for\ all\ atom\ u)\\(for\ all\ tuple\ y)\end{array}\left[not\ \left(eqmult(u,\ \langle\ \rangle,\ u\diamond y)\right)\right] \quad (empty\ insertion)$$

$$\begin{array}{l}(for\ all\ atom\ u)\\(for\ all\ tuple\ x)\end{array}\left[not\ \left(eqmult(u,\ u\diamond x,\ \langle\ \rangle)\right)\right] \quad (insertion\ empty)$$

$$\begin{array}{l}(for\ all\ atom\ u)\\(for\ all\ atom\ v)\\(for\ all\ tuple\ x)\\(for\ all\ tuple\ y)\end{array}\left[\begin{array}{l}eqmult(u,\ v\diamond x,\ v\diamond y)\\\quad if\ and\ only\ if\\eqmult(u,\ x,\ y)\end{array}\right] \qquad (equal\ insertion)$$

$$
\left|
\begin{array}{l}
(\textit{for all atom } u) \\
(\textit{for all atom } v) \\
(\textit{for all tuple } x) \\
(\textit{for all tuple } y)
\end{array}
\left[
\begin{array}{l}
\textit{if not } (u = v) \\
\quad \left[
\begin{array}{l}
eqmult(u,\ v \diamond x,\ y) \\
\quad \textit{if and only if} \\
eqmult(u,\ x,\ y)
\end{array}
\right] \\
\textit{then}
\end{array}
\right]
\right.
\qquad (\textit{left insertion})
$$

$$
\left|
\begin{array}{l}
(\textit{for all atom } u) \\
(\textit{for all atom } v) \\
(\textit{for all tuple } x) \\
(\textit{for all tuple } y)
\end{array}
\left[
\begin{array}{l}
\textit{if not } (u = v) \\
\quad \left[
\begin{array}{l}
eqmult(u,\ x,\ v \diamond y) \\
\quad \textit{if and only if} \\
eqmult(u,\ x,\ y)
\end{array}
\right] \\
\textit{then}
\end{array}
\right]
\right.
\qquad (\textit{right insertion})
$$

From these axioms we can establish the following properties:

$$
\begin{array}{l}
(\textit{for all atom } u) \\
(\textit{for all tuple } x) \\
(\textit{for all tuple } y)
\end{array}
\left[
\begin{array}{l}
eqmult(u,\ x,\ y) \\
\quad \textit{if and only if} \\
eqmult(u,\ y,\ x)
\end{array}
\right]
\qquad (\textit{symmetry})
$$

$$
\begin{array}{l}
(\textit{for all atom } u) \\
(\textit{for all tuple } x)
\end{array}
\Big[eqmult(u,\ x,\ x) \Big]
\qquad (\textit{reflexivity})
$$

$$
\begin{array}{l}
(\textit{for all atom } u) \\
(\textit{for all tuple } x) \\
(\textit{for all tuple } y)
\end{array}
\left[
\begin{array}{l}
\textit{if } eqmult(u,\ x,\ y) \\
\quad \left[
\begin{array}{l}
u \in x \\
\quad \textit{if and only if} \\
u \in y
\end{array}
\right] \\
\textit{then}
\end{array}
\right]
\qquad (\textit{member})
$$

$$
\begin{array}{r}
(\textit{for all tuple } x_1) \\
(\textit{for all atom } u)(\textit{for all tuple } x_2) \\
(\textit{for all atom } v)(\textit{for all tuple } y_1) \\
(\textit{for all tuple } y_2)
\end{array}
\left[
\begin{array}{l}
eqmult\big(u,\ x_1 \diamond \langle v \rangle \diamond x_2,\ y_1 \diamond \langle v \rangle \diamond y_2\big) \\
\quad \textit{if and only if} \\
eqmult(u,\ x_1 \diamond x_2,\ y_1 \diamond y_2)
\end{array}
\right]
$$
$$(\textit{append singleton})$$

The *append-singleton* property says that an atom u has the same multiplicity in two tuples with a common element v precisely when u has the same multiplicity in the tuples obtained by deleting v from each.

THE SUBTUPLE RELATION

The binary predicate symbol $x \subseteq y$ denotes the *subtuple* relation. We say that a tuple x is a subtuple of a tuple y if, for each occurrence of an element in x, there corresponds a distinct occurrence of the same element in y, and the elements occur in the same order. Thus

$$\langle A, \ C\rangle \ \subseteq \ \langle A, \ A, \ B, \ C\rangle,$$

but

$$not \quad \langle A, \ B, \ B\rangle \ \subseteq \ \langle A, \ A, \ B, \ C\rangle$$

$$not \quad \langle B, \ A\rangle \ \subseteq \ \langle A, \ A, \ B, \ C\rangle.$$

Note that we do not require the elements of the subtuple to occur contiguously in the larger tuple.

The *subtuple* relation is defined by the following four axioms:

$$(\textit{for all tuple } y)\left[\langle \ \rangle \ \subseteq \ y\right] \qquad\qquad (\textit{left empty})$$

$$\begin{array}{l}(\textit{for all atom } u)\\(\textit{for all tuple } x)\end{array}\left[not\ (u \diamond x \subseteq \langle \ \rangle)\right] \qquad (\textit{right empty})$$

$$\begin{array}{l}(\textit{for all atom } u)\\(\textit{for all tuple } x)\\(\textit{for all tuple } y)\end{array}\left[\begin{array}{l}u \diamond x \ \subseteq \ u \diamond y\\ \quad \textit{if and only if}\\ x \ \subseteq \ y\end{array}\right] \qquad (\textit{equal insertion})$$

$$\begin{array}{l}(\textit{for all atom } u)\\(\textit{for all atom } v)\\(\textit{for all tuple } x)\\(\textit{for all tuple } y)\end{array}\left[\begin{array}{l}\textit{if not } (u = v)\\ then \ \left[\begin{array}{l}u \diamond x \ \subseteq \ v \diamond y\\ \quad \textit{if and only if}\\ u \diamond x \ \subseteq \ y\end{array}\right]\end{array}\right] \ (\textit{nonequal insertion})$$

From these axioms we can establish the properties

$$\begin{array}{l}(\textit{for all tuple } x)\\(\textit{for all tuple } y)\end{array}\left[\begin{array}{l}\textit{if } x \subseteq y\\ then \ (\textit{for all atom } u) \left[\begin{array}{l}\textit{if } u \in x\\ then \ u \in y\end{array}\right]\end{array}\right] \quad (\textit{member})$$

$$\begin{array}{l}(\textit{for all atom } u)\\(\textit{for all tuple } x)\\(\textit{for all tuple } y)\end{array}\left[\begin{array}{l}\textit{if } u \diamond x \subseteq y\\ then \ u \in y \ \textit{and} \ x \subseteq y\end{array}\right] \qquad (\textit{left insertion})$$

The subtuple relation can be shown to be a weak partial ordering. Its irreflexive restriction, the *proper-subtuple* relation $x \subset y$, defined by the axiom

$$\begin{array}{l}(\textit{for all tuple } x)\\(\textit{for all tuple } y)\end{array}\left[\begin{array}{l}x \subset y\\ \quad \textit{if and only if}\\ x \subseteq y \ \textit{and not } (x = y)\end{array}\right] \qquad (\textit{proper subtuple})$$

is then a strict partial ordering.

The proper-subtuple relation can also be shown to satisfy the property

$$\begin{matrix} \textit{(for all atom } u) \\ \textit{(for all tuple } x) \end{matrix} \Big[x \; \subset \; (u \diamond x) \Big] \qquad\qquad \textit{(adjacent)}$$

12.2   NONNEGATIVE INTEGERS AND TUPLES

In this section we consider a combined theory of nonnegative integers and tuples.

THE LENGTH FUNCTION

In the combined theory of nonnegative integers and tuples, the unary function symbol $length(x)$ denotes the number of elements in the tuple x; for example,

$$length(\langle \text{A, A, B} \rangle) \; = \; 3.$$

The *length* function is defined by the axioms

$$\boxed{\begin{array}{ll} length(\langle \; \rangle) \; = \; 0 & \textit{(empty)} \\[2em] \begin{matrix} \textit{(for all atom } u) \\ \textit{(for all tuple } x) \end{matrix} \Big[length(u \diamond x) \; = \; length(x) + 1 \Big] & \textit{(insertion)} \end{array}}$$

From these axioms we can establish the following properties:

$$\textit{(for all tuple } x)\big[integer\,(length(x)) \big] \qquad\qquad\qquad \textit{(sort)}$$

$$\textit{(for all atom } u)\big[length\,(\langle u \rangle) = 1 \big] \qquad\qquad\qquad \textit{(singleton)}$$

$$\begin{matrix} \textit{(for all tuple } x) \\ \textit{(for all tuple } y) \end{matrix}\big[length(x \diamond y) \; = \; length(x) + length(y) \big] \qquad \textit{(append)}$$

$$\begin{matrix} \textit{(for all tuple } x) \\ \textit{(for all tuple } y) \end{matrix}\left[\begin{matrix} \textit{if } x \subset y \\ \textit{then } length(x) < length(y) \end{matrix} \right] \qquad \textit{(proper subtuple)}$$

THE COUNT FUNCTION

The binary function symbol $count(u, x)$ denotes the number of occurrences of the atom u in the tuple x. It is defined by the following axioms:

$$(for\ all\ atom\ u)\big[count\,(u,\ \langle\,\rangle)\ =\ 0\big] \qquad\qquad (empty)$$

$$\begin{matrix}(for\ all\ atom\ u)\\(for\ all\ tuple\ x)\end{matrix}\Big[count(u,\ u\diamond x)\ =\ count(u,\ x)+1\Big]$$

$$(equal\ insertion)$$

$$\begin{matrix}(for\ all\ atom\ u)\\(for\ all\ atom\ v)\\(for\ all\ tuple\ x)\end{matrix}\begin{bmatrix}if\ not\ (u=v)\\then\ \ count(u,\ v\diamond x)\ =\ count(u,\ x)\end{bmatrix}$$

$$(nonequal\ insertion)$$

In terms of the *count* function we can characterize the *member* relation by the property

$$\begin{matrix}(for\ all\ atom\ u)\\(for\ all\ tuple\ x)\end{matrix}\begin{bmatrix}u \in x\\if\ and\ only\ if\\not\,(count(u,\ x)=0)\end{bmatrix} \qquad (count\ of\ member)$$

We can also characterize the equal-multiplicity relation *eqmult* by the property

$$\begin{matrix}(for\ all\ atom\ u)\\(for\ all\ tuple\ x)\\(for\ all\ tuple\ y)\end{matrix}\begin{bmatrix}eqmult(u,\ x,\ y)\\if\ and\ only\ if\\count(u,\ x)\ =\ count(u,\ y)\end{bmatrix} \qquad (count\ of\ eqmult)$$

THE ELEMENT FUNCTION

The binary function symbol $[x]_z$ denotes the zth element of the tuple x, where z is a nonnegative integer. (Do not be confused: $[x]_z$ is our own personal notation for a standard binary predicate-logic function symbol, such as $f_{17}(x, z)$.) For example,

$$[\langle A,\ B,\ C\rangle]_0\ =\ A$$

$$[\langle A,\ B,\ C\rangle]_1\ =\ B$$

$$[\langle A,\ B,\ C\rangle]_2\ =\ C.$$

Note that we enumerate the elements of the tuple x beginning with 0, not 1.

The *element* function is defined by the axioms

$$
\begin{array}{l}
\textit{(for all atom u)} \\
\textit{(for all tuple x)}
\end{array}
\Big[[u \diamond x]_0 \;=\; u \Big]
\qquad\qquad \textit{(zero)}
$$

$$
\begin{array}{l}
\textit{(for all integer z)} \\
\quad\textit{(for all atom u)} \\
\quad\textit{(for all tuple x)}
\end{array}
\Big[[u \diamond x]_{z+1} \;=\; [x]_z \Big]
\qquad\qquad \textit{(successor)}
$$

Note that the axioms do not specify the value of $[y]_z$ if y is the empty tuple or, in general, if z is greater than or equal to $length(x)$. For example, they do not specify the value of $\big[\langle A,\ B,\ C\rangle\big]_3$.

The append function is related to the element function by the following two properties:

$$
\begin{array}{l}
\textit{(for all integer z)} \\
\quad\textit{(for all tuple x)} \\
\quad\textit{(for all tuple y)}
\end{array}
\left[
\begin{array}{l}
\textit{if } z < length(x) \\
\textit{then } [x \diamond y]_z \;=\; [x]_z
\end{array}
\right]
\qquad \textit{(left element)}
$$

$$
\begin{array}{l}
\textit{(for all integer z)} \\
\quad\textit{(for all tuple x)} \\
\quad\textit{(for all tuple y)}
\end{array}
\left[
\begin{array}{l}
\textit{if } z < length(y) \\
\textit{then } [x \diamond y]_{length(x)+z} \;=\; [y]_z
\end{array}
\right]
\qquad \textit{(right element)}
$$

The proof is left as an exercise (**Problem 12.2**).

THE ALTER FUNCTION

The ternary function symbol $alter(x, z, u)$ denotes the tuple obtained by replacing the zth element of the tuple x with the atom u, where z is a nonnegative integer. For example,

$$
alter\big(\langle A,\ B,\ B\rangle,\ 2,\ C\big) \;=\; \langle A,\ B,\ C\rangle.
$$

Here again we begin our enumeration of the elements of the tuple with 0, not 1.

The *alter* function is defined by the following axioms:

$$
\begin{array}{l}
\textit{(for all atom u)} \\
\textit{(for all tuple x)} \\
\textit{(for all atom v)}
\end{array}
\Big[alter(u \diamond x,\ 0,\ v) \;=\; v \diamond x \Big]
\qquad\qquad \textit{(zero)}
$$

$$
\begin{array}{l}
(\textit{for all atom } u) \\
(\textit{for all tuple } x) \\
(\textit{for all integer } z) \\
(\textit{for all atom } v)
\end{array}
\left[
\begin{array}{l}
aiter(u \diamond x,\; z+1,\; v) \\
= \\
u \diamond alter(x,\; z,\; v)
\end{array}
\right]
\qquad (\textit{successor})
$$

Note that these axioms specify the result $alter(x,\, z,\, v)$ of altering the zth element of a tuple x only if z is less than $length(x)$. For example, the values of $alter(\langle\,\rangle,\, 0,\, \mathrm{D})$ and of $alter(\langle \mathrm{A}, \mathrm{B}, \mathrm{C}\rangle,\, 3,\, \mathrm{D})$ are not specified.

From these axioms we can establish the following properties:

$$
\begin{array}{l}
(\textit{for all tuple } x) \\
(\textit{for all integer } z) \\
(\textit{for all atom } v)
\end{array}
\left[
\begin{array}{l}
\textit{if } z < length(x) \\
\textit{then } tuple\big(alter(x,\, z,\, v)\big)
\end{array}
\right]
\qquad (\textit{sort})
$$

$$
\begin{array}{l}
(\textit{for all tuple } x) \\
(\textit{for all integer } z) \\
(\textit{for all atom } v)
\end{array}
\left[
\begin{array}{l}
\textit{if } z < length(x) \\
\textit{then } [alter(x,\, z,\, v)]_z = v
\end{array}
\right]
\qquad (\textit{equal})
$$

$$
\begin{array}{l}
(\textit{for all tuple } x) \\
(\textit{for all integer } z) \\
(\textit{for all integer } z') \\
(\textit{for all atom } v)
\end{array}
\left[
\begin{array}{l}
\textit{if } z < length(x) \textit{ and } z' < length(x) \\
\textit{then if } not\,(z = z') \\
\qquad \textit{then } [alter(x,\, z,\, v)]_{z'} = [x]_{z'}
\end{array}
\right]
\qquad (\textit{nonequal})
$$

12.3   MAPPING TUPLES INTO SETS AND BAGS

Let us combine the theories of sets, bags, and tuples into one theory by identifying the atoms of the theories. This is expressed by using a single unary predicate symbol $atom(x)$ to characterize all of them. We augment this combined theory by introducing three unary function symbols, $bagtuple(x)$, $setbag(x)$, and $settuple(x)$, that map tuples into bags, bags into sets, and tuples into sets, respectively. They can be illustrated by the following diagram:

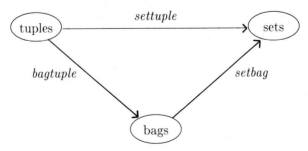

BAGTUPLE

The unary function symbol $bagtuple(x)$, which maps tuples into bags, is defined by the following axioms:

$$bagtuple(\langle\,\rangle) \;=\; [\![\,]\!] \hspace{4cm} (empty)$$

$$\begin{aligned}&(for\ all\ atom\ u)\\&(for\ all\ tuple\ x)\end{aligned}\Big[bagtuple(u \diamond x) \;=\; u \circ bagtuple(x)\Big] \quad (insertion)$$

Thus

$$bagtuple(\langle \text{A, B, B, C}\rangle) \;=\; [\![\text{A, B, B, C}]\!],$$

since

$$bagtuple(\langle \text{A, B, B, C}\rangle)$$

$$= \; bagtuple\big(\text{A} \diamond (\text{B} \diamond (\text{B} \diamond (\text{C} \diamond \langle\,\rangle)))\big)$$

$$= \; \text{A} \circ bagtuple\big(\text{B} \diamond (\text{B} \diamond (\text{C} \diamond \langle\,\rangle))\big)$$
(by the *insertion* axiom for *bagtuple*)

$$= \; \text{A} \circ \big(\text{B} \circ \big(\text{B} \circ \big(\text{C} \circ bagtuple(\langle\,\rangle)\big)\big)\big)$$
(by the *insertion* axiom for *bagtuple*,
three times more)

$$= \; \text{A} \circ \big(\text{B} \circ \big(\text{B} \circ \big(\text{C} \circ [\![\,]\!]\big)\big)\big)$$
(by the *empty* axiom for *bagtuple*)

$$= \; [\![\text{A, B, B, C}]\!].$$

SETBAG

The unary function symbol $setbag(x)$, which maps bags into sets, is defined by the following axioms:

$$setbag([\![\,]\!]) \;=\; \{\,\} \hspace{4cm} (empty)$$

$$\begin{aligned}&(for\ all\ atom\ u)\\&(for\ all\ bag\ x)\end{aligned}\Big[setbag(u \circ x) \;=\; u \circ setbag(x)\Big] \quad (insertion)$$

Thus

$$setbag(\llbracket A, B, B, C \rrbracket) \ = \ \{A, B, C\},$$

since

$$setbag(\llbracket A, B, B, C \rrbracket)$$

$$= \ setbag\big(A \circ (B \circ (B \circ (C \circ \llbracket \ \rrbracket))))$$

$$= \ A \circ setbag\big(B \circ (B \circ (C \circ \llbracket \ \rrbracket)))$$
(by the *insertion* axiom for *setbag*)

$$= \ A \circ \big(B \circ \big(B \circ \big(C \circ setbag(\llbracket \ \rrbracket))))$$
(by the *insertion* axiom for *setbag*,
three times more)

$$= \ A \circ \big(B \circ \big(B \circ \big(C \circ \{\ \}))))$$
(by the *empty* axiom for *setbag*)

$$= \ A \circ \big(B \circ \big(C \circ \{\ \})))$$
(by the *absorbtion* property of the insertion
function for sets, because $B \in (B \circ (C \circ \{\ \}))$)

$$= \ \{A, B, C\}.$$

SETTUPLE

The unary function symbol *settuple*(x), which maps tuples into sets, is defined by the following axioms:

$$settuple(\langle \ \rangle) \ = \ \{\ \} \qquad\qquad\qquad\qquad\qquad (empty)$$

$$(for \ all \ atom \ u) \atop (for \ all \ tuple \ x) \Big[settuple(u \diamond x) \ = \ u \circ settuple(x)\Big] \qquad (insertion)$$

Thus

$$settuple(\langle A, B, B, C \rangle) \ = \ \{A, B, C\}.$$

PROPERTIES OF THE MAPPING FUNCTIONS

Each of these functions can be shown to be "onto." For the *bagtuple* function, say, we have

$$(for\ all\ bag\ y)(for\ some\ tuple\ x)\big[bagtuple(x) = y\big] \qquad (onto)$$

that is, every bag is mapped onto by some tuple. The reader is requested to prove this in **Problem 12.3(a)**. Analogous properties hold for the *setbag* and *settuple* functions.

Each of the mapping functions preserves the elements of the object to which it is applied. In other words, for the *bagtuple* function, say, we have

$$\begin{array}{l}(for\ all\ atom\ u)\\(for\ all\ tuple\ x)\end{array}\left[\begin{array}{l}u \in x\\ \quad if\ and\ only\ if\\ u \in bagtuple(x)\end{array}\right] \qquad (member)$$

Analogous properties hold for the *setbag* and *settuple* functions.

The *bagtuple* function preserves the multiplicity of the tuple to which it is applied. In other words, we have

$$\begin{array}{l}(for\ all\ atom\ u)\\(for\ all\ tuple\ x)\\(for\ all\ tuple\ y)\end{array}\left[\begin{array}{l}eqmult(u,\ x,\ y)\\ \quad if\ and\ only\ if\\ eqmult\big(u,\ bagtuple(x),\ bagtuple(y)\big)\end{array}\right] \qquad (eqmult)$$

Note that there are no analogous *eqmult* properties for the *setbag* and *settuple* functions.

The mapping functions have a distributivity relationship with respect to the append function $\diamond$ for tuples, the sum function $\oplus$ for bags, and the union function $\cup$ for sets, expressed by the following properties:

$$\begin{array}{l}(for\ all\ tuple\ x)\\(for\ all\ tuple\ y)\end{array}\left[bagtuple(x \diamond y)\ =\ bagtuple(x) \oplus bagtuple(y)\right]$$
$$(append\text{-}sum)$$

$$\begin{array}{l}(for\ all\ bag\ x)\\(for\ all\ bag\ y)\end{array}\left[setbag(x \oplus y)\ =\ setbag(x)\ \cup\ setbag(y)\right]$$
$$(sum\text{-}union)$$

$$\begin{array}{l}(for\ all\ tuple\ x)\\(for\ all\ tuple\ y)\end{array}\left[settuple(x \diamond y)\ =\ settuple(x)\ \cup\ settuple(y)\right]$$
$$(append\text{-}union)$$

The basic relationship between the three mapping functions is expressed in the following result.

Proposition (composition)

The sentence

$$(for\ all\ tuple\ x)\big[settuple(x)\ =\ setbag\big(bagtuple(x)\big)\big] \qquad (composition)$$

is valid. ⏌

In other words, the result of applying the *settuple* function to a tuple x is the same as the result of first applying the *bagtuple* function to x and then applying the *setbag* function to the result. The proof is left as an exercise (**Problem 12.3(b)**).

Remark (not one to one)

The three mapping functions are not "one to one." In other words, for the *bagtuple* function, say, it is not the case that

$$\begin{matrix} (for\ all\ tuple\ x) \\ (for\ all\ tuple\ y) \end{matrix} \left[\begin{matrix} if\ bagtuple(x) = bagtuple(y) \\ then\ \ x = y \end{matrix}\right].$$

Analogous properties for the *setbag* and *settuple* functions do not hold either.

To see that the *bagtuple* function is not one to one, consider the case in which x is the tuple $A \diamond (B \diamond \langle\ \rangle)$, that is, $\langle A,\ B \rangle$, and y is the tuple $B \diamond (A \diamond \langle\ \rangle)$, that is, $\langle B,\ A \rangle$. Then (by the *insertion* and *empty* axioms for *bagtuple*)

$$bagtuple\big(A \diamond (B \diamond \langle\ \rangle)\big)\ =\ A \odot \big(B \odot [\![\ ]\!]\big)$$

and

$$bagtuple\big(B \diamond (A \diamond \langle\ \rangle)\big)\ =\ B \odot \big(A \odot [\![\ ]\!]\big).$$

But (by the *exchange* equality axiom for bags)

$$A \odot \big(B \odot [\![\ ]\!]\big)\ =\ B \odot \big(A \odot [\![\ ]\!]\big),$$

and therefore we have

$$bagtuple\big(A \diamond (B \diamond \langle\ \rangle)\big)\ =\ bagtuple\big(B \diamond (A \diamond \langle\ \rangle)\big).$$

On the other hand, because *not* $(A = B)$, we have (by the *insertion* uniqueness axiom for tuples)

$$not\ \ \ A \diamond (B \diamond \langle\ \rangle)\ =\ B \diamond (A \diamond \langle\ \rangle).\ \ \ ⏌$$

Remark (inverse mapping functions)

We cannot introduce mappings from the bags into tuples, the sets into bags, or the sets into tuples in an analogous way. For instance, if we define an inverse function *tuplebag*, say, by the axioms

$$tuplebag(\llbracket\ \rrbracket) \ = \ \langle\ \rangle \qquad\qquad\qquad (empty)$$

$$\begin{matrix}(for\ all\ atom\ u)\\(for\ all\ bag\ x)\end{matrix}\Big[tuplebag(u \odot x) \ = \ u \diamond tuplebag(x)\Big] \qquad (insertion)$$

the augmented theory would then be inconsistent. In particular, even if A and B are distinct atoms, we know that $A \odot (B \odot \llbracket\ \rrbracket) \ = \ B \odot (A \odot \llbracket\ \rrbracket)$, and therefore

$$tuplebag\big(A \odot (B \odot \llbracket\ \rrbracket)\big) \ = \ tuplebag\big(B \odot (A \odot \llbracket\ \rrbracket)\big).$$

But (by the *insertion* and *empty* axioms for *tuplebag*)

$$tuplebag\big(A \odot (B \odot \llbracket\ \rrbracket)\big) \ = \ A \diamond \big(B \diamond \langle\ \rangle\big)$$

and

$$tuplebag\big(B \odot (A \odot \llbracket\ \rrbracket)\big) \ = \ B \diamond \big(A \diamond \langle\ \rangle\big).$$

Hence

$$A \diamond \big(B \diamond \langle\ \rangle\big) \ = \ B \diamond \big(A \diamond \langle\ \rangle\big),$$

which is false (as we have seen in the previous remark).

Note however that we can obtain a consistent set of axioms for the inverse function *tuplebag* by replacing the *insertion* axiom above with the axiom

$$(for\ all\ bag\ x)\begin{bmatrix}if\ not\ (x = \llbracket\ \rrbracket)\\then\ tuplebag(x) \ = \ choice(x) \diamond \big(tuplebag\big(rest(x)\big)\big)\end{bmatrix}$$
$$(nonempty)$$

Inverse functions *bagset* and *tupleset* can be defined analogously.   ⌐

12.4   THE PERMUTATION RELATION

A tuple is said to be a *permutation* of another tuple if each can be obtained from the other simply by rearranging the elements; thus $\langle A, A, B \rangle$ is a permutation of $\langle B, A, A \rangle$ but not of $\langle A, A, C \rangle$, $\langle A, B \rangle$, or $\langle A, B, B \rangle$. Note that, for one tuple to be a permutation of another, any atom must have the same multiplicity in each tuple.

We define the permutation relation $perm(x, y)$ by the following three axioms:

$$perm(\langle\,\rangle, \langle\,\rangle) \hspace{4cm} (empty)$$

$$(for\ all\ atom\ u)$$
$$(for\ all\ tuple\ x_1)$$
$$(for\ all\ tuple\ x_2)$$
$$(for\ all\ tuple\ y_1)$$
$$(for\ all\ tuple\ y_2)$$
$$\left[\begin{array}{l} perm(x_1 \diamond \langle u \rangle \diamond x_2,\ y_1 \diamond \langle u \rangle \diamond y_2) \\ \quad if\ and\ only\ if \\ perm(x_1 \diamond x_2,\ y_1 \diamond y_2) \end{array}\right]$$

$$(append\ singleton)$$

The *append-singleton* axiom states that two tuples having a common element u are permutations precisely when the tuples obtained by deleting the element u from each of them are also permutations.

$$(for\ all\ tuple\ x)$$
$$(for\ all\ tuple\ y)$$
$$\left[\begin{array}{l} if\ perm(x, y) \\ then\ (for\ all\ atom\ u) \left[\begin{array}{l} u \in x \\ \quad if\ and\ only\ if \\ u \in y \end{array}\right] \end{array}\right] \ (member)$$

The *member* axiom states that if two tuples are permutations, they have the same elements.

These axioms suggest a method for computing whether two tuples x and y are permutations:

- If x and y are empty, they are indeed permutations (by the *empty* axiom).

- Otherwise, if x and y have a common element u, we delete u from each tuple (by the *append-singleton* axiom) and compute whether the resulting tuples are permutations.

- Otherwise, some element of one of the tuples is not an element of the other; therefore (by the contrapositive of the *member* axiom) the tuples are not permutations.

It is not immediately clear, however, that the relation defined by the axioms coincides with our intuitive notion of permutation. This is made more plausible by the following result.

Proposition (equal multiplicity)

The sentence

$$(\textit{for all tuple } x) \atop (\textit{for all tuple } y) \left[{perm(x,\ y) \atop \textit{if and only if} \atop (\textit{for all atom } u)[eqmult(u,\ x,\ y)]} \right] \qquad (\textit{eqmult})$$

is valid. ⏌

In other words, two tuples are permutations precisely when every atom has the same multiplicity in either tuple.

Proof

The proof is by induction on x, taking the inductive sentence to be

$$\mathcal{F}[x]: \quad (\textit{for all tuple } y) \left[{perm(x,\ y) \atop \textit{if and only if} \atop (\textit{for all atom } u)[eqmult(u,\ x,\ y)]} \right].$$

Base Case

We would like to show

$$\mathcal{F}[\langle\,\rangle]: \quad (\textit{for all tuple } y) \left[{perm(\langle\,\rangle,\ y) \atop \textit{if and only if} \atop (\textit{for all atom } u)[eqmult(u,\ \langle\,\rangle,\ y)]} \right].$$

Consider an arbitrary tuple y; we must show

$$perm(\langle\,\rangle,\ y)$$
$$\textit{if and only if}$$
$$(\textit{for all atom } u)[eqmult(u,\ \langle\,\rangle,\ y)].$$

We distinguish between two cases, according to whether or not y is empty.

Case: $y = \langle\,\rangle$

In this case, the left-hand side

$$perm(\langle\,\rangle,\ \langle\,\rangle)$$

is true (by the *empty* axiom for *perm*) and the right-hand side

$$(\textit{for all atom } u)[eqmult(u,\ \langle\,\rangle,\ \langle\,\rangle)]$$

is true (by the *empty* axiom for *eqmult*); therefore the entire equivalence is true.

Case: $not\ (y = \langle\ \rangle)$

Then (by the *decomposition* property of tuples) there exists an atom w and tuple y' such that

$$y\ =\ w \diamond y'.$$

Then the left-hand side

$$perm(\langle\ \rangle,\ w \diamond y')$$

is false (by the *member* axiom for *perm*, because $not\ (w \in \langle\ \rangle)$ and $w \in w \diamond y'$) and the right-hand side

$$(for\ all\ atom\ u)[eqmult(u,\ \langle\ \rangle,\ w \diamond y')]$$

is false (taking u to be w, by the *empty-insertion* axiom for *eqmult*). Therefore the entire equivalence is true.

Inductive Step

For an arbitrary atom v and tuple x, assume the induction hypothesis

$$\mathcal{F}[x]:\quad (for\ all\ tuple\ y)\left[\begin{array}{l} perm(x,\ y)\\ \quad if\ and\ only\ if\\ (for\ all\ atom\ u)[eqmult(u,\ x,\ y)]\end{array}\right].$$

We would like to show that then

$$\mathcal{F}[v \diamond x]:\quad (for\ all\ tuple\ y')\left[\begin{array}{l} perm(v \diamond x,\ y')\\ \quad if\ and\ only\ if\\ (for\ all\ atom\ u)[eqmult(u,\ v \diamond x,\ y')]\end{array}\right].$$

Consider an arbitrary tuple y'; we must show that

$$\begin{array}{l} perm(v \diamond x,\ y')\\ \quad if\ and\ only\ if\\ (for\ all\ atom\ u)[eqmult(u,\ v \diamond x,\ y')].\end{array}$$

We distinguish between two cases, depending on whether or not $v \in y'$.

Case: $v \in y'$

Then (by the *append-singleton* property of the member relation) there exist tuples y_1 and y_2 such that

$$y'\ =\ y_1 \diamond \langle v \rangle \diamond y_2.$$

The left-hand side of the desired equivalence in this case,

$$perm(v \diamond x, \; y_1 \diamond \langle v \rangle \diamond y_2),$$

holds precisely when (by the *singleton* property of append)

$$perm(\langle v \rangle \diamond x, \; y_1 \diamond \langle v \rangle \diamond y_2)$$

precisely when (by the *left-empty* axiom for append)

$$perm(\langle \, \rangle \diamond \langle v \rangle \diamond x, \; y_1 \diamond \langle v \rangle \diamond y_2)$$

precisely when (by the *append-singleton* axiom for *perm*)

$$perm(\langle \, \rangle \diamond x, \; y_1 \diamond y_2)$$

precisely when (by the *left-empty* axiom for append again)

$$perm(x, \; y_1 \diamond y_2).$$

On the other hand, the right-hand side of the desired equivalence in this case,

$$(for\ all\ atom\ u)\big[eqmult(u, \; v \diamond x, \; y_1 \diamond \langle v \rangle \diamond y_2)\big],$$

holds precisely when (by the *singleton* property of append)

$$(for\ all\ atom\ u)\big[eqmult(u, \; \langle v \rangle \diamond x, \; y_1 \diamond \langle v \rangle \diamond y_2)\big]$$

precisely when (by the *left-empty* axiom for append)

$$(for\ all\ atom\ u)\big[eqmult(u, \; \langle \, \rangle \diamond \langle v \rangle \diamond x, \; y_1 \diamond \langle v \rangle \diamond y_2)\big]$$

precisely when (by the *append-singleton* property of *eqmult*)

$$(for\ all\ atom\ u)\big[eqmult(u, \; \langle \, \rangle \diamond x, \; y_1 \diamond y_2)\big]$$

precisely when (by the *left-empty* axiom for append again)

$$(for\ all\ atom\ u)\big[eqmult(u, \; x, \; y_1 \diamond y_2)\big]$$

precisely when (by our induction hypothesis $\mathcal{F}[x]$, taking y to be $y_1 \diamond y_2$)

$$perm(x, \; y_1 \diamond y_2).$$

Therefore the desired equivalence is true in this case.

Case: $not\ (v \in y')$

Then the left-hand side of the desired equivalence,

$$perm(v \diamond x, \; y'),$$

is false (by the *member* axiom for *perm*, because $v \in (v \diamond x)$ and *not* $(v \in y')$).

But the right-hand side of the desired equivalence,

$$(\textit{for all atom } u)\big[eqmult(u, \ v \diamond x, \ y')\big],$$

is also false (taking u to be v, by the *member* property of *eqmult*, because we have $v \in (v \diamond x)$ and *not* $(v \in y')$).

Therefore the desired equivalence is true in this case too. ◢

Actually, the *eqmult* property of the permutation relation provides an alternative definition of the relation. The proof is requested as an exercise (**Problem 12.4**).

It is possible to establish that the permutation relation *perm* is an equivalence relation over the tuples, that is,

$$\begin{matrix}(\textit{for all tuple } x) \\ (\textit{for all tuple } y) \\ (\textit{for all tuple } z)\end{matrix}\left[\begin{matrix}\textit{if } perm(x, y) \ \textit{and} \ perm(y, z) \\ \textit{then } perm(x, z)\end{matrix}\right] \qquad (\textit{transitivity})$$

$$\begin{matrix}(\textit{for all tuple } x) \\ (\textit{for all tuple } y)\end{matrix}\left[\begin{matrix}\textit{if } perm(x, y) \\ \textit{then } perm(y, x)\end{matrix}\right] \qquad (\textit{symmetry})$$

$$(\textit{for all tuple } x)\big[perm(x, x)\big] \qquad (\textit{reflexivity})$$

We can also establish the following properties of the permutation relation:

$$\begin{matrix}(\textit{for all atom } u) \\ (\textit{for all atom } v) \\ (\textit{for all tuple } x)\end{matrix}\left[perm\big(u \diamond (v \diamond x), \ v \diamond (u \diamond x)\big)\right] \qquad (\textit{exchange})$$

$$\begin{matrix}(\textit{for all atom } u) \\ (\textit{for all tuple } x) \\ (\textit{for all tuple } y)\end{matrix}\left[\begin{matrix}perm(u \diamond x, \ u \diamond y) \\ \textit{if and only if} \\ perm(x, y)\end{matrix}\right] \qquad (\textit{equal insertion})$$

$$\begin{matrix}(\textit{for all tuple } x_1) \\ (\textit{for all tuple } y_1) \\ (\textit{for all tuple } x_2) \\ (\textit{for all tuple } y_2)\end{matrix}\left[\begin{matrix}\textit{if } perm(x_1, y_1) \ \textit{and} \\ perm(x_2, y_2) \\ \textit{then } perm(x_1 \diamond x_2, \ y_1 \diamond y_2)\end{matrix}\right] \qquad (\textit{append})$$

The proof of the *equal-insertion* property is straightforward; the proofs of the other two are left as an exercise (**Problem 12.5**).

In a combined theory of bags and tuples, in which we identify the atoms of each theory, we can characterize the permutation relation in terms of equality of bags by the property

$$(\textit{for all tuple } x) \;\; (\textit{for all tuple } y) \begin{bmatrix} perm(x, \, y) \\ \quad \textit{if and only if} \\ bagtuple(x) = bagtuple(y) \end{bmatrix} \qquad (\textit{bagtuple})$$

The proof is straightforward and does not require induction.

12.5   THE ORDERED RELATION

Consider a combined theory of the tuples and the nonnegative integers in which the atoms of the tuples are identified with the nonnegative integers. This is expressed by the axiom

$$(\textit{for all } x) \begin{bmatrix} atom(x) \\ \quad \textit{if and only if} \\ integer(x) \end{bmatrix}. \qquad (\textit{atom-integer})$$

We shall call this the theory of *tuples of nonnegative integers.*

A tuple in this combined theory is said to be *ordered* if its elements are (weakly) increasing; thus $\langle 2, \, 4, \, 4, \, 7 \rangle$ is ordered but $\langle 3, \, 2 \rangle$ is not. Note that an ordered tuple may have multiple occurrences of the same element.

The *ordered* relation is defined by the following axioms:

$$ordered(\langle \, \rangle) \qquad (\textit{empty})$$

$$(\textit{for all atom } u) \Big[ordered\big(u \diamond \langle \, \rangle\big) \Big] \qquad (\textit{singleton})$$

$$(\textit{for all atom } u) \;\; (\textit{for all atom } v) \;\; (\textit{for all tuple } x) \begin{bmatrix} ordered(u \diamond (v \diamond x)) \\ \quad \textit{if and only if} \\ u \leq v \;\; \textit{and} \;\; ordered(v \diamond x) \end{bmatrix} \qquad (\textit{double insertion})$$

Here $\leq$ is the weak less-than relation over the nonnegative integers.

From these axioms we can prove the following result.

Proposition (insertion)

The sentence

$$
(\textit{for all atom } u)
(\textit{for all tuple } x)
\left[
\begin{array}{l}
ordered(u \diamond x) \\
\quad \textit{if and only if} \\
\left[
\begin{array}{l}
ordered(x) \\
\quad \textit{and} \\
(\textit{for all atom } v)
\left[
\begin{array}{l}
\textit{if } v \in x \\
\textit{then } u \leq v
\end{array}
\right]
\end{array}
\right]
\end{array}
\right]
\qquad (\textit{insertion})
$$

is valid. ⌟

In other words, a nonempty tuple is ordered precisely when its tail is ordered and its head is less than or equal to every element of its tail.

Proof

The proof is by induction on x, taking our inductive sentence to be

$$
\mathcal{F}[x]: \quad (\textit{for all atom } u)
\left[
\begin{array}{l}
ordered(u \diamond x) \\
\quad \textit{if and only if} \\
\left[
\begin{array}{l}
ordered(x) \\
\quad \textit{and} \\
(\textit{for all atom } v)
\left[
\begin{array}{l}
\textit{if } v \in x \\
\textit{then } u \leq v
\end{array}
\right]
\end{array}
\right]
\end{array}
\right].
$$

Base Case

We would like to show

$$
\mathcal{F}[\langle\,\rangle]: \quad (\textit{for all atom } u)
\left[
\begin{array}{l}
ordered(u \diamond \langle\,\rangle) \\
\quad \textit{if and only if} \\
\left[
\begin{array}{l}
ordered(\langle\,\rangle) \\
\quad \textit{and} \\
(\textit{for all atom } v)
\left[
\begin{array}{l}
\textit{if } v \in \langle\,\rangle \\
\textit{then } u \leq v
\end{array}
\right]
\end{array}
\right]
\end{array}
\right].
$$

Consider an arbitrary atom u. The left-hand side,

$$
ordered(u \diamond \langle\,\rangle),
$$

is true (by the *singleton* axiom for the *ordered* relation).

The first conjunct of the right-hand side,

$$ordered(\langle\,\rangle),$$

holds (by the *empty* axiom for the *ordered* relation). The second conjunct,

$$(\textit{for all atom } v) \begin{bmatrix} \textit{if } v \in \langle\,\rangle \\ \textit{then } u \leq v \end{bmatrix},$$

is true vacuously, because, for any atom v, the antecedent $v \in \langle\,\rangle$ is false (by the *empty* axiom for the member relation).

Therefore the entire equivalence is true.

Inductive Step

For an arbitrary atom w and tuple x, assume as our induction hypothesis that

$$\mathcal{F}[x]: \quad (\textit{for all atom } u) \begin{bmatrix} ordered(u \diamond x) \\ \textit{if and only if} \\ \begin{bmatrix} ordered(x) \\ \textit{and} \\ (\textit{for all atom } v) \begin{bmatrix} \textit{if } v \in x \\ \textit{then } u \leq v \end{bmatrix} \end{bmatrix} \end{bmatrix}.$$

We would like to show that then

$$\mathcal{F}[w \diamond x]: \quad (\textit{for all atom } u') \begin{bmatrix} ordered(u' \diamond (w \diamond x)) \\ \textit{if and only if} \\ \begin{bmatrix} ordered(w \diamond x) \\ \textit{and} \\ (\textit{for all atom } v') \begin{bmatrix} \textit{if } v' \in (w \diamond x) \\ \textit{then } u' \leq v' \end{bmatrix} \end{bmatrix} \end{bmatrix}.$$

We prove only one direction of the equivalence. Consider an arbitrary atom u' and suppose that

$$ordered(u' \diamond (w \diamond x)).$$

We show that then

(†) $ordered(w \diamond x)$

and

(‡) $(\textit{for all atom } v') \begin{bmatrix} \textit{if } v' \in (w \diamond x) \\ \textit{then } u' \leq v' \end{bmatrix}.$

Because $ordered\big(u' \diamond (w \diamond x)\big)$, we have (by the *double-insertion* axiom for the ordered relation) that

$$u' \leq w$$

and

$$ordered(w \diamond x).$$

The latter sentence, $ordered(w \diamond x)$, is one of our desired conditions (†), and it also implies (by our induction hypothesis $\mathcal{F}[x]$, taking u to be w) that

$$ordered(x)$$

and

$$(*) \qquad (for\ all\ atom\ v) \begin{bmatrix} if\ v \in x \\ then\ w \leq v \end{bmatrix}.$$

To establish our remaining desired condition (‡), consider an arbitrary atom v', and suppose that

$$v' \in (w \diamond x).$$

We must show that then

$$u' \leq v'.$$

Because $v' \in (w \diamond x)$, we have (by the *insertion* axiom for the member relation) that

$$v' = w \ \ or \ \ v' \in x.$$

In the case in which $v' = w$, our earlier conclusion $u' \leq w$ implies the desired result $u' \leq v'$.

In the alternate case, in which $v' \in x$, we know (by our earlier conclusion $(*)$, taking v to be v') that

$$w \leq v'.$$

Therefore by our earlier conclusion $u' \leq w$, we have (by the transitivity of the less-than relation $\leq$) the desired result $u' \leq v'$.

This concludes the proof in one direction. The proof in the other direction, which is simpler, is omitted. ⌟

Remark (transitivity)

Although we have assumed initially that the elements of our tuples are identified with the nonnegative integers, the only property of the nonnegative integers we require in the proof of the *insertion* proposition is the *transitivity* property of the less-than relation $\leq$. Therefore we could establish the same results in an augmented theory of tuples in which $\leq$ is replaced by an arbitrary transitive relation $\prec$ over the atoms, without mentioning the nonnegative integers at all. ◢

The *empty* axiom and the *insertion* property actually provide an alternative definition of the *ordered* relation; the proof is left as an exercise (**Problem 12.6**).

A connection between the *ordered* relation and the append function is expressed in the property

$$
\begin{array}{l}
\textit{(for all tuple } x) \\
\textit{(for all tuple } y)
\end{array}
\left[
\begin{array}{l}
ordered(x \diamondsuit y) \\
\quad \textit{if and only if} \\
\left[
\begin{array}{l}
ordered(x) \ \textit{and} \ ordered(y) \\
\quad \textit{and} \\
\textit{(for all atom } u) \left[\textit{if } u \in x \ \textit{and} \ v \in y \right. \\
\textit{(for all atom } v) \left. \textit{then } u \leq v \right]
\end{array}
\right]
\end{array}
\right]
\qquad (append)
$$

In other words, the result of appending two tuples x and y is ordered precisely when the two tuples are themselves ordered and every element of x is less than or equal to every element of y. The proof is left as an exercise (**Problem 12.7**).

THE MINIMUM FUNCTION

Suppose we define a unary *minimum* function $mintuple(x)$, which is intended to produce the least element of a nonempty tuple x. The minimum function is defined over the tuples of nonnegative integers by the axioms

$$
\textit{(for all atom } u) \left[mintuple(u \diamondsuit \langle \, \rangle) = u \right]
\qquad (singleton)
$$

$$
\begin{array}{l}
\textit{(for all atom } u) \\
\textit{(for all tuple } x)
\end{array}
\left[
\begin{array}{l}
\textit{if not } (x = \langle \, \rangle) \\
\textit{then } \left[mintuple(u \diamondsuit x) =
\left\{
\begin{array}{l}
\textit{if } u \leq mintuple(x) \\
\textit{then } u \\
\textit{else } mintuple(x)
\end{array}
\right\}
\right]
\end{array}
\right]
$$

$$
(insertion)
$$

Note that these axioms do not specify any particular value for the term $mintuple(\langle\,\rangle)$.

We can establish that $mintuple(x)$ is indeed the least element of the nonempty tuple x, that is,

$$(\textit{for all tuple } x)\left[\begin{array}{l} \textit{if } \textit{not }(x = \langle\,\rangle) \\ \textit{then } \left[\begin{array}{l} mintuple(x) \in x \\ \textit{and} \\ (\textit{for all atom } u) \left[\begin{array}{l} \textit{if } u \in x \\ \textit{then } mintuple(x) \le u \end{array}\right] \end{array}\right] \end{array}\right] \quad (\textit{least})$$

The proof is left as an exercise (**Problem 12.8**).

12.6   THE SORT FUNCTION

Consider again the theory of tuples of nonnegative integers. We define a unary function symbol $sort(x)$ which, for any tuple x, produces a tuple whose elements are the same as those of x but rearranged into (weakly) increasing order. For example,

$$sort(\langle 4,\ 2,\ 1,\ 2\rangle)\ =\ \langle 1,\ 2,\ 2,\ 4\rangle.$$

Note that the multiplicity of each element in $sort(x)$ is the same as its multiplicity in x.

The *sort* function is defined in terms of an auxiliary binary function symbol $insert(u, y)$. If u is a nonnegative integer and y is a tuple already in increasing order, $insert(u, y)$ is the tuple obtained by inserting u in its place in order among the elements of y. For example,

$$insert(3,\ \langle 1,\ 2,\ 4\rangle)\ =\ \langle 1,\ 2,\ 3,\ 4\rangle$$

$$insert(2,\ \langle 1,\ 2,\ 4\rangle)\ =\ \langle 1,\ 2,\ 2,\ 4\rangle.$$

The *sort* function is defined by the axioms

$$\begin{array}{|lll|}\hline & & \\ sort(\langle\,\rangle)\ =\ \langle\,\rangle & & (\textit{empty}) \\ & & \\ \begin{array}{l}(\textit{for all atom } u)\\ (\textit{for all tuple } x)\end{array}\left[sort(u \diamond x)\ =\ insert(u,\ sort(x))\right] & & (\textit{insertion}) \\ & & \\ \hline\end{array}$$

In other words, if the given tuple is empty, the value of the *sort* function is also empty. On the other hand, if the given tuple is of form $u \diamond x$, the value of the *sort* function is obtained by arranging the elements of x in increasing order and inserting u in its place in order among them.

The auxiliary function *insert* is defined by the axioms

$$(\textit{for all atom } u)\left[insert\big(u,\ \langle\,\rangle\big)\ =\ u \diamond \langle\,\rangle\right] \qquad\qquad (\textit{empty})$$

$$
\begin{array}{l}
(\textit{for all atom } u) \\
(\textit{for all atom } v) \\
(\textit{for all tuple } x)
\end{array}
\left[insert(u,\ v \diamond x)\ =\
\left\{
\begin{array}{l}
\textit{if } u \leq v \\
\textit{then } u \diamond (v \diamond x) \\
\textit{else } v \diamond insert(u,\ x)
\end{array}
\right\}
\right]
$$
$$(\textit{insertion})$$

In other words, the result of inserting a nonnegative integer u in its place in the empty tuple $\langle\,\rangle$ is simply the singleton tuple $\langle u \rangle$. The result of inserting u in its place in the nonempty tuple $v \diamond x$ is obtained by putting u at the beginning, if $u \leq v$, and inserting u in its place in x otherwise.

The axioms for *sort* and *insert* suggest a method for sorting a given tuple, as illustrated in the next example.

Example (sorting)

Suppose we would like to sort the tuple $\langle 4,\ 1,\ 2 \rangle$, that is, $4 \diamond (1 \diamond (2 \diamond \langle\,\rangle))$. Then we have

$$sort\big(4 \diamond (1 \diamond (2 \diamond \langle\,\rangle))\big)$$

$$= insert\big(4,\ sort\big(1 \diamond (2 \diamond \langle\,\rangle))\big)\big)$$
(by the *insertion* axiom for *sort*)

$$= insert\big(4,\ insert\big(1,\ insert\big(2,\ sort(\langle\,\rangle))\big)\big)\big)$$
(by the *insertion* axiom for *sort*, twice more)

$$= insert\big(4,\ insert\big(1,\ insert\big(2,\ \langle\,\rangle)\big)\big)\big)$$
(by the *empty* axiom for *sort*)

$$= insert\big(4,\ insert\big(1,\ 2 \diamond \langle\,\rangle)\big)\big)$$
(by the *empty* axiom for *insert*)

$$= insert\big(4,\ 1 \diamond (2 \diamond \langle\,\rangle))\big)$$
(by the *insertion* axiom for *insert*, because $1 \leq 2$)

$$= 1 \diamond insert\big(4,\ 2 \diamond \langle\,\rangle)\big)$$
(by the *insertion* axiom for *insert*, because *not* $(4 \leq 1)$)

$$= 1 \diamond (2 \diamond insert(4, \langle \; \rangle))$$
(by the *insertion* axiom for *insert*, because *not* $(4 \leq 2)$)

$$= 1 \diamond (2 \diamond (4 \diamond \langle \; \rangle))$$
(by the *empty* axiom for *insert*).

In short,

$$sort(\langle 4, \, 1, \, 2 \rangle) \; = \; \langle 1, \, 2, \, 4 \rangle. \quad \blacksquare$$

We would like to show two properties of the *sort* function: that the tuple $sort(x)$ is in increasing order, that is,

$$(\textit{for all tuple } x)\big[ordered(sort(x))\big] \qquad\qquad (\textit{ordered})$$

and that the elements of the tuple $sort(x)$ are the same as those of the tuple x, that is,

$$(\textit{for all tuple } x)\big[perm(x, \; sort(x))\big] \qquad\qquad (\textit{permutation})$$

For this purpose we shall have to establish two corresponding properties of the auxiliary function *insert*: that if the tuple x is in increasing order, so is the tuple $insert(u, \, x)$, that is,

$$\begin{array}{l}(\textit{for all atom } u) \\ (\textit{for all tuple } x)\end{array}\left[\begin{array}{l}\textit{if } ordered(x) \\ \textit{then } ordered(insert(u, \, x))\end{array}\right] \qquad (\textit{ordered})$$

and that the elements of the tuple $insert(u, \, x)$ are precisely the atom u and the elements of the tuple x, that is,

$$\begin{array}{l}(\textit{for all atom } u) \\ (\textit{for all tuple } x)\end{array}\Big[perm(u \diamond x, \, insert(u, x))\Big] \qquad (\textit{permutation})$$

PROPERTIES OF INSERT

We first establish the required properties of the auxiliary function *insert*.

Lemma (insert)

The sentences

$$\begin{array}{l}(\textit{for all atom } u) \\ (\textit{for all tuple } x)\end{array}\left[\begin{array}{l}\textit{if } ordered(x) \\ \textit{then } ordered(insert(u, x))\end{array}\right] \qquad (\textit{ordered})$$

$$\begin{array}{l}(\textit{for all atom } u) \\ (\textit{for all tuple } x)\end{array}\Big[perm(u \diamond x, \; insert(u, \; x))\Big] \qquad (\textit{permutation})$$

are valid.   ◢

We establish the *permutation* property of the *insert* lemma first and then use it in the proof of the *ordered* property.

Proof (*permutation* of *insert*)

Consider an arbitrary atom u; we would like to establish

$$(for\ all\ tuple\ x)\left[perm\big(u \diamond x,\ insert(u,\ x)\big)\right].$$

The proof is by induction on x, taking the inductive sentence to be

$$\mathcal{F}[x]:\quad perm\big(u \diamond x,\ insert(u,\ x)\big).$$

Base Case

We would like to show

$$\mathcal{F}[\langle\ \rangle]:\quad perm\big(u \diamond \langle\ \rangle,\ insert(u,\ \langle\ \rangle)\big)$$

or, equivalently (by the *empty* axiom for *insert*),

$$perm\big(u \diamond \langle\ \rangle,\ u \diamond \langle\ \rangle\big).$$

But this is true (by the *reflexivity* property of *perm*).

Inductive Step

We would like to show

$$\begin{array}{l}(for\ all\ atom\ v)\\(for\ all\ tuple\ x)\end{array}\left[\begin{array}{l}if\ \mathcal{F}[x]\\then\ \mathcal{F}[v \diamond x]\end{array}\right].$$

For an arbitrary atom v and tuple x, assume the induction hypothesis

$$\mathcal{F}[x]:\quad perm\big(u \diamond x,\ insert(u,\ x)\big).$$

We must establish the desired conclusion

$$\mathcal{F}[v \diamond x]:\quad perm\big(u \diamond (v \diamond x),\ insert(u,\ v \diamond x)\big).$$

The proof distinguishes between two cases, depending on whether or not $u \leq v$.

Case: $u \leq v$

Then we have

$$perm\big(u \diamond (v \diamond x),\ insert(u,\ v \diamond x)\big)$$

precisely when (by the *insertion* axiom for *insert*, because $u \leq v$)

$$perm\big(u \diamond (v \diamond x), \ u \diamond (v \diamond x)\big),$$

which is true (by the *reflexivity* property of *perm*).

Case: not $(u \leq v)$

Then we have

$$perm\big(u \diamond (v \diamond x), \ insert(u, \ v \diamond x)\big)$$

precisely when (by the *insertion* axiom for *insert*, because *not* $(u \leq v)$)

$$perm\big(u \diamond (v \diamond x), \ v \diamond insert(u, \ x)\big)$$

precisely when (by the *exchange* and the *transitivity* properties of *perm*)

$$perm\big(v \diamond (u \diamond x), \ v \diamond insert(u, \ x)\big)$$

precisely when (by the *equal-insertion* property of *perm*)

$$perm\big(u \diamond x, \ insert(u, \ x)\big),$$

which is true (by our induction hypothesis $\mathcal{F}[x]$). ⌟

We can now establish the first part of the *insert* lemma, the *ordered* property of *insert*.

Proof (*ordered* of *insert*)

We would like to show

$$(\textit{for all atom } u) \ \begin{bmatrix} \textit{if } ordered(x) \\ (\textit{for all tuple } x) \end{bmatrix} \begin{bmatrix} \textit{if } ordered(x) \\ \textit{then } ordered\big(insert(u, \ x)\big) \end{bmatrix}.$$

Consider an arbitrary atom u; we must establish

$$(\textit{for all tuple } x) \begin{bmatrix} \textit{if } ordered(x) \\ \textit{then } ordered\big(insert(u, \ x)\big) \end{bmatrix}.$$

The proof is by induction on x, taking the inductive sentence to be

$$\mathcal{F}[x]: \quad \begin{array}{l} \textit{if } ordered(x) \\ \textit{then } ordered\big(insert(u, \ x)\big). \end{array}$$

Base Case

We would like to show

$$\mathcal{F}[\langle\,\rangle]: \quad \begin{array}{l} \textit{if } ordered(\langle\,\rangle) \\ \textit{then } ordered(insert(u, \ \langle\,\rangle)). \end{array}$$

But we have

$$ordered(insert(u, \langle \, \rangle))$$

precisely when (by the *empty* axiom for *insert*)

$$ordered(u \diamond \langle \, \rangle),$$

which is true (by the *singleton* axiom for the *ordered* relation).

Inductive Step

We would like to show

$$\begin{array}{l}(\textit{for all atom } v) \\ (\textit{for all tuple } x)\end{array} \left[\begin{array}{l}\textit{if } \mathcal{F}[x] \\ \textit{then } \mathcal{F}[v \diamond x]\end{array}\right].$$

For an arbitrary atom v and tuple x, assume the induction hypothesis

$$\mathcal{F}[x]: \quad \begin{array}{l}\textit{if } ordered(x) \\ \textit{then } ordered(insert(u, x)).\end{array}$$

We must establish the desired conclusion

$$\mathcal{F}[v \diamond x]: \quad \begin{array}{l}\textit{if } ordered(v \diamond x) \\ \textit{then } ordered(insert(u, v \diamond x)).\end{array}$$

Suppose that

$$(*) \qquad ordered(v \diamond x).$$

Then (by the *insertion* property of the *ordered* relation)

$$(\dagger) \qquad ordered(x)$$

and

$$(\ddagger) \qquad (\textit{for all atom } w) \left[\begin{array}{l}\textit{if } w \in x \\ \textit{then } v \leq w\end{array}\right].$$

We would like to show that

$$ordered(insert(u, v \diamond x)).$$

The proof distinguishes between two cases, depending on whether or not $u \leq v$.

Case: $u \leq v$

Then we have

$$ordered(insert(u, v \diamond x))$$

precisely when (by the *insertion* axiom for *insert*, because $u \leq v$)

$$ordered\big(u \diamond (v \diamond x)\big)$$

precisely when (by the *double-insertion* axiom for the *ordered* relation)

$$u \leq v \quad and \quad ordered(v \diamond x),$$

which is true by our case assumption and our supposition ($*$).

Case: *not* $(u \leq v)$

Then we have

$$ordered\big(insert(u, \, v \diamond x)\big)$$

precisely when (by the *insertion* axiom for *insert*, because *not* $(u \leq v)$)

$$ordered\big(v \diamond insert(u, \, x)\big)$$

precisely when (by the *insertion* property of the *ordered* relation)

$$ordered\big(insert(u, \, x)\big)$$

and

$$(for \; all \; atom \; w) \begin{bmatrix} if \; w \in insert(u, \, x) \\ then \; v \leq w \end{bmatrix}.$$

To show the first of these conditions, $ordered\big(insert(u, \, x)\big)$, it suffices (by our induction hypothesis $\mathcal{F}[x]$) to establish

$$ordered(x),$$

but this is our earlier conclusion (†).

To show the second of the above conditions, consider an arbitrary atom w and suppose that

$$w \in insert(u, \, x).$$

We would like to show that

$$v \leq w.$$

We know (by the *permutation* property of *insert*, which is the second part of this lemma) that

$$perm\big(u \diamond x, \, insert(u, \, x)\big).$$

Therefore (by the *member* axiom for *perm*, since $w \in insert(u, \, x)$ by our supposition) we have

$$w \in (u \diamond x)$$

and hence (by the *insertion* axiom for the member relation)

$$w = u \quad or \quad w \in x.$$

We distinguish between these two subcases.

Subcase: $w = u$

We would like to show $v \leq w$, that is,

$$v \leq u.$$

But this follows (by the *totality* of the less-than relation $\leq$) from our case assumption $not \, (u \leq v)$.

Subcase: $w \in x$

Then (by our earlier conclusion ($\ddagger$)) we have

$$v \leq w,$$

as we wanted to show. ⌐

PROPERTIES OF SORT

We are now ready to establish the desired properties of the *sort* function.

Proposition (sort)

The sentences

$$(\textit{for all tuple } x)\big[ordered\,(sort(x))\big] \qquad\qquad (\textit{ordered})$$

$$(\textit{for all tuple } x)\big[perm\,(x, \, sort(x))\big] \qquad\qquad (\textit{permutation})$$

are valid. ⌐

We establish the *ordered* property of the *sort* proposition first.

Proof (*ordered* of *sort*)

We would like to show

$$(for\ all\ tuple\ x)\big[ordered\big(sort(x)\big)\big].$$

The proof is by induction on x, taking our inductive sentence to be

$$\mathcal{F}[x]: \quad ordered\big(sort(x)\big).$$

Base Case

We would like to show

$$\mathcal{F}[\langle\,\rangle]: \quad ordered\big(sort(\langle\,\rangle)\big)$$

or, equivalently (by the *empty* axiom for *sort*),

$$ordered(\langle\,\rangle).$$

But this is true (by the *empty* axiom for *ordered*).

Inductive Step

For an arbitrary atom v and tuple x, assume the induction hypothesis

$$\mathcal{F}[x]: \quad ordered\big(sort(x)\big).$$

We must establish the desired conclusion

$$\mathcal{F}[v \diamond x]: \quad ordered\big(sort(v \diamond x)\big)$$

or, equivalently (by the *insertion* axiom for *sort*),

$$ordered\big(insert(v,\ sort(x))\big).$$

It suffices (by the *ordered* property of *insert*, proved in the lemma) to show that

$$ordered\big(sort(x)\big),$$

but this is precisely our induction hypothesis $\mathcal{F}[x]$. ◢

We next establish the second part of the *sort* proposition, the *permutation* property of *sort*.

Proof (*permutation* for *sort*)

We would like to show that

$$(for\ all\ tuple\ x)\big[perm\big(x,\ sort(x)\big)\big].$$

The proof is by induction on x, taking the inductive sentence to be

$$\mathcal{F}[x]: \quad perm\big(x,\ sort(x)\big).$$

Base Case

We would like to show

$$\mathcal{F}[\langle\ \rangle]: \quad perm\big(\langle\ \rangle,\ sort(\langle\ \rangle)\big)$$

or, equivalently (by the *empty* axiom for *sort*),

$$perm\big(\langle\ \rangle,\ \langle\ \rangle\big).$$

But this is true (by the *empty* axiom for *perm*).

Inductive Step

For an arbitrary atom v and tuple x, assume the induction hypothesis

$$\mathcal{F}[x]: \quad perm\big(x,\ sort(x)\big).$$

We must establish the desired conclusion

$$\mathcal{F}[v \diamond x]: \quad perm\big(v \diamond x,\ sort(v \diamond x)\big)$$

or, equivalently (by the *insertion* axiom for *sort*),

$$(*) \qquad perm\big(v \diamond x,\ insert(v,\ sort(x))\big).$$

We know (by our induction hypothesis $\mathcal{F}[x]$) that

$$perm\big(x,\ sort(x)\big).$$

Therefore (by the *equal-insertion* property of *perm*) we have

$$perm\big(v \diamond x,\ v \diamond sort(x)\big).$$

Also (by the *permutation* property of *insert*, proved in the lemma) we know

$$perm\big(v \diamond sort(x),\ insert(v,\ sort(x))\big).$$

Therefore (by the *transitivity* property of *perm*) we have

$$perm\big(v \diamond x,\ insert(v,\ sort(x))\big),$$

which is our desired result $(*)$. ∎

Remark

As in the section on the *ordered* relation, we have assumed initially that the atoms of our tuples are identified with the nonnegative integers; however, the only properties of the nonnegative integers we require for the proof of the *sort* proposition are the totality of the less-than relation $\leq$ (in the proof of the *ordered* property of *insert*) and its transitivity (in the proof of the *insertion* property of *ordered*). Therefore we could establish the same results in an augmented theory of tuples in which $\leq$ is replaced by an arbitrary transitive total relation $\prec$, without mentioning the nonnegative integers at all. ⌐

The *sort* function can be shown to be the only function that satisfies the *ordered* and *permutation* properties, that is,

$$(\text{for all tuple } x) \atop (\text{for all tuple } y) \left[\begin{matrix} \textit{if } ordered(y) \ \textit{and} \\ perm(x, y) \\ \textit{then } y = sort(x) \end{matrix} \right] \qquad (uniqueness)$$

Of course there are alternative definitions of the *sort* function.

We can also show that applying the *sort* function twice to a given tuple has the same effect as applying it once, that is,

$$(\textit{for all tuple } x)\big[sort\big(sort(x)\big) \ = \ sort(x)\big] \qquad (idempotence)$$

The proofs of the *uniqueness* and *idempotence* properties are requested in **Problem 12.9**.

The material in the next section is advanced and may be skipped on first reading.

12.7   RECURSIVE DEFINITION OF FUNCTIONS

In this section we use the theory of tuples of nonnegative integers to establish an important result about the nonnegative integers, that the systems of axioms we use to define new functions over the nonnegative integers do not lead to inconsistency in the theory.

In general, when we define a new function symbol by augmenting a given theory with a set of axioms, there is no guarantee that, in a model for the given theory, there actually exists a function over the domain that satisfies the new axioms. If there is no model in which such a function exists, the augmented theory will be inconsistent. We illustrate this with an example.

Example (bad)

Suppose we augment the theory of the nonnegative integers by introducing a new binary function symbol $bad(x, y)$, defined by the axioms

$$(for\ all\ integer\ x)[bad(x, 0) = 0] \qquad\qquad (zero)$$

$$\begin{array}{l}(for\ all\ integer\ x)\\(for\ all\ integer\ y)\end{array}\Big[bad(x, y + 1) = bad(x, y + 1) + 1\Big] \qquad (successor)$$

$$\begin{array}{l}(for\ all\ integer\ x)\\(for\ all\ integer\ y)\end{array}\Big[integer(bad(x, y))\Big] \qquad\qquad (sort)$$

Then the resulting theory is inconsistent. For suppose the augmented theory does have a model. Then for arbitrary domain elements x and y, we know (by the *sort* axiom for *bad*) that

$$integer(bad(x, y + 1)).$$

We know (by properties of the nonnegative integers) that

$$(for\ all\ integer\ u)\big[not\ (u = u + 1)\big]$$

is valid. Therefore (taking u to be the nonnegative integer $bad(x, y + 1)$)

$$not\ \big[bad(x, y + 1) = bad(x, y + 1) + 1)\big].$$

But this contradicts the *successor* axiom for *bad*. ◢

It is not always possible to detect whether a given set of axioms leads to an inconsistency. In the theory of the nonnegative integers, however, if the axioms for the new function are in a certain *recursive form*, we can guarantee that there exists a model for the augmented theory. In other words, there exists a function over the domain of the model that satisfies the axioms.

First let us make precise the notion of recursive form.

Definition (recursive form)

In the theory of the nonnegative integers, suppose that $s[x]$ and $t[x, y, z]$ are terms and a new binary function symbol $f(x, y)$ is defined by the following axioms:

$$(for\ all\ integer\ x)\big[f(x, 0) = s[x]\big] \qquad\qquad (zero)$$

$$\begin{array}{l}(for\ all\ integer\ x)\\(for\ all\ integer\ y)\end{array}\big[f(x, y + 1) = t[x, y, f(x, y)]\big] \qquad (successor)$$

Then these axioms are said to provide a *recursive definition* for f and the definition of f is said to be in *recursive form.* ⌐

The theory of the nonnegative integers we consider can actually be augmented by the definitions of other functions or relations. When we say that f is a "new" function symbol, we mean that f does not occur in $s[x]$, $t[x, y, z]$, or any of the other axioms for the augmented theory.

Example (multiplication)

The multiplication function was defined by the *right-zero* axiom

$$(for\ all\ integer\ x)[x \cdot 0 \ = \ 0]$$

and the *right-successor* axiom

$$\begin{matrix}(for\ all\ integer\ x)\\ (for\ all\ integer\ y)\end{matrix}\left[x \cdot (y + 1) \ = \ x \cdot y + x\right].$$

These axioms provide a recursive definition for the multiplication function, as we can see by taking

$s[x]$ to be 0

$t[x, y, z]$ to be $z + x$

in the definition of recursive form. ⌐

Note that axioms for the *bad* function defined earlier are not in recursive form.

Remark (computation of recursive definitions)

A recursive definition of a function f suggests a method for computing it, provided we have methods for computing the terms $s[x]$ and $t[x, y, z]$. For example, suppose we would like to compute the value of $f(x, 2)$, that is, $f\big(x, (0+1)+1\big)$. Then we have

$$f\big(x, (0 + 1) + 1\big) \ = \ t\big[x, \ 0 + 1, \ f(x, \ 0 + 1)\big]$$
$$\text{(by the } successor \text{ axiom for } f)$$

$$= \ t\big[x, \ 0 + 1, \ t\big[x, \ 0, \ f(x, \ 0)\big]\big]$$
$$\text{(by the } successor \text{ axiom for } f \text{ again)}$$

$$= \ t\big[x, \ 0 + 1, \ t\big[x, \ 0, \ s[x]\big]\big]$$
$$\text{(by the } zero \text{ axiom for } f),$$

which we can compute since we have methods for computing $s[x]$ and $t[x, y, z]$. ◢

We can now establish that, in the theory of the nonnegative integers, if the axioms for a function are in recursive form, then they cannot lead to an inconsistency in the theory.

Proposition (recursive definition)

Let I be a model for the theory of the nonnegative integers and let f be a new binary function symbol.

Then there exists a model I' for the theory under which the *zero* and *successor* axioms for f are true, where I' and I agree on all symbols except perhaps f. ◢

Again, the theory of the nonnegative integers we refer to may already include the definitions of other functions and relations. The proposition establishes that, if this theory is consistent, the theory augmented by the definition of f is also consistent.

For example, we have seen that the axioms for the multiplication function are in recursive form. The proposition establishes that if the theory of the nonnegative integers (including the definition of the addition function) is consistent, then the theory augmented by the definition of the multiplication function is also consistent. In fact, any model for the original theory can be converted into a model for the augmented theory simply by assigning the appropriate function to the new function symbol $x \cdot y$.

On the other hand, since the definition of the *bad* function was seen not to be of recursive form, the proposition does not establish that the theory of the nonnegative integers augmented by this definition is consistent; indeed we have shown it to be inconsistent.

Before proving the proposition we discuss a few related issues.

Remark (more general recursive definitions)

We have introduced the notion of recursive definition for a binary function symbol f; in fact, we can extend the notion to function symbols of any positive arity, and to predicate symbols as well, and establish a correspondingly extended *recursive-definition* proposition.

In the theory of the nonnegative integers, we often define functions with axioms that are not of recursive form. For instance, the greatest-common-divisor function $gcd(x, y)$ was defined by the axioms

$$(\text{for all integer } x)\big[gcd(x, 0) \ = \ x\big] \hspace{3cm} (zero)$$

$$\begin{array}{l}(\text{for all integer } x)\\(\text{for all positive } y)\end{array}\big[gcd(x, y) \ = \ gcd\big(y, \ rem(x, y)\big)\big] \hspace{1cm} (remainder)$$

These axioms are not in recursive form (as we have defined it) because the second axiom is not of form $f(x, y + 1) = t\big[x, \ y, \ f(x, y)\big]$. Nevertheless, the theory of the nonnegative integers is still consistent when augmented by these axioms, and the axioms do suggest a method for computing the function. In fact, one could introduce a more general notion of recursive definition and establish that such definitions also maintain the consistency of the theory of nonnegative integers, but we shall not do so. ◢

Remark (recursive definitions in other theories)

We have introduced the notion of recursive form and the *recursive-definition* proposition for the nonnegative integers. In fact, we can introduce an analogous notion of recursive form for the other theories, such as strings, lists, trees, sets, bags, and tuples. For most of these theories we can establish the corresponding *recursive-definition* proposition. For the theories of sets and bags, however, the analogous *recursive-definition* proposition does not hold: Augmenting the theory with axioms of recursive form may destroy the consistency of the theory. This is because these theories do not have the same uniqueness properties as the others.

For example, in the combined theory of bags and tuples, we discussed the possibility of defining a unary function symbol $tuplebag(x)$ by the *empty* axiom

$$tuplebag(\llbracket\,\rrbracket) \ = \ \langle\,\rangle$$

and the *insertion* axiom

$$\begin{array}{l}(\text{for all atom } u)\\(\text{for all bag } x)\end{array}\big[tuplebag(u \circ x) \ = \ u \diamond tuplebag(x)\big].$$

These axioms are in recursive form, as that notion is defined in the theory of bags. Nevertheless, introducing these axioms into the combined theory leads to an inconsistency; for example, we can show that

$$\langle A, B\rangle \ = \ tuplebag(\llbracket A, B\rrbracket) \ = \ tuplebag\big(\llbracket B, A\rrbracket\big) \ = \ \langle B, A\rangle,$$

but we know that

$$\text{not } \langle A, B\rangle = \langle B, A\rangle.$$

Similar inconsistencies can be obtained by adding recursive definitions to the theory of sets. In these theories, special care must be taken not to introduce inconsistencies in defining new functions and relations.   ⌐

We are ready to prove the proposition. Although the proposition itself does not mention the theory of tuples, the proof does rely on this theory.

Proof (recursive definition)

We do not give the precise proof of the proposition, which is lengthy and technical. The idea of the proof is as follows. The model I' we construct will be identical to the given model I except that the function symbol f will be assigned the function such that

$$f(x, 0) = s[x],$$

$$f(x, 1) = t[x, 0, s[x]] = t[x, 0, f(x, 0)],$$

$$f(x, 2) = t[x, 1, t[x, 0, s[x]]] = t[x, 1, f(x, 1)],$$

and so forth, are all true under I'.

To construct I', it turns out to be easier to first extend our model to include tuples of nonnegative integers and to define a binary function symbol g such that, for nonnegative integers x and y, the value of $g(x, y)$ is a tuple of $y+1$ nonnegative integers such that

$$[g(x, y)]_0 = s[x],$$

$$[g(x, y)]_1 = t[x, 0, s[x]],$$

$$[g(x, y)]_2 = t[x, 1, t[x, 0, s[x]]],$$

and so forth, under this model.

In other words, the desired function f will have the property that

$$g(x, y) = \langle f(x, 0), f(x, 1), \ldots, f(x, y) \rangle.$$

We can then define $f(x, y)$ to be the final element of $g(x, y)$, that is,

$$f(x, y) = [g(x, y)]_y.$$

The function f defined in this way can be shown to satisfy the desired *zero* and *successor* sentences.

This establishes the existence of an integer-valued function over the nonnegative integers satisfying the *zero* and *successor* sentences. The desired model I' can be taken to be the model over the nonnegative integers that assigns this function to f and that agrees with the original model $\mathcal{I}$ on all other symbols.

The function g itself is defined so that the sentence

$$tuple\big(g(x,\,y)\big)$$
$$and$$
$$length\big(g(x,\,y)\big)\ =\ y+1$$
$$and$$
$$(for\ all\ integer\ w)\begin{bmatrix} if\ w \leq y \\ then\ integer\big(\big[g(x,\,y)\big]_w\big) \end{bmatrix}$$
$$and$$
$$\big[g(x,\,y)\big]_0\ =\ s[x]$$
$$and$$
$$(for\ all\ integer\ w)\begin{bmatrix} if\ w < y \\ then\ \big[g(x,\,y)\big]_{w+1}\ =\ t\big[x,\,w,\,\big[g(x,\,y)\big]_w\big] \end{bmatrix}$$

is true for all nonnegative integers x and y. In other words, $g(x,\,y)$ is the tuple such that

$$\big[g(x,\,y)\big]_0\ =\ s[x],$$

$$\big[g(x,\,y)\big]_1\ =\ t\big[x,\,0,\,\big[g(x,\,y)\big]_0\big]\ =\ t\big[x,\,0,\,s[x]\big],$$

$$\big[g(x,\,y)\big]_2\ =\ t\big[x,\,1,\,\big[g(x,\,y)\big]_1\big]\ =\ t\big[x,\,1,\,t\big[x,\,0,\,s[x]\big]\big],$$

and so forth.

To show the existence of a suitable model in which such a function g exists, it suffices (by the *function-introduction* proposition of predicate logic) to show the truth of the sentence

$$\begin{matrix} (for\ all\ integer\ x) \\ (for\ all\ integer\ y) \end{matrix}(for\ some\ tuple\ z)$$

$$\begin{bmatrix} length(z)\ =\ y+1 \\ and \\ (for\ all\ integer\ w)\begin{bmatrix} if\ w \leq y \\ then\ integer\big([z]_w\big) \end{bmatrix} \\ and \\ [z]_0\ =\ s[x] \\ and \\ (for\ all\ integer\ w)\begin{bmatrix} if\ w < y \\ then\ [z]_{w+1}\ =\ t\big[x,\,w,\,[z]_w\big] \end{bmatrix} \end{bmatrix}$$

in the model $\mathcal{I}$ extended to include tuples of nonnegative integers. This establishes the existence of the desired function $g(x,\,y)$. The proof, which is by stepwise induction over the nonnegative integers, on y, is omitted. ◢

PROBLEMS

Problem 12.1 (the same relation) page 532

Establish that the following property provides an alternative definition for the *same* relation:

$$(for\ all\ tuple\ x) \begin{bmatrix} same(x) \\ if\ and\ only\ if \\ (for\ all\ atom\ u) \begin{bmatrix} if\ u \in x\ \ and\ \ v \in x \\ then\ \ u = v \end{bmatrix} \\ (for\ all\ atom\ v) \end{bmatrix} \quad (equality)$$

In other words

(a) Show that this property follows from the three axioms defining the *same* relation.

(b) Show that, if we replace the original three axioms for the *same* relation with this sentence, we can establish the validity of each of the original three axioms in the altered theory.

Problem 12.2 (element of append) page 538

In the combined theory of nonnegative integers and tuples, establish the properties that relate the append function and the element function; that is,

(a) *Left element*

$$\begin{matrix} (for\ all\ integer\ z) \\ (for\ all\ tuple\ x) \\ (for\ all\ tuple\ y) \end{matrix} \begin{bmatrix} if\ z < length(x) \\ then\ [x \diamond y]_z\ =\ [x]_z \end{bmatrix}$$

(b) *Right element*

$$\begin{matrix} (for\ all\ integer\ z) \\ (for\ all\ tuple\ x) \\ (for\ all\ tuple\ y) \end{matrix} \begin{bmatrix} if\ z < length(y) \\ then\ [x \diamond y]_{length(x)+z}\ =\ [y]_z \end{bmatrix}.$$

List all the new properties of the nonnegative integers you use; you need not prove them.

Problem 12.3 (mapping)   pages 542, 543

Establish the following properties of the mapping functions:

(a) *Onto*

Show that the *bagtuple* function, mapping tuples into bags, is onto, that is,

$$(\textit{for all bag } y)(\textit{for some tuple } x)\big[bagtuple(x) \;=\; y\big].$$

(b) *Composition*

Establish the *composition* property of the mapping functions, that is,

$$(\textit{for all tuple } x)\big[settuple(x) \;=\; setbag\,(bagtuple(x))\big].$$

Problem 12.4 (alternative definition of perm)   page 549

Show that the *eqmult* property of the permutation relation,

$$
\begin{array}{l}
(\textit{for all tuple } x) \\
(\textit{for all tuple } y)
\end{array}
\left[
\begin{array}{l}
perm(x,\ y) \\
\quad \textit{if and only if} \\
(\textit{for all atom } u)\big[eqmult(u,\ x,\ y)\big]
\end{array}
\right],
$$

provides an alternative definition for the relation. In other words, if we replace the three axioms for *perm*, i.e., the *empty*, *append-singleton*, and *member* axioms, with this sentence, we can establish the validity of each of the original three axioms in the altered theory.

Problem 12.5 (the permutation relation)   page 549

Establish the validity of the following properties of the permutation relation:

(a)   *Exchange*

$$
\begin{array}{l}
(\textit{for all atom } u) \\
(\textit{for all atom } v) \\
(\textit{for all tuple } x)
\end{array}
\left[perm\big(u \diamond (v \diamond x),\ v \diamond (u \diamond x)\big)\right].
$$

(b)   *Append*

$$
\begin{array}{l}
(\textit{for all tuple } x_1) \\
(\textit{for all tuple } y_1) \\
(\textit{for all tuple } x_2) \\
(\textit{for all tuple } y_2)
\end{array}
\left[
\begin{array}{l}
\textit{if } perm(x_1,\ y_1)\ \textit{ and} \\
\quad perm(x_2,\ y_2) \\
\textit{then } perm(x_1 \diamond x_2,\ y_1 \diamond y_2)
\end{array}
\right].
$$

Problem 12.6 (alternative definition of ordered)   page 554

Show that the *empty* axiom for *ordered*,

$$ordered(\langle\,\rangle),$$

and the *insertion* property of ordered,

$$
\begin{array}{ll}
(\textit{for all atom } u) \\
(\textit{for all tuple } x)
\end{array}
\left[
\begin{array}{l}
ordered(u \diamond x) \\
\quad \textit{if and only if} \\
\left[
\begin{array}{l}
ordered(x) \\
\quad and \\
(\textit{for all atom } v)
\left[
\begin{array}{l}
\textit{if } v \in x \\
\textit{then } u \le v
\end{array}
\right]
\end{array}
\right]
\end{array}
\right],
$$

provide an alternative definition of the ordered relation. In other words, if we replace the *singleton* and *double-insertion* axioms for *ordered* with the *insertion* property, we can establish the validity of the *singleton* and *double-insertion* axioms in the altered theory.

Problem 12.7 (the ordered relation)   page 554

In the theory of tuples of nonnegative integers, establish the *append* property of the *ordered* relation, that is,

$$
\begin{array}{ll}
(\textit{for all tuple } x) \\
(\textit{for all tuple } y)
\end{array}
\left[
\begin{array}{l}
ordered(x \diamond y) \\
\quad \textit{if and only if} \\
\left[
\begin{array}{l}
ordered(x) \;\; and \;\; ordered(y) \\
\quad and \\
(\textit{for all atom } u) \\
(\textit{for all atom } v)
\left[
\begin{array}{l}
\textit{if } u \in x \;\; and \;\; v \in y \\
\textit{then } u \le v
\end{array}
\right]
\end{array}
\right]
\end{array}
\right].
$$

Problem 12.8 (minimum function)   page 555

In the theory of tuples of nonnegative integers, establish the *least* property of the minimum function, that is,

$$
(\textit{for all tuple } x)
\left[
\begin{array}{l}
\textit{if not } (x = \langle\,\rangle) \\
\textit{then}
\left[
\begin{array}{l}
mintuple(x) \in x \\
\quad and \\
(\textit{for all atom } u)
\left[
\begin{array}{l}
\textit{if } u \in x \\
\textit{then } mintuple(x) \le u
\end{array}
\right]
\end{array}
\right]
\end{array}
\right].
$$

In other words, $mintuple(x)$ is the least element of a nonempty tuple x.

Problem 12.9 (the sort function)   page 565

In the theory of tuples of nonnegative integers, establish the validity of the following sentences:

(a)   *Ordered permutation*

$$(\textit{for all tuple } x)\ (\textit{for all tuple } y)\ \begin{bmatrix} \textit{if } perm(x,\,y)\ \textit{and} \\ ordered(x)\ \textit{and} \\ ordered(y) \\ \textit{then } x = y \end{bmatrix}$$

(b)   *Uniqueness of sort*

$$(\textit{for all tuple } x)\ (\textit{for all tuple } y)\ \begin{bmatrix} \textit{if } ordered(y)\ \textit{and} \\ perm(x,\,y) \\ \textit{then } y = sort(x) \end{bmatrix}$$

(c)   *Idempotence of sort*

$$(\textit{for all tuple } x)\,\big[sort\big(sort(x)\big) = sort(x)\big].$$

List all the new properties of the nonnegative integers you use; you need not prove them. As usual, you may use without proof the appropriate *sort* properties of the *insert* and *sort* functions.

Problem 12.10 (theory of integers — comprehensive problem)

(This problem is placed in this chapter not because it requires particular results from the theory of tuples, but because it demands the sophistication the reader has acquired by being exposed to many different theories.)

Design a theory of the integers. In other words, write a set of axioms for all the integers, including the negative integers. Try to make your axiom system concise and elegant (as well as correct and consistent).

In addition to some of the original symbols and the usual predicate and function symbols for the nonnegative integers, you may wish to define the following predicate and function symbols:

- *positive*(x): x is a (strictly) positive integer (i.e., $x > 0$)

- *negative*(x): x is a (strictly) negative integer (i.e., $x < 0$)

- *whole*(x): x is any integer, positive, negative, or zero

- $-x$: minus x.

Note that the minus function $-x$ is unary and is distinct from the subtraction function $x - y$, which is binary. Whereas in the theory of the nonnegative integers, the axioms did not specify the value of the subtraction function $x - y$ for $x < y$, the axioms for this theory should specify the value of $x - y$ for all integers x and y. Similarly, the value of x^- should be specified for all integers x.

Remember that you will need some form of induction axiom.

Within your system prove the following properties (unless they are already axioms):

(a) *Successor predecessor*

$$(\text{for all whole } x)\left[-(x^+) \ = \ (-x)^-\right]$$

(b) *Predecessor zero*

$$(\text{for all negative } x)\left[not\ (x^- = 0)\right]$$

(c) *Cancellation*

$$(\text{for all whole } x)\ \begin{bmatrix} x + y = z \\ \text{if and only if} \\ x = z - y \end{bmatrix}$$
$$(\text{for all whole } y)$$
$$(\text{for all whole } z)$$

(d) *Subtraction addition*

$$\begin{matrix}(\text{for all whole } x)\\(\text{for all whole } y)\end{matrix}\left[(x - y) + y \ = \ x\right]$$

(e) *Two*

$$not\ (2 = -2),$$

where 2 is $(0^+)^+$

(f) *Positive negative*

$$(\text{for all whole } x)\ \begin{bmatrix} if & \begin{bmatrix} positive(x) \\ \text{if and only if} \\ negative(x) \end{bmatrix} \\ then\ \ x = 0 \end{bmatrix}.$$

Problem 12.11 (parenthesis counting)

(This problem reflects a common method for detecting typographical errors in mathematical expressions. It does not rely on the theory of tuples, but it is included here because it uses the theory of integers of the previous problem. It is based on notions from the parsing example of Chapter 9.)

Consider a combined theory of trees, strings (in which the characters are the atoms of the trees and the three special characters $\widehat{(}$, $\widehat{)}$, and $\widehat{\bullet}$), and integers (of the previous problem). We define a unary function symbol $parcount(x)$ over the strings, which is intended to count the nonmatching parentheses in a string, by the axiom

$$(\textit{for all string } x)\big[parcount(x) \ = \ parcount2(x,\, 0)\big] \qquad (\textit{parcount})$$

where $parcount2(x,\, z)$ is a binary function, on a string x and an integer z, defined by the following axioms:

$$(\textit{for all whole } z)\big[parcount2(\Lambda,\, z) \ = \ z\big] \qquad (\textit{empty})$$

$$\begin{array}{l}(\textit{for all atom } u)\\(\textit{for all string } x)\\(\textit{for all whole } z)\end{array}\Big[parcount2(u * x,\, z) \ = \ parcount2(x,\, z)\Big] \qquad (\textit{atom})$$

$$\begin{array}{l}(\textit{for all string } x)\\(\textit{for all whole } z)\end{array}\Big[parcount2(\,\widehat{(}* x,\, z) \ = \ parcount2(x,\, z+1)\Big]$$

$$(\textit{left paren})$$

$$\begin{array}{l}(\textit{for all string } x)\\(\textit{for all whole } z)\end{array}\Big[parcount2(\,\widehat{)}* x,\, z) \ = \ parcount2(x,\, z-1)\Big]$$

$$(\textit{right paren})$$

$$\begin{array}{l}(\textit{for all string } x)\\(\textit{for all whole } z)\end{array}\Big[parcount2(\,\widehat{\bullet}* x,\, z) \ = \ parcount2(x,\, z)\Big]$$

$$(\textit{constructor})$$

Let the unary function symbol $generate(x)$ denote the function, defined in Chapter 9, that maps a tree x into its informal notation as a string.

Establish the following properties of the $parcount$ function:

(a) *Zero*

For an arbitrary tree z, the corresponding string representation $generate(z)$ has no nonmatching parentheses; that is,

$$(\textit{for all tree } z)\big[parcount(generate(z)) \ = \ 0\big].$$

(b) *Nonnegative-nonpositive*

Furthermore, any initial segment of $generate(z)$ has at least as many left parentheses as right; and any final segment of $generate(z)$ has at least as many right parentheses as left; that is,

$$
\begin{array}{l}
(for\ all\ tree\ z) \\
(for\ all\ string\ x) \\
(for\ all\ string\ y)
\end{array}
\left[
\begin{array}{l}
if\ \ generate(z) = x * y \\
then\ \ integer(parcount(x))\ \ and \\
\qquad not\ (positive(parcount(y)))
\end{array}
\right].
$$

Related Textbooks: a Selection

Introductions to logic from a mathematical point of view, with no computational emphasis:

A. CHURCH, *Introduction to Mathematical Logic*. Princeton: Princeton University Press, 1956.

H. B. ENDERTON, *A Mathematical Introduction to Logic*. New York: Academic Press, 1972.

S. C. KLEENE, *Mathematical Logic*. New York: John Wiley and Sons, 1967.

E. MENDELSON, *Introduction to Mathematical Logic*. New York: D. Van Nostrand, 1964.

More popular and informal introductions to logic:

D. R. HOFSTADTER, *Gödel, Escher, Bach: An Eternal Golden Braid*. New York: Basic Books, 1979.

R. SMULLYAN, *What Is the Name of This Book?* Englewood Cliffs, N. J.: Prentice-Hall, 1978.

Introductions to automatic theorem proving:

R. S. BOYER and J S. MOORE, *A Computational Logic*. New York: Academic Press, 1979.

C. L. CHANG and R. C. T. LEE, *Symbolic Logic and Mechanical Theorem Proving*. New York: Academic Press, 1973.

D. W. LOVELAND, *Automated Theorem Proving: A Logical Basis*. Amsterdam: North-Holland, 1978.

J. A. ROBINSON, *Logic: Form and Function*. New York: North-Holland, 1979.

L. WOS, R. OVERBEEK, E. LUSK, and J. BOYLE, *Automated Reasoning: Introduction and Application*. Englewood Cliffs, N. J.: Prentice-Hall, 1984.

Texts relating logic to the theory of computation:

H. R. LEWIS and C. H. PAPADIMITRIOU, *Elements of the Theory of Computation*. Englewood Cliffs, N. J: Prentice-Hall, 1981.

Z. MANNA, *Mathematical Theory of Computation*. New York: McGraw-Hill, 1974.

Books applying logic to the construction of correct computer programs:

R. L. CONSTABLE and M. J. O'DONNELL, *A Programming Logic*. Cambridge, Mass.: Winthrop, 1978.

E. W. DIJKSTRA, *A Discipline of Programming*. Englewood Cliffs, N. J.: Prentice-Hall, 1976.

D. GRIES, *The Science of Programming*. New York: Springer-Verlag, 1981.

J. C. REYNOLDS, *The Craft of Programming*. Englewood Cliffs, N. J.: Prentice-Hall International, 1981.

M. WAND, *Induction, Recursion, and Programming*. New York: North-Holland, 1980.

Texts applying logical techniques to problem solving and other topics in artificial intelligence:

R. KOWALSKI, *Logic for Problem Solving*. New York: North Holland, 1979.

N. J. NILSSON, *Principles of Artificial Intelligence*. Palo Alto, Calif.: Tioga, 1980.

Introductions to the logically oriented programming languages LISP and PROLOG:

W. F. CLOCKSIN and C. S. MELLISH, *Programming in Prolog*. Berlin: Springer-Verlag, 1981.

P. H. WINSTON and B. K. P. HORN, *LISP*. Reading, Mass.: Addison-Wesley, 1981.

W. A. WOLF, M. SHAW, P. N. HILFINGER, and L. FLON, *Fundamental Structures of Computer Science*, Reading, Mass.: Addison-Wesley, 1981.

Index of Symbols

ANNOTATIONS:

T: in proof by falsification, 28
   in semantic tree, 24
F: in proof by falsification, 28
   in semantic tree, 24
T_F: in proof by falsification, 29

BAGS:

$[\![\ ]\!]$: empty bag, 505
$[\![\ldots]\!]$: bag (informal notation), 506
$u \odot x$: insertion function, 506
$u \in x$: member relation, 506
$x \oplus y$: sum function, 522
$x \cup y$: union function, 522
$x \cap y$: intersection function, 523
$x \subset y$: proper subbag relation, 521
$x \subseteq y$: subbag relation, 520

GROUPS:

e: group identity, 249
$x \circ y$: group operation, 249
x^{-1}: group inverse, 249

INTERPRETATIONS:

$\langle P \leftarrow \tau \rangle \circ I$: extended interpretation (in
          propositional logic), 50
$\langle x \leftarrow d \rangle \circ I$: extended interpretation (in
          predicate logic), 89
$\langle P_1 \leftarrow \tau_1 \rangle \circ \ldots \circ \langle P_n \leftarrow \tau_n \rangle \circ I$:
    multiply extended interpretation
    (in propositional logic), 51
$\langle x_1 \leftarrow d_1 \rangle \circ \ldots \circ \langle x_n \leftarrow d_n \rangle \circ I$:
    multiply extended interpretation
    (in predicate logic), 91

LISTS:

$[\ ]$: empty list, 437
$[\ldots]$: list (informal notation), 438
$u \in x$: member relation, 444
$x \circ y$: insertion function, 437
$x \square y$: append function, 442

NONNEGATIVE INTEGERS:

0: zero constant, 285
1: as 0^+, 286
2: as $(0^+)^+$, 286
3: as $\big((0^+)^+\big)^+$, 286
x^+: successor function, 285
x^-: predecessor function, 312
$x!$: factorial function, 358
$-x$: minus function (for integers), 575
$x + y$: addition function, 291
$x \cdot y$: multiplication function, 304
x^y: exponentiation function, 305
$x - y$: subtraction function, 313
$x \mathbin{\dot{-}} y$: monus function, 314
$x < y$: strict less-than relation, 328
$x \leq y$: weak less-than relation, 321
$x > y$: strict greater-than relation, 329
$x \geq y$: weak greater-than relation, 325
$x \prec_{div} y$: proper divides relation, 343
$x \preceq_{div} y$: divides relation, 340

PAIRS:

$\langle x_1, x_2 \rangle$: pairing function, 256
$\langle x_1, x_2 \rangle \prec_{lex} \langle y_1, y_2 \rangle$: lexicographic rela-
    tion, 271

PARSING:

$\widehat{(}$: left parenthesis, 458
$\widehat{)}$: right parenthesis, 458
$\widehat{\bullet}$: constructor, 458

QUANTIFIERS:

(*for all x*): universal quantifier, 72
(*for some x*): existential quantifier, 72
(*for ... x*): universal or existential quantifier, 143
(*for all p x*): relativized universal quantifier, 266
(*for some p x*): relativized existential quantifier, 266
(*for all* *): universal closure, 108
(*for some* *): existential closure, 109

RELATIONS:

$x = y$: equality relation, 215
$x \approx y$: equivalence relation, 208
$x \prec y$: strict partial ordering, 201
    irreflexive restriction of $\preceq$, 232
$x \preceq y$: weak partial ordering, 229
$x \succ y$: inverse of strict partial ordering, 205
$x \succeq y$: inverse of weak partial ordering, 231
$x \prec\!\!\!\cdot\; y$: arbitrary binary relation, 232
$x \preceq\!\!\!\cdot\; y$: reflexive closure of $\prec\!\!\!\cdot$, 232
$\langle x_1, x_2 \rangle \prec\!\!\!\cdot_{lex} \langle y_1, y_2 \rangle$: lexicographic relation, 271

SETS:

$\{\ \}$: empty set, 471
$\{\ ...\ \}$: set (informal notation), 472
$u \circ x$: insertion function, 471
$u \in x$: member relation, 471
$x - u$: deletion function, 489
$x \cup y$: union function, 483
$x \cap y$: intersection function, 484
$x \sim y$: difference function, 490

$x \subset y$: proper subset relation, 492
$x \subseteq y$: subset relation, 491
$\{x : p(x)\}$: set constructor, 493

STRINGS:

Λ: empty string, 363
$u \bullet x$: prefix function, 363
$x * y$: concatenation function, 370
$x \preceq_{end} y$: end relation, 385
$x \prec_{init} y$: initial substring, 413
$x \preceq_{inter} y$: intersperse relation, 416
$x \prec_{string} y$: proper substring relation, 390
$x \preceq_{string} y$: substring relation, 389
$x \preceq_{string2} y$: substring2 relation, 414

SUBSTITUTIONS:

◄: total substitution (operator), 40, 46, 147, 151
◁: partial substitution (operator), 42, 46, 148, 151
$\mathcal{F}[\,...\,]$: total substitution (concise notation), 44, 48, 150, 152
$\mathcal{F}\langle\,...\,\rangle$: partial substitution (concise notation), 45, 49, 150, 152

TREES:

$x \bullet y$: construction function, 419
$x \prec_{tree} y$: proper subtree relation, 424
$x \preceq_{tree} y$: subtree relation, 424

TUPLES:

$\langle\ \rangle$: empty tuple, 530
$\langle\,...\,\rangle$: tuple (informal notation), 530
$\langle u \rangle$: singleton function, 532
$u \diamond x$: insertion function, 530
$u \in x$: member relation, 531
$x \diamondsuit y$: append function, 531
$x \subset y$: proper subtuple relation, 535
$x \subseteq y$: subtuple relation, 534
$[x]_z$: element function, 537

General Index

abelian group, 256
abnormal model (for equality), 219
absorption (for sets),
  of cardinality [property], 496
  of deletion [property], 490
  of insertion [property], 474
abstract sentence, 3, 68
Adam (in family theory) [axiom], 197
addition,
  for quotient [axiom], 331
  for remainder, [axiom] 331,
    [property] 404
  of divides [property], 340
  of subtraction [property], 314, 357
addition $x + y$ [function], 291, 354
  annihilation of [property], 303, 354
  associativity of [property], 303, 354
  commutativity of [property], 292, 302
  computation of, 296
  functional substitutivity for [axiom], 292
  left cancellation of [property], 303, 354
  left functional substitutivity for [axiom], 292
  left successor of [property], 292, 299
  left zero of [property], 292, 297
  right cancellation of [property], 303, 354
  right functional substitutivity for [axiom], 292
  right one of [property], 292, 293
  right successor for [axiom], 291
  right zero for [axiom], 291
  sort of [property], 292, 354
adjacent,
  of proper subtuple [property], 536

  of strict less-than [property], 329
affix (for lists) [function], 465
  decomposition of [property], 466
  empty for [axiom], 465
  front of [property], 466
  insertion for [axiom], 465
  last of [property], 466
agree on: see agreement
agreement (between interpretations),
  and multiply extended interpretation, 54, 97
  on expression, 95, 96
  on sentence, 52, 53
  on symbol, 95
agreement condition, of semantic rule for,
  existential closure, 114
  universal closure, 110
alphabet (for strings), 363
alter (for tuples) [function], 538
  equal of [property], 539
  nonequal of [property], 539
  sort of [property], 539
  successor for [axiom], 539
  zero for [axiom], 538
alternative definition,
  for *atoms* (for nonnegative integers and lists), 469
  for concatenation, 412
  for divides relation, 345, 359
  for exponential, 306
  for factorial, 357
  for *flatlist*, 467
  for *flattree*, 431, 434
  for *ordered*, 554, 574
  for *perm*, 549, 573
  for *reverse* (for strings), 377

for *same* (for tuples),   572
for set constructor,   501
for subset,   501
for substring,   413
for weak less-than,   358
and (connective),   6, 72
  conventional notation,   8
  multiple,   39, 74
  semantic rule,   11, 87
  truth table of,   12
and, of set constructor [property],   495
annihilation,
  of addition [property],   303, 354
  of concatenation [property],   372
annotation,
  in proof by falsification,   28
  in semantic tree,   24
antecedent (of implication),   6
antisymmetry,
  for weak partial ordering [axiom],
    229
  of divides [property],   341
  of reflexive closure [proposition],   237
  of subset [property],   492
  of substring [property],   390
  of subtree [property],   429
  of weak less-than [property],   325
append,
  of *flatlist*,   445
  of *length* (of tuples) [property],   536
  of *member* (for lists) [property],   444
  of *ordered* (for tuples of nonnegative
    integers) [property],   554, 574
  of *perm* (for tuples) [property],   549,
    573
append $x \square y$ (for lists) [function],   442,
  465
  associativity of [property],   443, 465
  head of [property],   443, 465
  left empty for [axiom],   443
  left insertion for [axiom],   443
  right empty of [property],   443, 465
  sort of [property],   443, 465
  tail of [property],   443, 465
  vs. insertion,   442
append $x \diamond y$ (for tuples) [function],
  531, 572
  associativity of [property],   532
  left element of [property],   538, 572

left empty for [axiom],   531
left insertion for [axiom],   531
member of [property],   532
right element of [property],   538, 572
right empty of [property],   532
singleton of [property],   533
append-singleton (for tuples),
  for *perm* [axiom],   545
  of *eqmult* [property],   534
  of member [property],   533
append-sum, of *bagtuple* [property],   542
append-union, of *settuple* [property],
  542
application semantic rule,   86
application (term),   70
arity,
  of function symbol,   70
  of predicate symbol,   70
associated relations, theory of,   232
associativity,
  for groups [axiom],   249
  of addition [property],   303, 354
  of append (for lists) [property],   443,
    465
  of append (for tuples) [property],
    532
  of concatenation (for strings) [prop-
    erty],   372, 410
  of intersection (for sets) [property],
    484
  of multiplication [property],   305, 355
  of union (for sets) [property],   483
associativity (valid sentence schema),
  36
asymmetry,
  of irreflexive restriction [proposition],
    237
  of lexicographic relation [property],
    276, 281
  of proper substring [property],   390
  of strict less-than [property],   328
  of strict partial ordering [proposition],
    203
  total (in theory of associated relations)
    [proposition],   248
atlist (for lists) [relation],   437
atlist generation (for lists) [axiom],   438
atom,
  for *atoms* (for nonnegative integers

and lists) [axiom], 469
for *atoms1* (for nonnegative integers
    and lists) [axiom], 469
for *depth* (for trees) [axiom], 435
for *flattree* [axiom], 430
for *flattree1* [axiom], 434
for *flattree2* [axiom], 431
for *generate* (for strings, trees, and
    lists) [axiom], 459
for *parcount2* (for parsing theory) [ax-
    iom], 577
for *parse2* [axiom], 460
for *proper* (for trees) [axiom], 451
for proper subtree [axiom], 425
for *size* (for trees) [axiom], 435
for subtree [property], 425
for *tips* (for trees) [axiom], 435
of pairs, 259
atom [relation],
    for bags, 505
    for lists, 437
    for pairs, 256
    for sets, 471
    for trees, 419
    for tuples, 530
atom affixation, of *revall* (for lists) [prop-
    erty], 467
atom construction,
    for *flattree1* [axiom], 434
    for *listtree* [axiom], 451
    for *proper* (for trees) [axiom], 451
atom generation (for trees) [axiom],
    420
atom insertion,
    for *atoms1* (for nonnegative integers
        and lists) [axiom], 469
    for *flatlist* [axiom], 445
    for *flatlist2* [axiom], 467
    for *revall* (for lists) [axiom], 467
    for *treelist* [axiom], 449
atom list (for lists) [property], 440
atom-integer, for tuples of nonnegative
    integers [axiom], 550
atom uniqueness,
    for lists [axiom], 438
    for trees [axiom], 420
atomℓ (for strings, trees, and lists) [rela-
    tion], 459
    atomℓ for [axiom], 459

atomic formula, 76
atoms,
    for bags, 505
    for lists, 437
    for sets, 471
    for trees, 419
    for tuples, 530
atoms (for nonnegative integers and
        lists) [function], 469
    alternative definition for, 469
    atom for [axiom], 469
    empty for [axiom], 469
    insertion for [axiom], 469
atoms1 (for nonnegative integers and
        lists), 469
    atom for [axiom], 469
    atom insertion for [axiom], 469
    empty for [axiom], 469
    empty insertion for [axiom], 469
    insertion insertion for [axiom], 469
augmented (theory), 196, 259
axiom (of theory), 189, 190
bad (for nonnegative integers) [function],
        566
    axioms not in recursive form, 565
    sort for [axiom], 566
    successor for [axiom], 566
    zero for [axiom], 566
bag, empty: see empty bag
bag [relation], 506
bags, 505
    and tuples and sets (combined the-
        ory), 539
    axioms for, 506
    induction principle for, 507
    finite vs. infinite, 505
bagtuple (mapping tuples into bags) [func-
    tion], 539, 540, 573
    and *settuple* and *setbag*, composition of
        [property], 543, 573
    append-sum of [property], 542
    empty for [axiom], 540
    eqmult of [property], 542
    insertion for [axiom], 540
    is not one to one, 543
    member of [property], 542
    onto of [property], 542, 573
bagtuple, of *perm* (for tuples) [property],
    550

base case: see also induction principle,
   287
  not in complete induction, 335
base zero, of exponentiation (x^y) [prop-
   erty], 306, 356
basic (valid sentence schemata), 35
basic semantic rule, 86
binary,
  function symbol, 70
  predicate symbol, 70
bound occurrence (of variable), 78
bound subexpression, 141, 143
  replacement of, 141
bound variable (in expression), 77, 79
  renaming of, 136, 139, 165
cancellation,
  for integers [property], 576
  of subtraction [property], 326
captured (variable by quantifier), 147
capturing, 145
card: see cardinality *card* (for sets)
cardinality *card* (for sets) [function],
   496, 502
  absorption of [property], 496
  empty for [axiom], 496
  insertion for [axiom], 496
  intersection of [property], 496, 502
  proper subset of [property], 496, 502
  sort of [property], 496
  union of [property], 496, 497
cardinality,
  of singleton (for sets) [property],
   499, 503
casting out nines, of *sum* (of digits of
   nonnegative integer) [proposition],
   403
catalog, of valid sentence schemata,
  for predicate logic, 121, 125
  for propositional logic, 35
chain of equivalences, 59, 66
char (for strings): see character *char*
character,
  equality (for strings) [axiom], 364
  for string representation of nonnegative integers [axiom], 402
  for strings, trees, and lists [axiom],
   458
  for *sum* (of digits of nonnegative integer) [axiom], 403

of concatenation (for strings) [prop-
   erty], 371, 410
of *head* (for strings) [property], 370,
   410
of *length* (for strings) [property], 400,
   414
of *reverse* [property], 375
of *tail* (for strings) [property], 370,
   410
character (for strings), 363
character atom,
  for strings and lists [axiom], 444
  for strings and trees [axiom], 430
  for strings, trees, and lists [axiom],
   468
character *char* (for strings) [relation],
   363
  predicate substitutivity for [axiom],
   366
character generation (for strings) [ax-
   iom], 364
choice (for bags) [function], and *rest*,
   520
  decomposition for [axiom], 520
  member of [property], 520
  sort for [axiom], 520
choice (for sets) [function] and *rest*, 481
  decomposition for [axiom], 481
  functional substitutivity for [axiom],
   482
  independence of axioms for, 482
  member of [property], 482
  nonmember for [axiom], 481
  sort for [axiom], 481
choice of variables, in inductive proof,
   299, 301
choice rest, of deletion (for sets) [prop-
   erty], 490, 501
class of sentences (sentence schema),
   119
closed sentence, 79
  consistent, 107
  contradictory, 107
  satisfiable, 107
  unsatisfiable, 107
closure, 108
  existential, 109
  distribution of, 134, 186
  duality of, 133

reflexive: see reflexive closure
satisfiability of, 113
universal, 108
validity of, 113
closure condition, of semantic rule for,
    existential closure, 113
    universal closure, 110
closure instantiation, 176
    existential, 176, 188
    universal, 176
combined theory, of strings and nonneg-
    ative integers, 398
common divisor, greatest: see greatest
    common divisor *gcd*
common divisor, of greatest common di-
    visor [property], 345, 351
commutative group, 256
commutativity,
    in propositional logic, 37
    of groups, 253
    valid sentence schema, 36
commutativity,
    of addition [property], 292, 304
    of groups [axiom], 256
    of intersection (for sets) [property],
        484
    of multiplication [property], 305, 355
    of union (for sets) [property], 483
complete induction principle (for non-
    negative integers) [proposition],
    329, 337
    and least-number principle, 353
    example of, 332
    vs. stepwise induction, 335, 348
complete induction principle (for strings)
    [proposition], 391
    example of, 393
    vs. stepwise induction, 398
component, of member (for sets) [prop-
    erty], 473
component (of sentence), 6
composition, of mappings (between bags,
    sets, and tuples) [property], 543,
    573
composition function (over permuta-
    tions), 254
composition introduction [proposition],
    227
composition permutation, 254

computation,
    of addition, 296
    of concatenation, 371
    of divides, 342
    of *eqmult* (for bags), 509
    of *exp3*, 307
    of factorial, 356
    of greatest common divisor, 344
    of monus, 315
    of *parse*, 461
    of *perm* (for tuples), 545
    of recursive definition, 567
    of *rev2*, 378
    of *reverse*, 374
    of *sort*, 556
    of subtraction, 313
    of substring, 389
    of weak less-than, 321
computer program, 296
conc2 (for strings) [function], 412
    left empty for [axiom], 413
    left suffix for [axiom], 413
concatenation,
    of end (for strings) [property], 386,
        413
    of intersperse (for strings) [property],
        416
    of *length* (for strings) [property], 400
    of *reverse* [property], 375
concatenation $x * y$ (for strings) [func-
    tion], 370, 410, 412
    alternative definition for, 412
    annihilation of [property], 372
    associativity of [property], 372, 410
    character of [property], 371, 410
    computation of, 371
    functional substitutivity for [axioms],
        371
    head of [property], 372, 410
    head-tail of [property], 386
    left empty of [axiom], 371
    left prefix of [axiom], 371
    prefix-suffix decomposition of [prop-
        erty], 393, 410
    right empty of [property], 371, 410
    sort of [property], 371, 410
    suffix decomposition for [property],
        372, 410
    suffix uniqueness for [property], 372,

410

tail of [property], 372, 410

conditional (connective): see also *if-then-else* sentence, 6, 63, 72

conditional (term), 71, 74

distribution of, 107

distributivity of [property], 226, 278

false of [property], 226, 278

true of [property], 226, 278

congruence-modulo-2 (a model for equivalence relation), 208

conjunct, 6

conjunction (connective): see also *and* (connective), 6, 72

multiple, 38, 74

connective, propositional, 6

consequent (of implication), 6

consistency: see consistent

consistent (axioms),

for addition, 292

for *bad*, 566

for *first* and *second* (for pairs) [proposition], 260

for greatest common divisor, 344, 569

for *inverse* [proposition], 206

for multiplication, 567

for recursive definition, 565

for *tuplebag*, 544, 569

consistent (sentences), 15, 107

and satisfiable, 19

consistent (theory), 192, 197

augmented theory, 206

constant, 69

semantic rule, 86

symbol, 69

constraint, on induction principle (for strings), 366, 417

construction,

for *depth* (for trees) [axiom], 435

for *flattree* [axiom], 430, 468

for *flattree1* [axiom], 434

for *flattree2* [axiom], 431

for proper subtree [axiom], 425

for *size* (for trees) [axiom], 435

for *tips* (for trees) [axiom], 435

construction $x \bullet y$ (for trees) [function], 419

construction generation (for trees) [axiom], 420

construction uniqueness (for trees) [axiom], 420

constructor,

for *generate* (for strings, trees, and lists) [axiom], 459

for *parcount2* (for parsing theory) [axiom], 577

for *parse2* [axiom], 460

constructor $\hat{\bullet}$ (special character, for parsing), 458

constructor, set: see set constructor

contained (in theory), 199

containment (for theories) [proposition], 199

contradiction (of sentence): see contradictory (sentence)

contradictory (sentence), 4, 15, 107

and valid, 17

truth-table method, 22

contrapositive law (valid sentence schema), 36

contrapositive (of implication), 38

conventional notation,

for propositional logic, 8

for predicate logic, 76

converse (of implication), 6

count,

of *eqmult* (for bags) [property], 519, 526

of *eqmult* (for tuples) [property], 537

of equality (for bags) [property], 519

of intersection (for bags) [property], 524, 527

of member (for bags) [property], 519

of member (for tuples) [property], 537

of subbag (for bags) [property], 521, 527

of sum (for bags) [property], 522, 527

of union (for bags) [property], 523, 527

count (multiplicity, for bags) [function], 518

empty for [axiom], 519

equal insertion for [axiom], 519

nonequal insertion for [axiom], 519

sort of [property], 519

count (multiplicity, for tuples) [function], 537
  empty for [axiom], 537
  equal insertion for [axiom], 537
  nonequal insertion for [axiom], 537
cycle permutation, 254
decomposition (for bags),
  for *choice* and *rest* [axiom], 520
decomposition (for lists),
  of *affix* [property], 466
  of *head* and *tail* [property], 441
decomposition (for nonnegative integers),
  of predecessor [property], 313, 357
  of subtraction [property], 326, 357
decomposition (for pairs) [proposition], 264
decomposition (for sets),
  for *choice* and *rest* [axiom], 481
  of deletion [property], 490
decomposition (for strings),
  of *front* and *last* [property], 412
  of *head* and *tail* [property], 370, 410
  prefix-suffix, of concatenation [property], 393, 411
  suffix, of concatenation [property], 372, 411
decomposition (for trees),
  of *left* and *right* [property], 423, 433
decomposition (in predecessor theory) [axiom], 317
decomposition [property],
  for bags, 507
  for lists, 440
  for nonnegative integers, 289, 360
  for sets, 481, 500
  for strings, 367
  for trees, 421
  for tuples, 531
decomposition induction (for lists) [property], 442
decomposition induction (for nonnegative integers) [proposition], 316, 361
  vs. generator induction, 317, 318, 320, 324
decomposition induction (for strings) [proposition], 383
  vs. generator induction, 385
decomposition induction (for trees) [prop-

erty], 423, 434
  vs. generator induction, 424
definition, alternative: see alternative definition
deletion $x - u$ (for sets) [function], 489, 500
  absorption of [property], 490
  choice rest of [property], 490, 501
  decomposition of [property], 490
  empty for [axiom], 489
  insertion for [axiom], 490
  member of [property], 490, 501
deletion, of set constructor [property], 495
depth (for trees) [function], 435
  atom for [axiom], 435
  construction for [axiom], 435
desired conclusion: see also induction principle, 287
diagram notation (for a binary relation), 104, 202
difference, of set constructor [property], 495
difference $x \sim y$ (for sets) [function], 490
  member of [property], 491
  right empty for [axiom], 491
  right insertion for [axiom], 491
digit, for *reduce* [axiom], 408
disjoint,
  for strings and nonnegative integers [axiom], 399
  of pairs [axiom], 257
  of sets [axiom], 489
disjoint (for sets) [relation], 489
  disjoint for [axiom], 489
  member of [property], 489
disjunct, 6
disjunction (connective): see also *or* (connective), 6, 72
  multiple, 39, 74
distinct, for extract (for bags) [axiom], 526
distribution,
  of closures [proposition], 134, 186
  of conditional terms, 107
  of quantifiers, 107, 122, 125
distributivity,
  intersection over union (for bags) [property], 524

intersection over union (for sets) [property], 485
  of conditional terms [property], 226, 278
  of relativized quantifiers [property], 281
  valid sentence schema, 37
divides $x \preceq_{div} y$ [relation], 340, 359
  addition of [property], 340
  alternative definition for, 343, 359
  antisymmetry of [property], 341
  computation of, 342
  divides for [axiom], 340
  greater-than of [property], 342, 359
  left zero of [property], 340, 359
  multiplication of [property], 341
  not total, 341
  reflexivity of [property], 341
  remainder of [property], 341
  right zero of [property], 340, 359
  subtraction of [property], 342, 359
  transitivity of, 341
divides, for divides [axiom], 340
divides, proper: see proper divides
divisibility by 9, test for [example], 408, 415
divisor, greatest common: see greatest common divisor
domain (of interpretation), 80, 83
  finite, 104
  two or three elements, 117
double induction, 510, 514
double insertion
  for *ordered* (for tuples of nonnegative integers) [axiom], 550
  for *same* (for tuples) [axiom], 532
double transitivity,
  of equality [property], 217
  of equivalence relation [property], 211
duality,
  of closures [proposition], 133
  of quantifiers, 97, 106, 124
  of relativized quantifier, 270
element $[x]_z$ (for tuples) [function], 537
  successor for [axiom], 538
  unspecified values for, 538
  zero for [axiom], 538
element, left and *right*, of append (for

tuples) [properties], 538, 572
elimination, of functions, 178, 180
else-clause (of conditional), 6
empty,
  bag ($[\![\ ]\!]$), 505
  interpretation, 9
  list ($[\ ]$), 437, 440, 449
  set ($\{\ \}$), 471
  string (Λ), 363, 367, 409
  tuple ($\langle\ \rangle$), 530
empty,
  of string representation of nonnegative integers [property], 403, 415
  of tree representations of lists [property], 449
empty-atom,
  for *flattree* [axiom], 468
  for lists and trees [axiom], 449
  for lists, strings, and trees [axiom], 468
empty (for bags),
  for *count* [axiom], 519
  for *eqmult* [axiom], 508
  for *extract* [axiom], 526
  for *member* [axiom], 506
  for *subbag* [axiom], 521
empty (for bags, sets and tuples),
  for *bagtuple* [axiom], 540
  for *setbag* [axiom], 540
  for *settuple* [axiom], 541
  for *tuplebag* [axiom], 544
empty (for lists),
  for *affix* [axiom], 465
  for *front* [axiom], 466
  for *last* [axiom], 465
  for *member* [axiom], 444
  for *parse2* [axiom], 460
  for *revall* [axiom], 467
empty (for lists and nonnegative integers),
  for *atoms* [axiom], 469
  for *atoms1* [axiom], 469
empty (for lists and strings),
  for *flatlist* [axiom], 445
  for *flatlist2* [axiom], 467
empty (for lists and trees),
  for *listtree* [axiom], 451
  for *treelist* [axiom], 449
empty (for nonnegative integers and tu-

ples),
  for *insert* [axiom], 556
  for *ordered* [axiom], 550, 574
  for *sort* [axiom], 555
empty (for parsing theory),
  for *parcount2* [axiom], 577
empty (for sets),
  for cardinality [axiom], 496
  for deletion [axiom], 489
  for intersection [axiom], 484
  for member [axiom], 472
  for set constructor [axiom schema],
    494, 502
  for union [axiom], 483
empty (for strings),
  for end [axiom], 386
  for *length* [axiom], 400
  for *reverse* [axiom], 374
empty (for tuples),
  for *count* [axiom], 537
  for *eqmult* [axiom], 533
  for *length* [axiom], 536
  for member [axiom], 531
  for *perm* [axiom], 545
  for *same* [axiom], 532
empty generation,
  for bags [axiom], 506
  for lists [axiom], 438
  for sets [axiom], 472
  for strings [axiom], 364
  for tuples [axiom], 530
empty insertion,
  for *atoms*1 (for lists and nonnegative
    integers) [axiom], 469
  for *eqmult* (for bags) [axiom], 508
  for *eqmult* (for tuples) [axiom], 533
empty uniqueness,
  for bags [property], 507
  for lists [axiom], 438
  for sets [property], 474
  for strings [axiom], 364
  for tuples [axiom], 530
end $x \preceq_{end} y$ (for strings) [relation],
    385
  concatenation for [property], 386, 413
  empty for [axiom], 386
  tail for [axiom], 386
end-concatenation [proposition], 386,
    413

eqmult,
  of *bagtuple* [property], 542
  of *perm* (for tuples) [property], 546,
    549, 573
eqmult (equal multiplicity, for bags) [re-
    lation], 507, 525
  computation of, 509
  count of [property], 519, 526
  empty for [axiom], 508
  empty insertion for [axiom], 508
  equal insertion for [axiom], 508
  equality of [property], 515
  insertion empty for [axiom], 508
  left insertion for [axiom], 508
  member of [property], 510, 525
  nonmember of [property], 510, 525
  reflexivity of [property], 510, 525
  right insertion for [axiom], 508
  symmetry of [property], 510
eqmult (equal multiplicity, for tuples)
    [relation], 533
  append singleton of [property], 534
  count of [property], 537
  empty for [axiom], 533
  empty insertion for [axiom], 533
  equal insertion for [axiom], 533
  insertion empty for [axiom], 533
  left insertion for [axiom], 534
  member of [property], 534
  reflexivity of [property], 534
  right insertion for [axiom], 534
  symmetry of [property], 534
equal,
  for *fact2* [axiom], 357
  of *alter* (for tuples) [property], 546
equal insertion (for bags),
  for *count* [axiom], 519
  for *eqmult* [axiom], 508
  for *subbag* [axiom], 521
equal insertion (for tuples),
  for *count* [axiom], 537
  for *eqmult* [axiom], 533
  for *subtuple* [axiom], 535
  of *perm* (for tuples) [property], 549
equal multiplicity (for bags) [relation]:
    see *eqmult* (for bags)
equal multiplicity (for tuples) [relation]:
    see *eqmult* (for tuples)
equal multiplicity [proposition],

for bags, 515
for tuples, 545
equal prefix, for initial substring [axiom],
    413
equality,
    of *eqmult* (for bags) [property], 515
    of *same* (for tuples) [property], 532,
        572
equality (for bags),
    count [property], 519
    exchange [axiom], 506
    extract [property], 526
    multiplicity [property], 515
    subbag [property], 521
equality (for groups),
    axioms, 250
equality (for lists),
    axioms, 440
equality (for nonnegative integers),
    axioms, 288
equality (for pairs),
    axioms, 258
equality (for sets),
    axioms, 472
    exchange [axiom], 473
    multiplicity [axiom], 473
    proposition, 477
equality (for strings),
    axioms, 366
    character [axiom], 364
equality $x = y$ [relation], 215
    abnormal model for, 219
    as equivalence relation, 217
    double transitivity of [property], 217
    functional substitutivity for [axiom
        schema], 216
    general replacement of [proposition],
        225
    implicit use of properties of, 296
    predicate substitutivity for [axiom schema],
        216
    reflexivity for [axiom], 216
    replacement of [proposition], 223
    semantic rule for [proposition], 218
    substitutivity of [proposition], 220
    symmetry for [axiom], 216
    theory with, 228
    transitivity for [axiom], 216
    uniqueness of [property], 228, 279

equality (=) rule, 218
equivalence,
    and validity, 56, 131, 185
    between sentences: see equivalent
        (sentences)
    between theories: see equivalent (the-
        ories)
    substitutivity of, 57, 143, 163
equivalence (connective): see also *if-and-
        only-if*, 6, 72
equivalence $x \approx y$ [relation], 208, 212
    double transitivity of [property], 211
    equality is an, 217
    examples, 208
    finite model for, 209
    independence of axioms for, 211
    perm is an, 549
    reflexivity for [axiom], 208
    symmetry for [axiom], 208
    theory of, 208
    transitivity for [axiom], 208
equivalences, chain of, 59, 66
equivalent (sentences, in theory), 192
equivalent (sentences, of predicate logic),
    129
    instance of equivalent propositional-
        logic sentence, 132
    replacement of [proposition], 134
    vs. implies, 123
equivalent (sentences, of propositional
    logic), 4, 15, 54, 131
    and implies, 19
    and valid, 18
    truth-table method, 22
equivalent (theories), 199, 200
exchange,
    for equality (for bags) [axiom], 506
    for equality (for sets) [axiom], 473
    of *perm* (for tuples) [property], 549,
        573
exclusive *or*, vs. inclusive, 13
exercises: see problems
existential,
    general replacement (of equality) [propo-
        sition], 226
    replacement (of equality) [proposi-
        tion], 228, 278
existential closure, 109
    instantiation, 176, 188

semantic rule for, 113
existential quantifier, 72
  conventional notation, 76
  instantiation, 169, 173
  multiple instantiation, 175
  semantic rule, 92
existential instantiation: see existential
    quantifier, instantiation
exp one, of exponentiation [property],
    306, 356
exp plus, of exponentiation [property],
    306, 356
exp times, of exponentiation [property],
    306, 356
exp zero, of exponentiation [axiom], 306
exp3 [function], 306
  computation of, 307
  successor for [axiom], 307
  zero for [axiom], 307
exponentiation x^y [function], 305, 356
  alternative definition for [proposition],
    306
  base zero of [property], 306, 356
  exp one of [property], 306, 356
  exp plus of [property], 306, 356
  exp times of [property], 306, 356
  exp zero for [axiom], 306
  functional substitutivity for [axioms],
    306
  sort of [property], 306, 356
  successor for [axiom], 306
expression, 75
  of theory, 190
extended interpretation,
  for predicate logic, 89
  for propositional logic, 49
  multiply: see multiply extended inter-
    pretation
extension condition, of semantic rule for,
  existential closure, 113
  universal closure, 110
extract [relation], 526
  and equality, 526
  distinct for [axiom], 526
  empty for [axiom], 526
  same for [axiom], 526
factorial $x!$ [function], 356
  alternative definition for, 356
  computation of, 356

successor for [axiom], 356
  zero for [axiom], 356
fact2 (for nonnegative integers) [func-
    tion], 357
  equal for [axiom], 357
  successor for [axiom], 357
fallacious induction principle, 360
false,
  of conditional terms [property], 226,
    278
  of set constructor [property], 495
  semantic rule, 11, 86
  truth symbol, 5, 69, 71
false (truth value), 9, 69
family interpretation, 192
family theory, 191, 212
father (in family theory) [axiom], 191
finite model,
  for associated relation, 237
  for equivalence relation, 209
  for strict partial ordering, 202
finite relation,
  for equivalence relation, 209
  for strict partial ordering, 202
first (for pairs) [function], 259
  consistency of axiom for [proposition],
    260
  first for [axiom], 259
  functional substitutivity for [axiom],
    259
  sort of [property], 264
flatlist (for lists) [function], 445, 467,
    468
  alternative definition for, 467
  and *flattree*, 468
  append of [property], 445
  atom insertion for [axiom], 445
  empty for [axiom], 445
  list insertion for [axiom], 445
  sort of [property], 445
flatlist-append [proposition], 445
flatlist2 (for lists) [function], 467
  atom insertion for [axiom], 467
  empty for [axiom], 467
  list insertion for [axiom], 467
flattree [function], 430, 434, 468
  alternative definition for, 431, 434
  and *flatlist*, 468
  atom for [axiom], 430

construction for [axiom],   430, 468
empty-atom for [axiom],   468
nonempty atom for [axiom],   468
sort of [property],   430
flattree1 [function],   434
  atom construction for [axiom],   434
  atom for [axiom],   434
  construction for [axiom],   434
flattree2 [function],   431
  atom for [axiom],   431
  construction for [axiom],   431
  sort of [property],   431
for-all (quantifier),   72
  conventional notation,   76
  semantic rule,   92
for-some (quantifier),   74
  conventional notation,   76
  semantic rule,   92
formula,
  atomic,   76
  well-formed,   76
free,
  occurrence (of variable),   78
  subexpression,   141, 144
  symbol,   80
  variable (in expression),   77, 79
frightful sentence [problem],   62
front (for lists) [function],   466
  empty for [axiom],   466
  nonempty for [axiom],   466
front (for strings) [function],   411
  and *last*, *decomposition* of [property],
    412
  front for [axiom],   411
  sort of [property],   412
  tail-reverse of [property],   412
front, of *affix* (for lists) [property],   466
function,
  elimination,   178, 180
  introduction,   178, 180
  symbol,   70
function-relation [lemma],   179
functional substitutivity (of equality) [ax-
  iom schema]: see also *left* and *right*
  functional substitutivity,   216
  for *choice* and *rest* functions (for sets)
    [axioms],   482
  for concatenation [axioms],   371
  for exponentiation [axioms],   306

for *first* (for pairs) [axiom],   259
for group inverse [axiom],   250
for *head* (for strings) [axiom],   370
for *second* (for pairs) [axiom],   259
for successor [axiom],   288
for *tail* (for strings) [axiom],   370
gcd: see greatest common divisor
general replacement (of equality) [propo-
  sition],   225
generalization (in inductive proof),
  306, 309, 349, 408, 431
generate (for parsing theory) [function],
  459, 577
  atom for [axiom],   459
  constructor for [axiom],   459
  of *parse* [property],   460
  of *parse2* [property],   461
generation axioms,
  for bags,   506
  for lists,   438
  for nonnegative integers,   286
  for sets,   472
  for strings,   364
  for trees,   420
  for tuples,   530
generator induction principle (for bags)
  [axiom schema],   507
generator induction principle (for lists)
  [axiom schema],   439
generator induction principle (for nonnegative integers) [axiom schema],
  287
  fallacious [problem],   360
  in altered theories [problem],   360
  vs. decomposition,   317, 318, 324
generator induction principle (for sets)
  [axiom schema],   473
  modified,   476
generator induction principle (for strings)
  [axiom schema],   365
  constraint,   366, 417
  vs. decomposition,   385
generator induction principle (for trees)
  [axiom schema],   421
  vs. decomposition,   424
generator induction principle (for tuples)
  [axiom schema],   530
grandfather (in family theory) [axiom],
  191

grandmother (in family theory) [axiom], 191

greater-than,
  for strict greater-than [axiom], 331
  of divides [property], 342, 359
  of maximum [property], 327, 358

greater-than, strict: see strict greater-than

greatest common divisor *gcd* [function], 343, 360
  axioms not in recursive form, 569
  alternative definition for, 351
  common divisor of [property], 345, 351
  computation of, 344
  consistency of axioms for, 344
  greatest of [property], 351, 360
  remainder for [axiom], 343
  zero for [axiom], 343

greatest, of greatest common divisor [property], 351, 360

group identity *e,* 249

group inverse x^{-1}, 249
  substitutivity for [axiom], 250

group operation $x \circ y$, 249
  left substitutivity for [axiom], 250
  right substitutivity for [axiom], 250

groups, 249, 280
  associativity for [axiom], 249
  commutative (abelian), 256
  commutativity of, 253
  left cancellation of [property], 253, 280
  left identity of [property], 253, 280
  left inverse of [property], 253, 280
  models for, 250
  nonidempotence of [property], 253, 280
  permutation model for, 254, 280
  right cancellation of [property], 251
  right identity for [axiom], 249
  right inverse for [axiom], 249

head,
  for append (for lists) [property], 443, 465
  of concatenation (for strings) [property], 372, 410
  of member (for lists) [property], 444

head (for lists) [function], 441

  and *tail,* of *decomposition* of [property], 441
  head of [axiom], 441
  sort of [property], 441

head (for strings) [function], 369, 409
  and *tail, decomposition* of [property], 370
  character of [property], 370, 410
  head for [axiom], 370
  unspecified values, 370
  functional substitutivity for [axiom], 370
  sort of [property], 370, 410

head-reverse, of *last* (for strings) [property], 412

head-tail, of concatenation (of strings) [property], 386

idempotence, of *sort* (for tuples of non-negative integers) [property], 565, 575

identity *e*: see group identity

identity permutation, 254

if-and-only-if (connective), 6, 72
  and equivalence, 18, 38
  conventional notation, 8
  semantic rule, 12, 87
  truth table of, 12

if-clause (of conditional), 6

if-then (connective), 6, 13, 72
  and implication, 18
  conventional notation, 8
  semantic rule, 12, 87
  truth table of, 12

if-then-else (connective), 6
  semantic rule, 12
  truth table of, 13

if-then-else sentence (connective), 72, 74
  semantic rule, 87

if-then-else term (operator), 71, 74
  semantic rule, 86
  vs. sentence, 76

implication (between sentences): see also implies,
  and validity [proposition], 54, 131, 185
  vs. equivalence, 123

implication (connective): see also *if-then*, 6, 72

implies (between sentences): see also
    implication, 15, 129
  and equivalent, 19
  and valid, 18
  in theory, 192
inclusive *or*, vs. exclusive, 13
incomplete (theory), 196
inconsistent, axioms for,
  family theory, 197
  tuplebag, 544, 569
inconsistent (theory), 197
independence, of axioms for,
  choice and *rest*, 482
  equivalence relation, 211, 212
  strict partial ordering, 203, 212
  weak partial ordering, 230, 279
induction hypothesis: see also induction
    principle, 287
induction principle: see generator induc-
    tion principle,
  complete: see complete induction
    principle
  decomposition: see decomposition in-
    duction principle
  stepwise: see stepwise induction
  suffix (for strings), 412
inductive proof,
  choice of variables in, 299, 301
  double induction in, 510, 514
  generalization in, 306, 309, 349, 408,
    431
  treatment of quantifiers in, 310, 377,
    381
inductive sentence: see also induction
    principle, 287
inductive step: see also induction princi-
    ple, 287
inductive variable: see also induction
    principle, 287
inequality relation, 203
initial substring $\preceq_{init}$ [relation], 413
  equal prefix for [axiom], 413
  left empty for [axiom], 413
  nonequal prefix for [axiom], 413
  right empty for [axiom], 413
insert (for tuples of nonnegative inte-
    gers) [function], 556
  empty for [axiom], 556
  insertion for [axiom], 556

ordered of [property], 557
permutation of [property], 557
insertion $u \odot x$ (for bags) [function], 506
insertion $x \circ y$ (for lists) [function], 437,
    464
  left nonidentity of [property], 464
  right nonidentity of [property], 464
  vs. append, 442
insertion $u \circ x$ (for sets) [function], 471
  absorption of [property], 474
insertion $u \diamond x$ (for tuples) [function],
    530
insertion (for bags),
  for member [axiom], 506
insertion (for lists and nonnegative inte-
    gers),
  for *atoms* [axiom], 469
insertion (for lists),
  for *affix* [axiom], 465
  for *last* [axiom], 465
  for member [axiom], 444
insertion (for sets),
  for cardinality [axiom], 496
  for deletion [axiom], 490
  for intersection [axiom], 484
  for member [axiom], 472
  for set constructor [axiom schema],
    494, 502
  for union [axiom], 483
insertion (for tuples),
  for *length* [axiom], 536
  for member [axiom], 531
insertion (for bags, sets and tuples),
  for *bagtuple* [axiom], 540
  for *setbag* [axiom], 540
  for *settuple* [axiom], 541
  for *tuplebag* [axiom], 544
insertion (for nonnegative integers and
    tuples),
  for *insert* [axiom], 556
  for *mintuple* [axiom], 554
  for *sort* [axiom], 555
  of *ordered* [property], 550, 574
insertion empty,
  for *eqmult* (for bags) [axiom], 508
  for *eqmult* (for tuples) [axiom], 533
insertion generation,
  for bags [axiom], 506
  for lists [axiom], 438

for sets [axiom], 472
for tuples [axiom], 530
insertion insertion, for *atoms*1 (for non-negative integers and lists) [axiom], 469
insertion uniqueness,
  for bags [axiom], 506
  for lists [axiom], 438
  for tuples [axiom], 530
instance,
  of (abstract) sentence, 3, 67
  of equivalent propositional-logic sentence, 132
  of sentence schema, 34, 120
  of valid propositional-logic sentence, 106, 123
  of value property [corollary], 159
instantiation,
  and partial substitution, 187
  existential closure, 176, 188
  existential quantifier, 168, 173, 175
  universal closure, 176
  universal quantifier, 168, 175, 294
integer [relation], 285
  predicate substitutivity for [axiom], 288
integer-string, of string representation of nonnegative integers [property], 403, 415
integers,
  including negative, 575, 577
  nonnegative: see nonnegative integers
interpretation (for family theory), 192
interpretation (for predicate logic), 68, 83, 115
  agreement between, 95
  extended, 89
  multiply extended, 91
  same (for value property), 162
interpretation (for propositional logic), 9
  agreement between, 52
  empty, 9
  extended, 49
  for several sentences, 10
  multiply extended, 51
intersection $x \cap y$ (for bags) [function], 523, 527
  count of [property], 524, 527

distributivity of [property], 524
left empty for [axiom], 524
member insertion for [axiom], 524
nonmember insertion for [axiom], 524
intersection $x \cap y$ (for sets) [function], 484
  associativity of [property], 484
  commutativity of [property], 484
  empty for [axiom], 484
  insertion for [axiom], 484
  member of [property], 484, 485
intersection (for sets),
  of cardinality [property], 496, 502
  of set constructor [property], 495
  of subset [property], 492
intersection absorption, of subset [property], 492
intersection-over-union distributivity,
  for bags [property], 524
  for sets [property], 485
intersperse $x \preceq_{inter} y$ (for strings) [relation], 416
  concatenation of [property], 416
  substring of [property], 416
introduction,
  of composition, 227
  of functions, 178, 180
  of quantifiers, 106
intuitive argument (in proof), 195
inverse,
  for strict partial ordering [axiom], 206
  for weak partial ordering [axiom], 231
inverse x^{-1} [function]: see group inverse
inverse $x \succ y$ (of strict partial ordering) [relation], 206
inverse $x \succeq y$ (of weak partial ordering) [relation], 231
  left substitutivity [axiom], 231
  right substitutivity [axiom], 231
inverse mapping functions (between bags, sets, and tuples), 544
inverse permutation, 255
invertibility of substitution, 223
irreflexive relation, 210
irreflexive restriction $x \prec y$ (in theory of associated relations), 232
  as a strict partial ordering [proposi-

tion], 242

asymmetry of [proposition], 237

irreflexivity condition of [proposition], 235

irreflexivity of [proposition], 234

left substitutivity for [axiom], 233

mixed transitivity of [proposition], 246, 279

of substring, 390

right substitutivity for [axiom], 233

transitivity of [proposition], 239

irreflexivity,

of irreflexive restriction, 234

of lexicographic relation [property], 277

of proper subset [property], 493

of proper substring [property], 390

of proper subtree [property], 425

of strict less-than [property], 328

of strict partial ordering [axiom], 201

irreflexivity condition, of irreflexive restriction [proposition], 235

land of liars and truth tellers [problem], 65

language,

of predicate logic, 68, 69

of propositional logic, 5, 68

of theory, 189

last,

for *affix* [property], 466

for *last* (for strings) [axiom], 411

last (for lists) [function], 466

empty for [axiom], 466

insertion for [axiom], 466

last (for strings) [function], 411

and *front*, *decomposition* of [property], 412

head-reverse of [property], 412

sort of [property], 412

law of negation (valid sentence schema), 37

leading zeroes, of string representation of nonnegative integers, 402

leading zeroes [property], 403, 415

least, of *mintuple* (for tuples of nonnegative integers) [property], 554, 574

least-number principle, 351

left addition,

of strict less-than [property], 329

of weak less-than [property], 322, 358

left cancellation,

of addition [property], 303, 354

of groups [property], 253, 280

left concatenation, of substring [property], 390

left construction, of proper subtree [property], 425

left distributivity, of multiplication [property], 305, 355

left element, of append (for tuples) [property], 538, 572

left empty,

for append (for lists) [axiom], 443

for append (for tuples) [axiom], 531

for concatenation [axiom], 371

for *conc2* (for strings) [axiom], 413

for initial substring [axiom], 413

for intersection (for bags) [axiom], 524

for *rev2* [axiom], 377

for subset [axiom], 491, 501

for subtuple [axiom], 535

for sum (for bags) [axiom], 522

for union (for bags) [axiom], 522

of substring [property], 390

left (for strings) [function], 416

and *right*, *length* of [property], 417

left (for trees) [function], 422, 433

and *right*, *decomposition* of [property], 423, 433

left of [axiom], 422

sort of [property], 423, 433

left functional substitutivity (of equality) [axiom schema], 216

for addition [axiom], 292

for group operation [axiom], 250

for multiplication [axiom], 304

for pairing function [axiom], 258

for prefix [axiom], 366

left identity, of groups [property], 253, 280

left insertion,

for append (for lists) [axiom], 443

for append (for tuples) [axiom], 531

for *eqmult* (for bags) [axiom], 508

for *eqmult* (for tuples) [axiom], 534

for subset [axiom], 491, 501
for *sum* (for bags) [axiom], 522
of subtuple [property], 535
left inverse, of groups [property], 253, 280
left mixed transitivity,
  of irreflexive restriction [proposition], 246, 279
  of proper substring [property], 391
  of reflexive closure [proposition], 244, 279
left nonidentity, of insertion (for lists) [property], 464
left one, of multiplication [property], 305, 355
left paren,
  for *parcount2* (for parsing theory) [axiom], 577
  for *parse2* [axiom], 460
left parenthesis ⌢ (special symbol, for parsing), 458
left-predicate substitutivity (of equality) [axiom schema], 216
  for binary relation [axiom], 232
  for inverse (of weak partial ordering) [axiom], 231
  for irreflexive restriction [axiom], 233
  for reflexive closure [axiom], 233
  for weak partial order [axiom], 229
left prefix,
  for concatenation [axiom], 371
  for *rev2* [axiom], 378
left substitutivity: see *left functional substitutivity* or *left predicate substitutivity*
left subtree, of proper subtree [property], 425
left succesor,
  of addition [property], 292, 299
  of multiplication [property], 305, 357
  of strict less-than [property], 329
left suffix, for *conc2* (for strings) [axiom], 413
left zero,
  for monus [axiom], 315
  of addition [property], 292, 297
  of divides [property], 340, 359
  of multiplication [property], 305, 355
  of strict less-than [property], 329

of weak less-than [property], 325
left-hand side (of equivalence), 6
length (for strings) [function], 398, 414
  character of [property], 400, 414
  concatenation of [property], 400
  empty for [axiom], 400
  prefix for [axiom], 400
  proper substring of, [property], 400, 414
  reverse of [property], 400, 414
  sort of [property], 400, 414
  zero of [property], 400, 414
length (for tuples) [function], 536
  append of [property], 536
  empty for [axiom], 536
  insertion for [axiom], 536
  proper subtuple of [property], 536
  singleton of [property], 536
  sort of [property], 536
length, of *left* and *right* [property], 417
less-than,
  for quotient [axiom], 331
  for remainder [axiom], 331
  for strict less than [axiom], 328
  of minimum [property], 327
  of monus [property], 326
less-than (strict): see strict less-than
less-than, weak: see weak less-than
lexicographic relation (in theory of pairs), 271, 281
  asymmetry of [property], 276, 281
  irreflexivity of [property], 277
  lexicographic relation for [axiom], 272
  over integers, 272
  transitivity of [property], 273
liars and truth tellers [problem], 65
list affixation, of *revall* (for lists) [property], 467
list insertion,
  for *flatlist* [axiom], 445
  for *flatlist2* [axiom], 467
  for *revall* (for lists) [axiom], 467
  for *treelist* [axiom], 449
list [relation], 437
lists, 437
  and strings (combined theory), 444
  and strings and trees (combined theory), 458, 468
  and trees (combined theory), 448

axioms for, 438
induction principles for, 439, 442
tree representation of, 448
uniqueness of, 457
vs. strings, 437
vs. trees, 437
list-tree-list, of *treelist* and *listtree* [property], 452
listtree [function], 450
  atom construction for [axiom], 451
  empty for [axiom], 451
  list-tree-list of [property], 452
  nonatom construction for [axiom], 451
  sort of [property], 452
love [problem], 64
mapping,
  bags into sets, 540
  bags into tuples, 544
  composition of [property], 543, 573
  lists into strings, 444, 468
  lists into trees, 449, 468
  trees into lists, 450
  trees into strings, 430, 468
  tuples into bags, 540, 573
  tuples into sets, 541, 543
mathematical induction principle, 285
mathematical logic, 3
max: see maximum *max*
maximin, of maximum and minimum [property], 327
maximum, for *max* [axiom], 327
maximum *max* [function], 326, 358
  greater-than of [property], 327, 358
  maximin of [property], 327
  minimax of [property], 327, 358
meaning (of sentence): see also interpretation, 9, 80
member,
  for difference (for sets) [property], 491
  for *perm* (for tuples) [axiom], 545
  for subbag [axiom], 521
  nonempty (for sets) [property], 478, 500
  of append (for tuples) [property], 532
  of *bagtuple* [property], 542
  of *choice* (for bags) [property], 520

of *choice* (for sets) [property], 482
of deletion (for sets) [property], 490, 501
of *disjoint* (for sets) [property], 489
of *eqmult* (for bags) [property], 510, 525
of *eqmult* (for tuples) [property], 534
of intersection (for sets) [property], 484, 485
of proper subset [property], 493
of set constructor [property], 494, 501
of subset [property], 491, 501
of subtuple [property], 535
of union (for sets) [property], 483, 500
member $u \in x$ (for bags) [relation], 506
  count of [property], 519
  empty for [axiom], 506
  insertion for [axiom], 506
member $u \in x$ (for lists) [relation], 443
  append of [property], 444
  empty for [axiom], 444
  head of [property], 444
  insertion for [axiom], 444
member $u \in x$ (for sets) [relation], 471
  component of [property], 473
  empty for [axiom], 472
  included in basic theory, 474
  insertion for [axiom], 472
member $u \in x$ (for tuples) [relation], 531
  append singleton of [property], 533
  count of [property], 537
  empty for [axiom], 531
  insertion for [axiom], 531
member decomposition,
  for bags [property], 507
  for sets [property], 478, 500
member insertion,
  for intersection (for bags) [axiom], 524
  for union (for bags) [axiom], 522
min: see minimum *min*
minimax, of maximum and minimum [property], 327, 358
minimum, for *min* [axiom], 329
minimum (of tuple of nonnegative integers): see *mintuple*

minimum *min* [function], 326, 358
  less-than of [property], 327
  maximin of [property], 327
  minimax of [property], 327, 358
mintuple (for tuple of nonnegative integers) [function], 554, 574
  insertion for [axiom], 554
  least of [property], 554, 574
  singleton for [axiom], 554
minus −*x* (for integers) [function], 575
mixed transitivity: see *left* and *right mixed transitivity*
model (for theory), 191
modified induction, generator (for sets) [proposition], 476
monotonicity (of theory) [proposition], 200
monotonicity, of *treelist* [property], 458, 468
monus *x* ∸ *y* [function], 314
  computation of, 315
  left zero for [axiom], 315
  less-than of [property], 326
  right zero for [axiom], 315
  sort of [property], 315
  subtraction of [property], 326
  successor for [axiom], 315
mother (in family theory) [axiom], 191
mother of us all [example], 103, 125
multiple,
  conjunction, 39, 74
  disjunction, 39, 74
  partial safe substitution, 151, 152
  partial substitution, 46, 48
  quantifier instantiation [proposition], 174
  relativized quantifier, 267
  safe substitution, 150
  substitution, 45
  total safe substitution, 151, 152
  total substitution, 46, 48
multiplication,
  of divides [property], 341
  of proper divides [property], 343
  of remainder [property], 404
multiplication *x* · *y* [function], 304, 355
  associativity of [property], 305, 355
  axioms in recursive form, 567
  commutativity of [property], 305, 355

functional substitutivity for [axioms], 304
left distributivity of [property], 305, 355
left functional substitutivity for [axiom], 304
left one of [property], 305, 355
left successor of [property], 305, 355
left zero of [property], 305, 355
right distributivity of [property], 305, 355
right functional substitutivity for [axiom], 304
right one of [property], 305, 355
right successor for [axiom], 304
right zero for [axiom], 304
sort of [property], 305, 355
multiplicity,
  for equality (for sets) [axiom], 473
  of equality (for bags) [property], 515
multiplicity, equal [relation],
  for bags: see *eqmult* (for bags)
  for tuples: see *eqmult* (for tuples)
multiplicity (for bags) [function]: see *count* (for bags) [function]
multiplicity, of elements,
  of bags, 505
  of sets, 471
  of tuples, 529
multiply extended interpretation, 51, 91
  and agreement, 54, 97
multiset: see bag, 505
necessity,
  for renaming, 172
  for side-conditions, 125
negation (connective): see also *not* (connective), 6, 72
negative (for integers) [relation], 575
negative, of subtraction [property], 357
nested quantifiers, 140
nine, test for divisibility by [example], 408, 415
nine test, of *reduce* [property], 408, 415
nonatom, of *treelist* [property], 450
nonatom construction,
  for *listtree* [axiom], 451
  for *proper* (for trees) [axiom], 451
nonempty,

for *front* (for lists) [axiom],   466
for *tuplebag* [axiom],   544
nonempty atom, for *flattree* [axiom],
   468
nonempty member (for sets) [property],
   478, 500
nonequal, of *alter* (for tuples) [property],
   546
nonequal insertion,
   for *count* (for bags) [axiom],   519
   for *count* (for tuples) [axiom],   537
   for subtuple [axiom],   535
nonequal prefix, for initial substring [ax-
   iom],   413
nonequivalence relation,   209
nonidempotence, of groups [property],
   253, 280
nonmember,
   for *choice* and *rest* (for sets) [axiom],
      481
   of *eqmult* (for bags) [property],   510,
      525
nonmember insertion,
   for intersection (for bags) [axiom],
      524
   for union (for bags) [axiom],   522
nonnegative integers,   285
   and strings (combined theory),   398
   and trees (combined theory),   435
   and tuples (combined theory),   536,
      550
   axioms for,   286
   induction principles for,   287, 316,
      329
   recursive definition for,   568
   represented as strings,   402
nonnegative-nonpositive, of *parcount* (for
   parsing theory) [property],   577
nonsymmetric relation,   210
nontransitive relation,   209
nonvalid (sentence),   17
   proof-by-falsification method,   34
nonvalidity, establishing,   101
normal model for equality,   219
not (connective),   6, 72
   conventional notation,   8
   semantic rule,   11, 87
   truth table of,   12
number interpretation (for family the-

ory),   192
occurrence (of subsentence),   7
occurrence (of variable),   77
   bound,   78
   free,   78
one-to-one (mapping),
   bagtuple is not,   543
   of *treelist* [property],   457
onto (mapping),
   of *bagtuple* [property],   542, 573
   of *treelist* [property],   457
operation ∘, of groups,   249
or (connective),   6, 72
   conventional notation,   8
   inclusive vs. exclusive,   13
   truth table of,   12
   multiple,   39, 74
   semantic rule,   11, 87
or, of set constructor [property],   495
order of elements,
   of bags,   505
   of sets,   471
   of tuples,   529
ordered,
   of *insert* (for tuples of nonnegative
      integers) [property],   557
   of *sort* (for tuples of nonnegative inte-
      gers) [property],   557, 562
ordered (for tuples of nonnegative inte-
      gers) [relation],   550, 574
   alternative definition for,   554, 574
   append of [property],   554, 574
   double insertion for [axiom],   550
   empty for [axiom],   550, 574
   insertion of [property],   551, 574
   singleton for [axiom],   550
ordered permutation (for tuples of non-
      negative integers) [property],   575
ordering, strict partial: see strict partial
      ordering
ordering, weak partial: see weak partial
      ordering
pair (of pairs) [relation],   256
   pair for [axiom],   257
   predicate substitutivity for [axiom],
      258
pairing ⟨x_1, x_2⟩ (of pairs) [function],
      256
   functional substitutivity for [axioms],

258
pairs, 256
  decomposition of [proposition], 264
  disjoint for [axiom], 257
  first function of, 259
  of integers, 258
  pair for [axiom], 257
  second function of, 259
  substitutivity axioms for, 258
  uniqueness for [axiom], 257
palin: see palindrome
palindrome *palin* (for strings) [relation],
    392, 414
  palindrome for [axiom], 392
  palindrome [proposition], 392, 414
parcount (for parsing theory) [function],
    577
  nonnegative-nonpositive of [property],
    577
  parcount of [property], 577
  zero of [property], 577
parcount2 (for parsing theory) [function],
    577
  atom for [axiom], 577
  constructor [axiom], 577
  empty for [axiom], 577
  left paren for [axiom], 577
  right paren for [axiom], 577
parenthesis counting, 576
parse (for lists, strings, and trees) [func-
    tion], 460
  computation of, 461
  generate of [property], 460
  parse [proposition], 460
  parse for [axiom], 460
parse2 (for lists, strings, and trees) [func-
    tion], 460
  atom for [axiom], 460
  constructor for [axiom], 460
  empty for [axiom], 460
  generate of [property], 460
  left paren for [axiom], 460
  parse2 [lemma], 461
  right paren for [axiom], 460
parsing (of strings), 458
  and parenthesis counting, 576
partial ordering,
  strict: see strict partial ordering
  weak: see weak partial ordering

partial safe substitution, 148
  concise notation, 150
  multiple: see multiple partial safe sub-
    stitution
partial substitution, 42
  and instantiation, 187
  concise notation, 45
  multiple: see multiple partial substitu-
    tion
  safe: see partial safe substitution
partial value [proposition], 154
  under same interpretation [corollary],
    162
perm (permutation, for tuples) [relation],
    544, 573
  alternative definition for, 549, 573
  append of [property], 549, 573
  append-singleton for [axiom], 545
  bagtuple of [property], 550
  computation of, 545
  empty for [axiom], 545
  eqmult of [property], 546, 573
  equal insertion of [property], 549
  equal-multiplicity for [property], 545
  exchange of [property], 549, 573
  is an equivalence relation, 549
  member for [axiom], 545
  reflexivity of [property], 549
  symmetry of [property], 549
  transitivity of [property], 549
permutation (for tuples): see *perm*
permutation (for tuples of nonnegative
    integers),
  of *insert* [property], 557
  of *sort* [property], 557, 562
  ordered, 575
permutation interpretation (model for
    group), 254, 280
plus interpretation (model for group),
    250
positive,
  for *positive* [axiom], 311
  in predecessor theory [axiom], 317
positive (for integers) [relation], 575
positive (for nonnegative integers) [rela-
    tion], 311
positive negative (for integers) [property],
    576
precisely when, 16

predecessor,
  for predecessor [axiom],   312
  in predecessor theory [axiom],   317
predecessor x^- [function],   312, 357
  decomposition of [property],   313, 357
  predecessor for [axiom],   312
  sort of [property],   313
  unspecified values,   312
predecessor theory,   317
predecessor zero (for integers) [property],
    576
predicate logic,
  advanced,   119
  basic,   67
  language of,   68, 69
predicate substitutivity (of equality) [ax-
    iom schema]: see also *left* and *right*
    predicate substitutivity,   216
  for *atom* [axiom],   258
  for *character* [axiom],   366
  for *integer* [axiom],   288
  for *pair* [axiom],   258
  for *string* [axiom],   367
predicate symbol,   70
prefix,
  for *length* (for strings) [axiom],   400
  for *reverse* [axiom],   374
prefix $u \bullet x$ (for strings) [function],   363
  functional substitutivity for [axiom],
    364
prefix adjacent, of proper substring [prop-
    erty],   391
prefix generator (for strings) [axiom],
    364
prefix-suffix decomposition of concatena-
    tion (for strings) [property],   393,
    411
prefix uniqueness (for strings) [axiom],
    366
principle of mathematical induction,
    285
problems,
  page references,   61
  use of previous results,   61
program,   296
proof-by-falsification method,   28
  vs. truth-table method,   30
proper,
  subexpression,   75

subsentence,   7, 75
subterm,   75
proper (for trees) [relation],   451
  atom construction for [axiom],   451
  atom for [axiom],   451
  nonatom construction for [axiom],
    451
proper divides $x \prec_{div} y$ [relation],   247,
    343
  multiplication of [property],   343
  proper divides for [axiom],   343
proper divides, for proper divides [ax-
    iom],   343
proper subbag $x \subset y$ [relation],   521
  is a strict partial ordering,   521
  rest of [property],   521
proper subset,
  for proper subset [axiom],   492
  of cardinality (for sets) [property],
    496, 502
proper subset $x \subset y$ [relation],   492
  irreflexivity of [property],   493
  is a strict partial ordering,   493
  member of [property],   493
  proper subset for [axiom],   492
  rest of [property],   493
  transitivity of [property],   493
proper substring,
  of *length* (for strings) [property],   400,
    414
  of proper substring [axiom],   390
proper substring $x \prec_{string} y$ [relation],
    390
  asymmetry of [property],   390
  irreflexivity of [property],   390
  is a strict partial ordering,   390
  left mixed transitivity of [property],
    391
  mixed transitivity of [property],   391
  prefix adjacent of [property],   391
  proper substring for [axiom],   390
  right empty of [property],   391
  right mixed transitivity of [property],
    391
  suffix adjacent of [property],   391
  transitivity of [property],   390
proper subtree $x \prec_{tree} y$ [relation],   424
  atom for [axiom],   425
  irreflexivity of [property],   428

is a strict partial ordering, 425, 429
left construction of [property], 425
left subtree of [property], 425
right construction of [property], 425
right mixed transitivity of [property], 425
right subtree of [property], 425
transitivity of [property], 428
proper subtuple,
for proper subtuple [axiom], 535
of *length* (for tuples) [property], 536
proper subtuple $x \subset y$ [relation], 535
adjacent of [property], 536
is a strict partial ordering, 536
proper subtuple of [axiom], 535
proper trees, 451
proposition, 5, 67, 71
semantic rule, 11, 87
propositional,
connective, 6
logic, 5, 67
symbol, 5
quantifier,
distribution of, 107, 122, 125
duality of, 97, 106, 122
existential: see existential quantifier
instantiation [proposition], 168
introduction of, 106
multiple relativized, 267
nested, 140
redundant, 106, 125
relativized: see relativized quantifier
removal of, 106
reversal of, 106, 122
scope of, 72
semantic rule for, 92
treatment of, in inductive proof, 310, 377, 381
universal: see universal quantifier
quot: see quotient *quot*
quotient *quot* [function], 331, 358
addition for [axiom], 331
and remainder, *uniqueness* of, 336, 359
less-than for [axiom], 331
quotient-remainder of [property], 332
sort of [property], 331, 358
smaller-than of [property], 404
unspecified values, 331

quotient-remainder, of quotient and remainder [property], 332
recursive definition, of functions,
and *bad*, 566
and *gcd*, 569
and multiplication function, 567
and *tuplebag*, 569
computation of, 567
consistency of, 565
for nonnegative integers [proposition], 568
for theories other than nonnegative integers, 569
successor for [axiom], 566
zero for [axiom], 566
recursive form, for axioms: see also recursive definition, 566
reduce (to test divisibility by nine) [function], 408
digit for [axiom], 408
nine-test of [property], 408, 415
sum for [axiom], 408
reduction law (valid sentence schema), 38
redundant quantifiers, 106, 125
reflexive closure, of strict less-than [property], 328
reflexive closure $x \preceq y$ (in theory of associated relations), 232
antisymmetry of [proposition], 237
as a weak partial ordering [proposition], 242
left substitutivity for [axiom], 233
mixed transitivity of [proposition], 244, 279
reflexivity condition of [proposition], 235
reflexivity of [proposition], 234
right substitutivity for [axiom], 233
totality of, 246
transitivity of [proposition], 239
reflexivity,
fallacious proof of, 212
for equality [axiom], 216
for equivalence relation [axiom], 208
for weak partial ordering [axiom], 229
of divides [property], 341
of *eqmult* (for bags) [property], 510,

525
of *eqmult* (for tuples) [property], 534
of *perm* (for tuples) [property], 549
of reflexive closure [proposition], 234
of subset [property], 492
of substring [property], 390
of subtree [property], 429
of weak less-than [property], 325
reflexivity condition, of reflexive closure
      [proposition], 235, 279
relativized quantifiers, 266, 281
   distributivity of [property], 281
   duality of [property], 270
   multiple, 267
   pitfall, 271
   reversal of [property], 269, 281
rem: see remainder *rem* [function]
remainder,
   for greatest common divisor [axiom],
      343
   of divides [property], 341
   of remainder [property], 404
remainder *rem* [function], 331, 358
   addition of, [axiom] 331, [property]
      404
   and quotient, *uniqueness* of, 336, 359
   less-than for [axiom], 331
   multiplication of [property], 404
   quotient-remainder of [property], 332
   remainder of [property], 404
   sort of [property], 331, 358
   unspecified values, 331
removal of quantifiers, 106
renaming,
   necessity for, 172
   of bound variables, 136, 139, 165
   of variables, 106
replacement,
   of bound subexpression, 141
   of equality [proposition], 223, 225
   of equivalent sentences, 134, 281
   safe, 150, 151
rest,
   of proper subbag [property], 521
   of proper subset [property], 493
   of singleton (for sets) [property],
      499, 503
rest (for bags) [function], and *choice*,
      520

decomposition for [axiom], 520
   sort for [axiom], 520
rest (for sets) [function], and *choice*,
      481
   decomposition for [axiom], 481
   functional substitutivity for [axiom],
      482
   independence of axioms for, 482
   nonmember for [axiom], 481
   sort for [axiom], 481
restriction, irreflexive: see irreflexive
      restriction
rev2 (for strings) [function], 377
   computation of, 378
   left empty for [axiom], 377
   left prefix for [axiom], 378
revall (for lists) [function], 466
   atom affixation of [property], 467
   atom insertion for [axiom], 467
   empty for [axiom], 467
   list affixation of [property], 467
   list insertion for [axiom], 467
   revall of [property], 467
revall, for *revall* (for lists) [property],
      467
reversal,
   of quantifiers, 106, 122
   of relativized quantifiers, 269, 281
reverse,
   of *length* (for strings) [property], 400,
      414
   of *reverse* (for strings) [property],
      375, 411
reverse (for strings) [function], 374, 411
   alternative definition for, 377
   character of [property], 375
   computation of, 374
   concatenation of [property], 375
   empty for [axiom], 374
   prefix for [axiom], 374
   reverse of [property], 375, 411
   sort of [property], 375
   suffix of [property], 375
right addition,
   of strict less than [property], 329
   of weak less than [property], 325,
      357
right cancellation,
   of addition [property], 303, 354

of groups [property], 251
right concatenation, of substring [property], 390
right construction, of proper subtree [property], 425
right distributivity, of multiplication [property], 305, 355
right element, of append (for tuples) [property], 538, 572
right empty,
  for append (for lists) [property], 443, 465
  for difference (for sets) [axiom], 491
  for initial substring [axiom], 413
  for substring2 [axiom], 414
  for subtuple [axiom], 535
  of append (for tuples) [property], 532
  of concatenation (for strings) [property], 371, 410
  of proper substring [property], 391
right (for strings) [function], 416
  and *left*, *length* of [property], 417
right (for trees) [function], 422, 433
  and *left*, *decomposition* of [property], 423, 433
  right of [axiom], 422
  sort of [property], 423, 433
right functional substitutivity (of equality) [axiom schema], 216
  for addition [axiom], 292
  for group operation [axiom], 250
  for multiplication [axiom], 304
  for pairing function [axiom], 258
  for prefix [axiom], 366
right-hand side (of equivalence), 6
right identity, for groups [axiom], 249
right insertion,
  for difference (for sets) [axiom], 491
  for *eqmult* (for bags) [axiom], 508
  for *eqmult* (for tuples) [axiom], 534
right inverse, for groups [axiom], 249
right mixed transitivity,
  of irreflexive restriction [proposition], 246, 279
  of proper substring [property], 391
  of reflexive closure [proposition], 244, 279
  of subtree [property], 425

right nonidentity, of insertion (for lists) [property], 464
right one,
  of addition [property], 292, 293
  of multiplication [property], 305, 355
  of subtraction [property], 314, 357
right paren,
  for *parcount2* (for parsing theory) [axiom], 577
  for *parse2* [axiom], 460
right parenthesis $\widehat{)}$ (special symbol, for parsing), 458
right predecessor, for weak less-than [axiom], 321
right predicate substitutivity (of equality) [axiom schema], 216
  for binary relation [axiom], 232
  for inverse (of weak partial ordering) [axiom], 231
  for irreflexive restriction [axiom], 233
  for reflexive closure [axiom], 233
  for weak partial ordering [axiom], 229
right prefix, for substring2 [axiom], 414
right substitutivity: see *right functional substitutivity* or *right predicate substitutivity*
right subtree, of proper subtree [property], 425
right successor,
  for addition [axiom], 291
  for multiplication [axiom], 304
  for weak less-than [alternative axiom], 358
  of strict less-than [property], 329
right zero,
  for addition [axiom], 292, 293
  for monus [axiom], 315
  for multiplication [axiom], 304
  for subtraction [axiom], 313
  for weak less-than [axiom], 321
  of divides [property], 340, 359
  of strict less-than [property], 329
rule, semantic: see semantic rule
safe substitution, 140, 147, 186
  concise notation for, 150, 152
  multiple, 150
  partial: see partial safe substitution
  total: see total safe substitution

safely replacing,   147, 149
same, for *extract* (for bags) [axiom],
       526
same (for tuples) [relation],   532, 572
   alternative definition for,   572
   double insertion for [axiom],   532
   empty for [axiom],   532
   equality of [property],   532, 572
   singleton for [axiom],   532
same interpretation (of value property)
       [corollary],   162
satisfiability,
   of closure [proposition],   114
   of sentence: see satisfiable (sentence)
satisfiable (sentence),   15, 107
   and consistent,   19
   and valid,   15
schema: see sentence schema
scope (of quantifiers),   72
script symbol (for sentence),   5, 35
second (for pairs) [function],   259
   consistency of axiom for [proposition],
       260
   functional substitutivity for [axiom],
       259
   second for [axiom],   259
   sort of [property],   264
semantic rule,
   basic,   86
   for equality [proposition],   218
   for existential closure [proposition],
       113
   for *false,*   11, 86
   for *if-and-only-if,*   12, 87
   for *if-then,*   12, 87
   for *if-then-else,*   12, 86, 87
   for multiple conjunction,   41
   for multiple disjunction,   41
   for *not,*   11, 87
   for *or,*   11, 87
   for propositional symbol,   11
   for quantifiers,   92
   for *true,*   11, 86
   for universal closure [proposition],
       110
   in predicate logic,   85
   in propositional logic,   10
semantic-tree method,   23
   vs. truth-table method,   27

semantics (of sentence),   9
sentence,   3, 6, 72
   abstract,   3, 68
   closed: see closed sentence
   consistent: see consistent (sentences)
   contradictory,   15
   equivalent: see equivalent (sentences)
   implies: see implies (between sen-
       tences)
   meaning of: see interpretation
   of theory,   190
   satisfiable: see satisfiable (sentence)
   substitutivity of equivalence for [propo-
       sition],   220
   valid: see valid (sentence)
sentence schema (class of sentences),
       34, 120
   instance of,   34, 120
   valid: see valid (sentence schema)
set constructor $\{x : p(x)\}$ [function],
       493, 501
   alternative definition for,   501
   and of [property],   495
   deletion of [property],   495
   difference of [property],   495
   empty for [axiom schema],   494, 502
   false of [property],   495
   insertion of [axiom schema],   494, 502
   intersection of [property],   495
   member of [property],   494, 501
   or of [property],   495
   true of [property],   495
set [relation],   471
set, empty: see empty set
setbag (mapping bags into sets) [func-
       tion],   539, 540
   and *settuple* and *bagtuple, composition*
       of [property],   543
   empty for [axiom],   540
   insertion for [axiom],   540
   sum-union of [property],   542
sets,   471
   and tuples and bags [combined the-
       ory],   539
   axioms for,   472
   finite vs. infinite,   471
   induction principles for,   473, 477
   nested,   471, 473
settuple (mapping tuples into sets) [func-

tion], 539, 541
and *setbag* and *bagtuple*, *composition* of [property], 543
append-union of [property], 542
empty for [axiom], 541
insertion for [axiom], 541
side conditions,
necessity for, 125
validity of schema under, 124
sing: see singleton (for sets) [relation]
singleton,
for *mintuple* (for nonnegative integers of tuples) [axiom], 554
for *ordered* (for tuples of nonnegative integers) [axiom], 550
for *same* (for tuples) [axiom], 532
for *singleton* (for sets) [axiom], 499
for *singleton* (for tuples) [axiom], 533
of append (for tuples) [property], 533
of *length* (of tuples) [property], 536
singleton (for sets) [relation], 499, 503
cardinality of [property], 499, 503
rest of [property], 499, 503
singleton for [axiom], 499
singleton (for sets) [axiom], 499
singleton (for tuples) [function], 532
size (for trees) [function], 435
atom for [axiom], 435
construction for [axiom], 435
smaller-than, for quotient [property], 404
Smullyan, R., 64
sort,
predicate, 264
property, 264
sort (for bags),
for *choice* and *rest* [axiom], 520
of *count* [property], 519
sort (for lists),
of append [property], 443, 465
of *head* [property], 441
of *tail* [property], 441
sort (for lists and strings),
of *flatlist* [property], 445
sort (for lists and trees),
of *listree* [property], 452
of *treelist* [property], 450
sort (for nonnegative integers),

for *bad* [axiom], 566
of addition [property], 292, 354
of exponentiation [property], 306, 356
of monus [property], 315
of multiplication [property], 305, 355
of predecessor [property], 313
of quotient [property], 331, 358
of remainder [property], 331, 358
of subtraction [property], 326
of successor [property], 312
sort (for pairs),
of *first* function [property], 264
of *second* function [property], 264
sort (for sets),
for *choice* and *rest* [axiom], 481
of cardinality [property], 496
sort (for strings),
of concatenation [property], 371, 410
of *front* [property], 412
of *head* [property], 370, 410
of *last* [property], 412
of *length* [property], 400, 414
of *reverse* [property], 375
of *tail* [property], 370, 410
sort (for strings and trees),
of *flattree* [property], 430
of *flattree2* [property], 431
sort (for trees),
of *left* [property], 423, 433
of *right* [property], 423, 433
sort (for tuples),
of *alter* [property], 539
of *length* [property], 536
sort (for tuples of nonnegative integers) [function], 555, 575
computation of, 556
empty for [axiom], 555
idempotence of [property], 565, 575
insertion for [axiom], 555
ordered of [property], 557, 562
permutation of [property], 557, 562
uniqueness of [property], 565, 575
sort conditions, omission of, 295
sorting function: see *sort* (for nonnegative integers and tuples) [function]
special theories, 189
splitting (of weak partial ordering) [property], 230

stepwise induction principle: see generator and decomposition induction
principle, 317
 vs. complete induction (for nonnegative integers), 335, 348
 vs. complete induction (for strings),
398
strict greater-than $x > y$ [relation], 329
 greater-than for [axiom], 329
strict less-than $x < y$ [relation], 327
 adjacent of [property], 329
 as an irreflexive restriction, 236
 asymmetry of [property], 328
 irreflexivity of [property], 328
 is a strict partial ordering, 202
 is total, 247
 left addition of [property], 329
 left successor of [property], 329
 left zero of [property], 329
 less-than for [axiom], 328
 reflexive closure of [property], 328
 right addition of [property], 329
 right successor of [property], 329
 right zero of [property], 329
 total asymmetry of [property], 328
 totality of [property], 328
 transitivity for [property], 328
strict partial ordering $x \prec y$, 201, 212
 asymmetry of [property], 203
 examples, 202
 finite model for, 202
 independence of axioms for, 203, 212
 inverse of, 205
 irreflexive restriction is a [proposi-
tion], 242
 irreflexivity for [axiom], 201
 proper subbag is a, 521
 proper substring is a, 390
 proper subtree is a, 425, 429
 proper subtuple is a, 536
 transitivity for [axiom], 201
string [relation], 364
 predicate substitutivity for [axiom],
367
string, empty: see empty string
string representation (of nonnegative
integers), 402, 415
 character for [axiom], 402
 empty of [property], 403, 415

integer-string of [property], 403, 415
 leading zeroes of [property], 403, 415
 suffix for [axiom], 402
strings, 363
 and integers and strings (combined
theory), 577
 and lists (combined theory), 444
 and lists and trees (combined theory),
458, 468
 and nonnegative integers (combined
theory), 398
 and trees (combined theory), 430,
435
 axioms for, 364
 induction principles for, 365, 383,
391
 vs. lists, 437
 vs. trees, 422
subbag, of equality [property], 521
subbag $x \subseteq y$ [relation], 520, 527
 count of [property], 521, 527
 empty for [axiom], 521
 equal insertion for [axiom], 521
 is a weak partial ordering, 521
 member for [axiom], 521
subexpression, 75
 bound, 141, 143
 free, 141, 144
 proper, 75
subsentence, 7, 75
 proper, 7, 75
subset, proper: see proper subset
subset $x \subseteq y$ [relation], 491, 501
 alternative definition for, 501
 antisymmetry of [property], 492
 intersection of [property], 492
 intersection absorption of [property],
492
 is a weak partial ordering, 492
 left empty for [axiom], 491, 501
 left insertion for [axiom], 491, 501
 member of [property], 491, 501
 reflexivity of [property], 492
 transitivity of [property], 492
 union absorption of [property], 492
 union of [property], 492
substitution, 40, 66
 and valid schemata, 163
 concise notation, 44

invertibility of, 223
multiple: see multiple substitution
partial safe: see partial safe substitution
partial: see partial substitution
safe: see safe substitution
total safe: see total safe substitution
total: see total substitution
substitutivity (of equality) [proposition], 220
   functional: see functional substitutivity
   predicate: see predicate substitutivity
substitutivity (of equivalence),
   for predicate logic, 141, 163
   for propositional logic, 57, 58
substring,
   for substring [axiom], 389
   of intersperse [property], 416
substring, proper: see proper substring
substring $x \preceq_{string} y$ [relation], 389, 413
   alternative definition for, 413
   antisymmetry of [property], 390
   computation of, 389
   irreflexive restriction of, 390
   is a weak-partial ordering, 390
   left concatenation of [property], 390
   left empty of [property], 390
   reflexivity of [property], 390
   right concatenation of [property], 390
   substring for [axiom], 389
   transitivity of [property], 390
substring2 $x \preceq_{string2} y$ (alternative definition for substring) [relation], 414
   right empty for [axiom], 414
   right prefix for [axiom], 414
subterm, 75
   proper, 75
subtraction $x - y$ [function], 313, 357
   addition of [property], 314, 357
   cancellation of [property], 326
   computation of, 313
   decomposition of [property], 326, 357
   negative of [property], 357
   right one of [property], 314, 357
   right zero for [axiom], 313
   sort of [property], 326

   successor for [axiom], 313
   unspecified values, 314
subtraction,
   of divides [property], 342, 359
   of monus [property], 326
subtraction addition (for integers) [property], 576
subtree,
   for subtree [axiom], 424
   left, of proper subtree [property], 425
   right, of proper subtree [property], 425
subtree, proper: see proper subtree
subtree $x \preceq_{tree} y$ [relation], 424
   antisymmetry of [property], 429
   atom of [property], 425
   is a weak partial ordering, 429
   reflexivity of [property], 429
   right mixed-transitivity of [property], 425
   subtree for [axiom], 424
   transitivity of [property], 429
subtuple $x \subseteq y$ [relation], 534
   equal insertion for [axiom], 535
   is a weak partial ordering, 535
   left empty for [axiom], 535
   left insertion of [property], 535
   member of [property], 535
   nonequal insertion for [axiom], 535
   right empty for [axiom], 535
successor,
   for *alter* (for tuples) [axiom], 539
   for *bad* (for nonnegative integers) [axiom], 566
   for element (for tuples) [axiom], 538
   for *exp3* [axiom], 307
   for exponentiation [axiom], 306
   for *fact2* [axiom], 357
   for factorial [axiom], 356
   for monus [axiom], 315
   for recursive definition [axiom], 566
   for subtraction [axiom], 313
successor [function], 285
   functional substitutivity for [axiom], 288
   sort of [property], 312
successor generation [axiom], 286
successor predecessor (for integers) [property], 576

successor uniqueness [axiom], 286
suffix,
    for string representation of nonnega-
        tive integers [axiom], 402
    for *sum* (of digits of nonnegative inte-
        ger) [axiom], 403
    of *reverse* [property], 375
suffix adjacent, of proper substring [prop-
    erty], 391
suffix decomposition, of concatenation
    (for strings) [property], 372, 411
suffix induction principle (for strings),
    412
suffix uniqueness, of concatenation (for
    strings) [property], 372, 411
sum, for *reduce* [axiom], 408
sum (of digits of nonnegative integer)
    [function], 403
    casting out nines of [property], 403
    character for [axiom], 403
    suffix for [axiom], 403
sum $x \oplus y$ (for bags) [function], 522,
    527
    count of [property], 522, 527
    left empty for [axiom], 522
    left insertion for [axiom], 522
sum-union, of *setbag* [property], 542
symbol,
    constant, 69
    free, 80
    function, 70
    of sentence, 5, 69
    predicate, 70
    propositional, 5
    truth, 5, 69
    variable, 70
symmetry,
    of *eqmult* (for bags) [property], 510
    of *eqmult* (for tuples) [property], 534
    of equality [axiom], 216
    of equivalence relation [axiom], 208
    of *perm* (for tuples) [property], 549
syntactic rule, 5, 69
tail (for lists) [function], 441
    and *head, decomposition* of [property],
        441
    sort of [property], 441
    tail of [property], 441
tail (for strings) [function], 369, 409

    and *head, decomposition* of [property],
        370
    character of [property], 370, 410
    functional substitutivity for [axiom],
        370
    sort of [property], 370, 410
    tail for [axiom], 370
    unspecified values, 370
tail,
    for append (for lists) [property], 443,
        465
    for end [axiom], 386
    of concatenation (for strings) [prop-
        erty], 372, 410
tail-reverse, of *front* (for strings) [prop-
    erty], 412
tardy bus [problem], 63
tautology (sentence), 15
term, 70
    application, 70
    conditional, 71
    of theory, 189
    substitutivity of equality for [proposi-
        tion], 220
ternary,
    function symbol, 70
    predicate symbol, 70
test for divisibility by 9 [example], 408,
    415
then-clause (of conditional), 6
theories,
    containment of, 199
    equivalence of, 199
theory, 189
    augmented, 196
    axioms of, 190
    consistent, 192
    incomplete, 196
    inconsistent, 197
    language of, 189
    model for, 191
    vocabulary of, 190
    of associated relations, 232
    of bags, 505
    of bags, sets, and tuples, 539
    of equality, 215
    of equivalence relations, 208
    of integers, 575
    of integers, strings, and trees, 577

of family, 191
of groups, 249, 280
of lists, 437
of lists and strings, 444
of lists and trees, 448
of lists, strings, and trees, 458, 468
of nonnegative integers, 285
of nonnegative integers and strings,
398
of nonnegative integers and trees,
430, 435
of nonnegative integers and tuples,
536, 550
of pairs, 256
of parsing, 458, 576
of sets, 471
of strict partial orderings, 201
of strings, 363
of trees, 419
of tuples, 529
of tuples of nonnegative integers, 550
of weak partial orderings, 229
predecessor, 317
with equality, 228
times interpretation (model for group),
250
times: see multiplication
tips (for trees) [function], 435
    atom for [axiom], 435
    construction for [axiom], 435
total asymmetry,
    in theory of associated relations [propo-
        sition], 248
    of strict less-than [property], 328
total relation (in theory of associated
    relations), 246
total safe substitution, 147
    concise notation for, 150
    multiple: see multiple total safe sub-
        stitution
total substitution, 40
    concise notation, 44
    multiple: see multiple total substitu-
        tion
    properties of, 41
    safe: see total safe substitution
total value [proposition], 154
    under same interpretation [corollary],
        162

totality,
    for relations [axiom], 246
    of proper-divides relation, 247
    of strict less-than, 247, 328
    of weak less-than, 325
transitivity,
    in propositional logic, 36
    in theory of associated relations, 244
    mixed: see mixed transitivity
    valid sentence schema, 36
transitivity,
    double (of equality) [property], 220
    for equality [axiom], 216
    for equivalence relation [axiom], 208
    for strict partial ordering [axiom],
        201
    for weak partial ordering [axiom],
        229
    of divides [property], 341
    of irreflexive restriction [proposition],
        239
    of lexicographic relation [property],
        273
    of *perm* (for tuples) [property], 549
    of proper subset [property], 493
    of proper substring [property], 390
    of proper subtree [property], 428
    of reflexive closure [proposition], 239
    of strict less-than [property], 328
    of subset [property], 492
    of substring [property], 390
    of subtree [property], 429
    of weak less than [property], 325
transposition permutation, 254
treatment of quantifiers (in inductive
    proof), 310, 377, 381
tree (for trees) [relation], 419
tree-list-tree, of *treelist* and *listtree* [prop-
    erty], 452
treelist [function], 449
    atom insertion for [axiom], 449
    empty for [axiom], 449
    list insertion for [axiom], 449
    list-tree-list of [property], 452
    monotonicity of [property], 458, 468
    nonatom of [property], 450
    one-to-one of [property], 457
    onto of [property], 457
    sort of [property], 450

trees,   419
  and integers and strings (combined
    theory),   577
  and lists (combined theory),   448
  and lists and strings (combined the-
    ory),   458, 468
  and nonnegative integers (combined
    theory),   430, 435
  and strings (combined theory),   430
  axioms for,   420
  induction principles for,   421, 423
  proper,   451
  representation of,   452, 457
  vs. lists,   437
  vs. strings,   422
true,
  of conditional terms [property],   226,
    278
  of set constructor [property],   405
  semantic rule,   11, 86
  truth symbol,   5, 69, 71
true (truth value),   9
true-false law (valid sentence schema),
  35
truth symbol,   5, 69
truth table (for connective),   12
  for *and*,   12
  for *if-and-only-if*,   12
  for *if-then*,   12
  for *if-then-else*,   13
  for *not*,   12
  for *or*,   12
truth-table method,   20
  vs. proof-by-falsification method,   30
  vs. semantic-tree method,   27
truth-value,   9, 10
tuplebag (mapping bags into tuples)
    [function],   544
  empty for [axiom],   544
  inconsistent axioms for,   544, 569
  insertion for [axiom],   544
  nonempty for [axiom],   544
tuple, empty: see empty tuple,   530
tuple (for tuples) [relation],   530
tuples,   529
  and bags and sets (combined theory),
    539
  and nonnegative integers (combined
    theory),   536, 550

axioms for,   530
  induction principle for,   530
  of nonnegative integers,   550
  vs. bags, lists, sets, and strings,   529
two (for integers) [property],   576
unary,
  function symbol,   70
  predicate symbol,   70
union,
  of cardinality (for sets) [property],
    496, 497
  of subset [property],   492
union $x \cup y$ (for bags) [function],   522,
    527
  count [property],   522, 527
  distributivity of [property],   524
  left empty for [axiom],   522
  member insertion for [axiom],   522
  nonmember insertion for [axiom],   522
union $x \cup y$ (for sets) [function],   483,
    500
  associativity of [property],   483
  commutativity of [property],   483
  empty for [axiom],   483
  insertion for [axiom],   483
  member of [property],   483, 500
union absorption, of subset [property],
    492
union-over-intersection distributivity
    [property],   485
uniqueness axioms,
  for bags,   506
  for lists,   438
  for nonnegative integers,   286
  for strings,   364
  for trees,   420
  for tuples,   530
  of tree representation of lists,   457
uniqueness,
  empty (for sets) [property],   474
  for pairs [axiom],   257
  of equality [proposition],   228, 279
  of quotient and remainder,   336
  of *sort* (for tuples of nonnegative inte-
    gers) [property],   565, 575
  suffix, of concatenation [property],
    372, 414
universal,
  general replacement (of equality) [propo-

sition], 226
replacement (of equality) [proposition], 223, 278
universal closure, 108
  instantiation, 176
  semantic rule for, 110
universal instantiation: see universal quantifier, instantiation
universal quantifier, 72
  conventional notation, 76
  instantiation, 168, 294
  multiple instantiation, 175
  semantic rule for, 92
unsatisfiable (sentence): see contradictory (sentence)
valid (in theory), 192
valid (sentence, of predicate logic), 97, 116, 119
  establishing, 97, 100
  examples of, 105
  instance of valid propositional-logic sentence, 124
valid (sentence, of propositional logic), 4, 15, 61
  and contradictory, 17
  and equivalence, 18
  and implies, 18
  and satisfiable, 17
  frightful, 62
  instance of, 123
  methods for establishing, 20, 23, 28
valid (sentence schema, of predicate logic), 116, 119
  catalog of, 121
  instance of, 120
  under side-conditions, 124, 185
  with substitution, 163
valid (sentence schema, of propositional logic), 33
  associativity, 36
  basic, 35
  catalog of, 35
  commutativity, 36
  contrapositive law, 36
  distributivity, 37
  instance of, 34
  law of negation, 37
  reduction law, 38
  transitivity, 36

true-false law, 35
validity,
  and equivalence, 56, 131, 185
  and implication, 54, 131, 185
  in theory, 192, 193
  of closures [proposition], 114
  of sentence: see valid (sentence)
  of sentence schema: see valid (sentence schema)
value [proposition], 154
value property, 154, 187
  instance [corollary], 159
  partial [proposition], 155
  same interpretation [corollary], 162
  total [proposition], 154
  variable [corollary], 161, 187
variable,
  bound (in expression), 76, 79
  captured, 147
  free (in expression), 76, 79
  of value property [corollary], 161
  renaming of, 106
  semantic rule, 86
  symbol, 70
vocabulary,
  for bags, 505
  for lists, 437
  for nonnegative integers, 285
  for sets, 471
  for strings, 363
  for trees, 419
  for tuples, 529
  of theory, 189
weak greater-than [axiom], 326
weak greater-than $x \geq y$ [relation], 325
weak less-than $x \leq y$ [relation], 321
  alternative definition of, 358
  antisymmetry of [property], 325
  as reflexive closure, 236
  computation of, 321
  left addition of [property], 322, 358
  left zero of [property], 325
  reflexivity of [property], 325
  right addition of [property], 325, 357
  right predecessor for [axiom], 321
  right successor for [alternative axiom], 358
  right zero for [axiom], 321
  totality of [property], 325

transitivity of [property], 325

weak partial ordering $x \preceq y$, 229, 279

   antisymmetry for [axiom], 229

   independence of axioms for, 230, 279

   inverse for [axiom], 231

   left substitutivity for [axiom], 229

   reflexive closure is a [proposition], 243

   reflexivity for [axiom], 229

   right substitutivity for [axiom], 229

   splitting of [property], 230

   subbag is a, 521

   subset is a, 492

   substring is a, 390

   subtree is a, 429

   subtuple is a, 535

   transitivity for [axiom], 229

well-formed formula, 76

whole (for integers) [relation], 575

zero (0), 285

zero,

   for *alter* (for tuples) [axiom], 538

   for *bad* (for nonnegative integers) [axiom], 566

   for element (for tuples) [axiom], 538

   for *exp3* [axiom], 307

   for factorial [axiom], 356

   for greatest common divisor [axiom], 343

   for recursive definition [axiom], 566

   of *length* (for strings) [property], 400, 414

   of *parcount* (for parsing theory) [property], 577

zeroes, leading, of string representation of nonnegative integers, 402

zero generation [axiom], 286

zero uniqueness [axiom], 286